LOM

the first jewish

compiled and edited by **Richard Siegel**

CREDITS

"editors" refers to Richard Siegel, Michael Strassfeld, Sharon Strassfeld

Symbols of the Home: editors and Stu Copans, Josh Heckelman

Kashrut: editors and Rabbi Joe Polak, Marvin Jussoy

Hallah: editors and Josh Heckelman, Sue Levi Elwell

Candles: editors

Kippah: Marian Sternstein, Karen Abramovitz

Tallit: editors and Rabbi Hershel Matt

Tefillin: editors

Shofar: Allan Lehmann

The Four Species: editors

Guide to Western Europe: Ruth Strassfeld

Guide to the Soviet Union: Debby Lipstadt

How to Travel Cheaply in Israel: Michael Paley

Aliyah: Deena Aziz

The Calendar: editors and Rabbi Everett Gendler

Shabbat: Murray Schaum, editors, and Rabbi Zalman Schachter

Festivals: editors and Sy Hefter, Rabbi Everett Gendler, Seymour Epstein, Jonathan Chipman

Berakhot: Rabbi Meyer Strassfeld and editors

Weddings: editors

Tumah and Taharah—Mikveh: Rachel Adler

Death and Burial: Josh Elkin

A Treatise on the Making of Hebrew Letters: Joel Rosenberg

A Practical Guide to Hebrew Calligraphy: Jay Greenspan, David Moss

The Calligraphy of the Classic Scribe: Rabbi Stuart Kelman

Gematria: editors

a do-it-yourself kit

catalog

Michael Strassfeld · Sharon Strassfeld

Philadelphia The Jewish Publication Society of America

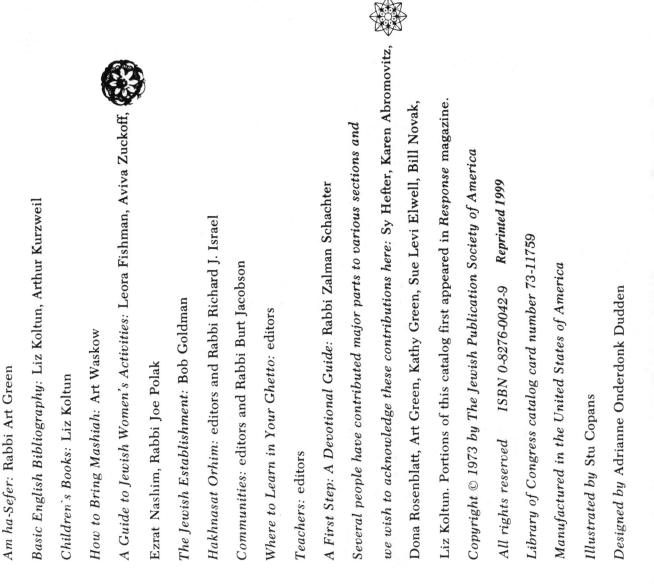

Music: George Savran

Film: Allan Sugarman

The Jewish Press and Periodicals: Velvel Young

Am ha-Sefer: Rabbi Art Green

Basic English Bibliography: Liz Koltun, Arthur Kurzweil

Children's Books: Liz Koltun

How to Bring Mashiah: Art Waskow

A Guide to Jewish Women's Activities: Leora Fishman, Aviva Zuckoff, Ezrat Nashim, Rabbi Joe Polak

The Jewish Establishment: Bob Goldman

Hakhnasat Orhim: editors and Rabbi Richard J. Israel

Communities: editors and Rabbi Burt Jacobson

Where to Learn in Your Ghetto: editors

Teachers: editors

A First Step: A Devotional Guide: Rabbi Zalman Schachter

Several people have contributed major parts to various sections and we wish to acknowledge these contributions here: Sy Hefter, Karen Abromovitz, Dona Rosenblatt, Art Green, Kathy Green, Sue Levi Elwell, Bill Novak, Liz Koltun. Portions of this catalog first appeared in *Response* magazine.

 ISBN 0-8276-0042-9 ***Reprinted 1999***

Library of Congress catalog card number 73-11759

Manufactured in the United States of America

Illustrated by Stu Copans

Designed by Adrianne Onderdonk Dudden

God's world is great and holy. Among the holy lands in the world is the Holy Land of Israel. In the land of Israel the holiest city is Jerusalem. In Jerusalem the holiest place was the Temple, and in the Temple the holiest spot was the holy of holies.

There are seventy peoples in the world. Among these holy peoples is the people of Israel. The holiest of the people of Israel is the tribe of Levi. In the tribe of Levi the holiest are the priests. Among the priests, the holiest was the high priest.

There are 354 days in the year. Among these the holidays are holy. Higher than these is the holiness of the Sabbath. Among Sabbaths the holiest is the Day of Atonement, the Sabbath of Sabbaths.

There are seventy languages in the world. Among the holy languages is the holy language of Hebrew. Holier than all else in this language is the holy

Torah, and in the Torah the holiest part is the Ten Commandments. In the Ten Commandments the holiest of all words is the Name of God.

And once during the year, at a certain hour, these four supreme sanctities of the world were joined with one another. That was on the Day of Atonement, when the high priest would enter the holy of holies and there utter the Name of God. And because this hour was beyond measure holy and awesome, it was the time of utmost peril not only for the high priest but for the whole of Israel. For if, in this hour, there had, God forbid, entered the mind of the high priest a false or sinful thought, the entire world would have been destroyed.

Every spot where a man raises his eyes to heaven is a holy of holies. Every man, having been created by God in His own image and likeness, is a high priest. Every day of a man's life is a Day of Atonement, and every word that a man speaks with sincerity is the Name of the Lord.

Folk tale adapted from a version in The Dybbuk *by Saul An-Ski*

word

We dedicate this book to an old rambling yellow house in Somerville, Mass.
to Krishna Kat
to those who daven and study there,
eat together
argue and love; to Havurat Shalom

In every generation, each person should search for his own Yavneh

This book was produced largely through the support and generous funding of the Jewish Student Projects and the Institute for Jewish Life.

The Institute for Jewish Life, a foundation involved in the promotion of projects for Jewish identity, was particularly instrumental in the critical final stages of compilation and production.

Jewish Student Projects, a funded subsidiary of the Combined Jewish Philanthropies of Boston, lent initial financial support to the project.

We deeply appreciate not only their financial support but also the confidence they showed in the project.

May He who blessed our fathers Abraham, Isaac, Jacob and our mothers Sarah, Rivkah, Leah, and Rachel bless

George Savran
Art Green
Kathy Green
Danny Margolis
Chaim Potok
Martha Cover
Kay Powell

for their assistance and encouragement in the preparation of this catalog. May *ha-Kadosh Baruch Hu* send blessing and prosperity on all the work of their hands together with all those who work for peace. AMEN.

Introduction

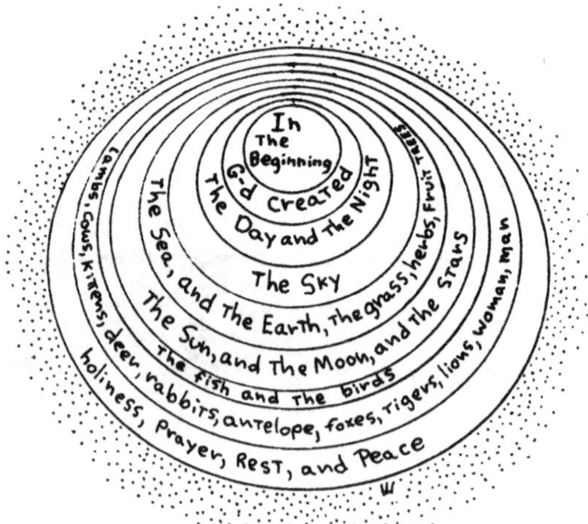

This is for those of you intrigued by backgrounds, orientations, and intentions. If you are not so inclined, skip to the last paragraph for suggestions on how to use this catalog.

וְדִבַּרְתָּ בָּם בְּשִׁבְתְּךָ בְּבֵיתֶךָ
וּבְלֶכְתְּךָ בַדֶּרֶךְ וּבְשָׁכְבְּךָ וּבְקוּמֶךָ׃

"Recite them when you stay at home and when you are away, when you lie down and when you get up" (Deuteronomy 6:7).

A few notes on using this catalog:

1. You should have a Bible and a good, complete Siddur as a companion—the Bible for checking the context of quotes, and the Siddur for the many cross-references made to it. (In addition, it contains a reservoir of material which we have not duplicated.)
2. Find out where the nearest *Encyclopaedia Judaica* is. Make frequent reference to it, as it has generally excellent supplementary material on many of the topics.

Perhaps the most difficult question we have been asked in the course of compiling this catalog has been, "What exactly is it?" Having realized quite early that there are no preexisting categories which would adequately satisfy this compulsion for definition, our rather vague response was generally, "It's a compendium of tools and resources for use in Jewish education and Jewish living in the fullest sense of these terms." Traditional Jewish compilations did not seem overly concerned with definitional precision or rigidity. To the extent that they were records and guides to life, they were wide-ranging and multifaceted. Thus, the Talmud interweaves stories and anecdotes with legalistic debate; the Rambam's commentary on the Mishnah includes a recipe for haroset; the *Shulhan Arukh* lists customs, variations, and kavvanot (intentions) along with ritual and legal prescriptions; and the *Siddur Kol Bo* ("the prayer book with everything in it") has alphabets, diagrams for tying tefillin, calendars, and even pictures of fruit juxtaposed with the traditional order of prayers. Not to be presumptuous, this catalog takes these earlier texts as models for its breadth, variations, uncategorizability, and necessary incompleteness.

A detailed analysis of the origin and development of this project is not crucial to the use of the catalog; however, a short summary may be appropriate. This can be seen largely as an outgrowth of the countercultural activity of the late 1960s—both in the secular and Jewish worlds. The move toward communal living, returning to the land, relearning the abilities and joys of "making it yourself," voicing social and political concern which characterized the general counterculture (see *The Making of a Counter Culture* by Theodore Roszak, Doubleday, 1969) was paralleled (a few years later, of course) by the development of a "Jewish counterculture" (see "The Making of a Jewish Counter-Culture" by Bill Novak, *Response* 4, no. 1 [Spring-Summer 1970]). What *The Whole Earth Catalog* (Portola Institute/Random House, 1969–71) was to the former, i.e., an access to tools and resources, this catalog was envisioned to be for the latter.

As the project developed, however, it became apparent that what was needed was not so much a cataloging of already existing resources but a guide or manual to the range of contemporary Jewish life—i.e., a resource in itself. The present volume thus represents an amalgam of the resource-retrieval catalog and the guide to Jewish life. (For a more complete description of the origins of the catalog, the attitude toward halakhah expressed in it, the traditional and contemporary models for it, and a rationale for the subject matter included and the audiences addressed, see "The Jewish Whole Earth Catalogue: Theory and Development," a master's thesis by George Savran and Richard Siegel—contact editors.)

Basically our intentions are (1) to give enough information to be immediately useful; (2) to direct those interested to additional resources; (3) to present the traditional dimensions of the subjects covered; and (4) to open options for personal creativity and contemporary utilization of these directives. We make no claim to be a repository of the whole past of Jewish ritual, law, folklore, crafts, and so on. This is a nonexhaustive selection of materials which offer the possibility for immediate application and integration into one's personal environment. (Hopefully, the needs of the community and the availability of other material will spur further investigation, increased communications, and additional compilations.) The orientation is to move away from the prefabricated, spoon-fed, nearsighted Judaism into the stream of possibilities for personal responsibility and physical participation. This entails a returning of the control of the Jewish environment to the hands of the individual—through accessible knowledge of the what, where, who, and how of contemporary Judaism.

To facilitate this process, we have collected material on a broad range of topics, investigated them from several aspects, and presented them from different perspectives. A large number of people have contributed to this work (see Credits). As will be apparent, they do not necessarily share approaches, life-styles, assumptions, or significance systems. Their attitudes, biases, inclinations, and orientations have generally not been edited out. This was an editorial decision which we felt was basic to the purpose and texture of the book. The present Jewish community is by no means monolithic. It is multifaceted, open, and pulsing with dynamism. To ignore the range of options and to limit ourselves to one orientation would have been to defeat the purpose of the book. Many opportunities are given for entrance. Many access routes to ritual, celebration, and the various facets of life are suggested through the interweaving of dynamics, laws, intentions, actions, possibilities, etc.

You can plug in wherever you want. Some people may be drawn to the halakhah and various types of halakhic observance within a mitzvah system. Others will be more concerned with the underlying psychological, mythical, spiritual levels and the vehicles which have developed within Judaism to express these. Still others will find the possibilities for physical expression within traditional forms—openings for the artist and craftsman. There is no need to be reductionist about this; many other orientations and needs can find expression within this work. The hope, in fact, is that the catalog will facilitate the development of a "repertoire of responses" so that a person can accommodate himself to the rapid pace of societal and environmental change—as well as to his own personal, emotional, and spiritual flux.

There are two potential drawbacks to this diversity, however.

1. The book reads unevenly. Solution: do not read it all at once.

2. An orientation to which you may respond in one section may not be evident in another. Solution: draw your own transference. If this book opens you to an awareness that there are manifold ways of approaching the facets of Judaism, it will have fulfilled an important function. It is up to you, however, to build on these flexibilities and extend them according to your own creativity.

Ultimately, however, our intentions or hopes for this book are irrelevant. You will or will not respond to what is included for reasons which are beyond our anticipation or our abilities to effect.

May this book serve to fulfill the intention of:

זֶה אֵלִי וְאַנְוֵהוּ

"This is my God and I will beautify Him."

3. If you are just entering into the ritual/celebratory aspects, find a supplement to the catalog in the form of another person. Much ritual simply cannot be translated, like a recipe, from reading to action; rather, you should be modeled for, guided, responded to personally—over time, gently.

4. Whatever value is found in this would probably be enhanced if discovered with a family, a community or another person—haver(ah).

5. For questions of halakhah consult a rabbi (or several) for full explanations and decisions. We perceive halakhah as a central input into our lives—to inform and set guidelines, to raise questions, to offer solutions, to provide inspirations, but not necessarily to dictate behavior as a monolithic law/rule. Thus, in all cases, we have researched the halakhah quite carefully and, though generally presenting the traditional opinions, have included defensible but not necessarily strict interpretations.

6. Be bold—and creative.

One final note:
We recognize the impossibility of our task. We would like to, but cannot, be everything for everyone. A book like this must be, by its very nature, incomplete. From your side it can be filled out with experiences, exposure to people, and further investigation. From our side, it is more difficult to rectify its incompleteness. Perhaps the pressures of time and necessity push it out before it is fully developed. As with all Jewish literature of this type, then, a tosefta—supplement—will follow if need and response warrant. If you have any comments, suggestions, or additions please send them to us directly:

Richard Siegel
115 North Country Rd.
Port Jefferson, N.Y. 11777

Michael and Sharon Strassfeld
220 W. 98th St., Apt. 3F
New York, N. Y. 10025

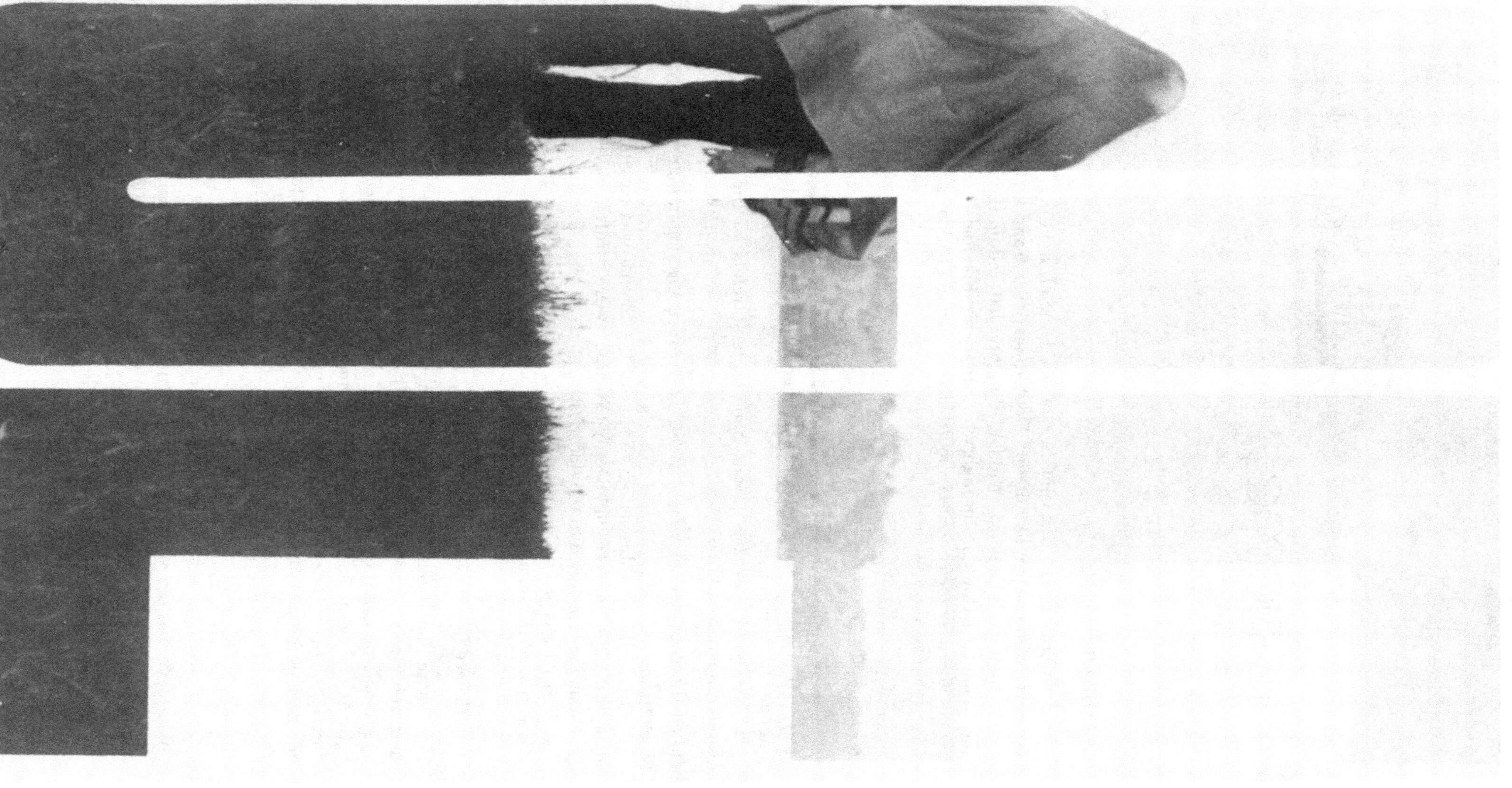

every spot where a man raises his eyes to heaven is a holy of holies

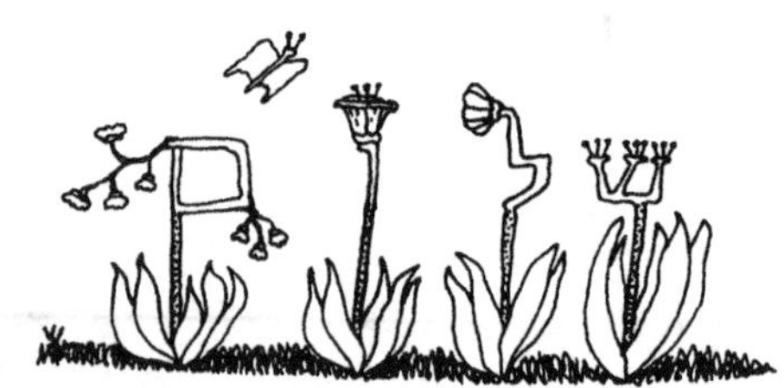

Symbols of the home

MEZUZAH

"There are many signs and symbols that identify a Jewish home—from the inside. From the outside, however, there is but one—the mezuzah" (Rabbi Hershel Matt).

The mezuzah consists of a container of wood, metal, stone, ceramic, or even paper containing a parchment with Deuteronomy 6:4–9 and 11:13–21 lettered on the front, and the word Shaddai (Almighty) lettered on the back. Usually the container has a hole through which the word Shaddai שדי can be seen. Otherwise the container should have the word Shaddai or the letter shin ש displayed on its front.

History

1. Many people date the mezuzah back to the time when we were slaves in Egypt. It is known that the Egyptians used to place a sacred document at the entrance to their houses.

2. The word mezuzah means doorpost and refers to the sentence in Deuteronomy 6:9, 11:20:

". . . inscribe them on the doorposts of your house and on your gates." וּכְתַבְתָּם עַל־מְזֻזוֹת בֵּיתֶךָ וּבִשְׁעָרֶיךָ:

3. Originally an abbreviated version of the Shema was carved into the doorpost. Later the present twenty-two lines were written on a piece of parchment and fastened to the doorpost.

4. Then it was placed in a hollow reed and attached to the doorpost. Finally it was placed in containers similar to those used at present.

Significance

1. There has been some disagreement over the significance of the mezuzah.

2. Some people think of it as an amulet which helps protect their house.

3. At one point kabbalistic symbols and inscriptions were added to the inscription in the mezuzah to enhance its protective function. The Shaddai on the back of the parchment is a remnant of this and was an abbreviation for

"guardian of the doors of Israel." שומר דלתות ישראל

4. A later view, more prevalent today, is that the mezuzah protects us not against external harm but against sinning. Eliezer ben Jacob said: "Whosoever has the tefillin on his head, the tefillin on his arm, the tzitzit on his garment, and the mezuzah on his doorpost is fortified against sinning."

5. Maimonides claimed that the mezuzah reminded us, each time we left our home and ventured into the world, that worldly affairs were unimportant.

By the commandment on the mezuzah, man is reminded, when entering or departing, of God's Unity, and is stirred into love for Him. He is awakened from his slumber and from his vain worldly thoughts to the knowledge that nothing endures in eternity like knowledge of the "Rock of the World." This contemplation brings him back to himself and leads him on to the right path.

Maimonides also claimed that to think of the mezuzah as an amulet was to distort and pervert its true meaning. "Fools pervert for temporal benefit the religious duty of mezuzah, of proclaiming the Unity of God and the love and service due Him, as though this were an amulet."

6. While having a mezuzah on your doorpost is a religious duty, it is considered a mitzvah to make mezuzot for others (see Scribal Arts).

Driftwood Mezuzah

R. Tanhum, son of R. Abba, explained: If one who has no property of his own practices charity and benevolence; if one who has no children pays fees to Bible and Mishnah teachers; if one who has no house makes a mezuzah for others; if one who has no tallit makes tzitzit for others; if one who has no tallit makes those of other people or prepares books and lends them to others– of such a one, the Holy One, blessed be He, says: "This man has been quick to perform My commandments before I gave him the means wherewith to fulfill them. I must repay him by giving him wealth and children who will read in books."

Some laws concerning the mezuzah (as found in the *Kitzur Shulhan Arukh* and selected by Rabbi Hershel Matt, with additions by Stu Copans)

1. A mezuzah is affixed to every door in the house. A room used for personal purposes such as a bathroom or lavatory needs no mezuzah on the door.
2. The mezuzah is affixed on the right-hand side as one enters.
3. The mezuzah is affixed within the upper third of the doorpost but must be no less than one handbreadth distant from the top.
4. The mezuzah is affixed in the following manner:
   a. Roll the parchment from the end of the sentence to the beginning, that is, from the last word—Ehad—toward the first word—Shema—so that the word Shema is on top.
   b. Put it in the tube.
   c. Fasten it with nails to the doorpost diagonally, having the top line containing the word Shema toward the house and the last word toward the outside. If the doorpost is not wide enough, the mezuzah may be fastened to it perpendicularly. The mezuzah is not considered valid if it is merely suspended; it must be fastened with nails at top and bottom.

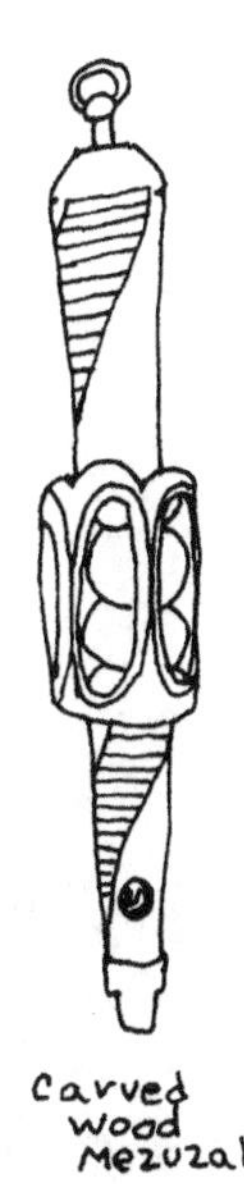

Carved Wood Mezuzah

5. Before affixing the mezuzah, say the blessing (below). If several mezuzot are to be affixed at one time, the saying of one blessing before affixing the first mezuzah will suffice for all. If a mezuzah happens to fall by itself from the doorpost, the blessing must be repeated when it is affixed again.
6. A building not used for a permanent residence needs no mezuzah. Therefore a sukkah (see Festivals) made for the holiday of Sukkot requires no mezuzah. It has become the custom today, however, to affix mezuzot to the entrance of public buildings, i.e., community centers and synagogues.
7. Every mezuzah must be inspected twice every seven years to be sure the writing is still legible. You must, therefore, make provision for opening the mezuzah to inspect the parchment.

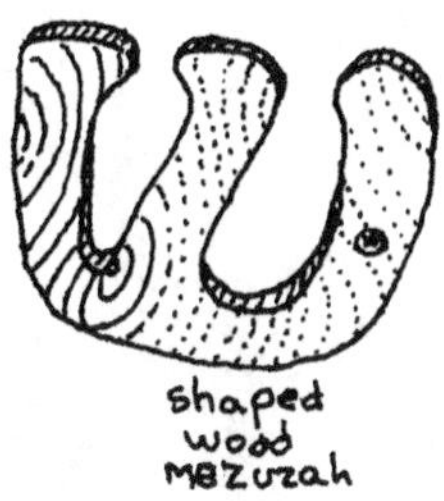

Shaped Wood Mezuzah

8. In the Diaspora, a mezuzah must be put up within thirty days of moving into a house.

9. In Israel, a mezuzah must be put up immediately on moving into a house.

10. The scroll in the mezuzah should be written on parchment by a scribe (see Scribal Arts).

11. If a house is sold or rented to a Jew, the mezuzah must be left on the doorpost. If the house is sold or rented to a gentile, it should be removed.

The blessings said for affixing the mezuzah are:

"Blessed are You, Lord our God, King of the Universe, who has sanctified us with His commandments, commanding us to affix the mezuzah."

בָּרוּךְ אַתָּה, יְיָ אֱלֹהֵינוּ, מֶלֶךְ הָעוֹלָם, אֲשֶׁר קִדְּשָׁנוּ בְּמִצְוֹתָיו, וְצִוָּנוּ לִקְבֹּעַ מְזוּזָה:

"Blessed are You, Lord our God, King of the Universe, who has kept us alive and sustained us and permitted us to reach this moment."

בָּרוּךְ אַתָּה, יְיָ אֱלֹהֵינוּ, מֶלֶךְ הָעוֹלָם, שֶׁהֶחֱיָנוּ, וְקִיְּמָנוּ, וְהִגִּיעָנוּ לַזְּמַן הַזֶּה:

12. Some have the custom of touching the mezuzah with their fingers and then bringing their fingers to their lips as they enter and leave. This reminds them of God's omnipresence.

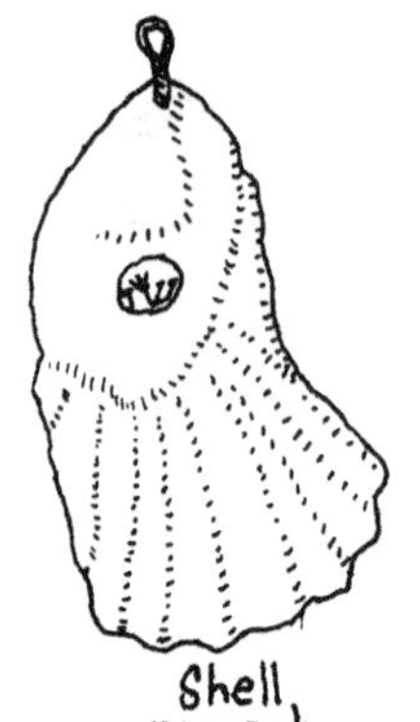
Shell mezuzah

Making mezuzot

1. In *Arts and Crafts the Year Round,* vol. 2 (United Synagogue Commission on Jewish Education, New York, 1965), Ruth Sharon suggests several methods for making mezuzot containers (pp. 96–103).

2. Very unusual mezuzot can be created out of clay, both firing clay and the self-hardening variety. Three-dimensional designs can be molded out of the clay itself. Paint or decorate with felt-tip pens.

Painted wood mezuzah (gessoed + painted)

3. Naomi Katz of Havurat Shalom led her sixth grade class in a mezuzah-making project. After much practice in Hebrew calligraphy, each youngster wrote out the Shema on a piece of paper. Then, by wetting the edges of each paper with water and burning them with a candle, they created a parchmentlike effect. The rolled up parchment was then inserted in a plastic toothbrush holder so that the Shema was still visible. Some students decorated the plastic containers with beads but made sure that their calligraphy was not hidden. The toothbrush holder can also be filled with beads or even peas and beans. Camp J.C.C. in Holden, Massachusetts, has lovely mezuzot filled with red lentils. These mezuzot are very easy to affix to the wall, for they have small display hooks on the top. (The plastic holders—complete with brushes—are available for about 20¢ or 30¢ each at discount houses.)

4. A small mezuzah can be made by gluing a walnut shell to a piece of heavy cardboard. Make sure to cut a slit in the back! Decorate with enamels, Magic Markers, or india ink.

5. Mezuzot can be whittled out of soft wood. Design a shin or the word Shaddai, and carve it in relief. Then hollow out the back. If there are places for nails at the top and bottom of the mezuzah, there is no need for a back, because the wood will hold the parchment securely against the doorpost.

6. For a soft mezuzah cover start with a square or rectangular piece of cloth. You can embroider an appropriate sign in the center. Fold the cloth in half—lengthwise and inside out. Sew up the long seam—opposite the fold. Pull through so that the right side is out. Roll seam to the middle. Fold or sew bottom. Insert the parchment and sew or fold back the top. It can be hung with two pretty thumbtacks or sewn to the door of your tent.

HANUKAT HABAYIT: DEDICATING A HOME

1. There is a reference in the Bible to the dedication of a new house (Deuteronomy 20:5):

"Then the officials shall address the troops, as follows: 'Is there anyone who has built a new house but has not dedicated it? Let him go back to his home, lest he die in battle and another dedicate it.' "	וְדִבְּרוּ הַשֹּׁטְרִים אֶל־הָעָם לֵאמֹר מִי־הָאִישׁ אֲשֶׁר בָּנָה בַיִת־חָדָשׁ וְלֹא חֲנָכוֹ יֵלֵךְ וְיָשֹׁב לְבֵיתוֹ פֶּן־יָמוּת בַּמִּלְחָמָה וְאִישׁ אַחֵר יַחְנְכֶנּוּ׃

2. It became a custom to have a Hanukat Habayit upon moving into a new apartment or home.

3. Some like to invite relatives, neighbors, and friends and have an open house.

4. There is no established form to the service for Hanukat Habayit aside from saying the appropriate blessings and affixing the mezuzah (see "Mezuzah").

5. A suggested order might be:
   a. The reciting of the blessings for mezuzah.
   b. The affixing of the mezuzah.
   c. Additional meditational material and singing.

6. Some suggested readings are:
   a. Psalm 15, which describes the Jewish ideal of human conduct.
   b. The following excerpts of Psalm 119, the first letters of which form the word berakhah—blessing.

"I have turned to You with all my heart; do not let me stray from Your commandments." (Psalms 119:10)	בְּכָל־לִבִּי דְרַשְׁתִּיךָ אַל־תַּשְׁגֵּנִי מִמִּצְוֺתֶיךָ׃
"Deliverance is far from the wicked, for they did not turn to Your laws." (Psalms 119:155)	רָחוֹק מֵרְשָׁעִים יְשׁוּעָה כִּי חֻקֶּיךָ לֹא דָרָשׁוּ׃
"I long for Your deliverance; I hope for Your word." (Psalms 119:81)	כָּלְתָה לִתְשׁוּעָתְךָ נַפְשִׁי לִדְבָרְךָ יִחָלְתִּי׃
"Teach me, O Lord, the way of Your laws; I will observe them to the utmost." (Psalms 119:33)	הוֹרֵנִי יְיָ דֶּרֶךְ חֻקֶּיךָ וְאֶצְּרֶנָּה עֵקֶב׃

7. The following is an excerpt from the prayer written by Dr. Adler which can be found in *The Daily Prayer Book* edited by Dr. Hertz and published by Bloch Publishing Co.

Sovereign of the universe! Look down from your holy habitation, and in mercy and favor accept the prayer and supplication of your children who are assembled here to consecrate this dwelling and to offer their thanksgiving unto you for all the loving kindness and truth you have shown to them. We beseech you, let not your loving kindness depart, nor the covenant of your peace be removed from them. Shield this their abode that no evil befall it. May sickness and sorrow not come unto it, nor the voice of lamentation be heard within its walls. Grant that the members of the household may dwell together in this, their habitation in brotherhood and fellowships, that they may love and fear you and cleave unto you, and may meditate in your Law, and be faithful to its precepts.

ADDITIONAL HOME CUSTOMS

1. Some people leave a small corner of their home or a wall free of decoration or adornment because of zeher lahurban—the remembrance of the destruction of the Temple.

2. Zalman Schachter of Manitoba also suggests creating "God's corner"—a special place reserved only for meditation, davening, etc. This might be an appropriate place to hang a shivviti (see below).

3. Some have the custom of bringing bread, candles, and salt to the new home before moving everything else in. The bread represents the hope that there should always be enough to eat, the candles symbolize the light and joy that should pervade your house, and the salt serves as a reminder of the Temple sacrifices (see Hallah).

MIZRAH

1. A mizrah is a plaque, watercolor, embroidered cloth, drawing, collage, or wall hanging which is hung on the eastern wall of the home so that one always knows where to face when praying.

2. This plaque or hanging always has the word מִזְרָח —mizrah, the Hebrew word for east—on it. The verse in Psalms 113:3 מִמִּזְרַח־שֶׁמֶשׁ עַד־מְבוֹאוֹ "From east to west"—is a frequent decorative motif.

3. Mizrahim were common in Eastern Europe. In Poland they were often made by cutting elaborate designs out of paper. At present they have virtually disappeared from the home.

4. There are no halakhic laws governing the hanging, design, or construction of a mizrah.

5. One should, however, always hang it on the eastern wall.

SHIVVITI

1. Similar to the mizrah is the shivviti, a votive wall hanging which was frequently hung in synagogues.

2. The term shivviti comes from Psalms 16:8: שִׁוִּיתִי יְהוָֹה לְנֶגְדִּי תָמִיד
"I am ever aware of the Lord's presence."

3. Because of its devotional nature, a shivviti generally has God's four-letter Name centrally displayed. Frequently other biblical verses or psalms surround and decorate the verse.

4. Although traditionally a shivviti was hung in a synagogue, people have recently begun to hang them in the home, feeling that one should *always* be conscious of God's presence.

Some suggestions for making a mizrah and shivviti:

1. The mizrah allows for infinite variation, from a carved wood plaque incorporated into macrame wall hanging to fine pen-and-ink drawings.

2. Suggested possibilities: pen and ink, paintings (acrylic, watercolor, oil, tempera, finger), ceramics, wood carving, wood burning, veneering and inlay, embroidery, needlepoint, weaving, macrame with plaque, etchings, woodcuts, and potato prints.

3. Directions for any of these processes can be found in a crafts manual.

4. Any designs may be used, though for the very traditional, human figures should be avoided.

5. Common designs include vases, flowers, quotations from Psalms, pictures of the Temple, menorot, and mythical beasts.

6. For papercuts, try using tinted paper and/or mounting it on a different colored background. To get a symmetrical design, fold the paper in half. For a circular or multilateral design, fold more than once. Fasten the paper with thin nails to a wooden board and cut out the design with a sharp knife. These can be made many different ways—without folding, asymmetrically, etc. Use your imagination.

Kashrut: food, eating, and wine-making

Explanation of Terms

KASHRUT: refers to the laws relating to kosher food
KOSHER: has a threefold meaning
(a) means "fit" or "proper"
(b) refers to foods that can be eaten in accordance with Jewish dietary laws, i.e., what categories of food are kosher and what categories are not
(c) refers to the separation of milk from meat
KASHERING: refers to
(a) the process of soaking and salting meat which removes the blood; or
(b) the process whereby a utensil which became treif is rendered kosher and fit for use again
TREIF: refers to
(a) any food which may not be eaten in accordance with Jewish dietary laws; or
(b) any utensil which may have become unfit for use
SHEHITAH: is the complex process of ritual slaughter of animals and fowl according to Jewish law
SHOHET: person specifically trained and authorized to perform shehitah
MILCHIK: any food which is or contains milk or any product derived from a milk substance
FLEISHIK: any food which contains meat or meat by-products or derivatives
PAREVE: any food product which has none of the above properties: a neutral food—a food having no gender (fruit, vegetables, etc.)

INTRODUCTION

Although there are many attitudes assumed regarding the observance of kashrut, three stand out predominantly. One of the most frequent explanations is that kashrut is a biblical injunction designed as an exercise in maintaining holiness before God. In Leviticus 11:1–43 we are informed as to which animals, fish, and fowl may be regarded as kosher. This is followed by verses 44–45: "For I the Lord am your God: you shall sanctify yourselves and be holy." Leviticus 20:25–26 states: "So you shall set apart the clean beast from the unclean. . . . You shall be holy to Me, for I the Lord am holy." (Clean and unclean refer to spiritual and not physical properties.) From this perspective, therefore, kashrut is observed primarily as a mitzvah—commandment—from God, intended both for man's ritual purity and for the maintenance of a proper relationship between God and man.

Another attitude toward kashrut is that through observance of this law we exercise, and hopefully gain control over, one of the basic activities of our lives—preparing and eating food. In effect, we are engaged in determining boundaries for ourselves within which we regulate our lives. The value of this is twofold. First, such self-control is in itself a form of personal growth. It is a paradoxical truth that through the acquisition of discipline and structure within an otherwise random and arbitrary life, freedom, spontaneity, and personal growth become possible. Second, such personal boundary-setting constantly confronts us with the knowledge and responsibility that we are, and must always be, the masters of our own lives—our selves and our bodies.

Finally, the laws of kashrut can lead to a reverence for life. It seems clear from Genesis 1:29—"God said, 'See, I give you every seed-bearing plant that is upon all the earth, and every tree that has seed-bearing fruit; they shall be yours for food' "—that man was originally intended to be vegetarian. In the course of history the eating of meat became an accepted part of human existence. Recognizing this development, the tradition sought to elevate it through sanctifying it. Killing and eating meat, however, was and is essentially a concession. Only God can take the life which only God can give. Originally this process was sanctified through the elaborate ritual of sacrifices—where, after offering to God first, man was *allowed* to partake. The sacrificial system no longer exists, but the need for sanctification remains. Kashrut, the process of separations, and shehitah, the process of religious ritual killing, preserve this sanctity within our own consciousnesses, within our homes, and on our tables. The killing of an animal with flesh, blood, and life, much like ours, is not necessarily cruel or inhumane, but it is certainly weighty. It is proper and fitting to the dignity of man that he does not just kill and eat, but takes responsibility for his food—before God and before life itself. It should be noted, however, that even with this procedure for sanctification there have always been great Jewish teachers who sought to limit or do without the eating of meat—and who found a basis for their actions from within the tradition.

This reverence for life is evidenced in two other aspects of kashrut. (1) Leviticus 17:11 states: "For the life of the flesh is in the blood." Since the blood *is* the life we are forbidden to eat the blood. Through the process of kashering, the blood must be removed from the animal before eating the meat. (2) "You shall not boil a kid in its mother's milk" (Exodus 23:19; 34:26; Deuteronomy 14:21) is stated and restated because of the basic cruelty involved in combining the life-giving element of an animal—its milk—with the death element—its flesh. Over time, this separation of milk and meat was expanded to prohibit any preparing, cooking, and/or eating of the two elements together.

It is very important to remember that this section is not, and makes no pretense of being, an exhaustive approach to kashrut. Thousands of pages have been written about the subject. This section has tried only to point to a general direction—to make available the major issues and to direct the reader to more detailed material.

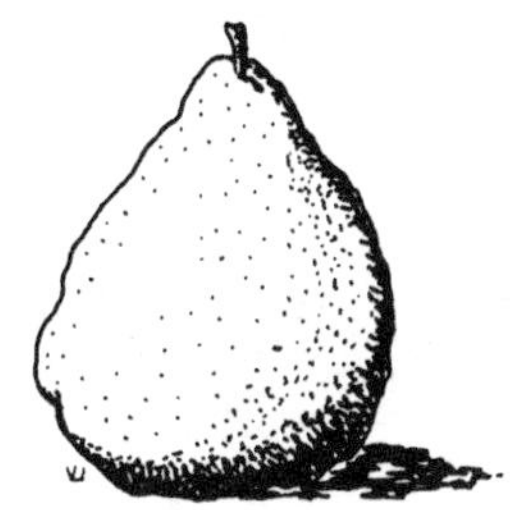

Vegetables

In accordance with Genesis 1:29, quoted above, all vegetables and fruits are kosher. Not only that, they are genderless and may be served with either milk or meat foods. The only thing to worry about is that insects haven't invaded your food, since food invaded by insects should not be eaten. For further elucidation see *A Guide to the Jewish Dietary Laws* by Rabbi Dr. Y. Kemelman. It is best to treat vegetables cooked in a milchik pot as milchik and vice versa.

Fish

Any variety of fish that has *both* fins and scales is considered kosher. A list of some common kosher fish and some common treif fish follows. In addition, although fish is regarded as pareve, one may not cook fish together with meat. Fish may, however, be cooked in or with milk.

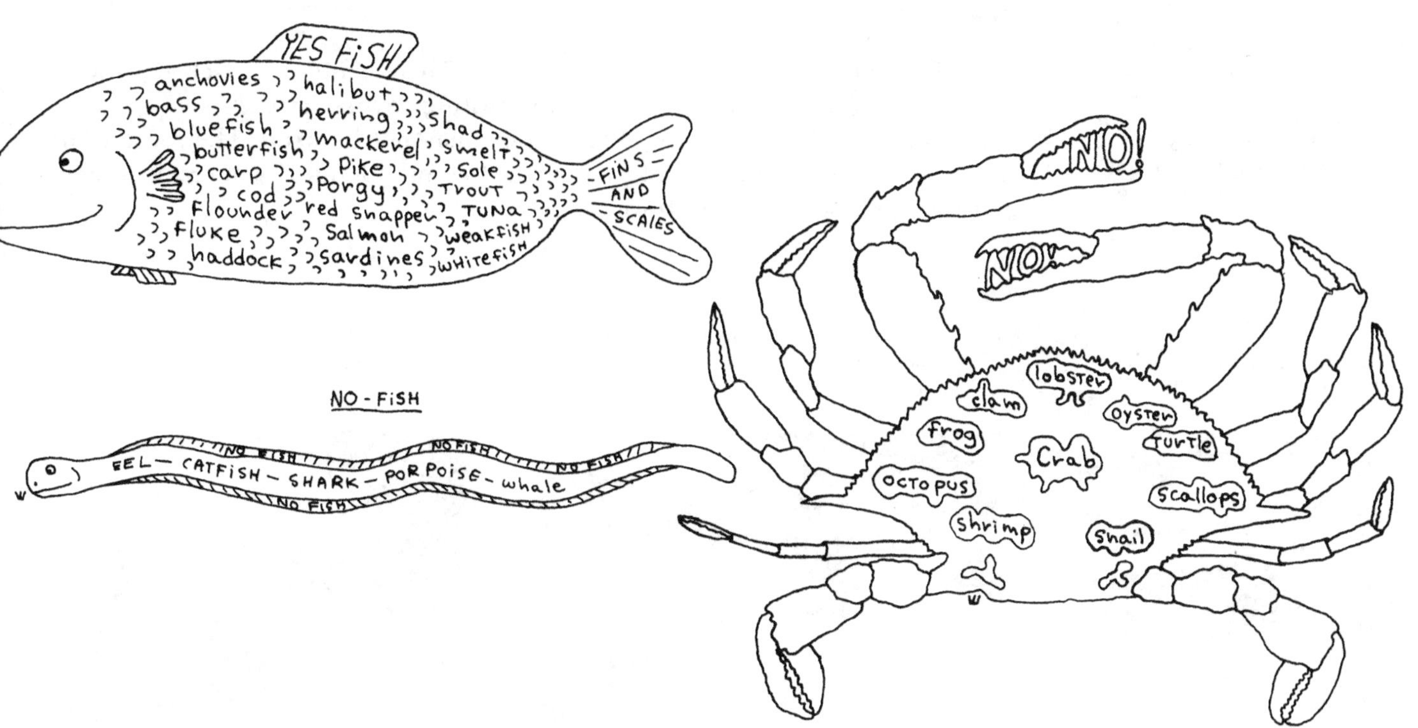

Fowl: Birds

Most domestic fowl are kosher. This includes:

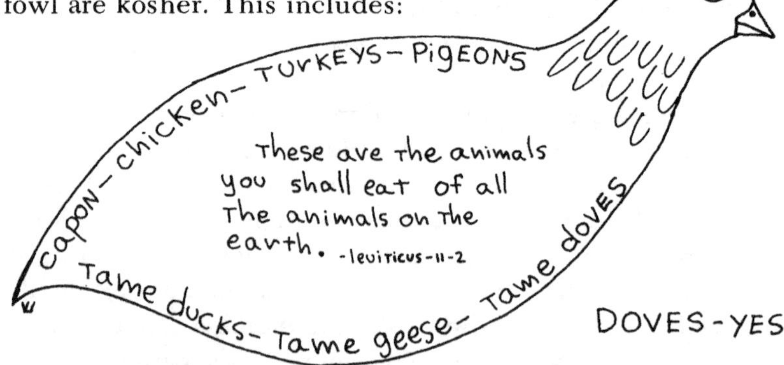

Wild birds and birds of prey are treif. There are twenty-four varieties listed in the Bible and among these treif varieties are such interesting species as:

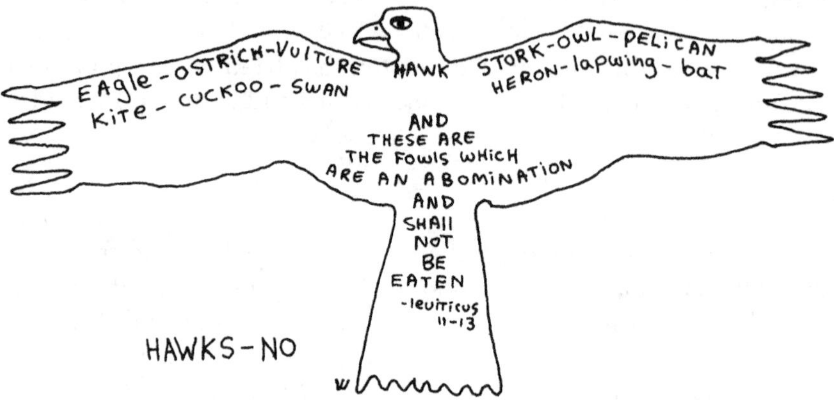

EAgle-OSTRICH-VULTURE
KITE-CUCKOO-SWAN
HAWK
STORK-OWL-PELICAN
HERON-lapwing-bat
AND THESE ARE THE FOWLS WHICH ARE AN ABOMINATION AND SHALL NOT BE EATEN
-leviticus 11-13
HAWKS-NO

As in the case of meat, fowl and birds must be ritually slaughtered by a qualified shohet in order to be kosher. Any animal or fowl that is killed in any other way or that dies a natural death is not kosher.

Fowl in general is kashered according to the rules given in the next section for meat. First, though, for fowl:

a. remove all innards from the center cavity
b. remove neck

If you plan on kashering the feet, remove claws and skin from them.

HINT: Generally, the best policy is, if you have a number of eggs to crack, crack them one by one into a glass. As you crack each egg, check it for blood spots and then add it to the rest of your recipe. This process will eliminate the "Contaminating Egg Syndrome." This refers to the unfortunate occurrence of needing eight eggs for a recipe, breaking seven in a row into the glass and finding that the eighth (by now floating cheerfully in the bowl with the other seven) is bloodspotted. In case it hasn't dawned on you yet, that means you have to throw out all eight eggs since the one contaminates the many.

Eggs

Eggs from nonkosher birds are not kosher. This includes ostrich eggs and seagull eggs (add that to your list of Interesting Jewish Trivia).

In addition, eggs containing blood spots may not be used. The reason for this is a corollary to the prohibition against eating blood. If you crack an egg and find a blood spot in it, throw it away.

1. *Soaking*—Meat is soaked a full half hour before salting.

2. *Preparation for salting*—Meat is placed on inclined or perforated surface.

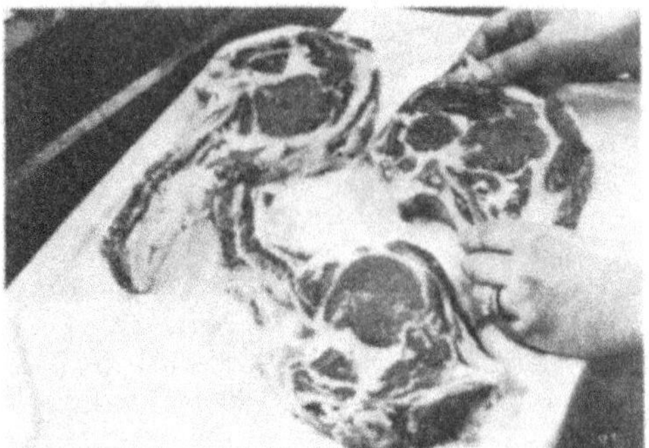

3. *Salting*—All sides and surfaces are liberally sprinkled with koshering salt.

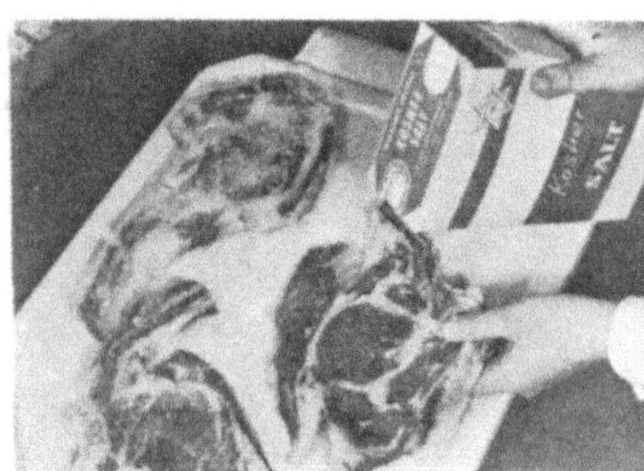

Meat

1. All animals which both chew their cud and have a split hoof are kosher. This includes cattle, sheep, goats, and deer. Animals that are treif include horses, donkeys, camels, and pigs.

2. Meat must be killed according to the laws of shehitah; otherwise it is not regarded as kosher. This means that eating Colonel Sanders' chicken is a no-no.

3. Such properly slaughtered meat is available at a kosher butcher. Sometimes your local supermarket may carry a limited stock of kosher foods, among which might be EMPIRE chickens, MORRISON and SCHIFF, BARNET and BRODIE, HEBREW NATIONAL hot dogs, salami, bologna, etc.

4. Once the meat is properly slaughtered, it must be kashered—i.e., soaked and salted to remove excess blood. Frequently a kosher butcher will perform this service for you, but if he hasn't, it is up to you to do it. By doing the kashering yourself, you gain the advantage of caring for your own meat and taking a part in the kashrut process.

How to kasher meat

The process of kashering is really much simpler than you might believe. It takes only an hour and a half and requires the following four objects: coarse "kosher" salt, water, a deep tub for soaking, and an inclined board.

1. Rinse the meat thoroughly and put it in the tub with enough cold tap water so that all the meat is covered. Include soup bones, which might appear to be meatless but which must be kashered too. This process of soaking softens the tissue in the meat.
2. After a half hour, drain the meat and lay it on the inclined board so that the blood will be able to drain away from the meat.
3. Salt the meat on both sides with a fine covering of the coarse salt. Include all crevices, nooks, crannies, and hidden caverns that the meat might contain. The salt will draw the blood from the meat.
4. Let the meat drain, untouched, on the board for an hour.
5. At the end of that time, wash off the salt.

That's all there is to it.

ADDENDUM: The heart must be cut and rinsed free of all blood before salting.

Liver

While we're on the subject of kashering, there is a special way to kasher liver. It's even simpler than kashering meat. Simply take a shallow pan and buy a top for it that has holes at regularly spaced intervals (a grid or broiling pan is excellent). Rinse the liver and score it in different directions. Salt the liver thoroughly with the coarse salt and place on the pan with the holes. The blood will drip into the pan below as the liver broils. Broil until all the blood is drained from the liver and the meat is edible (it should have a crust on the outside). Incidentally, the utensils used for this purpose should be set aside and used only for kashering and nothing else. The liver may be broiled to the point of edibility and then cooked any way you want.

The reason for treating liver in a manner different from other meats is that liver has an excess of blood, and the most effective way to remove blood is by broiling it away. Which brings us to our next point. . . .

Broiling: salt-free diets

Any meat you broil need not be soaked and salted. For people on salt-free diets, simply broil the meat to the point of edibility (using a grid as indicated above) and enjoy.

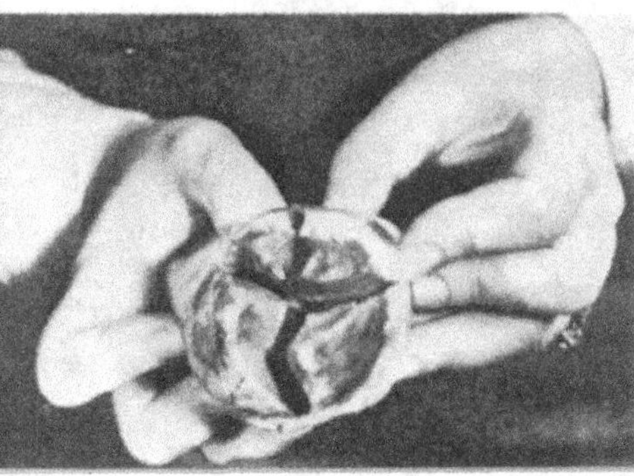

4. *Heart*—Heart must be cut and rinsed free of blood before salting.

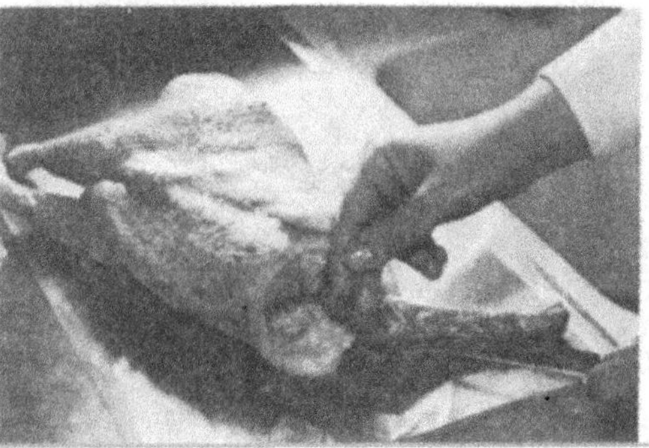

5. *Artery*—The artery in neck of fowl is removed before salting.

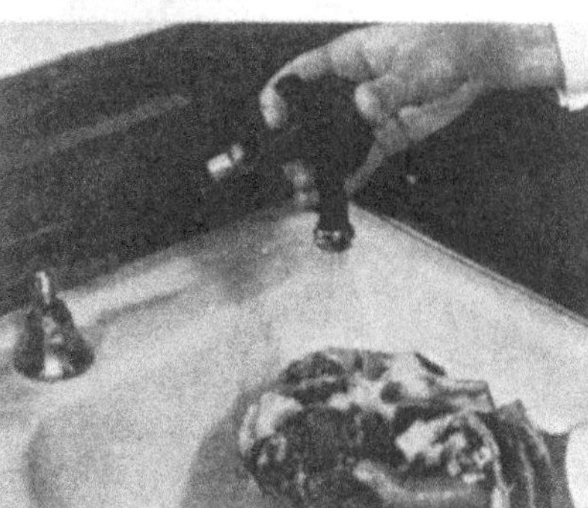

6. *Washing*—Salt is removed by washing under freely flowing faucet.

Separation of milk and meat

1. The separation of milk and meat utensils as well as the separation of milk and dairy foods from meat ones is as important as eating kosher meat.

2. For this reason you should check all the products you use in order to ascertain their gender. For example, many white breads, even if kosher, can contain milk or milk products. You should therefore beware of serving them at a meal where meat is served.

3. Margarine is not always pareve—unless specifically stated. Very frequently if you check the ingredients you will discover that milk, milk by-products, or nonfat milk is used.

4. Lactose, lactic acid, sodium caseinate, and whey may be milk derivatives. BEWARE!

5. The custom is to create a further separation between meat and milk by waiting a certain specified amount of time after eating meat before eating dairy foods. The amount of time varies, depending on where your zaydeh came from in Europe and what your family tradition is. German Jews generally wait three hours, East European Jews wait six hours, and Dutch Jews wait one hour. There are many variations, but these seem to be the most widely accepted waiting periods. If you do not have a family tradition, create one of your own (with appropriate attention to how often you get hungry).

KOSHER SYMBOLS ON FOODS

There are four symbols to look for in determining the kashrut of a product.

1. First there is the Ⓤ.

This is the symbol used by:

Union of Orthodox Jewish Congregations of America
84 Fifth Ave.
New York, N.Y. 10011

and is very reliable. The thing to be careful about with the Ⓤ symbol is that there is rarely an indication as to whether the product is pareve. They provide a Kosher Products Guide free on request.

2. ꟽ is a symbol used by the Vaad Harabonim in Boston. This symbol is found mostly on products in and around Massachusetts, Rhode Island, etc. Rabbi Samuel Korff is the rabbinic administrator and he will supply information about kashrut on request. The Vaad Harabonim is located at:

177 Tremont St.
Boston, Mass. 02215

3. The Organized Kashrus Laboratories symbolized by the Ⓚ is administered by Rabbi B. Levy. It too publishes a Kosher Products Newsletter, which is available free on request. It is located at:

1692 52nd St.
Brooklyn, N. Y.

4. Finally, the K. The problem with the use of the letter K as a kashrut symbol is, of course, that a letter of the alphabet is not a copyrighted symbol. While it is true that a K is a symbol attesting to the kashrut of a product, it is often wise to inquire of the manufacturer for more specific information about actual rabbinic supervision.

SETTING UP A KOSHER HOME

Setting up a kosher home is not at all difficult once one gets the hang of what one is and is not allowed to do and eat. There is sometimes an unfortunate tendency among those just beginning to keep kosher to make the process as complicated as possible. One of the best ways to decomplicate the issue is to visit someone who has a kosher home and request a guided tour of the kitchen. Shortcuts and maneuverability areas become clearer and the whole process somehow simplifies itself.

a. You should have two sets of dishes and two sets of silverware—stored separately: one for meat meals and one for dairy meals. These should never be mixed—this rule includes washing, storing, etc.

b. It is preferable to have different dish towels for meat and milk dishes.

c. Two sets of dish drainers and sink liners are advisable (the greatest invention ever for keeping kosher was the double sink). Use kosher soaps and detergents to wash dishes. You absolutely need sink liners so that your utensils don't come in contact with the sink. Never wash meat and milk utensils together.

Kashering utensils

This section was written with the help of Rabbi Joe Polak (see Teachers), who has made himself available to answer any questions or problems you can come up with about kashrut. Write him at

233 Bay State Rd.
Boston, Mass. 02215

The following are general rules for kashering. Consult a rabbi for more detailed explanations.

How to kasher a sink

If it's made of metal, a sink can be kashered. Rinse every square inch of sink with boiling water (the water must be boiling *while* you pour, so your best bet is an electric kettle still plugged in—*be careful!!!*).

How to kasher an oven

Method one: blowtorch

Clean it out thoroughly with a kosher oven cleaner. Then slowly, deliberately, and carefully, go over the entire interior surface of the stove with one of those (lit) portable propane blowtorches that you can pick up at your local hardware store for less than five dollars (no Jewish home should be without one). *Before* propaning the stove this way, *check it for gas leaks.* Borrow and use a welder's mask and gloves (stoves have been known to blow up in people's faces).

Method two: heating

Another approach is to clean out the oven thoroughly and then heat the oven to the highest degree for a full half hour.

How to kasher silverware: boiling

If the utensil is made of one piece of metal, it can be kashered. However, any utensil with a plastic or bone handle which might be damaged by boiling water cannot be kashered. Don't use the utensil for twenty-four hours prior to kashering. After this waiting period, clean it thoroughly of food and rust. Now kasher it by immersing it completely in a vat or pot of boiling water. Make sure that

1. the water is actually boiling in the vat (e.g., placing the utensil in the vat lowers the temperature of the water if the former is too cold);
2. the utensil being kashered is not touching *anything* while immersed in the boiling water, i.e., that all its surfaces come in contact with the boiling water (not necessarily simultaneously);
3. dairy items are kashered in a dairy vat and meat items in a meat vat.

How to kasher pots and pans

1. Pots and pans not used for frying which can be thoroughly cleaned can be kashered by the boiling method described above.
2. Frying pots and pans can be kashered by a blowtorch as described above.

How to kasher counters

Counters made of nonporous material can be kashered. (Anything porous, like butcher-block counters, cannot be kashered.) Simply follow the procedure applicable to sinks above.

How to kasher porcelain dishes

You can't. Consult a rabbi on how to dispose of them.

CONTROVERSIES

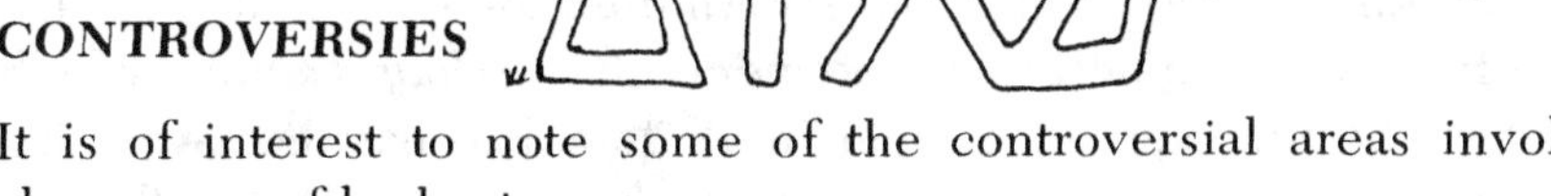

It is of interest to note some of the controversial areas involved in the observance of kashrut.

The great American cheese freeze

Orthodox opinion A kashrut question attaches to the use of hard cheese not made under rabbinic supervision (this includes American, Muenster, Gouda, Swiss). Essentially, in its most nonscientific form, the issue is the following:

1. *Most hard cheese uses a product called rennet as a curdling agent. This cuts down on production time since the milk need not sour naturally if rennet is used. In addition, this solidifies the milk (hence the title of this section: "Cheese Freeze") so that it is ready to be made into hard cheese. BUT, here's the catch:*

2. *Most rennet is a secretion which comes from the stomach lining of pigs, calves, and other animals. It is accordingly unacceptable on those terms to some people.*

3. *If rennet is to be used in cheese that is to be acceptable to these people, it must come from kosher animals which have been ritually slaughtered.*

4. *Some companies producing such cheese are:*

Dellwood	*Millers*	*Tuxedo*	*Raskas*
Farmlea	*Raskins*	*Sante*	*Migdal*

List of chemical additives which, besides probably poisoning your body, may be unkosher

Depending on what rabbi or authority you ask and what positions you adhere to, some of the following may be treif for you. The best policy is to consult a rabbi who likes to eat the same things you do.

Mono-glyceride	Glycine
Di-glyceride	Emulsifiers
Stearates	Gelatin
Stearic acid	Lipids
Softeners	Rennet
Argol	Pepsin

Non-Orthodox opinion 1. In using rennet an interesting phenomenon occurs. The substance gets reduced to its basic chemical components and no longer has any relationship to the animal from which it came.

2. Rabbi Isaac Klein of Buffalo elucidates this by referring to the Rabbinical Assembly Law Archives, which point out that many authorities claim that since the rennet used comes from the thoroughly dried-up wall of the stomach, it has ceased to be a food.

3. The substance can no longer be identified with the substance from which it comes—and it is no longer forbidden to us.

Swordfish–sturgeon

A major (fish)bone of contention between the Orthodox and Conservative is over the question of whether or not swordfish is a kosher species of fish.

Orthodox Essentially the Orthodox opinion set forth by Dr. Moshe Tendler is that the swordfish never grows real scales, but instead has "bony tubercles or expanded compressed platelike bodies." These are not, according to Dr. Tendler, the scales referred to in the Torah as essential elements of a kosher fish. Dr. Tendler's second point is that even if these protrusions are accepted as real scales, they are shed by the time the fish becomes an adult. No halakhic authority, according to Rabbi Tendler, permits as kosher a fish which drops its scales before reaching maturity.

Conservative The Conservative opinion, set forth by Rabbi Isaac Klein, quotes the passage in the Torah which states that in order for a fish to be kosher it must have fins and scales *while it swims in the streams or rivers.* He further quotes an assistant laboratory director of the Bureau of Fisheries of the United States Department of the Interior who says that swordfish retain their scales as juveniles but lose them after they are approximately four feet long. Rabbi Klein's position is that these protrusions are indeed scales. He then quotes from rabbinic sources which have permitted swordfish in the past. Rabbi Klein offers as a support the statement in *Darchay Tshuva* which maintains: "It is the widespread custom in all Israel to eat the swordfish called 'fish ispada' even though it has no scales when it comes out of the sea because it is said that as a result of its excitement it shakes and sheds its scales." Seymour E. Freedman, in his volume *The Book of Kashruth*, deals cogently with both arguments (pp. 130–32).

Glass

Because glass is a nonporous material, it is generally accepted that glass utensils (glasses, etc.) may be used for both milk and meat foods (although not simultaneously!). Most authorities agree that one should nonetheless have two separate sets of dishes. Pyrex, Corning Ware, etc. should not be used for both milk and meat.

RECIPES

We're including some of the more traditional Jewish foods and variations on the recipes.

Cholent

Cholent is a sort of stew which came into existence through the ingenuity of Jewish housewives in Europe who were faced with the necessity of preparing a hot meal for Shabbat afternoon in spite of the injunction against beginning to cook foods on Shabbat itself. The stew was begun well before Shabbat and allowed to cook all Friday afternoon. Before Shabbat it was put into a big communal oven and allowed to simmer until lunch the next day. Today this once-lowly dish is considered a "gastronomical pleasure" and is served on State Occasions.

Our first recipe comes from Eva Epstein, who actually remembers the entire process being done in Hungary, where she was born.

CHOLENT 1 (will serve ten normal people or two Hungarians)

1½ cups navy beans
¾ cup medium white pearl barley
2 medium onions
2 cloves garlic
3 medium potatoes (this is a non-Hungarian addition demanded by my husband who is a nice boy but not one of us)
pepper
paprika
salt
flanken (or other fatty meat *with* bones)

Soak the beans overnight. When ready to use, wash them well. Place barley and beans in a large ovenproof pot (earthenware is the real thing). Cover them with water. Dice onions and garlic and add to above. Add potatoes, spices, and salt to taste (start with ¾ tablespoon and adjust later). Set to boiling, then lower flame. Continue to cook; as the water is absorbed, keep adding more so that there is plenty in the pot at all times. Add the meat about half an hour before Shabbat. The entire cholent should be just covered with water when you place it in the oven for Shabbat. Make sure it doesn't dry out by the morning but don't fall into the trap of making soggy cholent (YECH!). By morning there should be a nice crust on top. Leave in the oven at 200° or, if your oven is slow, leave it at 250°.

NOTE: A piece of kishke or knaidel cooked in the cholent overnight can be unbelievably good.

Our second recipe comes from Ms. Frieda S. Siegel, who serves her cholent in chicken soup. Richie says his mother's cholent is the best in the world.

CHOLENT 2

5 pounds potatoes
flour
2 or 3 onions
pepper
paprika
salt
¼ cup ketchup
1 cup water
3 pounds untrimmed second-cut brisket
2 cans kidney beans

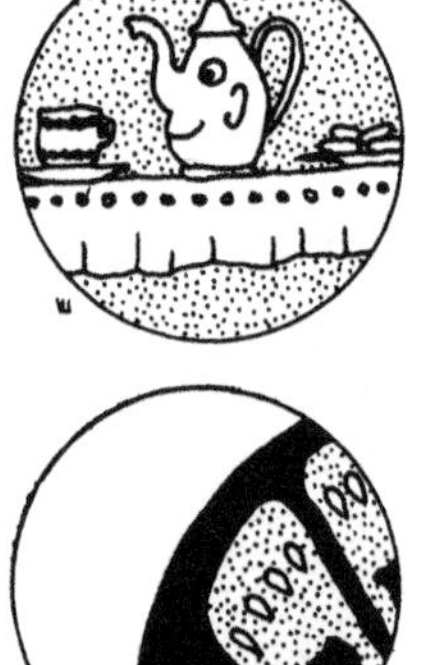

Pare and quarter the potatoes. Place in a large roasting pan (a tub if using a peck of potatoes). Sprinkle flour over the potatoes, making sure all potatoes are completely covered (this makes a delicious crust over the potatoes). Dice onions and toss over the potatoes. Sprinkle salt, pepper, and paprika all over the ingredients. Add ¼ cup of ketchup to 1 cup of water and add to the roasting pan. (This quantity is for about five pounds of potatoes, so if more potatoes are used, increase the amount of ketchup and water.) Place a fat piece of meat–about three pounds of brisket (untrimmed)–plus additional pieces of beef fat over the potatoes. Salt and pepper meat and fat. Cover the roaster and place in a 250° oven. Plan to keep roast in oven for at least eight hours (the longer the better). Check every couple of hours and add a bit of water, if necessary. Add cans of undrained kidney beans the last two hours. If there is too much liquid in pan, remove lid and roast uncovered until most of the liquid is absorbed.

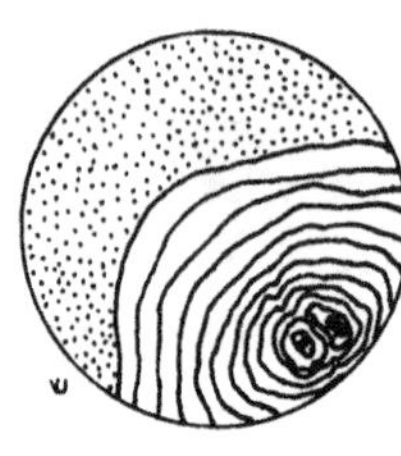

Tzimmes

A tzimmes is, essentially, a mishmash of different foods. Sometimes tzimmes includes only carrots and is called a carrot tzimmes. Sometimes tzimmes includes meat, sweet potatoes, prunes, and is called a gantze tzimmes. In any case, tzimmes is always sweet and always has carrots in it (and in a rapidly changing world such reassurances are important!). Here is Eva's recipe for a carrot tzimmes.

NOTE: Eva says to resist all efforts to make this more complicated!

CARROT TZIMMES

1 bunch tender new carrots
oil
salt
honey
flour

Cut carrots into thin slices. Sauté carrots lightly in oil (absolutely without burning them). Add ¼ cup water and let simmer until carrots are almost soft. Add a pinch of salt and honey to taste. By now it should have a sauce. If not, add another ¼ cup water. Simmer and thicken by adding a little flour. Simmer one minute more.

Our gantze tzimmes recipe comes from Ruth Nulman, who makes a whole meal out of it.

GANTZE TZIMMES

2-4 pounds deckle brisket
2 onions diced
oil or chicken fat
1½ teaspoons salt
¼ teaspoon pepper
4 sweet potatoes peeled and quartered
2 white potatoes peeled and quartered
½-¾ cup honey to taste
½ teaspoon cinnamon
½ teaspoon allspice
4 carrots peeled and sliced

Brown meat and onions in oil or fat. Use a big heavy pan. Cook over low heat for one hour, adding one cup of water after the meat is browned. If the water boils out, add more. Add salt and pepper, both kinds of potatoes and rest of the ingredients. Add water and simmer at least two more hours until all is soft. Keep adding water as necessary but don't create a soup. When done, tzimmes should hold together and be soft.

Fallafel

Anyone who has ever been to Israel knows what fallafel is. It is a concoction of sauce, salad, chick-pea balls all stuffed into Syrian bread (available in most supermarkets). It is the classic Agony and Ecstasy food—an agony to make, an ecstasy to eat.

FALLAFEL BALLS

2 cups canned chick-peas which have been drained and mashed
½ teaspoon salt
¼ teaspoon hot pepper sauce
shortening for deep fat frying
¼ teaspoon pepper
2 cups fine dry bread crumbs
2 tablespoons melted shortening
2 eggs

To mashed chick-peas, add all ingredients except melted shortening and eggs. Stir thoroughly. Add eggs which have been beaten. Stir in melted shortening. Shape mix into balls about ½-¾ inch in diameter. Roll balls in crumbs. Fry a few at a time in deep hot fat for two or three minutes until golden brown. Remove with slotted spoon and dry on absorbent paper. Makes 15 balls.

TECHINA SAUCE FOR FALLAFEL

In a supermarket buy a can of techina sauce (sometimes called "tehina," it can usually be found in Jewish or exotic foods or health foods section) and dilute the contents with a little lemon juice and a little oil until consistency of thin sour cream has been achieved.

TO MAKE THE FALLAFEL

Cut off one end of the Syrian bread. You now have a pocket of bread. Fill this pocket with lettuce, tomatoes, cucumbers, hot fallafel balls, and techina sauce. A slice of pickle may be added to top off this ambrosia.

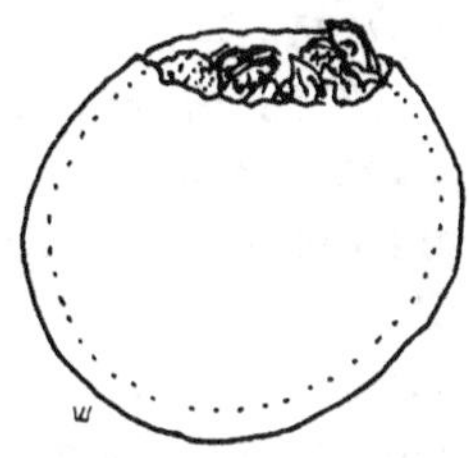

Houmous (an Israeli dip that is delicious with Syrian bread)

1 can chick-peas, drained
¼ can techina—sesame seed butter (¼ cup oil or other nut butters can be substituted for the techina)
lemon juice
1 clove crushed garlic

Mash chick-peas until smooth. Add techina and mix until all is smooth. Add lemon juice and garlic to taste.

Gefilte Fish (Ms. Siegel's recipe; makes about 10–12 pieces)

3 pounds white fish
2 medium onions
3 eggs
½ cup bread crumbs or matzah meal
1 cup water
¾ teaspoon salt
¼ teaspoon pepper (white preferably)

Grind the fish and onions together. Add all the other ingredients to the fish. Place in a wooden mixing bowl. Chop all ingredients until mixture is spongy and of a consistency to handle easily. Keep hands wet as fish is shaped into flat oval croquettes or into patties. Place into boiling fish stock, which should be kept boiling until all the fish balls are shaped and put into stock. Lower heat and cook for about 1½ hours. It will be noted that the stock will stop boiling as the fish balls are added to it. Do not add more fish until the stock comes to a boil again. In this way the gefilte fish will be easier to remove from the stock when they are finished cooking.

STOCK

fish skins and heads (eyes removed)
2 onions, quartered
2 carrots, scraped
1 tablespoon salt
½ teaspoon pepper

Clean fish skins and heads. Place in large kettle with onions, carrots, salt, and pepper. Add water to cover all the ingredients; the pot should be about half full. Bring to a boil, then simmer for two hours. Strain stock. Remove carrots to garnish the cooked fish. (This makes a very rich fish stock and may be diluted with water.)

NOTE: After fish is finished cooking, do not throw out fish stock. It is excellent used as a base for fish chowder. Add diced potatoes, celery, and any other vegetables as desired (peas, string beans, etc.) plus the carrots. Rice, barley, or farfel may be added to thicken chowder.

We're including Ms. Siegel's recipe for matzah balls. Actually what we're including is a recipe for knaidlech, but Ms. Siegel comes from Russia so we won't argue. Maybe they do it differently there.

Matzah balls

3 eggs, separated
1½ teaspoons salt
1–1½ cups matzah meal

Separate eggs. Beat yolks light and frothy. Beat whites stiff and dry. Fold whites carefully into yolks. Add ½ teaspoon salt. Add matzah meal very slowly to the egg mixture. Place in refrigerator for several hours. Bring large kettle of water to a rolling boil, add 1 teaspoon salt. Wet hands and shape matzah meal mixture into small balls about 1 inch in diameter. Add to boiling water. Don't add the matzah balls until the earlier ones surface. It is important not to add too many matzah balls at one time to the boiling water and to make sure that the water continues to boil. Cook for about half an hour. Remove from water with slotted spoon. (If mixture is too loose to shape, or if the matzah balls fall apart in the water, add small quantities of matzah meal until of proper consistency.)

This is Ms. Siegel's receipe for kreplach and they are light and delicious.

Kreplach (makes about 30 small kreplach)

DOUGH

1 cup flour
1 egg
pinch of salt
¼ cup water, (if you have no measuring cup, use an eggshell full of water)

Mix all ingredients well and set aside to rest.

FILLING

boiled chicken (usually left over from chicken soup) *or*
leftover brisket *or*
leftover boiled meat from vegetable soup
1 onion sautéed in margarine
1 egg
salt and pepper to taste

Grind or chop the meat and add the rest of the ingredients. (This also makes a delicious sandwich spread if you don't want to make kreplach.) Take part of the dough and add enough flour to roll it out very thin. If you don't have a rolling pin, you can use any round object: an empty wine bottle or even a full one will do, and if the kreplach don't come out good, you can always drink the wine.

Using a juice glass or cookie cutter about 1½ inches in diameter, cut circles out of the dough. Put together the dough that is left over with the unused dough and use it for the next batch. Put about a half teaspoon or small ball of filling in the middle of the circle and then paste the ends together in a semicircle and then draw the two ends together so that it forms somewhat of a circle.

After all the dough is filled, fill a large pot with water, add a teaspoon of salt, and bring it to a rolling boil. Drop the kreplach into the water. Do not drop more than twelve kreplach at a time into the water. Boil for about 20 minutes. If any dough is left over, roll it very thin, let it dry thoroughly, cut it in strips, and you will have noodles . . . delicious!

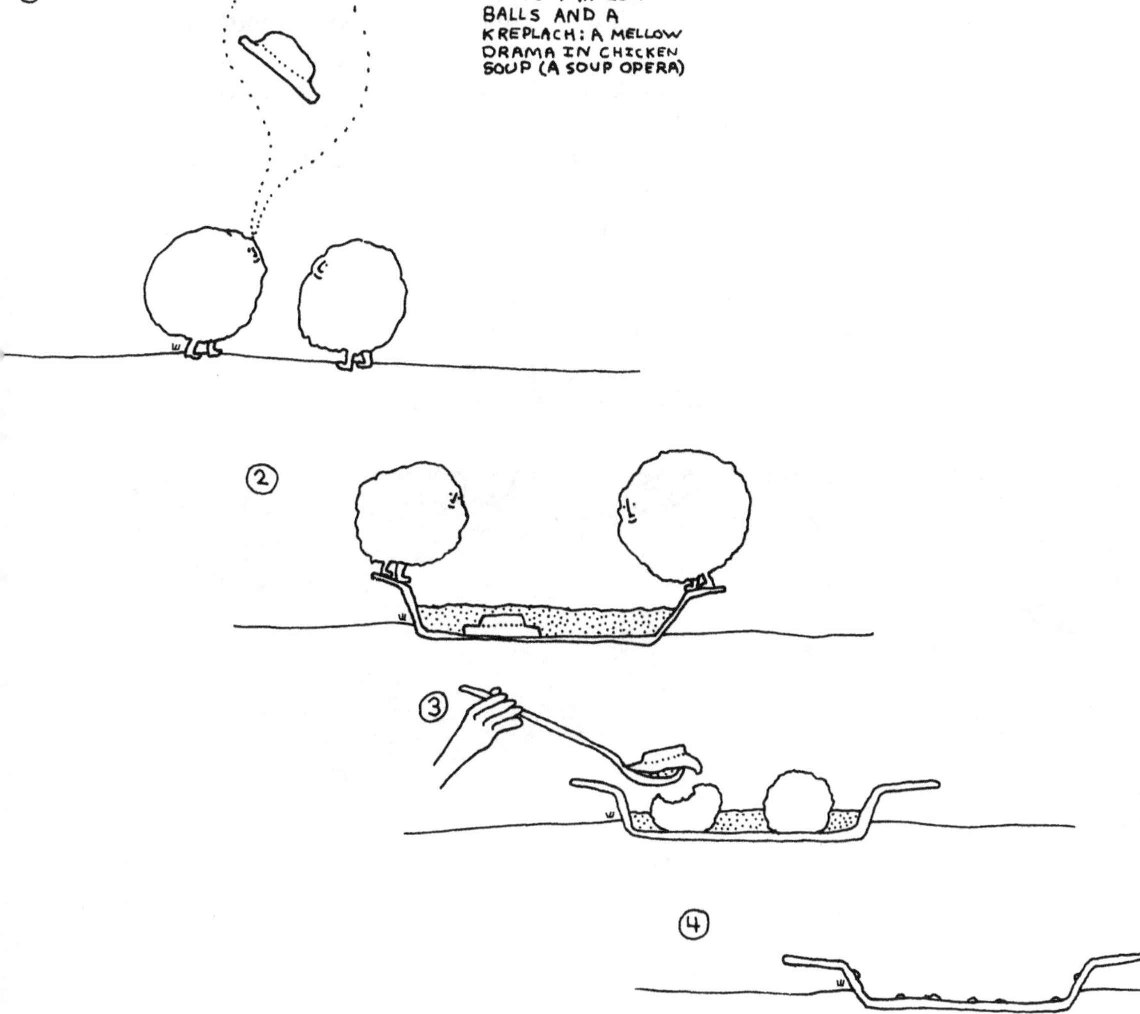

①
TWO MATZOH BALLS AND A KREPLACH: A MELLOW DRAMA IN CHICKEN SOUP (A SOUP OPERA)
②
③
④

For those initiatès into the mystique of Yiddish and its many variations, halipkes, halishkes, prakes, galuptze, and stuffed cabbage all mean what Eva calls "cabbage rolls." (Honestly, these Americans!)

Cabbage rolls (this recipe can serve 8 to 10 people)

Use two small healthy cabbages with greenish leaves. (This is crucial).

FILLING *(I don't use ground meat because I have become accustomed to cubed chuck and prefer it–but usually ground beef is used)*

3 or 4 onions diced
oil
3 or 4 garlic cloves diced
1½–2 pounds beef ground or cubed in small pieces (chuck is good)
¾ cup long-grained rice, preferably brown
about ½ tablespoon of salt
freshly ground pepper—about ¼ teaspoon
paprika
2 small cabbages
sauerkraut (optional)
onion, sliced
1 green pepper
¾ tablespoon salt
2 tablespoons brown sugar
tomato sauce or tomato paste

Sauté all those onions in oil, and when they are becoming translucent add the garlic cloves and sauté them also for 1 minute. Add the beef and the rice, and sauté these well until the meat is browned. Stir it well to blend the flavors. Season with spices and salt. When the filling is well sautéed, separate the cabbage into individual leaves and steam each leaf for about one minute (if the leaf is green, less than one minute). Fill the leaves (cut off any fibrous parts–veins or skin) with the filling, rolling it so that each bundle will remain secure. Use a very large pot–enameled is best; place chopped pieces of green cabbage on the bottom, then a layer of sauerkraut (this is original, but I like the flavor it adds), then add a layer of stuffed cabbage.

Add a sliced onion–not sautéed among the cabbage rolls. Cover with another layer of sauerkraut and raw cabbage and one sliced green pepper. Add water until the pot is ¾ full. Add ¾ tablespoon salt and 2 tablespoons brown sugar. If you don't use sauerkraut, add a tablespoon of vinegar or lemon juice. Bring water to a slow boil, and then simmer very slowly for one hour. Add tomato sauce or two cans of tomato paste. Simmer for ¾ hour. (You do this last part in 375° oven.) The rice will absorb the water and you should be left with a small amount of sauce only.

We've included the panacea to the ills of the world—Chicken Soup. Please! We know your mother makes it differently and hers is the best soup you've ever eaten. Nonetheless, this is a good basic recipe which so far has been proven to cure headache, flu, and asthma.

Chicken soup

one stewing chicken or portion thereof
1 tablespoon salt
1 onion
4 celery tops
2 carrots
2 bunches of parsley leaves
optional: for variety try some of the following additions:
1 beef bone or turkey giblet
1 garlic clove
1 parsnip
1 small potato
half a kohlrabi
a cluster of cauliflower

Clean the chicken. Cover the chicken in a pot (4–5 qts.) with water. Add salt and bring this to a boil. Simmer for an hour. Add the vegetables and simmer another hour. Let the soup stand until it gets cold and skim off the top.

WINE-MAKING—a little like your zaydeh used to do it

For everyone wanting to go back to the shtetl in one fashion or another, making sweet kosher wine is a relatively easy way to do it. All the equipment mentioned can be obtained by mail from:

Wine Art
4324 Geary Blvd.
San Francisco, Cal. 94118

but there may be a similar wine-making store in your ghetto, e.g.:

Wine Hobby U. S. A.
100 N. 9th St.
Allentown, Pa. 18102

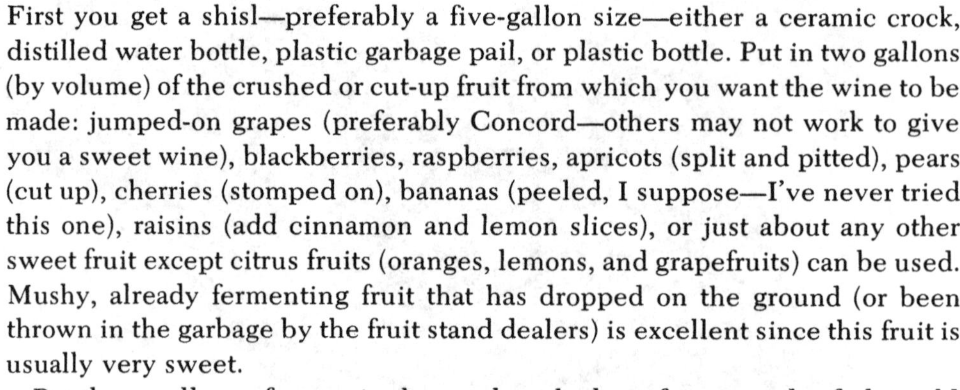

First you get a shisl—preferably a five-gallon size—either a ceramic crock, distilled water bottle, plastic garbage pail, or plastic bottle. Put in two gallons (by volume) of the crushed or cut-up fruit from which you want the wine to be made: jumped-on grapes (preferably Concord—others may not work to give you a sweet wine), blackberries, raspberries, apricots (split and pitted), pears (cut up), cherries (stomped on), bananas (peeled, I suppose—I've never tried this one), raisins (add cinnamon and lemon slices), or just about any other sweet fruit except citrus fruits (oranges, lemons, and grapefruits) can be used. Mushy, already fermenting fruit that has dropped on the ground (or been thrown in the garbage by the fruit stand dealers) is excellent since this fruit is usually very sweet.

Put three gallons of water in the crock with about four pounds of plain old granulated sugar. (Food freaks drop out here, since I can't find anything natural other than sugar which can be used to make good wine. Any suggestions on that score will be appreciated.) Stir up the mess and say an appropriate incantation. Sprinkle on top of this a package (about one ounce by weight) of *wine* yeast, *not* brewer's yeast, which is used for home brew beer.

NOTE: For Passover wine, don't put in any yeast but leave the wine-to-be exposed to the air, where it will pick up yeast and start fermenting on its own in a few days. Wine yeast is hametz for Pesah. Wine for Pesah also has to be kept away from any hametz, and there are other restrictions concerning the utensils you use, etc. Before embarking on the project of making kosher wine for Pesah, it is best to consult with a liberal Orthodox rabbi, preferably one that likes wine. The wine yeast yields a higher alcoholic content than the air variety, since what happens is that the sugar is changed to alcohol by the yeast, which then is killed off as the alcohol content reaches about 15% for the wine yeast but somewhat less for the air variety.

The wine people recommend that you put a trap on this mess. This trap can be just a tube with a one-hole stopper on one end and a glass full of water on the other. The stopper is put into your narrow-necked bottle (where else did you think, dummy) and this has the effect of letting the gases (mostly carbon dioxide) escape from the now foaming mess without letting oxygen in. I suppose that there is a reason for it (I once knew a girl who wrote a Ph.D. thesis on it—no kidding), but I've made wine with bottles trapped and untrapped with no perceptible difference. In fact, if you put enough love into the wine, and HaShem smiles on you, and it comes out good, there is no perceptible difference after a few glasses anyway. The trap also keeps the smell down, which is fine if you don't want your pad to smell like a brewery.

Getting back to the brewery, let it go bloop, bloop for about a week to ten days. Taste it and add sugar (about a cup at a time) if it starts getting sour—otherwise you will end up with wine vinegar, which is groovy too, but not the name of the game. After about ten days, you will have a smelly, cruddy-looking mess on top (the fruit) and a smelly, cruddy-looking mess on the bottom (the yeast). (This brings us to the true test of a wife or girl friend. If your woman will let you keep this mess in the kitchen, she is truly your soul mate and should be valued above all else.) It is best to siphon out the juice in the middle of the vat into another bottle. Otherwise the yeast taste will begin to affect the wine taste and confuse you. During the siphoning (and straining) operation, enough yeast will be carried over to the second vat to continue the fermentation process, since the yeasties are fertile little beasties. Again, trap the secondary fermentation jug if you want, and keep tasting and sweetening. Make a berakhah—you never can tell who is listening. What happens eventually is that the wine will be sweet (to your taste), alcoholic, and the trap will stop blooping. The end of fermentation is harder to determine if you use an open crock, but you can purchase a hydrometer to indicate the specific gravity of the wine (which is a measure of the fermentation process) or try (very difficult) to see any small bubbles in the fluid (absence of bubbles=end of fermentation).

This is the key part. It had better be *sweet, alcoholic,* and the *fermentation ended* or there will be a disaster. The fermentation process is exponential and I've waited two to three months for fermentation to end. (Keeping the vat in a warm area such as the kitchen or on a heated waterbed will speed up the process.) At this stage you are ready for bottling. Carefully siphon out the clear liquid (there will be some crud at the bottom of the secondary fermentation vat also) and bottle. Don't forget to make a fancy label. What I do is to siphon out the wine from the secondary five-gallon container to five one-gallon containers (apple-cider type) and let these sit for one day. This lets any stirred-up solids settle out where they can be seen and avoided. To play safe you can purchase some Campden tablets (sulphur dioxide) to put in (instructions are on the package) to kill any yeast which is not dead yet. However, if the thought of killing bugs you, then this step can be skipped if you have let the fermentation process run its course.

The wine is drinkable now but rough. Six months in a bottle mellows it considerably. I've used the above method to make delicious wine with a little love and prayer along with each step. Whatever you do, don't talk to anyone at the wine-making stores as they are the biggest bunch of fussbudgets I have ever seen. Good luck in your wine-making, and l'Chaim to all.

Marvin Jussoy
3169 Washington St.
San Francisco, Cal. 94115

P.S. To avoid legal hassles, fill out I. R. S. Form 1541 and mail it in. This form registers the wine you make for home family consumption only. I've never heard of any recent wine busts, however, and in the only case that I know that ever came to court, the judge fined the victim one dollar and asked for his recipe.

For other recipes check out one of the many excellent wine books now readily available. *Successful Wine Making at Home* by H. E. Bravery (Gramercy Publishing Co., New York) seems to be a concise, clear, uncomplicated, complete, and inexpensive book of this type (it is often found on remaindered-book shelves).

Although not as involving, the home wine-making kits are somewhat easier and may serve as a good starting point on a career of wine-making.

Larry Laufman of Havurat Shalom, long a friend of wine-makers, would offer this l'Chaim (in one breath) before drinking:

לְחַיִּים טוֹבִים, פַּרְנָסָה קַלָּה, כַּלְכָּלָה יָפָה, לִימוּדִים טוֹבִים, בְּחִינוֹת קַלּוֹת, כָּל טוּב, וּדְרִישַׁת שָׁלוֹם לַמִּשְׁפָּחָה.

"To a good life, easy work, nice employment, good studies, easy exams, goodness in everything, and regards to the family."

P. P. S. The best homemade wine I have ever tasted was made by Mordechai and Esther (he seemed to be a character out of Sholem Aleichem) who had a store at 9 David Allon Street, Jerusalem, near the main shuk (marketplace). The store was dirty and he poured the wine into a bottle from an old army gasoline can, but the wine was what Adam made Kiddush over on the first Shabbat. Since my Hebrew and Yiddish were nonexistent and Mordechai wasn't doing English, we couldn't communicate, but there will be a reward for anyone getting his recipe to me.

RETREATS: food and advice

In the last few years it has become very important to some people to "retreat" every now and then for a Shabbat or a few days. Basically a retreat involves a small group of people who go away to the country (although sometimes they're held in the city at someone's house) to pray, eat, play, talk, and relax together. If planned in advance—and that means *both* program and food—it can be a wonderfully relaxing, learning, living kind of experience. If you are thinking about trying it, some possible places to consider are Ramah camps, most or all of which are winterized, or Christian retreat houses, which can frequently be rented at a reasonable fee.

Retreat food planning:

The important thing to remember on retreats is to think simple. Don't plan elaborate menus and don't get headaches about it. Incidentally, it is of value to remember that all the food contained herein can be made ahead and warmed up later. Thinking simple might include a meal of a few selections from the following list:

baked potatoes
cheese
egg salad
tuna salad
yogurt salad (recipe follows)
eggplant salad (recipe follows)
cauliflower and broccoli casserole
cottage cheese
macaroni salad
potato and cheese casserole
cole slaw
vegetable salad
potato salad

Big one-meal-in-a-pot things include:

cholent
tzimmes
stew
chicken pies, tuna pies
chicken and rice
eggplant parmigiana
cheese and lukshen kugel (recipe follows)
koos koos

Other possibilities:

ITALIAN MEAL
spaghetti
homemade meatless sauce
cheese
big salad
hot Italian bread
fruit or melon in season

CHINESE MEAL
rice
chow mein or Chinese vegetables
chow mein noodles
soy sauce
fortune cookies

YOGURT SALAD (30-35 people, give or take a couple)

2 or 3 superlarge containers of yogurt
6 unpeeled apples cut up into small pieces
4 bananas in small slices
1 cup raisins
1 cup walnuts, chopped
honey to taste

Mix this all up and refrigerate.

EGGPLANT SALAD (30–35 people)

6 eggplants
4 onions
6–8 hardboiled eggs (optional)
mayonnaise

Pierce eggplants with a fork and bake in 350° oven for an hour until soft. Peel immediately. Chop fine. Add one chopped onion and six chopped eggs. Sauté three onions until brown and add. Add about two tablespoons of mayonnaise, more if needed. Can be eaten with black or whole wheat bread.

LUKSHEN KUGEL (8 people; multiply accordingly)

There are a million ways to make kugel. This is a milchik recipe containing plenty of protein, so that with a salad this can be a fine meal.

1 pound wide egg noodles
6–8 eggs
sugar to taste
¼ cup oil
1 small container (1 pound) cottage cheese
6–8 slices American cheese
salt
optional: ¾ cup raisins
2 unpeeled apples cut up in small pieces
¾ cup chopped walnuts

Boil noodles in salted water until soft. Drain and rinse with cold water. Add six beaten eggs, sugar, and rest of ingredients. Mix thoroughly. Put in well-oiled casserole. Bake at 350° for 50 minutes until set. May be eaten warm or cold.

SALAD (for 25 people)

2 heads lettuce
5 or 6 tomatoes
3 cucumbers
3 peppers

Some advice about retreats

1. Try to make cleanups and meal preparation as simple as possible. Depending on how strongly you feel about ecology, it may be reasonable to think about using aluminum foil, disposable pans, and/or paper dishes.

2. Don't forget to bring such staples as:
   coffee, tea
   sugar
   salt
   spices
   knives, vegetable peelers, serving utensils, and any other kitchenware to cook with.

3. If you are doing a Shabbat retreat, remember to provide for Kiddush cup, hallah cover, candles, prayer books, wine, hallot, and any other religious paraphernalia you might need.

4. Depending on how you organize it, cooking at home and bringing prepared food to the retreat is often an excellent idea. It saves some people spending lots of time in the kitchen when they might prefer to be basket-weaving or meditating.

5. Again, depending on how you prefer to organize it, a suggestion from Havurat Shalom. Set up a work list before you get to the retreat so that three or four different people are responsible for every meal. Responsible means cooking, setting tables, serving, and cleaning up. They also use a final worksheet on the last night of a retreat. Every person has one job (some jobs may require more than one person), and the retreat center can be left as spotless as it was when you got there. Jobs can range from sweeping floors to packing away food and cleaning stoves, etc.

6. People like to "nosh" on retreats. Remember to get fresh fruits, dried fruits, raisins, nuts, cookies, etc.—whatever people dig.

One last thing—retreats are really wonderful inventions. Enjoy.

BIBLIOGRAPHY FOR KASHRUT

1. Dresner, Samuel H., and Siegel, Seymour. *The Jewish Dietary Laws.* New York: Burning Bush, 1959.

In general, a clearcut approach to the observance of kashrut. The "Guide to Observance" section is especially well written and provides an easy reference guide for the basic Jewish laws.

2. Freedman, Seymour E. *The Book of Kashruth.* New York: Bloch Publishing Co., 1970.

This book is an interesting combination of an Orthodox approach interspersed with knowledge of the Conservative deviations from that approach. This is a good book for learning about the history of kashrut and frauds and fantasies in kashrut. Also includes an excellent list of colleges and universities where kosher food is available. This is not the best book to choose for a simple guide to observance but the material that is dealt with is covered coherently and with humor.

3. Kitov, Eliyahu. *The Jew and His Home.* New York: Shengold Publishers, Inc., 1963.

A strictly fundamentalist approach to Judaism. Very self-righteous and rather preachy in tone, it is, nonetheless, authoritative. Not the easiest or best reading on this subject.

4. Levi, Shonie B., and Kaplan, Sylvia R. *Guide for the Jewish Homemaker.* New York: Schocken, 1964. The cloth edition was published under the title *Across the Threshold: A Guide for the Jewish Homemaker.*

The authors have a warm and sensitive approach to their material. This book covers everything from kashrut to holidays to camps to recipes. A thoroughly approachable book.

5. Gordon, Rabbi Irwin, and Geller, Victor B. *Kashruth.* New York: Union of Orthodox Jewish Congregations of America, 1965.

A short Orthodox approach to kashrut. Gives a clear picture, although the rationale for the laws is omitted.

6. Kemelman, Rabbi Dr. Y. *A Guide to the Jewish Dietary Laws.* The Central Synagogue, Jewish Pocket Library. Sydney, Australia.

Brief and to the point, this pamphlet has a very traditional approach to the material.

There are many Jewish cookbooks on the market. Most are reasonably good. One of the best sources for Jewish recipes is the Sisterhood cookbooks that so many congregations publish. These invariably contain a variety of easy and practical dishes. What's more, if a recipe doesn't work out for you, you can always call the lady whose recipe you used and vent your spleen immediately.

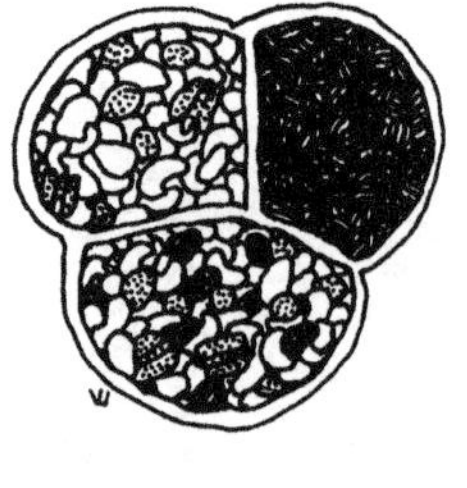

Two excellent commercial cookbooks are:

1. Grossinger, Jennie. *The Art of Jewish Cooking.* New York: Bantam Books, 1958.

This contains a variety of good, easy, and delicious traditional Jewish foods. A classic cookbook that really does belong in any home.

2. Kasdan, Sarah. *Love and Knishes.* New York: The Vanguard Press, 1957.

A cute book that contains at least as many stories as it does recipes. Good for light reading and you'll learn something about Jewish cooking along the way.

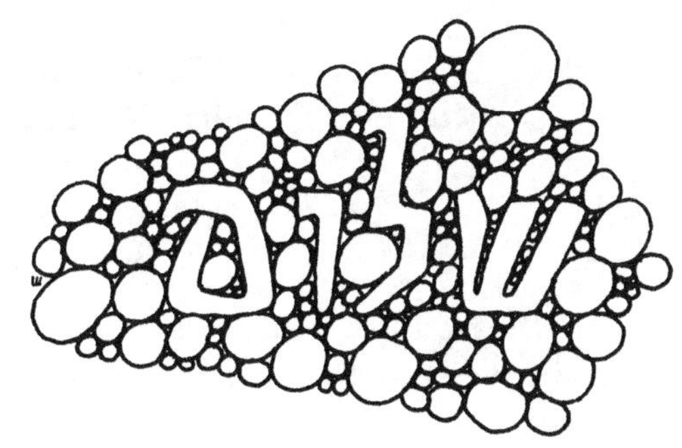

Hallah

INTRODUCTION

Hallah is the traditional braided bread eaten on Shabbat and holidays. Recently the new awareness and concern for doing things naturally and simply has led many of us back to the timeless tradition of baking our own hallah for Shabbat. Fresh warm hallah is food for the gods. The smooth, even texture and warm, rich taste call up visions of Shabbat as the "taste of the world-to-come."

If you have ever baked bread, hallah is not any more difficult. As a preface to the perfect warmth and tranquillity of Shabbat, there is no better activity. Hallah baking draws you in to the world of Shabbat, demanding your presence, urging you on in anticipation and love. The dough requires love, warmth, and caring—and somehow hallah made this way has no equal.

LAWS AND CUSTOMS ABOUT HALLAH

1. In the Torah, there is a mitzvah (law) that the rosh—head—of the dough be separated and given to the priests.
2. Since the destruction of the Temple we have fulfilled this mitzvah by removing from the dough a small piece, about the size of an olive, before baking.
3. This portion is burnt in the oven, both in lieu of giving it to the priests and also as a contemporary sacrifice. We diminish our joy in memory of the destruction of the Temple.
4. The word hallah means dough, and refers specifically to the bread from which the dough has been separated.
5. Only breads made from five specific grains need be separated: wheat, barley, maize, spelt, and oats. In Europe, where these were the grains of the rich man's bread, hallah came to be eaten only on Shabbat and festivals. Even the poor are rich on Shabbat. The custom has remained of eating hallah only on Shabbat and festivals.
6. As the hallah is separated and a piece of it thrown into the oven, the following blessing is recited:

"Blessed are You, Lord our God, King of the Universe, who has sanctified us with His commandments and commanded us to separate hallah."

בָּרוּךְ אַתָּה, יְיָ אֱלֹהֵינוּ, מֶלֶךְ הָעוֹלָם, אֲשֶׁר קִדְּשָׁנוּ
בְּמִצְוֹתָיו, וְצִוָּנוּ לְהַפְרִישׁ חַלָּה:

7. If one has forgotten to separate the dough before the hallah is baked, a piece can be broken off and discarded later.

8. Since the destruction of the Temple, the table of the Jew has been his altar. We use two hallot which reflect the shewbreads of the Temple. These also reflect the double portion of manna which was received in the desert on Fridays to provide for Shabbat, when no manna fell.

9. Before breaking and eating them, the hallot are blessed as follows:

"Blessed are you, Lord our God, King of the Universe, who takes bread out of the earth."

בָּרוּךְ אַתָּה, יְיָ אֱלֹהֵינוּ, מֶלֶךְ הָעוֹלָם, הַמּוֹצִיא לֶחֶם מִן הָאָרֶץ:

10. Knives on the table may be covered before this blessing. There is a tradition not to use a hallah knife at all on Friday night as a reflection of Isaiah's prophecy: "And they shall beat their swords into plowshares and their spears into pruning hooks" (Isaiah 2:4). In addition, the stone altar consecrated to God was not built of hewn stones, "for by wielding your tools upon them you have profaned them" (Exodus 20:22). Rather than cut the hallah with a knife—a weapon of war—which thereby profanes the altar and the offering, the custom has developed to break the hallah apart with your hands.

11. After the blessing and before eating the hallah, one should salt the bread. This both reflects the Temple sacrifices ritual and recalls that "by the sweat of your brow shall you get bread to eat" (Genesis 3:19).

12. There is a custom not to hand the pieces of bread directly to those at the table, but rather to put them on a plate and pass the plate around, or to place each piece of bread on the person's plate. It is not from man that we receive our bread.

13. When the blessing is made over the wine, the hallah should be kept covered. It is sensitive and may be offended by being placed second to the wine. A story is told about a famous rabbi who once visited a man for Shabbat. The man, trying to impress the rabbi, set out an elaborate meal in honor of Shabbat. He became annoyed when he noticed his wife had forgotten the hallah cover, and he began to berate her. The rabbi turned to the man and rebuked him, saying, "The purpose of covering the hallah is to shield its sensitive feelings. This teaches us concern for the feeling of even inanimate objects. How much more so should we be sensitive to another human being!"

14. Some have the custom of sprinkling poppy or sesame seeds on the hallah before it is baked. This symbolizes the manna which fell in the desert.

Basic hallah recipe

RECIPE # 1

This classic hallah recipe is from Jeanette Schreiber of Seattle, Washington. It is quite simple and most *reliable, producing lovely, even-textured loaves for every Shabbat.*

½ cup oil	2 packages dry yeast
4 teaspoons salt	⅓ cup warm water
1 tablespoon sugar	3 eggs
1 cup boiling water	7 cups flour
½ cup cold water	sesame or poppy seeds

Pour the oil, salt, and sugar into a large mixing bowl. Add 1 cup boiling water and stir; add ½ cup cold water. Dissolve 2 packages dry yeast in ⅓ cup warm water. Beat 3 eggs, and add to oil and water mixture, saving 1 tablespoon of beaten egg to be brushed on loaves before baking. Add dissolved yeast and stir. Add seven cups of unbleached flour and mix well.

Turn out on floured board and knead until dough does not stick to board or

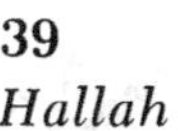

hands. Add more flour if necessary. Return dough to bowl and cover with a clean towel. Place in oven that has been preheated for 1 minute and then turned off. Let dough rise for 1 hour; it will double in bulk. If poked with finger, the hole will remain.

Turn dough out on lightly floured board and knead for about 1 minute. Cut into 12 equal pieces and knead each piece with a little flour until it is not sticky. Let rest while you grease a cookie sheet with vegetable shortening. Roll each piece of dough into a strand about 8 inches long. Make four braided loaves.

Place on baking sheet and let rise for 45 minutes at room temperature. Brush tops of loaves with beaten egg and sprinkle with sesame or poppy seeds. Bake in 375° oven for 40 minutes; remove loaves to racks to cool.

Extra loaves may be stored in the freezer. Frozen loaves should be thawed and placed in the oven for 5 to 10 minutes to restore their fresh flavor.

Shabbat Shalom!

RECIPE #2

The following is the Sharon Strassfeld adaptation of the Kathy Green adaptation of the Terri Sokol hallah recipe. It is a very rich, very moist variety of hallah.

2 cups lukewarm water
3 packages yeast
8 cups flour
1½ cups sugar
1½ teaspoons salt
2 sticks (½ pound) margarine or butter
5 eggs, beaten (reserve one for glaze)

Mix water and yeast in a superhuge bowl. Add three cups flour and 1 cup sugar. Stir with a fork and let rise a half hour in a warm place.

Meanwhile, in another bowl measure in five cups of flour, salt, and half a cup of sugar. Add margarine and cut in with a knife until mixture resembles coarse meal. At end of half hour, add 4 beaten eggs to yeast mixture and stir well. (Mix will decrease in volume.) Add flour-margarine mixture to yeast mixture and work in bowl. If sticky, add up to two more cups of flour. Knead well on floured board until smooth and elastic. Put in oiled bowl and cover with towel. Put in warm place and let rise two hours (or until doubled). Punch down. Knead lightly for a minute or two.

Divide dough into parts (depending on how many hallot you want). This recipe makes:

4 smallish-medium loaves
3 medium loaves
2 large loaves
1 superhugie wedding special

Braid the loaves. Place in oiled loaf pans. Cover and let rise in warm place as long as possible *(3 or 4 or 5 hours is fine.) THIS IS IMPORTANT: the longer you let it rise (being careful not to kill the yeast), the lighter your loaves will be. When it is done rising, brush top with beaten egg and bake at 350°for 45 minutes.*

Hints and variations: notes on successful hallah-baking

1. I often begin making hallah at seven or eight on Thursday night. By eleven P.M. the loaves are braided and ready for the final rising. You can leave the covered loaf pans in your unheated oven overnight for the final rising IF you have no pilot light burning and IF you bake the loaves by 7:30 the next morning. By experimentation I have learned that the yeast dies shortly after 7:30 (it smothers in too much air, I've been told) and your bread will be like concrete if you bake it after that time.
2. You can also make bubka from this recipe. Instead of braiding the loaves, mix together about half a cup of a cinnamon sugar mixture and spread this on a flattened slab of dough. Sprinkle liberally with raisins and roll up as for jelly roll. Pinch ends together to form a smooth circle of bread and let rise as usual. Instead of glazing with egg, spread with margarine and a little cinnamon and sugar.
3. More sugar can be added for sweeter hallah.
4. Use unbleached flour. You'll find that bread made from bleached flour looks washed out when compared with the healthier hue of unbleached-flour bread.
5. If you have an oilcloth table covering, don't bother to use a board for kneading. Simply scrub your oilcloth very well and sprinkle liberally with flour before kneading bread.
6. A good way to insure an even and symmetrical braid is to weigh the individual strands on a kitchen scale before braiding.
7. About kneading: the most successful kneading involves not only your hands and arms, but your whole body, and we're convinced that the rhythmic sway that accompanies the most serious kneading enriches the final product.
8. Debby Fine suggests the following baking times for various sizes of loaves at 350°:
   4 medium: 30 minutes
   3 medium-large: 30–45 minutes
   2 big-hugies: 45–50 minutes
   1 supergigantic: 50–55 minutes
9. Josh Heckelman discovered this variation: instead of eggs, use 1 tablespoon liquid lecithin, and make a flour mixture of 1 part whole wheat flour, 1 part whole wheat pastry flour, and a pinch of soy flour.
10. For a delightful variation to all the hallah recipes above, add raisins or currants during first kneading.

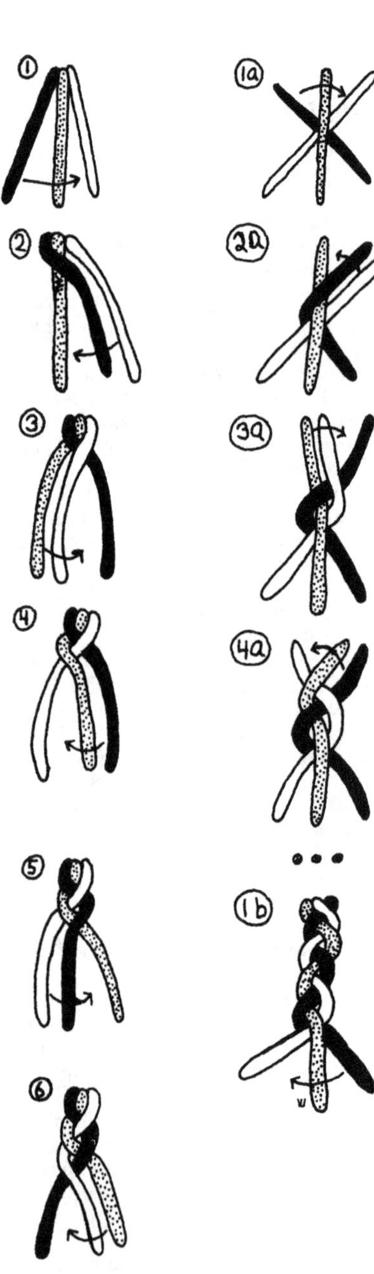

Braiding

Braiding allows for the expression of your artistic abilities. The first enjoyment of the baked hallah is visual—the browned crust, the shiny glaze, and the voluptuous curves of the interlocking braids. Each person relates to this phase uniquely, bringing to it his mood, personality, and fancy. The varieties of braiding forms listed here represent a basic structure, and serve only to give an indication of what the hallah may finally look like. Ultimately, your personal touches and the spirits of the oven will determine the beauty, smell, texture, and taste of your bread.

Basic three-strand braid Divide dough into three parts. Roll each into a long snake of even thickness. Then pinch together the ends and braid as you do hair; *or* overlap braids in the center and braid toward the ends. This gives a more symmetrical figure to the bread.

Round Form the three-strand braid into a spiral form and pinch together the ends.

Braiding with a crown (a) For long hallah: on top of a long three-strand braid, place a smaller one.
(b) For round hallah: form unbraided dough into a circle; place a small three-strand braid in a circle on top of the round.

Birds Divide dough into 8 parts (half recipe; 16 parts for whole recipe). Roll each part into 6-inch snakes.

Flatten long end and slice like feathers. On short end pinch out beak and put two whole cloves or allspice for eyes. Brush with diluted egg yolk and baste till brown. Fun for kids or to use on round High Holiday hallot.

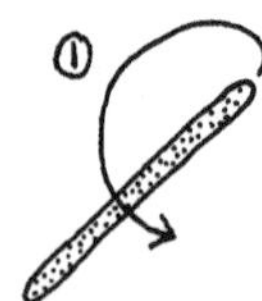

Hallah covers: some suggestions

1. Karen Abromovitz suggests a variety of methods. Her first is a very easy one. Simply take a square of permanent press cloth with a pretty pattern and fringe the edges (ravel about 1 inch around).

2. If you use a piece of satin, Karen suggests the following method. Draw out a design on paper. Use carbon paper and trace directly onto the satin. One fun idea is drawing "open" Hebrew letters:

These can then be decorated on the inside of the letters with flowers, leaves, insects, animals, designs, etc. Karen made one hallah cover decorated with a lamed which became an enormous kneeling lion. Your imagination is your limit. Finish it off with a lining (cotton or Dacron blend) to keep it from sliding off the hallah. Attach the lining thus:

a. Put lining and cover right sides together and sew around, leaving opening on one side.

b. Trim seams to ¼ inch and cut corners diagonally.

c. Turn right-side-out and press.

d. You can, if you wish, sew commercial fringe around the edges. Otherwise, with a blind stitch, close the opening.

3. For needlepoint hallah covers, draw a design on graph paper. Work out the design with each square equaling one stitch on canvas. Line with satin or corduroy (blends would be too light). You will not need fringe or, in fact, any other decoration. Experiment with pattern needlepoint stitches.

4. To do needlepoint on other material, take canvas and baste carefully to cloth—velvet, satin, brocade, etc. Work the design and then carefully remove canvas by pulling it out strand by strand from the "underwork." Line as for satin hallah cover and fringe if you wish.

5. Dona Rosenblatt suggests embroidering as you would over satin, but instead use a piece of material you have tie-dyed earlier. For tie-dyeing, use white or off-white cotton or synthetic material. Follow the instructions on the dye package (use Rit or any other commercial dye). One thing to remember is that once you put one color over another, you will get a combination of the two, so plan accordingly (e.g., red over yellow gives you orange).

6. Dona also recommends block printing your hallah cover. Cut a linoleum tile or a potato as you would to print on paper. Use non-water-soluble printing ink, or Inko dye (a specially prepared textile dye).

7. You can also use Inko dyes for hand painting a design on a piece of fabric. When using Inko dyes, be sure to follow the directions explicitly.

8. Finally, Dona suggests you might try batik. Many crafts books have batik instruction but you should use the wax-resist batik method.

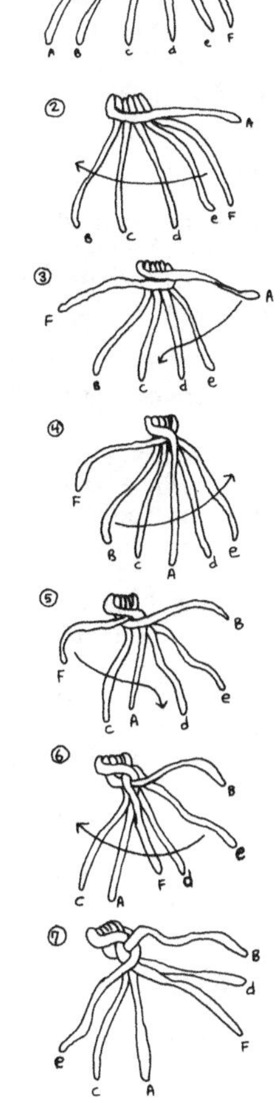

4 braid

basic Rule- under two, over one alternating outermost strands on the right and left

① 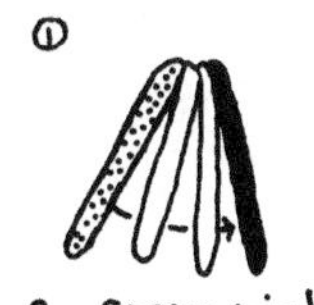
under 2 from right

② 
over 1

③ 
under 2 from left

④ 
over one

⑤ 
begin again

Candles and candle-making

וְהָיָה בָּעֵת הַהִיא אֲחַפֵּשׂ
אֶת־יְרוּשָׁלַםִ בַּנֵּרוֹת

"And it shall come to pass at that time, that I will search Jerusalem with lamps" (Zephaniah 1:12).

As a ceremonial object or art, the candle is generally overlooked; yet it has great significance. Whether intended for practical purposes—such as providing light—or for more evocative, quasi-magical ends—such as rekindling the winter sun—almost every festival and celebration incorporates the use of candles at some point.

Fire is universally recognized as one of the basic elements of the world. It is mysterious, frightening, mesmerizing. Its attraction is almost irresistible. (See *Psychoanalysis of Fire* by Gaston Bachelard, Beacon Press Paperback, 1964.) In the Kabbalah, the image of a multicolored flame emanating from a candle is taken as a metaphor for God's relation to the world and man. The flame is a single entity, yet it appears to be undergoing constant change. The flame adheres to, relies on, and appears to emanate from the candle, yet is a distinct and separate entity. The white interior of the flame is constant, but its exterior is always in motion and changes color.

Reducing fire to a few metaphors, however, robs it of its natural power and mystique. Fortunately the tradition, by incorporating the lighting of candles into the celebratory cycle in a number of different ways, left open the possibilities for recognizing the many potentialities of fire. It is for us to rediscover those potentialities and allow them to "illumine our eyes."

Prayer of a Jewish Woman before Lighting the Candles

O God of Your people Israel:
You are holy
And You have made the Sabbath and the people of Israel holy.
You have called upon us to honor the Sabbath with light,
With joy
And with peace—
As a king and queen give love to one another;
As a bride and her bridegroom—
So have we kindled these two lights for love of your daughter,
The Sabbath day.
Almighty God,
Grant me and all my loved ones
A chance to truly rest on this Sabbath day.
May the light of the candles drive out from among us
The spirit of anger, the spirit of harm,
Send Your blessings to my children,
That they may walk in the ways of Your Torah, Your light.
May You ever be their God
And mine, O Lord,
My Creator and my Redeemer.
Amen.
—Translated from the Yiddish by Arthur Green

SHABBAT CANDLES

1. On Friday night, one is required to light candles *in the house* for the sake of shalom bayit (harmony in the home) and oneg Shabbat (Sabbath Joy). The candles ought to be in the room where the Sabbath meal is to be eaten.

2. It is the woman who lights the candles, but men may light them when no woman is present.

3. Candles may be lit, at the earliest, 1¼ hours before sunset (see The Calendar), but the usual time is up to 18 minutes before sunset. Check a Jewish calendar for precise time of sunset (see The Calendar). If the time limit cannot be met, candles may be lit during the 18 minutes immediately preceding sunset.

4. At least two candles must be lit. These represent " שָׁמוֹר " and " זָכוֹר ": the first words of the commandments concerning Shabbat (Exodus 20:8; Deuteronomy 5:12). They also symbolize the unity underlying all apparent duality, such as man and woman, body and soul, speech and silence, creation and revelation.

5. It is permissible to light more than two candles. In fact, it is considered particularly meritorious to do so. This is implied in an interpretation on "And God blessed the seventh day: What did he bless it with? Light."

6. Some people light an additional candle for each child in the family. Once you've lit a certain number, it is a custom never to decrease that number.

7. Students away from home should light candles for themselves, as they are no longer within the household of their parents.

8. The ritual of lighting candles involves:
   a. the actual lighting of the candles
   b. drawing the hands around the candles and toward the face—from one to seven times (three is most common)
   c. covering the eyes with the hands
   d. saying the blessing

9. The halakhah for this is a bit complicated. A blessing must be said *before* an act. However, since the blessing over the Shabbat candles is also the act which initiates Shabbat, it is forbidden to light a fire after the blessing is said. To get over this bind, one lights the candles and then covers one's eyes while saying the blessing. When the eyes are opened, the already lit candles are enjoyed for the first time, as it were, therefore both completing the blessing and not violating the Shabbat.

10. There are several intentions associated with the waving of the hands around the candles: it serves to usher in the Shabbat Bride (see Shabbat) as the light of Shabbat fills the room and surrounds the person; it symbolizes the culmination of the six days of creation into the seventh day of rest; it draws the warmth and light inside oneself.

11. After saying the blessing, you can softly utter prayers for yourself or others.

12. You should make use of the light (e.g., by eating or reading by it); otherwise it is a wasted and invalidated blessing.

13. If there are no candles available, you can make the blessing over electric lights or gas (e.g., camping lanterns).

14. Candles are lit on all yomim tovim and Yom Kippur. The blessing for Shabbat is:

"Blessed are You, Lord our God, King of the Universe, who has sanctified us with His commandments, and commanded us to light the Shabbat candles."

בָּרוּךְ אַתָּה, יְיָ אֱלֹהֵינוּ, מֶלֶךְ הָעוֹלָם, אֲשֶׁר קִדְּשָׁנוּ
בְּמִצְוֹתָיו, וְצִוָּנוּ לְהַדְלִיק נֵר שֶׁל־שַׁבָּת:

The blessing for yom tov is:

"Blessed are You, Lord our God, King of the Universe, who has sanctified us with His commandments and commanded us to light the holiday candles."

בָּרוּךְ אַתָּה, יְיָ אֱלֹהֵינוּ, מֶלֶךְ הָעוֹלָם, אֲשֶׁר קִדְּשָׁנוּ
בְּמִצְוֹתָיו, וְצִוָּנוּ לְהַדְלִיק נֵר שֶׁל (On Friday add שַׁבָּת וְ) יוֹם
טוֹב:

The blessing for Yom Kippur is:

"Blessed are You, Lord our God, King of the Universe, who has sanctified us with His commandments and commanded us to light the Yom Kippur candles."

בָּרוּךְ אַתָּה, יְיָ אֱלֹהֵינוּ, מֶלֶךְ הָעוֹלָם, אֲשֶׁר קִדְּשָׁנוּ
בְּמִצְוֹתָיו, וְצִוָּנוּ לְהַדְלִיק נֵר שֶׁל (On Friday add שַׁבָּת וְשֶׁל)
יוֹם הַכִּפּוּרִים:

HAVDALAH

1. Since light cannot be lit throughout all of Shabbat or Yom Kippur, the conclusion of these days and their separation from all others is marked by the lighting of candles. Since fire can be lit from fire on yom tov, there is no lighting of candles at the conclusion of those days.

2. You need an avukah—torch—e.g., a candle with at least two wicks because it gives off a lot of light. This signifies, as well, the final bringing together of the separate lights lit on Erev Shabbat.

3. The blessing recited during the service is:

"Blessed are You, Lord our God, King of the Universe, Creator of the light of the fire."

בָּרוּךְ אַתָּה, יְיָ אֱלֹהֵינוּ, מֶלֶךְ הָעוֹלָם, בּוֹרֵא מְאוֹרֵי הָאֵשׁ:

4. While saying the blessing, it is customary to look at the palms, hands, and nails in the light of the candles. Some bend the fingers over the palms in order to see both. Several reasons have been offered for this custom:

a. Being able to differentiate between palm and nails is a sign that there is enough light.

b. Nails are a sign of blessing because they are continually growing.

c. The neshamah yetairah—"super" soul—which each person receives on Shabbat leaves from the nails and you should be aware of it for the longest time possible.

d. The interplay of shadow and light between the palm and the nails is a symbolic parallel of the havdalah (separation) between Shabbat and the weekdays. If the hands are cupped so that the light hits the nails, then the palms will be in shadow.

5. After the Havdalah Service, pour out a little wine and extinguish the candle in it. This shows that the candle was lit specifically for the mitzvah of the Havdalah Service.

6. If you do not have a Havdalah candle, use the stars.

7. If you have neither a Havdalah candle nor stars, you can put together two single candles or two matches (if they are long enough and you can pray fast enough). Electric light and gas lights may also be used if necessary. (See Shabbat for more about Havdalah.)

HANUKKAH CANDLES

1. The Hanukkah candles should be lit on each of the eight nights of the festival.

2. Either wax candles or oil lamps can be used for the lights.

3. Process of lighting:

a. Although there is a talmudic dispute regarding this, the now accepted custom is to increase the candles from one to eight as the festival progresses. (Obviously, the other opinion was to decrease from eight to one. However, since we should be constantly increasing joy and light in the world, rather than diminishing it, the former opinion is superior.)

b. The candles should be placed in the menorah beginning from the right side and moving to the left with each day.

c. Light the shammash (an additional candle used to light the others) and recite the two blessings:

"Blessed are You, Lord our God, King of the Universe, who has sanctified us with His commandments and commanded us to kindle the light of Hanukkah."

בָּרוּךְ אַתָּה, יְיָ אֱלֹהֵינוּ, מֶלֶךְ הָעוֹלָם, אֲשֶׁר קִדְּשָׁנוּ בְּמִצְוֹתָיו, וְצִוָּנוּ לְהַדְלִיק נֵר שֶׁל חֲנֻכָּה:

"Blessed are You, Lord our God, King of the Universe, who performed miracles for our fathers in those days, at this time."

בָּרוּךְ אַתָּה, יְיָ אֱלֹהֵינוּ, מֶלֶךְ הָעוֹלָם, שֶׁעָשָׂה נִסִּים לַאֲבוֹתֵינוּ, בַּיָּמִים הָהֵם, בַּזְּמַן הַזֶּה:

d. On the first night recite:

"Blessed are You, Lord our God, King of the Universe, who has granted us life and sustenance and permitted us to reach this season."

בָּרוּךְ אַתָּה, יְיָ אֱלֹהֵינוּ, מֶלֶךְ הָעוֹלָם, שֶׁהֶחֱיָנוּ, וְקִיְּמָנוּ, וְהִגִּיעָנוּ לַזְּמַן הַזֶּה:

e. Light the candles with the shammash from left to right—so that the new candle is lit first.

f. Place the shammash in its special holder on the menorah.

g. It is customary to say/sing "Ha-Nerot Halalu," "We kindle these lights . . ." and "Maoz Tzur," "Rock of Ages"—following the lighting.

4. According to some authorities, each person in a household should light his own candles. Traditionally, women as well as men are obligated to light Hanukkah candles.

5. It was customary to light the candles in the doorway, but now they are commonly lit in a window facing the street. This should be on the opposite side of the doorway from the mezuzah. Lighting by a window or in the doorway is based both on a common custom of midwinter fire festivals, and on the principle of pirsum ha-nes—making known the miracle. In either case, it is important that people passing by be able to see the lights and know by their number which night it is.

6. The candles should be lit soon after sunset; if necessary, one can light them anytime during the night.

7. They should burn for at least half an hour.

8. The light of the Hanukkah candles should not be used for any purpose. (See margin, "We kindle these lights. . . .")

We kindle these lights on account of the miracles, wonders, and deliverances which You performed for our fathers in those days at this time, by means of Your holy priests. These lights are sacred throughout all the eight days of Hanukkah; we are not permitted to make any use of them; but we are only to look at them, in order to give thanks to Your great Name for Your miracles, deliverances, and wonders.

9. On Friday night the Hanukkah lights are kindled before the Shabbat candles. On Saturday night the Hanukkah lights are kindled before Havdalah in the synagogue, but at home Havdalah is said first.

10. Forty-four candles are needed for the entire festival. You can buy the candles at Hebrew bookstores or through a local synagogue. Or they can be made quite easily (see below).

(See Festivals for more on Hanukkah.)

NER TAMID—ETERNAL LIGHT:

The children of Israel were commanded to set up a menorah in the desert Tabernacle and to maintain a light there constantly (or regularly). This commandment was then transferred to the Temple in Jerusalem. Now it applies to the synagogue, which is referred to as a "lesser Temple" (Megillah 29a).

"You shall further instruct the Israelites to bring you clear oil of beaten olives for lighting, for kindling lamps regularly [or: for kindling lamps always]. Aaron and his sons shall set them up in the Tent of Meeting, outside the curtain which is over the Pact, [to burn] from evening to morning before the Lord. It shall be a due from the Israelites for all time, throughout the ages" (Exodus 27:20-21; Leviticus 24:2-4).

The eternal light should be lit either on the west side of the synagogue—or, as is the contemporary custom, in front of the holy ark. Minimally, the light should be lit during times of prayer. Maximally, of course, it should burn continually.

It is not inappropriate to set up a ner tamid in your house—to be used for times of prayer and meditation for Shabbat and yom tov, or for all times as a continual reminder of God's presence.

How to make a ner tamid

Of the many possibilities and varieties of materials, a brief selection follows:

1. Use a Yahrzeit candle for the light itself, as it burns for at least twenty-five hours.

For containers:

a. Easiest is to buy an Indian or oriental oil censer and suspend it from the ceiling. Insert the candle.

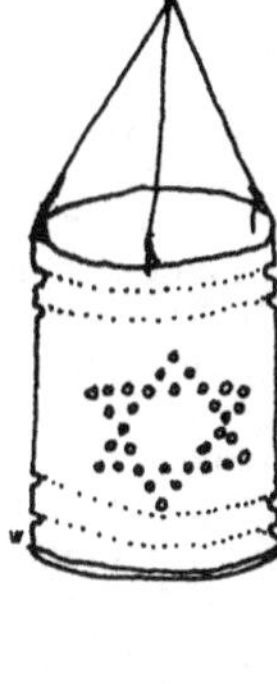

b. A simple way to fashion one yourself is as follows:

Take a tin can with one end left intact. Fill the can with water and place it in the freezer. When the water is frozen, take the can out, and cover it with a sheet of paper on which you have drawn a design. With hammer and nail,

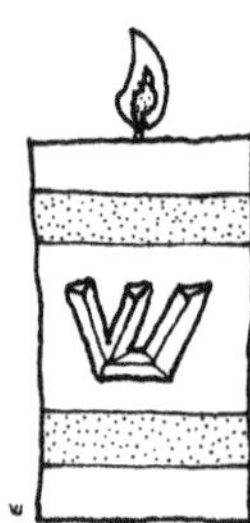

punch holes in the can until the design is completed. (The ice prevents the can from collapsing. Tightly packed sand may also be used.) Remove paper and attach wire to the top of the can. Suspend it from the ceiling and insert the candle. The perforated design will produce a lattice effect on the walls as the candlelight shines through.

2. For those with the mechanical ingenuity and proper aesthetic sense, a mesmerizing, intricate, and unorthodox ner tamid can be made as an adaptation of an electric light box. This involves:

a. getting or making a transparent container, e.g., a large, clear plastic refrigerator box;

b. setting into this cardboard partitions in a predetermined pattern, i.e., as interlocking flames or, more radically, in the form of the Tetragrammaton;

c. attaching to each section one of a string of variously colored lights on a random-flashing sequence chain. Make sure to insulate against electrical fires. Plug it in. This is a particularly appropriate contemporary metaphor and extension of the ner tamid.

(For more specific directions, questions, and variations, write to Zalman Schachter—see Teachers.)

YAHRZEIT: ANNIVERSARY OF A DEATH

When a person's soul leaves him, candles should be lit and placed by his head.

During the seven days of mourning (see Death and Burial), candles should burn continually in the house of mourning.

Each year on the anniversary of the death (according to the Hebrew calendar) a candle should be lit and burn all day in the house of the mourner.

Underlying this is the verse from Proverbs 20:27:

"The spirit of man is the lamp of the Lord." נֵר יְהוָה נִשְׁמַת אָדָם

"Man is composed of four fundamental elements—Fire, Wind, Earth, Water—and Fire is at the head of the others" (Ketubbot 23).

Special Yahrzeit candles which burn at least twenty-five hours can be purchased at Hebrew bookstores and even at some food stores which carry kosher products.

Several different types of Yahrzeit candles have been designed recently. Of particular note is one designed by Chana Wolpert Richard. The candle (replaceable) is placed inside a glass casing which has the verse

נֵר יְהוָה נִשְׁמַת אָדָם

inscribed upon it. It is available for $5.50 from:

Ludwig Wolpert
c/o The Jewish Museum
Tobe Pascher Workshop
1109 Fifth Ave.
New York, N.Y. 10028

ON CANDLE-MAKING

There are basically three ways of making candles (at least for Jewish ceremonial purposes):

1. pouring hot wax
2. rolling thin sheets of wax
3. burning oil

Additional customs involving candles

1. It is a custom to light a candle in the synagogue on Yom Kippur with the intention that this will help bring atonement to the נפש —soul (the initials of נ"ר פ"תילה ש"מן light=wick=oil).
2. It is customary to light candles on the occasion of a circumcision as a mark of honor and joy.
3. The attendants who bring the groom to the huppah should hold in their hands two lit candles—because the word נר —candle—in gematria, doubled, is equivalent to the numerical value of פרו ורבו "be fruitful and multiply." And this is a good sign.
4. In some places there is the custom that the first time the father brings his son to the synagogue, he brings a wax candle to light there.

For melted wax candles you need:

MOLD—a paper cup, food containers like milk cartons or yogurt containers, juice cans, glasses, etc.

WICK—available at crafts stores; heavy cotton twine can be used but candle wicking is preferable

PARAFFIN—available at craft stores or even at some supermarkets (look for boxes of Gulfwax)

COLORING AGENTS—dyes available at crafts stores, or crayons (although these do not produce a true color)

a couple of SMALL POTS

optional are SCENTS, HARDENING AGENTS, SMOOTHING AGENTS—available at crafts stores

CAUTION: There is a question as to whether the paraffin used for making candles (or particular paraffins) is kosher. If in doubt, ask. If still in doubt, it may be a good idea to get a special set of cheap pots to do the melting in. Otherwise, if you use kosher pots, they may end up being nonkosher.

Put some water in one pot (about 2 inches) and bring to a boil. Rest the other pot inside the first in the semblance of a double boiler (you can also use a double boiler). Place the paraffin in the top pot—a bit at a time. Allow it to melt. Coloring and scents should be added here. Suspend the wick in the center of the mold. The easiest way of doing this is to tie it to a stick and rest the stick across the mold.

Pour the melted colored wax into the mold. Place the mold in the refrigerator or freezer to harden. When fully hardened, remove the mold, trim the wick, and there you are.

Experiment with different molds, layers of colors, putting ice in the mold before pouring the wax, etc.

This is basically the process for pouring candles. Crafts books and crafts stores will supply information which can embellish this outline tremendously. Unfortunately, there are few ceremonial purposes for which candles made in this way can be used. The reason is that, basically, they are too big and burn too long. Since you are not allowed to extinguish Shabbat candles, if you use candles made in this way, you may end up with a lot of melted wax around. (This long-burning quality, however, makes them excellent for use as Yahrzeit candles.) Two alternatives:

1. Try to devise some kind of a taper mold so that the candles will end up long and thin.

2. Try *dipping* the wicks in the wax rather than pouring the candle into the mold. IDEA: Place paraffin in the bottom of a metal ice cube tray and rest it over the pot of boiling water. Adjust the heat so that the wax in the ice cube tray is melted but just at the point of hardening. Holding the ends of the wick in either hand, dip it into the wax. As you raise the wick out, it will harden around it. With repeated dippings, additional layers will build up. Continue until it reaches the size taper you want. (An alternative is to solder two coffee cans together, fill with wax and dip the wicks vertically.)

Dipping Havdalah candles: Follow the above procedure for dipping—but only build up relatively thin, long tapers. Do this for three (or as many tapers as you want in your candle). If you do this quickly enough, or if a few people are working on the separate tapers at the same time, or if you have a few pots going, the tapers will still be soft enough to mold, braid, or twist. If one or two have hardened before the others were ready, simply heat the hardened ones for a bit over the boiler and then braid them together. Make your first candle with a simple three-braid. Put embellishments on later ones. Remember, the Havdalah candle does not have to be made in any one way. It just must have more than one wick and resemble a torch somewhat. An embellishment: after braiding or twisting, dip the whole candle into the melted wax to glaze it and give it a soft, textured effect.

For honeycomb beeswax candles

This wax comes in thin rectangular sheets (approximately 8″× 12″) pressed to the texture of a honeycomb. It is very easy to work with, safe, requires no melting, and is tremendously versatile. The sheets come in a wide range of colors. To work with it, cut with scissors or knife to the length you want. Place a length of wick along one edge. Beginning with that edge, fold the wax tightly around the wick and roll tightly. Press the other edge lightly so that it adheres to the rest of the candle. Cut off the wick on the bottom. Trim the wick at the top. There is a basic candle. An elegant variation: instead of using a rectangle, begin with a triangular piece of wax. Place the wick along one edge. When you finish rolling, the candle will have a spiral, tapered appearance.

Practice with the wax to gain an idea of how much wax is needed for what size and thickness.

Be imaginative. Explore the possibilities of this medium. Fortunately, this process can be adapted for making a number of ceremonial candles.

a. Since you can make these candles virtually any thickness or size, you can easily gauge them to the size of your Hanukkah menorah. Also, these candles are perfect for homemade menorot—particularly those made from wood you have gleaned from forests (see Festivals, "Hanukkah"). Red, yellow, and orange emphasize the flame motif.

b. Use white sheets rolled into simple candles—tapers for Shabbat or yom tov.

c. Even Havdalah candles can be made from honeycomb wax, but you must do it carefully. Use the entire length of the sheet but only roll a thin taper. Roll three tapers. *Carefully* braid the three together. The wax is bound to crack a bit in the process. This can be patched up. If you hold the tapers over a hot stove while braiding them, you will increase their flexibility. For a final touch, if you happen to have some melted wax around dip the final braided candle into the wax so as to give it a glaze and seal any cracks which may have occurred while rolling. Also, the effect of the glaze over the honeycomb wax is wonderful.

NOTE: Honeycomb wax is available from local crafts shops. For some reason, however, it is becoming more and more difficult to find. If you discover a supply, it may be worth your while to stock up on it. Price is generally 35c a sheet—less for quantities.

For oil candles:

These are probably the oldest and simplest type of candles. Fill a small (unbreakable) vessel with olive oil, stick a wick in it, light the wick.

Many Hanukkah menorot from Israel are made of brass with oil cups instead of candle holders. Rather than let these serve simply as ornaments in your house, try using them the way they were originally intended.

An idea for an oil float or menorah Take a large glass bowl or goblet. Pour in a layer of water—approximately 2 inches, but this will vary with the size of the bowl. (This is just to douse the flame when the oil runs out.) Pour in a top layer of olive oil (the oil will float on top of the water).

Cut out small triangles of tin (available in thin sheets from a hardware store or simply cut up a disposable aluminum pan). Punch a small hole into the center of the triangle. Extend a piece of wick through the hole. Take small pieces of cork and attach them to the corners of the triangle. These triangles will now float in the pot. Simply light the wick and it will continue to burn until the oil runs out. Then the water will extinguish the flame.

For Hanukkah: Each night you can add another one of these triangles—and allow them to float around in the bowl.

For Shabbat or yom tov: Each member of the family can put his/her own candle into the float.

The beauty of this, besides the obvious aesthetic, is that all the flames, though separate, share the same source. SHALOM

Kippah

INTRODUCTION

Throughout Jewish history, the attitude toward covering the head has varied. Drawings from the third century C. E. depict Jews without hats. In the Middle Ages, many Jews wore hats only during prayer and study. Gradually it became a binding custom to wear hats at all times.

The Talmud records two opposing attitudes about the issue of covering the head. In tractate Nedarim (30b), the wearing of a hat is considered optional and a matter of custom. In tractate Shabbat (156b), it is stated that covering a child's head insures his piety. For those who favored covering the head, it was seen as a sign of modesty before God as well as an acknowledgment of the kingship of God.

In the modern period, covering the head became a matter of debate between those who considered it obligatory and those who either were opposed to it or who considered it optional even during services. A middle-of-the-road path was adopted by others, who considered it obligatory only for services.

The use of a kippah—skullcap or yarmulka—instead of a hat is of posttalmudic origin. Lately, kippot have become a symbol for Jewish identification and are often worn for that reason alone.

While it is possible to buy cloth, velvet, or satin kippot, we are including some suggestions on how to make your own crocheted ones.

Note: Each square =1 stitch. Different markings indicate different colors.

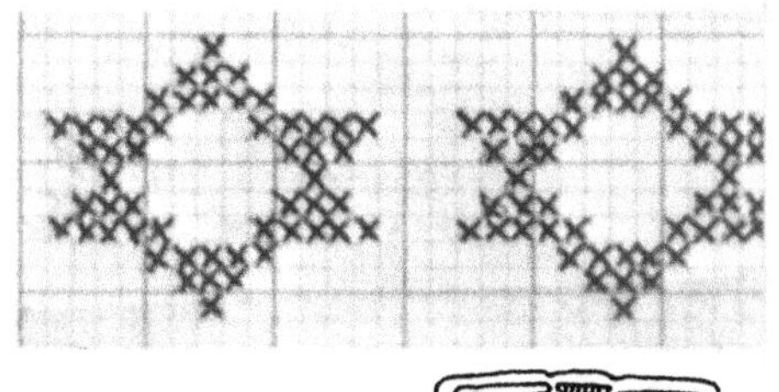

CROCHETING KIPPOT

Crocheting kippot is a creative and enjoyable art. With relatively little practice, you can create beautiful and original kippot. There are a few basics which must be kept in mind.

1. If you want your patterns to come oui really sharp and clear, use heavy-duty thread. I use J. & P. Coats Knit-Cro-Sheen, but any thread of the same weight will do as well. You do not have to be overly concerned with brand names.

2. The smaller the needle, the tighter and firmer-holding your kippah will be. I would suggest a size 10 or 12 for beginners. For some of the more intricate patterns you may need a size 15.

3. I usually start with five single chain stitches and then loop them into a circle. Beginning with too many chain stitches will cause a big hole in the center.

4. Once you have your circle, continue crocheting around and around. Although you can do the kippah in double crochets, if you want it really firm always use a single crochet. The pattern *must* be done in single crochet or it will be blurry.

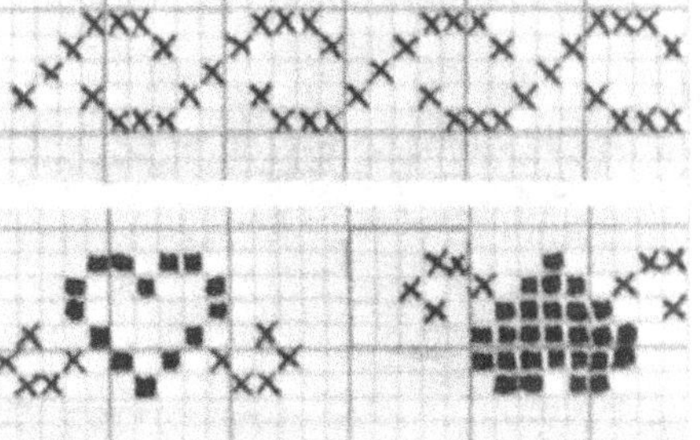

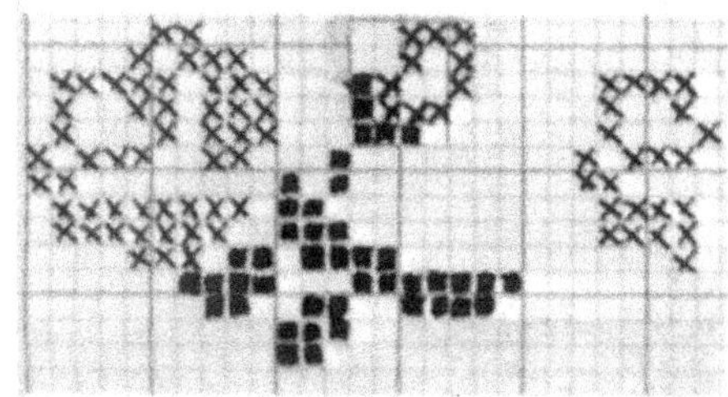

5. Increasing: In the first row, inorease once for every stitch you crochet. For the second and third rows, increase once every other stitch. For the fourth and fifth rows, increase every third stitch. Increasing after that point will depend upon how tight you crochet. All I can tell you is that if your kippah begins to look like a nose-warmer, you aren't increasing enough, and if it ripples, it means you are increasing too much. You determine the shape of your kippah by how often you increase. Remember, it is very difficult to increase during the pattern, so count on the brim drawing in the kippah a little.

6. Size: There is no universally recognized size for kippot. The best method I have found for determining how large a kippah should be is simply to ask the person for whom you are making it. Since he will be wearing it, let his preference determine the size.

7. One final step: Wash the kippah. This serves two purposes. The first and most obvious is to get rid of the dirt it accumulates during the creation. Secondly, when you wash it, you can set the shape. It is just like blocking out a sweater or a scarf. While it is still wet, put the kippah on your head or a bowl and shape it. Then just let it dry. You will have a perfectly shaped and beautiful kippah.

A final word about designing patterns. There are infinite possibilities. All you need is some graph paper and colored pens. Anything can serve as a model: a pattern in a book or on material, a wall hanging, or even a doodle on a piece of paper. If you can block it out on graph paper, you can put it on a kippah. Once you have made up a pattern, keep a copy of it. The most important thing to keep in mind is the taste of the person for whom you are making it. A kippah lasts a long time and is meant to be enjoyed.

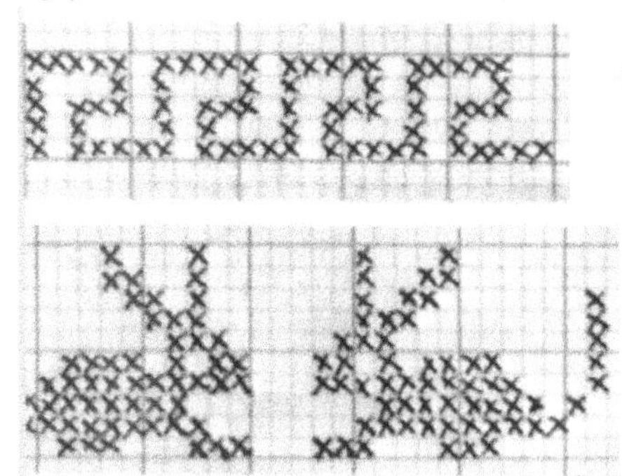

Border designs

The following are patterns suggested by:

Marian Sternstein
300 Lynn Shore Dr.
Lynn, Mass. 01901

and

Karen Abramovitz
Road 4, Box 454E
North Brunswick, N.J. 08902

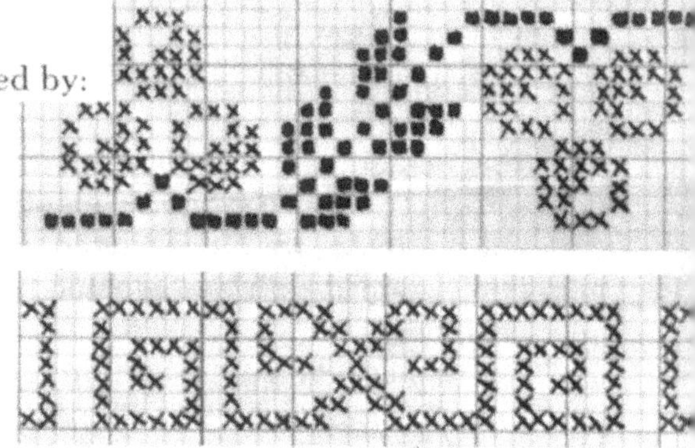

Both of them are highly talented and will answer questions on crocheting. Marian has collected a large book of patterns which she will share if contacted in person.

Karen uses the following patterns between names.

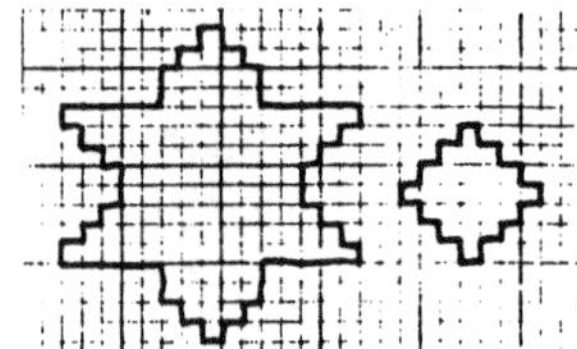

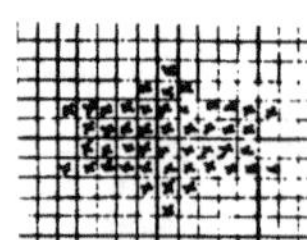

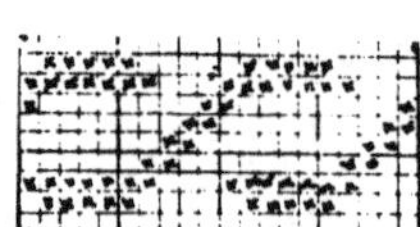

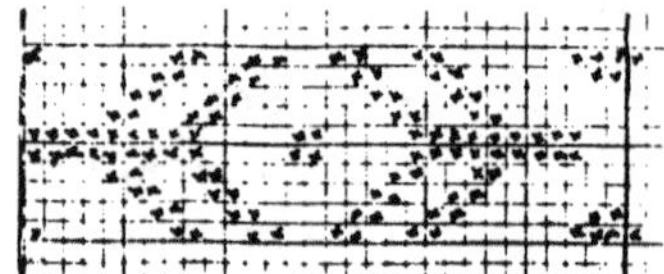

The following are alphabets suggested by Karen for crocheting names along the border of the kippah.

Tallit

The tallit is the prayer shawl worn by married men in Orthodox synagogues, and by all males past the age of Bar Mitzvah in Conservative and Reform synagogues. It is a composite garment consisting of two main parts, the garment itself and the tzitzit—fringes on the corners which transform the garment from a piece of cloth to a tallit.

LAWS AND CUSTOMS

The tallit is worn by congregants for the Shaharit (Morning) and Musaf (Additional) Services; by the leader of the tefillot at the Minhah (Afternoon) Services; some also have the leader wear it for the Maariv (Evening) Services of Shabbat, festivals, and holy days.

Originally the tallit was made out of either linen or wool, but now silk is also acceptable. With regard to the material, there is the concept of shatnez—which is the biblical prohibition against mixing together certain distinct species. Specifically, it is forbidden to wear a garment made of both linen and wool. If you wish to observe this you should be careful about the material you select as well as the material with which the tzitzit are made. Silk goes with everything.

The size of the manufactured silk tallitot commonly found in synagogues today is approximately five feet by two feet. This is by no means a standard for what the size should be. Traditionally, the large tallit was approximately six feet by three or four feet. There are certain advantages to this size:

1. You feel that you are wearing a garment and not a scarf.
2. You can more easily feel enwrapped by it.
3. The symbolisms mentioned later become much more applicable. The size as well as the design—as will be seen later—are ultimately determined by the wearer.

Although there are differing opinions, the commonly accepted custom is to put the tallit on before the tefillin. The reason for this is that (1) the mitzvah of tzitzit is equal to all the mitzvot together, and (2) because wearing a tallit is a more regular ritual than putting on tefillin. You wear the tallit during the week, on Shabbat, and on holidays, while the tefillin are worn neither on Shabbat nor on holidays. Where there is a question of performing two acts, one regular and one not, the regular act is performed first, i.e., tallit before tefillin.

Women are not obligated to wear a tallit, nor are they prohibited from wearing one. The importance and need for a prayer robe in which to wrap and immerse yourself during tefillah is certainly equal for both men and women. It is often difficult, however, for women who have been raised in a tradition where only men wear tallitot to readily accept the same type of tallit for themselves. Since any four-cornered garment with tzitzit can be used as a tallit, there are a variety of forms and options available to women. Some are suggested later, but these suggestions are by no means exhaustive. The imagination, creativity, sensitivities, and taste of the wearer are the criteria for making a tallit.

LAWS AND CUSTOMS REGARDING THE TZITZIT

It is a positive commandment to put tzitzit on any four-cornered garment that you wear, as it says in Numbers 15:37-41:

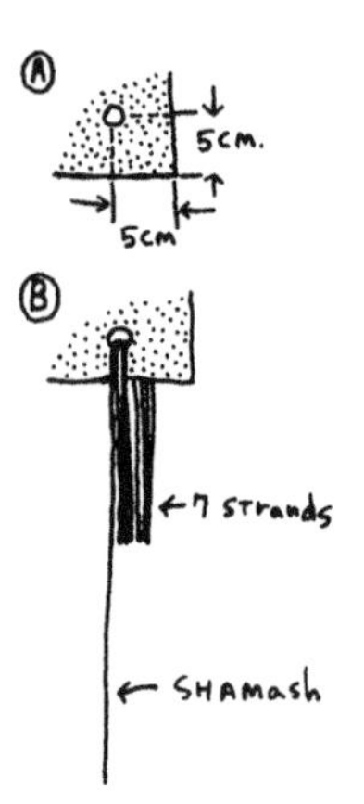

The Lord said to Moses as follows: Speak to the Israelite people and instruct them to make for themselves fringes on the corners of their garments throughout the ages; let them attach a cord of blue to the fringe at each corner. That shall be your fringe; look at it and recall all the commandments of the Lord and observe them, so that you do not follow your heart and eyes in your lustful urge. Thus you shall be reminded to observe all My commandments and to be holy to your God. I the Lord am your God, who brought you out of the land of Egypt to be your God: I, the Lord your God.

As is apparent, this mitzvah is given in order to remember God, His great love, all of His commandments—and to do them.

While the large tallit is used specifically for prayer, it is a mitzvah in itself to wear a garment with tzitzit *all day*. Traditional Jews, therefore, wear a tallit katan—small tallit—all day and a large tallit just for morning prayers.

The tallit is not worn at night because the mitzvah stipulates that one should *see* the tzitzit. (The implication is that this should be seen by light of day, not by artificial light.)

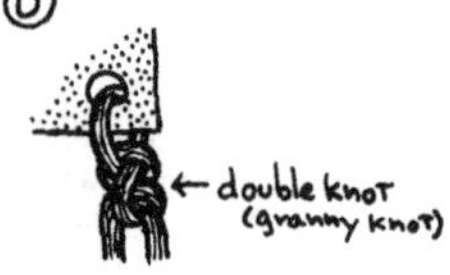

The tzitzit have to be at the corners; but there is a question as to where the corner is on a four-cornered piece of material. A general guide is that the hole be three or four fingerbreadths from the corner edges.

There is an opinion that the tzitzit should hang on the side of the corner and not on the bottom toward the ground.

There is a custom not to cut the tzitzit to shorten them, but to bite them with your teeth.

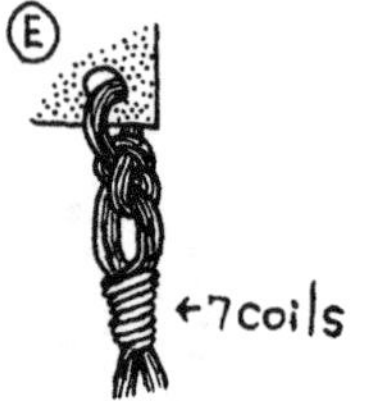

How to tie tzitzit: ritual macrame

Before you try tying tzitzit to your tallit, it is advisable to practice with twine or heavy string looped around a chair leg.

Although you can spin or devise your own tzitzit strands, it is easier to buy a tzitzit pack, which is available at most Hebrew bookstores.

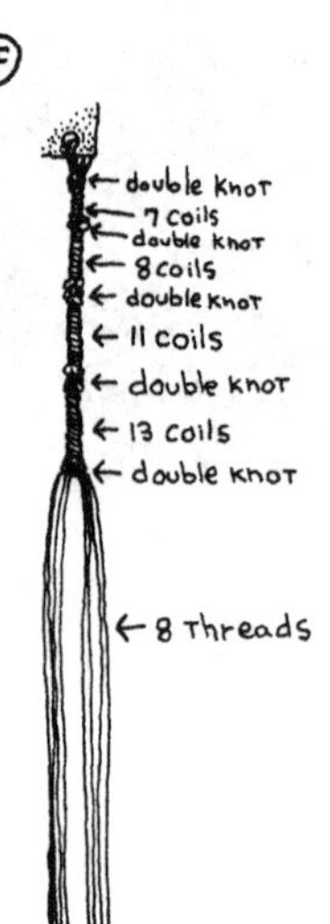

There will be sixteen strands in the pack—four long ones and twelve short ones. Separate these into four groups with one long and three short in each. The longer strand is called the shammash and is the one used for the winding.

Even up the four strands at one end and push the group through one of the corner holes in the tallit.

Even up seven of the eight strands (the four being doubled) and leave the extra length of the shammash hanging to one side.

With four strands in one hand and the other four in the other hand, make a double knot near the edge of the material. Take the shammash and wind it around the other seven strands in a spiral—seven turns. Be sure you end the winding where you began—otherwise you may end up with 7½ or 6½ winds. Make another double knot at this point (four over four).

Spiral the shammash eight times around. Double knot. Spiral the shammash eleven times around. Double knot. Spiral the shammash thirteen times around. Final double knot.

This is the common, and halakhically precise type of tying. There are, however, two variations on this:

1. A Sephardic tying adds another dimension to the pattern: each time the shammash is brought around, take it *under* the previous wind before winding it further. This will produce a curving ridge around the tzitzit. This, too, should be practiced before trying it on the tallit.

2. Although not in strict accordance with the halakhah, some tie the tzitzit with the shammash spiraling 10-5-6-5 times respectively.

The symbolism for the numbers is central to the overall symbolism of the tallit. Seven and eight equals fifteen, which in gematria (numerology) is equal to the two letters yod and heh—the first two letters of the Name of God. Eleven is the equivalent of vav and heh—the last two letters of the Name of God. The total—twenty-six—is thus equivalent and representative of YHVH—the four-letter Name of God. Thirteen is equivalent to the Hebrew word Ehad—alef, het, dalet—which means One. So to look at the tzitzit is to remember and know that "God is One."

According to the second way of winding, each section is a different letter of God's four-letter Name.

The central commandment surrounding tzitzit is:

"And you should see it and remember all of God's commandments and do them."

וּרְאִיתֶם אֹתוֹ וּזְכַרְתֶּם אֶת־כָּל־מִצְוֹת יְיָ, וַעֲשִׂיתֶם אֹתָם.

How do the tzitzit do this?

In gematria, tzitzit = six hundred. In addition there are eight strands plus five knots. The total is six hundred and thirteen—which, according to tradition, is the exact number of commandments—mitzvot—in the Torah. Just to look at them, therefore, is to remember all the mitzvot.

WRAPPING ONESELF IN THE TALLIT

In the process of putting on and wearing the tallit, its many levels of symbolism become apparent. Only some of this symbolism can be alluded to here. Keep these symbols in mind as you put on and wear the tallit. Other associations will probably occur to you. Nurture them.

There are three steps to putting on the tallit.

1. Before putting on the tallit, inspect the tzitzit to insure that they are still intact and correct. To heighten your awareness of the act, the following verses are said (Psalms 104:1-2):

"Bless the Lord, O my soul; O Lord, my God, You are very great; *You are clothed* in glory and majesty, *wrapped in a robe* of light; You spread the heavens like a tent cloth."

A kabbalistic meditation follows this which leads to greater kavvanah—intention and centering:

For the purpose of unifying the Holy One, blessed be He and His presence—with a mixture of fear and love, for the purpose of unifying the YH of God's Name (masculine) with the VH of God's Name (feminine) in one complete Unity, in the name of all of Israel, I wrap myself in this tallit with tzitzit. So should my soul and my 248 limbs and my 365 veins be wrapped in the light of the tzitzit which is 613. And just as I am covered by a tallit in this world so should I be worthy of a dignified cloak and beautiful tallit in the world to come–in the Garden of Eden. And through the fulfillment of this command may my soul, spirit, holy spark, and prayer be saved from obstructions. May the tallit spread its wings over them and save them "As an eagle that stirs its nestlings, fluttering over its chicks." And the doing of this mitzvah should be considered by the Holy One, blessed be He, to be as important as fulfilling in all particulars, details, and intentions, the six hundred thirteen mitzvot that depend upon it. Amen, Selah.

אמן

2. Immediately before putting on the tallit, hold it out spread open before you and say the berakhah:

"Blessed are You, Lord our God, King of the Universe, who has sanctified us with His commandments, and commanded us to enwrap ourselves in [a tallit with] tzitzit."

בָּרוּךְ אַתָּה, יְיָ אֱלֹהֵינוּ, מֶלֶךְ הָעוֹלָם, אֲשֶׁר קִדְּשָׁנוּ בְּמִצְוֹתָיו, וְצִוָּנוּ לְהִתְעַטֵּף בַּצִּיצִת:

(Some have the custom of kissing the ends of the crown at this point).

3. After this, bring the tallit around behind you (like a cape) and, before letting it rest on your shoulders, cover your head with it and allow yourself to feel totally enwrapped, sheltered, and protected. The following is a traditional meditation said at this point:

How precious is Your kindness, God. Man can take refuge in the shadow of Your wings. He is sated with the fat of Your house and from the stream of Your delight he drinks. Because with You is the fountain of life and in Your light do we see light. Send Your kindness to those who (try to) know You and Your righteousness to the good-hearted.

At this point, bring the tallit to your shoulders and wear it well and consciously.

There is one other part in the service in which the tallit is actively used—at the reciting of the Shema.

During the prayer immediately preceding the Shema—the Ahava—the tzitzit are gathered together and held around one finger.

The symbolism for this is at least twofold:

1. It represents the coming together of the "four corners of the earth." You should try to gather the tzitzit as you say: "Hurry, and quickly bring upon us blessing and peace from the four corners of the earth."

2. As the numerical value of the windings of each tzitzit is "God is One," the bringing together is a form of expressing the complete unification of God, and all that this implies. There is a hint of this in the words that come right before the Shema: "You have brought us close to Your great Name, with love and with truth, so that we can praise You and unite You and be in love through Your Name." Immediately following this is the Shema—which is the affirmation of the *actuality* of God's Oneness.

In the third paragraph of the Shema—va-Yomer—for each time that the tzitzit are mentioned (three times) there is a custom to look at them and kiss them. Some even elaborate on this by kissing the tzitzit four times each time—for the four letters of God's Name; or, when wearing tefillin to first touch the shel yad with the tzitzit, kiss them, then the shel rosh, and kiss them again—for each time. When the final words, Adonai Eloheikhem Emet, are repeated by the leader of the service, the tzitzit are kissed for the *fourth* time. (When davening alone, the three words El Melekh Ne-eman preface the Shema. When you have reached the final word, Eloheikhem, then you kiss the tzitzit.)

Following this, the tzitzit should not be immediately dropped, but should be held for a while. They should be released sometime before Ezrat Avotainu, as this deals with the drowning of the Egyptians and indicates a separation —the reality of the divided world as opposed to the unification effected by bringing together the tzitzit.

Some people have the custom of drawing the tallit over the head during various parts of the service to inspire extra kavvanah.

Creating a tallit

As mentioned before, there are no limitations as to the size, or decoration of the tallit—except for the taste, sensitivities, and personality of the person who is going to wear it. (Within this, you are free to explore the range of your creativity and imagination.) Some suggestions follow, but these are meant as guides or structures upon which you are invited to impose yourself.

1. The simplest and often the most elegant way to make a tallit is as follows:

Carefully search out a piece of material which appeals to you and in which you would like to wrap yourself. Buy it. Hem the ends, if necessary. Attach the tzitzit. Wear it beautifully.

Some refinements on the theme

a. If you are concerned with shatnez (see earlier) check the composition of the material. If in real doubt, send a piece of it to a shatnez lab:

Shatnez Laboratory
203 Lee Ave.
Brooklyn, N.Y. 11206
(EV7-8520)

b. When selecting material, pay attention to the weight and lay of the cloth. Since it takes a lot of material to make a tallit, if it is too heavy it becomes uncomfortable. If it is not flexible, it is difficult to wear.

c. It is probably best to get a double-sided piece of material (referring to the print or design), since both the inside and outside of the tallit are visible.

d. A good size is: length—the span of your arms; width—36–48″.

e. If the material is unravelable, you might want to pull threads for three inches on each end, then gather ten to twenty threads and make a knot, as extra fringe. This, however, is *not* necessary fringe for the tallit.

f. If you want this fringe but either cannot or do not want to unravel the ends, you can buy fringing at fabric stores and sew this to the ends.

g. If you want neither to buy a print nor to use a plain color, there are many possibilities for embellishment and personal creativity.

Fabric stores sell various-sized colored, designed hemming material (ribbon) which is perfect for use as stripes. Simply decide the progression and spacing you want and sew them to the material. This should be done carefully to insure that the stripe will lie straight. One disadvantage of this method is that the stitches show through to the other side.

Many people like to embroider the stripes—an obviously more difficult and intricate process. Karen Abromovitz recommends using a white or off-white basket weave or other large weave as the base material so that you can use the threads as a grid for the embroidery.

Other methods can be tried:

tie-dyeing   batiking

We have heard of the possibility of silkscreening stripes. If you know of any success with this, please tell us about it.

h. An atarah—or crown—is often placed on the edge of one side for the purpose of providing some spatial orientation for the tallit (or tallit-wearer).

This can be made from bought material—hemming ribbon, brocade, velvet—or silver and gold crowns can be purchased at most Hebrew bookstores. Or this piece can be embroidered. It is often effective and beautiful to embroider the blessing, or one of the many phrases from the ritual for putting on the tallit, or any other Hebrew phrase which you feel would deepen the wearer's kavvanah.

i. If you buy a little extra material, you can cut out patches for the corners. This both reinforces the area and gives a clear indication of the corner. These also can be embroidered—with inscriptions, flowers, ritual symbols, or any decoration.

2. A much more difficult way of making a tallit is by weaving it yourself.

a. Mrs. Hoisington of Dayton, N.J., has been weaving what is called the Bnai Or (Children of Light) tallit for several years. This is an off-white woolen tallit with several bands of deep, vibrant, brilliant colors used in the ancient Temple—royal blue, purple, red. She will take commissions for these tallitot. Write:

Mrs. E. E. Hoisington
Box 206
Mendham, N.J. 07945

Mrs. Hoisington's specifications for the weaving follow below (these instructions assume a prior knowledge of the art of weaving). The tallitot are woven from a very fine (20/2′) wool—which she imports from:

Hyslop
Bathgate & Co.
Galashiels, Scotland

A wonderful weaver of tallitot is:

Reverend Sydney Fisher
640 Bok Rd.
Nazareth, Pa. 18064

whose prize-winning work is superb.

Try also:

F. L. Fawcett, Inc.
129 South St.
Boston, Mass.

She weaves in four sizes (all dimensions in inches): 40 x 84, 20 x 84, 12 x 84 and 8 x 84. These are made with reinforced corners and buttonholes in each (so the tzitzit can be added). She knots the end threads across to make the extra fringe.

b. The base tallit material for the Bnai Or tallit—made from Orlon—without tzitzit or lining is also available from:

Zalman Schachter
c/o Judaics Department
University of Manitoba
Winnipeg, Manitoba

Price available upon request.

Additional suggestions for the proper observance of the mitzvah of tzitzit (from a pamphlet *The Fringed Garment* by Rabbi Hershel Matt):

1. Try to provide yourself with your own tallit, for use in public worship (even if your synagogue provides a tallit for each worshiper) and for use in private worship, at home or away from home. Make sure that it is large enough to cover most of your body and that it is beautiful enough to be considered by you as an adornment. Provide yourself with a tallit bag also.
2. Consider using two tallitot, one for weekdays and one for Shabbat and holidays.
3. At the conclusion of your morning prayer, remove the tallit gently, reluctantly; fold it neatly; and return it carefully to the tallit bag.
4. Keep your tallit in an appropriate place.
5. Check periodically to see whether your tallit needs to be laundered, or to have its fringes replaced, or to be entirely replaced.
6. Although not considered to be holy in the same sense as books or parchments containing God's Name, fringes or tallitot, when no longer usable, should not be crudely discarded but should rather be put aside for eventual burial in a cemetery. (Most synagogues have a place for keeping such objects until burial.)
7. Leave instructions that when you die you wish to be buried in your tallit.
8. Consider giving a tallit as a gift—to a friend whose tallit needs replacing, or to one who owns no tallit but would cherish one. It is a worthy and lovely custom for the bride or her family to give the groom a tallit as a wedding present.

c. An interesting project was begun at the Jewish Community Center in Wilkes-Barre. Several women and men have been weaving tallitot for their sons' Bar Mitzvahs. Over eighty-five tallitot have been woven to date, and there are already reservations for years in the future. A set of plans for starting such a program is available from:

Sy Hefter
Educational Director
Jewish Community Center
60 S. River St.
Wilkes-Barre, Pa. 18702

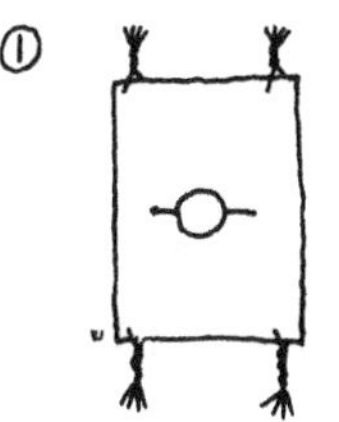

All of the preceding deals with the traditional style-form of the tallit. There are, however, many varieties possible which stay within the confines of a four-cornered garment. As mentioned before, this is particularly advantageous for women who want to wear a prayer robe but have difficulty with the associations of the traditional tallit. The following are a few of the alternative forms. We would be interested in hearing about other designs.

1. If you cut a hole in the middle, you will have the form of a poncho. (This is actually an expansion of the idea of a tallit katan which is worn under your clothes.) If you have a poncho already, you can attach tzitzit to it and convert it into a tallit. This can be of two sizes:
   a. just extending to the shoulders
   b. extending down the arms

   Both can be belted with a sash of some kind. By doing this to "B" in diagram you will create bell-shaped sleeves. The garment should be long enough for the tzitzit to be readily accessible.
2. A bit more complicated is a form which resembles a shepherd's coat:
3. This is also a possibility—as a combination poncho-shawl:

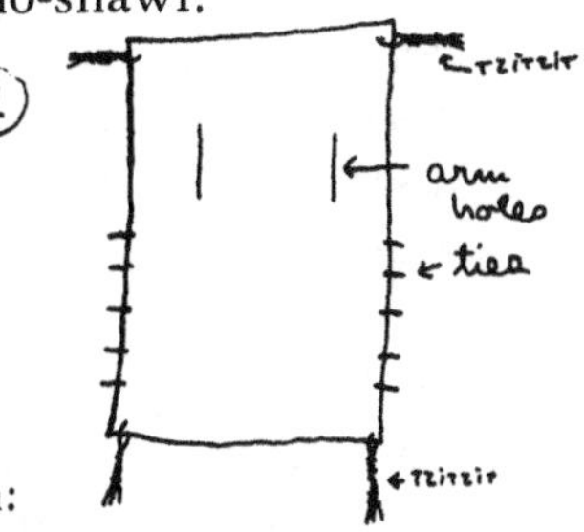

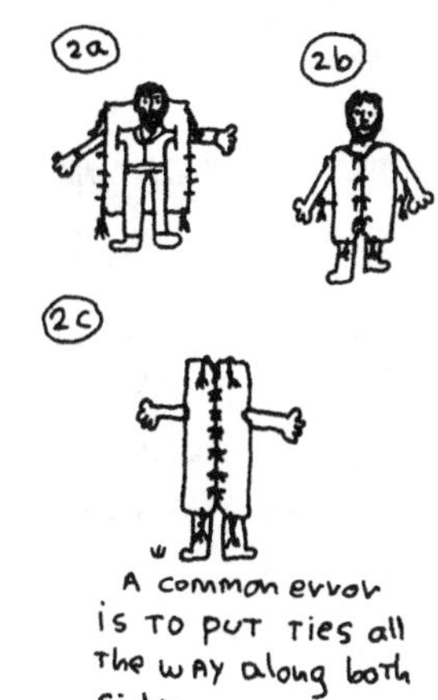

A common error is to put ties all the way along both sides.

KITEL

A white linen garment bound by a white belt and worn:

1. by some during the services of the High Holidays—Rosh ha-Shanah and Yom Kippur;
2. by the leader of the Pesah Seder;
3. by the groom at his wedding; and
4. as the shroud for the dead.

Because it is worn at such diverse occasions, the kitel is virtually a paradigmatic symbol of the admixture of joy and sorrow in all rites of passage.

The purity of rebirth and beginnings—i.e., the wedding and the Seder—is linked and identified with the purity of atonement and endings—i.e., Rosh ha-Shanah/Yom Kippur and death.

To extend the paradox, the day of the wedding is considered as a Yom Kippur for the couple. During the first year of marriage the kitel does not have to be worn for the High Holidays because there was already a calling to repentance and atonement.

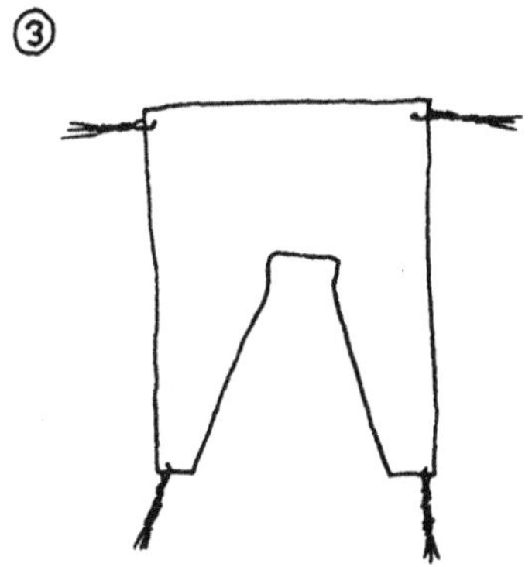

In terms of completing life cycles, it is quite fitting that the kitel, which is symbolic of the purity of birth, be a man's wedding garment as well as his burial shroud.

The kitel can be made fairly easily by using a shirt pattern and elongating it. It can be either a pullover or button/zipper front. The white belt should be made from the same material.

Tefillin

וְהָיָה לְךָ לְאוֹת עַל־יָדְךָ וּלְזִכָּרוֹן
בֵּין עֵינֶיךָ לְמַעַן תִּהְיֶה תּוֹרַת
יְהוָה בְּפִיךָ כִּי בְּיָד חֲזָקָה הוֹצִאֲךָ
יְהוָה מִמִּצְרָיִם׃

"And this shall serve you as a sign on your hand and as a reminder on your forehead—in order that the teachings of the Lord may be in your mouth—that with a mighty hand the Lord freed you from Egypt" (Exodus 13:9).

וְהָיָה לְאוֹת עַל־יָדְכָה וּלְטוֹטָפֹת
בֵּין עֵינֶיךָ כִּי בְּחֹזֶק יָד הוֹצִיאָנוּ
יְהוָה מִמִּצְרָיִם׃

"And so it shall be as a sign upon your hand and as a symbol on your forehead that with a mighty hand the Lord freed us from Egypt" (Exodus 13:16).

וּקְשַׁרְתָּם לְאוֹת עַל־יָדֶךָ וְהָיוּ
לְטֹטָפֹת בֵּין עֵינֶיךָ׃

"Bind them as a sign on your hand and let them serve as a symbol on your forehead" (Deuteronomy 6:8).

וְשַׂמְתֶּם אֶת־דְּבָרַי אֵלֶּה
עַל־לְבַבְכֶם וְעַל־נַפְשְׁכֶם,
וּקְשַׁרְתֶּם אֹתָם לְאוֹת עַל־יֶדְכֶם וְהָיוּ
לְטוֹטָפֹת בֵּין עֵינֵיכֶם׃

"Therefore impress these my words upon your very heart: bind them as a sign on your hand and let them serve as a symbol on your forehead" (Deuteronomy 11:18).

INTRODUCTION

These passages are the sources for the mitzvah of tefillin, phylacteries. The tefillin are worn on the arm and head every weekday morning, during Shaharit—the Morning Service.

PARTS OF TEFILLIN

Tefillin are composed of two main parts:

1. tefillin shel yad—the tefillin that are wound around your arm and hand; and
2. tefillin shel rosh—the tefillin that are placed on your head.

Tefillin have the following components:

1. *Bayit (pl. batim)—box.* Each part has a bayit. There are, however, basic differences between the bayit shel yad and the bayit shel rosh.

Shel yad: has one compartment

Shel rosh: has four separate compartments, though placed tightly together. Also the shel rosh has the Hebrew letter shin ש on two of its sides. One is a three-pronged ש ; the other is a four-pronged ש . Some see these letters as an allusion to the three patriarchs and four matriarchs. Others say that since the gematria (see Gematria) of ש is 300, the letters serve us as a reminder that 300 out of 354 days of the year tefillin are worn. The unusual four-pronged ש , tradition says, was used on the Ten Commandments. The commandments were engraved all the way through the tablets so they could be read from either side. For a shin to be read both ways it has to be four-pronged so there are three spaces in between. To understand this, hold up four fingers and see how the spaces in between the fingers form a shin.

The bayit is made from the skin of a kosher animal and is in the shape of a perfect square. The corners should form sharp points. With "superduper" tefillin, each bayit is made from a single piece of leather.

2. *Parshiyot—portions from the Torah.* There is one set of four portions, i.e., Exodus 13:1–10; 13:11–16; Deuteronomy 6:4–9; 11:13–21, enclosed in each bayit. These portions deal with the mitzvah of tefillin.

The portions are written on parchment by a scribe (see Scribal Arts). The parshiyot are tightly rolled and tied with the hairs of an animal. They are then enclosed in another piece of parchment and again bound with hairs. For the shel yad, the parshiyot are written on one long piece of parchment. For the shel rosh, each parshah is written on a different piece of parchment and each parchment is put in a different compartment. The binding hairs are drawn through the bayit of the shel rosh and should be visible on the outside. This is one sign that the pair of tefillin is a good one.

3. *Titora—the square base* (length and width, not height). It should be larger than two fingers by two fingers (width, not height) and smaller than 4 x 4 fingers.

4. *Maabarta—a leather protrusion from the back of the bayit.* It is a hollow extension through which the strap is passed.

5. *Giddin—threads made from the fibers of the hip muscle tissue of kosher animals.* These are used for sewing closed the bayit. Twelve holes are made in a square around the sides of the bayit and the titora, which are then sewn together with the giddin.

6. *Retzuah—strap.* One long retzuah is attached (through the maabarta) to the shel yad. It is knotted in the shape of the letter yod and should always be close to the bayit. It is also shaped in the form of a noose so it can be tightened on the arm. One long retzuah is attached to the shel rosh. It forms a circlet which is adjusted to fit the head. The knot which forms the circlet is made in the shape of the letter dalet or double dalet—a square shape. The ends of the straps should be long enough to hang down slightly below the waist.

TO PUT ON TEFILLIN

The best and easiest way is to have someone show you, but if no one is available, the general order is to:

1. put on the shel yad;
2. put on the shel rosh;
3. finish tying the strap around your hand and fingers. Reverse this order when taking off the tefillin. Tefillin are put on and taken off while standing.

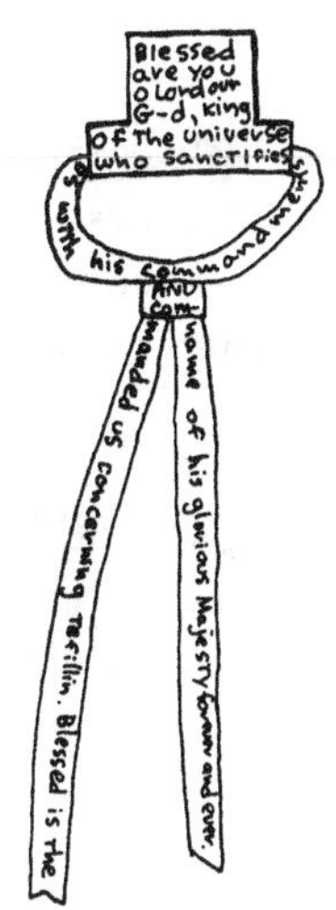

The tefillin shel yad is put on your "weak" hand—that is, your left hand if you are right-handed. This is done because of Exodus 13:16, which says: "And so it shall be as a sign upon your hand." The Hebrew word for "your hand" has an extra Hebrew letter heh attached to it. The rabbis felt that the extra letter alludes to one's weak hand יד כהה (יד כהה=ידכה) The left hand is closer to your heart and this fits the symbolism of the biblical statement: "And you shall place these words upon your heart." Nonetheless, if you are a lefty, wear the tefillin on your weak hand, i.e., your right.

To begin:

1. Roll up your sleeve (if you have one) to above your muscle. This is done because there can be nothing between the tefillin and your skin. For this reason, watches should be taken off or put on your other hand.

2. Unwrap the straps of the tefillin shel yad. Place the bayit on the muscle of your arm. The maabarta should be on the side closest to your shoulder. Also, the knot should be both next to the bayit and on the side closest to your body. The bayit should be placed on top of your muscle, not on the side or the bottom. If you put your arm down to your side, the tefillin will be both facing toward and on the same level with your heart.

When everything is in place, say the blessing:

"Blessed are You, Lord our God, King of the Universe, who has sanctified us with His commandments and commanded us to wear tefillin."

בָּרוּךְ אַתָּה, יְיָ אֱלֹהֵינוּ, מֶלֶךְ הָעוֹלָם, אֲשֶׁר קִדְּשָׁנוּ בְּמִצְוֹתָיו, וְצִוָּנוּ לְהָנִיחַ תְּפִלִּין:

Pull on the strap until the tefillin are tightly bound to your arm. With practice you will learn how tightly you have to pull to keep it from slipping. At

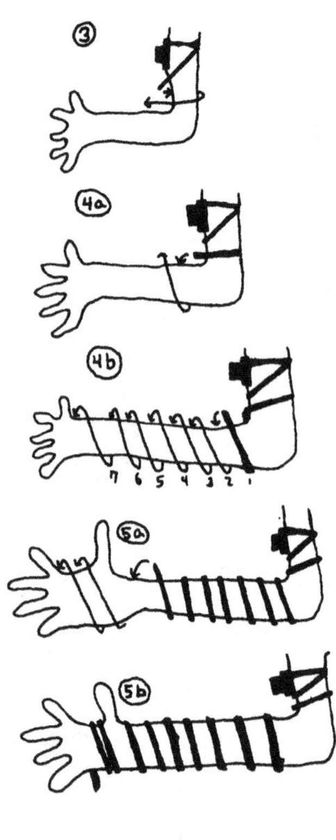

first it is better to pull very tightly, for it has a tendency to slip off. However, tefillin are not supposed to cut off your circulation. Do not let the knot loosen while you wind the rest of the strap.

3. Many people wind the strap at least once around the upper arm to help keep the bayit in place.

4. Wind the strap seven times around your arm between your elbow and your wrist. Ashkenazic Jews wind the strap counterclockwise. Sephardic Jews wind it clockwise. The black side of the strap should always face outward.

5. After the seventh time, bring the strap around the outside of your hand to your palm and then wrap the rest around the middle of your palm, i.e., the space between your thumb and index finger. Tuck the end of the strap underneath this middle coil to prevent the strap from unwinding.

6. Unwrap the tefillin shel rosh. Hold the bayit and place the bayit on the top of your head above the forehead. The maabarta should be on the side away from your face and thus toward the middle of your head. The opposite end of the bayit should rest at the beginning of your hairline. The bayit should not hang over your forehead. It should be centered between your eyes, as it says: "And they shall be a sign between your eyes."

7. Place the knot on the back of your head, i.e., on the nape of your neck. Check to see that the strap is not twisted. The strap ends should be brought forward to hang down over your chest. Make sure the black side is facing out.

8. Before you have the whole thing in place say the berakhah:

"Blessed are You, Lord our God, King of the Universe, who has sanctified us with His commandments and commanded us concerning the precept of tefillin."

בָּרוּךְ אַתָּה, יְיָ אֱלֹהֵינוּ, מֶלֶךְ הָעוֹלָם, אֲשֶׁר קִדְּשָׁנוּ בְּמִצְוֹתָיו, וְצִוָּנוּ עַל מִצְוַת תְּפִלִּין:

This should be followed by:

"Blessed be the Name of His glorious majesty forever and ever."

בָּרוּךְ שֵׁם כְּבוֹד מַלְכוּתוֹ לְעוֹלָם וָעֶד:

This is said because of an involved halakhic question. Very briefly, there is doubt whether the second blessing is superfluous because you have already said the first blessing. Saying unnecessary blessings is frowned upon; so in case the second blessing is unnecessary, you say, "Blessed be the Name . . ." which "neutralizes" the second blessing.

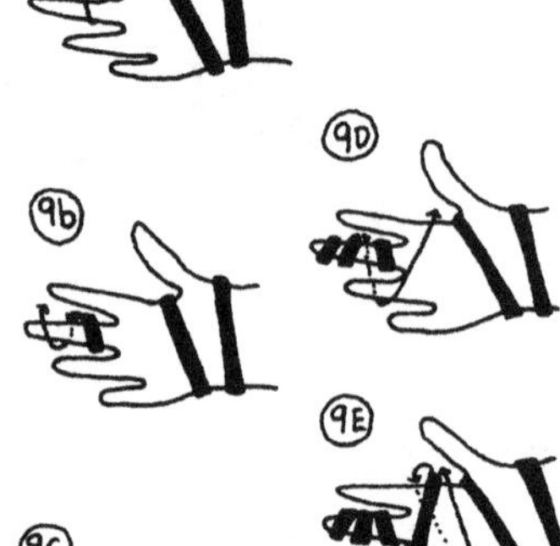

9. Finally you unwind the part of the strap wrapped about the middle of your palm (leaving in place the coil from your wrist to your palm). According to Ashkenazic custom, you then wrap it three times around your middle finger, twice around the lower part of that finger (i.e., the part closest to the knuckle), and once around the middle part of the finger. While this is done, Hosea 2:21–22 is said: "And I will betroth thee unto Me for ever; yea, I will betroth thee unto Me in righteousness and in justice, and in lovingkindness, and in compassion. And I will betroth thee unto Me in faithfulness; and thou shalt know the Lord." The remainder of the strap is brought under the ring finger and over the outside of the hand, forming a V. Then the strap is once again wound around the middle of the palm, forming a shin. Any extra strap is wound around this middle coil and again the end of the strap is tucked under this coil. The winding around the finger forms the Hebrew letter dalet.

10. To take the tefillin off, reverse the order—take apart the dalet and shin on your hand, wrapping the strap around the middle of the palm. Then take off the shel rosh and wrap up the straps. Loosen and unwind the strap on the hand; take off the shel yad and wrap up the straps. There is no prescribed way

of wrapping the tefillin. Many people wrap the straps around the batim. Try various ways and see which one you like.

KAVVANOT

There is a multilevel symbolism involved in this mitzvah, often working in sets of three.

1. The central theme of the tefillin is the act of binding.

The tefillin bind you not only physically, but spiritually.

The shel yad binds your arm—that is, your body. The shel yad also binds your heart, as it says: ". . . impress these My words upon your very heart: bind them . . ." (Deuteronomy 11:18).

The shel rosh binds your mind.

Thus, mind-heart-body, your total self, is bound together to worship God. The tefillin also reminds us to use mind-heart-body for good and not for evil.

Mind-body-heart — thoughts-actions-will — thoughts-possessions-feelings. Some base this trichotomy on the three words used in the Bible to refer to tefillin:

(a) זִכָּרוֹן memorial (mind);
(b) אוֹת sign (heart);
(c) טוֹטָפוֹת frontlets (body).

2. The tefillin are a memorial, a remembrance (mind) of the most important event of our collective past—the exodus from Egypt. As it says: ". . . and as a reminder on your forehead . . . that with a mighty hand the Lord freed you from Egypt" (Exodus 13:9). Thus we are reminded of leaving the binding to the slavery of Pharaoh for the binding to the service of God—the leaving of the leather thongs of the lash for the leather straps of the tefillin.

They are also to remind us of the mitzvot, as it says: " . . . that the teachings of the Lord may be in your mouth" (Exodus 13:9). We received at Sinai the mitzvot which bind us to the service of God.

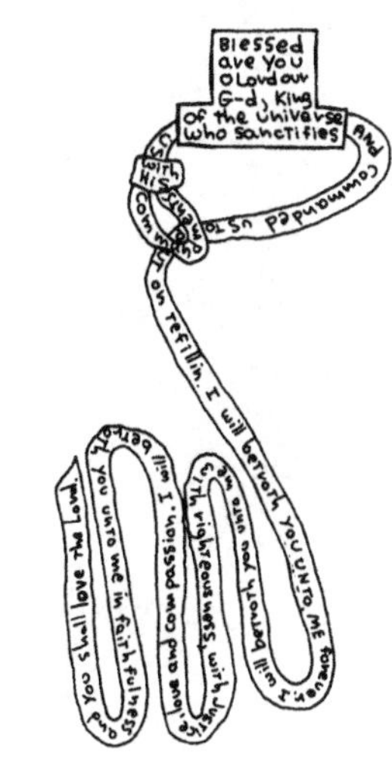

3. The tefillin are a sign of where we have been (Egypt), who we are (the nation which stood at Sinai), and where we are going (the permanent duty of service to God). Thus the tefillin shel rosh, in particular, is seen as a sign to the nations "that the Lord's name is proclaimed over you" (Deuteronomy 28:10). Therefore, it is not covered when it is worn.

4. The tefillin are especially a sign of our recognition of God. This is symbolized in the very construction of the tefillin, for one of God's names, שדי (Shaddai), is formed by the tefillin. That is, the ש (shin) on the hand or on the bayit of the shel rosh, the ד (dalet) on the fingers or the knot on the back of the head, the י (yod) is the knot next to the bayit of the shel yad or the end of the strap of the shel rosh.

Thus the tefillin help us in our feeling and awareness of the presence of Shaddai—Almighty God. The tefillin are a sign of our desire and will to worship God.

5. The frontlets, that is, the physical tefillin themselves—the physical act of binding—the touch of leather on skin—the parshiyot and their contents—"Hear O Israel, the Lord your God, the Lord is One. And you shall love the Lord your God with all your heart, and with all your soul [mind], and with all your might"—these, too, are part of the mitzvah of tefillin.

6. The binding theme is finally carried through in the verses from Hosea (mentioned above) which are said while winding the strap around your finger. "And I will betroth thee unto Me for ever . . . and thou shalt know the Lord. . . ." Daat in the Bible means "to know" in an experiential rather than an academic sense. For example, it is also used to mean sexual intercourse,

the deepest kind of human knowing. It is this kind of profound experiential knowing that Hosea meant. These verses consummate the binding in a betrothal between man and God.

7. Finally, the importance of the tefillin is further emphasized by a discussion in the Talmud. R. Abin . . . says, How do you know that the Holy One . . . puts on *tefillin?* For it is said: *The Lord hath sworn by His right hand, and by the arm of His strength. . . . "And by the arm of His strength":* this is the *tefillin. . . .* R. Nahman b. Isaac said to R. Hiyya b. Abin: What is written in the *tefillin* of the Lord of the Universe?—He replied to Him: *And who is like Thy people Israel, a nation one in the earth. . . .* The Holy One . . . said to Israel: You have made me a unique entity in the world . . . as it is said: *Hear, O Israel, the Lord our God, the Lord is One.* 'And I shall make you a unique entity in the world,' as it is said: *And who is like Thy people Israel, a nation one in the earth*" (Berakhot 6a).

Surrounded by the tallit and bound by the tefillin, man is ready to worship with God.

SOME LAWS AND CUSTOMS

1. Tefillin are usually worn during Shaharait, though one can fulfill the mitzvah by putting them on any time during the day. If put on at times other than Shaharit, it is customary to say the three paragraphs of the Shema.

2. Tefillin are worn when one reaches physical maturity, for men age thirteen, for women age twelve. Traditionally only men wore tefillin, though there were cases of women wearing them (e.g., Rashi's daughters). They can be worn before these ages for the purpose of learning how to put them on correctly.

3. Tefillin are not worn on Shabbat or holidays (i.e., Rosh ha-Shanah, Yom Kippur, the first and last days of Sukkot, Passover, and Shavuot). These days are also considered an אות , a sign, and so the wearing of tefillin, which are also a sign, is considered superfluous.

4. Tefillin are considered an adornment and so are not worn the morning of Tisha b'Av (they are worn during Minhah), by the bereaved before the funeral, or the bridegroom on his wedding day (see Weddings).

5. There are three opinions concerning the wearing of tefillin during Hol ha-Moed (intermediate festival days). The doubt exists because of the ambiguous status of the intermediate days as partial holidays.

a. The first opinion is not to wear tefillin.

b. The second opinion is to wear them but not to say the berakhot.

c. The third opinion is to wear them and say the berakhot quietly. One follows the custom of his family or, especially, his synagogue.

6. For Shaharit, the tallit is put on before the tefillin. This is because the tallit is worn every day of the year while tefillin are worn only on weekdays (as explained above). A mitzvah done consistently is performed before one that is performed less frequently. The tallit is removed after you take off your tefillin.

7. There are two kinds of tefillin: tefillin according to Rashi's opinion and tefillin according to Rabbenu Tam's opinion. Nearly all Jews wear Rashi tefillin. Some people wear Rashi tefillin for Shaharit and then take them off and put on R. Tam's tefillin and say the three paragraphs of the Shema. Others wear both at once. The only difference between the two kinds of tefillin is in the order of the parshiyot in the shel rosh. Rashi's order is Exodus 13:1–10; 13:11–16; Deuteronomy 6:4–9; 11:13–21, following the order they appear in the Bible. R. Tam's order is Exodus 13:1–10; 13:11–16; Deuteronomy 11:13-21; and 6:4-9, switching the place of the last two parshiyot. This

disagreement precedes Rashi and R. Tam, who lived in the Middle Ages and goes back at least to the first century C. E. This has been shown by pairs of tefillin dating from that period found at Qumran in Israel.

8. There is a custom to touch the batim with the fingers and then bring the fingers to the lips as a kiss when you say, ". . . bind them for a sign . . ." during the Shema.

9. Some people take off the shel rosh with their left hands to show their reluctance in removing the tefillin. It is also a custom to turn to one side so as not to face the ark directly. Both reflect the desire not to leave the level of kedushah, sanctity, attained while wearing the tefillin.

10. On Rosh Hodesh (New Month) tefillin are taken off before the Musaf Service. If worn on Hol ha-Moed, they are removed after the Shaharit Amidah.

11. When wrapping the strap around the arm seven times, some people say:

"You open Your hand and satisfy every living thing with favor."

פּוֹתֵחַ אֶת יָדֶךָ, וּמַשְׂבִּיעַ לְכָל חַי רָצוֹן:

Caring for your tefillin

1. You should keep your tefillin in a cloth bag. These can be handmade or bought at a Jewish bookstore. It should be a separate bag from your tallit bag so that the tefillin can be put aside for Shabbat and holidays. Because the tefillin are not worn those days, they are not supposed to be touched.

2. You can buy cases that are made to fit around your batim and help to protect them. These can be obtained from the same place you buy your tefillin. With more expensive tefillin, these cases are usually included in the price.

3. Your tefillin should be taken to a sofer, scribe, twice in seven years. They should be checked for the squareness of the batim, the blackness of the straps and batim, and especially the correctness of the parshiyot. The latter are checked to see if the writing has faded, etc. If the sofer will check them while you are around, you can get a chance to see the inside of the batim and get a good idea of how the tefillin are made. If you want, you can buy the special black ink used for dying the tefillin. This can be bought from a sofer or a Jewish bookstore. In this way, you can see to it that your straps and batim are always black.

To buy tefillin

The purchase of tefillin should be done with great care. The best thing is to take someone along who knows about tefillin. It is especially important to purchase tefillin from a reliable Hebrew bookstore. You must rely on the dealer for the kashrut of the parchments. For this reason some people have a scribe check their tefillin right after they buy them. The best place to buy tefillin is in Israel. Most tefillin are made in Israel anyway and are somewhat cheaper there than elsewhere. However, tefillin can be bought from any Hebrew bookstore. The price can range anywhere from $18 to $150.

Finally, for more information about the practical aspects of tefillin, you should obtain *The Tefillin Manual* by S. Rubenstein, edited by R. Posner and available ($2.85 in U.S. and Canada, $3.10 elsewhere) from:

S. Rabinowitz
30 Canal St.
New York, N.Y. 10002

This pamphlet is very highly recommended. It describes in great detail how tefillin are made. It also gives directions for (a) making the shel rosh headband larger or smaller; (b) making the knot of the shel rosh; (c) making the knot of the shel yad both for lefties and righties. All the above is accompanied by diagrams.

Shofar

INTRODUCTION

Certainly one of the strangest pieces of ritual paraphernalia is the shofar. Even though there are several other religious objects that never seem to lose their potential for surprising and amazing people, in some ways the shofar still stands alone. The smoothly curved ram's horn has an aura of the primitive about it; for people saturated with sophisticated technology, the shofar appears to be a throwback to hoary antiquity. And perhaps this is precisely why the shofar is so exciting and stirring—it brings us back to places inside ourselves that are very basic and primitive, very near the root of our being. Since the shofar is used mainly around the time of the year when it is most important to be in touch with ourselves, finding those places is crucial.

BUYING A SHOFAR

First, let's understand the practical stuff. No thoughts, no matter how lofty, will get you off on shofar unless there's a shofar around to serve as object of such inspiration. If you're a self-reliant, living-off-the-land-naturally type, you can make your own shofar with little more than a raw ram's horn and a couple of elementary power tools (see below). If, however, you are in the market for a store-bought shofar, here's how to do it and what to look for.

First, it helps a lot to be in close proximity to either Jerusalem or (not to mention the two in the same breath) New York. If you are so situated, head for Meah Shearim or its diasporic equivalent, the Lower East Side. Look for Jewish bookstores (see Bibliography, "Jewish Bookstores"). But before you go, be ready. If you're a guy, make sure your head is covered. If you are a woman, there are further complications. First of all, if you are married, wear a hat or a kerchief on your head. Wear a skirt—not a short one (below your knees if possible)—and by all means do not wear a sleeveless top. Shofar merchants tend to be very Orthodox types and they might be offended and not take you seriously if you dress improperly.

When you get to a likely store, ask to see a selection of shofarot. If they don't have any, ask where you can find a place that does. (An important note of caution: Jewish capitalism, like any other kind, is run on ideas of supply and demand. That means that people usually think about a shofar during the months preceding Rosh ha-Shanah, and you are not likely to find a huge selection in March.) When selecting a shofar, check for two major things: appearance and sound. It should be curved, smooth, and not cracked or split. It can be as big as you want, remembering that the smaller shofarot often sound best; but there is a minimum size. It must be big enough so that when you hold it in your hand, both ends protrude. But don't worry too much; I've never yet come across a too-small shofar. No artificial mouthpiece may be attached. A shofar with a trumpet mouthpiece is not considered a real shofar, since in such an instance the shofar is only amplifying the sound that is really coming from the mouthpiece.

But most important, check how it sounds. Try out as many as you can. Even if the reason you are buying one in the first place is because you don't know how to blow and want to learn, try them out anyway. Remember, the basic technique is to place the shofar against your lips in the right corner of your mouth and emit into it a compressed high-pitched Bronx cheer. What you are doing is forcing air through your pursed lips (for further elucidation, ask a friend who plays the tuba or bugle). You want a shofar from which YOU can get the best sound. The guy in the store can probably get an ear-splitting blast out of a plastic Barton's toy shofar, or maybe even a live ram. It's his business. It's not that you shouldn't trust him, but who are you buying it for anyway—you or him? Which brings up another possible complication. If you are a female and want to try out a shofar, you might really freak out the seller, who, shall we say, may not yet have sufficiently raised his consciousness. You can dodge the problem by bringing a male friend along. But if you run into any difficulty, remind the fellow that the *Shulhan Arukh* (Orah Hayyim 589:6) specifically allows women to blow a shofar.

Jews live almost everywhere, and you, dear reader, might be reading this in Butte, Montana, Donaldsville, Louisiana, or some other exotic place west of the Hudson, and unable to reach the above-mentioned stores. Don't give up. The first place to try is the *local* Jewish bookstore, if such exists. Otherwise, see if you can get the local rabbi, Hillel director, or Sisterhood giftshop chairman to order a shofar for you from New York. If for some reason that is impossible, you can order one yourself. Write to some of the bookstores (again, see Bibliography, "Jewish Bookstores," for listing) and see what they can do for you. And remember, if all else fails, you can always make your own.

PRACTICING THE BLASTS

Once you have your shofar, you'd better start practicing. It's not at all complicated: there are only four notes to learn, but practice will make you a real baal tekiah (a master blaster). Fortunately, our tradition provides us with a built-in training period. Beginning with the first day of the month of Elul (the month before Rosh ha-Shanah), it is customary to blow the shofar each morning, sounding one sequence of the calls tekiah, shevarim, teruah, tekiah (more about the specific calls later). This is done every day of Elul except Shabbat and the day before Rosh ha-Shanah. That day is skipped to make a clear distinction between the shofar blasts of Elul, which are a minhag, custom, and those of Rosh ha-Shanah itself, which are in fulfillment of a mitzvah—a commandment from the Torah—to hear the sound of the shofar. During Elul, the shofar is sounded at the conclusion of the Morning Service. "With the beginning of Elul, one awakens to teshuvah— repentance—turning back to the path" (Minhagei Maharil). Hearing the shofar helps to make for such an awakening. But such a month of official shofar practice can be great preparation for the novice.

The specific calls are not very complicated.

1. The first one, and the one most often sounded, is tekiah, which means "blast" and is exactly that—one long blast with as clear a tone as possible.
2. Shevarim, "broken" sound, is three short calls, together being as long as one tekiah.

3. Teruah, "alarm," is a rapid series of very short notes, at least nine of them, that also should together equal one tekiah.

4. Finally, tekiah gedolah—the "great tekiah"—is just what its name says it is: a single unbroken tekiah blast that is stretched out and held for as long as your breath holds out.

If you have never heard the shofar blown, this description is probably meaningless, in which case you'll have to ask someone how it sounds. But since you probably at least vaguely remember how it's supposed to sound, these lengths should be helpful.

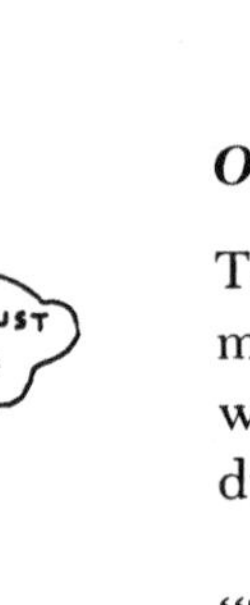

Order of blowing

To the untrained eye, it would seem that the Torah gives no instruction in the matter of how the shofar is to be blown. To come to understand how the rabbis were able to derive our present system is to receive an enlightening introduction into how statements of the Torah were concretized into halakhah.

To begin, the procedure of shofar-blowing is deduced from Leviticus 25:9: "Then you shall sound the horn loud[teruah]; in the seventh month, on the tenth day of the month—the Day of Atonement—you shall have the horn sounded throughout your land."

Since the word teruah is preceded and followed by the word shofar, teruah is sounded in between two plain shofar blasts, or tekiot. Thus, tekiah teruah tekiah.

Because there are three verses ordaining the blowing of the shofar —Leviticus 25:9, plus Leviticus 23:24 and Numbers 29:1—each with the word teruah, it is understood that tekiah teruah tekiah should be sounded three times.

As I said before, tekiah is a plain single blast. Teruah is more complicated, and a story in itself. The rabbis understood teruah as "wailing." Over the years, differing traditions arose as to what sort of wailing was indicated. Some maintained it to be a ululation, an Indian war-whoop type of howl which anyone who has ever attended a Moroccan Bar Mitzvah or funeral has heard. Others preferred a thrice-repeated loud groan. Still others sounded a combination of the two. Before matters became more confusing, it was decided that such differences in shofar melody were divisive, and all three forms were incorporated into what was to become the universal custom of giving equal time to the three teruah versions. The ululation was called teruah, the groan was called shevarim, and the combination was called shevarim-teruah (what else?).

The three sets of tekiah teruah tekiah having been expanded threefold results in the sounding three times each of tekiah shevarim teruah tekiah, tekiah shevarim tekiah, and tekiah teruah tekiah; this yields a total (so far) of 12+9+9=30 calls.

Now let's see how this fits into the Rosh ha-Shanah liturgy. After the Torah and haftarah have been read, Seder Tekiat Shofar—the Order of the Blowing of the Shofar—begins. Preliminary verses from Psalms are read, and the shofar-blower makes two berakhot:

"Blessed are You, Lord our God, King of the Universe, who has sanctified us by Your commandments and has instructed us to hear the call of the shofar."

בָּרוּךְ אַתָּה, יְיָ אֱלֹהֵינוּ, מֶלֶךְ הָעוֹלָם, אֲשֶׁר קִדְּשָׁנוּ
בְּמִצְוֹתָיו, וְצִוָּנוּ לִשְׁמֹעַ קוֹל שׁוֹפָר:

"Blessed are You, Lord our God, King of the Universe, who has granted us life, sustenance, and permitted us to reach this day."

בָּרוּךְ אַתָּה, יְיָ אֱלֹהֵינוּ, מֶלֶךְ הָעוֹלָם, שֶׁהֶחֱיָנוּ, וְקִיְּמָנוּ, וְהִגִּיעָנוּ לַזְּמַן הַזֶּה:

All this time the shofar-blower is concealing the shofar in the folds of his tallit. Then the person who has been designated as the caller calls out, "Tekiah," and tekiah is sounded; "Shevarim teruah," and that is sounded; again, "Tekiah," and tekiah is blown. This is repeated three times. This is followed by the next cycle, three repetitions of tekiah shevarim tekiah, carried out in the same manner. The third cycle, tekiah teruah tekiah, is done the same way, except for the case of the very last tekiah. This time, the caller says, "Tekiah gedolah," and the shofar-blower holds the note as long as he can. The shofar-blowing is followed by more verses of Psalms.

An absolute prerequisite to fulfill the mitzvah of hearing the sound of the shofar is for the hearer to intend to do the mitzvah by hearing that particular shofar sound, and for the baal tekiah to intend that his blowings fulfill the hearer's obligation to hear (blow) the shofar. Practically speaking, the shofar-blower must think to himself that he intends by his blowing to fulfill the mitzvah for anyone hearing. In such a way, even people he can't see but who are within earshot will be included. The hearer must not only listen, but must think to himself that he is listening for the purpose of fulfilling the precept. Minimally, this is done by answering "Amen" to the baal tekiah's berakhot.

אמן

After Torah scrolls are returned to the ark, the Musaf (Additional) Service begins. The Musaf for Rosh ha-Shanah, like other Musafim, consists of a silent individual recitation of the prayer followed by a repetition by the hazan, including numerous medieval poetic additions called piyyutim. The most striking aspect of the Rosh ha-Shanah Musaf Amidah are three special sections called Malkhuyot (Kingships), using the metaphor of king to proclaim God's sovereignty over the universe; Zikhronot (Remembrances), asking God to remember the merit of the fathers and the hesed (love) that He had in making His berit (covenant) with them; and Shofarot, reminding us of beginnings and ends, the shofarlike thundering at the giving of the Torah at Mount Sinai, and the great shofar to be sounded heralding the arrival of the Messiah.

At the end of each of the three sections, the shofar is sounded. There are surprisingly many local customs governing the order of the blasts. Usually each mahzor contains its own minhag, custom, but some of the more all-encompassing editions present a veritable smorgasbord from which a minhag can be chosen.

The simplest minhag for the shofar-sounding of Musaf is that of Rabbenu Tam (the Tosaphist and grandson of Rashi). According to him, tekiah shevarim teruah tekiah is sounded once following all three sections. Another way is to blow tekiah shevarim teruah tekiah after Malkhuyot, tekiah shevarim tekiah after Zikhronot, and tekiah teruah tekiah after Shofarot. Others repeat the above three times. Still another minhag is to sound tekiah shevarim teruah tekiah three times, tekiah shevarim tekiah three times, and tekiah teruah tekiah three times after each of the three blessings. It is important to caution here that when a community has an established minhag for these shofar calls, that is the minhag to be employed. Individual and communal minhagim are precious bits of oral tradition, and those that have survived until today should be jealously guarded.

Many Hasidim, Sephardim, and kabbalists practice the custom of blowing the Musaf tekiot twice, in the silent Amidah as well as in the repetition. In such cases, the shofar is sounded without the caller calling the notes. The shofar is blown when the baal tekiah arrives in his prayer at the places for shofar-blowing.

Although, as we have already seen, the basic mitzvah of the Torah is fulfilled by hearing nine sounds, or thirty when you follow the three teruah methods, it has become a custom to sound one hundred notes. Additional blasts are added at the end of the service to reach one hundred. One way of doing this is to blow an additional thirty sounds in the middle of the Full Kaddish after Musaf, between the paragraphs Titkabbel and Yehei Shelamah, and the balance (according to this minhag, ten—tekiah shevarim teruah tekiah, tekiah shevarim tekiah, tekiah teruah tekiah) before "Adon Olam" at the very end of the service.

Other than the fact that it is a very round number, I could find no probable origin for the custom of the one hundred sounds. There is, however, an interesting midrash that explains the custom. Remember when I said that the rabbis interpreted teruah as "wailing"? They did so because the Aramaic translation of the word is from the same root as "wailed" from Judges 5:28, "Through the window she looked forth, and peered [and wailed]"; the reference is to General Sisera's mother's distress at his not returning home because he had been killed. She is comforted by the wisest of her princesses who tell her that they must be abducting women and taking spoils. The answer satisfied her, and this fact was seen by the rabbis as proof of her incredible cruelty—that her anguish for her son could be assuaged in the thought that he must be in the process of making other mothers childless. Now if you add up the letters of the verse describing the scene, namely Judges 5:28–29, you come up with one hundred and one. Thus the shofar, sound of mercy, can erase all of the wails which were all shrieks of cruelty—all except one. Even among the cruelest of people, there is at least a shred of a feeling of mercy in the pain that a mother feels for her child. That one merciful wail is not blotted out by the shofar. So one hundred shofar blasts are sounded for the one hundred cruel wails.

Kavvanot

Now you know basically what you need to know about how, when, and where to go about blowing the shofar. All this should not be dismissed as mere mechanics, for it is the core, the substance of the mitzvah, around which you can develop ideas and kavvanot. Now we can explore some of the varieties of these ideas and kavvanot.

The command to blow the shofar is given in the Torah without explanation. Even so, according to Maimonides, there is a message implicit within the practice:

Sleepers, awake from your sleep! Slumberers, rouse yourselves from your slumber! Search your deeds and return to teshuvah [*repentance, literally, returning*] *and remember your Creator. Those forgetters of the truth in the vanities of time and those who stray all their year in vanity and emptiness which can neither help nor save—look to your souls, better your ways and deeds. Let each one of you abandon your evil way and your thoughts which are not good.*

—Hilkhot Teshuvah, chapter 3

Here the shofar is seen as a reminder of the major motif of the Days of Awe—teshuvah. We commemorate the beginning of the world by trying to make new beginnings within ourselves, by *returning* to the beginning of the path. According to Maimonides, it is for this purpose that the shofar is blown.

Saadia Gaon gave ten reasons for the shofar. They are cited by Agnon in his book *Days of Awe* (Schocken Books, New York, 1965). Among these are:

. . . because Rosh ha-Shanah marks the beginning of creation, on which the Holy One, blessed, created the world and reigned over it. Kings do the same, who have trumpets and horns blown to let it be known and heard everywhere when the anniversary of the beginning of their reign falls. So we, on Rosh ha-Shanah, accept the kingship of the Creator, be blessed. Thus said David: "With trumpets and sound of the horn shout you before the King the Lord" [*Psalms 98:6*].

The second reason is that since Rosh ha-Shanah is the first of the ten days of teshuvah, the ram's horn is blown to announce their beginning, as though to warn: Let all who desire to turn in teshuvah, turn now: and if you do not, you will have no reason to cry injustice. Kings do the same: first they warn the populace in their decree, and whoever violates the decrees after the warning complains unheeded.

The third reason is to remind us of our stand at the foot of Mount Sinai, as it is said [*Exodus 19:19*]: *"The voice of the horn waxed louder and louder," in order that we may take upon ourselves that which our forefathers took upon themselves when they said* [*Exodus 24:7*]: *"We will do and obey.". . .*

The sixth reason is to remind us of the Binding of Isaac, who offered himself to heaven. So ought we to be ready at all times to offer our lives for the sanctification of His name. And may our remembrance rise before Him for our benefit.

The seventh reason is that, when we hear the blowing of the ram's horn, we fear and tremble and bend our will to the will of the Creator—for such is the effect of the ram's horn, which causes shaking and trembling, as it is written [*Amos 3:6*]: *"Shall the horn be blown in a city, and the people not tremble?"*

. . .

The ninth reason is to remind us of the gathering of the dispersed of Israel, that we may passionately long for it, as it is said [*Isaiah 27:13*]: *"And it shall come to pass in that day, that a great horn shall be blown; and they shall come that were lost in the land of Assyria."*

Saadia Gaon's ten reasons for the shofar focus our attention on the aspects of existence that, taken together, include all of life—from beginning to end of time and space, with the most dramatic of archetypal mythic events in between. The shofar teaches past, present, and future. It heightens consciousness and awareness of self—the self alone as well as the self in relation to the universe.

A Hasidic rebbe asked one of his Hasidim to be his baal tekiah. "Rebbe, I cannot. I am not learned in the secrets of the mystical kavvanot for the shofar blasts." This was no excuse for the rebbe, who had his reasons for his choice, so he taught his disciple the kavvanot. After being fully versed in the esoteric knowledge the Hasid again refused his rebbe's wish, this time saying, "Rebbe, I cannot. Now I know the kavvanot."

Having proper kavvanah for the shofar is a theme which runs through many Hasidic stories. Rabbi Zev Kitkes was the caller for the Baal Shem Tov, and so was ordered by his master to learn the secret meanings. So afraid was Rabbi Zev that he would forget what he had learned that he wrote it all down on a crib sheet, which he hid in his sleeve. When it came time to blow the shofar, he looked for his notes and they were nowhere to be found. Stunned, he began to weep uncontrollably, and brokenheartedly called the notes for the shofar. The Baal Shem said later, "In the palace of the king there are many chambers, and each one needs a different key to enter. But there is a master key which can open all the doors—the ax. The shofar is similar. The secret meanings are the keys, and each one opens a different door. But when a man passionately breaks his heart before God, he can crash any gate in the palace of the Holy One."

According to one tradition, the shofar is sounded in order to confuse Satan. Satan, it seems, hates the sound of the shofar because of all it represents. After all, when the Messiah comes, the great shofar will be sounded, heralding, among other things, Satan's ultimate defeat. So Satan, who on Rosh ha-Shanah is the chief prosecutor against Israel, is completely disoriented when he hears the shofar blown; hopefully that will help assure a positive judgment.

There is a verse in Psalms which expresses this idea of the shofar being efficacious in moving God from justice toward mercy. "God [Elohim] ascends midst acclamation [be-teruah]; the Lord [YHVH] to the blasts of the horn [shofar]" (Psalms 47:6). In kabbalistic symbolism, Elohim represents the side of God's stern judgment, and the unpronounceable Name YHVH stands for His infinite mercy. Thus the verse can be explained as God getting up from His throne of judgment, as it were, when He hears Israel blowing the shofar, and moving to the throne of mercy.

The word shofar itself comes from the root sh-p-r, which has the basic meaning of hollowness. The shofar is an empty instrument that becomes important only when a man's breath enters it. Then it becomes supremely important, able even to move worlds. Thus man should see himself, especially on Rosh ha-Shanah, as a shofar—an empty vessel that is worthless by itself, but potentially capable of divinity.

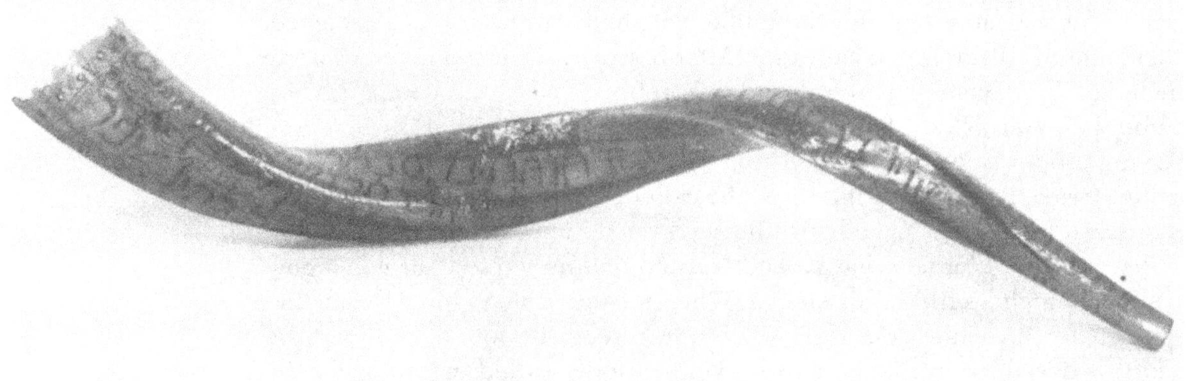

MAKING A SHOFAR

(Sy Hefter's description of how a shofar-making project began in his community of Wilkes-Barre, Pa.)

This is where we began. Two years ago, we learned that there were several Jewish patients in a local Catholic hospital who could not be home for the High Holidays. The Jewish Community Center arranged for a ten-year-old member who was a trumpet player to borrow a shofar from one of the synagogues. He went with his father to the hospital on the first afternoon of Rosh ha-Shanah and sounded the shofar for each Jewish patient. It was easy to arrange and worked out very well.

The following summer, a shofar was brought to day camp and it was sounded every Friday afternoon before the oneg Shabbat, to announce the forthcoming Shabbat. In some parts of Israel, this is done. Seven boys were interested in learning to blow the shofar. Each one who could make a sound was given a raw shofar, provided he agreed to come with his father early in the fall to drill and carve the shofar.

Early last fall, the boys and their fathers came to the center on a Sunday afternoon. With the help of a college boy who was excellent with tools, with some research on the laws of construction of shofars, and with some practice on the notes, the five boys completed the making of their own instruments and learned the notes. Arrangements were made for these boys to go with their parents to every hospital in the area on Rosh ha-Shanah to sound their homemade authentic shofars. In addition, the boys were asked to visit Jewish shut-ins on the same day. "Clans" that assembled in the homes of the great-grandparents for the holiday were honored to hear the sounding of the shofar. Next year, six more boys will make their own shofars and join in the honor of helping people hear the shofar on Rosh ha-Shanah.

Four important elements of this project bear out the mystical sense of rebirth that is inherent in our Rosh ha-Shanah celebration. First of all, boys who could sound a note on a raw shofar were the ones privileged to carve them. Second, the project called for cooperation between father and son. Third, the father-son team actually created an instrument out of a ram's horn. Last, the shofars were blown for the sick and the elderly, people who would not otherwise have heard a shofar. Thus this project offered a primal challenge to each boy. If he passed the test, he and his father, his guide, would together create a vehicle for song, the most basic form of communication. And this song of the glory of the Lord was blown for the grandparents, the honored elders, the ones who give to the young an inkling of that very mystery of life and rebirth.

Directions for making a shofar

The shofar can be made of the horn of a ram, antelope, gazelle, goat, or Rocky Mountain goat. These horns are not solid bone, but contain cartilage which can be removed. The word shofar means "hollow." The above animals are kosher since they have split hooves and chew their cud.

Ram's horns can be obtained from slaughterhouses. Butcher store owners may be able to get them from their suppliers.

"Traditionally a ram's horn is sounded . . . because of its connection with the sacrifice of Isaac, the story of which is in the Torah reading for the second day [of Rosh ha-Shanah]. Conversely, a cow's horn may not be used because of the incident of the golden calf" *(Encyclopaedia Judaica).*

STEP 1

Boil the shofar in water for at least two hours and probably as long as five. A bit of washing soda added to the water facilitates later cleaning. The cartilage can be pulled out with the aid of a pick. If the horns are small, the cartilage can be removed in about half an hour.

STEP 2

With a soft wire, measure how far the hollow of the shofar extends. Measure one inch farther on the outside and cut the tip off with a coping saw or hacksaw. The horn should completely dry before cutting.

STEP 3

Drill a ⅛" hole with an electric drill from the sawed-off end until the bit reaches the hollow of the horn.

STEP 4

Using various bits from an electric modeling set (we use the Dremel Model #2 Moto-Tool Set, which looks like a light-weight electric hand drill and comes with about 24 attachments), carve a bell-shaped mouthpiece at the end of the shofar, similar to the one on a trumpet. Smooth the edges of the mouthpiece with the electric model tool. The mouthpiece may require modification in size and shape for each shofar and person. An experienced shofar-blower or trumpet player can test out the shofars.

The electric modeling tool can also be used to carve designs on the outer edge of the shofar as well as on the body of the shofar. There must be no holes in the sides of the shofar and no paint or anything added to the shofar.

Thus far we have not been successful in reshaping the curves of the shofar. We used them as they came naturally.

With the electric tool, the outside and inside surfaces of the shofar can be smoothed. We do not smooth over shofars; they are rough and uneven. However, when blown properly, the shofars sound beautiful.

The Four Species

It is a positive commandment from the Torah to gather together the Four Species during Sukkot:

"On the first day you shall take the product of *hadar* [goodly] trees, branches of palm trees, boughs of leafy trees, and willows of the brook, and you shall rejoice before the Lord your God seven days" (Leviticus 23:40).

"The first day" refers to the first day of Sukkot.
"Fruit of goodly trees" refers to the etrog (citron).
"Branches of palm trees" refers to the lulav.
"Boughs of leafy trees" refers to the myrtle.
"Willows of the brook" refers to the aravot or hoshanot.

The four are lumped together under the inclusive term lulav since the lulav is the largest and most prominent. Thus, while the mitzvah is to wave the lulav, this actually refers to the four taken together as one.

HOW THE FOUR FIT TOGETHER

The lulav is a single palm branch and occupies the central position in the grouping. It comes with a holderlike contraption (made from its own leaves) which has two extensions. With the backbone (the solid spine) of the lulav facing you and this holder in place near the bottom, two willow branches are placed in the left extension and three myrtle branches are placed in the right. The myrtle should extend to a greater height than the willows.

This whole cluster is held in the right hand, the etrog is held in the left, and the two should be touching one another. Some have the custom of picking up the etrog first and then the lulav—reversing the order when putting them down—because the etrog is referred to before the others in the biblical verse.

Waving the lulav

It is a mitzvah to wave the lulav on each of the first seven days of Sukkot. The proper time is in the morning—either before the Morning Service or during the service immediately before the Hallel. A meditation (found in the Siddur) is recited prior to the blessing (this has many kabbalistic secrets concealed within it). The blessing is:

"Blessed are You, Lord our God, King of the Universe, who has sanctified us with His commandments and has commanded us concerning the waving of the lulav."

בָּרוּךְ אַתָּה, יְיָ אֱלֹהֵינוּ, מֶלֶךְ הָעוֹלָם, אֲשֶׁר קִדְּשָׁנוּ בְּמִצְוֹתָיו, וְצִוָּנוּ עַל־נְטִילַת לוּלָב:

On the first day of waving add:

"Blessed are You, Lord our God, King of the Universe, who has granted us life, sustenance, and permitted us to reach this season."

בָּרוּךְ אַתָּה, יְיָ אֱלֹהֵינוּ, מֶלֶךְ הָעוֹלָם, שֶׁהֶחֱיָנוּ, וְקִיְּמָנוּ, וְהִגִּיעָנוּ לַזְּמַן הַזֶּה:

Before the blessing, the etrog is held with its pittam (stemlike protrusion) pointed downward. After the blessing, it is inverted so that the pittam faces up.

At this point you wave/shake the lulav (together with the other three) in the following manner:

1. Stand facing east.
2. Hold the lulav out to the east (in front of you) and shake it three times. Each time the motion of shaking should be a drawing in to you—i.e., reach out and draw in, reach out and draw in, reach out and draw in.
3. Repeat the same motion three times to your right (south), behind you, over your shoulder (west), to your left (north), raising it up above you, and lowering it down below you.
4. All of these should be done slowly and deliberately—concentrating on the symbolisms and intentions of the act. The lulav is also waved during Hallel while saying:

"Give thanks to the Lord for He is good, for His lovingkindness endures forever."

FRONT RIGHT BACK LEFT UP DOWN

הוֹדוּ לַיְיָ כִּי־טוֹב. כִּי לְעוֹלָם חַסְדּוֹ:

This verse occurs twice during Hallel.

The lulav is again waved while saying:

"Let Israel say that His lovingkindness endures forever."

FRONT RIGHT BACK LEFT UP DOWN

יֹאמַר־נָא יִשְׂרָאֵל. כִּי לְעוֹלָם חַסְדּוֹ:

And it is waved again while saying:

"We implore You, Lord, save us."

FRONT RIGHT BACK LEFT UP DOWN

אָנָּא יְיָ, הוֹשִׁיעָה נָּא:

אָנָּא יְיָ, הוֹשִׁיעָה נָּא:

For the Four Species

1. The four represent the four-letter Name of God—with the lulav being the vav which channels the divine energy into the world and man. If for no other reason, the four must be held together while waving for the Unity of the Name.

2. There is a masculine-feminine symbolism within the Four Species —besides that represented within God's Name. The lulav is obviously a masculine symbol and the etrog, with the form of a breast, is obviously feminine. Since these are conduits of divine flow, it is important that they be perfect and whole. The necessity of having the pittam intact makes ultimate sense in this context (cf. *Sefer Sefat Emet,* the comment on Sukkot).

3. Each of the species is a hint or allusion to God, according to a midrash found in Leviticus Rabbah, 83:

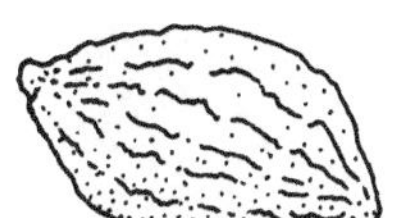

Etrog—because it is written (Psalms 104:1): "You are clothed in glory and majesty."

Palm—because it is written (Psalms 92:13): "The righteous bloom like a date-palm."

Myrtle—because it is written (Zechariah 1:8): "And he stood among the myrtle-trees."

Willow—because it is written (Psalms 68:5): "Extol Him who rides on the clouds [aravot], the Lord is His name."

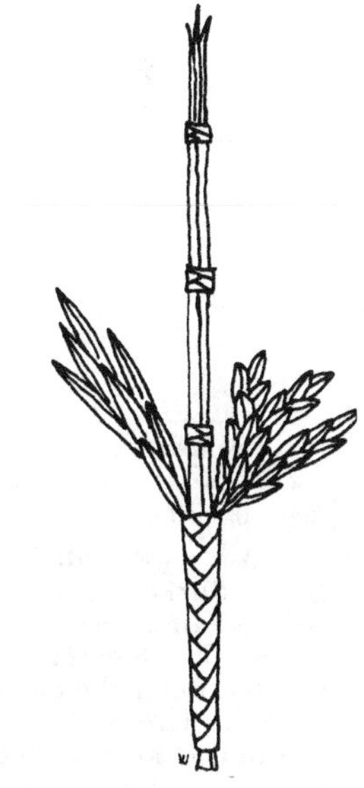

4. Each of the four relates to a particular limb through which man is to serve God (cf. *Sefer ha-Hinukh, #285*):

Etrog—refers to the heart, the place of understanding and wisdom.

Lulav—refers to the backbone, uprightness.

Myrtle—corresponds to the eyes, enlightenment.

Willow—represents the lips, the service of the lips (prayer).

5. Taste represents learning. Smell represents good deeds. The etrog has both taste and smell. The lulav has taste but not fragrance. The myrtle has smell but no taste. And the willow has neither. Each represents a different type of man. Some have both learning and good deeds; some have one without the other; and some have neither. Real community is found in their being bound together and brought under one roof.

For the wavings

The motion and order of the wavings is highly significant.

1. On a basic level there is simply the arousal of our joy, thanksgiving, and praise of God at the time of the final fruit harvest.

2. The directions are symbolic of divine rule over nature.

3. There is the representation of the fertility of the land and the desire for rain.

4. This is also representative of our complete immersion in the holiday. On one level, we are *surrounded* by the sukkah. On another level, through this motion (of bringing in toward us), Sukkot enters us. The lulav becomes a conduit of peace and God's presence from every direction. Transcendence and immanence. We gather in and are gathered in.

Through all of these, the themes of Sukkot are played out and interwoven beautifully: redemption, universal peace and brotherhood, completion.

Additional laws and customs

1. The lulav is not shaken on Shabbat—because perhaps you may carry it

(e.g., to the synagogue) and thereby violate the prohibition against carrying an object more than four amot (approximately eighty inches) in the public domain during Shabbat.

2. All of the Four Species must be fresh—i.e., not dried up.

3. Everyone must have his own lulav (set) since the commandment is to take them to *you*. You cannot borrow a lulav to use, but you can receive it as a gift—even if it was given as a gift on the condition that you return it.

HOW TO SELECT AND BUY THE FOUR SPECIES

With regard to selecting the lulav and etrog, there is an operative principle involved called hiddur mitzvah. This is a bit difficult to explain. Essentially it entails going beyond the specification for the "legal" minimum—to select the most beautiful, elegant, and as nearly perfect fruits as possible. Thus, although there are relatively few categories of absolutely unacceptable species, there are many criteria—we'll discuss these soon—relating to the level of beauty of the species. Much of the fun of buying sets is in making your own evaluations and selecting the best among large varieties. After knowing what the criteria are, choose what *you* like. You are the one who is going to have to live with your lulav and etrog for seven days.

Where to buy 1. Hebrew bookstores generally carry a stock of lulavim and etrogim. In less heavily Jewish populated areas, the store may only get a small number from which you can choose—but the same standards should be applied and the same care taken in selection as is outlined below. Check with the store owner well before Sukkot to see whether he supplies only for those who preorder or whether he stocks a general supply.

2. Most synagogues arrange to buy sets for their members or others in the community. Although convenient, you generally do not have control over the selection or price.

Here, as in a small store, there are a few points which you should keep in mind:

a. Most important. The closer it gets to Sukkot, the lower the prices will be. In a small store, this also means that the selection will be smaller. But in the Lower East Side market, there is little worry about finding beautiful species right down to the last minute. If you have the patience and self-control to wait until the last few hours—or at least until the late morning—of the day before Sukkot, you will find a phenomenal stock of fruits for a fraction of the price they originally sold at. Remember, the unsold, unused etrog is of no value to the vendor once Sukkot begins, so it is to *his* advantage to sell it to you for a price you are willing to pay (classic supply-and-demand theory).

b. Take your time. Look at each species carefully. Savor it. Comment on it. Ask questions about it. Hold it. Wave it. Test the balance. Ask other people's advice. Do not buy the first one you see. Act as if you know what you are doing. Not only will your bargaining position be better—but you will appreciate your lulav and etrog more after going through a careful examination and decision process.

3. If you are in New York, you can have a unique bargaining experience from what seem to be hundreds of street vendors who set up stands and stalls in the market area of the Lower East Side during the few weeks preceding Sukkot. There are both advantages and disadvantages to this setup. Advantages:

a. a huge, almost unending selection and price range;

b. the opportunity to bargain because of the highly competitive market (particularly if you are buying in quantity);

c. the incomparable flavor of the area.

The major disadvantage is that if you are not a bold bargainer you may get taken (in fact, you probably will get taken). Most of the sellers are excellent bargainers and use every trick they can during the transaction. Tricks range from intimidation to presenting only a small percentage of their stock (and claiming that this is "the last"). Also, the business is a quasi-cooperative —so the competition factor and the bargaining tolerances are less than would be expected. There is real joy, though, in taking up this challenge.

What to look for

The etrog You must pay the greatest attention to the selection of the etrog. Compared to selecting an etrog, choosing a lulav is like an afterthought. Begin the buying process with the selection of the etrog, then the lulav, then the myrtle, then the willows. It is with the etrog that the greatest variation exists and the greatest obligation for hiddur mitzvah—beauty—applies (based on the etrog being "the product of the *hadar* [beautiful] trees").

It must have a pittam; there are some varieties which do not grow a pittam to begin with and are therefore usable. But if you have an etrog without a pittam, make sure that it is from such a variety and that the pittam did not simply fall off.

It should be a good yellow color.

It should have a pleasing, basically symmetrical, oblong shape.

It should *not* have little black spots on it or any permanent discoloration or disfiguration (rub your nail over it to see if spots will come off). An etrog without any discoloration or black spots at all is very expensive and almost impossible to find. Still, these imperfections should definitely be avoided around the top third of the fruit (toward the side of the pittam).

For even greater elegance, there should be lengthwise ridges extending from the bottom toward the pittam. It is also good if the skin is sort of evenly bumpy. Again, the choice is yours as to what is and is not a beautiful etrog—color, shape, size, smell, weight, etc.

The lulav It should be fresh—i.e., not dried up.

It should be at least four tefahim (approximately 14") long so that it will shake well.

Its backbone—a solid ridge from which the leaves spread—ideally should extend from the bottom all the way to the top.

So that the leaves of the palm do not spread out obtrusively, the lulav should be bound at three points along its length. The bands are made from its leaves. If they are not already on the lulav, you can ask the seller to bind them for you, or you can improvise a bind yourself. (The three bands represent Abraham, Isaac, and Jacob; creation, revelation, redemption. . . .) Aside from this, it should have a good feel in your hand and possess whatever other qualities *you* feel a lulav should possess—e.g., good spring, length, tight leaves, loose leaves, a thick backbone, a thin backbone.

When you buy it ask for a plastic bag to keep it in. This will be used to preserve its freshness and protect it throughout the holiday.

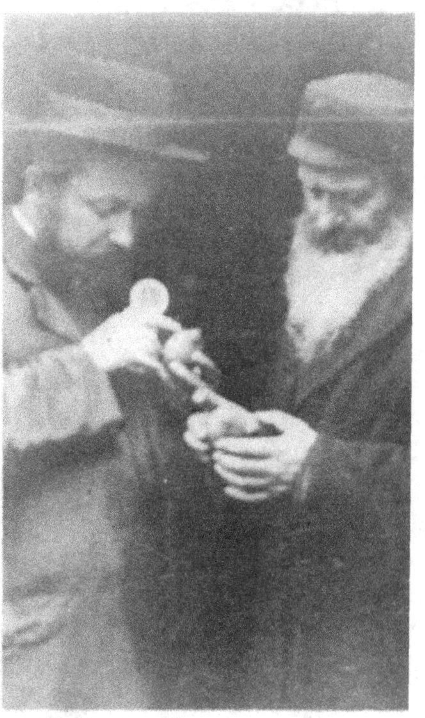

The myrtle They should be at least three tefahim (approximately 10") long.

There must be three branches.

The leaves of the myrtle, ideally, should grow in clusters of three at every spot on the stem. Often, however, the three leaves do not emanate from the exact same spot on the stem. You should select myrtle branches which have *at least* three clusters of three emanating from single spots—preferably near the top.

The willow They should be at least three tefahim (approximately 10") long.

There must be two branches.

The leaves of the willow, ideally, should grow in clusters of two at every spot on the stem. Often, however, the two leaves do not emanate from the exact same spot on the stem. You should select willow branches which have *at least* two clusters of two emanating from single spots—preferably near the top.

How to care for the species

Until you have to assemble them, store the parts separately. The etrog will come wrapped in a padding material and enclosed in a box. Make sure to keep it wrapped in this, with the pittam well protected. If you have a separate etrog box, store it there. Otherwise, keep it in its box and in a safe place. It is advisable, although not necessary, to keep it in the refrigerator. The etrog has an amazing quality: it will not rot. It will dry up, but not spoil.

The myrtle and willow will spoil and should be kept in the refrigerator wrapped in a wet towel. These will dry up and the leaves will fall off. So handle them with care. Avoid overhandling them. Once they are squeezed into the little holder gadget that comes with the lulav, it is best not to remove them, as this will generally rip the lower leaves off. Rather than do this, either:

1. take off the entire holder, wrap the leaves in a wet towel, and store in the refrigerator; *or*
2. slip the whole lulav with the holder and branches into the plastic bag, put a little bit of water in the bottom of the bag, seal (tie) the top. It can be left out as is or stored in the refrigerator.

The lulav will generally stay fresh for at least the seven days without any special care required of it.

What to do with it afterwards

Virtually nothing can be done with the myrtle and willow. Until it dries up, the myrtle can be used for besamim, spices, during Havdalah. If anyone knows some use for them besides a decorative one, please write us about it. The lulav can be:

1. Used for decoration. It has a certain slim elegance and graceful dignity to it.
2. Saved and waved on Hanukkah (see 2 Maccabees 10:5–8).
3. Saved and used in place of a feather for searching out the hametz before Pesah. Then burn it with the hametz.

The etrog has a number of wonderful uses after its need during the holiday is exhausted:

1. Collect etrogim from friends and make etrog marmalade: Slice etrog into thin cross-sections. Place in a pot or bowl of water for four days or so. Change the water every day. This serves to take out some of the abundant bitterness and acidity of the etrog. For the curious, try tasting a bit of the water on the second or third day. After this process, proceed with any marmalade, jelly, or preserves recipe. You may have to add oranges for volume. Even if the etrog is but a small part of the whole, it is worth the effort.
2. Collect etrogim from friends and make etrog wine.
3. Stick a lot of whole cloves into the etrog. Cover totally with powdered cinnamon and let dry for a few weeks. You will then have a wonderful spice essence. Use it for Havdalah. Let it cast its fragrance in a closet. Give it to a friend.

SHALOM

Jewish travel

What particular difficulties does the observant Jewish traveler face? In my experience, I have found two major potential trouble areas—kashrut and the observance of Shabbat. I hope to be able to pass on to you some hints which have proved valuable to me so that no observant Jew need be deterred from traveling.

KASHRUT

The entire kashrut problem has been made immeasurably easier by the upsurge of vegetarianism. Most major cities in Europe have at least one good vegetarian restaurant, as do many of the smaller cities. They are generally clean, serve interesting and healthful food, and are far less expensive than other restaurants. The atmosphere is almost invariably friendly and informal, a far cry from the ordinary situation in normal restaurants. One can find a list of these restaurants in the *Jewish Travel Guide,* published by Jewish Chronicle Publications and distributed by Bloch Publishing Company. For a more complete list write to:

A note of warning:
Everyone has differing standards of kashrut and I in no way intend this section to be taken as a pesak halakhah—a halakhic decree. If you do not eat cooked food in restaurants, ignore what I have to say about it. What I am trying to include is simply a few hints for making *your own* particular level of observance easier in a foreign country.

National Health Food Society
1615 North Wilcox
Box 432
Los Angeles, Cal. 90028

You might also want to refer to *The Vegetarian and Macrobiotic Guide to Europe, 1973,* by Howie Simkowitz, available for $1.25 from:

Craftsbury Publishers
Craftsbury, Vt. 05826

It offers maps and descriptions of health food restaurants in Europe.

I would think that even strictly traditional kashrut observers can be fully satisfied with the kashrut of these restaurants, as, in my experience, they do not serve fish or any other animal foods.

In addition, in most major European cities there are kosher restaurants. They vary in quality from city to city; however, one thing remains constant—the high prices. In justification, I suppose that this is necessary since so few people patronize them; however, such rationalizations do nothing to alleviate the strain on your purse. Nonetheless, for the strictly observant these restaurants are certainly a mainstay. I feel they deserve the patronage of all who care about kashrut.

In any case, if you choose to eat gefilte fish in five different languages, then you can have it in England, Italy, Spain, Holland, and France. As you might guess, it has been my experience that generally these restaurants serve more Jewish food than the cuisine of the particular country in which they are located. One exception that I have found is the kosher restaurant in Florence, located right next door to the exquisite synagogue. This restaurant served excellent Italian food.

Another alternative, and one which is often more satisfying than restaurant eating, is to do your own shopping in the local stores. Fruits, vegetables, canned salmon and sardines, bread and butter, etc. are convenient to eat if you carry a few plastic forks and knives and a can opener with you. It is always nice to have a picnic in your room or someplace on the open road. This has certain other added advantages:

1. It enables you to discover the market areas in the city.
2. You get a chance to compare products and prices.
3. It provides you with an opportunity for striking up conversations with the natives.

Incidentally, we have always found that shopkeepers, waiters, etc. were cooperative once we could make them understand what we wanted. A word of caution: you are better off not trying to explain about kashrut. If you say you are a vegetarian, everyone will understand what that means and will help you choose foods accordingly.

For anyone traveling in Ireland, there are the castle banquets given at various castles throughout the country. Having been told that they were really delightful (albeit a bit touristy), we decided to attend and not eat. When we sat at the banquet not eating, but thoroughly enthralled by the atmosphere and the entertainment, the people in charge inquired why we were not eating. We explained that we were vegetarians, and they insisted on fixing us plates of bread and butter, lox, and salad. This kind of concern and cooperation is, I find, generally the norm throughout Europe and renders your eating peculiarities considerably less of a problem.

All in all, observing kashrut may require a bit of planning and ingenuity, but it is certainly possible and should not deter people from traveling.

SHABBAT

Shabbat, depending upon your own personal level of observance, may present some problems.

In a large city where there is a synagogue and a rabbi, the first thing to do always is to contact the rabbi. This may frequently result in an invitation to the home of either the rabbi or one of the local congregants. There are, occasionally, other alternatives which the rabbi will know about. As we found in Dublin, there was a lady who served kosher Shabbat meals for tourists in her home. We spent a very pleasant Shabbat afternoon there and made some fine acquaintances.

For the most part, however, when you have made no other arrangements, make it a habit to buy food on Erev Shabbat. If you have a refrigerator in your room or can use space in the hotel's refrigerator, you can often buy food at the kosher restaurant and eat it cold on Shabbat. If you are in a place where there are no kosher restaurants, you can buy canned foods and bread and crackers. You will eat a most un-Shabbat-like meal, I will admit, but one which, under the circumstances, will certainly be adequate.

The larger problem is really how to spend the day. This is especially true in northern Europe, where Shabbat is not over during the summer until ten or eleven o'clock at night.

If you are in a city with a synagogue, by all means attend the Shabbat services. This is your best link with the Jewish community. Here you will be able to see and feel the pitiful decline of European Jewry. In many of these former flourishing Jewish centers there are but a handful of Jews, many of whose children emigrate to Israel.

It is of interest to notice the differences in the synagogue services from country to country. At times these distinctions may be minor, but they are always fascinating.

Shabbat is a great time for taking walks and really poking about a city. It is also a good time to catch up on your much-needed rest after a week of sightseeing and touring. Depending on your own inclination, it can be a good idea to visit the museums on Shabbat, many of which are free. If there is an admission fee, you can try to arrange to pay before Shabbat begins; but the explanation may not always be worth the trouble.

These are really only a few ideas; but, as I have sometimes found Shabbat to go on interminably, I would be happy to hear from anyone who has other suggestions.

GUIDE TO WESTERN EUROPE

There are three good books listed in the Bibliography, all of which give the reader a detailed account of what points of Jewish interest there are in the various countries. These books are very complete and well written and I need not repeat what they say. I should like, however, to add a few things which I have found particularly meaningful as a Jew, and which often are not mentioned in these books.

The first European country I visited was Denmark. This was my own private way of expressing gratitude to the Danes, one of the few peoples to engage in an all-out effort to save the Jews in 1943. Aside from all the charm, beauty, and friendliness of this country, there is a museum of major interest to all Jews. The Museum of the Danish Resistance, part of the National Museum, is a small museum located on the Esplanade near the lovely little mermaid. The museum illustrates the conditions under which the Danish people carried out their struggle for freedom during World War II. A special section is devoted to the Jews and displays photographs depicting Jewish persecution at the hands of the Nazis, the efforts of the Danes to effect their escape, and the help provided by the Swedes.

For those visiting Rotterdam, a city which was entirely destroyed by the Nazis, the monument erected to commemorate that destruction is a chilling sight. The monument, symbolizing the death of a city, depicts a man without a heart.

On a visit to London, don't miss Hyde Park corner on a Sunday afternoon. There are always speakers representing all shades and varieties of opinions, from the serious to the ridiculous. You can move from speaker to speaker and hear views on vegetarianism, Scottish home rule, and, of course, the Israel and Arab situation.

Students interested in visiting England should write to the London Hillel House, which publishes a brochure offering tips and hospitality to visiting students. Write to:

Rabbi Cyril K. Harris
Bnai Brith Hillel Foundation
1 Endsleigh St.
London WC1H ODS
England

Should your travels take you to Glasgow, you may hear the only Jewish pipe band in the world, with headquarters at:

65 Albert Rd.
Glasgow, Scotland

Their repertoire includes both Scottish and Hebrew numbers. The Glasgow Jewish Lads Brigade has been playing the pipes and drums and doing highland dancing since 1921.

In Florence, make a special effort to visit the synagogue because it is particularly beautiful. The exquisite Venetian mosaics make it a unique work of art. It took eight years to build and, of course, it was heavily damaged during World War II. It was restored with government help.

There is much of artistic interest to Jews that can be found in the various museums of Florence, and these are listed in the books I have mentioned. However, I would like to call your attention to the truly magnificent pair of bronze doors of the baptistery of San Giovanni done by Ghiberti. The ten panels depict scenes of the Bible.

In Venice, be sure to visit the ghetto, which was the first ghetto in Europe. There are five beautiful synagogues there, only two of which are in use. In addition, located there is an exhibition of ritual art, an old age home, and a kosher restaurant.

In this ghetto there exists one of the most unique shops I have ever seen. The owner creates and sells small figurines of blown Venetian glass which depict Jewish scenes. I have seen figurines of a Jew holding a Torah, a marriage scene, and a man holding a lulav and etrog. They are really exquisite and the small ones make excellent gifts. If you arrive at the right time and are really lucky, you may find the owner in the process of blowing the glass for the figurines. The name and address of this shop is:

Tosi Gianni
Ghetto Nuovo 2884
30121 Venezia

These are a few of the places of interest I have found. If you travel at all, you will have additions from your own list of favorites which I hope you will share with me.

GUIDE TO THE SOVIET UNION

Travel arrangements

You must work through American Express, Cooks, or one of the other travel agencies that are affiliated with INtourist (the Soviet travel agency). It is best to make arrangements with one of the bigger agencies since they are more likely to have representatives in Moscow. It is also best to travel with one or two other people. As soon as you are in a large group you are much less mobile and will find it harder to break away and meet people. When making arrangements for connections between cities, especially if they are distant cities, insist on plane connections and not train. Train rides can be very long (even if two cities appear to be adjacent on a map) and tiring. If there appear to be any discrepancies in your itinerary, e.g., if you are to spend two nights on a train even though the two cities are close to one another, have your travel agent check it out BEFORE YOU LEAVE. It is almost impossible to change your itinerary once you arrive in the Soviet Union. (When I tried to change mine I was emphatically informed by the head of INtourist in one city, "This is our country. You will see it our way or you won't see it at all.")

Before you leave make a Xerox copy of your visa and voucher. If you are made to pay any additional fees upon arrival get exact receipts for all payments.

Things to take to the Soviet Union

Jewish paraphernalia You are allowed to bring into the Soviet Union religious items for your own personal use. Instead of bringing many pieces of one item bring an assorted range of materials. If you are checked at customs when you enter you might have a hard time explaining why you need six prayer shawls or seven copies of the same Siddur. Instead you might take the following:

a prayer shawl (tallit)
a Siddur
a mahzor (festival prayer book)
a skullcap (you can take more than one of these)
phylacteries (tefillin)
small Bible (Hebrew-Russian if available)
Haggadah
Jewish calendar
hallah cover
Kiddush cup
Sabbath candlesticks
Jewish stars on a chain (you can bring a number of these)

If you are searched at customs when you enter the country DO NOT LET THE OFFICIALS TAKE THESE ITEMS AWAY FROM YOU. BE POLITE BUT ADAMANT.

Tell the customs official that they are for your own personal use and you know that it is the law that you are allowed to bring them in with you. The most that they might do is write on your visa that you brought them in and say that they will check to make sure you take them out. If, perchance, you don't have them when you leave, you can say that you lost them or that you left them in your hotel room and when you came back they were gone.

Books Bring modern works of fiction, specifically those with a Jewish theme *(The Source, the Fixer, Night, The Slave, The Chosen).* You will probably meet people who speak English well and are anxious to improve their reading knowledge. They are very happy to receive books of this nature.

A useful book of your own to have is a small pocket English-Russian dictionary.

Clothing Gifts of clothing are very much appreciated. Women's pantyhose are a very valuable gift, as are jeans, sweaters, men's knit shirts, and most other American articles of clothing.

Maps Good street maps of Russian cities are not easily available in the Soviet Union. They are obtainable in the West. Though it might take some legwork, try to buy them before you leave.

Phone numbers and use of the phone Get all phone numbers that you might need before you leave. It is very difficult to find a phone book in the Soviet Union. All phone calls from your hotel must go through the switchboard. If you are calling a private home, it is better to make the call from a phone booth outside the hotel. You will need a two-kopeck piece for the telephone. The phones operate backwards from the ones owned by "Ma Bell" in the United States; you deposit the two-kopeck piece, wait for a click, and *then* you pick up the receiver.

NOTE: Phones tend to work in the Soviet Union, and trains run on time.

Food If you observe dietary laws you might want to take certain portable and easily prepared food with you, such as powdered soup mixes, cans of fish, etc. If you are going during Passover take your own matzah because you are not going to find it for sale in the Soviet Union. Also helpful for Passover travelers are gerry tubes. These are plastic tubes used by hikers and campers and available in most camping supply stores. You fill these with anything squeezable (honey, jam, mayonnaise, ketchup, applesauce, haroset, etc.) and then you seal the bottom with a clasp that comes with the tube. Though this may seem to be a minor matter, remember that there will be little available on Passover that you can eat. In many cities fruits and vegetables are hard to obtain, so do not assume that you will be able to live on them. You can buy a hot plate in large department stores (e.g., GUM in Moscow) or in an electrical supply store, so that you will be able to warm up food, soup, and make tea and coffee. If you have your own guide take him/her along to help you make the purchase.

Film Take lots of film with you and a flash attachment. People will often let you take their picture indoors but not outdoors. Before you take someone's picture, ask him/her if it is all right.

Miscellaneous 1. Take a few small snapshots of yourself. They are nice mementos to leave with people you meet.

2. You will constantly be asked for your name and address. If available take the sticky mailing labels with your name and address already on them (the kind sent out by philanthropic organizations). This way you can give out your address discreetly and without delay. If you can't get these labels, then write your name and address on a few slips of paper each morning before you leave your hotel. Keep them handy and be ready to give them to someone if asked. This is particularly important on days when you will be visiting the synagogue.

3. Though your hotel room will probably NOT be bugged it pays to be careful about what you say in the room—or for that matter in any room or building. A handy thing to have in this case is a child's slate, the type with the plastic cover that erases when you lift up the plastic. This is much simpler than writing notes and tearing them up and makes a nice gift for a child at the end of your visit.

4. Chewing gum is very much coveted by Russian children and will be greatly appreciated (by children if not by their parents). If you are morally opposed to giving out gum then cheap ballpoint pens also are nice gifts for children.

5. Russians are heavy smokers and drinkers, and American cigarettes and liquor are good gifts.

Languages If you can, take along a working knowledge of Hebrew, Yiddish, and Russian (in addition to English and hand signals). Many young Russians have taught themselves Hebrew, and others, particularly university-educated ones, know English. If you don't know Russian, try at least to familiarize yourself with the Cyrillic alphabet so that you will be able to read the street signs.

How to meet Jews in the Soviet Union

The guide and the INtourist officials may ask why you want to visit it or tell you that there is no reason for you to go. DO NOT LET INTOURIST OFFICIALS DISSUADE YOU OR FRIGHTEN YOU INTO NOT GOING.

Synagogue The easiest place to find Jews in the Soviet Union is at the synagogue. Try to get the address and general location of the synagogue before your trip. If you did not do that, do not be afraid to ask your guide for the address and instructions on how to find it.

Ironically, sometimes INtourist is very happy to arrange a tour of the synagogue for you. After showing you the building and introducing you to the sexton and rabbi, if there is one, they will probably say something like this: "You see, Jews have a place to pray and books and religious leaders. Now you know that their protests are unjustified."

When to go to the synagogue In order to meet Jews at the synagogue, it is best to go on Friday evening or Saturday morning. It is important that you go without a guide. The more often you are seen at the synagogue the less hesitant Jews will be about approaching you and talking to you. Therefore, if possible, try to attend daily services. Young people, specifically those interested in emigrating, gather there on Saturday mornings. The synagogue is one of the few places where it is not necessary to hide the fact that one is a Jew. It serves the Russian Jews, the younger people in particular, as a Jewish club (moadone) or Jewish Community Center, at the same time offering them an opportunity to manifest their religious-national affiliation.

How to act in the synagogue Upon entering the synagogue the gabbai (sexton) will attempt to shepherd you up front to a special section reserved for important guests. If you sit there, few Jews will be able or willing to approach you in order to talk. Try, therefore, to find a seat in the back as soon as you enter and politely decline to move if requested to do so. However, do not be overly adamant about not moving if the gabbai insists upon it.

Women will be made to sit in the women's section and be asked to cover their heads whether they are married or not. Be sure to have a scarf or some sort of hat with you. Men will be expected to wear a kippah or hat.

If you are offered an honor, accept it and try to read or sing your blessing in as loud and clear a voice as possible. If you know how to pray and know Hebrew, it is important that you pray aloud and even shuckle and shake some. This may seem like a minor detail or may appear to be false piety, but it is very important and reassuring to the Russian Jew to know that Jews in other countries, especially young ones, know Hebrew and are familiar and comfortable with the service.

There will probably be people in the synagogue who will want to talk with you but will be afraid to approach you. When services are over, hang around the building and walk around the area very slowly in order to make it easier for others to make contact with you. On important holidays, e.g., Simhat Torah, Rosh ha-Shanah, Pesah, when the synagogue is crowded, many people will stand outside in the vestibule or on the street. Go outside and stand in the crowd, for at times such as these, people are less reticent and reserved.

Do not accept anything in writing from anyone in the synagogue or, for that matter, anyone at all other than a name and address of a person who might wish to correspond with you or the name and address of a relative he/she might wish you to contact. If you wish to give someone a prayer book or any other type of printed material, try not to give it to him in the synagogue. If you cannot arrange to meet him at another time or place, then be very discreet about handing anything to anyone. Do not give your prayer book or any Judaica to the rabbi or gabbai. Remember that not everyone in the synagogue can be trusted and that it pays to be careful about what you say about Israel, the Soviet government, the struggle for Soviet Jewry, and so forth. There is nothing wrong with telling people about the activities that are going on in their behalf in the free world, e.g., rallies, protest marches, congressional amendments; but do not express opinions about the Soviet authorities or system.

The Jewish cemetery Ask to be taken to the Jewish cemetery. Do not let your guide tell you that there is none. Any town that had a Jewish community and a synagogue had a cemetery. If you are asked why you wish to visit it say that you are looking for relatives' graves (the Russian people, by and large, are sensitive to the problem of separation of families because of war). While you are in the cemetery, ask to be shown the fraternal grave (the group grave used for those victims of Nazi mass killings) and request that the inscription on the grave be translated. There will probably be no mention of Jews in it (it might say something like: "Here lie the remains of 1,000 victims of the Nazis"). It is Soviet policy to make as little mention of *Jewish* victims of the Nazis as possible in order not to provide any motive for heightening religious-national consciousness.

If you are in Kiev, ask to be taken to Babi Yar. It is about ten minutes by car from the city. You will probably be told by your guide that it is very far from the city. IT IS NOT. It is very important that INtourist be aware of the fact that foreigners are concerned about these places and want to visit them.

Private homes (can anything in a Communist state be called private?) If you are invited to a home—accept. You will be treated as an honored guest and give the Russian family you are visiting a great sense of pride and pleasure. Your hosts will know whether it is safe for you to come or not. Follow the same rules here that you follow in the synagogue and in your hotel room. Be careful about what you say, do not be critical of the Soviet system or leaders, and try to listen more than you talk. Do not be afraid, however, of telling people what is known about them in the free world and about Jewish life in other places.

The street Other than in the synagogue and Jewish cemetery, Russian Jews will have to find you. To make the identification process easier wear a large and rather ostentatious Jewish star (the kind you might never wear in the United States) or a hai charm. You might also carry an El Al flight bag or a Yiddish or Hebrew newspaper. Whenever you have free time, walk up and down the street and meander slowly in order to give people an opportunity to approach at their discretion.

Information you should have and questions you will be asked by Russian Jews

People will want to know how much the outside world knows about the specifics of their struggle. Try to familiarize yourself with as many names and general details of recent cases of Russian Jews, especially from the cities you are visiting; e.g., if there was a sit-in in Kiev shortly before you arrived, try to know the names of the leaders and as many of the participants as possible. It is a tremendous morale-booster to Russian Jews if they know that the world Jewish community is aware of them.

The National Conference on Soviet Jewry
11 West 42nd St.
New York, N.Y. 10036

or your local Jewish Community Council should be able to provide you with the information which you need.

You will be asked questions about Jewish life in America: How many Jews are there? How many synagogues are there? How many Jewish children attend Jewish schools? How many yeshivot or day schools are there? How many schools for rabbis are there? Can you study Jewish history and Jewish philosophy in the university? (This is a question that you may not be asked, since to a Russian Jew such study in a university will seem to be an unbelievable state of affairs. If they don't ask, tell them that Judaic Studies Departments are being established by many private and public universities.) Is there any anti-Semitism in America (how are you going to answer that one?)? How many Jewish members of Congress are there? Does every synagogue

For additional information

An excellent booklet has been published by the American Jewish Congress, *How to Find and Meet Russian Jews: A Briefing Kit for Travelers to the U.S.S.R.* It can be ordered at $1.25 a copy from:

American Jewish Congress
15 East 84th St.
New York, N.Y. 10028

It includes street maps for finding synagogues and facts on Soviet Jewry as well as information that will facilitate meeting Russian Jews.

Check the Soviet Jewry section in the Bibliography for a list of books that will give you some background information.

have a rabbi? Do American Jews want to live in Israel? Do you want to live in Israel?

They will ask questions about Israel: What is life in Israel like? How many universities are there? Is it hard to get a good job? If I go to Israel will I be able to live wherever I want? Is it hard to learn Hebrew? How many Russian Jews have left Israel? Why did they leave? Do Israelis want Russian Jews to come to Israel? What is the weather like?

HOW TO TRAVEL CHEAPLY IN ISRAEL

Getting there

If you want to make the entire trip as inexpensive as possible, the first thing you should do is find a cheap flight. Generally, you can tell that a flight is the cheapest if it's a charter that stops in 43 different countries, each one of which makes you go through customs twice and doesn't even leave you time to change enough money to buy a postcard. If all these stops occur in the middle of the night, just when you are settling down to go to sleep, the flight is probably fifty dollars cheaper!

For all of this you'll need a student card, which you can obtain from any student travel service and can use not only for the flight but also for discounts on all public transportation as well as meals.

Your first night

If you have followed my advice about choosing a flight, you will no doubt arrive in Israel in the middle of the night when even your own mother wouldn't wait around in the airport to meet you. Don't take a cab anywhere—it's expensive. If not taking a cab to get where you're going means sleeping in the airport overnight—sleep in the airport. It's better to start off on the right foot anyway. Take out the sleeping bag that you were astute enough to pack and forget your inhibitions. Sack out right in the middle of customs and wait for the buses to start in the morning.

The country runs a hotel information service where they will put you in a cab at the airport (along with other people so it'll be a little cheaper) and get you a reservation at a hotel in Tel Aviv. This might be a worthwhile alternative for some people to consider, having been awake for six days now making all those midnight stops in those 43 countries. It can be costly—even more so if you share a room with friendly foreigners, since friendly foreigners abroad sometimes have this annoying habit of ripping off your travelers checks or money. Which brings me to my Hint of the Century: When in airports, hotels, restaurants, etc., put a bicycle chain lock on your wallet. A good idea can be to carry your wallet in your front pocket instead of your back pocket since I have been told that it is harder to unobtrusively empty a front pocket than a back one.

Arranging your base

Pick a city that you would like to spend time in. If you want to practice your Hebrew pick a small city, preferably one with a beach; if you're into sand (?) try the desert; if you want to be able to get around in English, stick to a big city.

After you have chosen your "base" city, take a bus there. Go to the nearest shul for a service (preferably Shabbat). Make yourself look as lonely, poor, and miserable as possible. Nine times out of ten someone will invite you home for Shabbat. (If nothing else, Israelis are famed for their hospitality.) If no one invites you for Shabbat, go to the rabbi and quote the following verse from *Pirkei Avot:* "And no man ever said to his friend: I have no place to sleep in Jerusalem" (5:7).

You have now arranged for a place to eat. While eating dinner with your newfound benefactors, casually mention that you have little money, it's your first time in Israel, you want to practice your Hebrew, you're very lonely, and you're a very undemanding person. Emphasize the undemanding part, since this will undoubtably render you a member of the less objectionable class of American tourists. If they don't suggest a place to stay for the rest of the summer, be it their own or a neighbor's, gently guide them into the discussion and tell them you'd be willing to pay $100 (or whatever you can afford) to share a room or sleep on the couch. This latter suggestion will not make your nights as uncomfortable as you might guess, since all Israeli beds are terrible anyway. Share anything! Ask for breakfast but no other meal. Breakfast you'll get anyway because no mother in Israel can resist force-feeding any live animal within a radius of three miles. They'll probably also force you to accept lunch and dinner periodically, to which offers you will say that really you shouldn't, which makes you seem uncomplaining and makes them happy and they'll feed you anyway

The $100 investment is the best of the summer for a number of reasons. First, it will give you a hold on a real Israeli family, and they'll try to help you as much as they can throughout the summer. For that $100 you'll not only get a bed and breakfast, you'll also get the most competent tour guides that any travel bureau can provide, plus, in many cases, transportation on your sightseeing tours with your adopted family and friends in the neighborhood when they take trips. Also, and equally important, you get exposure to real Israeli society. You will be invited to their parties. Their friends will become your friends. Their family will become your family. You will become an integral part of their society—the "dream" of any American student tourist.

If you fall in love with the family as much as they inevitably will fall in love with you, then it may even be worthwhile to spend more time at your base than in touring.

If this does become the case—settle in. Buy a very cheap bicycle for *no more* than $15, on which you can get $12 back when you resell it at the end of the summer (unless you connive a little, whereupon you may be able to sell it for $20).

Jobs while you're there

At all costs try to get a job. You can try working in some phase of what the family does, or teaching in the neighborhood, or working at a local American food chain joint (Wimpy's, fallafel stands, etc.). Don't get a full-time job—all you want is a morning or an afternoon job. There's always a need for people who can speak English and Hebrew in Israel. You can become cheap labor.

Two things can result from this. First, any expenses you had in the beginning are taken care of, and you can work at making back the flight money. Second, and more important, this gives you a chance to talk to the people with whom you will work; you will also be gratified by all the nachas people feel when they see an American working in Israel. The community accepts you and makes you feel much more at home. They will feel free to offer you hints and to laugh at your mistakes and experiences (another good sign of acceptance anywhere). If you are really extraordinary and they truly like you, they will yell at you for messing up the place, wasting time, wasting too much water in the shower, etc.

Hints

1. Get a haircut; Israelis are wary of foreign "hippies."
2. Travel light. Take one large bag and one small one for short trips.
3. Wear long pants in most cities because you never know when you will want to visit a holy place where they don't allow shorts.
4. Learn as much Hebrew as possible before you leave and be willing to learn more when you get there.
5. Take as many addresses of friends as you can—even ones that you don't think you will use.
6. Bring a sleeping bag (lightweight).
7. Before you go, contact the Israeli government tourist office for literature, information, etc. They can also give you information about visiting a kibbutz, should you be interested in that aspect of Israeli life. If there is no office in your city, contact Israeli Government Tourist Office:

   8929 Wilshire Blvd.
   Los Angeles, Cal. 90211

   31 St. James Ave.
   Suite 450
   Boston, Mass. 02116

   5 S. Wabash Ave.
   Chicago, Ill. 60603

   1118 St. Catherine St. W.
   Montreal, 110, Quebec
   Canada

   488 Madison Ave.
   New York, N.Y. 10022

   805 Peachtree St. N.E.
   Atlanta, Ga. 30308
8. For guides to Israeli travel, see Jewish Travel, bibliography.
9. When traveling through Israel, don't buy soft drinks when you are thirsty—buy watermelon. It's cheaper and healthier.
10. Also, when traveling try to buy your food in the shuk, market, before you leave. Buying food en route to anywhere is always expensive.

Ask as many questions as your fertile little brain can think up. Ask about the history of the land (something every self-respecting Israeli knows backward and forward). Ask about places to visit. Ask about anything you might be interested in. Ask about things you're not interested in. Ask about emigration, study, chickens, diamonds, trees, politics, etc.

In addition, every self-respecting Israeli will tell you his life history at the drop of a hat. Wherever you are in Israel, at any given moment there will be someone within a radius of two feet from you who is (a) an Iraqi who escaped while bullets flew over his head; (b) an Egyptian who dug a tunnel to freedom through the same 43 countries you stopped at on the way over; or (c) a Moroccan who smuggled in his 25 brothers and sisters, all of whom had glaucoma and would now be dead if it weren't for Israel. The thing is, all these stories are true and tucked away among them are fascinating and authentic personal histories. You will frequently meet Holocaust survivors, many of whose life histories can be terribly moving. Encourage these people to talk. You will be the wiser for it.

Traveling through the cities

Take as many independent short afternoon, evening, and day trips as you can (on your own). The bulk of Israel's population lives in an area roughly the size of New Jersey and therefore nothing is very far away from anything else. Netanya is only half an hour from Tel Aviv. Jerusalem is about one hour from Tel Aviv. Haifa is an hour from Netanya, and Herzlia is even closer to Netanya. So it's worthwhile to visit these places for an afternoon or evening.

There are many things to do; one of the best is just to walk. The important thing is to relax. If you feel like seeing a movie, see a movie. If you feel like idling the night away in a café, idle the night away in a café—they're abundant all over Israel. The best thing to help you decide what to do on these junkets is (besides referring to your trusty guidebook) to ask your adopted Israeli family and your newfound Israeli friends. More often than not, if they see that you show an interest in these short trips, they will not only accompany you, they will drive you there as well, since Israelis are compulsive about their land. After a while you'll become a haver (buddy) and can then make fun of American tourists as much as they do.

Things to see

It is not my intention to repeat that information already available in many guidebooks (see Jewish Travel, bibliography). Israel is full of cultural, historical, and aesthetic sites, and I strongly advise you to read a good history of Israel before you get there and to take along a guidebook when you go.

Gifts

As your summer ends you will remember that one of the main reasons your summer was so cheap was that you forgot to buy any presents for all your loved ones at home. Therefore, you will scurry off to a large city and in one day completely blow all the money you have managed to save by not eating

11. Israeli soldiers tend to have misconceptions about the morality of American women.
12. Watch your money and carry your wallet in your front pocket.
13. Bargain in the shuk and while bargaining, speak any language but English since everyone knows that all Americans are so wealthy that they can afford any exorbitant price that the Israelis can dream up!
14. Bring a gift with you for your future family in Israel. A good idea is to get it on the plane or at the duty-free shop. Also, bringing home an occasional watermelon or such can only endear you more to your family.
15. Buy postcards instead of taking pictures. Cameras only make you look and feel touristy, and with the price of film and the quality of picture you are likely to take, you're better off forgetting the whole thing.
16. Have a good trip!!!

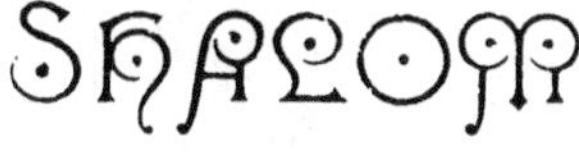

the whole summer. Unfortunately, this is where my advice breaks down, for try as I might I can see no way out of this bind. Sooner or later you will have to buy gifts for every member of your family or their feelings will be so hurt you will have to spend more money on another trip just to rest your nerves. You can try to buy gifts from people that you know in your base city so that at least they can also serve as mementos for you, but this will still cost you the rest of your savings. Another piece of advice is to get objects that are as unusual and as indicative of your travels as possible so that you will have a lot of material for Show and Tell when you relate your wild tales of the summer at home. If you are close to spending your last agurot on the last day of your summer, spend it and then plead with your loving family to drive you and your now overweight knapsack to the airport for your 3 A.M. flight home.

ALIYAH

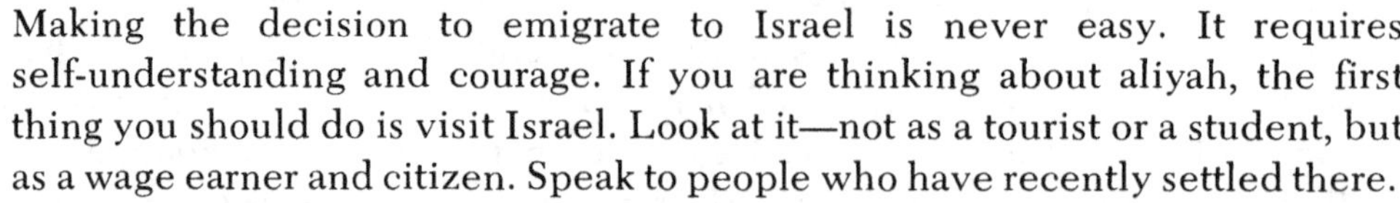

Making the decision to emigrate to Israel is never easy. It requires self-understanding and courage. If you are thinking about aliyah, the first thing you should do is visit Israel. Look at it—not as a tourist or a student, but as a wage earner and citizen. Speak to people who have recently settled there.

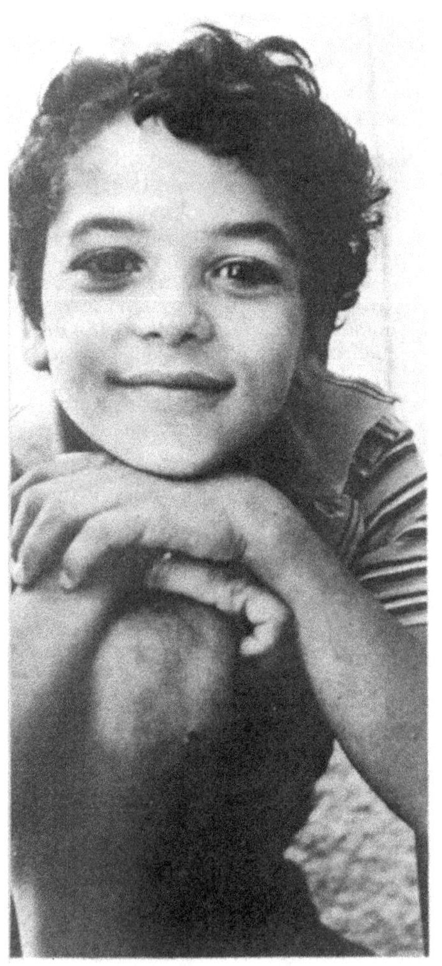

Aliyah is difficult. A person emigrating from America is leaving one of the most industrialized and civilized countries in the world. (Only when you leave it do you realize what you have been taking for granted for so long.) For some, this may be a reason for leaving; but if you are heading for Israel, you may find yourself disappointed.

Disappointments are due to improper preparation for aliyah, both mentally and financially. If you know what you are getting yourself into—exactly what profession you'll follow, where your apartment is, what to expect in the way of bureaucracy, standard of living, take-home pay, and life-style—then your aliyah and absorption into Israeli life and society will be easier, more pleasant, and more successful.

Every immigrant, whether he chose to emigrate or was forced to, reminisces about "the old country" and how good life was there. Inevitably, comparisons are made between "the old country" and Israel. These comparisons can be unfair, especially between America and Israel. Israel is, after all, only twenty-five years old, and although she is doing relatively well in the fields of science, technology, industry, etc., one cannot compare her standard of living to America's.

Rather than talk about what she is not, let's mention what Israel is. Israel is a good place to bring up kids—if you don't mind their picking up Israeli hutzpah along with the language. It's a place to live a slower, simpler life—if you don't mind working six days a week. It's a beautiful country—if you can see beyond the intense building all over the country. In addition, it's a wonderful place to be during holidays—religious and secular, major and minor. It commands a tremendous sense of unity during times of national trouble and joy.

For example:

1. The day before Yom Haatzmaut—Independence Day—is a day of national mourning for all those who gave their lives for the state. The nationwide siren goes off at the close of this day for two minutes of silence. At other times the siren is sounded in solidarity with the Jews of Russia. These times give rise to a tremendous sense of unity among the Jewish people.

2. On several celebrations of the New Month and one of the intermediate days of Passover and Sukkot, there is a mass "blessing by the

kohanim"—blessing by the priests at the Western Wall, with kohanim coming from all parts of the country to participate.

3. There is also the annual aliyat haregel—the traditional pilgrimage to Jerusalem on the three major festivals.

4. Every Hanukkah, the Flame of the Maccabees is lit in Modiin (home of the ancient Maccabees) and carried to all parts of the Jewish community.

5. Purim is celebrated all over the country—everyone, even the bus driver, wears costumes.

However, while times like these stir up those old Zionist feelings you had while living in galut, exile, these feelings somehow get lost and buried beneath the reality of aliyah.

Life in Israel on a day-to-day basis is what you make it. It can be just like it was in the United States—housework, business, studying, working, etc. But one of the nice things about Israel is that, somehow, all those things you never did before become more possible here. For instance, you might enjoy yourself by enjoying the country: join the local "nature preservation society" and go on hikes or tours. You could give a little of your time and help out. Visit patients in a hospital, institution, or orphanage. Tutor underprivileged kids from a slum area in English. Teach a new or old immigrant how to read Hebrew. Meet new Russian immigrants at the airport. Share in their happiness and befriend them. You could make use of the fact that you are from America and begin to introduce some good old American know-how into ecology, traffic control, consumer protection, education, national recreation and physical fitness, culture and the arts, youth group work, community and synagogue groups for education, socializing or volunteer work. You know how to do these things because you have seen them done.

Bureaucracy

There is a rabbinic saying that the land of Israel can only be gained through much difficulty and hardship. The Jewish Agency tries very hard to enable every immigrant to feel that he has participated in fulfilling this prophecy.

The Jewish Agency
515 Park Ave.
New York, N.Y. 10022

is in charge of the absorption of the new immigrant, so it—unfortunately—becomes the new immigrant's first contact with Israelis and Israeli bureaucracy.

Israel is almost Kafkaesque in its bureaucracy, and the most important thing the new immigrant can have when dealing with it is patience. The joke about it having taken 2,000 years for the State of Israel to have come about, so what's another day (week, month, year!) is no joke here.

All countries have immigration laws and all kinds of red tape one has to go through, and Israel is no exception. To the new immigrant from a Western country, this will probably be his first acquaintance with all the formalities of becoming a new citizen and so he plunges into Israeli bureaucracy. Everything happens in a relatively short period of time: arranging suitable temporary and permanent living accommodations, finding suitable jobs, registering in schools, changing status, changing money, getting loans and a mortgage, buying furniture, appliances, etc., in addition to learning the language and getting used to living in a new, foreign, and somewhat primitive environment. You need plenty of patience, a sense of humor, and a few sympathetic friends. Once you make it over the "initiation period," which runs anywhere from one to three years, you can settle down to a comfortable, uncomplicated life.

Some pointers

Aliyah is not easy. Many Americans go back—because they can't make a go of it economically (no job available for their specific skill) or socially (life on the kibbutz and/or living with Israelis or even putting up with the bureaucracy is hard). But then there are those Americans who, in spite of it all, stick it out and actually enjoy living in Israel and can be considered an important, productive part of this up-and-coming Israeli society.

If you keep a few things in mind, you can help make your own aliyah and integration into Israeli life much easier and smoother.

1. Your reasons for coming to Israel must be as clear to you as your reasons for leaving America. You must realize what you are coming to and not be drawn by naive idealism, or you will be quickly and unhappily disillusioned.

2. That is why a visit or "pilot" trip ("Tour Ve Aleh," arranged through the World Zionist Organization and the Jewish Agency) is so necessary. While here, make sure to speak to Americans who have recently come on aliyah; speak especially to those in your profession or field of interest.

3. An excellent organization, the only one of its kind, is the Association of Americans and Canadians for Aliyah (AACA). The address is:

515 Park Ave.
New York, N.Y. 10022

In Israel it is known as the Association of Americans and Canadians in Israel (AACI). Its head office is at:

76A Ben Yehuda St.
Tel Aviv

It is an industrious organization working for new Americans and Canadians in Israel. It has brochures and booklets available with information about packing, shipping, appliances, furniture, clothing, etc. for the potential oleh (immigrant) gathered from the experiences of Americans and Canadians who have emigrated. Once in Israel, you can get information from this organization about all sorts of things, including ulpans (study centers for rapid assimilation of Hebrew), job placement, tours, educational and social programs. It is becoming active in such areas as consumer protection, education, and immigration rights. It is a place where you can find a sympathetic ear when the going gets too rough and you feel like leaving. It's a worthwhile organization to join because its aim is to help you.

4. The Jewish Agency has aliyah offices all over the United States, and it would be worthwhile checking with them for job and housing possibilities, as well as for shipping and housing loans.

5. Unless you have spent time in Israel as something other than a tourist, you are probably unaware of the term zechuyot, privileges. As a new immigrant you are entitled to certain privileges for three years. For example, you can take to or buy in Israel one of each electric appliance without paying a luxury tax, you can receive packages from abroad without tax, you can leave the country without paying a travel tax, you can have a gradual income tax, six months' free health care, etc. These privileges are constantly being revised and changed, as is the whole matter of status (what you are considered when you enter the country—tourist, student, temporary resident, new immigrant). Each one needs a different type of visa and has its own advantages and disadvantages regarding privileges. It is all very confusing, so check with both the Jewish Agency and the AACA/AACI.

6. A last word of advice: *Get things in writing!* The promise of a job or an apartment from a representative in the U.S. of the Jewish Agency or any company, the clarification of status and privileges from Ministry of the

Interior—all this is valid only if you have it in writing. This is absolutely necessary because there is a communication gap between many branches of the government and between sections in Israel and abroad. As long as you are a potential oleh who still resides in the U.S., people will promise you almost anything to get you to Israel. Whenever possible, check into the validity of these promises and get them in writing.

Literature

1. As mentioned earlier, check with the AACA/AACI for their helpful and informative brochures.

2. More information is available in the form of two books put out by the owner of a duty-free appliance store and a building and finance company, both with offices in Tel Aviv and New York. A 100-page book entitled *How To Be an Oleh: Things the Jewish Agency Never Told You* by Murray S. Greenfield, is available for $2 from the author at:

21 W. 39th St.
New York, N.Y. 10018

3. A pamphlet entitled "How to Live on $450 (IȽ 1, 890) a Month without Even Trying" is available from:

Isralom, Israel Home and Real Estate Corp., Ltd.
71A Ben Yehuda St.
Tel Aviv; *or*
P.O.B. 3450
Tel Aviv

Finally . . .

Even if you know what to expect, if you follow everyone's good advice, and nothing of a serious nature goes wrong with your trip over, daily life in Israel takes a lot of getting used to and a lot of putting up with.

You're bound to hear a lot of complaints. You'll meet a lot of dissatisfied people. But you'll also meet a lot of people who are doing things to eliminate the complaints and dissatisfaction. Many people feel that there is something special about Israel that makes it really their "home." It's true for me; maybe it will be true for you. Shalom!

BIBLIOGRAPHY FOR JEWISH TRAVEL

1. Bazak, ed. *Israel Guide.* New York: Harper & Row, 1972. $3.95.
Includes wonderful walking tours of cities as well as good descriptions of restaurants, including a rating system.

2. Fodor, Eugene. *Israel 1973.* New York: McKay, 1973. $7.95.
Very detailed, comprehensive guide to the country.

3. Freedman, Warren. *The Selective Guide for the Jewish Traveler.* New York: Macmillan, 1972. $6.95.
Includes Jewish historical background—interesting reading.

4. *Green Flag.* Compiled by *The Jewish Travel Guide,* Jewish Chronicle Publications, 1972. $3.45.
Lists synagogues, kosher restaurants, kosher butchers, rabbis, etc., in all the communities.

5. Lieber, Joel. *Israel on $5 and $10 a Day, 1970–1971.* New York: Arthur Frommer, 1970. $2.50.
Grand for a person who wants to travel economically.

6. Postal, Bernard and Abramson, Samuel. *The Landmarks of a People–A Guide to Jewish Sites in Europe.* New York: Hill & Wang, 1971. $4.95 paperback.
Good descriptions of Jewish sites in each country.

7. Postal, Bernard, and Koppman, Lionel. *A Jewish Tourist's Guide to the United States.* Philadelphia: Jewish Publication Society, 1954.
The only Jewish guide to the United States, informative, authoritative; now out of print.

8. Rand, Abby. *American Traveler's Guide to Israel.* New York: Scribners, 1972. $4.50.
An honest and approachable guide.

תאומים

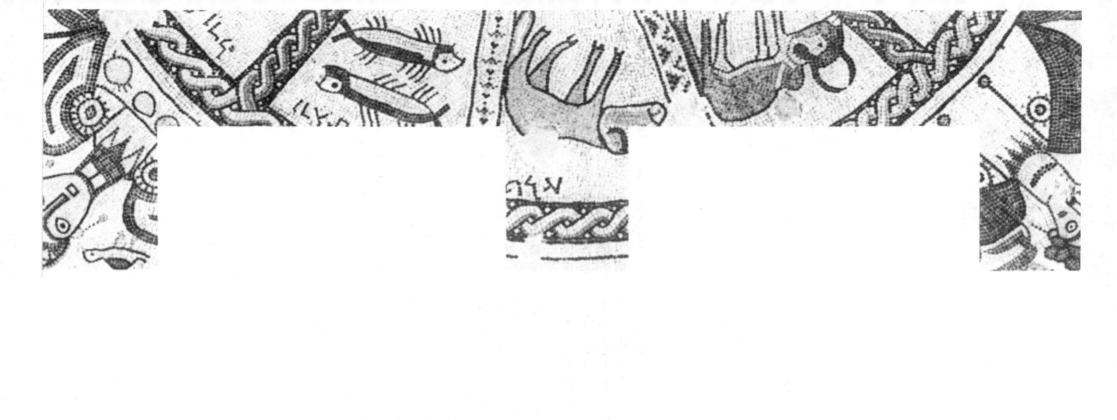

every day of a man's life is a Day of *Atonement*

The calendar

"Oh, what a catastrophe for man when he cut himself off from the rhythm of the year, from his union with the sun and the earth. Oh, what a catastrophe, what a maiming of love when it was a personal, merely personal feeling taken away from the rising and setting of the sun, and cut off from the magic connection of the solstice and the equinox!

"That is what is the matter with us.

"We are bleeding at the roots, because we are cut off from the earth and sun and stars, and love is a grinning mockery, because, poor blossom, we plucked it from its stem on the tree of Life, and expected it to keep on blooming in our civilized vase on the table' (D.H. Lawrence).

"The sun is always the same, always itself, never in any sense 'becoming.' The moon, on the other hand, is a body which waxes, wanes, and disappears, a body whose existence is subject to the universal law of becoming, of birth and death. . . . For three nights the starry sky is without a moon. But this 'death' is followed by a rebirth: the 'new moon.' . . . This perpetual return to its beginning, and this ever-recurring cycle make the moon the heavenly body above all others concerned with the rhythms of life. . . . They reveal life repeating itself rhythmically. . . . It might be said that the moon shows man his true human condition; that in a sense man looks at himself, and finds himself anew in the life of the moon" (Mircea Eliade, *Patterns in Comparative Religion*).

INTRODUCTION

Naturally, Jews have their own time (generally fifteen minutes late!). This affects the time units of years, months, weeks, and days. Jews follow a lunar-solar calendar which uses the moon for its basic calculations, but makes adjustments according to the solar seasons. The United States, on the other hand, uses a strictly solar calendar.

THE MOON

The moon waxes and wanes and so reflects the fluctuating fate of Israel. Yet, like Israel, the moon is always renewed. As such, it was seen as a sign of Israel's redemption, and so was a comfort during periods of persecution. Much of the Blessing of the New Moon ceremony (see below) speaks of the hope for redemption and the restoration of the Davidic kingdom.

R. Simeon b. Pazzi pointed out a contradiction [*between verses*]. *One verse says,* And God made the two great lights [*Genesis 1:16*], *and immediately the verse continues,* The greater light . . . and the lesser light. *The moon said unto the Holy One, blessed be He, "Sovereign of the Universe! Is it possible for two kings to wear one crown?" He answered, "Go then and make thyself smaller." "Sovereign of the Universe!" cried the moon, "Because I have suggested that which is proper must I then make myself smaller?" He replied, "Go and thou wilt rule by day and by night." "But what is the value of this?" cried the moon; "Of what use is a lamp in broad daylight?" He replied, "Go. Israel shall reckon by thee the days and the years." "But it is impossible," said the moon, "to do without the sun for the reckoning of the seasons, as it is written,* And let them be for signs, and for seasons, and for days and years [*Genesis 1:14*]." *"Go. The righteous shall be named after thee as we find, Jacob the Small* [*cf. Amos 7:2*], *Samuel the Small, David the Small (cf. 1 Samuel 17:14)." On seeing that it would not be consoled the Holy One, blessed be He, said, "Bring an atonement for Me for making the moon smaller."*

—*Talmud Babli, Hullin 60b*

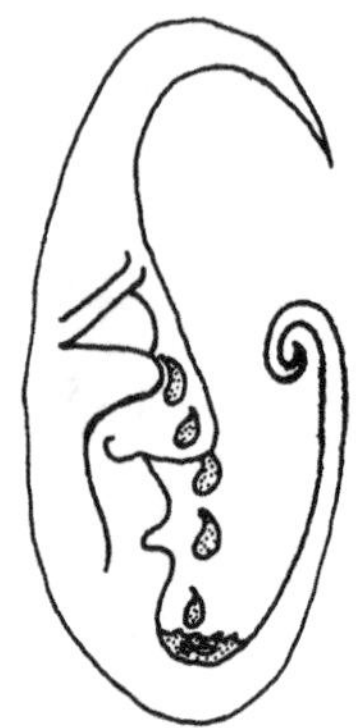

During the Blessing of the Moon, we ask for the restoration of the moon to its pristine brightness. In that time, Israel, too, will achieve its final redemption.

Traditionally the moon is also seen as symbolic of the feminine: it receives its light from the sun—receptiveness; and, more important, it has a monthly rhythm. Kabbalistically the moon is seen as representative of the feminine aspect of the divine—the Shekhinah.

Moon-watching

The difference between calculated and observed time is immeasurable. Calculated time is a mathematical product of the mind alone; observed time is the fruit of eye-and-mind involvement with the moon. Calculated time is homogeneous and repetitious: each day is twenty-four hours. Observed time is different each night: the moon manifests birth and growth, fullness and fading, death and rebirth.

Judaism, blessings upon it and us, did not abandon observed time despite the development of the calculated calendar. The importance of ancient moon-watching, reflected in the quite exciting material of Mishnah Rosh ha-Shanah, chapters 1 and 2, persists in the ceremony of Kiddush ha-Levanah or Birkhat ha-Levanah.

מראות הלבנה במשך החודש.
בעיגול החיצוני, מסומן בלבן, החלק של הלבנה המואר על־ידי השמש.
בעיגול הפנימי, מסומן בלבן, החלק המואר של הלבנה הנראה לעינינו.

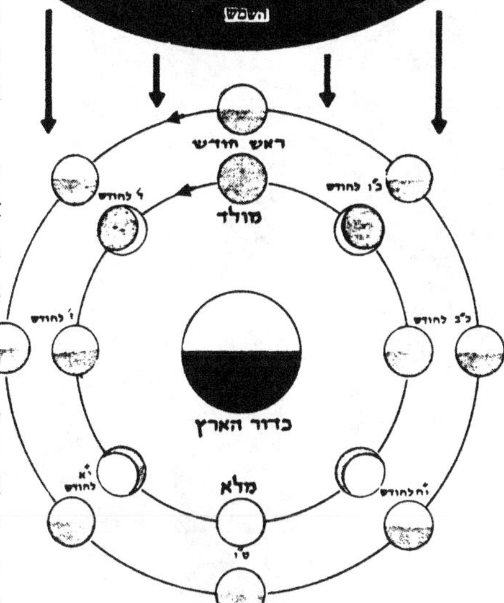

How to find and follow her To our eyes the moon, like all heavenly bodies, appears to move from east to west, but she travels more slowly than the sun. One might say that she lags behind the sun about 48 minutes per day. Around Rosh Hodesh—the beginning of the lunar month—she sets in the west shortly after sunset, and each day she sets some 45–50 minutes later. By full moon she is rising in the east at about the time the sun is setting in the west. (Hence Pesah, Sukkot, Tu b'Shevat, and Purim are fine times to see an almost simultaneous sunset-moonrise in the evening and moonset-sunrise in the morning.)

Lagging further and further behind the sun, near the end of the lunar month she is rising in the east nearer and nearer to sunrise. Finally, for three days she rises and sets so close to the sun that she is quite invisible (see Blessing of the Moon, below). Following which she is a new moon once more, and eyes again turn westward just after sunset. Moon-watch a few months and feel what you see, then see what you feel and let thinking follow!

The lunar year *generally* has twelve months. At one time these did not have names but instead had numbers; the first month, the second month, etc. Later, names were given to the months: Nisan, Iyyar, Sivan, Tammuz, Av, Elul, Tishri, Heshvan, Kislev, Tevet, Shevat, Adar. Nisan is the first month of the year, yet Rosh ha-Shanah—the New Year—occurs in Tishri, the seventh month. Rosh ha-Shanah marks the creation of the world—a different celebration from the first month of the year.

The determination of a month is dependent on the phases of the moon, which completes its cycle every 29½ days (approximately). Since this is uneven, one month may have 29 days (this is called חסר , lacking) and the next may have thirty days (called מלא , full).

Rosh Hodesh

"And on your joyous occasions, your fixed festivals and new moon days, you shall sound the trumpets over your burnt offerings and your sacrifices of well-being. They shall be a reminder of you before the Lord your God" (Numbers 10:10).

Rosh Hodesh celebrates the new moon, and, therefore, the new month. For thirty-day months there are two days of Rosh Hodesh: one on the 30th day of the old month and one on the first day of the new month. Since the months are actually only 29½ days, part of the 30th day is, in reality, a new month and is celebrated as such. On the other hand, a month having only 29 days will be followed by a one-day Rosh Hodesh for the new month. Nisan, Sivan, Av, Tishri, Shevat, and in leap years (see below) Adar I are 30-day months. Iyyar, Tammuz, Elul, Tevet, and Adar (Adar II in leap years) are 29-day months. Heshvan and Kislev vary.

Rosh Hodesh is commemorated by a special Musaf, the saying of יעלה ויבוא in the Amidah, part of Hallel, and a Torah reading of Numbers 28:1–15. In the Bible it was a day of festive meals, visiting prophets, and not doing business. The Shabbat before Rosh Hodesh is called Shabbat Mevarekhim. The exact time of the new moon in the coming week is announced and certain prayers are said. Some people have the custom of singing some part of the order of prayers to a melody associated with the month, e.g., "Maoz Tzur" for Kislev—the month when Hanukkah occurs.

Some people used to light candles both at the synagogue and at home, and prepared a festive meal to celebrate Rosh Hodesh. These are nice ways to sharpen one's appreciation for Rosh Hodesh and the moon's rebirth.

For kabbalists, the day before each Rosh Hodesh was a day of atonement and was called Yom Kippur katan—a minor Day of Atonement.

Those women who feel that it is important to be able to express womanliness in Jewish ways should take note of an interesting custom associated with Rosh Hodesh. Traditionally women did not work on Rosh Hodesh. This was seen as a reward, because after the exodus from Egypt the women refused to volunteer their jewelry for the making of the golden calf. This, once again, reinforces the feminine imagery so apparent in the moon and Rosh Hodesh and can help make this day a real celebration of the feminine.

"Had Israel merited no other privilege than to greet the presence of their Heavenly Father once a month [by reciting the blessing over the new moon], it would have been sufficient" (Talmud Babli, Sanhedrin 42a).

Blessing the New Moon: Birkhat ha-Levanah

1. It is a custom to bless the new moon. This is in remembrance of the way the new moon was publicly announced. In ancient times, any two witnesses would see the new moon and report it to the Sanhedrin—the ancient supreme court of the Jews—which would then proclaim the new month. Today, however, the whole procedure is done by calculation.

2. The Blessing of the New Moon should be done, however, between the third and fourteenth days of the new month, at which time the moon begins to diminish. The blessing is delayed until the third day because one should be able to see a significant portion of the new moon's light before blessing it.

"Whoever pronounces the benediction over the new moon in its due time welcomes, as it were, the presence of the Shekhinah" (Sanhedrin 42a).

3. The Blessing of the New Moon is usually done after Havdalah on Saturday night (see Candles and Candle-making). It is recommended that it be recited at that time because one is still in a festive mood and well dressed. However, it can be said any night during this period, even by oneself (i.e., without a minyan, quorum). The ceremony is found in the Siddur after the Shabbat Maariv—the Evening Service that ends the Shabbat.

4. The ceremony should be said (a) in the open air; (b) in a standing position; (c) with the moon visible.

5. It is customary to say "Shalom Aleichem" to three different people who answer back "Aleichem Shalom."

6. Since it was customary to dance at the announcement of the new moon, we rise on our tiptoes three times when we say, "Just as I dance before you and cannot touch you. . . ." Some actually do dance.

7. Everett Gendler suggests the following additions to the traditional ceremony:

   a. The reading of ha-Maariv Aravim either in Hebrew or in this translation:

You abound in blessings, Lord our God, Source of all Creations:
shading evenings with intent, brightening morning by design,
causing time to pass and seasons to alternate,
setting stars in their courses in rhythmic sway.
You are the Source of day and night
rolling light before darkness and dark before light,
passing on day and bringing on night,
yet always distinguishing day from night.
Lord-of-Heavenly-Hosts is His Name!
O God of Life, living eternally,
sway us too through time without end.
You abound in blessings, Lord,
shading skies as evenings descend.

—translated by E. Gendler

b. Among the traditional readings might be included the singing of:
"Kol Dodi"
"Dodi Li"
"Ha-Le-Lu-Hu B'tzil-tz'le Sha-ma" (Psalm 150)
"David Meleh Yisrael"
"Esa Enai" (Shlomo Carlebach's version)

c. The following free rendering of "M'Ha-desh Ho-da-shim" might be read:

Praise to You, Lord our God,
  King of the endless universe.
You chanted a word,
  and that word became–heaven!
You smiled and breathed forth suns and stars!
Seasons and cycles You gave to them;
  they ever waltz
    in their rhythmic courses.
They sing and rejoice
  as they dance their Lover's will:
"God is our architect,
His plan is good!"

To the moon He called:
"Polish yourself
bright and new!
Be a crown
for My lovely people!
One day
they'll polish themselves
and be bright as you.
I'll be their King.
They'll be My crown!"
Be praised then, Lord,
for renewing the months of moons.

—translated by Burt Jacobson

d. In addition, waving lighted sticks of incense yields a very nice effect as the lighted tips trace vivid patterns against the darkened sky.

BECAUSE OF THE EQUAL-TIME LAW, WE BRING YOU A WORD FROM THE SUN . . .

The sun, too, has a blessing which is so special that it only occurs once every twenty-eight years. This service is hard to find since it is not in most prayer books, so we'll give you a brief résumé.

In this service, the sun is blessed in thanksgiving for its creation and its being set into motion in the firmament on the fourth day of creation. The service is said after Shaharit on the first Wednesday of tekufat Nisan, when the sun is almost 90° above the eastern horizon. The date is based on the calculations of Abbaye, a talmudic sage, according to whom the vernal equinox cycle begins at this time. This method of calculation is now known to be inaccurate but is still used. The service consists of the following:

Psalms 84:12; 72:5; 75:2
Malachi 3:20
Psalms 97:6
Psalm 148

These are followed by the benediction "Praised be the Maker of creation . . ." (see Berakhot). Then follow Psalms 19 and 121, "El Adon," and the section by Abbaye from Berakhot 59b. The service ends with a short thanksgiving prayer which expresses our gratitude for sustaining us until this day and our hope that we may live to see the Messianic Age when "and the light of the sun shall become sevenfold, like the light of the seven days" (Isaiah 30:26).

The next occurrence of this celebration is April 8, 1981. Don't miss it!

RAMIFICATIONS OF THE LUNAR YEAR; OR, PASSOVER IN OCTOBER?

1. The lunar year has only 354 days, while the solar year has 365 days.

2. If we were to use a wholly lunar calendar for each solar year, the Jewish holidays would fall approximately eleven days earlier each year. Eventually, Passover would end up in the middle of winter and Sukkot would occur in July, despite the fact that Passover is called the festival of spring. For that matter, Shavuot, Sukkot, and Passover all are connected with the planting-harvest cycle.

3. To keep the holidays in their appropriate seasons, therefore, an extra month is periodically added to the lunar calendar.

4. This "leap month"—called Adar II, is added seven times in a nineteen-year cycle and serves to keep the discrepancy between the lunar and solar calendars at a minimum. It is added in the 3rd, 6th, 8th, 11th, 14th, 17th, and 19th years of the cycle.

5. Because of the slight discrepancy, Jewish holidays do change according to the non-Jewish calendar. Rosh ha-Shanah can, for example, occur anywhere from the first to the last week in September.

LENGTH OF THE DAY; OR, WHEN IS AN HOUR NOT AN HOUR?

There is concern in determining the actual length of the daylight hours.

1. The hours referred to above are not 60-minute hours. To calculate a Jewish "hour," take the total time from sunrise to sunset and divide by 12. The 12 equal units of daylight are called hours. Note that Jewish hours vary greatly in length from long summer days to short winter ones.

2. For example, if the sun were to rise at 5:30 A.M. and set at 8:30 P.M., the day would consist of 900 minutes, which, divided by 12 would yield 75 minutes per "hour."

3. This determination primarily affects the proper time for prayers. For example, the Talmud says that the morning Shema can be said only until the end of the third hour after sunrise; according to our example this would be

9:15 A.M. Shaharit can be said only until the fourth hour after sunrise (10:30 A.M.); Musaf may be said all day; Minhah can be started anytime after the sixth hour (1:38 P.M.) and can be said until sunset, although the preferred time is 2½ hours before sunset (5:22 P.M.). Maariv can be said all night starting at sunset (some however do not begin Maariv until 42 minutes after sunset (see "Period of Twilight").

5739/40 **1979** תשל"ט ׀ תש"מ

	January	February	March	April	May	June	July	August	September	October	November	December
1	2 Tevet Hanukkah 8	4	2	4	4	6 Shavuot	6	8	9 Ki Teze	10 Yom Kippur	11	11 Va-Yeze
2	3	5	3	5	5 Yom ha-Azma'ut	7	7	9 Tishah be-Av	10	11	12	12
3	4	6 Bo	4 Terumah	6	6	8	8	10	11	12	13 Lekh Lekha	13
4	5	7	5	7	7	9	9	11 Va-Ethannan	12	13	14	14
5	6	8	6	8	8 Aharei Mot Kedoshim	10	10	12	13	14	15	15
6	7 Va-Yiggash	9	7	9	9	11	11	13	14	15 Sukkot	16	16
7	8	10	8	10 Zav Shabbat ha-Gadol	10	12	12 Hukkat Balak	14	15	16	17	17
8	9	11	9	11	11	13	13	15	16 Ki Tavo	17	18	18 Va-Yishlah
9	10 Fast	12	10	12	12	14 Naso	14	16	17	18 Hol ha-Mo'ed	19	19
10	11	13 Be-Shallah	11 Tezavveh Zakhor	13	13	15	15	17	18	19	20 Va-Yera	20
11	12	14	12	14	14	16	16	18 Ekev	19	20	21	21
12	13	15	13 Ta'anit Esther	15 Pesah	15 Emor	17	17 Fast	19	20	21 Hoshana Rabba	22	22
13	14 Va-Yehi	16	14 Purim	16 Omer	16	18	18	20	21	22 Shemini Azeret	23	23
14	15	17	15 Shushan Purim	17	17	19	19 Pinhas	21	22	23 Simhat Torah Ve-Zot Ha-Berakhah	24	24
15	16	18	16	18 Hol ha-Mo'ed	18 Lag ba-Omer	20	20	22	23 Nizzavim Va-Yelekh	24	25	25 Va-Yeshev Hanukkah 1
16	17	19	17	19	19	21 Be-Ha'alotkha	21	23	24	25	26	26 2
17	18	20 Yitro	18 Ki Tissa Parah	20	20	22	22	24	25	26	27 Hayyei Sarah	27 3
18	19	21	19	21 Pesah	21	23	23	25 Re'eh	26	27	28	28 4
19	20	22	20	22	22 Be-Har Be-Hukkotai	24	24	26	27	28	29	29 5
20	21 Shemot	23	21	23	23	25	25	27	28	29 Bereshit	30 R H	30 R H 6
21	22	24	22	24 Shemini	24	26	26 Mattot Masei	28	29	30 R H	1 Kislev R H	1 Tevet R H 7
22	23	25	23	25	25	27	27	29	1 Tishri Rosh Ha-Shanah	1 Heshvan R H	2	2 Mi-Kez 8
23	24	26	24	26	26	28 Shelah	28	30 R H	2	2	3	3
24	25	27 Mishpatim Shekalim	25 Va-Yakhel Pekudei Ha-Hodesh	27	27	29	29	1 Elul R H	3 Fast	3	4 Toledot	4
25	26	28	26	28	28	30 R H	1 Av R H	2 Shofetim	4	4	5	5
26	27	29	27	29	29 Be-Midbar	1 Tammuz R H	2	3	5	5	6	6
27	28 Va-Era	30 R H	28	30 R H	1 Sivan R H	2	3	4	6	6 No'ah	7	7
28	29	1 Adar R H	29	1 Iyyar R H Tazri'a Mezora	2	3	4 Devarim	5	7	7	8	8
29	1 Shevat R H		1 Nisan R H	2	3	4	5	6	8 Ha'azinu Shabbat Shuvah	8	9	9 Va-Yiggash
30	2		2	3	4	5 Korah	6	7	9	9	10	10 Fast
31	3		3 Va-Yikra		5		7	8		10		11

5740/41 **1980** תש"מ ׀ תשמ"א

	January	February	March	April	May	June	July	August	September	October	November	December
1	12 Tevet	14	13 Tezavveh Zakhor	15 Pesah	15	17	17 Fast	19	20	21 Hoshana Rabba	22 Hayyei Sarah	23
2	13	15 Be-Shallah	14 Purim	16 Omer	16	18	18	20 Ekev	21	22 Shemini Azeret	23	24
3	14	16	15 Shushan Purim	17	17 Emor	19	19	21	22	23 Simhat Torah Ve-Zot Ha-Berakhah	24	25 Hanukkah 1
4	15	17	16	18 Hol ha-Mo'ed	18 Lag ba-Omer	20	20	22	23	24 Bereshit	25	26 2
5	16 Va-Yehi	18	17	19	19	21	21 Pinhas	23	24	25	26	27 3
6	17	19	18	20	20	22	22	24	25 Nizzavim Va-Yelekh	26	27	28 Mi-Kez 4
7	18	20	19	21 Pesah	21	23 Shelah	23	25	26	27	28	29 5
8	19	21	20 Ki Tissa Parah	22	22	24	24	26	27	28	29 Toledot	1 Tevet R H 6
9	20	22 Yitro	21	23	23	25	25	27 Re'eh	28	29	1 Kislev R H	2 7
10	21	23	22	24	24 Be-Har Be-Hukkotai	26	26	28	29	30 R H	2	3 8
11	22	24	23	25	25	27	27	29	1 Tishri Rosh Ha-Shanah	1 Heshvan R H No'ah	3	4
12	23 Shemot	25	24	26 Shemini	26	28	28 Mattot Masei	30 R H	2	2	4	5
13	24	26	25	27	27	29	29	1 Elul R H	3 Ha'azinu Shabbat Shuvah	3	5	6 Va-Yiggash
14	25	27	26	28	28	30 R H Korah	1 Av R H	2	4 Fast	4	6	7
15	26	28	27 Va-Yakhel Pekudei Ha-Hodesh	29	29	1 Tammuz R H	2	3	5	5	7 Va-Yeze	8
16	27	29 Mishpatim Shekalim	28	30 R H	1 Sivan R H	2	3	4 Shofetim	6	6	8	9
17	28	30 R H	29	1 Iyyar R H	2 Be-Midbar	3	4	5	7	7	9	10 Fast
18	29	1 Adar R H	1 Nisan R H	2	3	4	5	6	8	8 Lekh Lekha	10	11
19	1 Shevat R H Va-Era	2	2	3 Tazri'a Mezora	4	5	6 Devarim	7	9	9	11	12
20	2	3	3	4	5	6	7	8	10 Yom Kippur	10	12	13 Va-Yehi
21	3	4	4	5 Yom ha-Azma'ut	6 Shavuot	7 Hukkat	8	9	11	11	13	14
22	4	5	5 Va-Yikra	6	7	8	9 Tishah be-Av	10	12	12	14 Va-Yishlah	15
23	5	6 Terumah	6	7	8	9	10	11 Ki Teze	13	13	15	16
24	6	7	7	8	9 Naso	10	11	12	14	14	16	17
25	7	8	8	9	10	11	12	13	15 Sukkot	15 Va-Yera	17	18
26	8 Bo	9	9	10 Aharei Mot Kedoshim	11	12	13 Va-Ethannan	14	16	16	18	19
27	9	10	10	11	12	13	14	15	17	17	19	20 Shemot
28	10	11 Ta'anit Esther	11	12	13	14 Balak	15	16	18 Hol ha-Mo'ed	18	20	21
29	11	12	12 Zav Shabbat ha-Gadol	13	14	15	16	17	19	19	21 Va-Yeshev	22
30	12		13	14	15	16	17	18 Ki Tavo	20	20	22	23
31	13		14		16 Be-Ha'alotkha		18	19		21		24

NOTE: The days do not have names in the Hebrew calendar. They have numbers, i.e., Sunday is the first day, Monday is the second day, etc. Only Shabbat has its own name (although it is sometimes called the seventh day). This emphasizes the notion that all the weekdays are only an anticipation of the Shabbat.

4. This method of hour calculation is also used with regard to the laws about hametz—leavened bread—on the day before Passover. One can eat hametz until the end of the third hour after sunrise, and hametz may be in your possession until the end of the fourth hour (see Festivals). However, this method of calculation is not used for other issues; for example, the time one waits to eat dairy after eating meat (see Kashrut). These hours refer to 60-minute hours.

Period of twilight

1. A question emerges concerning the period of twilight. Exactly what is it—day? night? or both? Although the question may seem hypothetical at first, it takes on significance if one realizes that such problems as the proper time to begin and end Shabbat and holidays all rest on this issue.

2. There are two opinions about the duration of twilight: (a) 13½ to 18 minutes before sunset through sunset; *or* (b) from sunset to 42 to 50 minutes after sunset, i.e., until the time that three stars are visible.

3. Because of twilight's ambiguity, and concern for the observance of Shabbat, both opinions are observed. Since the 18 minutes before sunset could be night, Shabbat candles are lit Friday afternoon 18 minutes before sunset. Since 42 minutes after sunset could still be day, Havdalah is made at least 42 minutes after sunset on Saturday night.

4. Some people believe that twilight continues not 42 but 72 minutes after sunset, and so they wait 72 minutes before making Havdalah on Saturday night.

5. It is, however, not only a concern for twilight's ambiguous status that is involved in this issue. There is also a desire to lengthen the Shabbat and the holidays to make them last as long as possible before beginning the mundane week.

As time flies . . .

One can get a Jewish wall calendar (i.e., one with the Hebrew months, holidays, etc.) from many places, especially from kosher butchers. Many Jewish organizations put out a combination pocket calendar and appointment book. Ask around. If you cannot find one anywhere for free (try Jewish businesses—Morrison and Schiff sometimes gives them away), go to a Jewish bookstore (see Bibliography). Remember, these calendars run from September to September, not from January 1, so get your new one at the appropriate time.

There are also 100-year calendars which are good for those who like to plan ahead or for those who want to find out what their Hebrew birthdays were in 1953 or 1922, etc. Interesting trivia. One of the 100-year calendars around is *The Comprehensive Calendar, 1900–2000,* by Arthur Spier (published in 1952 by Behrman House).

Another 1920–2020 calendar can be found in the first volume of the *Encyclopaedia Judaica.*

A shul luach—synagogue calendar—gives much information, including changes in the liturgy because of holidays, exact times of the new month, etc. This comes either in booklet form or as a large wall hanging. Either can be obtained inexpensively from a Jewish bookstore (see Bibliography) or from:

Ziontalis Manufacturing Company, Inc.
48 Eldridge St.
New York, N. Y. 10002

Shabbat

Shabbat is a day so precious, so extraordinary, that to write about it seems an almost superhuman task—or perhaps a sacrilege. It is to explain a period of timelessness set off from the week, when our moving frenetic activities come to a slow halt and a sense of unutterable peace, soul-calm, and tranquillity can begin to be felt.

This period, from twilight on Friday to Saturday evening, gives us the opportunity to begin to let ourselves feel intense love and joy and appreciate that which we are often too busy to notice during the week. We can let our emotions come out—acknowledge them, examine them, know them so intensely that each moment becomes a complete experience.

It is not easy to begin to know Shabbat. But understanding what she is and what she is not can help. Indeed, understanding what the rest of the week is and is not can help too. Put it all in perspective. Figure out who is the master and who is the slave. Does your telephone (mail, work, study, office, house, car) control you or do you control it?

UNDERSTANDING THE OTHER SIX DAYS

What exactly happens in our lives during the other six days of the week? It's an interesting question and one that deserves some serious thought.

God commands us to work. "Six days you shall labor" (Exodus 20:9). The activities we do during those six days have an important place in our lives.

But there is danger in human productivity.

First, man paradoxically tends to become dependent upon the very instruments he has fashioned to free and serve him. . . . Second, the danger is very real in modern industrial society that man, as worker, becomes de-personalized and functions merely as a human cog in a vast assembly line. Above all, however, there is the opposite danger—the danger that man, aware of his power and success in dominating nature, will begin to regard himself as the measure of what is right and the yardstick of the good. "Beware," warned Moses thirty centuries ago, ". . . lest when thou hast eaten and art satisfied, and hast built goodly houses (probably split-level ones), and dwelt therein and thy silver and thy gold is multiplied . . . (when thine industrial plants and commercial enterprises have multiplied) then thy heart be lifted up, and thou forget the Lord thy God . . . and thou say in thy heart: My power and the might of hand hath gotten me this wealth!" Men are singularly susceptible to these spiritual foibles.

—*Norman Frimer, pp. 258–59*

[see Bibliography for Shabbat for complete references]

The point is, we should try to guide the world around us—positively and creatively. The very effort involved in doing this makes us understand the value of a "realm of time where the goal is not to *have* but to *be*, not to own but to give, not to control but to share, not to subdue but to be in accord" (Abraham Heschel, p. 3).

MENUHAH—SHABBAT REST

Throughout Jewish history, Shabbat has had an almost supernatural power.

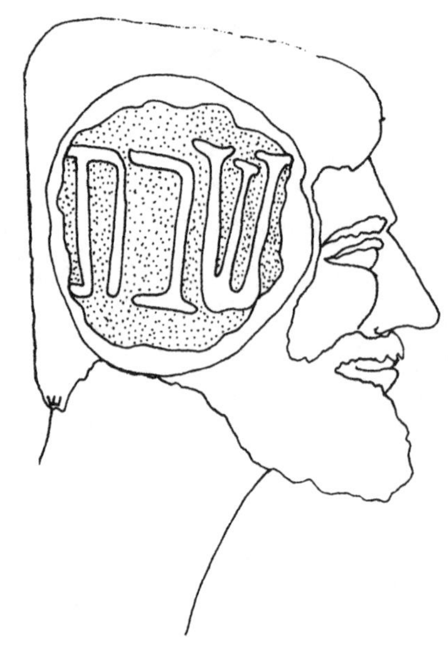

Within its bounds [is] one of the surest means of finding peace in the war-torn realm of the soul. It is one of the basic institutions of humanity—an idea with infinite potentiality, infinite power, infinite hope. . . . Through the Sabbath, Judaism has succeeded in turning its greatest teachings into a day. Out of a remote world of profound thoughts, grand dreams and fond hopes—all of which seem so distant, so intangible and so unrealizeable—the Sabbath has forged a living reality which can be seen and tasted and felt at least once a week.

—*Samuel Dresner, p. 14*

To help us achieve this state of menuhah, tradition forbids us to engage in many of our everyday activities. Refraining from these activities frees us for other activities, and a day of rest can then say to us: You can slow your life down. You can have the time to rediscover your family and friends. You can take a long walk, sing songs, dance, make love, have a feast, take a long time to pray, meditate, study, etc. You can talk, smile, laugh, sl-o-w-l-y—with intense care and joy. A yom menuhah frees us in the most basic sense of that word—to rediscover places inside ourselves that can get rusty without use.

Rest in the sense of the traditional Sabbath concept is quite different from "rest" being defined as not working, or not making an effort (just as "peace"—shalom—in the prophetic tradition is more than merely the absence of war; it expresses harmony, wholeness). On the Sabbath, man ceases completely to be an animal whose main occupation is to fight for survival and to sustain his biological life. On the Sabbath, man is fully man, with no task other than to be human.

—*Erich Fromm, pp. 195–98*

MELAKHAH—THE MEANING OF WORK

"The seventh day is a sabbath of the Lord your God: you shall not do any work [melakhah]" (Exodus 20:10).

The word melakhah is a puzzling one. It means work (this is its basic literal meaning). But it means work in a very different way from what we usually conceive of it. Not doing melakhah on Shabbat means not doing those acts which were necessary for the construction and furnishing of the mishkan—the sanctuary—in the desert. As Heschel wrote: "The Sabbath itself is a sanctuary which we build, *a sanctuary in time*" (p. 29). Therefore, the work involved in building the sanctuary was forbidden on Shabbat. These acts have been interpreted and expanded as new problems in society arose, but all concepts of melakhah stem from the original 39 forbidden acts.

As an example of how these melakhot were later interpreted, the prohibition against reaping came to include a prohibition against any severing of a natural growing plant from its place of growth; accordingly, picking flowers, breaking tree branches, plucking up grass all came to be forbidden.

In addition, Shabbat itself is the testimony that God is the Supreme Creator of heaven and earth. Our lives revolve around mastering our world—controlling God's creation. The more we try to control, the more we are in danger of forgetting just where we fit into the world. We too are dependent on God. We are beloved by Him, and share that love on the day of rest. Anyone who has ever tasted Shabbat knows the relief of laying down the burden for a while. The melakhah that we abstain from on Shabbat includes any "act that shows man's mastery over the world by the constructive exercise of his intelligence and skill" (I. Grunfeld, p. 19).

The prohibition against melakhah, then, means refraining from interfering in the physical world. We let the physical world rest for a while, and it lets us rest for a while.

The Sabbath is the day of complete harmony between man and nature. "Work" is any kind of disturbance of the man-nature equilibrium. On the basis of this general definition, we can understand the Sabbath ritual. . . . The Sabbath symbolizes a state of union between man and nature and between man and man. By not working—that is to say, by not participating in the process of natural and social change—man is free from the chains of time.

—*Fromm, pp. 195–98*

The 39 forbidden acts are:

Ploughing
Sowing
Reaping
Sheaf-making
Threshing
Winnowing
Selecting
Sifting
Grinding
Kneading
Baking
Sheep-shearing
Bleaching
Combing raw material
Dyeing
Spinning
Inserting thread into a loom
Weaving
Removing the finished article
Separating into threads
Tying a knot
Untying a knot
Sewing
Tearing
Trapping
Slaughtering
Skinning or flaying
Tanning
Scraping
Marking out
Cutting to shape
Writing
Erasing
Building
Demolishing
Kindling a fire
Extinguishing a fire
The final hammer blow
Carrying in a public place

THE WEEK REVOLVES AROUND SHABBAT

How do we move into Shabbat?

We cannot suddenly tune into Shabbat without preparation. We cannot all at once blot out the week, our work, our weekday thoughts and habits. The week must become a preparation, a path leading to the orchard of Shabbat.

The week surrounding Shabbat begins on Wednesday and ends the following Tuesday night. This is reflected in the halakhah of Havdalah, the ceremony which ends Shabbat. One is permitted to recite the Havdalah up until Tuesday night, because Sunday, Monday, and Tuesday belong to the past Shabbat; Wednesday, Thursday, and Friday belong to the coming Shabbat.

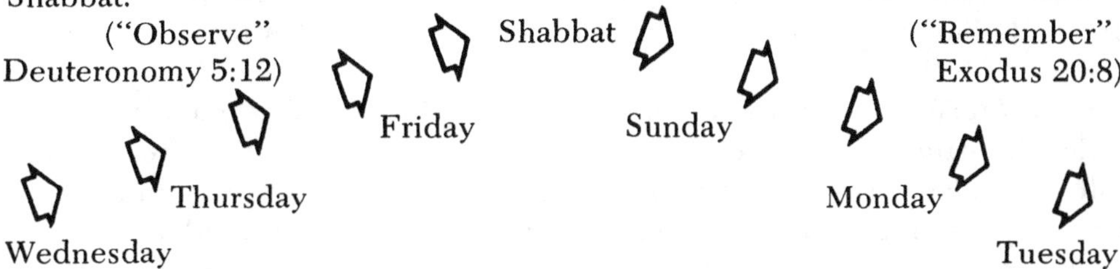

The week has a psychological and physical dynamic to it. First of all, the whole week, Sunday to Friday, can be viewed as preparatory for the coming Shabbat. Special foods are put away for Shabbat, the Shabbat tablecloths are cleaned, guests are invited (it is a mitzvah to have guests for Shabbat). Second, the week moves away from one Shabbat toward another. The days of the week exist only because of Shabbat. This is reflected in the fact that in Hebrew the days of the week do not have independent names, but rather are named in their relation to Shabbat. Sunday is "the first day to the Shabbat," Monday is "the second . . . ," and so on.

Shabbat
6. Friday
5. Thursday
4. Wednesday
3. Tuesday
2. Monday
1. Sunday

Each day of the week has a different "mood" which is determined by its distance from the Shabbat. Sunday is "the day after," the beginning of the week. On the Shabbat we had a taste of messianic life. Sunday is the day *after* the Messiah came: "Nu, where do we go from here?" On Sunday we try to pull some of the kedushah—holiness—of Shabbat into the week.

On Monday the Torah portion is chanted in the synagogue. The Torah gives additional strength to maintain the Shabbat feelings and to keep the kedushah in the week. By nightfall of Tuesday, however, the last vestige of Shabbat finally slips away. We cannot hold onto Shabbat any longer.

Wednesday begins the new Shabbat. Each day of the week has a special psalm, and at the end of the psalm for Wednesday, three extra verses are added. These verses are from the beginning of Psalm 95, the beginning psalm of the Kabbalat Shabbat Service. The aura of the new Shabbat has begun.

Thursday the Torah is read again—to gather strength for the coming Shabbat. And finally Friday arrives—"the sixth day in the Shabbat"—Erev Shabbat. Friday should be set aside as a special day of preparation.

Friday as Preparation

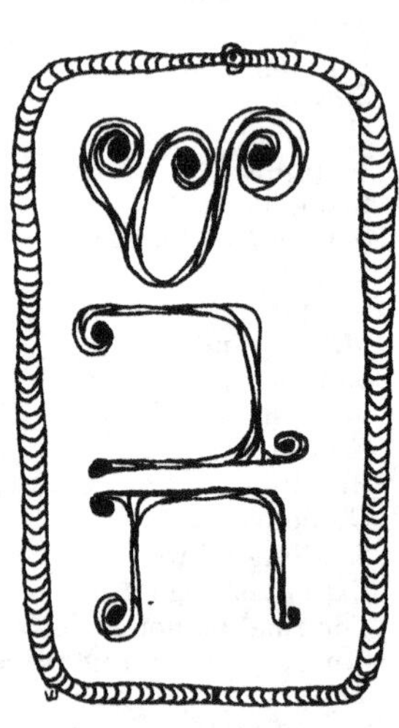

Physical Preparation Much work should be done Erev Shabbat. The house should be cleaned and the food cooked. The stove should be set so that food will be kept warm but will not cook. If you do not use electricity, the lights must be set—some to be left on, some possibly to be regulated by a timer. Muktzah—objects which cannot be used on Shabbat—must be put away (see Grunfeld, pp. 69–71, for further details). Hallot must be baked or bought, along with any other special Shabbat foods. The table has to be set, the candlesticks polished and set up. . . . All in all, we work up a frantic sweat on Friday. Finally toward evening it is time to wash up and put on fresh Shabbat clothes—and begin to unwind. It is customary to wear good clothing for Shabbat. If new clothes were bought during the week, they should be worn for the first time on Shabbat. On Friday it is good not to eat too much, so that when Shabbat finally arrives, you are not only thoroughly exhausted but also sufficiently hungry to truly enjoy and appreciate the Shabbat meal.

Spiritual Preparation Spiritual preparation on Friday is as important as physical preparation. To enter fully into Shabbat, the mind should be empty of all "weekday" thoughts; we should be at ease with ourselves and with others. All pressing "matters of consequence" must be left behind.

Spiritual preparation can take many forms, all depending upon the individual. Some people immerse themselves in a mikveh, a ritual immersion bath (see Tumah and Taharah—Mikveh). Such immersion spiritually cleanses a person so that he emerges with a "clean" soul—with a new life, as it were.

Many people set aside time to study the parshat ha-shavuah, the Torah portion of the week. This may be prepared simply by reading the portion in Hebrew or in translation or by more in-depth study utilizing one of the various commentaries. (Hertz, Hirsch, Rashi, and parts of Ramban are in English.)

It is good to set aside some money for tzedakhah, charity, on Friday afternoon.

As a further preparation, immediately before the Shabbat begins, some people spend time in meditation—reflecting upon the week, reviewing the past week day by day, relieving the mind of the "weekday mentality." It can be quite a beautiful experience to allow 15 minutes to an hour for this type of meditation each Erev Shabbat. As the week falls into perspective, it can become less of a weight and mental burden. You can then begin to enter Shabbat.

RESOULING THE WORLD

Dynamics—mood and setting The world is resouled every Shabbat, and the person who observes it gains a neshamah yetairah, an additional soul. The sages say that the neshamah yetairah brings with it that highest form of spiritual happiness created by Shabbat. These words are not empty ones; if one experiences a *real* Shabbat he will certainly feel the neshamah yetairah enter on Friday night and depart at the close of the Shabbat.

"Every seventh day a miracle comes to pass, the resurrection of the soul, of the soul of man and of the soul of all things. A medieval sage declared: The world which was created in six days was a world without a soul. This is why it is said: 'and on the seventh day He rested, *vayinnafash'* (Exodus 31:17): nefesh means a soul" (Heschel, p. 83).

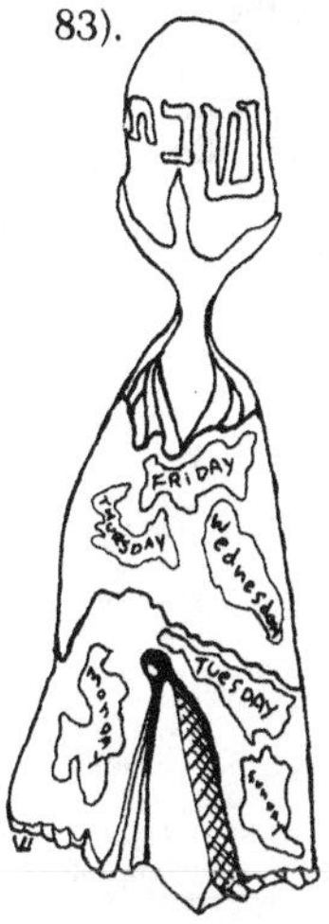

The basic theme of Friday night is creation. Shabbat is a remembrance of God's act of creation and of *God's* rest from that act. In our observance of the Shabbat, we bear witness to and affirm the creation. Specifically, on Friday night the creation motif appears in the Kiddush, in certain references in the Evening Service, in songs, and also in the propitiousness (according to tradition) of intercourse (natural creation) with one's spouse.

Creation, the physical world, is seen as feminine. The indwelling presence of God, the Shekhinah, is the feminine aspect of God. She rests with and within us on Friday night. The mystics extended this symbolism further, viewing Shabbat (Friday night) as the time of the holy wedding of the Holy One, blessed be He, with the Shekhinah—this being concomitant with the wedding of God and Israel, and with the wedding of Israel and Shabbat.

During the Friday evening service we say "and may Israel rest in *her.*" Shabbat herself is here conceived of as feminine. She is referred to both as Kallah—Bride—and as Malkah—Queen.

Shabbat as Kallah

This theme of Shabbat as bride is found extensively throughout the Friday night liturgy. Heschel wrote:

In the Friday evening service we say Thou hast sanctified the seventh day, *referring to the marriage of the bride to the groom [sanctification is the Hebrew word for marriage]. In the morning prayer we say:* Moses rejoiced in the gift [*of the Sabbath*] *bestowed upon him which corresponds to the groom's rejoicing with the bride. In the additional prayer we make mention of* the two lambs, the fine flour for a meal offering, mingled with oil and the drink thereof, *referring to the meat, the bread, the wine, and the oil used in the wedding banquet.* [*In the last hour of the day we say*] Thou art One *to parallel the consummation of the marriage by which the bride and groom are united.*

—Heschel, p. 55

"The symbol of a bride is love, devotion, and joy—an inward feeling. It is the peculiar inward feeling of the Jew which characterizes the Sabbath day. To him the Sabbath is a bride. Just as one prepares for a bride with the utmost care and meticulous detail, so the Sabbath is preceded by careful preparation. Just as one yearns for the arrival of a bride, so is the Sabbath met and welcomed. Just as the presence of the bride elicits tender concern, so does the Sabbath evoke love and devotion. Just as the departure of a bride occasions sadness, so is the departure of the Sabbath in darkness and regret" (Dresner, p. 17).

The sixteenth-century mystics of Safed created the Kabbalat Shabbat Friday evening service. Among the prayers is a beautiful song, "L'Kha Dodi," an excerpt of which is:

Come my beloved to meet the Bride.
Let us welcome the presence of the Sabbath
Come in peace . . . and come in joy . . .
Come, O Bride! Come, O Bride!

To the mystics of Safed,

the synagogue was not grand enough to receive the Sabbath: its walls were too limiting, its presence too confining. So they would go out into the open fields, dressed in white, the color of the wedding garment, and there chant psalms and sing Lekhah Dodi, accompanying the Shabbat Bride into their synagogue. Still today, when the last verse of the prayer is sung . . . the congregation turns from the Ark, faces the entrance and bows to the Bride who is about to enter.

—*Dresner, p. 19*

Shabbat as Malkah

Since all of Israel are princes and princesses, the Shabbat is not just a Bride, but a *royal* Bride, a Queen.

The Kallah symbolizes love.
The Malkah is law.
The Kallah evokes devotion.
The Malkah demands obedience.
The Kallah stands for feeling.
The Malkah represents observance.

"Inwardness, important though it may be, is not enough. There must likewise be an outward form, a pattern of conduct, a definite way" (Dresner, p. 21). Shabbat observance follows a general pattern which insures Shabbat "success." This pattern of behavior is symbolized by the Shabbat Queen.

Shabbat must be both Kallah and Malkah. A person's mood is easily subject to change—the Malkah comes to provide stability, to guarantee the mood; she lends permanence to Shabbat feelings.

"On the other hand, the law of the Malkah without the love of the Kallah would mean a harsh, officious, legalistic day" (Dresner, p. 26). Therefore, we have both Malkah and Kallah. The rabbis say that the two commandments of the Shabbat, "Remember the sabbath day" (Exodus 20:8) and "Observe the sabbath day" (Deuteronomy 5:12) were spoken by God as one command. " 'Remember the Sabbath day'—in your heart and soul with joy and love and inner peace; 'Keep [Observe] the Sabbath day'—keep its laws and statutes with devotion and loyalty and steadfastness. The Sabbath is both Bride and Queen, both remembering and keeping, both inward feeling and outward observance" (Dresner, p. 26).

NOTE: The sections on observance should not be taken as strict decisions of halakhah. They are intended merely as introduction to the basics of some Shabbat rituals, laws, and customs.

With the mood of Friday evening being gently feminine and infused with the aura of a wedding, it is a particularly sensual time—replete with good food, dim candlelight, songs, quiet talk, and enjoyment of both the physical and spiritual love of the family. It is a time for the spiritual growth of the family and the community. The communal aspect of Friday evening, indeed, of all of Shabbat, should be emphasized. Shabbat is best celebrated and most fully experienced from within a community. Particularly if you are just beginning to come to Shabbat—search out a community or communities with whom to explore it.

FURTHER NOTE: One point must be stressed. A person with little or no Shabbat background should *not* attempt to observe immediately all the Shabbat laws and customs in all their detail. Shabbat observance should grow gradually. Add something each week. Experience Shabbat with different people who have established their own modes. Again, seek out a community to grow with.

Friday Night

1. Lighting Shabbat candles. This marks the formal initiation of Shabbat. (See Candles and Candle-making for laws, customs, and rituals.)

2. Kabbalat Shabbat. This is a mystical prayer service made up of six introductory psalms (which represent the six weekdays as well as the kingship motif), "L'Kha Dodi" (representing the coming of Shabbat and the queenship motif), and the psalm for the Sabbath day.

The Maariv—Evening Service—follows. In the Amidah is the central reference to creation (Genesis 2:1–3). At the conclusion, it is customary to wish everyone else a Gut Shabbos or a Shabbat Shalom—a good and peaceful Shabbat.

3. Blessing of the children. After Kabbalat Shabbat, on arrival home, it is customary for the father to bless his children. The traditional blessing is, "May God make you like Ephraim and Menasheh" (for the males) and "May God make you like Sarah, Rebekah, Rachel, and Leah" (for the females). The

father places his lips on the child's forehead and holds the child while blessing him/her.

4. "Shalom Aleichem." The family or community, at the table, sing "Shalom Aleichem"—"Peace Be unto You" (found in the Siddur). This is a welcoming and an offer of hospitality to the angels who accompany us and the Bride during Shabbat. "Angels of peace, may your coming be in peace; bless me with peace, and bless my prepared table. May your departure be in peace, from now and forever. Amen."

5. Woman of valor. The husband sings to his wife the verses from Proverbs 31:10–31, extolling her virtues and declaring his love and appreciation. Although this has fallen into some disuse and has come under considerable attack contentwise, it can be a quite significant and beautiful ritual.

6. Kiddush—Sanctification. This is recited over a full (brimming) large cup of wine. The wine symbolizes joy—and the full cup symbolizes overflowing joy and bounty. On Shabbat there should be nothing missing from total physical and spiritual completion. Kiddush may be recited and drunk while (a) standing, (b) sitting, or (c) standing while reciting and sitting while drinking. There are a number of variations for holding the cup. Of particular note: place the cup in the palm of the right hand with the five fingers curled upward holding it. This symbolizes the five-petaled rose, the symbol of perfection, of longing for God (the petals reach upward), of the people of Israel.

The text of the Kiddush can be found in the Siddur. The first half is an account of the completion of creation on the seventh day—Genesis 1:31—2:1–3. The introductory phrase וַיְהִי־עֶרֶב וַיְהִי־בֹקֶר —"And there was evening and there was morning"—is said in a low tone. This allows the emphasis to fall on the first four words יוֹם הַשִּׁשִּׁי: וַיְכֻלּוּ הַשָּׁמַיִם —"the sixth day. The heaven and the earth were finished"—the first letters of which form the Tetragrammaton, the holy four-letter Name of God.

After this we recite the blessing over the wine.

The second half of the Kiddush recalls both the creation and the exodus from Egypt, the paradigm for all physical and spiritual redemptions and rebirths—and concludes with the blessing on the sanctification of the Shab-

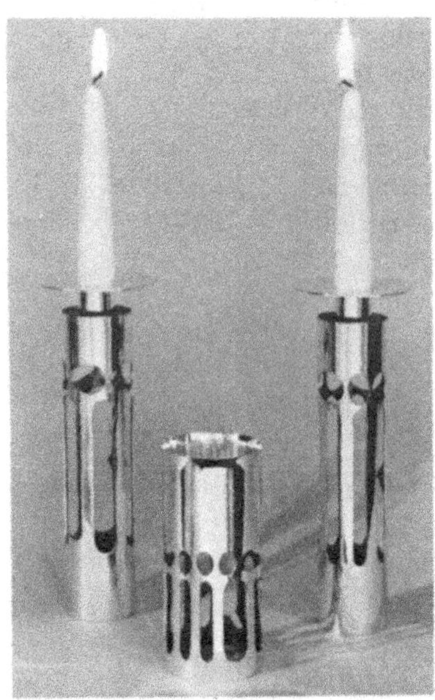

bat. If wine is not available, the Kiddush can be recited over the twin hallot. Simply substitute the blessing over the bread for the one over the wine.

7. Hallah. Following the Kiddush, the hands should be washed in the ritually prescribed manner. When everyone is reseated, the hallah cover is removed from the hallot, and ha-Motzi—the blessing over the bread—is recited. The hallah is then cut or broken, and distributed to each person. (For specifics regarding the full ritual, symbolisms, and intention behind this, see Hallah.)

8. The first meal—zemirot. It is a mitzvah to eat three meals on Shabbat: one on Friday night, one on Saturday after the Morning Service, and one late Saturday afternoon, before Shabbat ends. The first meal is a large one, with many courses. Before partaking of each course, some people say, "Likhvod ha-Shabbat"—for the honor of Shabbat—as a kavvanah, intention, to the act of eating. During and after the meal, traditional songs—zemirot—are sung. Some of these may be found in the Siddur. These zemirot for Friday night are quite beautiful, and while reflecting the mood and feeling of Shabbat, also add an important element to the setting. Sing a lot. Sing other songs (Hebrew, Yiddish, English) as well, if they fit in and contribute to the Shabbat mood. The zemirot on Friday night are generally in ¾ time—the grand waltz. Following the meal is the Birkhat ha-Mazon—Grace after Meals—(see Berakhot) with the special additions for Shabbat.

9. The night. After the meal, the time before going to sleep is usually spent talking to family or friends, and/or in the study of Torah.

Shabbat is the crowning glory in the life of the Jew. Countless generations of Jews followed the advice of Shammai the Elder who, whenever he found some especially tasty bit of food, would set it aside to be eaten on Shabbat. Jews who lived in poverty would deprive themselves all week in order to honor the Sabbath with light, wine, and proper food.

Why are Shabbat meals considered so important? If the Sabbath is a time of spiritual joy, why the concern with eating and drinking? The tale is told of a king who invited one of his subjects to come and dwell in the royal palace. Said the subject to the king, "I have a friend whom I love so dearly that I never allow myself to dwell apart from him. Only if you invite him to be with me can I accept your invitation. The soul refuses to leave the body; true joy can happen only when they rejoice together as one."

Two disciples once came before the master, filled with worry. "Is it really the Sabbath that we love?" they exclaimed, "or is it only the food and drink, the fine garments, and words of Torah?" The master had them set up a test, preparing all the material things as they would for Shabbat, and then enjoying them on a weekday. When the feeling they had seemed to them exactly like that of Shabbat, they came back to their teacher filled with woe; indeed, they must be sunk in the love of material things. The master's answer: "On the contrary—the Sabbath foods you eat and the Sabbath garments you wear are so filled with holiness that they stormed the gates of heaven and forced Shabbat to come to earth right in the middle of the week!"

God, the Sabbath, and the Jew are partners in a special bond of love. Testimony always requires two witnesses. In the Kiddush, God and Israel testify together that Shabbat is holy. In the Shabbat afternoon prayer, God and Shabbat testify together to the uniqueness of Israel. And all of Shabbat is a testimony by the Jew and his beloved day that God is One, and that the world is filled with His glory.

Shabbat is the Queen in God's kingdom, but she is also the Bride of Israel.

Shabbat Morning

Dynamics—mood and setting The central theme on Shabbat morning is revelation. The Torah, God's revelation to man, is read in the synagogue. The mood is quiet, more intellectual; we learn and teach Torah. We awaken to the unchanging reality of God and His Torah.

The Shabbat morning changes from the feminine imagery of Friday night to the masculine aspect of Shabbat. During the morning service, we say, "And may Israel rest in Him."

Observance—rituals and customs 1. It is generally preferable to pray with a minyan, a quorum of ten men, in a synagogue where there is a Torah, since the Torah reading is central to the service—dynamically and thematically. Both the Morning Service as well as Musaf, the Additional Service based on the ancient Temple sacrifices, are included in the davening.

2. After services, before the meal, Kiddush is recited, usually over wine, but another beverage may be used as well. The text of this Kiddush is quite different from the one recited on Friday night and is essentially just the blessing over the wine. (Check a Siddur for the full text.)

3. The ha-Motzi is made over the hallot again as on Friday night.

4. This meal usually consists of meat dishes—although some people prefer

to keep it light and serve dairy.

5. There should be singing at this meal also—reflective of the particular mood of Shabbat morning. The tempo is generally 4/4—march time.

6. Some people have the custom of always having some divrei Torah, words of Torah, taught during the meal.

7. Birkhat ha-Mazon is the same as on Friday night.

8. The period after the meal is a good time to take a short nap, learn some Torah, take a walk, visit friends, etc.

9. As the afternoon wears on, one should try to engage in some learning of Torah, whether in a group or individually. *Pirkei Avot* (Ethics of the Fathers) is a favorite for Shabbat afternoon. One does not need any background to study *Pirkei Avot,* and it can be found in most Siddurim translated and annotated. Although normally studied after Minhah—the Afternoon Service—it may be studied before as well.

Minhah–the final hours

Dynamics and observance The Shabbat may be viewed as a ladder of spiritual consciousness. As the time for Minhah, the Afternoon Service, approaches, we are on the highest rungs.

1. At Minhah, the first section of the following week's Torah portion is chanted.

2. "Abraham is glad, Isaac rejoices, Jacob and his sons find menuhah in *them.*" Shabbat now wears the aura of *them,* the holy union of the masculine and feminine aspects. The ecstasy of this union is felt on a spiritual level. The third meal, eaten after Minhah, is traditionally dairy, light and quite small, perhaps just some cake. Whereas on Friday night, at the beginning of the Shabbat, we needed sensual stimuli to "get into" it, by Minhah we no longer need physical stimulation. We are "high" on God.

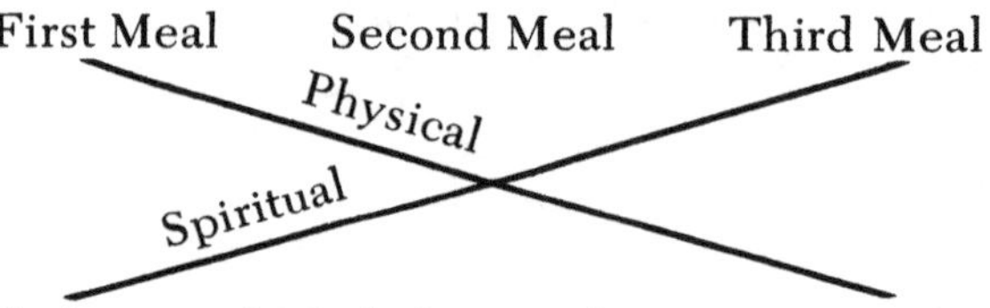

It is said that the Messiah will not come on Shabbat—because he is already present.

3. The central theme of Minhah is redemption—"and a redeemer will come unto Zion." The feelings are of the messianic time, when the Messiah will redeem the world and bring universal peace and rest. If we have really lived Shabbat, we now experience the complete or perfect rest of the messianic time to come. We usually say, "In *that* day (in the messianic future) will the Lord be One and His Name One" (everyone will truly recognize the Oneness of God). However, at Minhah we say to God, "Thou art One." At Minhah on Shabbat, God truly becomes One in the world, for this period is the true paradigm of the messianic future.

4. The mood is yearning, longing, mercy, and beauty. We are "Torah-dreamy." We become aware of man's inherent potential to bring the Messiah. The zemirot are slow and are sung over and over again. Many have reference to the messianic time. Words of Torah are usually spoken at the meal.

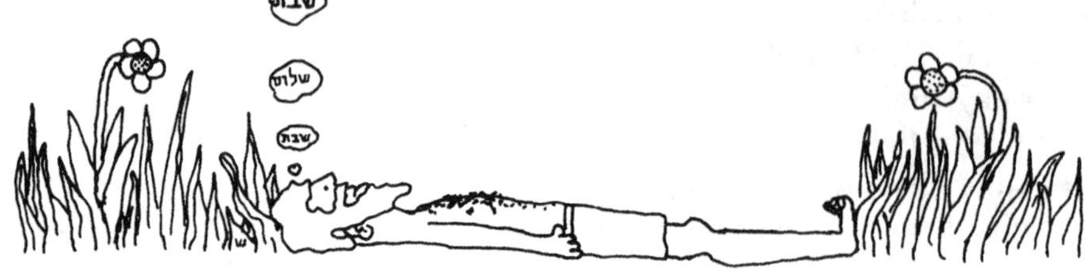

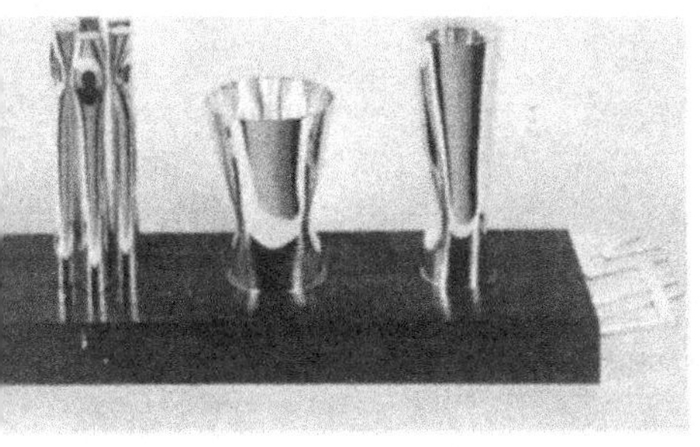

Havdalah

Dynamics and observance After the third meal, when the sky is already dark (approximately 42 minutes after sunset) Maariv, the Evening Service, is said. In this we say: *You have made a distinction, O Lord our God, between the holy and the profane, between light and darkness, between Israel and the nations, between the seventh day and the six of work.* These several divisions or distinctions are of profound significance.

That which is set apart from other things as "holy" is so distinguished only in order that it may imbue with holiness and consecration also every phase of life taking place beyond its confines. Light is set apart from darkness only so that it may give life and growth to the forces and materials that have gathered in the darkness, . . . In the same manner, the Seventh Day was set apart from the six working days only so that its Sabbath spirit might permeate all of weekday life.

—*Hirsch Siddur, p. 567*

These same distinctions are mentioned in the Havdalah, Separation, ceremony itself which follows the Maariv prayer.

1. Havdalah is recited using (a) one candle made up of at least two separate wicks and usually 6–8 inches long; (b) a full large cup of wine or other beverage; (c) a spice box usually filled with cloves, but any fragrant spice or flowers may be used.

2. The cup of wine has the same symbolic significance as in the Friday night Kiddush.

3. The Havdalah candle is lit before the Havdalah ceremony begins. The candle, usually held by a young child, must be one candle with at least two wicks, in contradistinction to the Shabbat candles, which have to be at least two separate candles with single wicks. (See Candles and Candle-making for specifics regarding the ritual, intentions, and symbolisms.) "Creation" and "redemption," the two ends of sacred history, the two extremes of Shabbat, become one. This is how we enter the week—i.e., *with* the experience of Shabbat. We try to make the forthcoming week a good week, a peaceful week, a holy week—a "shabbasdik" week.

The light of the candle is the symbol of the divine in man. The Lord is our Light and our Redeemer. Light brings the Shabbat to us and it ushers out the rest and peace of Shabbat.

Fire is the symbol of civilization, of man's conquest of the natural forces. Making a fire is our first act of creation after Shabbat. The Midrash states that fire was created on the first Saturday night. Fire is a neutral element; it can be used for constructive or destructive purposes. Man has the power to make fire and to use it as he sees fit. Therefore, fire also symbolizes the coming week: the week is in our hands to do with as we wish.

4. The spices symbolize the spiritual riches of Shabbat. We smell a pleasant fragrance to enliven our spirits, to dispel our sadness over the departure of the Shabbat Queen. The neshamah yetairah, the additional soul, also leaves us until next Shabbat. The spices refresh our souls.

5. The text of Havdalah can be found in a Siddur. After an introductory paragraph, the blessing over the wine is said, but the wine is not drunk. Then the blessing before the smelling of spices is recited, at which point the spices are smelled and passed around to the others present. The blessing over the light of the fire follows this. When the blessing over the flame is recited, we spread out our hands toward the candlelight, and see the light reflected in our fingernails with the shadow projected onto our palms. This symbolizes both the receiving of the light and the division between light and dark. The last paragraph of Havdalah recalls the distinctions cited above in the Maariv Service.

NOTE: If you use brandy (also a wine) and warm it beforehand, it will flame when the candle is extinguished in it. This produces a quite desirable meditative atmosphere for the passing of Shabbat.

6. Finally, the one reciting the Havdalah drinks the entire cup or passes it around for all to sip. A few drops of the wine, however, should be poured onto a dish and the candle extinguished in the wine.

7. There is a custom to touch your index fingers to the remaining drops of wine and then brush them across your (or a friend's) eyebrows and pockets—symbolizing the wish for enlightenment, wisdom, and prosperity for the coming week.

8. During the Havdalah ceremony, all lights should be off except for the candle.

The complete Shabbat

"The Jew bids a plaintive farewell to this great day, but with zeal replenished and faith renewed. For his eyes are now lifted to a new Shabbat, a distant yet beckoning Shabbat, when life will be holy and one, humanity whole and one, and God's Name perfect and one. He sees from afar the day of the mizmor shir leyom ha-Shabbat, mizmor shir leatid lavo, the day when the Sabbath will in and of itself be a psalm of song, a hymn to the future that can be. What kind of future? A yom she-kulah Shabbat umenukah lehayei haolamim, a day which is totally Sabbath and tranquility unto all eternity!" (Frimer, p. 268).

9. After Havdalah it is customary to wish everyone a shavuah tov or a gut vawch (Hebrew and Yiddish for "a good week"). The song "Eliahu ha-Navi" ("May the prophet Elijah come soon, heralding the coming of the Messiah") and other zemirot are often sung at this time.

10. In some communities, a Melaveh Malkah—Escorting of the Queen—is held. This is a meal or party through which the Shabbat Queen is escorted out with beauty, dignity, and triumph. In so doing, we are also prolonging her stay beyond the end of Shabbat. This is in the tradition of prolonging Shabbat as long as possible—we are reluctant to let her go. In some Hasidic communities, Shabbat is prolonged for several hours after nightfall. We add some "weekday" to the Shabbat; we make a bit of the "profane" holy.

May the whole world soon sing the song of the Sabbath of Sabbaths!

BIBLIOGRAPHY FOR SHABBAT

Dresner, Samuel H. *The Sabbath.* New York: Burning Bush Press, 1970.

Frimer, Norman E. "Law as Living Discipline: The Sabbath as Paradigm." *Tradition and Contemporary Experience: Essays on Jewish Thought and Life,* ed. Alfred Jospe. New York: Schocken Books, 1970, pp. 257–68.

Fromm, Erich. *You Shall Be as Gods.* New York: Holt Rinehart & Winston, 1966.

———. *The Forgotten Language.* New York: Holt Rinehart & Winston, 1951. See chapter on "Symbolic Language."

Grunfeld, I. *The Sabbath: A Guide to Its Understanding and Observance.* Jerusalem: Feldheim Publishers, 1972.

Heschel, Abraham Joshua. *The Sabbath: Its Meaning for Modern Man* (expanded edition includes *The Earth Is the Lord's).* New York: Harper Torchbooks, 1966.

Rosenzweig, Franz. *The Star of Redemption.* Boston: Beacon, 1972, pp. 310–15.

A Schematic Description of Sabbath Meals and Time-Periods

	Friday Night Meal and Prayers	Sabbath A.M.	Sabbath P.M.	Saturday Night
Mood and setting	Gentle, expansive At home Eating with much singing (¾ time) Great variety of food Celebrating the body All together Open joy Love talk JAPA-BHAKTI	Quiet, reflective intellectual Reviewing history sub specie aeternitatis Teaching Torah Stately melodies (4/4 time) Calm, head-joy Cholent and kugel Contemplation JNANA	Yearning, longing Torah-dreaming about the good life Melody: slow and recitative Food: meager and in the synagogue Togetherness Tarrying Preparation of motivation for action KARMA	Hopeful Story, ballad In group at shul or at one home to which all come Relaxed and buoyant The fellowship of comrades LILA
Intentions	Homecoming Transformation from dog to prince Nostalgia The haven of the old way Harmony in the home (candles) PAST	Awakening to unchanging realities God is all; He is "the soul of all that lives" The perfect order unimpeded EVER-PRESENT	Realization of what correction is needed Celebration of man's inherent possibility "None is like your people Israel, one nation on earth" PRESENT-FUTURE	Charge up weekday resources Seek vision of Elijah and his help and advice in involvement in world
Program	Recovering the good past History, patriarchs THE LORD WAS KING	Anchoring the essential self in unchanging transcendence Millennium Messiah THE LORD IS KING	Promise of possible correction Seek God's will: in the present, e.g., in ecology, in technology THE LORD WILL BE KING	Specific action directives to further God's kingdom on earth
The archetypal person in ascendancy	Abraham Grace Generosity Hospitality IMMANENCE FIRST TEMPLE THESIS	Isaac Rigor and intensity Profundity Ideological clarity SECOND TEMPLE ANTITHESIS	Jacob Mercy, beauty Integrity THIRD MESSIANIC TEMPLE SYNTHESIS	"David King of Israel alive existing" Majesty
Antagonists and dangers	Ishmael Idolatry Fertility cult Hospitality without discrimination	Esau Divisiveness Baseless hatred	None All Jacob's children Israelites	
From the *Zohar* and from the writings of Rabbi Isaac Luria (16th century)	Shekhinah or feminine aspect of God "Holy orchard" Lower paradise Holy wedding: union of heh, vav, and heh	"Ancient of Days" "Eyn-Sof" Transcendent aspect of God Upper paradise God withdrawn into His yod	The impatient lover Masculine aspect Paradise on earth God immanent in redemptive strivings Vav	Shekhinah extending sustenance for next week ADNY
From *The Star of Redemption*, Franz Rosensweig (1887–1929) Services	Creation "in remembrance of the act of creation"	Revelation "Moses rejoiced" The Sinai-gift	Redemption "And the Redeemer will come to Zion" "Jacob and his children rest thereon"	"Into Life"
Relation	Divine-World	Divine-Man	Man-World	Integration of two triangles ▲▲
Meal celebrates primarily	Israel	Torah	God	INTO ✡

The festivals: some home customs and rituals

A BIT OF AN EXPLANATION. DILEMMA:

1. This being a compendium of Jewish resources, it would be a gross and obvious oversight to omit a section on the festivals and celebratory cycle.

2. On the other hand, there are (a) so many holidays; (b) so many aspects to them—history, folklore, ritual, custom, halakhah, kavvanah . . .; (c) so much already written about them; and (d) so much that needs to be written about them that we despaired of providing any useful materials on the subject. Ideally this should be the content matter for an entire catalog in and of itself—as indeed it may be at some time. But at this time the question is how to handle this material in a limited yet still useful manner.

3. Our resolution—both necessary and frustrating—is to provide (a) short, broad synopses of the festivals; (b) highlight the ritual peculiarities centered in the home; (c) make reference to the multitude of variously qualified material around—to fill in the areas in which we are deficient; and (d) provide some ideas and assistance for entering into the festivals in a personal way through taking responsibility for creating the environment, atmosphere, and ingredients with which and within which to celebrate the festival.

BOOKS ON THE HOLIDAYS

In English

Gaster, Theodore. *Festivals of the Jewish Year,* New York: William Morrow and Co., 1953. $2.95.

An excellent interpretation of the holidays. Approaches them from folkloristic, seasonal, agricultural, historic, and religious origins. Tries to show the unique way in which Judaism molds and adapts what are often commonly shared symbols and festivals. Good source for some lost customs.

Schauss, Haim. *Guide to Jewish Holy Days.* New York: Schocken, 1962. $1.95.

A guide and interpretation, much like Gaster's, but not as penetrating, daring, or exciting.

Kitov, Eliyahu. *The Book of Our Heritage: The Jewish Year and Its Days of Significance.* 3 vols. New York: Feldheim, 1970. $20.

Complete analysis and description of the customs and rituals of the celebratory cycle.

Vainstein, Yaacov. *The Cycle of the Jewish Year.* Jerusalem: The Department for Torah Education and Culture in the Diaspora, The World Zionist Organization, 1953. $3.95.

Brief, basic sketches of the home and synagogue rituals for the holidays.

Glatzer, Nahum, ed. *Franz Rosenzweig: His Life and Times,* Schocken Books, New York. 1961. $2.95.

See the section "The Jewish Year"—also in *The Star of Redemption*—for Rosenzweig's interpretation of the Jewish year based on the recurrent themes of creation-revelation-redemption.

Hirsch, S. R. *Horeb.* Translated by I. Grunfeld. Vol. 1. London: Soncino, 1962.

See section "On the Jewish Year" for Hirsch's schematic and thematic working through the cycle of the year.

Series

The Jewish Chronicle Publications
25 Furnival St.
London, England, EC4

A Guide to Sabbath by Rabbi Soloman Goldman.
Shavuoth by Rabbi Chaim Pearl.
Succoth by Rabbi Isaac N. Fabricant.
The Minor Festivals and Fasts by Rabbi Chaim Pearl.
Rosh Ha-Shanah by Rabbi Louis Jacobs.
Hanukah and Purim by Rabbi Lehrman.
Yom Kippur by Rabbi Louis Jacobs.
Passover by Rabbi Isaac Levy.

This is a generally excellent series—each (small) volume covering history, ritual, customs. The volumes are available separately at $2.45 each or as a boxed set.

The Jewish Publication Society Anthology Series
1528 Walnut St.
Philadelphia, Pa. 19102

Yom Kippur Anthology by Philip Goodman, 1971, illus. $7.50.
Rosh Hashanah Anthology by Philip Goodman, 1970, illus. $6.
Sabbath: The Day of Delight, edited by Abraham E. Millgram, 1965, illus. $5.
Purim Anthology by Philip Goodman, 1949, illus. $5.
Hanukah Anthology by Emily Solis-Cohen, 1937, illus. $5.
Passover Anthology by Philip Goodman, 1961, illus. $5.
Sukkot and Simhat Torah Anthology by Philip Goodman, 1973, illus. $7.50.

These are generally good, comprehensive collections. Each volume includes stories, legends, and other extras beyond the presentation of ritual and custom.

The National Conference of Synagogue Youth (N.C.S.Y.) pamphlets on the holidays

Union of Orthodox Congregations of America
116 E. 27th St.
New York, N.Y. 10016

Concise and informative guides to the holidays—with little embellishment. 18¢ each.

In Hebrew

Eisenstein, J. D. *Otzar Dinim u-Minhagim (A Digest of Jewish Laws and Customs).* New York: Hebrew Publishing Co., 1917.

Excellent. A succinct, learned, and halakhically reliable treatment of the holidays, and almost everything else. Source for many interesting but neglected customs.

Sefer ha-Moadim (Book of the Festivals).

Individual volumes as per the holiday. Includes many stories, legends, poems, etc.

Zevin, Rav Shlomo Yosef. *Moadim b'Halacha.* Tel Aviv: Abraham Tsioni, 1957.

One volume. Deals with laws of the holidays.

For Hanukkah, Sukkot, and Shavuot:

Issica Gaon in conjunction with the Youth and Hechalutz Department of the World Zionist Organization, Jerusalem, has compiled an excellent manual for each of these holidays. Included in each is historical background, varieties of customs, program suggestions, and instructions for creating the various ceremonial objects associated with the festivals. Each set contains excellent photographs, illustrations, and instructional diagrams. Its format is loose-leaf enclosed in a paper binder. There is not a large supply, but additional reprintings will be initiated based on demand. At present they are free. Write:

Shlomo Ketko, Director
Youth and Hechalutz Dept.
World Zionist Org.
Keren Hayesod 19a, P.O.B. 92
Jerusalem, Israel

or:

Mr. Natan Yanai
American Zionist Youth Foundation
515 Park Ave.
New York, N. Y. 10022

Crafts and ceremonial art

Sharon, Ruth. *Arts and Crafts the Year Round.* 2 vols. New York: United Synagogue Commission on Jewish Education, 1965. $20.

Arts and Crafts the Year Round is perhaps the best book available in the area. In the two two-hundred-page volumes, Ms. Sharon covers almost every conceivable application of arts and crafts techniques in the Jewish school. Her directions are clear, and the diagrams are easy to adapt to one's own project. The book is most useful as a storehouse of ideas and not necessarily as a manual of execution of those ideas.

Freehof, Lillian S. and King, Bucky. *Embroideries and Fabrics for Synagogue and Home.* New York: Hearthside Press Inc., 1966. $10.

An excellent compendium of instructions, designs, ideas, and pictures for handworked ceremonial art relating both to the synagogue and the individual. There is an extensive bibliography of books and articles relating to ceremonial art in the back.

Rockland, Mae Shafter. *The Work of Our Hands: Jewish Needlecraft for Today.* New York: Schocken Books, 1973. $10.

An instruction manual for the beginner and an idea reservoir for the advanced. History, design, method, and inspiration.

WHERE TO LEARN AND DO CEREMONIAL ART

Many cities or communities have small groups of people involved in creating ceremonial art. In Washington, check with the Fabrengen; in Boston, Havurat Shalom or Boston University Hillel; in San Francisco, the House of Love and Prayer (addresses in Where to Learn).

The only full-time workshop for the design and creation of contemporary ceremonial objects is:

The Tobe Pascher Workshop
Jewish Museum
1109 Fifth Ave.
New York, N.Y. 10028

Both of its directors, Moshe Zabari and Ludwig Wolper, are excellent full-time craftsmen of Jewish ceremonial art. Mr. Zabari runs evening classes at the workshop for a limited number of students—working basically with silver. In addition, pieces can be commissioned from the workshop. Contact Moshe Zabari for additional information.

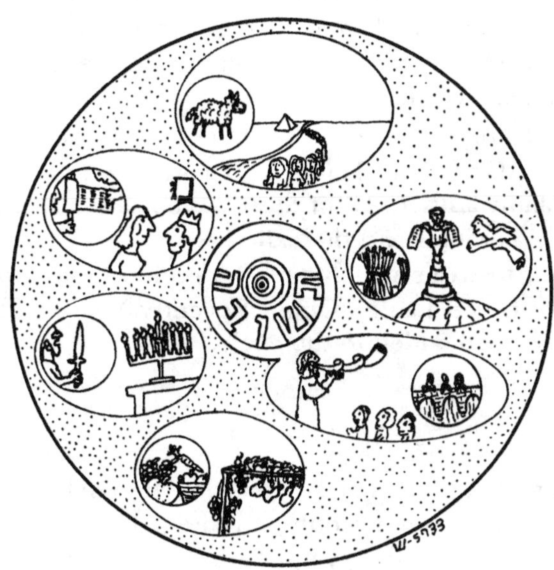

The major festivals are made up of two groups:

1. the Pilgrim Festivals, which include Pesah, Shavuot, and Sukkot (including Shemini Atzeret and Simhat Torah); and

2. the High Holidays: Rosh ha-Shanah and Yom Kippur (which is also a fast day).

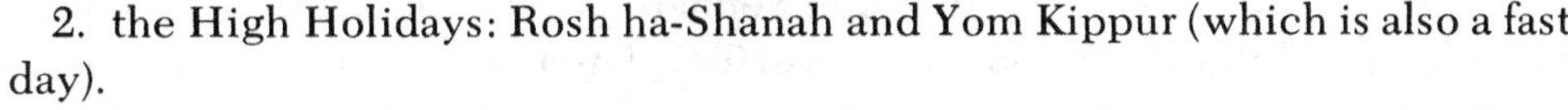

Although these holidays have many of the same observances as Shabbat, like the prohibition of work and the recitation of the Kiddush, they do have differences (beyond the basic differences in the individual character of each festival). For instance:

a. the prohibition of work is basically the same as on Shabbat except that one is allowed to cook, increase a flame, and carry in the public domain. Yom Kippur is the exception since it is observed as strictly as Shabbat.

b. The Kiddush is recited on these festivals with the wording changed to include a reference to yom tov—a festive day. The same is true of the blessing over the candle-lighting. The blessing She-heheyanu is recited after the Kiddush and candle-lighting except on the last day(s) of Pesah (see Berakhot).

c. Yizkor—the prayer for the dead—is said during the festivals.

d. Rather than the three meals of Shabbat, a minimum of two are eaten on festivals. As is the Shabbat custom, however, the blessing is said over two loaves of bread at each meal.

e. Havdalah is recited without the blessings for

(1) fire (since, unlike Shabbat, fire can be used on festivals);

(2) spices (this is traditionally interpreted as needed to revive one after the departure of the extra soul at the end of Shabbat). Since there is no extra soul on festivals, the blessing is not recited (see Shabbat).

There is a difference between Jews of Israel and some Diaspora Jews in the observance of festivals. In Israel all festivals except Rosh ha-Shanah are observed for one day. In the Diaspora they are all observed for two days. This divergence of practice arose before the calendar was established. The months were declared by the Sanhedrin in Jerusalem on the basis of witnesses. The Sanhedrin would then send out runners to announce the new month. The runners could not reach the distant Diaspora before the beginning of the festivals. Since the new moon could occur on the twenty-ninth or thirtieth day of the month (see Calendar), there was doubt as to which day any festival would fall. To be safe, two days of the festival were observed. This practice continued even after the calendar was mathematically calculated and the exact date of the festival was known. Today Orthodox and some Conservative Jews observe two days, while Reform and some Conservative Jews observe only one day in the Diaspora. For an excellent discussion of the issues involved see *Conservative Judaism*, Winter 1970.

NOTE: Intermediate days are those between the first and last days of Pesah and Sukkot. They are considered semiholidays (i.e., work is permitted, but one still eats in the sukkah, etc.).

Another kind of special days are the fast days based on occurrences in the Bible. These are the Fast of Gedaliah, Tenth of Tevet, Seventeenth of Tammuz, Tisha b'Av, and Taanit Esther. All of these except the last are related to the destruction of the Temples and the exile.

Finally, there are the minor festivals which have no prohibition of work: Purim, Hanukkah, Tu b'Shevat, and Lag ba-Omer. Recently Yom ha-Shoah and Israel Independence Day were added to the cycle.

THE HIGH HOLIDAYS

The Hebrew month of Elul, which immediately precedes the High Holiday period, is seen as a period of preparation. Emotionally and psychologically it is intended for introspection, review of the year, and preparation for repentance. There is the recognition that teshuvah—returning—does not happen at will or instantaneously but only with great effort, direction, and time.

Ritually, it is marked primarily by the recitation of Psalm 27 after Aleinu in the Shaharit and Maariv Services (the Sephardim say it after Minhah) and by the blowing of the shofar after Shaharit. This latter is a call for the people to awake and prepare.

During this period it is customary to visit the graves of relatives and teachers—to remember the sanctity of their lives and to gain inspiration for the coming year.

The blessing le-Shana Tovah should be included in all letters. In addition, many people prepare special Rosh ha-Shanah cards (see below).

Selihot—penitential prayers—are recited beginning the Saturday night before Rosh ha-Shanah. Selihot must be said for a minimum of four days. If Rosh ha-Shanah occurs on a Monday or Tuesday, therefore, Selihot are begun the week before. On the first night these are said at midnight. On each following day they are said immediately before sunrise while it is still dark. The times, however, are flexible. People have been known to say these before Shaharit or late at night. In any event, with the beginning of Selihot, the tenor of the High Holiday period intensifies.

Calendar of Festivals and Fasts of the Jewish Year

TISHRI	HESHVAN	KISLEV	TEVET	SHEVAT	ADAR	NISAN	IYYAR	SIVAN	TAMMUZ	AV	ELUL
1 ROSH HA-SHANAH (New Year)			1				16	45			O
2 ROSH HA-SHANAH (New Year)			2				17	46			O
3 Fast of Gedaliah							18	47			O
							19	48		Nine Days	O
							5 YOM HA'AZMA'UT (Independence Day)	49			O
Ten Days of Penitence							21	6 SHAVUOT (Pentecost)			O
							22	7			O
							23				O
							24			9 Fast of Tishah be-Av	O
10 YOM KIPPUR (Day of Atonement)			10 Fast of Tenth of Tevet				25				O
							26				O
							27				O
					13 Fast of Esther		28				O
					14 PURIM	14 Fast of the Firstborn	29				O
15 SUKKOT (Tabernacles)				15 Tu bi-Shevat	15 Shushan Purim	15 PESAH (Passover)	30			15 Fifteenth of Av	O
16						16 *	31				O
17 ḥol ha-mo'ed						17 ḥol ha-mo'ed 2	32		17 Fast of Seventeenth of Tammuz		O
18						18 3	18 Lag ba-Omer 33				O
19						19	34				O
20						20 5	35				O
21 Hoshanah Rabba						21 PESAH Last Day 6	36		Three Weeks of Mourning		O
22 SHEMINI AZERET SIMHAT TORAH[1]						22 7	37				O
23 SIMHAT TORAH						8	38				O
						9	39				O
		25 ḤANUKKAH				10	40				O
		26				11	41				O
		27				27 Yom ha-Sho'ah (Day of Holocaust)	42				O
		28				13	43				O
		29				14	44				O
		30				15					

MAJOR HOLIDAY | MINOR HOLIDAY | Second day holiday in Diaspora only | Pilgrimage festivals | * Counting of the Omer (Sefirah period) begins | O Seliḥot prayer | [1] Simḥat Torah in Israel only

Rosh ha-Shanah (New Year)

Alias, Yom ha-Din (Day of Judgment), Yom ha-Zikkaron (Day of Memorial), Yom Teruah (Day of Shofar-sounding).

There is some ambiguity as to the mood of Rosh ha-Shanah. On one hand, it is the Day of Judgment—a solemn time of reconciliation and confronting the year past. On the other hand, it is New Year's Day and, although not as frivolous as January 1, it is still Yom Harat Olam—the Birthday of the World—a joyous remembrance of the creation.

Danny Matt often questions his students: "How do we know on what day of the year the world was created? Because the first word of the Torah is בראשית —which when changed around reads א' בתשרי —the First of Tishri 'God began to create the heaven and the earth.' "

Meals On the first night, after the Kiddush and ha-Motzi (see Berakhot), it is customary to dip an apple in honey and say:

"Blessed are You, Lord our God, King of the Universe, who creates the fruit of the tree."

בָּרוּךְ אַתָּה, יְיָ אֱלֹהֵינוּ, מֶלֶךְ הָעוֹלָם, בּוֹרֵא פְּרִי הָעֵץ:

After eating the apple and honey, the following is then said:

"May it be Your will, God and God of our fathers, to renew on us a good and sweet year."

יְהִי רָצוֹן מִלְּפָנֶיךָ, יְיָ אֱלֹהֵינוּ וֵאלֹהֵי אֲבוֹתֵינוּ, שֶׁתְּחַדֵּשׁ עָלֵינוּ שָׁנָה טוֹבָה וּמְתוּקָה:

On the second night, it is customary to eat a new fruit—not yet eaten that season—and to recite the blessing over it. Many people accompany all meals during this period with apples and honey, as a sign and hope for sweetness in the year to come. The apple, aside from being a primary fruit of the season, also symbolizes the Shekhinah—the Divine Presence—which is often referred to as an apple orchard in kabbalistic literature.

Hallah is prepared for these holiday meals—just as for Shabbat—but these hallot are generally round in shape to symbolize a crown—in consonance with the kingship motif of the day. Some form a ladder across the hallah or form the entire hallah in the shape of a ladder. There are two explanations for this:

1. We are reminded of the ladder of Jacob's dream, which connected heaven and earth (Genesis 28:10–22)—a link-up which is hopefully reestablished during this period.

2. A theme in the liturgy is "who will be made poor and who will be made rich. . . ." There is the sense that on Rosh ha-Shanah God forms ladders. He raises up this man and lowers that one.

Although the table should be spread with good foods—red apples, white grapes, white figs—some people refrain from eating nuts, as אגוז —nut—in gematria is equivalent to חטא —sin (minus one!).

Beginning with Rosh ha-Shanah and continuing throughout the following ten days, the following blessing should be offered when greeting or taking leave of another person: "Shanah tovah tikkatevu, le-shanah tovah u-metukah—May you be inscribed for a good (or sweet) year."

Tashlikh On the afternoon of the first day—or on that of the second, if the first falls on Shabbat or is rainy—it is customary to walk to a river or spring, preferably one with fish in it, and recite special penitential prayers. The essence of these is:

"You will cast all their sins into the depths of the sea, and may You cast all the sins of Your people, the house of Israel, into a place where they shall be no more remembered or visited or ever come to mind."

וְתַשְׁלִיךְ בִּמְצוּלוֹת יָם כָּל־חַטֹּאתָם: וְכָל־חַטֹּאת עַמְּךָ, בֵּית יִשְׂרָאֵל, תַּשְׁלִיךְ בִּמְקוֹם אֲשֶׁר לֹא יִזָּכְרוּ וְלֹא יִפָּקְדוּ, וְלֹא יַעֲלוּ עַל־לֵב לְעוֹלָם:

This Tashlikh is accompanied by either an emptying of one's pockets and hems or a casting of bread crumbs into the water—symbolic of our casting off our sins and beginning afresh.

Ten days of turning The ten days beginning with Rosh ha-Shanah and ending with Yom Kippur mark a concentrated form of introspection and reconciliation. It is customary to ask forgiveness of other people whom we have slighted or hurt during the year—since the atonement of Yom Kippur is between man and God alone. Only in directly confronting the other person can we approach forgiveness or reconciliation with others. It should be noted that even more difficult and often more important than asking forgiveness is being able to give it. It is difficult to make *spiritual* return when shackled with unresolved guilt and resentments.

The intermediate Shabbat is called Shabbat Shuvah—the Shabbat of Return—based on the predominant theme of the period and on the opening words of the haftarah portion (Hosea 14:2–10) beginning: "Return, O Israel, unto the Lord thy God." It is customary for the leader of the services to give a *long* sermon on this day. In Europe, the rabbis gave sermons only twice a year (it should only happen in our days)—on Shabbat Shuvah and on Shabbat ha-Gadol (before Pesah).

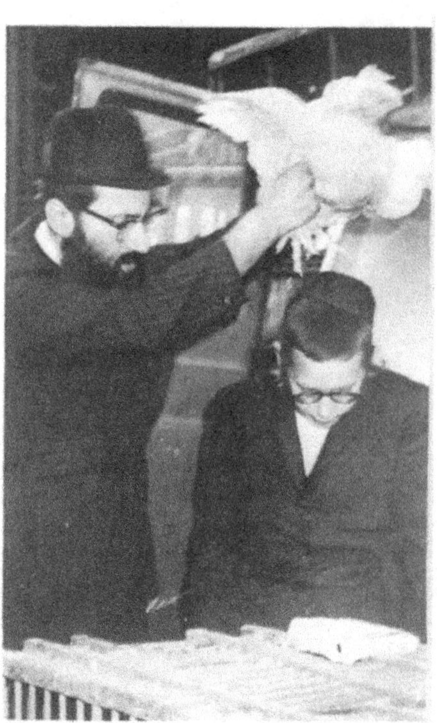

Yom Kippur

The tenth of Tishri.

Yom Kippur is the culmination of the entire High Holiday period. After this, hopefully, the old year is ended and the new one begun.

Kapparot There was once a custom called kapparot. It is practiced now only by very Orthodox Jews on the day before Yom Kippur. It entails swinging a chicken around one's head as a means or symbol of expiating sins. The chicken is then slaughtered and given to the poor for the final meal that evening. A more popularly observed remnant of this custom exists in the form of tying money in a handkerchief (many people give a "hai"—18) and swinging it around the head three times while saying:

Female:

זֹאת חֲלִיפָתֵנוּ, זֹאת תְּמוּרָתֵנוּ, זֹאת כַּפָּרָתֵנוּ, זֹאת הַתַּרְנְגֹלֶת תֵּלֵךְ לְמִיתָה, וַאֲנַחְנוּ נִכָּנֵס וְנֵלֵךְ לְחַיִּים טוֹבִים אֲרוּכִים וּלְשָׁלוֹם:

"This is my change, this is my compensation, this is my redemption. This cock is going to be killed, and I shall enter upon a long, happy and peaceful life."

Male:

זֶה חֲלִיפָתֵנוּ, זֶה תְּמוּרָתֵנוּ, זֶה כַּפָּרָתֵנוּ, זֶה הַתַּרְנְגוֹל יֵלֵךְ לְמִיתָה, וַאֲנַחְנוּ נִכָּנֵס וְנֵלֵךְ לְחַיִּים טוֹבִים אֲרוּכִים וּלְשָׁלוֹם:

(A pregnant woman and people saying this for themselves and another should use the plural form.) There is a meditation before this which is symbolically repeated three times. Following this whole process, the money should be given to tzedakhah.

Before all holidays, it is good to give tzedakhah, but it is particularly important to do so before Yom Kippur. Tzedakhah along with prayer and returning represents a central theme and the moral/spiritual quality for the day (and, by extension, throughout one's life).

In the afternoon it is customary for men (why not women?) to go to the mikveh, for symbolic purification (see Tumah and Taharah—Mikveh).

The meal immediately preceding Yom Kippur should be big and joyous. In fact, this is often regarded as an obligation. The hallot baked for this meal are often formed in the shape of birds with wings or have this figure on top of them. This symbolizes both the aspiration and opportunity of man to attain the level of the angels, and the sheltering protection of God (see Isaiah 31:5).

The abstinence involves:

1. Total fasting—those who are sick and/or weak are exempt from this.
2. No wearing of leather shoes.
3. No major washing of the body.
4. Abstaining from sexual intercourse.
5. No anointing any part of the body or wearing cosmetics.

Yom Kippur itself is marked by physical abstinence. This is regarded ambivalently. Some say that the abstinence is for the sake of physical mortification and purgation; others say that on Yom Kippur man is so close to God he can forget about his body (or vice versa—through forgetting the body, man can concentrate on the spiritual all the more intensely and gloriously).

The Maariv Service, during which Kol Nidrei is chanted, is begun before sunset. Unlike any other Maariv Service, the tallit is worn. It is also customary to wear the white kitel as symbol of the purity (Isaiah 1:18) and equality of all people before God (see Tallit).

The greeting used during this day is "Gemar Hatimah Tovah—May you be finally sealed for good (in the Book of Life)," although some people consciously avoid using this phrase because it implies that the good verdict is hanging until the final moments.

Although the Book of Jonah is read at Minhah, some have the interesting custom of reading the Book of Job (otherwise left out of the synagogue reading cycle) during the earlier part of the afternoon.

The final element—the ultimate culmination of the entire process begun a month and a half earlier in Elul—is the loud, long, piercing shofar blast which comes at the end of Neilah, the Closing Service, which marks the final sealing of the heavenly gates.

That evening, it is a custom to recite the Kiddush ha-Levanah (see The Calendar) and also to begin constructing the sukkah—as a reaffirmation of the continuity of the year.

On Rosh ha-Shanah cards

The custom of sending friends and relatives special wishes for a good and happy New Year can be quite personal and meaningful, if you wish to make it so.

1. There are some selections of preprinted cards which are attractive, appropriate, and adaptable for personal additions:

UNICEF Cards
c/o United States Committee
331 E. 38th St.
New York, N.Y. 10016
(boxes of 12 for $2)
Jewish Museum
1109 5th Ave.
New York, N.Y. 10028
(varied prices from 15c–50c)

2. Creating your own cards is obviously more personal, generally more exciting, and certainly more creative. You do not have to be an artist or craftsman to do this as all the techniques are easily acquired. As with hallah, so with this area of artistic endeavor—almost any design done by yourself has that special character and beauty which even the most satisfying "other"-produced cards lack.

a. Set up a paste-up collage and Xerox it. Although this will be on regular paper, it is easy, inexpensive, and open to many options and varieties.

b. Linoleum-cutting or silk-screening on card stock. Both require some knowledge, materials, and practice. The former can be fairly easy and inexpensive, the latter a bit more complicated. Materials can be purchased at any art supply store. Instructions are available either at the art store or in crafts manuals.

c. Photography. Have a picture printed which reflects some aspect of how you relate to this period and simply stick it to a plain white card. If you have access to a darkroom and the know-how, print directly on to a lightweight photographic paper, which when folded can serve as the card itself.

d. Hand-calligraph onto card stock (see Scribal Arts).

There are many more possibilities—for technique, design, and content. Although often regarded lightly, creating and sending these cards can be an important means of entering into the atmosphere of the period and the process of teshuvah, returning or re-turning.

Bibliography for the high holidays

Agnon, S.Y. *Days of Awe.* New York: Schocken, paperback.

Arzt, Max. *Justice and Mercy.* New York: Holt, Rinehart & Winston, 1963.

Rambam. *Mishneh Torah.* "Hilkhot Teshuvah," available in English from the Yale Judaica Series.

Mahzorim and Supplementary Prayer Materials

Birnbaum, Phillip, ed. *High Holyday Prayer Book.* New York: Hebrew Publishing Co., 1951.

Harlow, Jules, ed. *Machzor for Rosh Hashanah and Yom Kippur.* New York: Rabbinical Assembly, 1972.

High Holiday Prayer Book. New York: Jewish Reconstructionist Foundation, Inc., 1948.

Mahzor Kol Bo, Ashkenaz or Sephard. New York: Hebrew Publishing Co., 1926.

Reimer, Jack, ed. *New Prayers for the High Holidays.* Hartford: Media Judaica, 1970.

Sugarman, Allan and Greenberg, Sidney, eds. *A Contemporary High Holiday Service for Teenagers . . .* Hartford: Prayer Book Press, 1970.

Union Prayerbook for Jewish Worship. New York: Central Conference of American Rabbis, 1961.

Sukkot

This is actually a composite of several holidays. It begins two weeks after Rosh ha-Shanah on the same day of the week and lasts nine days (eight in Israel). It falls on the 15th–22nd of Tishri.

Full Hallel is recited on all of the days. On the intermediate Shabbat, Kohelet (Ecclesiastes) is read.

As with many of the holidays, Sukkot has dual origins—being both a historical and agricultural festival. Historically, it represents the journey of Israel through the desert after the exodus from Egypt—during which time the people lived in booths of an obviously impermanent nature. Agriculturally, the holiday celebrates the final gathering of fruit and produce of the year. In this aspect it is referred to as Hag ha-Asif—the Holiday of the In-Gathering.

Unlike Pesah and Shavuot, the two other major festivals, Sukkot is referred to as Zeman Simhatenu—the Season of Our Joy. The singular nature of the festival is further emphasized in its being known simply as He-Hag—*The* Holiday. During this period (1) the verse הַזֹּרְעִים בְּדִמְעָה בְּרִנָּה יִקְצֹרוּ: —"He who sows in tears reaps in joy"—is fulfilled; and (2) the High Holiday period of introspection and penitence is *finally* completed. As such, the essence of Sukkot is sheer joy. People go to extra great lengths to make the environment and ritual aspects of the festival beautiful and joyous (hiddur mitzvah). This joy, however, is somewhat dampened by our awareness that we are in the autumn of the year. The land has yielded its fruit; the days are shorter; winter (death) approaches. Ritually, as well, the joy is tempered at various points—we say Yizkor, we plead for life-giving rain. The holiday is thus in some ways a microcosm of the entire celebratory cycle which mixes and moves from joy to sorrow, fast to slow, high to low with little transition or insulation.

Preparation for Sukkot should be begun immediately after Yom Kippur—with the construction of the sukkah. During the few days that follow, the sukkah should be completed and the lulav and etrog purchased.

The basic mitzvot regarding Sukkot—to dwell in the sukkah Minimally, this means eating in the sukkah. Even more minimally, it means saying, while inside, ha-Motzi (see Berakhot), Kiddush and the blessing:

"Blessed are You, Lord our God, King of the Universe, who has sanctified us through His commandments and commanded us to sit in the sukkah."

בָּרוּךְ אַתָּה, יְיָ אֱלֹהֵינוּ, מֶלֶךְ הָעוֹלָם, אֲשֶׁר קִדְּשָׁנוּ בְּמִצְוֹתָיו, וְצִוָּנוּ לֵישֵׁב בַּסֻּכָּה:

Maximally, the commandment includes sleeping in it as well.

Ushpizin–Hospitality Sukkot is a tremendously universalistic holiday. In that it comes at the veritable end of time—at least the timeline of the year—it is symbolic and anticipatory of the messianic time. All the seventy nations are to participate in it as a foretaste or initiation of peace throughout the world. Thirteen bullocks were to have been offered as sacrifices on the first day, twelve on the second, and so on, up to seven on the seventh for a total of seventy—one for each of the nations. And in the haftarah of the first day, the following passages from Zechariah are read: "And it shall come to pass, that every one that is left of all the nations that came against Jerusalem shall go up from year to year to worship the King, the Lord of Hosts, and to keep the feast of tabernacles" (Zechariah 14:16). "And the Lord shall be King over all the earth; in that day shall the Lord be One, and His name one" (Zechariah 14:9).

In an analogy to harvesting, just as we gather our fruits together into the sukkah, so God gathers all His fruits together under His great sukkah—the Sukkat Shalom, the All-embracing Covering of Peace. An essential element of the holiday, then, is the extending of hospitality and taking in guests. In a symbolic form, we ask a different biblical person to visit our sukkah and sit with us each night—Abraham, Isaac, Jacob, Joseph, Moses, Aaron, and David. (There is a custom at Havurat Shalom to invite both the man and his wife.) It is this ritual process which is called ushpizin. The formula for this can be found in the Siddur or on wall-chart decorations sold specifically for the walls of the sukkah. These charts often have neat little pictures of all the guys, paintings of Jerusalem, diagrams of the Temple. They are available at Jewish bookstores, generally. It is a nice custom to read one of the beggar's stories from Rabbi Nahman's "The Seven Beggars" each night. (See *Classic Hassidic Tales* by Meyer Levin or the *Tales of Rabbi Nahman* by Martin Buber.) There is an almost universal custom of inviting at least one poor person or one person who has no sukkah of his/her own to join in the meals. The essence of hospitality can be learned from Abraham, who did not sit down to eat while there were guests needing his attention and care.

Arbaah Minim–Four Species "On the first day you shall take the product of *hadar* [goodly] trees, branches of palm trees, boughs of leafy trees and willows of the brook, and you shall rejoice before the Lord your God seven days" (Leviticus 23:40). For a full explanation of these, their symbolism, how to buy them, and what to do with them, see Four Species.

Hoshanot On each day there is an addition to the synagogue service called Hoshanot. "Save, we beseech You. For Your sake, our God, save, we beseech You." These are prayers of supplication recited while circling the synagogue (either inside or, if you are in the country, possibly outside as well), waving the lulav and etrog. Hoshanot are a reminder of the processions around the altar in the time of the ancient Temple. It is customary to wear the tallit over one's head during the procession. On a subjective and spiritual level, this ceremony can be extremely powerful, although strange and unsettling. The rhythm of the ritual and the expressiveness of the plea can immerse you in a sense of timelessness and frighteningly direct confrontation.

Hoshana Rabba

The seventh day of Sukkot is a semifestival in itself, called Hoshana Rabba—the Great Hosanna—or Yom ha-Shevii shel Aravah, the Seventh Day of the Willow. On this day seven circuits are made around the synagogue, while carrying a bunch of aravot, willows, as well as the lulav. As a counterpoint to the prevailing mood of joy during Sukkot, Hoshana Rabba is regarded as an extension of Yom Kippur, with its concomitant mood and atmosphere. It is on this day that the gates of judgment *finally* close—both an allowance for final, tardy petition and a caution against taking Sukkot as Zeman Simhatenu too frivolously. After the final circuits, the willows are taken and beaten off their stems—a final beating off of our sins, a final supplication, a hope for rain—to water next year's willows, and our lives, both physically and spiritually.

Shemini Atzeret: The eighth day

This is a holiday in itself although its contemporary function is unclear. It is essentially a conclusion and is primarily marked by the insertion of the Prayer for Rain—Tefillat Geshem. As this is the *beginning* of the season which determines the fertility of the land in the year to come, Geshem is recited in the manner of a supplication. Having lived through the past year, we are able to rejoice. About to live another, we already face the fear and uncertainty and hopes which the future engenders.

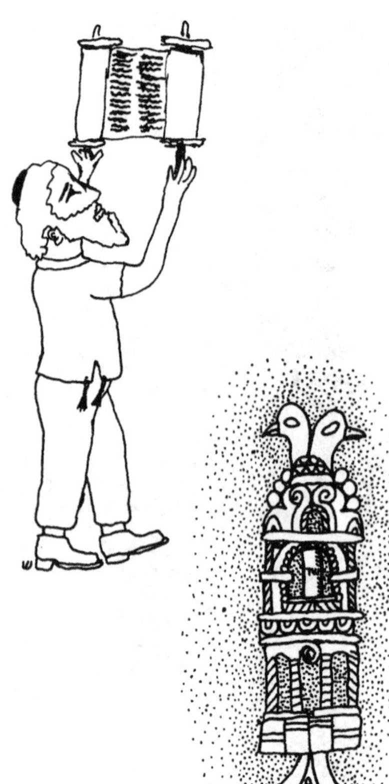

Simhat Torah

Simhat Torah, the Rejoicing with the Torah, is associated with Sukkot but is actually an independent holiday falling on the day after. In the Diaspora this occurs on the ninth day, while in Israel it is combined with Shemini Atzeret. Although this is basically a synagogue festival, some of its customs should be noted.

Basically, it is a grand simha involving the entire community, young and old.

The Maariv Service is often done as a parody—not quite as farcically as on Purim, but still with humor and joy. Some have the custom of using different melodies from the year for each part of the service.

After the Amidah, various verses beginning with Attah Hareita (see the Siddur for the specifics) are recited aloud by selected members of the congregation—and then repeated by everyone. Some congregations have the custom of auctioning off these verses.

At this point, all the Torah scrolls are taken out and are carried around the synagogue in a series of processions—hakkafot—accompanied with singing and little kids with flags and apples. Alphabetical verses are recited to start off with, but as these finish there is the opportunity for much additional singing and dancing—with the Torah and with each other. It can take quite a while to complete each hakkafah—and there are seven of them. Since to some it is praiseworthy to get drunk at this time, and since drinking improves one's ability to dance—the whole process can become extended, exhilarating, and exhausting. (Not all synagogues have top-quality exuberance, elaboration, or participation. Generally each city has one or two shuls which are known for their Simhat Torah celebrations. If you want a full experience, try to attend one of these.)

When the seven circuits are completed, all but one of the Torah scrolls are returned to the ark. The last section of Deuteronomy is then read out of the remaining Torah. This is the only time the Torah is read in the synagogue at night!

On the following morning the hakkafot are repeated. This has been compared by one apikoras—unbeliever—to drinking a Bloody Mary in order to work off a hangover. After the circuits, three Torah scrolls are left out of the ark. From the first scroll, the last portion of the Torah is read, Deuteronomy 33–34. It is customary for everyone in the congregation to be called up for an aliyah. The fifth aliyah is traditionally given to all children as a group. This is called Kol ha-Nearim—All the Children. A large tallit is spread over their heads as they recite together the blessings over the Torah. The person who is called for the last aliyah of this section is called Hatan Torah, the Groom of the Torah—a special honor, as he completes the Torah-reading cycle for the year. After this the second Torah replaces the first and Genesis 1:1—2:3 is read. This aliyah is called Hatan Bereshit—the Groom of the Beginning. From the third scroll Numbers 29:35—30:4 is read. Finally, Joshua is read as the haftarah to indicate the continuity of the people and leadership after the death of Moses and the "completion" of the Torah.

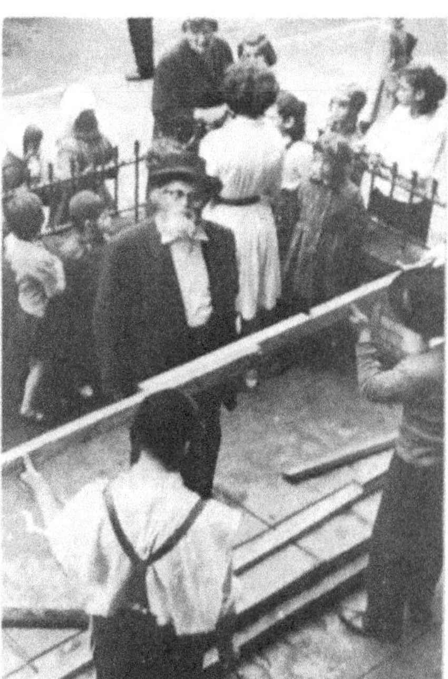

Then winter sets in and there are no holidays until Hanukkah—which is as much a reflection of winter as a time of hibernation as it is of the need to rest and recuperate after the long holiday cycle of the fall.

Sukkah-building If you can get into this mitzvah you will probably find great joy in it. Start building as soon after Yom Kippur as possible. One of the good things about a sukkah is that you should build your own. Even if you buy the prefab variety, you should erect it yourself. Most of us live in houses or apartments built by others. Most of us eat bread baked by professionals. Like hallah-baking, sukkah-building gives us the chance to enjoy the fruits of our own labor. The sukkah should not be an elegant structure. A rough shack built by hand is the ideal.

PLANS The easiest way to build a sukkah is with cement blocks, 2 x 4 standards, and improvised walls. Remember that the number of walls required is related to the forms of the Hebrew letters of the word sukkah.

2½ walls

3 walls

4 walls

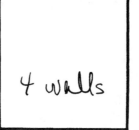

All of these are permissible. If you can use the back wall of a house or garage as one of the walls, do so. Stack 3 cement blocks in each corner and insert 7-foot 2 x 4's into the air holes of the blocks. Connect the 2 x 4's with 1 x 2's across the middle and the top. Stretch cloth (or nail 1/4-inch plywood, if you can afford it) over the frame and one wall is complete. One wall can serve as the entrance if covered with cloth on a wire track. Place some 1 x 1's running in both directions on the roof and cover that with rushes or pine boughs. The entire roof must be made of organic material. Remember to let the stars shine through! A sample sukkah might be a 7-foot cube, for which the following materials would be necessary:

12 cement blocks
4 pieces of 2" x 2" x 7½'
7 pieces of 1" x 2" x 7½'
8 pieces of 1" x 1" x 8'
enough cloth or plywood to cover 3 walls
cloth drape for entrance wall
nails
binding twine
greens for roofing

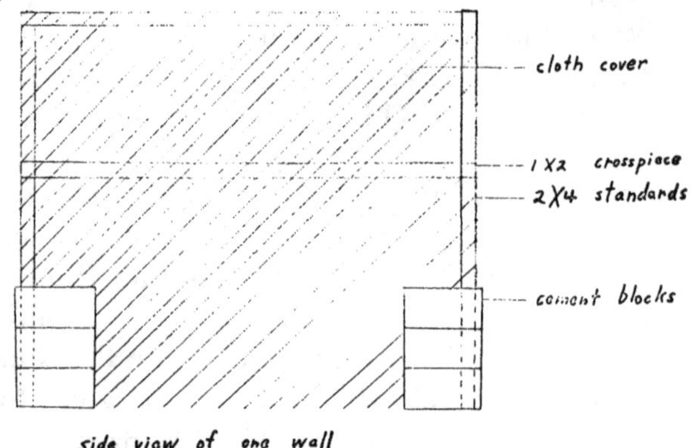

Remember never to make the sukkah overly comfortable. It should shake in the wind. One last thing—once you build it, use it. Eat every meal there (including breakfast). Sleep in it if you can. Invite guests to your sukkah and share it with all who have none. Always invite the guest of the day according to the ushpizin ritual. When you finally break it down, store the material for next year's festival with the understanding and hope that you may not need it again. For if the Messiah comes before next Sukkot, we will all sit together under the Sukkah of Shalom and partake of the Great Feast of Leviathan.

You might want the challenge of not using nails, and binding with rope at all joints. It can be done and a fine binding is a beautiful thing to see.

DECORATIONS Here you can do as you please. Everything's possible from traditional fruit hanging to ushpizin posters to printed murals to strung macaroni, gourds, origami, paper chains, etc. Some way should be found not to waste too much fruit in these days of hungry nations. People with families should perhaps divide the sukkah into areas, with one person decorating each area. Put in a carpet—that adds a lot of class. An electric light can be installed. Use a garage-style rubber-insulated socket.

Hanukkah (Dedication)–the Festival of Lights

Hanukkah is an eight-day festival beginning on the 25th of Kislev and lasting through the 2nd of Tevet.

As with other festivals in the cycle of the Jewish year, there seems to be a dual origin to Hanukkah—seasonal and historical. The historical story is quite well known. Judah the Maccabee lead a revolt against the Hellenistic Syrians who occupied the land of Israel around 165 B.C.E.—and for some reason he was victorious. There is a miracle associated with this victory. Some say that when the Temple was to be rededicated only one cruse of sacramental oil was found. Although this was only supposed to burn for one day, it miraculously lasted for eight full days, during which time other oil was prepared. Others maintain that the victory in itself constitutes the miracle.

The seasonal referents of Hanukkah are much less known and, in some ways, much more stimulating. Long before the Maccabees, there was some kind of established winter festival at this season of the year (see Babylonian Talmud, Avodah Zarah 8b.). The motifs were several. One had to do with the gradual increase in daylight after the ominous, steadily darkening days of late autumn. A number of legends connect Hanukkah with the winter solstice, which occurs during the holiday. Another motif had to do with the kindling of fire, reported as an ancient Jewish custom at the dedication of the Temple altar, and related to the event described in 2 Maccabees 1:18–22. A third was a festive act, related to Sukkot, which included the carrying of wands wreathed with leaves, branches with their fruit, and palm fronds (see 2 Maccabees 10:5–8). Possibly a fourth was some sort of camping-out custom, also related to the Sukkot theme. (In the Chicago translation of 2 Maccabees, the Sukkot reference is rendered as "the Camping-out Festival." See 2 Maccabees 1:18.)

Whether Hanukkah draws its source from the historic, the seasonal, or, as is most likely, from some combination of the two, it is clear that the central motif is light. The only special mitzvah related to the holiday is to kindle the lights each night. (For the ritual and further significance see Candles and Candle-making.)

Additional prayers
A section called Al ha-Nissim—For the Miracles—is added to the Amidah and Grace after Meals during the holiday. In addition, Hallel is said during Shaharit.

A few customs In Turkey there was the custom of weaving the candlewicks from the fibers in which the etrog of Sukkot was wrapped. Following the holiday, the candle remains were formed into another candle which was then used for searching for leaven before Passover. This effects a beautiful continuity to the holidays.

In Kurdistan, dolls or effigies of Antiochus were carried around by children asking for Hanukkah money. At the end of the day the effigy would be set on fire to the cries of, "Antiochus, Antiochus."

In many parts of the world it is customary to devote time to communal and charitable affairs during Hanukkah.

There is, of course, the widespread custom of giving Hanukkah gelt (money) or, more recently, presents to children and students. The intentions behind this include spreading light and joy, giving incentive to study, and hastening the coming of the Messiah. This custom is actually quite old and independent of the parallel custom of giving presents on Christmas.

Food Many have the custom of eating dairy foods, e.g., cheese blintzes on Hanukkah. Also common are dishes cooked in oil. The most widespread food for the holiday is potato latkes.

There is a long tradition of playing games of chance during the evenings of the holiday. Although this custom was often under attack by rabbinic leadership, it remained a central element of the celebration. The most widely played game is dreidel—a derivative of an old German gambling game. At present it is played with a four-sided top—on each side of which is one of the letters nun, נ, gimmel, ג, heh, ה, and shin, ש. Although these represent various gambling terms, they have been reinterpreted to mean נֵס גָּדוֹל הָיָה שָׁם a great miracle happened here. In gematria, these letters have the numerical equivalent of 358, which is the same as Messiah— משיח, as well as the phrase יְיָ מֶלֶךְ, יְיָ מָלָךְ, יְיָ יִמְלֹךְ —God is King, God was King, God will be King.

How to make the dreidel Plastic store-bought dreidels are acceptable and certainly usable, but there is a challenge and joy in being able to make one yourself. Possibilities for design and material are extensive. Probably the easiest would be to "make it out of clay." But also consider plaster of paris or wood. An interesting idea would be to whittle or carve it from a nice tree branch garnered from the woods. The Jewish Community Center in Wilkes-Barre, Pa., among its other crafts projects, has one directed at making dreidels for the community. The following are instructions explaining how they crafted their dreidels—as submitted by Richard Rabin, the program director:

The base of the dreidel is a block of hardwood—1″ x 1″ x 1″—with a 5/16″ hole drilled. According to my expert, the preferable hardwood is maple because it takes ink better than some of the other woods.

The holes were drilled by one of our fathers who had a power drill, for which he made a special jig, into which he placed the blocks one after another. This enabled him to center the hole in most cases. It would, of course, be possible to do this by hand, but the supply would be severely limited and your ability to center the hole would be severely curtailed. If the hole is not centered, the "spinability" is sharply reduced.

The blocks were also cut by one of the adults, since in order to make them uniform it needs power saws and the hand of an expert. Again, it is possible for older boys to do this by hand.

The dowel is 5/16″, cut to a length of about 2½″ each. These the children were easily able to do. A special jig was made up in which you could lay the long pieces of dowel and place the saw, enabling us to have the same lengths of dowel. In order to put a point on the dowel stick, we used first an electric sharpener and then a hand pencil sharpener. I believe there are heavy-duty pencil sharpeners which can be used, but this should be done carefully because it is possible to burn them out on hardwood.

The dowel should not be sharpened to a point. It should be left with about ⅛″ of flat bottom, which can then be sanded to give you a curved bottom. This makes for better spinning.

The blocks are then sanded. This can be done either by machine or hand, though for a large number of dreidels this can become pretty tedious, and the kids begin to get a little bored if they have to sand a lot. They should be sanded on all sides. This makes them smoother and finer-looking and also enables them to take the ink in a much clearer fashion.

The next step is to insert the dowels in the blocks. This is a simple operation and one which all the children enjoyed. A wooden mallet and a vise are all that is needed, and they loved to knock them in. You'll have to determine how far you want them to knock the dowels in, and actually check the dreidels a little to determine how well they spin at this point.

The stamping can be done either before or after the dowels are inserted —possibly it might be better to do it before the dowels are put in. I leave this up to you. We went to a stamp-maker who made us a simple rubber stamp. We gave him an example from a Hebrew schoolbook, which had nice big letters, and they made us a number of rubber stamps just that size. This operation went very quickly. You line up a number of children with sufficient stamps and ink pads and each one can work a different letter, and before you know it you have all four letters stamped. Sometimes the children have to be watched during stamping. They tend to get a little careless, with the result that some of the letters would be upside down, some would be off center, or otherwise poorly stamped.

The next process was dipping. We secured a good semigloss clear varnish and placed it in a number of wide-mouthed cups or jars. A thumbtack was inserted into the end of each dreidel. We then took paper clips and opened

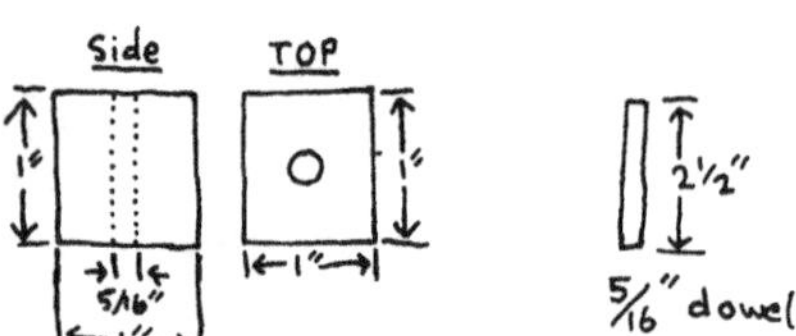

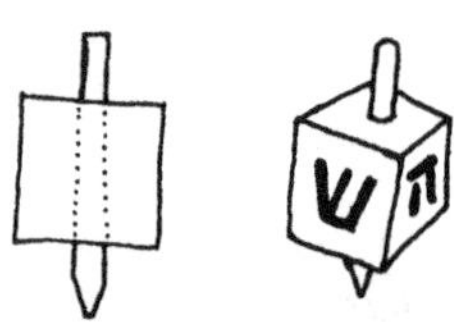

How to play dreidel

Everyone in the game starts with 10 or 15 pennies (nuts, raisins, matchsticks, etc.).

Each player puts one of these in the middle (called The Pot).

The dreidel is spun by one player at a time.

Whether he wins or loses depends on which face of the dreidel is up when it falls.

Nun means nisht or "nothing." Player does nothing.

Gimmel means gantz or "all." Player takes everything in The Pot.

Heh, means halb or "half." Player takes half of what is in The Pot.

Shin means shtel or "put in." Player adds two objects to The Pot.

When only one object or none is left in The Pot, every player adds one. When an odd number of objects are in The Pot, the player rolling heh, "half," takes half the total plus one.

When one person has won everything the game is over.

A note about the dreidel: Apart from the fun-and-games aspect, what could be better than a spinning top to suggest the shifting of the sun, the succession of the seasons, and the spinning (and wobbling) of the earth on its axis?

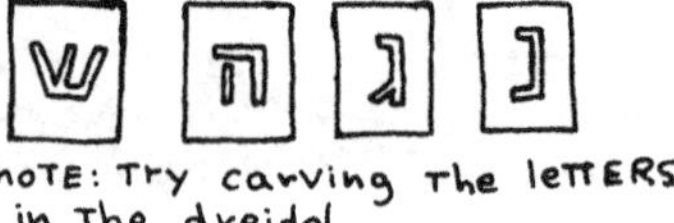

NOTE: Try carving the letters in the dreidel

them up so that one end could go around the thumbtack and the other could be hung over string so that they could dry. We then, by hand, dipped them into the jar of varnish, let the varnish drip off as much as possible, and then hung them on the line (string or wire) that extended across the room. We tried to put paper underneath them to absorb any of the dripping, and some of us would take a brush and go around and take off any of the bubbles or drops that might form. It would take anywhere from 24 to 48 hours for the varnish to dry. We then took them down and checked them—for placement of letters and for ability to spin. A number of the dreidels required a little sanding on the point in order to make them spin better. I should add that at every stage of manufacture we would be checking, and at each point we would catch dreidels that had double letters, wrong letters, letters missed, or upside-down letters, or were not well balanced, so that we could guarantee that every dreidel that came out of the "factory" was able to spin. If they are to be hand-sanded, we would suggest that you take sandpaper and tack it to a piece of board, so that the children can take the blocks and run them across the sand-board.

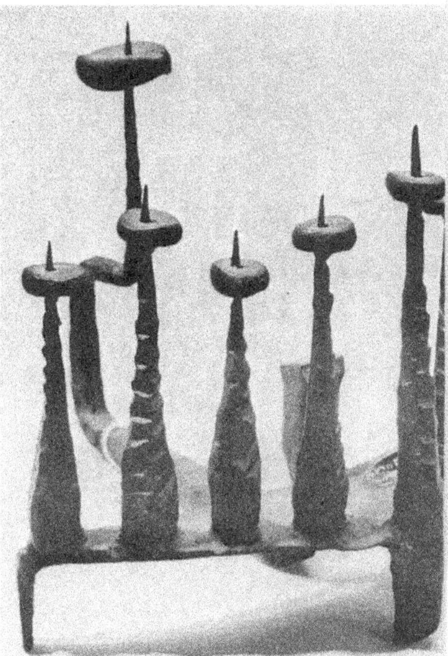

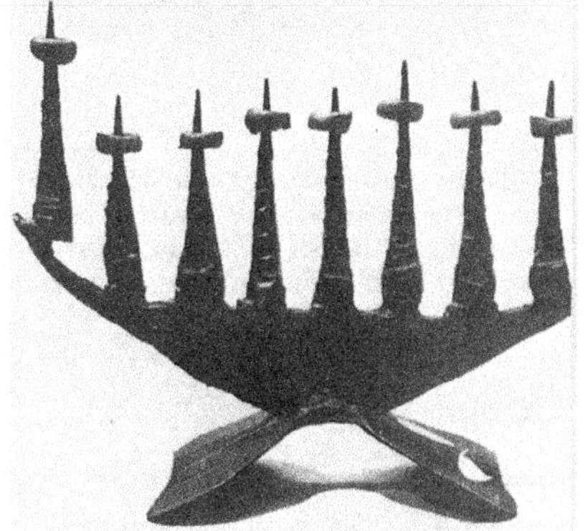

How to make a menorah What shape should the menorah be? As long as the flames are kept distinct and do not merge to form a bonfire, one has a choice of shapes: straight line, semicircle, curve, up-and-down, spiral, etc.

Here again, the possibilities for material and design are extensive. Some possibilities: wooden spools glued to boards are easy to assemble, easy to paint, and well within the capacities of even young children. However, one must watch when the candlewick burns below the wood level. If you roll your own, of course, you simply start the wick ½" up from the bottom of the wax so that it will go out before it reaches the wood (See Candles and Candle-making).

Clay is also easy to work with, and it can yield a menorah which can burn olive oil with wicks as well as the usual candles.

An interesting and somewhat ambitious idea is to carve the menorah out of soapstone. This will require wood or metal files for carving or refining the shape, metal or masonry drill bits to drill the holes, sandpaper to smooth it, wax or linseed oil to bring out the grain in the stone. (This idea was submitted by Paul Ruttkay of the Fabrengen.)

Highly recommended: forage in the woods to find your own menorah. First of all it is a nice reason to go to the woods—if you need a reason. Second, it is very much in the spirit of the Sukkot–vegetation–camping-out motif of Hanukkah. Finally, the result is likely to be quite striking.

The exposed root of a fallen tree, fingers pointing in various directions, is striking and lends itself beautifully to adaption as a menorah. The points will nicely accommodate the soft wax of the hand-rolled beeswax candles, and if you saw the root off carefully from the trunk, you should have a flat, even surface on which to rest it.

Another natural shape which serves well is a weathered branch of a tree, preferably one which can lie flat. Using a simple hand or power drill with a drill bit to match the size of the candles you will be lighting (or shape the candles to fit your drill bit—⅜" or ½" are likely sizes), you can drill nine holes in various parts of the branch to hold the candles. Care must be taken, of course, to select the places for drilling with an eye to spacing, height, succession, etc.

Yet a third possibility is to find a sizable log and nine smaller sticks or branches. Peg onto the bottom of the log a couple of pieces of wood to hold it steady, drill nine holes to accommodate the smaller sticks or branches, and drill holes in the top of each stick to hold the candle. This too can be quite handsome.

Kavvanot and suggestions for further reading For a deeper sense of what Hanukkah and some of its motifs may be about, several further references may be helpful.

Erwin R. Goodenough has a marvelously suggestive, illuminating, and well-documented discussion of the menorah in his *Jewish Symbols in the Greco-Roman Period* (Bollingen-Princeton University Press, 1953), 4:71–98.

Another richly suggestive work, difficult but well worth the effort, is Morton Smith's essay "The Image of God: Notes on the Hellenization of Judaism . . . ," in *Bulletin of the John Rylands Library* 40 (1957–1958): 473–512.

Taken together, the Smith and Goodenough pieces strongly suggest that the menorah may be understood as a stylized tree which bears light. This symbol of the Divine, combining the vegetation and light motifs in an organic growth with the elements so naturally intertwined, can function as a powerful stimulus to the personal religious imagination as the candelabrum radiates light amid surrounding darkness. So it serves weekly on Shabbat, and so it serves annually on Hanukkah. In the latter case its nightly increase in illumination anticipates the significant and profoundly reassuring seasonal shift in the sun.

For comparison, contrast, and general delight, folk material from Great Britain on candles and fires, flames, and feasts of light, charmingly written and of considerable historical value, is to be found in John Brand's *Observations on Popular Antiquities.* The three-volume work, printed in England in 1841 and reprinted numerous times since, is likely to be in the reference room of any good college library. The articles on the Yule Log or block, the word Yule, Candlemas Day, and summer solstice are a good place to begin.

Tu b'Shevat–the Fifteenth of Shevat

"In the future each man will have to give account for having seen wonderful foods—and not having eaten them" (Talmud Yerushalmi, Yuhasin, ch. 10).

Rosh ha-Shanah le-Ilanot–the New Year for Trees Agriculturally, this holiday marked the date from which to count the age of a tree for reasons of the tithe and for indication of the maturation of the fruit of the tree. (Fruit could not be eaten until the fourth year. This standardizes the birthday of trees.)

Seasonally, this is the approximate time when the sap begins to flow once again—marking the refructification and rebirth, as it were, of the tree following its winter hibernation.

There are few customs associated with Tu b'Shevat. Most common is the eating of fruit from trees—and in particular, fruit from trees which grow in Israel, especially the carob (boxer, St.-John's-bread). Some stay up almost the entire night—reciting and studying passages from the Bible, Mishnah, Talmud, and Zohar which speak about fruit and trees. Between study sessions, they eat from the fruits which they have just studied about. More recently it has become a form of Arbor Day—when it is the custom to plant trees, or provide money for the planting of trees in Israel. It is certainly within the intent of the day to offer money to the Trees for Vietnam project as well (see How to Bring Mashiah).

Kabbalistically, some interesting things are done with the festival. There is a play on the talmudic reference to Tu b'Shevat not as Rosh ha-Shanah le-Ilanot—New Year for Trees—but as Rosh ha-Shanah le-*Ilan*—New Year for *the Tree* (Rosh Hashanah 14a). Which tree? The Tree of Life and/or the inverted treelike figure which represents God's emanations flowing through creation (roots above, limbs below). The day marks the refructification of the earthly tree through the flow received from the divine Tree. By eating of the various fruits—and reciting the appropriate blessing—the flow is maintained. A person who enjoys the pleasures of this world without a blessing is called a thief—because the blessing is what causes the continuation of the divine flow into the world. In the kabbalistic text *Peri Ez Hadar* (The fruit of the goodly tree) Rabbi Chaim Vital set out an elaborate structure and ritual for the eating of the fruits. There are three groups of fruits, with ten fruit in each group. The ten represent the ten sefirot (emanations) through which creation is channeled. Each group represents one of the worlds of creation:

1. Assiyah: our level of physical creation—the lowest
2. Yezirah: formation—second lowest level
3. Beriah: creation—next to the highest level.

The highest and purest level—azilut—emanation—is beyond any representation by fruit. In beriah, the fruit are closest to pure emanation and therefore need no protection or shells, either inside or outside. The entire fruit can be eaten (carob, apples, oranges, grapes, figs, etc.). As yezirah is a little lower, it needs some reinforcement and protection—not totally, but just around its heart. These fruits, thus, have an inedible pit (peaches, plums, dates, olives, etc.). In the lowest world, assiyah, there is the greatest need for protection. It is a greater risk to open up, to peel off protective shells. These fruits thus have an inedible outer shell (nuts, coconuts, pomegranates, etc.) Try working out a Tu b'Shevat "Seder" using these symbols—plus the natural enjoyment of eating good fruit.

Purim–Feast of Lots

The festival is ostensibly purely historical in origin; however, it bears striking resemblances to holidays of other folk cultures held at about this same time—i.e., the emergence of spring (see Theodore Gaster, *Festivals of the Jewish Year,* "Purim"). The history, as written in Megillat Esther—the Scroll of Esther—involves a plot by wicked Haman (ptui, ptui, ptui . . .) against the Jews and his eventual defeat and demise through the efforts of that great uncle-niece team of Mordehai and Esther (Marduke and Ishtar?). The Jews were saved, wrong was righted, and everyone joined together in celebration. In commemoration of this event we similarly gather to read the story—and, particularly, to celebrate.

Adar 14—if there are two months of Adar in the year (i.e., a leap year), Purim falls during Adar II.

In consonance with the tradition of not leaving any joy (or sorrow) unadulterated, the day before Purim (Adar 13) is a fast day—the Fast of Esther. It begins with sunrise (as opposed to other types of fasts, which begin the previous sunset).

Joy and celebration, however, are the central elements of the day. Purim festivities begin with the Maariv Service. This service is often done as a spoof or parody of the other services of the year—using melodies particular to the various holidays and exaggerating them or putting them in unexpected places. It is customary to collect half a shekel (50c) either before the service or before the Megillah reading. This money is then given to charity, and serves as a remembrance of the half-shekel tax collected in biblical times from every adult male for support of the Temple.

The Megillah At the conclusion of the Maariv Service (and again the next morning) the Megillah is read. It is traditionally written on a scroll of parchment. Unlike the Torah, though, it has a wood winder on only one end (actually, it need not have a winder at all). An interesting aspect of the Megillah of Esther is that it is the only book of the Bible in which the Name of God is not mentioned at all. Because of this, it is possible to have elaborate decorations or pictures accompany the text—as there can be no claim of making an image of God. It would be a worthwhile project to try to write and decorate your own scroll (see Scribal Arts).

The reading is often done in a comical way—with different voices and impromptu dramatics. Esther 1:7 (the first six words), 3:15, and 7:4 are sung to the trope for Lamentations. Verses 2.5 and 8.16 are recited by the congregation before the reader. Where the ten sons of Haman are listed, they must all be read in one breath.

For a complete account of all the special verses, secret meanings, and other assorted trivia fascinatum, see the Tikkun for Megillat Esther (occasionally available with English), available at Hebrew bookstores (see list in Bibliography).

Of course, the most famous and delightful part of the reading involves the obligation to "blot out" Haman's name. Every time the name is pronounced by the reader, it is an obligation to make noise, yell, stamp your feet, etc. The traditional instrument for this is the grager (see below); however, other tools can be used as well.

It is *obligatory* to eat, drink, drink, and be merry on Purim. The actual requirement is to get so drunk that you cannot distinguish between "bless Mordehai and curse Haman."

Some suggestions Write Haman's name on the bottom of your shoes and then kick and stamp. Bang together rocks with his name on them. Blow a shofar. Blow a trumpet. Play appropriate organ music. Play inappropriate organ music. Beat on a drum, pots and pans, etc. Shake a tin can full of nails (this can be devastating). Be imaginative. Use your head. There is also the custom to make a dummy Haman and beat it, hang it, burn it.

But Remember . . .

It should be kept in mind, that the mitzvah involved with the reading of the Megillah is to *hear* it. Traditionally, every single word must be heard. The reader should wait until all the noise dies down before continuing—or you should try to get a seat close to the reader(s).

A section called "Al ha-Nissim"—For the Miracles—is added to the Amidah and Grace after Meals during Purim.

Purim is notorious for its plays and parodies. No one, not even the most learned and pious of scholars, is free from scathing attack. Parodies of the Talmud and other religious writings have been combined into a virtual "liturgy" for the day.

Aside from the drunken ecstacy, Purim is also a time of general good feeling for one another. It is a mitzvah to give presents to at least two poor people during the holiday. In addition, there is the custom of shalakhmones. Every person is supposed to send presents of at least two kinds of fruit, cookies, or candies to at least one friend. It is customary, however, to give extensively. This is one of the most delightful of Jewish customs. It is fun to visit heavily Jewish parts of New York (e.g., Williamsburg) and see hundreds of children in costumes delivering shalakhmones.

Traditionally, there is a Purim seudah (feast) in the afternoon of the day. Often relatives and friends gather together for this feast.

The traditional Purim food is hamantashen—a tricornered dough cookie generally filled with poppy seed (mohn). Kreplach, three-cornered meat-filled dough, is also customarily eaten. The triangular shape supposedly is representative of Haman's hat.

Purim project

Please help to spread the word that as Adar arrives, joy is heightened in the cosmos. Print BE HAPPY—IT'S ADAR on white 8½" x 11" sheets of paper—right in the middle of the page—and mail them to heads of government, friends, enemies, etc. Post them in laundromats, on telephone poles, in shul lobbies, and such.

They make people smile and that's good (especially in Adar).

Ushering in Adar

(Talmud Babli, Ta-anit 29a) מִשֶּׁנִּכְנַס אֲדָר מַרְבִּים בְּשִׂמְחָה

With the beginning of Adar, we make much joy. Because Purim is such a joyous, uninhibited holiday—with wonderful overtones of friendship and sharing—it is considered meritorious to anticipate it eagerly. Thus the tradition informs us that whoever is attentive to the coming of Adar brings greater joy into the world—because he will assuredly not forget to rejoice on Purim. With this in mind, Seymour Epstein has initiated a Purim project both simple and fun.

BE HAPPY
IT'S ADAR

How to make a grager Aside from the noisemakers mentioned earlier, there is a great variety of homemade gragers. For kids, try putting some stones or hard beans between two paper bowls or aluminum foil cups. Seal the circumference with staples and decorate.

It may be possible to buy a large wooden grager (much noisier than the metal ones) that is just like one of those that were used in the old country. These often disguise themselves as "police rattles" (which were used to call other policemen) and hide out in antique stores.

If you are a bit more ambitious, you might want to make a Franklin Grager [designed by Leon Franklin, member, JCC, Wilkes-Barre, Pa.—ed.]. This was another of the crafts projects undertaken at the Wilkes-Barre, Pa. Jewish Community Center under the direction of Sy Hefter.

Jewish Community Center
60 S. River St.
Wilkes-Barre, Pa. 18701

Instructions for making the Franklin Grager

TOOLS NEEDED
Electric drill with ½″ and 1/16″ bits
Coping saw, jigsaw, or band saw to cut gear
Hammer, plane, sandpaper
Hand saw

SUPPLIES NEEDED (estimated cost of materials for 24 gragers approximately $5)
One dowel 1/16 x 1″ (for locking pin)
One tongue depressor ¾″ x 6¼″ (available from doctor or drugstore)
One dowel ½″ x 5½″ (for handle)
Two pieces soft white pine lath 9¾″ x 1⅜″ x ¼″
One block soft white pine 3⅛″ x 1⅜″ x ¾″
Four brads
One wooden spool 1½″ diameter and ¾″ wide with a ½″ center hole, hardwood (for gear). Available from shoe factory, usually discarded, called the center spool from a ¾″ shoe gear.

PROCEDURE FOR MAKING THE FRANKLIN GRAGER

1. Cut two pieces of lath to length.
2. Mark center line and drill ½″ hole through both lath pieces.
3. Mark spool and cut for eight teeth. Use jig, coping, or band saw.
4. Position spool on dowel and drill 1/16″ hole through both.

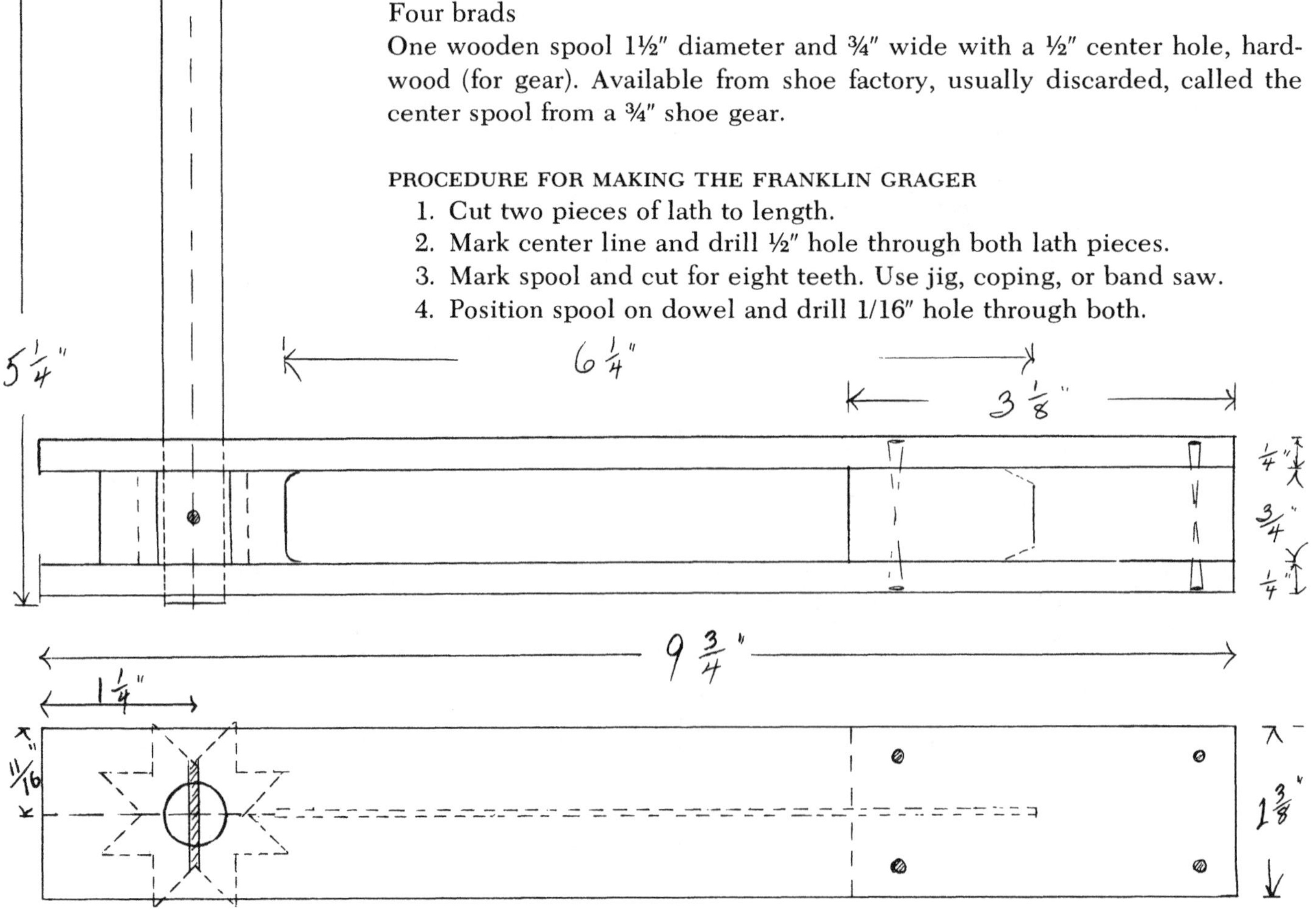

5. Insert 1/16″ dowel in hole to pin gear to ½″ dowel. Cut off excess.
6. Mark center on 1⅜″ side of block and cut 1½″ slot with hand saw (to hold depressor).
7. Insert tongue depressor into slot. Force fit. DO NOT NAIL.
8. Assemble:
   a. Place lath pieces on both sides of gear through ½″ holes. Check for free movement. If too tight, ream ½″ hole.
   b. Place block with tongue depressor between laths and adjust so that the gear will turn with the tongue depressor at its maximum.
      (1) Be certain that tongue depressor is perfectly centered.
      (2) Hold in this position and put 4 brads through each side into base block.
9. Finish by planing or cutting off excess wood edges, sand to fine finish, paint or stain. Design and colors can be as original as possible.

Pesah—Passover

15 Nisan–22 Nisan. Song of Songs is read on the intermediate Shabbat; Hallel on first two days; Half Hallel on the other days; prayer of Tal said on second day (first day in Israel); Yizkor on last day.

As with all of the major festivals, Pesah has both agricultural and historical origins. Agriculturally there are two distinct roots, as indicated by the two names for the holiday: Hag ha-Pesah—Festival of the Pascal Sacrifice, and Hag ha-Matzot—Festival of Matzah. With regard to the first, it seems that early spring is the time when cows begin to calve. The pascal sacrifice was an offering of firstfruits, as it were, by the cattle-ranchers. The Festival of Matzah was a parallel offering of firstfruits by the farmers—the grain offering. Historically Pesah commemorates the exodus from Egypt and the release from slavery. The pascal sacrifice thus refers to the meal which God commanded the Israelites to eat the evening before, while the matzah refers to the type of bread which the Jews had to eat in their hasty flight from Egypt.

Although redemption is the primary theme of the holiday, a secondary theme, paradoxically, is creation. Pesah is a New Year festival—the new year that is signified by spring: rebirth and revival. According to the traditional counting of the months, Nisan is the first month of the Jewish calendar. Thematically this is borne out as well, this being the beginning of the agricultural cycle and also the period during which the people Israel (as a people) was created. A careful examination of the motifs of the exodus and creation stories will show striking parallels—which lead to a comparison of the two primal events. This is certainly recognized by the tradition; for example, on Friday night—the paradigmatic moment of creation—the Kiddush refers both to the completion of creation *and* to the exodus from Egypt. (Try also playing with the ideas of movement from chaos to order, from potential to actual, from the womb to the open world, etc.)

There is a powerful midrashic-Hasidic understanding of Pesah which has become almost normative. We are told that each one of us is to regard himself as if he personally had gone out of Egypt. This is an interesting flight of the imagination and an effective means of eternalizing the event; however, in a physical, practical sense, it is quite difficult to achieve. The Hasidic move is to psychologize this directive. מִצְרַיִם—Egypt—stems from the root word צר—which means narrow, constrained, inhibited. Thus, to say that we must leave Egypt is to say that each one of us must struggle to break out of his narrownesses, free himself to attain his full potential—spiritual, emotional, psychological. (It is perhaps instructive that even after leaving Egypt, the Jews wandered for forty years in the desert before reaching the land of milk and honey.)

Preparation Dietary regulations for Pesah are quite strict and require an extensive and thorough preparation. The basis for these restrictions lies in the absolute prohibition against eating any leaven during the eight days—in remembrance of the hasty departure from Egypt, during which there was no opportunity for bread to rise. Only unleavened bread—matzah—is permitted. Beyond not *eating* leaven, however, the prohibition extends to not even *owning* any—i.e., having any within your legal possession (see Exodus 13:6–7; 12:17–20). Preparation thus has two aspects:

1. removing all traces of leaven from your house; and
2. making certain that whatever utensils or cookware you use are kosher-for-Pesah—free from any hametz, leaven residue. The strict laws pertaining to these processes are quite complex. If in doubt, consult a rabbi.

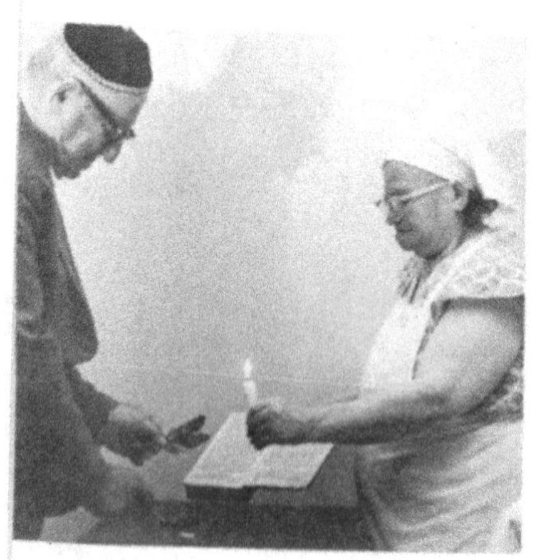

1. Removing leaven: As much as possible of those foods not packaged under specifications of kashrut-for-Passover should be eaten prior to the holiday. That which is not eaten should be put aside in a special place (closet, cupboard, etc.), sealed off, and marked as out-of-bounds. This must then be sold to a non-Jew, so that for all intents and purposes it is his property and not yours. After Pesah a purchase is effected to reacquire the foods and reinstate them as your property. Underlying this is the specification that any hametz which has not been removed from your possession cannot be eaten even *after* the holiday. It is also prohibited, as mentioned, to have hametz in your possession during Passover. Because of the complexities involved in the sale, it is often effected through a rabbi.

The final search for the hametz takes place the night before Pesah. Refer to any Haggadah for the specific details of the ritual. Traditionally, a candle, wooden spoon, feather, and bag are used for this search. ("Searching sets" are available at Hebrew bookstores. Some people form the remnants of the Hanukkah candles into the candle for the search. Some also use a leaf of the lulav from Sukkot in place of the feather—and then burn the lulav with the hametz on the following morning.) Ten pieces of bread (actually any number can be used) should be placed in different parts of the house. The blessing preceding the search is said, the candle lit, and the search begun. Every place where hametz *could* be found should be searched out. Minimally, of course, the ten pieces of bread must be collected. Afterwards, the renouncement of all unfound hametz is recited and the collected hametz is tied up to be burnt in the morning. On the following morning it is forbidden to eat leaven after approximately 9:30 (see The Calendar)—and the hametz collected from the previous night should be burnt, with the renunciation recited once again after the burning.

NOTE: Although hametz cannot be eaten after 9:30, it is customary *not* to eat any matzah either—reserving the first taste for the Seder.

2. Kashering for Pesah: This is an extremely complicated procedure and should be looked into carefully—both regarding the Law and the extent of your fervor (or fanaticism, depending on your perspective). Perhaps "easiest" is to have a special set of dishes, silverware, and cooking utensils reserved only for use on Pesah. Scour and cover all eating and food preparation surfaces with foil. Thoroughly clean the refrigerator, table, sink, etc. In order to use your oven and stove during Pesah, follow the directions for stove kashering found in Kashrut. In addition, during Pesah some people cover the burners so that no Pesah pot touches the parts of the stove used every other day. Make certain that the foods you bring in after this procedure are kosher-for-Pesah (this labeling is another large area of contention and confusion).

NOTE: For a concise, halakhically accurate presentation of the laws pertaining to preparation, as well as a rundown on acceptable foods, medicines, drugs, and pharmaceuticals, write for the *Passover Handbook* edited by Rabbi Jacob Hecht:
National Committee for Furtherance of Jewish Education
824 Eastern Pkwy.
Brooklyn, N.Y. 11213.
ee.

Each year the Union of Orthodox Jewish Congregations of America publishes a Passover Products Directory listing all foods that are kosher-for-

Passover. For a free copy send a stamped, self-addressed envelope to:

Dept. A, Orthodox Union
116 E. 27th St.
New York, N.Y. 10016

Fast of the Firstborn When the firstborn of Egypt were slain during the final plague, the firstborn of Israel were saved. In appreciation for this, it is incumbent upon Jewish firstborn to fast on the day before Pesah. This is customarily circumvented, however, by the participation in a Seudat Mitzvah—a festive meal celebrating the performance of a mitzvah such as the completion of a tractate of Talmud. This meal supersedes the fast. Thus, if the firstborn participates in a final study session (even of someone else—notably the local rabbi) after the Morning Service, he can partake of that meal and be freed of the obligation to fast.

The Seder Participation in a Seder—a highly ritualized feast—is central to the celebration of the festival. The Seder is entirely and exclusively a *home* ritual. Its origins stem both from the description of the meal which the Israelites prepared before the exodus from Egypt (Exodus 12:3–11) and from the prescription repeated four times in the Bible adjuring the father to tell the story of the exodus to his children (Exodus 12:26–27; 13:8; 13:14; Deuteronomy 6:20–21). The Seder (and by extension the whole of Pesah) is a time when the entire extended family comes together. The psychological roots underlying this penetrate quite deeply. Many generations should be represented: each has a particular role to fulfill. We are to experience the exodus ourselves at this time; thus, the symbolism of the Seder must reach the adults. The children must understand; thus, great care and concern should be taken that they participate and receive proper explanations. Aside from family, it is customary—some even say obligatory—to invite others who have no Seder for themselves, particularly the poor in the community. The words "Let all who are hungry come and eat" should be taken quite seriously. This is the night when Elijah is to visit each house, and, as legend relates, Elijah likes to dress himself as a beggar to see if he will be received—to see if the world is yet ready and worthy of the Messiah.

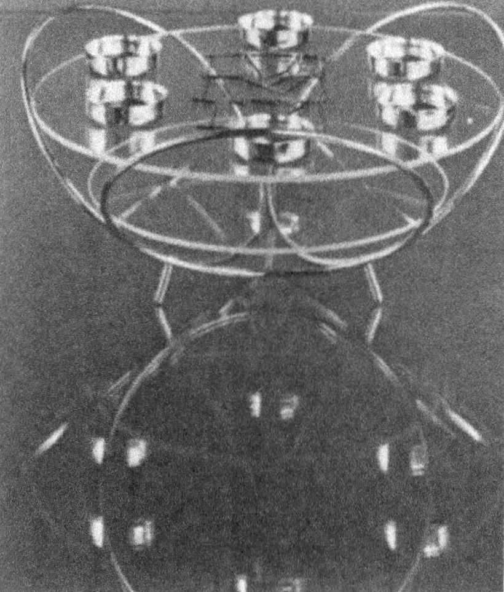

The intricate ritual of the Seder is explained in detail in the Haggadah, the text for the Seder. Since space does not permit an in-depth explanation of each ritual, only the structure will be outlined here, along with some variations. It is advisable to study the Haggadah for some time prior to Pesah so that its structure, organization, problems, and possibilities will be clear to you before the start of the Seder.

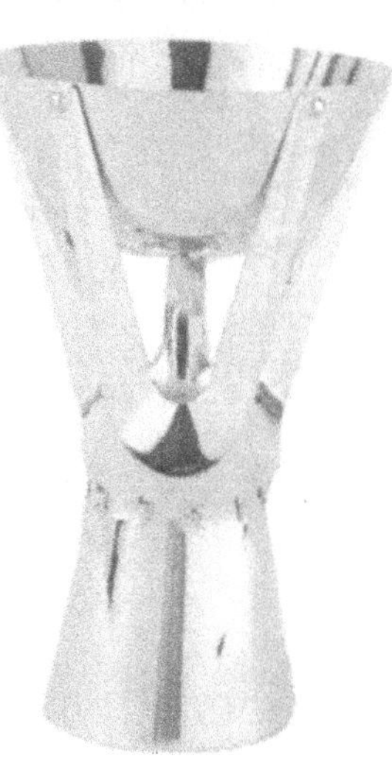

WHAT YOU NEED FOR THE SEDER

1. Haggadot for all participants. People unfamiliar with the running of a Seder should use similarly paginated standard Haggadot.

2. Seder plate with all its ingredients–i.e., a hard-boiled egg, a roasted lamb bone, greens, bitter herbs, salt water, haroset.

3. Salt water—for dipping by all the celebrants.

4. Greens—parsley, celery—for all.

5. Bitter herbs—horseradish or romaine lettuce—for all.

6. Haroset—a special nut, apple, wine mixture—for all.

7. Matzah and a special three-layer matzah cover or plate.

8. Wine—enough for four cups for everyone.

9. Pillows—to recline on.

10. A cup for Elijah.

THE ORDER

A few alternative suggestions

The ritual, although complete and highly structured, offers a number of opportunities for embellishment or the insertion of personal interpretation.

1. For vegetarians, who may object to using a lamb bone on the Seder plate (as a remembrance of the pascal sacrifice): it is halakhically acceptable to use a broiled beet as a replacement.

2. If your observance level allows you to light fire on yom tov, an interesting idea is to light some small charcoals and throw some powdered frankincense and myrrh on them (also as a remembrance of the Temple sacrifice) during the telling about the pascal sacrifice and at other suitable moments.

3. At the asking of the Four Questions allow time for both the children and the adults to ask *additional* questions which they may have regarding the Seder or the holiday in general. Try to answer them—as a group. The Four Questions were only meant as suggestions, not as an exhaustive or restrictive list.

4. At the telling of the story: for a variation, try going around the room asking everyone to reconstruct a part of the story from memory. This does not have to be, and probably will not be, sequential. Begin by asking, "What do you remember about your leaving Egypt?"

5. Allow time and opportunity to discuss issues and questions which may arise in the course of the evening.

1. Kaddesh—Kiddush over the first cup of wine. Drink in a reclining position.

2. Urchatz—Wash the hands without a blessing; it is an old custom to wash prior to dipping food in liquid.

3. Karpas—Eat the greens dipped in salt water. The green is symbolic of spring; the salt water is symbolic of a slave people's tears of bitterness.

4. Yahatz—Break the middle of the three matzot; half is for the afikomen—guard it carefully; kids have been known to steal it and demand ransom!

5. Maggid—Telling the story of Passover as embellished by rabbinic commentary. This is the bulk of the Haggadah text and includes everyone's favorite parts—the Four Questions, the Four Sons, the Ten Plagues. . . . This ends with the second cup of wine. Drink in a reclining position.

6. Rahtzah—Wash the hands before the meal, with a blessing.

7-8. Motzi, Matzah—The double blessing said over the matzah just prior to the meal. Eat the matzah (top and middle of the three matzot) in a reclining position.

9. Maror—The bitter herbs. Eat straight horseradish with a blessing. Many people dip the bitter herbs in the haroset to mitigate the sharp taste.

10. Korekh—Eat a sandwich made of matzah and horseradish; use the bottom one of the three matzot. This is called the Hillel sandwich.

11. Shulhan Orekh—The meal. Eat and sing.

12. Tzafun—Eat the afikomen as the desert. The question is: If it is hidden, how is it eaten? There are two variations about why the afikomen is never around when you want it. Either

a. the kids try to steal it from the leader, or

b. the leader hides it sometime during the Seder and the kids try to find it.

If one or all of the kids produce the afikomen, the leader must either give them a present for it, or, more traditionally, bargain with them for something which they feel to be of equivalent value. Following this, the afikomen is broken up and eaten.

13. Barekh—Grace after the Meal, said over the third cup of wine (recline).

14. Hallel—Reciting/singing the Hallel psalms; at the end, drink the fourth cup of wine in a reclining position; then pour Elijah's cup and have the children open the door for him.

15. Nirtzeh, Conclusion—"Next year in Jerusalem!" More singing. Beginning with the second night of Pesah, the omer is counted.

The following are some editions of especially beautiful Haggadot.

Glatzer, Nahum N., ed. *The Passover Haggadah.* New York: Schocken, 1967. Text with notes. $1.95

Harris, Joel, and Schuldenfrei, Jack. *Fourth World Haggadah.* London: WUJS, 1973. Available from Network, 36 W. 37th St., New York, N.Y. 10018. Text with readings. $3.50

Kasher, Rabbi M. *Israel Passover Haggadah.* New York: Schulsinger, 1950. Text with extensive notes. $6.50

Podwall, Mark, ed. *Let My People Go Haggadah.* New York: Macmillan, 1972. Introduction by Theodore Bikel. Excellent and evocative illustrations. $7.95. Paperback available from SSSJ, 2460 Stanley St., Montreal 112, Que., Canada. $3.95 plus 50c postage.

Raphael, Haim. *A Feast of History.* New York: Simon & Schuster, 1972. History of Passover. $12.50

Shahn, Ben. *Ben Shahn's Haggadah.* Boston: Little Brown, 1965. Artistic. $10

Waskow, Arthur. *The Freedom Seder: A New Haggadah for Passover.* New York: Holt Rinehart & Winston, Micah, 1970. Radical/political. Paperback $1.50

Zuckoff, Aviva. *Jewish Liberation Hagada.* 1970. Available from Jewish Liberation Project, Rm. 700, 150 5th Ave., New York, N.Y. 10011. A radical Zionist Haggadah. $2 plus 25c postage.

On matzah Since the prescription regarding the eating of matzah in place of hametz is repeated several times in the Torah (see Exodus 12), it has come to be observed with extreme strictness—particularly on the first two nights (Seder nights). There are several types of matzah, varying in their strictness:

1. Shemurah (watched). Hand-made. The wheat is watched from the time of harvesting until the final baking to insure that no water, heat, or other natural processes cause it to begin fermentation. It is hand-made, constantly observed, and the utensils used for making it are washed every eighteen minutes (the time when fermentation can begin, according to halakhah).

2. Shemurah (machine-baked). Same as above but baked by mechanical processes. Although this is kosher in all ways, some have questions as to whether the introduction of machinery necessitates revision in the laws.

3. Not shemurah. This is the supermarket matzah. It is only watched from the time of grinding (as opposed to the time of harvesting). Although this is also kosher, many people prefer to use the shemurah matzah to fulfill the mitzvah during the Seder, and use this for regular consumption during Pesah.

4. Egg matzah. Matzah baked with egg, milk, wine, or fruit extracts. It is called "unleavened bread prepared in a rich manner." Eating this will not fulfill the obligation of eating matzah at the Seder.

How to bake matzot

INGREDIENTS AND TOOLS

special Passover flour, or whole-grain wheat
cold spring water
a baker's oven
smooth working surfaces—preferably glass or marble slabs
1 kneading tub
rolling pins
sandpaper
matzah-perforating machine (you may have to improvise this: it looks like a rolling pin with spikes)
long wooden poles
6 or more people

NOTE: This is intended as a general description of the method by which matzot may be baked for Passover. Before actually baking, a competent rabbinic authority should be consulted to find out whether the equipment and procedure you intend to use are suitable or not. As will be seen, several of the requirements for matzah, particularly the temperature of the oven, make it virtually impossible to bake matzot in a home setting.

THE BASIC PROBLEM

Hametz, which is forbidden during the entire holiday of Passover, is defined as any fermented grain product (specifically, from one of the "five grains" mentioned in rabbinic literature: wheat, spelt, barley, oats, and rye; rice, millet, and beans, while not explicitly forbidden in the Talmud, are not eaten by any Ashkenazic Jews because they undergo a process similar to fermentation). Fermentation is presumed to take place within eighteen minutes after the exposure of the cut grain to moisture. Matzah, which is required as the central element at the Seder and which is the staple food throughout the week of Passover, is defined as the bread made from grain and water dough without fermentation. The problem, of course, is how to make such a dough without causing fermentation. This is accomplished by three means.

1. Protecting the ingredients from moisture and heat prior to mixing.
2. Preparing the dough very rapidly.
3. Baking at extremely high temperatures.

THE STARTING INGREDIENTS

The flour must be absolutely dry, and stored in a cool, dark place. According to the strictest interpretation, it should have been watched from the time of reaping to ascertain that it was never exposed to moisture. Such flour, known as shemurah flour, may be purchased from one of the shemurah matzah bakeries in New York. According to a more lenient view, it is sufficient if the flour was watched from the time of milling. In the latter case, you may purchase whole grain for matzah at any grain store and mill it yourself, making sure that your mill is kosher-for-Passover before you start.

The water must be drawn from a spring and allowed to settle overnight in a cool, dark, place. This is done so the water will not be warm. The vessel in which it is stored should be perfectly clean and kosher-for-Passover. Tap water or bottled spring water may not be used.

THE KNEADING

Before starting, make certain that the boards, rolling pins, etc., which you are using are kosher-for-Passover. Everyone who will be handling dough should wash his/her hands in cold water before beginning to work, and between each batch of dough he handles, and then dry his hands thoroughly. The flour and water are mixed in a tub at a ratio of 3¼ to 1. The maximum amount of flour to be used at any one time is 3 pounds, but unless one has a small army of people working together it's advisable to use much less. Once

the dough is made, it should be cut into small pieces, no bigger than the palm of your hand, and distributed for kneading. Each piece should be worked continuously—it may not sit on the table, even for a brief period. Kneading prevents the dough from rising. The small teyglekh, or balls of dough, should be kneaded until they are of uniform consistency—perhaps for 60 or 90 seconds—and then rolled out into a pancake shape. While the matzot are being rolled they should be constantly picked up, to make certain that the dough does not stick to the table. One reason that this is important is that, unlike kneading bread, one may not sprinkle additional flour on the kneading board. Once the dough has become very thin, and has reached a diameter of 6 or 8 inches, it should be carried on the rolling pin to a special place where the matzah is perforated with holes by means of a special machine. From here the dough is taken to the oven.

Between batches of dough, several people should be assigned to clean off each work spot and every rolling pin. Because water might produce hametz, sandpaper is probably best for this purpose.

BAKING

As noted above, it is probably necessary to use a baker's oven to make matzah, in order to reach temperatures of 600° to 800°F. The oven should be stoked up from 2 to 4 hours or more before baking begins. The perforated matzot are placed in the oven with long wooden poles and should bake within 2 to 3 minutes. The total time elapsed, from the beginning of the kneading till the matzot are placed in the oven, should in no event be more than 18 minutes.

After baking is completed, a small portion is separated, using the same blessing as in baking hallah (see Hallah), and this is burnt up completely.

THE RESULT

Brown, crisp matzot, suitable for eating at the Seder and celebrating true freedom SHALOM

On haroset An interesting note: The Rambam, Moses Maimonides, included in his explanation to the Mishnah Pesahim (chapter 10) a recipe for haroset. It differs a bit from what is normally eaten today, but with some variation it could be palatable:

A mixture in which there is some sourness, and has an appearance of straw in remembrance of the mortar. And this is how we make it: soak dates or figs, cook/boil them, grind them until they are soft, and knead them with vinegar. Added to this are various spices (which along with some kind of corn, are a bit obscure) and unground cinnamon.

Omer period

A period of forty-nine days (seven full weeks—7 × 7), beginning with the second night of Pesah and ending with Shavuot—thereby linking the exodus (rebirth of the people) with the revelation (encounter between the people and God). It is a mitzvah from the Bible to actively count these days.

"And from the day on which you bring the sheaf of wave offering—the day after the sabbath—you shall count off seven weeks. They must be complete." (Leviticus 23:15).

The ritual for counting can be found in any complete prayer book. Its basic outline is as follows:

a. A preliminary meditation and kavvanah

b. The blessing:

"Blessed are You, Lord our God, King of the Universe, who has sanctified us through His commandments, and commanded us concerning the counting of the omer."

בָּרוּךְ אַתָּה, יְיָ אֱלֹהֵינוּ, מֶלֶךְ הָעוֹלָם, אֲשֶׁר קִדְּשָׁנוּ בְּמִצְוֹתָיו, וְצִוָּנוּ עַל סְפִירַת הָעֹמֶר:

c. The counting done in a formulaic manner:

"Today is the *(19th)* day, which is *(2)* weeks and *(5)* days in the omer."

הַיּוֹם, תִּשְׁעָה עָשָׂר יוֹם, שֶׁהֵם שְׁנֵי שָׁבוּעוֹת וַחֲמִשָּׁה יָמִים, לָעֹמֶר:

הוד שבתפארת

d. One psalm and one meditation/prayer follow this. These have the interesting characteristic of being composed of forty-nine words (each representing one day). In addition, one of the lines in the psalm has forty-nine letters—again each representing one day:

"Nations will exult and shout for joy, for You rule the peoples with equity, guide the nations of the earth. Selah" (Psalms 67:5).

יִשְׂמְחוּ וִירַנְּנוּ לְאֻמִּים, כִּי תִשְׁפֹּט עַמִּים מִישֹׁר, וּלְאֻמִּים בָּאָרֶץ תַּנְחֵם, סֶלָה:

For kabbalists (and would-be mystics) there are further levels of meaning in this ritual. Seven is an extremely powerful number—primarily representing the days of creation but appearing in other contexts as well. Seven times seven is even more so. Beyond this, the word sefirah—counting—is also the word for the ten levels of divine emanation (sefirot). Only the lower *seven* of these are within our apprehension. Each day thus takes on the character not just of one sefirah but of the combined power of one sefirah within another (hesed—love; gevurah—power; tiferet—beauty; netzah—victory; hod—majesty; yesod—foundation; Malkut—Queen-mother. Thus the 19th day is hod she-be-Tiferet—majesty which is in beauty.)

The counting is generally said while standing. Traditionally it is done in the evening after sunset, but it may also be said the following morning without a blessing. If you lapse in your counting for a whole day and then resume, it is customary to continue from that point (of resumption) but without the blessing.

"Sefirah counters" can be bought at Jewish bookstores, or can be made quite easily by marking out the days on a calendar and putting it in a prominent place, so that you will not forget. It is a great challenge to see if you can remember to do this forty-nine days in a row. It certainly builds up an anticipation for Shavuot.

The prevailing mood for this entire period is one of semimourning. Weddings are not supposed to take place; you should not cut your hair, etc. This is explained variously as

1. a period of apprehensive anticipation of approaching Mount Sinai and the revelation of God;
2. the critical time when the fate of the season's crops is determined; and
3. traditionally, a period in remembrance of the plague which killed many of Rabbi Akiba's students (2nd century C.E.).

The 33rd day of this period—Lag ba-Omer (Iyyar 18)—is a special day of celebration. This also is interpreted either as a rite of spring or as the day when the plague lifted. In any event, it is a day of outings and midnight bonfires. There are no specific rituals associated with it, but the prohibitions relating to mourning are lifted.

Shavuot—Feast of Weeks

Alias, Yom ha-Bikkurim—Festival of the Firstfruits; Hag ha-Katzir—Festival of the Harvest; Atzeret—Convocation; Zeman Mattan Torahtenu—The Time of Giving of Our Torah.

Sixth and seventh of Sivan; the Book of Ruth is read; Full Hallel is recited on both days; Yizkor is said on the second day.

It is connected to Pesah in both its agricultural and historical aspects:

1. as the end of the grain harvest; and
2. the receiving of the Torah (which was the raison d'être of the exodus, in spite of what it says in Dayyeinu). Although it is only a two-day festival and has little ritual associated with it, it is still quite significant and can be highly powerful—representing, as it does, the greatest epiphany in the history of the cosmos: God revealing Himself directly to 600,000 people. According to tradition, we all stood at Sinai — we all stand at Sinai to receive the Torah directly.

Some of the most wonderful customs of the year are associated with Shavuot:

1. It is customary to decorate both the home and synagogue with branches, greens, and flowers.
2. Some spread grass on the floor of the synagogue—representative of the grass upon which Israel stood while receiving the Torah. (You would probably have to take off your shoes to feel the true impact of this.)
3. The shammash of the synagogue should give out sweet-smelling herbs and grasses during services.
4. Some weave a crown of flowers and branches and place it over the Torah (a combination of both themes).

Tikkun Leil Shavuot It is customary to stay up the entire night of Shavuot, studying and discussing Torah. The traditional Tikkun involves studying a small section from every book of the Bible and every section of Talmud in order to study symbolically the entire body of Jewish religious writings. Nontraditionally, the study matter is a matter of choice by whatever group is engaging in the Tikkun. It should, however, be thought out and prepared in advance (with time given to wake-up games and exercises). At least two reasons are given for the Tikkun:

1. Because the Israelites fell asleep during the night before the receiving of the Torah—and had to be awakened by Moses. To show our eagerness (and because we do not have Moses to awaken us) we stay up all night.
2. As Sinai is the marriage of Israel and God—and of heaven and earth—we stay up all night as is the custom for the attendants to a bride before her wedding. The Torah, in this schema, becomes the ketubbah, the wedding contract.

It is said that the heavens open up at midnight on Shavuot, making it a propitious time for our prayers and thoughts to ascend. There is an undefinable beauty in staying up all night studying, and then greeting the sunrise —and receiving the Torah.

Food It is customary to eat dairy foods during Shavuot—especially blintzes and cheesecake: (a) because after Sinai the Jews did not want to spend a lot of time preparing a meat meal—which involves slaughtering the animal, koshering the meat, etc.; (b) because Torah is like milk and honey; (c) because when receiving the Ten Commandments we should not be reminded of the golden calf and the subsequent breaking of the first tablets.

Twin hallot are baked—representative of the two tablets or reminiscent of

It is also customary to eat kreplach on Shavuot (see Kashrut). Kreplach have three sides, representative of:

1. God, Israel, Torah;
2. Abraham, Isaac and Jacob—because of whom we received the Torah;
3. the Bible, which has three parts (Torah, Prophets, Writings), given to
4. Israel, which has three parts (priests, Levites, Israelites);
5. the Torah was given on the sixth day (2×3) of the third month.

the two loaves of bread which were offered in the Temple. Some add a ladder of seven rungs, symbolic of the seven layers of heaven which God rent as He descended onto Sinai. Also סלם —ladder—is equivalent to סיני —Sinai—in gematria.

In Europe it was customary to begin a child's education on Shavuot. This was a major occasion for both the parents and the child—and was surrounded by many rituals. One particularly interesting custom was to coat the first letters the child was taught with honey or candy. This was meant to encourage the child in his studies and to express the wish that the words of Torah should be sweet to his lips. In today's Hebrew schools kids bring their own candy—every day.

Tisha b'Av—the Ninth of Av

This marks the end of a three-week period of semimourning beginning with the 17th of Tammuz, also a fast day. The nine days from the beginning of Av to Tisha b'Av mark an intensified mourning period; many people abstain from meat and wine, refrain from shaving, from buying new clothes, and from various forms of entertainment.

Tisha b'Av is a fast day in commemoration of the various disasters and tragedies which have befallen the Jewish people throughout history. The central mourning is over the destruction of the Temple—an event which marked the initiation of the exile. This has both physical as well as spiritual dimensions. As Israel was divided from the land, so too was the Shekhinah—the Divine Presence. To the kabbalists the day represented the nature of the world's incompleteness and the great need for tikkun—repair (returning the Shekhinah to her place). Although there is a temptation to concentrate on the Holocaust, this should be resisted, so as not to blur distinctions or lose sight of the essence of the day.

Aspects of the day

The fast begins at sundown.

No leather is worn.

The Book of Lamentations is read at night while sitting on the floor or on low stools. Candlelight is used for the reading.

After the chanting, kinot—a form of dirge—are said. These are also said in the morning.

Tallit and tefillin are not worn for Shaharit.

At Minhah, tallit and tefillin are put on and there is a Torah reading.

In both services, there is addition to the Amidah that makes special reference to Tisha b'Av.

One is supposed to study on Tisha b'Av only those sections of the Talmud which deal with the destruction of the Temple.

TWO RECENT ADDITIONS TO THE CELEBRATORY CYCLE

Yom ha-Shoah—Day in Commemoration of the Holocaust

27th of Nisan. This day is a recent addition to the Jewish calendar, and is still in the state of development—from the point of view of rituals, liturgy, and customs. There is not yet enough perspective on the event to know what to say about it or how to respond to it. The event itself is still too real to be symbolic.

The best attempt at a liturgy-ritual for the day is *Nightwords* by David

Roskies, published by Bnai Brith Hillel and available at:

1640 R.I. Ave. N.W.
Washington, D.C. 20036

Also available is a collection of readings on the Holocaust edited by Muki Tsur and Nathan Yanai, available through:

Educational Offices, American Zionist Youth Foundation
515 Park Ave.
New York, N.Y. 10022

Israel Independence Day

Celebration of the founding of the State of Israel in 1948. Celebrated mostly with a military parade (in Israel) and children's parades (in the Diaspora). Very few people view this day religiously beyond seeing it as resulting from God's having performed a miracle in creating the state. There are, as yet, no religious (or any other) customs (except parades), and attempts at additions to the liturgy have been pitiful (e.g., saying Hallel without the blessings).

Berakhot-blessings

"A person who enjoys the pleasures of this world without a blessing is called a thief because the blessing is what causes the continuation of the divine flow into the world" *(Peri Ez Hadar).*

"Our sages regarded it as their duty not only to call us from the turmoil of life to a gathering to God, but to approach us in life itself, to make us realize that everything emanates from Him, and that in dedicating ourselves to His service, according to His dictates, we thus bring Berakhah, blessing, to God—which really means that we fulfill His will" (Samson R. Hirsh).

The berakhot, blessings or benedictions, are attributed to the men of the Great Assembly (c. 400–300 B.C.E.). These blessings can be said in any language as long as they convey the same thoughts as the Hebrew text and include the basic formula of God and King of the Universe. Also, it is required that the blessing be followed immediately by the pertinent action, such as eating, smelling, or by the performance of the mitzvah.

According to Maimonides, there are three types of berakhot.

1. Blessings recited prior to enjoying food, drink or scent—Birkhot ha-Nehenin.

2. Blessings recited prior to the performance of a mitzvah—Birkhot ha-Mitzvot.

3. Blessings that express praise of and gratitude to God, and that petition Him—Birkhot Hodaah (from Berakhot 1:4).

BIRKHOT HA-NEHENIN

The basic form of the Birkhot ha-Nehenin, as established by the sages, reads as follows: "Blessed are You, Lord our God, King of the Universe. . . ." The Birkhot ha-Nehenin basically deal with the enjoyment of the five senses, i.e., eating, smelling, viewing natural phenomena, hearing good news, and wearing a new garment.

Taste

On partaking of bread When bread is to be eaten at the meal, one should first wash the hands, reciting the blessing Al Netilat Yadayim (see below), and then recite ha-Motzi, the blessing over bread. The ha-Motzi blessing frees one from saying any other blessing at that meal. The berakhah is:

"Blessed are You, Lord our God, King of the Universe, who brings forth bread from the earth."

בָּרוּךְ אַתָּה, יְיָ אֱלֹהֵינוּ, מֶלֶךְ הָעוֹלָם, הַמּוֹצִיא לֶחֶם מִן הָאָרֶץ:

On drinking wine or grape juice

"Blessed. . . . Universe, who creates the fruit of the vine."

בָּרוּךְ אַתָּה, יְיָ אֱלֹהֵינוּ, מֶלֶךְ הָעוֹלָם, בּוֹרֵא פְּרִי הַגָּפֶן:

This blessing is part of Kiddush and Havdalah recited on Shabbat and holidays as well as part of the wedding ceremony.

NOTE: Since the beginning part of the blessing is the same, we have left it out of the translation; for an example of a complete blessing, see the blessing for bread above.

On eating cakes or cookies

"Blessed . . . Universe, who creates various kinds of foods."

בָּרוּךְ אַתָּה, יְיָ אֱלֹהֵינוּ, מֶלֶךְ הָעוֹלָם, בּוֹרֵא מִינֵי מְזוֹנוֹת:

On eating fruit of the trees

"Blessed . . . Universe, who creates the fruit of the tree."

בָּרוּךְ אַתָּה, יְיָ אֱלֹהֵינוּ, מֶלֶךְ הָעוֹלָם, בּוֹרֵא פְּרִי הָעֵץ:

On eating vegetables

"Blessed . . . Universe, who creates the fruit of the earth."

בָּרוּךְ אַתָּה, יְיָ אֱלֹהֵינוּ, מֶלֶךְ הָעוֹלָם, בּוֹרֵא פְּרִי הָאֲדָמָה:

On partaking of any other food (e.g., most liquids, meat, fish, chocolate, ice cream, etc.)

"Blessed . . . Universe, by whose word all things come into being."

בָּרוּךְ אַתָּה, יְיָ אֱלֹהֵינוּ, מֶלֶךְ הָעוֹלָם, שֶׁהַכֹּל נִהְיָה בִּדְבָרוֹ:

This blessing is applicable to all foods, and therefore is used when one is in doubt about the proper blessing.

These are the six berakhot said before eating or drinking food. The rules concerning which blessing to say on a particular food are very complicated. For instance, one does not say the blessing for vegetables on potato chips even though one generally says it for potatoes. It would be nice to say that the rule is: borei peri ha-adamah applies to a vegetable in its natural state, and she-ha-kol applies to a vegetable after it has been cooked or processed. However, this is not exactly true. Often the blessing depends on whether the rabbis thought it was natural to cook a food. By this reasoning cooked apples are still peri ha-ez, while cooked nuts are she-ha-kol. The laws apparently have not kept up with changing food styles and thus often appear illogical.

Other complicated questions involve the mixture of types of foods, e.g., vegetable soup, and eating more than one kind of food at a time, e.g., cookies and milk. One should remember that (a) she-ha-kol can be said over any food, and (b) all food eaten in a meal begun by eating bread does not need an additional blessing.

An excellent and inexpensive booklet dealing with many of these problems is *A Guide to Blessings*, edited by Mosad Eliezer Hoffman, available for $1 from:

National Conference of Synagogue Youth
116 E. 27th St.
New York, N.Y. 10016

It also has a long alphabetical list of foods and their respective berakhot. One word of reservation: it often follows the most strict opinion in order to avoid any possibility of error.

In case of doubt, ask a rabbi.

Smell

On smelling fragrant woods or barks

"Blessed . . . Universe, who creates fragrant woods."

בָּרוּךְ אַתָּה, יְיָ אֱלֹהֵינוּ, מֶלֶךְ הָעוֹלָם, בּוֹרֵא עֲצֵי בְשָׂמִים:

On smelling fragrant fruits

"Blessed . . . Universe, who gives a pleasant scent to fruits."

בָּרוּךְ אַתָּה, יְיָ אֱלֹהֵינוּ, מֶלֶךְ הָעוֹלָם, הַנּוֹתֵן רֵיחַ טוֹב בַּפֵּרוֹת:

On smelling any other fragrance

"Blessed . . . Universe, who creates various kinds of spices."

בָּרוּךְ אַתָּה, יְיָ אֱלֹהֵינוּ, מֶלֶךְ הָעוֹלָם, בּוֹרֵא מִינֵי בְשָׂמִים:

Sight

These are blessings to be recited on witnessing natural phenomena or unusual sights and on various occasions and events. They are meant to remind us of God and of our debt to Him, the Creator and controller of the world.

On seeing lightning, shooting stars, great deserts, high mountains, or a sunrise

"Blessed . . . Universe, who does the workings of creation."

בָּרוּךְ אַתָּה, יְיָ אֱלֹהֵינוּ, מֶלֶךְ הָעוֹלָם, עֹשֶׂה מַעֲשֵׂה בְרֵאשִׁית:

On seeing a rainbow

"Blessed . . . Universe, who remembers the covenant and who is faithful to His covenant and keeps His promise."

בָּרוּךְ אַתָּה, יְיָ אֱלֹהֵינוּ, מֶלֶךְ הָעוֹלָם, זוֹכֵר הַבְּרִית וְנֶאֱמָן בִּבְרִיתוֹ, וְקַיָּם בְּמַאֲמָרוֹ:

NOTE: The covenant refers to God's promise given to Noah after the flood.

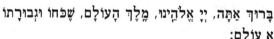

On seeing trees blooming for the first time in the year

"Blessed . . . Universe, who has withheld nothing from this world and has created beautiful creatures and beautiful trees in it, so that man may delight in them."

בָּרוּךְ אַתָּה, יְיָ אֱלֹהֵינוּ, מֶלֶךְ הָעוֹלָם, שֶׁלֹּא חִסַּר בְּעוֹלָמוֹ דָּבָר, וּבָרָא בוֹ בְּרִיּוֹת טוֹבוֹת וְאִילָנוֹת טוֹבִים לְהַנּוֹת בָּהֶם בְּנֵי אָדָם:

On seeing the ocean

"Blessed . . . Universe, who has made the great sea."

בָּרוּךְ אַתָּה, יְיָ אֱלֹהֵינוּ, מֶלֶךְ הָעוֹלָם, שֶׁעָשָׂה אֶת־הַיָּם הַגָּדוֹל:

On seeing a king

"Blessed . . . Universe, who has given of His glory to flesh and man."

בָּרוּךְ אַתָּה, יְיָ אֱלֹהֵינוּ, מֶלֶךְ הָעוֹלָם, שֶׁנָּתַן מִכְּבוֹדוֹ לְבָשָׂר וָדָם:

When Agnon received the Nobel Prize for literature in the presence of the king of Sweden, he recited this blessing.

On seeing a scholar

"Blessed . . . Universe, who has given of His wisdom to flesh and blood."

בָּרוּךְ אַתָּה, יְיָ אֱלֹהֵינוּ, מֶלֶךְ הָעוֹלָם, שֶׁנָּתַן מֵחָכְמָתוֹ לְבָשָׂר וָדָם:

Sound

On hearing thunder

"Blessed . . . Universe, whose strength and might fill the world."

בָּרוּךְ אַתָּה, יְיָ אֱלֹהֵינוּ, מֶלֶךְ הָעוֹלָם, שֶׁכֹּחוֹ וּגְבוּרָתוֹ מָלֵא עוֹלָם:

On hearing good news

"Blessed . . . Universe, who is good and does good."

בָּרוּךְ אַתָּה, יְיָ אֱלֹהֵינוּ, מֶלֶךְ הָעוֹלָם, הַטּוֹב וְהַמֵּטִיב:

On hearing bad news

"Blessed . . . Universe, the true Judge."

בָּרוּךְ אַתָּה, יְיָ אֱלֹהֵינוּ, מֶלֶךְ הָעוֹלָם, דַּיַּן הָאֱמֶת:

This blessing is also said when tearing a garment during mourning (see Death and Burial).

Touch

On putting on a new garment

"Blessed . . . Universe, who clothes the naked."

בָּרוּךְ אַתָּה, יְיָ אֱלֹהֵינוּ, מֶלֶךְ הָעוֹלָם, מַלְבִּישׁ עֲרֻמִּים:

This is followed by the She-heheyanu (see below).

This is not meant to be an exhaustive list of this type of berakhot. See the Hertz Siddur for additional blessings.

Berakhot of Thanksgiving after eating food

There are three distinct blessings recited after partaking of food. These blessings are based on the verse

"When you have eaten your fill, give thanks to the Lord your God for the good land which He has given you" (Deuteronomy 8:10).

וְאָכַלְתָּ וְשָׂבָעְתָּ וּבֵרַכְתָּ אֶת יְיָ אֱלֹהֶיךָ עַל הָאָרֶץ הַטּוֹבָה אֲשֶׁר נָתַן לָךְ

1. בִּרְכַּת הַמָּזוֹן —Birkhat ha-Mazon—Grace after Meals.
This is recited after a meal which began with the blessing over bread. It consists of three ancient blessings to which a fourth was added after the defeat of Bar Kokhba (about 135 C.E.). According to the Talmud (Berakhot 48b), the first paragraph (Birkhat ha-Zan) was composed by Moses at the time of the manna. The next blessing, consisting of two paragraphs (Birkhat ha-Arez), was composed by Joshua. The next blessing, consisting of two paragraphs (Boneih Yerushalayim), was composed by David and Solomon. The fourth blessing (ha-Tov ve-ha-Metiv) was composed by the sages of Yavneh, because they were allowed to bury the bodies, which had miraculously not decomposed, of those who fell at Betar. At first, the Romans had refused to allow the burials as further punishment for Bar Kokhba's revolt.

A. When at least three people eat together, they constitute a mezuman; one is asked to call the others to bentsh—say grace—through an introductory formula which is found in a Siddur. If there are ten people eating together, the same formula is used with the addition of the word Eloheinu—our God. It is said as follows:

The leader says:
"Let us say grace."

רַבּוֹתַי נְבָרֵךְ:

The others respond:
"Blessed be the name of the Lord from this time forth and forever."

יְהִי שֵׁם יְיָ מְבֹרָךְ מֵעַתָּה וְעַד עוֹלָם:

The leader repeats this and adds:
"With the permission of those present, we will bless (our) God, whose food we have eaten."

בִּרְשׁוּת מָרָנָן וְרַבָּנָן וְרַבּוֹתַי, נְבָרֵךְ (אֱלֹהֵינוּ) שֶׁאָכַלְנוּ מִשֶּׁלּוֹ:

The others respond:
"Blessed be (our) God, whose food we have eaten and through whose goodness we live."

בָּרוּךְ (אֱלֹהֵינוּ) שֶׁאָכַלְנוּ מִשֶּׁלּוֹ וּבְטוּבוֹ חָיִינוּ:

The leader repeats this
And then all say:
"Blessed be He and blessed be His Name."

בָּרוּךְ הוּא וּבָרוּךְ שְׁמוֹ:

b. It is customary to give the honor of leading to a guest; the ha-Motzi blessing is usually recited by the host. This order is followed because the host will distribute the bread more generously than a guest. The guest, however, has the opportunity to thank and bless the host during the grace.

c. Prayers for Shabbat, holidays, Rosh Hodesh, Purim, and Hanukkah were added later. Petitions beginning with ha-Rahaman—May the All-Merciful—were added at a much later date and are not obligatory. The Rabbinical Assembly (Conservative) has introduced an abbreviated Birkhat ha-Mazon covering some parts of the basic blessings. The Hertz Siddur (page 980) also contains a shorter form of the grace.

d. The Hertz Siddur (page 982) also contains specific changes that are made in the Birkhat ha-Mazon when it is said in the house of a mourner.

e. Before the grace, it is appropriate to clear the table of all utensils, especially the knives, and leave just a piece of bread. The piece of bread is symbolic of the hope that there should never be a lack of food. The knives are removed because they can be used as weapons of war and the table is considered an altar, a place of harmony and peace. Just as the stones used for the Temple in Jerusalem were not hewn by iron, so too we remove knives from our symbolic altar.

f. When there is a mezuman, it is often the custom to lead the grace over a cup of wine. This is thought of as a kos shel berakhah—a cup of blessing—which is distributed to all assembled at the table. The cup is held in the hand during the introductory formula. At the end of the grace, one says the blessing over wine, drinks it, and then passes it.

g. Little booklets containing Grace after Meals and other berakhot can be bought at any Jewish bookstore (see Bibliography).

2. The long berakhah aharonah is recited after partaking of cakes, wine, or certain other foods. These foods are the seven species for which the land of Israel is praised in the Torah: ". . . a land of wheat and barley, of vines, figs and pomegranates, a land of olive trees and honey" (Deuteronomy 8:8). This blessing is an abridged version of the themes of Birkhat ha-Mazon found in its three basic blessings. This also can be found in a Siddur.

3. בּוֹרֵא נְפָשׁוֹת —Borei Nefashot—who creates living beings. This blessing is recited after all other foods not included above. In cases where one does not have a Siddur and does not know the long berakhah aharonah by heart, you can say this berakhah:

"Blessed are You, Lord our God, King of the Universe, who creates innumerable living beings and their needs, for all the things You have created to sustain every living being. Blessed are You who are the life of the universe."

בָּרוּךְ אַתָּה, יְיָ אֱלֹהֵינוּ, מֶלֶךְ הָעוֹלָם, בּוֹרֵא נְפָשׁוֹת רַבּוֹת, וְחֶסְרוֹנָן עַל כָּל מַה שֶׁבָּרָא, לְהַחֲיוֹת בָּהֶם נֶפֶשׁ כָּל חָי, בָּרוּךְ חֵי הָעוֹלָמִים:

Thank you, oh Lord, for The dawn and the Twilight, The months and The Seasons, The Stars, The moon, The sun and The Planets.

BIRKHOT HA-MITZVOT

These blessings, which are recited before the performance of a mitzvah, are intended to show that these practices are divinely ordained and are part of the elaborate mitzvah-discipline system of Judaism. They stress the fact that we owe gratitude to God not merely for supplying our daily needs and creating a beautiful world, but also for sanctifying us and our actions through His commandments.

The basic structure of these blessings is:

"Blessed are You, Lord our God, King of the Universe, who has sanctified us through His commandments, and commanded us. . . ."

בָּרוּךְ אַתָּה, יְיָ אֱלֹהֵינוּ, מֶלֶךְ הָעוֹלָם, אֲשֶׁר קִדְּשָׁנוּ בְּמִצְוֹתָיו וְצִוָּנוּ

We list but a few examples. Other examples—such as, the blessing for the lighting of Hanukkah, Shabbat and holiday candles, before the blowing of the shofar, blessing at a wedding ceremony, over the Four Species, etc.—can be found throughout this book and in any Siddur.

On washing one's hands

"Blessed. . . . Universe, who has sanctified us through His commandments and commanded us concerning the washing of the hands."

בָּרוּךְ אַתָּה, יְיָ אֱלֹהֵינוּ, מֶלֶךְ הָעוֹלָם, אֲשֶׁר קִדְּשָׁנוּ
בְּמִצְוֹתָיו, וְצִוָּנוּ עַל נְטִילַת יָדָיִם:

Besides washing one's hands before eating bread, one washes the hands upon awakening in the morning. This washing of the hands, in addition to its sanitary importance, also serves to "dedicate" our hands, and through them our whole physical being, for a life of renewed active service to God. In fact, the term netilat yadayim literally means "a lifting up" of the hands.

It is also because of this interpretation that one washes one's hands and recites this blessing before a meal at which bread is served. This lifts up the gratification of a bodily need to a higher level. As mentioned, the sages considered the table at which a meal is eaten as if it were an altar.

On reciting the Hallel

"Blessed . . . Universe, who has commanded us to read the Hallel."

בָּרוּךְ אַתָּה, יְיָ אֱלֹהֵינוּ, מֶלֶךְ הָעוֹלָם, אֲשֶׁר קִדְּשָׁנוּ
בְּמִצְוֹתָיו, וְצִוָּנוּ לִקְרֹא אֶת־הַהַלֵּל:

BIRKHOT HODAAH

This third category, according to Maimonides, is intended to praise, petition, and express gratitude to God, so that one will constantly remember the Creator. This category, therefore, includes many portions of the Siddur, such as the nineteen blessings of the Amidah.

The Amidah or Shemoneh Esreh is the central prayer in the three daily services. Originally it contained eighteen blessings, hence the name Shemoneh Esreh (meaning "eighteen" in English). Later, a nineteenth blessing was added. It is a matter of scholarly debate whether the nineteenth blessing was the blessing concerning slanderers or the one concerning the reestablishment of the Davidic kingdom.

According to the Talmud, the Amidah may be divided into three sections. The worshiper may be compared to a servant who, in the first three blessings, offers homage to his master. In the middle blessings, he asks his master for support and sustenance, while in the final three blessings he takes his leave in gratitude (Talmud, Berakhot 34a).

The first three blessings and the last three blessings are the same for every Amidah, whether daily, Shabbat, or holidays. The middle section, however, varies. Only on weekdays, the middle paragraphs contain petitions for the fulfillment of spiritual and material needs. We ask God for wisdom, repentance, forgiveness, personal freedom, healing, prosperity, ingathering of the dispersed, restoration of justice, retribution to the wicked, protection of the pious, rebuilding of Jerusalem, the coming of the Messiah, and the acceptance of our prayers.

Birkhot Ha-Shahar

These morning benedictions, filled with thanksgiving for life, were originally recited at home as one awoke, washed, dressed and prepared for another day. Later, they were included in the first section of Shaharit. These blessings include thanks to God for the gift of sight, our clothing, the use of our limbs, etc.

Birkhat Ha-Torah

When the Torah is read in synagogue, members of the congregation are called for an aliyah—a going up to the Torah. When you are honored with an aliyah, mount the bimah where the Torah is being read. The scroll is open, and the reader will point out the place. Take the end of your tallit in your right hand and touch it to the place in the Torah. Lift the tallit and kiss it. Then say aloud:

"Bless the Lord, who is blessed."

בָּרְכוּ אֶת־יְיָ, הַמְבֹרָךְ:

The congregation will respond:

"Blessed be the Lord, who is blessed forever and ever."

בָּרוּךְ יְיָ, הַמְבֹרָךְ לְעוֹלָם וָעֶד:

You then repeat the above and add:

"Blessed are You, Lord our God, King of the Universe, who has chosen us from all peoples and has given us Your Torah. Blessed are You, Lord, giver of the Torah."

בָּרוּךְ אַתָּה, יְיָ אֱלֹהֵינוּ, מֶלֶךְ הָעוֹלָם, אֲשֶׁר בָּחַר־בָּנוּ מִכָּל־הָעַמִּים, וְנָתַן־לָנוּ אֶת־תּוֹרָתוֹ. בָּרוּךְ אַתָּה, יְיָ, נוֹתֵן הַתּוֹרָה:

The congregation and the reader will respond, "Amen." When the reader begins to read the portion, hold the right handle of the scroll with your right hand until the portion is completed. If you can, read along quietly. The reader, when finished, will again indicate the place. Kiss the Torah as you did before and then hold the handles of the scroll with both hands and say:

"Blessed are You, Lord our God, King of the Universe, who has given us the Torah of truth, and has planted eternal life in our midst. Blessed are You, Lord, giver of the Torah."

בָּרוּךְ אַתָּה, יְיָ אֱלֹהֵינוּ, מֶלֶךְ הָעוֹלָם, אֲשֶׁר נָתַן־לָנוּ תּוֹרַת אֱמֶת, וְחַיֵּי עוֹלָם נָטַע בְּתוֹכֵנוּ. בָּרוּךְ אַתָּה, יְיָ, נוֹתֵן הַתּוֹרָה:

Remain on the bimah until the reading of the next portion has been completed. This shows one's reluctance to leave the Torah quickly.

These two blessings have twenty words each, making a total of forty, which is equal to the forty days that Moses spent on Mount Sinai before he returned with the Ten Commandments.

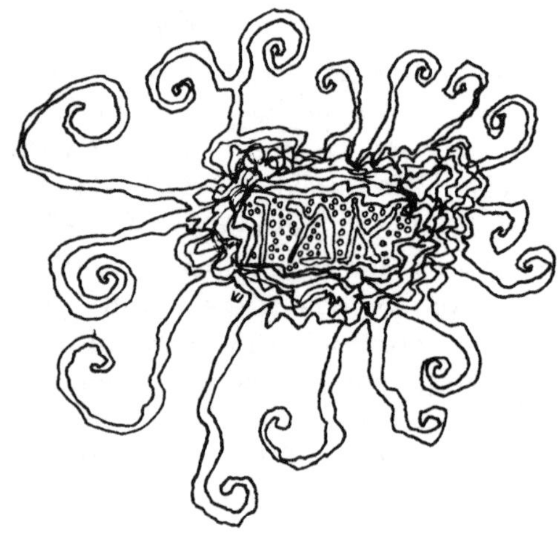

Birkhat Ha-Gomeil

Jewish tradition requires those who have safely returned from a lengthy voyage, recovered from a serious illness, or who have been released from imprisonment to recite Birkhat ha-Gomeil following their aliyah at the public Torah reading. The tradition for this is based on the talmudic interpretation of Psalm 107 (see Talmud, Berakhot 54b). As a general rule, whenever one has escaped from danger, this blessing of thanksgiving is said.

"Blessed are You, Lord, our God, King of the Universe, who bestows favor upon the undeserving just as he has bestowed favor upon me."

בָּרוּךְ אַתָּה, יְיָ אֱלֹהֵינוּ, מֶלֶךְ הָעוֹלָם, הַגּוֹמֵל לְחַיָּבִים טוֹבוֹת. שֶׁגְּמָלַנִי כָּל טוֹב:

The congregation responds:

"May He who has shown you every kindness continue to deal kindly with you."

מִי שֶׁגְּמָלְךָ כָּל־טוֹב, הוּא יִגְמָלְךָ כָּל־טוֹב סֶלָה.

She-Heheyanu

"Blessed are You, Lord, our God, King of the Universe, who has kept us alive and preserved us and enabled us to reach this season."

בָּרוּךְ אַתָּה, יְיָ אֱלֹהֵינוּ, מֶלֶךְ הָעוֹלָם, שֶׁהֶחֱיָנוּ וְקִיְּמָנוּ וְהִגִּיעָנוּ לַזְּמַן הַזֶּה:

This blessing is recited at the end of the Kiddush for every festival except the last two nights of Pesah. It is also recited when one lights the candles on the first two nights of all festivals, including Shemini Atzeret and Simhat Torah; when one lights the first Hanukkah candle; when the shofar is sounded on Rosh ha-Shanah; the first time the etrog and lulav are used on Sukkot; and before the reading of the Megillah on Purim.

In addition, it is also said when one takes possession of a new home, acquires new clothing or household effects, or tastes any fruit for the first time of the season. It is not said over a pair of new shoes made of animal skin. In general, the She-heheyanu celebrates the opportunity to do something new or something not done in so long that it feels new. It is a joyous expression of thanksgiving for being alive.

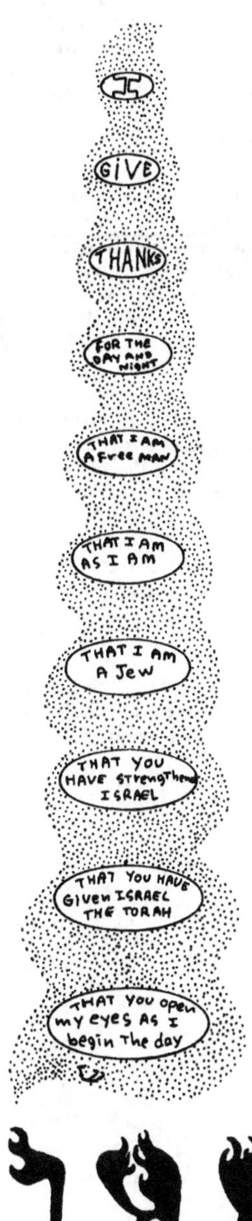

Weddings

"From every human being there rises a light that reaches straight to heaven. And when two souls that are destined to be together find each other, their streams of light flow together, and a single brighter light goes forth from their united being" (Baal Shem Tov).

"Perhaps it is so too with all the enduring forces of the universe and the foundations of all existence, both the hidden as well as the revealed, the far and the near, the great and the small from the hosts of the heavens to the dust of the earth, from the drops of rain to the winds and storms, all of them God made twain, male and female. In them all He planted the desire, the passion to be joined one to the other and to become one. From afar they are drawn to each other, they are attracted to each other, they are ever pursuing and being pursued, moving restlessly to and fro and they know no rest. For such is love, magnificent and conquering, implanted by a mighty God, the soul of every being and its living spirit, a fire pent up within the world's confines, filling all creation so that there is no place free of it—without end, without limit" (H. N. Bialik).

INTRODUCTION

Talmudic law provided for three methods of establishing a marriage. All three had to be performed in the presence of acceptable witnesses. The first was the act of cohabitation. This, however, was generally frowned upon as not being a fitting way to get married. The second method was the delivery of a document by the man to the woman and her acceptance of it. The third was the presentation to the woman of some article of established value and her acceptance of it.

The structure of the present-day wedding ceremony symbolically involves all three. At the wedding ceremony the groom presents his bride with both a wedding band and a marriage contract. After the ceremony they retire in private to a room for yihud (see below).

MAKING MARRIAGES

Once a Roman matron asked Rabbi Jose bar Halafta:

"How long did it take the Holy One, blessed be He, to create the world?"

He said to her: "Six days."

"And from then until now what has He been doing?"

"The Holy One, blessed be He, is occupied in making marriages."

"And is that His occupation?" the woman asked. "Even I can do that. I have many men slaves and women slaves and in one short hour I can marry them off."

"Though it may appear easy in your eyes," he said, "yet every marriage is as difficult for the Holy One, blessed be He, as the dividing of the Red Sea." Then Rabbi Jose left her and went on his way.

What did the matron do? She took a thousand men slaves and a thousand women slaves, placed them in two rows and said: "This one should wed that one, and this one should wed that one." In one night she married them all. The next day they came before her—one with wounded head, one with a bruised eye, another with a fractured arm and one with a broken foot.

"What is the matter with you?" she asked.

Each one said: "I do not want the one you gave me."

Immediately the woman sent for Rabbi Jose bar Halafta and said to him: "Rabbi, your Torah is true, beautiful and praiseworthy."

"Indeed a suitable match may seem easy to make, yet God considers it as difficult a task as dividing the Red Sea," Rabbi Jose acknowledged.

—Genesis Rabbah 68.4

Rejoicing

1. The wonderful obligation of being מְשַׂמֵּחַ חָתָן וְכַלָּה. causing the groom and the bride to rejoice, is one of the most important commandments. At traditional weddings, following the ceremony, the bride and groom are lifted on chairs by their friends, who sing and dance with joy.

2. One of the nice ways of helping out with last-minute details at the wedding is to make sure that there is a goblet, wine, and a Siddur under the huppah. Also, check to make sure that *someone* has the ring!

3. Most of all, the best way to rejoice with the bride and groom is to express your joy and love for them in whatever way is you.

Planning a wedding can be an extraordinarily exhilarating experience if you don't let the hassles of parents, relatives, and other people's opinions get to you. This section is a short guide to planning a wedding as well as a review of the basic structure of the ceremony.

Invitations

1. You can always go to your local printer and get him to print up your invitations.

You might consider having the printing done on the inside of cards rather than on your printer's normal stock. You can go to any art gallery or card store to choose a card and then order them in quantity.

2. If you know anyone who can do Hebrew calligraphy, you might like to have him do the invitation on a sheet of paper which can then be photocopied onto the invitations. There is a list of professional Hebrew calligraphers in Scribal Arts. These people are skilled in designing invitations and can be contacted through the addresses given.

3. Although the common invitation is English-on-the-outside—Hebrew-on-the-inside, you might consider printing up one set of English and one set of Hebrew.

Ring

Traditionally, the ring used for the wedding ceremony must be a band of metal with no holes going through it, i.e., one solid piece. The reason for this is to eliminate any misunderstanding about the value of the ring. If a stone were to be set in the ring, the wife might overestimate its worth and this might invalidate her acceptance of it. Another reason given for the plain band is that, Jewishly, a union of two people involves the achievement of shlaymut —wholeness—represented by the wholeness of the wedding band. This tradition, incidentally, need not limit your choice of a wedding ring since one can be married in a plain band and then afterwards wear a different ring. The important thing to remember is that under the huppah, the ring presented to the bride by the groom must belong to the groom and to no one else. It must also be worth at least a perutah—about a dime—and have some established monetary value.

There are lots of jewelers in Israel who do lovely wedding rings. In the United States there are about twenty importers of Israeli jewelry. A complete list can be found in the United Synagogue of America's *1972 Yearbook Directory and Buyers' Guide* available from:

United Synagogue of America
3080 Broadway
New York, N.Y. 10027

Any good jeweler can imitate Hebrew lettering and can design to your specifications. In addition there are a number of jewelers in New York and Boston who design original creative Hebrew jewelry. Some of the ones we know about are:

1. **Nissim Hizme**
   89 Canal St.
   New York, N. Y. 10002

2. **Peter Ehrenthal**
   Moriah Artcraft, Inc.
   28 W. 46th St.
   New York, N. Y. 10036

3. **Wolf Hecker**
   43 W. 61st St.
   New York, N. Y. 10023

4. **The Wedding Ring**
   50 W. 8th St.
   New York, N. Y. 10011

5. **Ben Kupferman**
   5 Babcock St.
   Brookline, Mass. 02146

Music

Everyone knows that the best place to get a band that is familiar with traditional Jewish music is New York. The possibilities there are endless. Among the ones we have heard and liked recently are:

Rudy Tepel
1921 Avenue K
Brooklyn, N. Y. 11230

Bernie Marinbach
1311 44th St.
Brooklyn, N. Y. 11219
(212-871-6223)

The Wakely Band
120 Elm
Tenafly, N. J. 07670
(New York phone 212-898-2400)

Epstein Brothers
211 W. 53rd St.
New York, N. Y. 10019

Beyond this there is everyone's favorite singer, "meise" teller, and all around loving person, Shlomo Carlebach, who can be reached through:

The Jewish Welfare Board
15 E. 26th St.
New York, N. Y. 10010
(212-532-4949)

All the above groups have standard rates which are not cheap. If your finances are limited, an alternative is to tape lots of the music you like and use that. Also, with the help of these tapes any good local band ought to be able to pick up the tunes. In addition, there are books which give the music for traditional Jewish melodies (see Music).

Food

1. One short suggestion for an alternative to "The-Great-Kosher-Caterers-Shakedown": Depending on the size of your wedding, a lovely alternative to hiring a caterer is to get some friends together a month or so before the wedding to do a cook-and-freeze thing. You can fill in this menu with "bought" food if necessary, and you can hire a few waitresses to serve at the feast. This makes a wonderfully personal wedding gift to you from your friends.

2. One other alternative is to investigate a new phenomenon called accommodators. Accomodators are usually one or two women who do cooking, hire a few waitresses, and can cater a simple affair quite beautifully. They're much cheaper than caterers and often do milchik (dairy) menus.

Huppah

The marriage ceremony takes place under a canopy supported by four poles. This huppah formerly referred to the chamber reserved for the bride on her wedding day. The custom of using a huppah canopy originated with the rabbis in the Middle Ages. Traditionally, the wedding ceremony took place outdoors as an omen that the marriage should be blessed with as many children as "the stars of the heaven." To separate the ceremony from the marketplace surrounding it, the rabbis sanctioned the use of a huppah, and thus provided a more modest setting for the wedding.

Lately, among the more lavish Jewish weddings, the custom has been for a huppah to be created from huge floral arrangements. While this is elaborate and expensive (and presumably awe-inspiring), nonetheless the loveliest huppot I have ever seen have been plain tallitot supported by four poles. You might consider making your own tallit out of a material you choose and using that as your huppah (see Tallit). Another lovely custom is to have friends hold the huppah poles. There is something very warm and beautiful about getting married surrounded by one's friends.

Ketubbah

For explanation, discussion, and suggestions, see Scribal Arts.

Witnesses

1. One of the most essential elements to any Jewish legal proceeding is the proper presence of witnesses.

2. There are a number of times in the course of the wedding where it is traditional or necessary (according to requirements of halakhah) that witnesses observe the proceedings.

3. Such times include the signing of all documents, that is, both engagement and marriage contracts, the actual legal ceremony when the groom places the ring on the bride's finger and recites the formula, and the yihud, when they watch the couple enter the room, guard their privacy, and witness their emergence.

Structure of the wedding

The basic procedure for getting married Jewishly goes something like this:

Oyfrufn 1. On the Shabbat morning before the wedding the hatan—groom

—is honored by being called up to the reading of the Torah in the synagogue.

2. The tradition for this is so old that the Talmud tells how King Solomon built a gate in the Temple where residents of Jerusalem would sit on Shabbat to perform kindnesses to bridegrooms who came there. When the Temple was destroyed, the custom arose of honoring the groom in the synagogue.

3. After the groom recites the final blessings, it is the custom to throw candy and raisins at him to insure a sweet life to him and his bride.

4. We strongly advise putting the candy in bags before throwing it. Otherwise, the likelihood is that three years after the oyfrufn you'll still be scraping up raisins which got ground into the carpet.

Fasting the day of the wedding 1. On the wedding day, tradition has it that all past sins are forgiven the couple as they begin a new life together.

2. Accordingly, the wedding took on a certain similarity to Yom Kippur.

3. This similarity is signified by the recitation in the Afternoon Service of Viddui, the confessional of Yom Kippur.

4. To further emphasize this similarity, the bridegroom and bride fast on their wedding day until after the ceremony.

5. It became the custom to be married in the late afternoon so that the fast might last as close to a complete day as possible.

Kitel Tied in with this Yom Kippur theme is the tradition for the bride and groom to wear white at the wedding as a symbol of purity.

The bride accordingly wears a white gown and the groom wears a white kitel which is also worn on Yom Kippur. Some wait until they are standing under the huppah before donning the kitel (see Tallit).

Tenaim 1. The betrothal is created by the writing of tenaim—a legal document binding on both parties.

2. Because the tenaim are as binding as a marriage contract—that is, they are dissoluble only through divorce or death—the custom of signing tenaim a year before the wedding has, in general, given way to the custom of signing them immediately before the actual wedding takes place.

Kinyan After the ketubbah is prepared, the groom is asked if he is prepared to fulfill his obligations as stated in the ketubbah. The groom formally accepts his obligation by taking hold of a handkerchief or some other object given him by the rabbi. This is the traditional method by which an agreement is considered binding: it is performed in the presence of witnesses, who later sign the ketubbah.

Bedeken 1. While the bride, assisted by her attendants, is preparing herself for the wedding, the male members of the wedding party are at the groom's table, completing and signing the documents needed for the ceremony.

2. When they finish this process, the men surround the groom and dance with him toward the bride, who sits regally on a throne.

3. The groom lifts the veil over the bride's face while the rabbi recites the phrase:

"O sister! May you grow into [be the mother of] thousands of myriads" (Genesis 24:60).

אֲחֹתֵנוּ אַתְּ הֲיִי לְאַלְפֵי רְבָבָה.

4. The bedeken supposedly originated to prevent a repetition of the deceit which was practiced on Jacob. Jacob thought he was marrying Rachel but, not having seen her before the ceremony, discovered he had married Leah. The

custom, therefore, arose for the hatan to look at his bride's face before the ceremony.

Processional 1. The custom of escorting the bride and groom to the huppah is an ancient one.

2. It was felt, traditionally, that the bride and groom on their wedding day are compared to a queen and a king and should therefore be accompanied with an entourage to the huppah.

3. Usually the parents of the groom escort him to the huppah, followed by the bride accompanied by her parents.

Circling the groom 1. The custom has arisen that under the huppah the bride (either alone or with the two mothers) circles the groom anywhere from two to thirteen times, depending on one's tradition.

2. The origin of the custom stems from the verse in Jeremiah 31:22: "A woman shall court [go around] a man."

3. The number seven seems to be the most widely accepted number; it corresponds with the seven times in the Bible where it is written "and when a man takes a wife."

4. One of the most beautiful of explanations for this mystical number is that in so circling him, she is entering the seven spheres of her beloved's soul.

Procedure 1. As a prelude to the ceremony the rabbi recites Psalms 118: 26–29.

2. After the couple arrives under the huppah, a medieval hymn is sung:

He who is strong above all else
He who is blessed above all else
He who is great above all else
May He bless the bridegroom and bride.

3. The blessing over wine and then this betrothal benediction is recited:

"Blessed are You, Lord our God, who has made us holy through Your commandments and has commanded us concerning marriages that are forbidden and those that are permitted when carried out under the canopy and with the sacred wedding ceremonies.

בָּרוּךְ אַתָּה, יְיָ אֱלֹהֵינוּ, מֶלֶךְ הָעוֹלָם, אֲשֶׁר קִדְּשָׁנוּ בְּמִצְוֹתָיו, וְצִוָּנוּ עַל הָעֲרָיוֹת, וְאָסַר לָנוּ אֶת הָאֲרוּסוֹת, וְהִתִּיר לָנוּ אֶת הַנְּשׂוּאוֹת לָנוּ עַל יְדֵי חֻפָּה וְקִדּוּשִׁין.

"Blessed are You, Lord our God, who makes Your people Israel holy through this rite of the canopy and the sacred bond of marriage."

בָּרוּךְ אַתָּה יְיָ, מְקַדֵּשׁ עַמּוֹ יִשְׂרָאֵל עַל יְדֵי חֻפָּה וְקִדּוּשִׁין.

4. These are recited over a cup of wine since "there is no joy without wine," and the bridegroom and bride both drink from the goblet.

5. The most important act of the entire marriage ceremony then occurs. The groom puts the ring on the index finger of the bride's right hand and recites:

"Behold you are consecrated to me with this ring according to the Law of Moses and Israel."

הֲרֵי אַתְּ מְקֻדֶּשֶׁת לִי בְּטַבַּעַת זוּ, כְּדַת משֶׁה וְיִשְׂרָאֵל.

Digression: This statement is the essence of the ceremony and legalizes the marriage. All the rest is deeply rooted in tradition and plays a significant role in the overall ritual of the ceremony but possesses no legal status. It is *crucial* to understand the seriousness of this act. *A marriage has taken place halakhically* anytime:

a. a man hands a woman an object worth more than a dime; and
b. she accepts it knowingly; and
c. he recites " הֲרֵי אַתְּ מְקֻדֶּשֶׁת לִי בְּטַבַּעַת זוּ, כְּדַת משֶׁה וְיִשְׂרָאֵל. "; and

d. there are at least two acceptable witnesses.

And this means anywhere, anytime, with or without a rabbi, license, huppah, etc. No one should joke around with this ritual.

6. The reason that the index finger is chosen is that this is the finger used for pointing and the ring can easily be shown to the witnesses.

7. After this the marriage contract is read and presented to the bride by the groom. This document belongs to the bride and she is charged with taking care of it.

8. The seven blessings are then recited. The custom has arisen that friends or honored guests are called upon, each to recite one of these blessings.

Breaking the glass 1. It is customary for the groom to smash a glass by stamping on it at the conclusion of the ceremony.

2. This serves as a recollection of our grief at the destruction of the Temple.

3. Another interpretation given is that the smashing of a glass is irrevocable and permanent. So, too, may the marriage last an infinity of time.

Yihud 1. It is customary for the bride and groom to retire to a private room right after the ceremony for a short time.

2. Traditionally, this had one essential function. This used to be the time when the marriage was consummated.

3. Today, this has become the traditional time when the bride and groom break their fast together.

4. Again, according to the old tradition, their yihud or solitude is guarded by two witnesses.

5. When the couple emerge, they are greeted with music, dancing, and joy.

Everett Gendler suggests a rather nice procedure, which is to invite the couple to think in advance of people—family or close friends—whose expression of good wishes at the wedding itself would mean something to them. They then speak to these persons, six in number, and ask them either to offer a blessing in their own words, share a bit of poetry or a brief reading of special meaning to them, or recite one of the traditional concluding seven blessings. Most often the latter is the preference, for these blessings still serve beautifully as transmitters of deep, transpersonal, yet personal feeling.

The following slightly modified versions of the first six blessings have been written by Everett (who says he usually recites the seventh when he is officiating):

1. You abound in blessings, Lord our God, Source of all creation, Creator of the fruit of the vine, symbol of human joy.

2. You abound in blessings, Lord our God, Source of all creation, all of whose creations reflect Your glory.

3. You abound in blessings, Lord our God, Source of all creation, Creator of human beings.

4. You abound in blessings, Lord our God, Source of all creation, who created man and woman in Your image that they might live, love, and so perpetuate life. You abound in blessings, Lord, Creator of human beings.

5. We all rejoice as these two persons, overcoming separateness, unite in joy. You abound in blessings, Lord, permitting us to share in others' joy.

6. May these lovers rejoice as did the first man and woman in the primordial Garden of Eden. You abound in blessings, Lord, Source of joy for bride and groom.

On mutualizing the wedding ceremony

A contemporary problem. On the one hand, modern sensitivities often see marriage as a mutual bonding involving equal responsibility for entering, maintaining, and, God forbid, ending the relationship. On the other hand, the traditional ceremony still preserves the sense of the man effecting a contract for the acquisition of the woman. Tradition *does* demand that the woman consent and noticeably express her consent—but there is no role for her in the process/ritual itself aside from accepting the ring and ketubbah. For people who do feel the pressure or tension of this dichotomy, there are possibilities for working some degree of mutuality into the ceremony. How far you can go before jeopardizing the validity of the marriage from a Judaic/legal point of view (as opposed to the civil law) is dependant largely on the attitude of your rabbi and your own tolerance for risk. Possible additions are:

1. The wife giving the husband a ring—fairly common.

2. Saying pesukim (biblical verses) to one another—less common but not unusual.

3. Revising the ketubbah—very tricky and should be approached with great caution.

In any event, the best thing to do is to speak with the rabbi who will be officiating and determine his position and tolerances. If you do not have a rabbi already in mind, then inquire as to who might share your sensitivities. For further information on creative possibilities contact the following (see Teachers):

Rabbi Al Axelrad
Rabbi Larry Kushner
Rabbi Everett Gendler

כתובה

ב___ בשבת ___ לחדש ___ שנת
חמשת אלפים ושבע מאות ו___ לבריאת
העולם למנין שאנו מונים כאן ___

אמר מר ___
בן ___
ו___ החתן
לכלת ___
בת ___
ו___ הכלה
הוי לי לאשתי כדת משה
וישראל ואני אוקיר
ואכבד אותך כדרך
בני ישראל המוקירים
ומכבדים את נשיהם
באמונה ובישר

הכלה ___
בת ___
ו___ אמרה
ל___
בן ___
ו___ החתן
היה לי לאישי כדת משה
וישראל ואני אוקיר
ואכבד אותך כדרך
בנות ישראל המוקירות
ומכבדות את אנשיהן
באמונה ובישר

החתן והכלה הבטיחו חגיגית זה לזה לשאוף
ולהשיג את המטרות הבאות משך חייהם
המשותפים להגיע לגילוי לב הדדי אשר
יאפשר להם להשתתף בשלימותם את מחשבותיהם
הרגשותיהם והויותיהם

להיות ערים ופתוחים האחד לכל צרכי השני
לשאוף להגיע להגשמה הדדית של צרכי השכל
הרגש הגוף והנפש לנצור את נחלת
היהדות ועם ישראל בביתם בחיי משפחתם
ובקשריהם החברתיים

הנשואים האלו אושרו גם כן על ידי השלטונות
האזרחיים ב___

והכל שריר וקיים

עד ___ עד ___
החתן ___ הכלה ___
הרב ___

On the ___ day of the week the ___ day of ___
Five thousand seven hundred ___ since the creation
of the world as we reckon time here in ___

The bride ___
daughter of ___
and ___
promised ___ the groom
son of ___
and ___
You are my husband according to the tradition of Moses and Israel I shall cherish you and honor you as is customary among the daughters of Israel who have cherished and honored their husbands in faithfulness and in integrity

The groom ___
son of ___
and ___
promised ___ the bride
daughter of ___
and ___
You are my wife according to the tradition of Moses and Israel I shall cherish you and honor you as is customary among the sons of Israel who have cherished and honored their wives in faithfulness and in integrity

The groom and bride have also promised each other to strive throughout their lives together to achieve an openness which will enable them to share their thoughts their feelings and their experiences

To be sensitive at all times to each others needs to attain mutual intellectual emotional physical and spiritual fulfillment to work for the perpetuation of Judaism and of the Jewish people in their home in their family life and in their communal endeavors

This marriage has been authorized also by the civil authorities of ___

It is valid and binding

witness ___ witness ___
bride ___ groom ___
rabbi ___

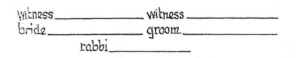

Here is a sample of an equalized ketubbah.

Grace after the wedding feast

1. Following the wedding feast, the traditional Grace after Meals is recited but with a special introduction:

Lord, drive away sadness and anger
And let even those who cannot speak break into song;
Guide us in the path of right;
Accept the blessing of the children of Jeshurun, the sons of Aaron.

דְּוַי הָסֵר וְגַם חָרוֹן,
וְאָז אִלֵּם בְּשִׁיר יָרוֹן,
נְחֵנוּ בְּמַעְגְּלֵי צֶדֶק
שְׁעֵה בִּרְכַּת בְּנֵי יְשֻׁרוּן, בְּנֵי אַהֲרֹן.

With permission of all here, we will bless our God, who gives men joy everywhere and Whose gifts of food we have eaten.

בִּרְשׁוּת מָרָנָן וְרַבָּנָן וְרַבּוֹתַי, נְבָרֵךְ אֱלֹהֵינוּ שֶׁהַשִּׂמְחָה בִּמְעוֹנוֹ וְשֶׁאָכַלְנוּ מִשֶּׁלּוֹ.

Bless God, who gives men joy everywhere and whose gifts of food we have eaten and because of whose goodness we live.

בָּרוּךְ אֱלֹהֵינוּ שֶׁהַשִּׂמְחָה בִּמְעוֹנוֹ, וְשֶׁאָכַלְנוּ מִשֶּׁלּוֹ וּבְטוּבוֹ חָיִינוּ.

2. The grace ends with the recitation of the seven blessings. Once again, the members of the family, friends, or guests can be honored by being given one of these blessings to recite.

Seven days of feasting

1. The custom of observing seven days of feasting after the wedding originates with Jacob, who made a seven-day banquet when he married Leah.

2. Many people still observe the custom of preparing festival meals for the bride and groom during the wedding week.

3. If ten people are present, the seven blessings are recited following each Grace after Meals.

!!!!!!!!!!!MAZEL TOV!!!!!!!!!!!!

Some interesting customs

1. There is a custom that the bride give the groom a tallit (see Tallit) on the day of the wedding. One reason is that a tallit represents the number 32, which is the number of fringes on the shawl. This number is the numerical equivalent of the word לֵב heart.

2. In Europe a badhen—jester—was hired for any reasonably large wedding. His job was to be actor, singer, poet, philosophizer, and master of ceremonies. A skilled badhen could move the guests to tears one moment and laughter the next. Nowadays we have caterers who can do the same thing.

3. Another important personage in the European shtetl was the shadhen—the matchmaker. It was the shadhen who determined the social stature of a family and so matched the children. For greater explanation and discussion of both shadhen and badhen, see *Life Is with People,* by Mark Zborowski and Elizabeth Herzog (New York: Schocken, 1962, $2.25).

4. A Sephardic custom which is becoming widespread is that the bride and groom be married enwrapped together by a single tallit.

5. The custom of setting a wedding date for a Tuesday is a very strong one because on the third day of creation the Bible repeats twice: "and God saw how good this was." It is thought that to be married on a Tuesday is a good omen for a new marriage.

6. The week before the wedding is, traditionally, a time for serious thought by the couple. Accordingly, tradition has it that the couple do not see each other at all for that week to allow each of them time to think about this most important step in their lives.

Tumah and taharah-mikveh

All things die and are reborn continually. The plant which bows its head to the earth leaves its life capsulized in the dormant seed. In our own bodies, death and regeneration proceed cell by cell. Our fingernails grow, die, and are discarded; our hair also. Our skins slough off dead cells, while a tender new layer forms below the surface. Within us our organs repair and renew themselves repeatedly. Throughout each teeming and dying body, moreover, flows an undying spirit. It is confined to no single area but, as the sages taught, it "fills the body as the ocean fills its bed." That spirit is the soul. Only a conscious being has a soul. Of what is such a being conscious? He is aware of himself. He is aware also of his own growth processes and of his history. Our consciousness tells us that we are created beings and so are mortal. Our soul tells us that we are the image of the Creator and so cannot be mortal. Our knowledge of ourselves, then, is paradoxical. How do we reconcile it and make ourselves whole? Jews solve the paradox with the ritual cycle of tumah and taharah, in which we act out our death and resurrection.

"A polluted person is always in the wrong. He has developed some wrong condition or simply crossed some line which should not have been crossed and this displacement unleashes danger for someone" (Mary Douglas, Purity and Danger).

Tumah is the result of our confrontation with the fact of our own mortality. It is the going down into darkness. Taharah is the result of our reaffirmation of our own immortality. It is the reentry into light. Tumah is evil or frightening only when there is no further life. Otherwise, tumah is simply part of the human cycle. To be tameh is not wrong or bad. Often it is necessary and sometimes it is mandatory.

It was not so for the primitive religions, the soil out of which our tumah and taharah symbolism grew. For them, tumah was pollution. The source of pollution was a source of danger, and a polluted person was both endangered and dangerous.

Thus the menstruant woman might have the power to cause illness or death. The corpse, in some societies, was so dangerous that the dying had to be carried outside the village to breathe their last. Or the corpse had to be mutilated to prevent it from doing harm. In other societies, those who had the task of burying the dead were permanently polluted.

In a Jewish society, however, tumah was not perceived as causing physical consequences, nor was it viewed as dangerous in any way. Since some of the basic human functions and behaviors caused tumah, every member of the society regularly underwent the cycle from tumah to taharah. Nor were even the most intense sources of tumah, such as a corpse, treated with dread and

And death shall have no dominion
Dead men naked they shall be one
With the man in the wind and the west moon;
When their bones are picked clean and the clean bones gone,
They shall have stars at elbow and foot;
Though they go mad they shall be sane,
Though they sink through the sea they shall rise again;
Though lovers be lost love shall not;
And death shall have no dominion.
—Dylan Thomas

"In water everything is 'dissolved,' every 'form' is broken up, everything that has happened ceases to exist; nothing that was before remains after immersion in water, not an outline, not a 'sign,' not an event. Immersion is the equivalent, at the human level, of death at the cosmic level, of the cataclysm (the Flood) which periodically dissolves the world into the primeval ocean. Breaking up all forms, doing away with the past, water possesses the power of purifying, of regenerating, of giving new birth. . . . Water purifies and regenerates because it nullifies the past, and restores —even if only for a moment—the integrity of the dawn of things" (Mircea Eliade).

O dark dark dark. They all go into the dark,
The vacant interstellar spaces, the vacant into the vacant.
—T. S. Eliot

avoidance. Everyone, even the kohen, who otherwise had to avoid the tumah of corpses, was obligated by the Torah to participate in the burial of a parent, sibling, spouse, or child. Similarly, it was a special mitzvah to bury an unburied corpse which one found. If no other person was available to perform this mitzvah, a kohen was obligated to do so. The kohen also contracted special forms of tumah in the purification rituals in which he officiated. Thus tumah was an accepted component of the human condition. Neither fear nor disgust is associated with tumah in Jewish law. The prophets made such associations only when they saw the tumah as detached from its place in the cycle. They saw a tumah for which there seemed to be no taharah, and they hid their eyes before the vision of everlasting darkness.

How, then, does one contract tumah? Its most powerful source is a human corpse. Touching this inanimate shell, we recall that a person inhabited it, willing it to sing, to make love, to pray. Whoever touches a human corpse sees in its face his own. Whoever is in the presence of death is in the presence of his own death. For that reason, whoever comes into contact with a corpse or is in the same room with one himself becomes a source of tumah and imparts tumah to others upon contact. An animal carcass also is a source of tumah, although its tumah is less powerful than that of the corpse. Nevertheless, it breathed, it moved upon the earth, and now it is still. We recognize its stillness as our own. Tumah is also caused by the biblical disease tzaraat, usually (inaccurately) translated "leprosy." The person who had tzaraat had to withdraw from society until he was cured, and that, perhaps, is why the sages compared him to a dead man.

"In my beginning is my end," writes T. S. Eliot. In all creation is the seed of destruction. All that is born dies, and all that begets. Begetting and birth are the nexus points at which life and death are coupled. They are the beginnings which point to an end. Menstruation, too, is a nexus point. It is an end which points to a beginning. At the nexus points, the begetter becomes tameh. The fluids on which new life depends—the semen, the rich uteral lining which sustains embryonic life—the departure of these from the body leaves the giver tameh. The menstrual blood, which inside the womb was a potential nutriment, is a token of dying when it is shed. Menstruation is an autumn within, the dying which makes room for new birth. Semen has always symbolized man's vital force. That is why in so many cultures the idea existed (and still exists) that a man's semen supply is limited, and when it is depleted he will die. Men may have associated this folk belief with the feeling of exhaustion which follows sexual intercourse; or perhaps it is simply the feeling of one's consciousness being yielded up and borne on an overwhelming tide which has caused poets of all nations and all times to link love and death. Such an association must underlie the Elizabethan slang term for orgasm: "dying."

The nexus points are those in which there appears to be a departure or a transfer of vital force. One of the most powerful nexus points, therefore, is childbirth. The infant who passes from the womb into the world undergoes a transition from potential life into life itself. The womb of woman is associated with the womb of earth. Living things grow out of the earth, dead things return to it and are buried in it. Seeds must be buried to bring them to life. The womb is the dark warm place in which we do not live, but live *in potentia*. We think of death as a return to the womb because the womb is the place of birth.

What we call the beginning is often the end
And to make an end is to make a beginning.
The end is where we start from . . .
. . . and any action
Is a step to the block, to the fire, down the sea's throat,
Or to an illegible stone: and that is where we start.
We die with the dying:
See, they depart and we go with them.
We are born with the dead:
See, they return, and bring us with them.

—T. S. Eliot

What were the practical consequences of tumah? When one became tameh, he acted out his own death by withdrawing from the great life-affirming Jewish symbols. A niddah, a menstruating woman, could not engage in sexual intercourse, a person with tzaraat was isolated from human society, and no person in any category of tumah could enter the Great Temple at Jerusalem. It is easy to see why the Great Temple would have been interdicted for the tameh. There was the dwelling of the Master of time, the God whose dread and unarticulated Name meant "was-is-will be." Who but the deathless can stand in the presence of the undying King? The laws of taharah teach men to impersonate immortality. It is a mask we assume, this taharah, just as tumah is a mask of death. Even after the Israelites and the sanctuary have been readied for the Shekhinah by means of the rites of taharah, the Torah still speaks of the Tent of Meeting—the earthly resting place of the Shekhinah—as abiding "with them in the midst of their uncleanness [tumah]" (Leviticus 16:16). Ultimately, our taharah is but a mime of taharah, a shadow of the taharah of God, a semblance of our own taharah which is to be.

The duration of tumah is divided into two parts: the duration of contact with that which renders one tameh, and a period of dormancy whose length is determined by the type of tumah contracted. At the end of the dormancy, the one who is tameh immerses himself in a mikveh. For those with tzaraat or the tumah of corpses, there was an additional purification ritual which is no longer extant.[1] The mikveh is what is referred to in the Bible as mayim

1. The purification rituals for corpse tumah and tzaraat present excellent examples of symbolism using life-death nexus. These two types of tumah represent the most concrete experiences of death, and therefore, immersion in a mikveh, while necessary, is in itself insufficient to remove the tumah. The ceremony for removing the tumah of corpses utilizes the ashes of a red heifer which was slaughtered and burned with scarlet wool, cedar, and hyssop added to the fire. The ashes were mixed with mayim hayyim, "living water," and sprinkled upon the tameh with a spray of hyssop. Among those things which are burned, the color red predominates. Red is the color of blood, which itself symbolizes both life and death. Blood is the vehicle through which life pulsates through the living body. To kill someone is to "shed his blood." Ashes, a death symbol, are mixed with mikveh water, a life symbol. Hyssop is a plant, and probably symbolizes vegetative life. The mixture itself, then, becomes one of the fluids associated with the life-death nexus, and thus it creates a bridge over which the dead travel toward life and the living toward death. That is why the tameh person who is sprinkled with the mixture becomes tahor, while the tahor who sprinkles or touches it becomes tameh.

Similarly, the purification ritual for tzaraat utilizes nexus symbolism. The kohen was to take two birds of a tahor species. One bird was to be killed and its blood mixed with "living water." Then the kohen was to take scarlet, cedar, hyssop, and the living bird, dip them in the blood and water, and sprinkle the tzaraat victim with the mixture. The living bird was then freed and allowed to fly away. Clearly the two birds represent life and death. The cedar and scarlet wool both enhance the blood symbolism. The mixture of blood and "living water" is another life-death amalgam, while the hyssop, again, may represent vegetative life.

hayyim—literally, "living water"; that is, running water as opposed to stagnant water. Any natural gathering of water at least forty sah in volume constitutes a natural mikveh. (Blackman [Mishnayoth, 1:20] estimates a sah to be approximately 13,222 cubic centimeters.) This would include ponds, lakes, rivers, and seas.

There is also a way to make a legally valid approximation of a natural mikveh, using water collected only through the force of gravity. The water, usually rainwater, is permitted to fall into a huge container called the bor, or pit, since it usually extends beneath the ground surface. A building is constructed around this bor. The building contains small sunken pools. Each pool shares a wall with the bor. Each shared wall has a hole cut in it which can be plugged up or left open. In order to make the adjoining pools into legally valid mikvaot, they are "seeded" with bor water and then filled with regular tap water. When the hole between the pool and the bor is unplugged so that the waters are touching (or as the sources put it, "kissing"), the pool becomes a valid mikveh.

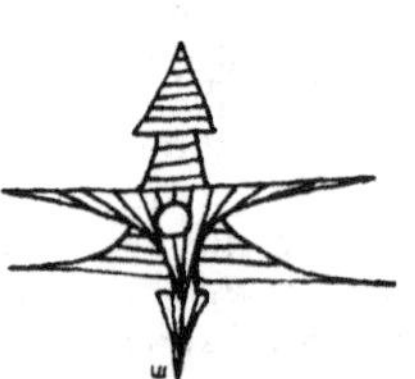

"Rabbi Akiva said: Happy are you, Israel! Before whom do you make yourselves tahor, and who makes you tahor? Your Father in heaven. As it is written, 'The mikveh of Israel is the Lord' (Jeremiah 17:13). Just as the mikveh makes tahor those who are tameh, so the Holy One makes Israel tahor" (Mishnah Yoma 8:9).

The mikveh simulates the original living water, the primal sea from which all life comes, the womb of the world, the amniotic tide on which the unborn child is rocked. To be reborn, one must reenter this womb and "drown" in living water. We enter the mikveh naked as an infant enters the world. We stand in the water, feet slightly apart, arms outstretched frontward and fingers spread. The lips, too, should be loosely compressed and the eyes loosely closed. Then we bend the knees so that the entire body, including the head and all the hair, is covered by water. Then we reemerge. At this point, a niddah says a blessing. So does a convert, since immersion in a mikveh is the final step in conversion, the rebirth of a gentile as a Jew. The blessing is followed by a second immersion. We emerge from the mikveh tahor, having confronted and experienced our own death and resurrection. Taharah is the end beyond the end, which constitutes a beginning, just as the messianic "end of days" is in actuality the beginning of days.

LAWS AND CUSTOMS

Most of the laws of tumah and taharah have not been in effect since the destruction of the Temple. The additional purification rituals which rid one of the tumah of corpses and of the biblical disease tzaraat are also no longer extant. According to most views, it is a custom, but not a law, for a man who has had a seminal emission to immerse himself in a mikveh before engaging in prayer or Torah study. Nevertheless, because the mikveh is one of the most powerful Jewish symbols, Jewish men have been loath to relinquish it and so have developed many customs involving immersion. Some men go to the mikveh before Yom Kippur, some before every holiday, some before Shabbat, and some every day. The *legal obligation* to go to the mikveh, however, is nowadays confined to women. Rabbinic law permits only married women to attend the mikveh.

According to Torah law, it is forbidden for men and women to have intercourse when the woman is a niddah. The state of niddah includes the duration of the menstrual flow, for which one must count a minimum of five days, plus a "dormancy period" of seven days during which there is absolutely no bleeding. To count these seven days, a woman should examine herself in the morning and late afternoon, using a tampon to determine that there is no blood in the vaginal passage. The days are counted from sundown to sundown. After the seventh consecutive day which is free of bleeding the woman goes to the mikveh. That is, if the first blood-free day begins Thursday at sundown, the woman goes to the mikveh the following Thursday *after* sundown. Since seven full sundown-to-sundown days must be counted, women always go to the mikveh at night, after the end of the seventh sundown. The seven blood-free days must be consecutive. Finding a spot of blood obligates one to start counting from the beginning.

Before going into a mikveh, a person should bathe or shower thoroughly. Hair should be washed and combed free of tangles. Any foreign substance adhering to the body, such as adhesive bandages, nail polish, paint, makeup, or dried blood, should be removed. Fingernails and toenails should be cleaned with special care, and all rings, earrings, and jewelry should be taken off. Most mikvaot provide tubs, showers, soap, and washcloths. Many also have hair dryers and similar conveniences. Women should have someone watch their immersions to tell them if their hair floated or they were otherwise improperly immersed. Most mikvaot employ a woman to supervise immersions. The mikveh, bathing facilities, and dressing room are *private,* for the use of only one woman at a time. You sit in a waiting room until the mikveh is free. The berakhah which women say after the first immersion and prior to the second is:

"Blessed are You, Lord our God, King of the Universe, who has made us holy with Your commandments and commanded us concerning immersion."

בָּרוּךְ אַתָּה, יְיָ אֱלֹהֵינוּ, מֶלֶךְ הָעוֹלָם, אֲשֶׁר קִדְּשָׁנוּ בְּמִצְוֹתָיו וְצִוָּנוּ עַל הַטְּבִילָה:

Some women have the custom of immersing themselves twice or three times before and after the blessing. In addition, some women say a kavvanah, a prayer which focuses their minds on the mitzvah they are about to perform. In any case, it is good to stop a minute and think about the mitzvah and its meaning before immersion.

After immersion a couple can resume their normal sex life. As a precautionary measure, however, it is customary to stop having intercourse twelve hours before the menstrual period is expected.

Because childbirth is the most powerful of the nexus points, the duration of the tumah is longer than that of menstruation. After bearing a male child, one must count a minimum of seven days for bleeding plus seven blood-free days. After bearing a female child, one must count fourteen days for bleeding plus seven blood-free days. These durations are given in Leviticus 12.[2] No one seems to understand the meaning of the sexual distinction. We know that the more powerful the life-death nexus, the longer in duration the tumah. Perhaps, then, the time of tumah is doubled if one gives birth to another potential birth-giver.

Practical questions involving niddah or immersion should be addressed to a halakhically observant rabbi. Any observant Jew in your community will be able to direct you to the local mikveh.

2. The long "dormancy" periods prescribed in Leviticus 12 for taharah after childbirth apply only when there is a Temple in Jerusalem, although many people keep them as a custom.

Sources

Biblical
- Leviticus 12:1–18; 13; 14; 15:1–33
- Numbers 19:1–22

Talmudic
- Mishnayot Negaim, Parah, and Niddah

Posttalmudic
- Maimonides *Mishneh Torah,* Book of Taharah: esp. Hilkhot Tum'at Met, Hilkhot Tzaraat, Hilkhot M'tameh Mishkav u-Moshav, and Hilkhot Mikvaot.
- Shulhan Arukh: Yoreh Deah: Hilkhot Niddah, sec. 183–200.

NOTE: I have not discovered any book in English on the laws of niddah and mikveh which was written for people above the intellectual level of a cretin. People would therefore be better off consulting one of the observant resource people listed in this catalog.

Death and burial

INTRODUCTION

"Man's days are like grass; he blooms like the flower of the field; a wind passes by and it is no more, its own no longer knows it" (Psalms 103:15-16).

Generally speaking, death has been a rather suppressed topic in contemporary society. A person who begins to discuss anything related to death is usually considered to be morbid. All the other major rites of passage have elaborate preparations associated with them, for example, birth, initiation, and marriage; however, death often occurs with little prior discussion or confrontation on the part of the dying person, his family, or relatives and friends.

Fortunately, within the past five or ten years the interest in death has grown substantially. A sizable number of publications have recently appeared dealing with issues related to death (see the bibliography at the end of this section); many medical schools have begun to offer courses about death and the dying; and psychologists are tackling the complex psychological problems associated with death.

Within most Jewish communities, however, matters related to death are still left undiscussed until a death has actually occurred. Many Jews find themselves unprepared to face the crisis. In addition, ignorance of the Jewish traditions surrounding death leaves many Jews at the mercy of funeral directors whose commitment to Jewish practice is often questionable.

This section on death, burial, and mourning is written with a number of purposes in mind: (1) to stimulate interest and discussion about the subject of death; (2) to acquaint the reader with some aspects of the extensive Jewish tradition surrounding death, and to lead him, hopefully, to an appreciation of its meaningfulness and sensitivity; (3) to encourage people to study what goes on in their own community when a death occurs, and to act wherever necessary to change funeral and burial practices so that they are more in keeping with Jewish tradition; and (4) to make accessible an annotated bibliography of traditional and contemporary sources that contain material on the many facets of death, burial, and mourning, from both a Jewish and a general perspective.

SOME PRELIMINARY HISTORICAL BACKGROUND

In order to gain an understanding of Jewish practice in death and burial, one needs a bit of historical perspective. The mitzvah of preparing and burying a person's body is highly valued within all of Jewish tradition because it is an act performed without any possible ulterior motive, such as hope of recompense. The funeral and burial arrangements were traditionally seen as a community responsibility. Each community had its own Hevra Kadisha (Holy Brotherhood) that was responsible for all aspects of the preparation for burial and the burial itself. It was considered a great honor to be a member of the Hevra Kadisha. With the existence of a Hevra Kadisha, no one made money on death; the hevra was totally nonprofit, as is the case in communities today that have a Hevra Kadisha. (For further information on the Hevra Kadisha, see numbers 9, 11 and 14 in the bibliography.)

The existence of a profit-making funeral home is a relatively recent phenomenon in Jewish life. The very thought of making money through performing this essential mitzvah is totally foreign to the Jewish tradition. Nevertheless, Jews are faced with a situation where funeral homes are fairly well established. Acknowledging the alien character of a funeral home, it is still possible to strive to educate and inform ourselves about our heritage so that we can know enough to request a funeral and burial that are in keeping with the value system and guidelines found within the Jewish experience.

AN OVERVIEW OF SELECTED JEWISH PRACTICES IN DEATH, BURIAL, AND MOURNING

A few preliminary notes:

1. This section is organized chronologically from the moment of death until the mourning period and after.
2. The approach described is deliberately very traditional in an effort to provide maximum exposure to the Jewish law; however, the general principles of simplicity and equality in death are guidelines to which *all Jews* should commit themselves.
3. A general outline of this sort does not permit a discussion of the complex distinctions and interactions between laws and customs.
4. The single contemporary volume that is the most highly recommended to the reader is Maurice Lamm's *The Jewish Way in Death and Mourning* (see the bibliography).

THE MOMENT OF DEATH

1. During the last minutes of life, it is customary that one should not leave the room out of respect to the dying person (see bibliography, number 2, section 339).
2. The confession recited before death is: "Understand O Israel, the Lord our God is One. I acknowledge before Thee, my God, God of my fathers, that my recovery and my death are in Your hand. May it be Your will to heal me completely, but if I should die, may my death be an atonement for all sins that I have committed."
3. On witnessing or hearing of a death, one should say the following berakhah (though it is often said at the funeral itself):

"Blessed are You, Lord our God, King of the Universe, the true Judge."

בָּרוּךְ אַתָּה, יְיָ אֱלֹהֵינוּ, מֶלֶךְ הָעוֹלָם, דַּיַּן הָאֱמֶת:

4. At the moment of death (or else at the funeral, as is customary today) the immediate relatives—son, daughter, father, mother, brother, sister, and spouse—should perform the traditional Jewish act of mourning and grief, keriah:the tearing of a garment. The tearing can provide a needed outlet for the pentup anguish and emotion that a mourner feels (see bibliography, number 2, section 340).

Tradition calls upon us to tear our *garments, to put the mark of the broken heart on* our *clothing—and not to vent our feelings on a meaningless and impersonal strip of cloth pinned on us by a stranger.*

–*The Jewish Way in Death and Mourning*, p. 43

5. In the house of mourning, "mirrors should be covered to de-emphasize the beauty and ornamentation of the flesh at a time when another person's body has begun to decay" *(The Jewish Way in Death and Mourning*, p. 4; bibliography, number 3, p. 261).

6. In accordance with the highest degree of respect for the deceased, the body may not be left alone from the moment of death until the burial. The family should arrange for someone to be at the side of the deceased at all times, reciting psalms (see bibliography, number 2, sections 339, 341).

7. Because they are distraught, mourners are not obligated to perform any positive commandments (regarding, e.g., tefillin) until after the funeral.

Taharah

The practice of taharah, the ritual washing of the body, is an absolute requirement of Jewish law. The specific steps of the taharah are performed by the funeral home or by the Hevra Kadisha, if the community has one. It is wise to check to be sure that the funeral home director is acquainted with the details of the ceremony for washing. The taharah is accompanied by the recitation of prayers and psalms appropriate to the situation. The body is washed thoroughly from head to foot, and the deceased's face is never allowed to look downward out of respect to the deceased. A detailed and concise description of the taharah procedure, as well as other duties of the Hevra Kadisha, can be found in Lamm, pp. 239–40. These pages are highly recommended.

The dressing of the body and the casket

Formerly, they used to bring food to the house of mourning, the rich in baskets of gold and silver, the poor in baskets of willow twigs; and the poor felt ashamed. Therefore, a law was instituted that all should use baskets of willow twigs. . . .

Formerly they used to bring out the deceased for burial, the rich on a tall state bed, ornamented and covered with rich coverlets, the poor on a plain bier (or box); and the poor felt ashamed. Therefore, a law was instituted that all should be brought out on a plain bier. . . .

Formerly the expense of the burial was harder to bear by the family than the death itself, so that sometimes they fled to escape the expense. This was so until Rabban Gamaliel insisted that he be buried in a plain linen shroud instead of costly garments. And since then we follow the principle of burial in a simple manner.

—*Talmud Babli, Moed Katan 27a–b*

This quotation from the Talmud embodies the values of simplicity and equality that dominate the Jewish approach to burial and funeral arrangements.

Dressing the body

Jewish tradition recognizes the egalitarian nature of death. The tradition states that all Jews, rich and poor alike, should be buried in the same garment. The quotation from the Talmud speaks of Rabban Gamaliel, who insisted on equality and simplicity in response to a situation where the poor were made to feel ashamed. The traditional garment, as it was originally prescribed by Rabban Gamaliel, is takhrikhin, shrouds—simple, handmade, perfectly white and clean. The shrouds symbolize purity and dignity. Shrouds have no pockets, and so no material wealth can be placed in them. "Not a man's possessions but his soul is of importance"*(The Jewish Way in Death and Mourning*, p. 7). Men should be buried with a tallit over the shroud; some authorities state that one of the fringes should be cut.

The aron (casket)

"For dust you are, and to dust you shall return" (Genesis 3:19) serves as a guide in the choosing of a casket. The purpose of burial is so that the body can decompose and return naturally to the earth. In Israel, the practice is to bury the deceased on a bed of intertwined reeds. In the United States, where the practice is to bury with a coffin, the basic requirement is a coffin made entirely of wood, usually pine. The use of an all-wood coffin facilitates the decomposition of the body and is thereby in accord with the biblical injunction. The same coffin should be used by all. In Jewish tradition, wealth and elegance are not recognized as means for showing respect to the deceased.

The funeral

It has been Jewish practice for the funeral to take place within twenty-four hours after the moment of death, though it is permissible to wait a bit longer for relatives to arrive (their attendance at the funeral being seen as additional honor to the deceased). The speedy funeral aids the mourners in confronting the finality of death fairly quickly, and it is also in keeping with the implication of the biblical statement that the body should return to its natural course of decomposition as soon as possible. The prompt funeral and burial is also part of kvod ha-met, respect for the deceased; it was considered a great humiliation to the dead to leave them unburied.

A service takes place at the funeral home during which psalms and the prayer אֵל מָלֵא רַחֲמִים. —Lord Who Is Full of Mercy—is recited and eulogies are given.

Friends of the deceased carry the coffin from the funeral home to the hearse and from the hearse to the burial site. This act is considered a hesed shel emet—an act of truthful and pure lovingkindness—because there cannot possibly be any ulterior motive involved; the dead person can never repay the people for their assistance in his burial.

The burial

A common practice is to stop seven times with the coffin while en route to the grave site. The number seven is symbolic of the seven times that the word hevel —utter futility— occurs in the Book of Ecclesiastes (Talmud, Baba Batra 100b).

During the burial service, after the coffin has been placed in the grave, the following is recited: "May he (she) come to his place in peace." The traditional requirement is that a few spadefuls of earth be dropped on the coffin. The sound of the first fall of earth on the coffin is very important for the mourners to hear; it has an air of finality, leaving no doubt that the person has

indeed died. It is customary to remain at the grave site at least until the coffin is completely covered, and some remain until the grave is filled. However painful it may be, remaining until the burial is complete increases the reality of the death, and enables friends and relatives to participate in the mitzvah. After leaving the grave, it is customary to wash one's hands.

After the burial—the meal and the shivah period

The mourners' first meal after the funeral and burial is known as Seudat Havraah—the Meal of Consolation. This meal is provided by friends and neighbors so that the mourners will not have to be bothered at such a moment with the preparation of food. According to tradition, the meal should consist of hard-boiled eggs. In ancient times, the egg was regarded as a symbol of fertility and life—the mourners' return from the cemetery marking their return to life after a direct confrontation with death. Some see the egg as a symbol for the round wheel of fate; we must all die.

Shivah, the seven-day period that starts after the funeral, is observed in order to carry the mourners over the painful period until they can resume some degree of normal life.

Shivah is the designated time for the mourning family to talk with close friends and relatives who help in the acceptance of the reality of the death. It is a time for comforting the mourners, as opposed to the prefuneral time when no comforting is permitted, the mourners being left alone to grieve and cry. A candle should burn in the home of the mourners for the entire seven-day period. The mourners should refrain from using cosmetics and leather, and from bathing and cutting the hair. Also, it is the custom not to sit on chairs but on low stools during this time.

It must be stressed that paying a call to a mourner's home during the shivah period is an important mitzvah. One must realize the purpose involved in the observance of shivah and act accordingly. The often partylike atmosphere that prevails at some mourners' homes during shivah is totally incongruous with the proper observance of shivah. A visitor during shivah should not expect a party, or even any sort of food, when paying his call. In fact, the custom is not to speak to the mourner until he speaks to you.

It is the custom that a minyan gather in the house of a mourner for the daily services.

Traditionally the mourners come to the synagogue the first Shabbat after the conclusion of shivah. They are welcomed by the congregation during the Kabbalat Shabbat service at the conclusion of the "L'Kha Dodi," the song that welcomes the Shabbat. The traditional greeting is:

"May the Lord comfort and sustain you among the other mourners for Zion and Jerusalem."

הַמָּקוֹם יְנַחֵם אֶתְכֶם בְּתוֹךְ שְׁאָר אֲבֵלֵי צִיּוֹן וִירוּשָׁלָיִם:

This phrase is also said before leaving the house when visiting during shivah.

Kaddish, Sheloshim, Yahrzeit, and Yizkor

One who mourns for a parent recites the Kaddish at all public services for eleven months. The Kaddish is the traditional Jewish statement in which the mourner affirms the justice of God and the meaningfulness of life.

The Kaddish contains no reference to the dead. The earliest allusion to the Kaddish as a mourners' prayer is found in *Mahzor Vitry*, dated 1208, where it is said plainly: "The lad rises and recites the Kaddish." One may safely assume that since the Kaddish has as its underlying thought the hope for the redemption and ultimate healing of suffering mankind, the power of redeeming the dead from the sufferings of Gehinnom—hell—came to be ascribed in the course of time to the recitation of this sublime doxology. Formerly, the Kaddish was recited during the entire year of mourning, so as to rescue the souls of one's parents from the torture of Gehinnom, where the wicked are said to spend no less than twelve months. In order not to count one's own parents among the wicked, the period for reciting the Kaddish was later reduced to eleven months.

After shivah, for a period of thirty days (sheloshim) following the burial, the mourner returns to work but continues to observe certain restrictions as a sign of mourning. He may not attend festive gatherings, such as weddings, dances, parties, or any other form of merriment. When mourning for parents, one observes these restrictions for a year.

Jewish tradition adds a further ritual to help meet the crisis of bereavement—the commemoration of the day of death. Each year, on the anniversary of the death, Yahrzeit is observed, a day of solemn remembering in prayer and meditation. The chief expressions of the Yahrzeit are the lighting of a twenty-four-hour candle and the recitation of the Kaddish.

In addition to the Yahrzeit, the dead are remembered throughout the Jewish calendar year at the festival times. The short Yizkor service, which takes place right after the haftarah, is recited on Yom Kippur, Shemini Atzeret, the eighth day of Pesah, and the second day of Shavuot. The juxtaposition of Yizkor with the three joyous festivals is very characteristic of Judaism's attitude toward life. The happy and the sad are both integral parts of living and, therefore, Yizkor is made a part of the service on festivals.

Finally, the rabbis discouraged excessive mourning, referring to the verse in Jeremiah 22:10: "Weep ye not [in excess] for the dead, neither bemoan him [too much]."

THE CONDITION OF JEWISH FUNERALS TODAY—WHAT CAN WE DO?

Knowledge of traditional Jewish practices is only the first step toward re-Judaizing the procedures surrounding death, burial, and mourning. The next steps are fraught with difficulty. Given the enormous power and influence of funeral home directors and the all too few communities with a Hevra Kadisha, what plan of action can a person undertake to insure a funeral in keeping with the simplicity prescribed by the Jewish heritage? The following is a suggestion for action, beginning with the individual and moving to the collective.

Individual

1. Read about Jewish practices before a death takes place. See the annotated bibliography for particular suggestions. The Lamm book and the material by Isaac Klein are especially recommended.
2. Try to stimulate interest in forming study groups and classes with rabbis and other community leaders to further study the whole area of death and mourning in Judaism.
3. Check to see if there is a Hevra Kadisha in your community. If there is, support it and maybe even try to become a member and take part in this extremely important mitzvah. See the bibliography, number 9, for a good article on the Hevra Kadisha today.
4. Where there is no Hevra Kadisha, become acquainted with your local

funeral home *before* being confronted with the death of a relative. Find out if the director has simple pine coffins and shrouds, and if he is familiar with the laws of taharah. Request assistance from your rabbi in this research endeavor, as well as in all aspects and issues relating to death.

Such advance preparation and study can avert a situation where a mourner is at the mercy of a profit-seeking funeral director.

Collective

Realistically speaking, it is often very difficult to make any significant impact on funeral homes. They are extremely powerful and persuasive in coaxing people to spend more and more money, supposedly in "honoring" the dead despite the fact that this is not honor in accordance with the Jewish value system. In order to entertain seriously the possibility of simple and uniform funerals in a community that has a funeral home, it is usually necessary to speak about collective action. The best single essay on the subject is "The Scandal of the Jewish Funeral" by Rabbi Samuel Dresner (see the bibliography). Dresner describes in graphic terms the state of Jewish funerals in general in 1963. He then proceeds to describe what happened in his community of Springfield, Massachusetts. This case is quoted at length in the hope that it can serve as a model for other communities.

These present-day abuses of funeral and mourning practice moved some of the rabbis and congregations of Springfield to action. Orthodox, Conservative, and Reform were equally concerned. The following are the regulations regarding funeral and mourning practices for the Jewish community of Springfield:

1) In keeping with Jewish tradition which teaches the equality of all men, and that, therefore, there should be no distinction at the time of death between rich and poor, there will be one uniform casket used for all funerals. This casket will be draped with a cover of the congregation.

2) In keeping with the above tradition, no flowers will be permitted at funerals. Instead, friends and relatives will be encouraged to contribute to the charities of their congregations and other worthy causes.

3) The casket will remain closed at all times. The living should be helped to remember the departed as they were in life, not with the image of death.

4) Out of respect to the departed, the body should never be left alone; a shomer (guard) should remain with the departed at all times until the funeral. During this period Psalms should be recited.

5) Rather than engage in idle conversation, visitors to the place where the departed reposes should be encouraged to recite from the Book of Psalms and other literature which should be made available for this purpose.

6) According to Jewish tradition, it is not required to visit the funeral parlor prior to the funeral, or that the family be available for such visits at the funeral parlor. It is, however, a mitzvah to be present at the funeral services and to visit the family during the shivah period.

7) No special gloves shall be provided to the pallbearers.

*8) Meals provided by mourners for those attending shivah services should be discouraged as an imposition on the family.**

The above eight proposals which were drawn up and presented to our respective congregations could have been enlarged upon, but we wanted to establish an approach which would be acceptable to all wings of Jewry. For example, Conservative and Orthodox congregations also require ritual washing of the body and the garbing in shrouds in accordance with Jewish law.

**As of this date [December 1962], these rules, with varying changes, have been approved by the cemetery committees and boards of the Conservative, Reform and the largest Orthodox congregations of Springfield. The changes made by the Conservative congregation are in rule 1 which now "recommends" a single casket, and 7, which is broadened to read: "The introduction [by the funeral director] of any new practices in the funeral service must have the approval of the Rabbi, Hevra Kadisha and the Board" [see bibliography, number 7, pp. 27–28].*

Dresner goes on to describe the reactions to the Springfield case. His essay is must reading for anyone who feels that he is ready to engage in collective action to rectify the inequities and extravagances of Jewish funerals.

Dresner calls on rabbinic and lay leaders and interested parties to remedy the situation. He cites other cases similar to the one in Springfield, (e.g., Lancaster, Pennsylvania), and he readily acknowledges that the Springfield proposal is only one possibility. "The re-establishment of communal nonprofit funeral parlors should be the central goal for all" (*The Jew in American Life*, p. 48).

Dresner concludes with four concrete proposals toward which all concerned people should direct their attention and energies.

1. Reassertion by the synagogue of its authority and the authority of Jewish law and tradition in all matters dealing with burial and mourning.
2. Establishment of an ongoing educational program directed to members of the congregation to acquaint them with what Jewish law and tradition teaches regarding burial and mourning, and their relevance today.
3. Drawing up a code of funeral practice which would apply to all members of the congregation or those to be buried in the congregation cemetery.
4. The establishment (especially in large communities) of communal nonprofit funeral establishments, preferably sponsored by all branches of American Jewry (p. 49).

Summary

1. Study the tradition.
2. Research your own community.
3. Educate others and draw up a code of practice for all.
4. Bind together in forceful collective action, leading hopefully to nonprofit funeral establishments.

"He will destroy death forever. My Lord God will wipe the tears away from all faces" (Isaiah 25:8).

BIBLIOGRAPHY FOR DEATH AND BURIAL

A. Jewish material–traditional texts–available only in Hebrew

1. *Arbaah Turim*, Yoreh Deah, sections 335–403.

The precursor of the *Shulhan Arukh;* a code that preserves the many varied practices of the Jewish community up until the fourteenth century.

2. *Shulhan Arukh*, Yoreh Deah, sections 335–403.

This source is written in fairly straightforward Hebrew. It is probably the major source for the Jewish law in matters of death, burial, and mourning.

3. Greenwald, Yekutiel. *Kol Bo Al Avelut.* New York: Philipp Feldheim, Inc., 1947.

This volume is an excellent compendium of all recent customs and practices related to death, as well as most of the traditional material. The author has pulled together all the references to each aspect of death, burial, and mourning.

B. Jewish material–traditional texts–Hebrew and English

4. Maimonides. *Mishneh Torah.* The Laws of Mourning (found in the fourteenth and last book, very near the end).

His section on the laws of mourning is written in his usual clear and lucid style.

KEY TO INFORMATION

Historical background
Hevra Kadisha: see numbers 9, 11, and 14
Moment of death
Number 2, sections 339-41
Taharah
Number 11, pp. 239-40
Dressing the body and the casket
Number 2, section 352
The funeral
Number 2, section 357
Number 11, pp. 26–34
Number 10, p. 13
The burial
Number 11, p. 65
After the burial
Number 2, sections
375, 378, 380, 382, 390
Number 10, pp. 2, 6
Number 11, pp. 140–41
Kaddish, sheloshim, Yahrzeit, and Yizkor
Number 10, p. 7
Number 2, section 376

5. Zlotnick, Dov, ed. and trans. *Mourning* [Semahot]. New Haven: Yale University Press, 1966.

A rabbinic tractate (posttalmudic) that contains a compendium of very early references to death, burial, and mourning. The volume is carefully edited and translated, with an introduction and notes, and offers both the Hebrew text and the translation.

6. Ganzfried, Solomon. *Code of Jewish Law* [Kitzur Shulhan Arukh]. Translated by Hyman E. Goldin. New York: Hebrew Publishing Company, 1961.

An abridged code of Jewish law, based on Karo's *Shulhan Arukh.*

C. Jewish material–contemporary publications and articles

7. Dresner, Samuel. *The Jew in American Life.* New York: Crown Publishers, 1963. Chapter 2, "The Scandal of the Jewish Funeral."

This essay is unquestionably one of the best statements on the corruption and extravagance involved in Jewish funerals, and what can be done to try to rectify the situation.

8. Feldman, Emanuel. "Death as Estrangement: The Halakhah of Mourning." *Judaism,* Winter 1971, pp. 59–66.

A focused and interesting view of the laws that affect the mourner. Feldman argues that the laws function to estrange the mourner from life, and to enable him to participate, as it were, in a temporary "death."

9. *Genesis II,* issue of February 17, 1972, especially the article by Jonathan Chipman on the Hevra Kadisha. (Available by writing to the newspaper, 298 Harvard Street, Cambridge, Mass. 02138.)

The entire issue was devoted to the theme of death. Chipman's article is especially interesting because he writes of his own experiences in a Hevra Kadisha now in existence in the Boston area.

10. Klein, Isaac. "Course in Jewish Life and Practice," units 16 and 17 entitled "The Laws of Mourning."

Unpublished pamphlets used in a course on Jewish life and practice, under the auspices of the Rabbinical Department of the Jewish Theological Seminary of America. Klein has attempted to provide a fairly thorough, readable, and concise guide to the practices for traditional but not necessarily Orthodox people.

11. Lamm, Maurice. *The Jewish Way in Death and Mourning.* New York: Jonathan David, 1969.

This volume is unquestionably the best single-volume English source for the practices and their explanations. The presentation is clear; it is well worth reading. (Now available in paperback, $2.95.)

12. Rabinowicz, Harry. *Guide to Life: Jewish Laws and Customs of Mourning.* London: Jewish Chronicle Publications, 1964.

A short and fairly simple summary of the basic laws.

13. Rozwaski, Chaim Z. "On Jewish Mourning Psychology." *Judaism* 17, no. 3 (Summer 1968): 335–46.

The literature on mourning psychology is vast. This is one of the few recent articles that deals with the psychological issues from a distinctively Jewish vantage point.

14. Zborowski, Mark, and Herzog, Elizabeth. *Life Is with People: The Culture of the Shtetl.* New York: Schocken Books, 1962 (pp. 201–5, 376–80).

The ten pages that are cited provide a quick look at the duties and workings of a Hevra Kadisha in Eastern Europe during the past few centuries.

D. General material

15. Dempsey, D. "Learning How to Die." *New York Times Magazine,* November 14, 1971.

16. Grollman, Earl, ed. *Explaining Death to Children.* Boston: Beacon Press, 1967.

This book is probably the only collection of articles on this particular topic.

17. Grollman, Earl. *Talking about Death to Children.* Boston: Beacon Press, 1970.

This short (32 pp.) book is superbly and sensitively written, with very expressive artistic work. The text of the book is a proposal for what a mother should say to her little child when the child's grandfather has died. The last page of the book contains some general guidelines that should be closely followed when talking about death with a child.

18. Kubler-Ross, Elisabeth. *Death and Dying.* New York: Macmillan, 1970.

The author is a doctor who relates her experiences while working with terminally ill patients. A significant section of the book contains accounts of actual conversations with people who were about to die.

19. Mitchell, Marjorie. *The Child's Attitude to Death.* New York: Schocken Books, 1967.

20. *Psychology Today,* issue of August 1970.

This issue contains a lead article on death. There is also a rather interesting attitude questionnaire about various matters relating to death and dying. The questions are quite stimulating.

21. Ruitenbeck, Henrik M. *Death: Interpretations.* New York: Dell, 1969.

22. Schrank, Jeffrey. *Teaching Human Beings.* Boston: Beacon Press, 1972. Chapter 5, "Learning about Death."

His chapter on the teaching and learning about death is possibly the only thing of its kind—a series of practical suggestions for handling the subject of death in an educational situation. His suggestions include projects, books, and films.

ר בשושן לעשות כדת היום וא
רת בני המן יתלו על העץ ויאמר
לך להעשות כן ותנתן דת בשושן
ת עשרת בני המן תלו ויקהלו
הודיים אשר בשושן גם ביום
בעה עשר לח
ושן שלש מא
לחו את ידם ו
מדינות המלך
שם ונוח מאיב
משה ושבעי
י המן בן המ
רגו ובבזה לא
הוא בא מספ
בירה לפני ה
אסתר המלכה ב
הודים ואבד ח
שרת בני המן ב
ה עשו ומה ש
קשתך עוד ותע
ל המלך טוב י
שר בשושן ל
שרת בני המן
מלך להעשות
את עשרת בנ
יהודיים אשר
רבעה עשר לו
ושן שלש מא
לחו את ידם ו
מדינות המלך
שם ונוח מאיב
משה ושבעי
י המן בן הב
רגו ובבזה לא
הוא בא מספ
בירה לפני ה
אסתר המלכה ו
יהודים ואבד ח
שרת בני המן ב
ה עשו ומה ש
קשתך עוד ותע

ש אדר ויהרגו
איש ובבזה לא
י היהודים אשר
הלכו ועמד על
והרוג בשנאיהם
לך ובבזה לא
נא צרר היהודים
לחו את ידם ביום
הרוגים בשושן
ר ויאמר המלך
ישן הבירה הרגו
מאות איש ואת
אר מדינות המלך
תך וינתן לך ומה
תאמר אסתר אם
גם מחר ליהודים
ת כדת היום ואת
על העץ ויאמר
ותנתן דת בשושן
מן תלו ויקהלו
שושן גם ביום
ש אדר ויהרגו
איש ובבזה לא
ר היהודים אשר
הלכו ועמד על
ו והרוג בשנאיהם
לך ובבזה לא
נא צרר היהודים
לחו את ידם ביום
הרוגים בשושן
ר ויאמר המלך
ושן הבירה הרגו
מאות איש ואת
אר מדינות המלך
תך וינתן לך ומה
ותאמר אסתר אם
ל המלך טוב ינתן גם מחר ליהודים
שר בשושן לעשות כדת היום ואת
שרת בני המן יתלו על העץ ויאמר
מלך להעשות כן ותנתן דת בשוש
ית עשרת בני המן תלו ויקה

לאביונים וקבל ז
החלו לעשות ואו
אליהם כי המן ב
צרר כל היהודים
אבדם והפל פור
לאבדם ובבאה ל
ספר ישוב מחש
שב על היהודי
נו ואת בניו על ז
מים האלה פורי
כן על כל דברי
ו על ככה ומה ה
על היהודים על
כל הנלוים עלי
ות עשים את ש
תבם וכזמנם בכ
ימים האלה נזכר
ודור משפחה ו

: אשר לאביונים
: מרדכי והחלו לעשי
א האגגי אליהם כ
היהודים צרר כל ה
ל להמם לאבדם וה
אמר עם ולאבדם וב
עה אשר הספר ישו
אשו ותלו וחשב על ז
כן קראו אתו ואת בנ
שם הפור לימים האל
ת הזאת ומה על כן על כ
וכליהם קימו וראו על ככה
ועל זרעם וקבל היהו
ולא יעבור ועל כל הנלו
ימים האלה להיות עשים
שנה ושנה ככתבם וכזמ
ונעשים בכל והימים האלה
משפחה מדינה דור ודור מש

רים את אשו
שר כתב מרדי
המדתא האג
שב על היהודי
וא הגורל להמ
י המלך אמר ע
בתו הרעה אש
ז על ראשו ותל
העץ על כן קרא
ים על שם הפו
י האגרת הזאת ו
הגיע אליהם קי
עליהם ועל זרי
עליהם ולא יעב
שני הימים הא
בכל שנה וש
זכרים ונעשים ב
זה ומשפחה מד

נה ועיר ועיר ויב הפורים האלה ומדינה ועיר ו יר וימי הפורים ה
עברו מתוך היה דים וזכרם לא לא יעברו מתו - היהודים וזכרו
ת מנות איש לרעהו ומתנות ומשלוח מנות איש לרעהו ומד
ים וקבל היהודים את אשר לאביונים וקבל היהודים את א
עשות ואת אשר כתב מרדכי החלו לעשות ואת אשר כתב מ
ז כי המן בן המדתא האגגי אליהם כי המן בן המדתא ז
ל היהודים חשב על היהודים צרר כל היהודים חשב על הי
ז והפל פור הוא הגורל להמנ לאבדם והפל פור הוא הגורל
ם ובבאה לפני המלך אמר ע לאבדם ובבאה לפני המלך א

שוב מח, שבתו הרעה אש
ל היהודים על ראשו ותי
נ בניו על העץ על כן קר
אלה פורים על שם הפ
כל דברי האגרת הזאת ו
ככה ומה הגיע אליהם ק
הודים עליהם ועל זר
נלוים עליהם ולא יע
ים את שני הימים הא
כזמנם בכל שנה וש
אלה נזכרים ונעשים
משפחה ומשפחה כ
יר ועיר וימי הפורים
מתוך היהודים וזכו
יו על העץ על כן
ה פורים על שם
ל דברי האגרת הז
ומה הגיע אליו
ים עליהם ו

ספר ישוב מחשבתו הרעה
שב על היהודים על ראש
נו ואת בניו על העץ על כ
מים האלה פורים על ש
כן על כל דברי האגרת ה
ו על ככה ומה הגיע אליו
כל היהודים עליהם וע
כל הנלוים עליהם ולא
ת עשים את שני הימי
בם וכזמנם בכל שנ
ים האלה נזכרים ונע
דור משפחה ומשפ
ה ועיר ועיר וימי הפו
ברו מתוך היהודים
עשים את שני הי
ם וכזמנם בכל ש
האלה נזכרים ונ
ור משפחה ומש

every word that a man speaks with sincerity is the Name of the Lord

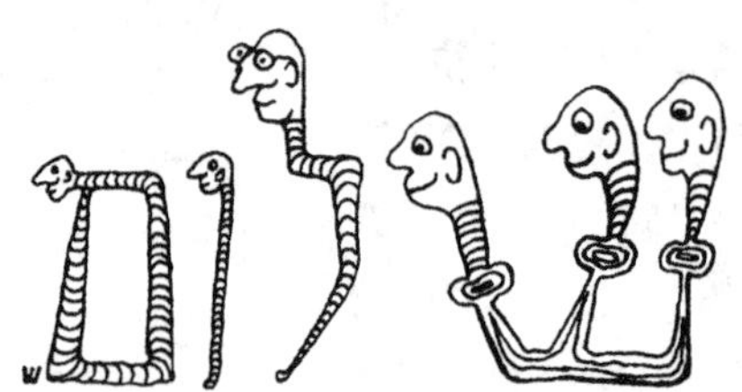

Scribal arts

The art of Hebrew calligraphy has an ancient history (as old as the written Torah), a huge scope, and a surprisingly easy accessibility, yet relatively little has been written about it. The articles which follow represent three distinct aspects of the art—the imaginative, the practical, and the classical. It is hoped that together they present a fairly comprehensive view of the art. Where one author's material has overlapped the material of another, we (the editors) have transposed it from where it originally appeared and appended it to where it relates. The consequent notes or comments are much in the tradition of talmudic discussion—which would often take place over centuries and without direct contact between the discussants. These comments do not so much show disagreement as indicate the spectrum of approaches and the opportunity for the input of personal preference. They serve to signify clearly that even within this exact structure and discipline, the individual calligrapher has the latitude to impose his own personality.

A TREATISE ON THE MAKING OF HEBREW LETTERS: Joel Rosenberg

The experience of letters

Do you remember back to when you learned the alphabet? My first memories are of a children's puzzle where I had to fit the letters into cut-out frames. But it was a world unto itself. Each letter was a gate, which opened into moods and palaces and stages of a journey. "G," for example, was filled with solemn expectation, all because it was the last one on the first row of letters, and it opened, as with a burst of energy, onto "H" and "I" and "J," which seemed to go downhill, then level out into "K" and "L" and "M." "M" and "N" were always turning into one another. They would argue with each other about who they were, and each claimed to be the middle of the alphabet—or, as they might have put it, the middle of the world. It was not until I was older that I learned that "M" (mem, mayim) meant "water," and "N" (nun) meant "fish," and that it was even more understandable that they should struggle with each other over which of them was more basic. A story of creation says that the world was once surrounded by the waters of the deep (tehom) as if girded by a gigantic serpent-fish. Do you begin to see what I mean about letters?

When I was still older, I would imagine *myself* as letters of the alphabet. An "A," however, was more than a shape; it was a landscape. I imagined clouds and mountains, rivers, sunsets, trees, and animals, all assembled in the *mood* or *state* of "A," and "B," and so on.

The significance of letters

You have to be (need this be said at all?) a little crazy to get into letters. You have to break down the meanings of words and treat the component letters as magic formulas, as tools for getting into the primal power of the world. The Hebrew word for letter—ot—is made up of the three signs:

alef א
vav ו
and taw— ת
the first (א)
and the last (ת)

letters of the alphabet joined by the sign for "and" (ו). It could be a contraction for AlphabeT, or it could mean, ideogrammatically, "first-and-last," i.e., "everything." A letter (ot) is also a sign (ot), in the double sense of oracle and cause for wonder. The word *ot*—אות—is conceivably related to the particle *et*—את—signifying transitive action. When we were taught the alphabet, we were given forces that were checked only by our innocence, by our natural inclination to CELEBRATE rather than to USE, to dance amid the world of letters and combine them playfully, without imagining that this combining could move the world and open gates. When we were taught to read we were made to forget the letters as we combined them, to forget their elemental power, to turn them into bloodless, abstract codes, to cool it and pretend they no longer existed in themselves but only as parts of WORDS—words we built and combined like building blocks, like sunbaked bricks for Pharaoh's pyramids and towers of babble, like computer cards: homogeneous, comparable, portable, and dead; words we multiplied like smoke, like garbage, like money; words we INFLATED, recombined. We used letters up, until their power was gone. Yes, you have to be a little crazy to get into letters. You have to slay words, and be prepared to have the walls you built with them come tumbling down.

To be concerned with letters is to make the world unwieldy, to fill the world with pictures, hieroglyphs, monsters. It is to render information UNUSABLE. A letter is a living being, a spirit. It cannot be trundled around at will, cannot be stuck away on cupboard shelves. In a world that has demythologized and devitalized information, penned the magicians and the storytellers up in bureaus and retirement homes, how dangerous is the RECOVERY OF LETTERS.

The letter is a means of calling out: the inhabitants of Babel, before they built their tower, had the power of letters in the rhythms of their speech:

Come now,
let us bake bricks and let us burn
them to burning.

Like the speech of God Himself: "I will multiply, multiply your seed as the stars in the heavens and as the sand which is on the shores of the sea" (borrowed from Everett Fox's "In the Beginning," *Response*, Summer 1972).

Like Moses. Moses stuttered, says tradition. He was a born magician. Alliteration was built into everything he said. He could make each word a prayer. He was UNWILLING TO LEAVE BEHIND A WORD, but would throw his whole being into THE INITIAL LETTER and get stuck there. Thus, the Hasidim said, with regard to prayer:

Know that each letter is a complete living being.
And when one does not put his whole strength into it, it is like a creature with a missing limb. . . .

If one reads a prayer, and sees the lights within the letters, even if he does not understand the meanings of the words, God approves. . . .

One should be prepared to die upon each letter from exhaustion.

–adapted somewhat liberally from *Sefer Liqqutim Yekarim* (reprinted privately, Brooklyn, N.Y., 1963)

The letter is the spiritual substance of the thing. The world is made of thirty-two pathways, i.e., twenty-two letters of the alphabet, ten sefirot (emanations of God). Their combinations produce all things, make up the HEART (lev, לב =32) of the thing. The Hebrew language knows this. Each word, a family of letters. Each word, its physiognomy. The letters of the word, in their unique combinations, are its essence. To pronounce a letter is to invoke its essence. Although a source of potential chaos, letters have staying powers: they hold a thing together. When Moses broke the first stone tablets of the Ten Commandments, the letters of the commandments hovered in the air, then fled. The letters of the Divine Name, engraved upon the Foundation Stone of the Temple, held back the waters of tehom (and do they flow today?). All things are not only called into being by their letters, but sustained in being.

A combination of letters in Hebrew does not form a word in the English sense—a new unit whose components are forgotten—but a tevah ("word" and also "ark"), a fragile boundary (taw, taavah), bearing, longing, and desire (taavah), bearing redemption-in-infancy (Noah, Moses, the tablets of the Law). Every word is the bearer of a covenant between the elements, a specific AGREEMENT TO COMBINE against chaos.

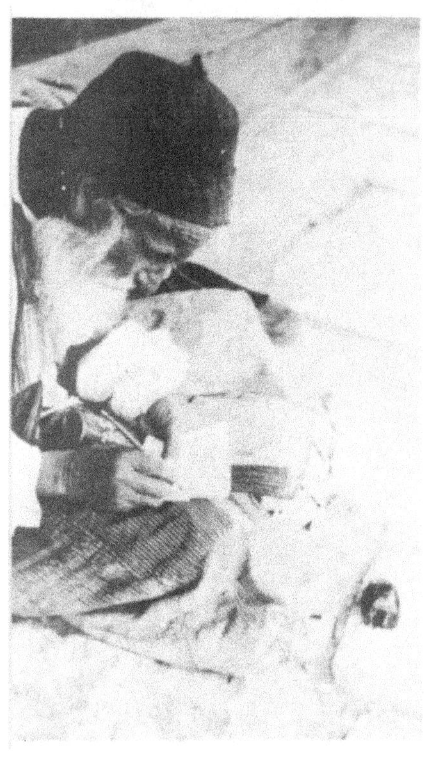

Yet letters are ambivalent. The Midrash says that each letter pleaded to God to let it be the one through which the world would be created. Yet each one bore a virtue and a fault. Shin ש, for example, was the letter for Shaddai—a name of God—and shalom, and also for sheker (falsehood). No letter has a pure value. The shin comes from the name for tooth (ve-shinnantam le-vanekha, "Impress [or hone or bite] them upon your children," Deuteronomy 6:7). But it is also a tree, an upraised hand, a flame, a candelabrum, a vine, etc.

We are midway between East and West. We do not have a purely hieroglyphic sense of letters. Every word rings with many echoes, many possible values of its component letters. The Syrophoenician alphabet (and thus, the Hebrew, the Greek, the Roman), like the Semitic peoples in general, bridged worlds, created movement and worldly business out of imagery rooted in the eternal, the mythic. The *I-Ching*, with its binary form of combination, is more static, more eternal, its internal movements more archetypal. To create an alphabet is to bridge the distance between memory and forgetting, between eternity and movement. A letter is a HALF-forgotten picture. Sounding it in alliteration, a HALF-effective magic. The calligrapher's art is a form of suggestion that can bestir, awaken, summon, but never carry to conclusion. Our involvement with letters must not—like that of Chonnan, the hero of the film *The Dybbuk*, who drives himself mad with the mystical preoccupation with letters—become deadly serious. The calligrapher must call us to memory, without immersing us totally. His art is an art of selection. An art of play.

The making of letters

The sofer—scribe—is the spiritual ancestor of the sage. The act of writing down, of accounting and recounting (sefirah), became the basis of religious knowledge. To be a scribe requires knowing how to select, knowing what to make large and what to reduce. A scribe who sees the lights within the letters, i.e., one who ILLUMINATES the manuscript, must bridge the gap between the narrative and the picture, between word and hieroglyph.

Not everything can attain prominence in the assemblage of letters. A scribe must toy with memory and be at home in a world where FORGETTING IS OF THE ESSENCE. His job is to facilitate communication, but also to slow the process down just slightly, long enough for preverbal memories to register, delicately enough that it does not prevent the worldly message from being transmitted.

Every world of script is unique. A Chinese scribe can make a HORIZON 一 into a sign for ASCENT 上 or DESCENT 下, or for DAWN 旦, or RAIN 雨 or . . . one who bridges heaven and earth, a KING 王. He can make visible a sound: 轟, the RUMBLING OF CARRIAGES. In short, the versatility of the Chinese sign-system for the use of words iconographically is unparalleled.

The Arab scribe, by contrast, like all workers of a Western alphabet, is limited to the use of ciphers whose pictorial content has become fixed and abstract. But he can, nevertheless, make of a sentence a TEXTURE that transcends the individual words:

شربنا على ذكر الحبيب مدامة سكرنا بها من قبل أن يحلق الكرم

But a Hebrew scribe, too, has his own unique world, a world born of letters, yet a world destined to be limited to words. His trade is the selection of words that carry echoes of their primary letters. His discipline is one of facing and enduring the hard questions of existence. He creates illumination as a musician at a wedding produces tears and laughter, as a badhen—jester—produces smiles and wisdom, as one who reminds us we are always MIDWAY between life and death, between tragedy and mirth.

The Basic Strokes

There are SIX basic strokes. The significance of the number will be apparent in time. The SIX STROKES are:

(1) the *yod* ׳
(2) the *vav* ו
(3) the *resh* ר
(4) the *short vertical* |
(5) the *bottom horizontal* —
(6) the *diagonal* \

(Now, don't go counting the ones I left out. The apparent exceptions—a stroke in the ayin or shin, for example—grow out of the above family in certain specific ways, and as the scribe develops his art he will begin to develop his own ways, his own sense of discretion, his own elaborations.) Whether one accepts the foregoing family as his own is not the important thing. I am speaking only of the necessity for FUNDAMENTAL PRINCIPLES. [See A Practical Guide to Hebrew Calligraphy for a different analysis of strokes.] But let me explain why THESE SIX.

The yod is, in some way, the embryo of all letters. Each of the twenty-two letters of the Hebrew alphabet contains and conceals a yod. In Kabbalah, the yod is the symbol for the origin of light in the world, a pinpoint, a nekudah, a beginning musical note of a niggun, a fine point within the human being that lives in the Holy Image, the pintele Yid. One who would begin to learn the making of letters—who would really BEGIN—will spend the first day, even more, if necessary, writing NOTHING BUT YODS. The hieroglyph from which

ב״ה
עוד ישמע בערי יהודה
ובחוצות ירושלים
קול ששון וקול שמחה
קול חתן וקול כלה
שמואל דב קולטן ורעיתו
הורי הכלה
זאב קלמן ורעיתו
הורי החתן
מתכבדים להזמינכם להשתתף
בשמחת כלולת בניהם
החתן שלום לב נ״י
עב״ל
הכלה אביבה חוה שתחיה
החופה תתקיים אי״ה
ביום א׳ פ׳ שמות, ט״ז בטבת תשכ״ה
בשעה 12
ב״שטו ד׳אור״
2560 אושין אבניו, ברוקלין, ניו יורק

the yod is developed is the sign for hand, yad: concentration on the yod will enable the scribe to develop his hand, and, too, to learn something of the secrets of the MIGHTY HAND that with an outstretched arm brought us out of Egypt and sustained us through the generations. Numerically, the yod is 10, the number of the sefirot, the stages of divine unfolding, and thus, because it begins the scribal art, the name (sefirah, sofrut) for the art itself.

The vav is essentially the stroke that connects upper and lower. Kabbalistically, the vav is a symbol for the CHANNELING OF LIGHT, the central letter of the NAME, the bridge between heaven and earth, the number SIX. Now, what about this number SIX? Why have I insisted that SIX is the number of the nuclear family of scribal strokes? Because it expresses so much about Israel, about her role in the world, and, too, the world itself, which I see as a kind of analogue to Israel, since both stand MIDWAY between CHAOS (tohu va-vohu, תוהו ובהו) and LIGHT (or, אור). Thus, SIX: six days of creation, six thousand years between creation and the Messiah, six pairs of Israelite tribes (that is why, in part, Jacob, the father of the tribes and the archetypal Israelite, stands kabbalistically for the vav in the NAME), six hundred thousand who stood at Mount Sinai, and . . . yes, it must be said, as well: six million martyred in our time. Six is also the number of points in a Star of David, the number of months between the month of Pesah and the month of Rosh ha-Shanah, and vice versa, the number of orders of the Mishnah and the Talmud, and the date in Sivan when Israel received the Torah. But, above all: the number of days BETWEEN the Sabbaths. The BETWEENNESS of the vav! It is no wonder that it is also the word for "and" in Hebrew, the letter of connection. But a vav is not merely a static link. Grammatically, it can transform past into future and future into past (i.e., the vav-consecutive)—as the Jew, between the Sabbaths, is commanded to TRANSFORM the world. Get into this letter. Learn to breathe it. Learn to hold it deep inside your expanded lungs and feel its power working inside you.

A wonderful new book that will get you into the mystery and midrash of Hebrew letters is Lawrence Kushner's *The Book of Letters* (New York: Harper & Row, 1975), which sells for $6.95. It's a terrific gift, too.

The resh is nothing more than an exaggerated vav. But I have chosen to call it a basic stroke because it composes so many letters, and because it incorporates so much movement, horizontal, circular, and vertical. It is a canopy of heaven, a huppah (marriage canopy), the hieroglyph for HEAD (rosh), thus, a sign for reshit, "beginning," in some ways, too, an oversized yod, also called "beginning." Like the resh of Rosh ha-Shanah, the stroke resembles a SHOFAR which summons a community to holy convocation. As "beginning," it closes the past, just as a letter with the resh in its makeup appears to ignore the letter preceding it, turns THE BACK OF THE HEAD to it, even as it looks forward to the back of the head of the letter to come. This does not mean that we are made for waiting in lines. We are made for FACING (that is, after all, the root meaning of our two most important terms in Hebrew for works of the creative imaginations, HAGGADAH and KABBALAH). But during those times when we HAPPEN to be waiting in line, we may dwell on the secret of the resh: the rabbis discouraged esoteric speculation by insisting that our vision must be trained AHEAD, to the future. Likewise, God says to Moses at Mount Sinai:

I will make all My goodness pass before you, and I will proclaim before you the name Lord, and the grace that I grant and the compassion that I show. But . . . you cannot see My face, for man may not see Me and live. . . . See, there is a place near Me. Station yourself on the rock and, as My Presence passes by, I will put you in a cleft of the rock and shield you with My hand until I have passed by. Then I will take My hand away and you will see My back; but My face must not be seen.

—*Exodus 33:19–23*

The short vertical is a vav without a yod. It is weak and in need. It cannot stand alone as a letter or a sign. But it helps other letters come into being, like the heh ה , and the zayin ז , and (a little elongated, and sometimes curved a bit) alef א , so it can be thought of as the PROP par excellence. Thus, that which began as weak and in need ends by providing support for others. Sometimes, as we shall see below, it can be rendered as an upside-down yod ┗ or, as I prefer to call it, "the helping hand."

The bottom horizontal, as in Chinese, functions as an EARTH, a HORIZON ("nor [ask] what is below"). The foundation of all houses. Combined with resh, the canopy or roof and its support, it forms a bet ב , the sign of HOUSE, also the sign of BINAH (discernment), the wise mother who contains all seminal wisdom and nurtures it and makes it grow. This ENCLOSURE is SECURE without being RESTRICTIVE. The door of the house, even one whole wall, is open. Our rabbis have said, as we have already noted, that we should be open toward the FUTURE, meaning, perhaps, that our position in the world is one of hope. But the bet is also a MOVING SCOOP, a hand which sweeps along, intensifying reality, filling to the brim with life, and overflowing, like a cup, into the WORLD TO COME. This is, then, the MODEL FOR A HOUSEHOLD. This is why the Torah began with the letter bet, why ketubbot (marriage deeds, about which more later) likewise begin with the letter bet, and why tractates of the Talmud always begin on page two, i.e., bet ("to teach us," someone said, "that we have never gotten to page one, no matter how much we learn"; still, bet has a wisdom of its own).

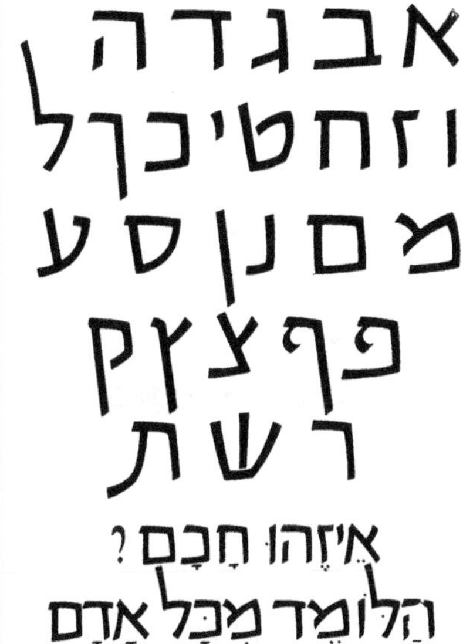

The diagonal is used principally in the alef, and, depending on the individual discretion of the scribe, for other letters, such as the downstroke of the tsade. Its infrequency might disqualify it for status as a BASIC stroke, but because it is so IMPOSING and expresses so many things, I have chosen to include it in the family. It is interesting that the alef א , unlike the Arabic alif, which is a straight vertical | , is NOT a BASIC stroke. Though in some forms of haggadic and kabbalistic thought the alef is the BEGINNING of ALL (this is why the bet points back to it). It is, nevertheless, only discovered GRADUALLY, after much training and experience and discernment. It is perhaps the HARDEST letter to perform, just as it is the hardest letter to PRONOUNCE (except when we are not trying). In any case, the diagonal of the alef may be taken as a symbol, on the one hand, for FALL FROM A DEGREE, i.e., suffering, exile, etc., and, on the other hand, the FLOW OF BLESSING from the upper worlds to lower. Now, alef is also the sign of ayin, אין , nothingness (please note: this ayin is spelled with an alef, and is not to be confused with עין , eye). Here is contained the secret of secrets. A NOTHING more real than any SOMETHING we could dream of, a NOTHING because it is NO THING. It is the sign of ani, אני , "I," the inversion of "nothing," the assertion of SELF, the emergence into the world of individual self-consciousness. We should think of ani as an alef with the first-person-singular direct-object suffix—ni, ני —thus: the NOTHING-WHICH-FILLS-ME. Alef is also the initial of anokhi (I or I-AM), the first divine word to Israel at Mount Sinai, thus the emergence of His own Selfhood, as it were, His first word with the people of HIS DESTINY. Some rabbis are of the opinion that only the first LETTER of the first word of the Commandments was actually spoken aloud at Mount Sinai. But alef, we know, is a silent letter, a glottal stop that underlies a vowel. God's elemental speech in the world: a prebeginning, pure intent, potential silence, humility. A silence which contains all commandment. The alef, as we have observed, is the hardest of the letters to form. It is arrived at only after much practice and experience. A descending line of suffering and blessing, held with care between two hands, thus:

All letters represent a numerical value, a being in nature, a sound in nature, a man-made object, an event in creation, an event in Israel's history, a phase of divine unfolding.

To repeat the cardinal rule of scribal art: it is up to the scribe to SELECT, not expand infinitely, what is inherent in the letters that he works with. As the Creator diminished the MOON that the world not be FLOODED with light, so the maker of letters must diminish the importance of all but a few of his letters, lest he flood the page with light and turn the world to chaos and madness.

In my effort to reduce the BASIC strokes to SIX, I also hope to suggest that the forming of letters is SIMPLE, that the scribe, especially in the early days of practice, should work for the simplest, cleanest, most UNADORNED letters. It is for Rabbi Akiba to place tagin—crowns—on the letters. It is for us to master the letter itself.

This short treatise is only a sample of what is to be learned about the making of letters. My own knowledge is quite limited. I suggest that you pursue further reading (see bibliography below).

[For Joel's suggestions on the practical aspects of Hebrew Calligraphy, see his notes appended to "A Practical Guide. . . ."]

A PRACTICAL GUIDE TO HEBREW CALLIGRAPHY: Jay Greenspan

Introduction

MATERIALS
Essential: a good working surface, either a desk, table, or drafting board; a pad of paper on the working surface; a cloth or rag
Extremely helpful: T-square, triangle, masking tape, erasers (ink and pencil), soft pencils (HB, B), a ruler
Suggested: a good compass (with a sharp point—useful in scoring lines onto the paper you are writing on); a french curve; razor blades or X-acto knife

This is intended to be a short, basic guide to the fundamentals and techniques of Hebrew calligraphy. It is not exhaustive. I hope to be suggestive and helpful about approaches to the art of Hebrew calligraphy.

Indeed, this is intended to be a springboard for the user. Its goal is to develop creative expression through suggestion.

Discipline, however, is sometimes helpful in developing creativity. Practice develops skill and art.

There is a certain beauty and joy in writing Hebrew. The letters imbue me with a sense of holiness and purity, joy and excitement. At times I feel restricted and confined by the letters; at other times I feel released from all bounds and filled with heightened awareness.

Use this guide in whatever good paths your own needs and creative expressions lead you.

The writing tool

NOTE: Left-handed writers have an advantage in writing Hebrew. Since Hebrew is written from right to left, your left hand enables you to see where you've been and makes it easier to prevent smudging of the letters at the beginning of the line, a problem right-handers often have.

This guide does not include special directions for left-handed calligraphers. If you have particular problems write to David Moss or Mark Loeb (see below).

It is possible to use anything from a fountain pen to a good sable brush in Hebrew calligraphy; freedom of style is not dictated by the materials one uses. I like to use an Osmiroid pen. I use the Osmiroid "65" and interchangeable nibs that fit the holder. (Pen is $2 to $3; nibs $1 each.) I prefer the Osmiroid because it gives a constant uninterrupted and steady flow of ink. This is useful so that you won't find some letters looking very dark and some looking very light—and you won't have to keep dipping the pen. Good nibs are the broadest: B-2, B-3, and B-4. If you are left-handed, there are left-handed nibs available, as well as oblique nibs, but they are not as broad as the "B" series nibs. Since Hebrew calligraphy is best written with the "B" series nibs, I know several excellent left-handed calligraphers who never have used the left-handed nibs.

You may prefer to use either the Speedball "C" series of points and holder; or you may prefer to buy the Mitchell pen and points. Both sets are cheaper, but I believe they have disadvantages (although they can be advantageous in certain types of Hebrew calligraphy). I still prefer the Osmiroid. Each to his own style and temperament.

If you are using the Osmiroid pen, you should use either Artone Inks (Fountain Pen India) or Pelikan Schwarz Fount. You can even use regular fountain pen ink, but with the Osmiroid pen, it is essential that you use *nonwaterproof inks*. Waterproof inks will corrode the rubber in the barrel and clog the pen after a while. (For extra thickness of line, you might want to use Artone Extra Dense Black.)

Generally, clean points provide sharper letters. Whatever pen you use, it's a good idea to keep the points clean. Soak them in water often. After each sitting wipe them dry of as much excess ink as possible. Be careful not to let the Osmiroid sit unused too long without a good cleaning.

[Joel suggests that the best tool for the initial practice of Hebrew calligraphy is a stiff brush, preferably of a material that absorbs inks well, ¼ to ½ inch in thickness, with a flat edge. In other words, the brush should be a kind of exaggerated version of an italic pen nib, which also possesses a flat edge enabling the calligrapher to vary the thickness of a letter. He prefers starting people out on a brush rather than a pen for several reasons: first, because all scribal art is fundamentally a form of painting; second, because the letters will come out larger: this will enable the neophyte (and teacher, if any is available) to study the letter more carefully, to comment and correct more effectively; it will also produce an immediate array of bold, decorative letters that can be mounted on walls to provide pleasure and edification; finally, brush writing, if it is done with a dry enough brush, leaves blank streaks in the body of the letter which reveal its sinews and lines of force; this again is both pleasurable to behold and instructive.]

What to write on

You can write on anything from plain paper to good parchment. The choice of paper depends on the type of manuscript you will be producing. For just general work or practice, any bond paper will do. Graph paper (10 squares to the inch) is especially helpful because it provides visual cues for height, length, and consistency of letters. For good manuscript writing, you might want to use poster board, mat board, Strathmore Bond, parchment paper, or even oak tag. For writing something special, like a ketubbah or a special quote, you might want to use real parchment. (But be careful—it's expensive and is a little more difficult to work with than paper.)

Keep in mind that Hebrew calligraphy needs nothing more than someone willing to use some type of writing instrument on some type of surface. The beauty of Hebrew letters cannot be confined to a beautiful piece of paper done by special pen.

Once you develop, you will be making letters on the back of lunch bags and on the corners of telephone book pages; you will be writing with quill pens and Papermate ballpoints. There is, in other words, no limit to the ways in which you might develop, or the unseemly tools you might redeem.

Before you begin

There are some miscellaneous notes that might be helpful before you start writing. Take a good look at the Hebrew alphabet in a Siddur or Torah or even a ketubbah. Study the alphabet. Notice how the letters are shaped, the directions of the strokes, the proportion, form, and structure of each letter. Study the letters as they relate to each other. Get a good picture of how the Hebrew alphabet looks on paper. This will help you when *you* try to put it on paper.

Sit comfortably in a good position at your writing surface. You might want to use a paper guard to prevent the smearing of previously written letters.

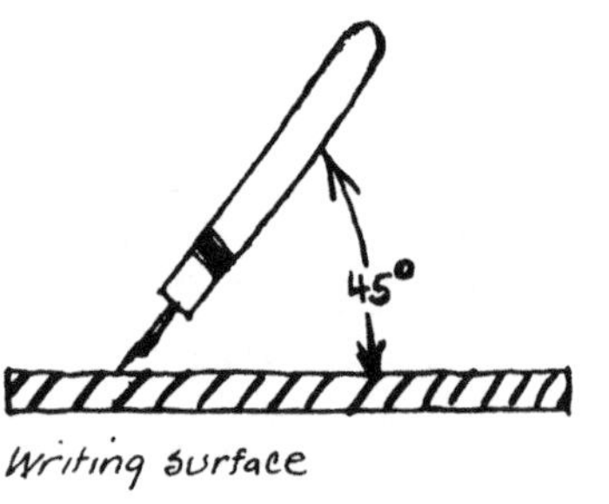

Now, hold the pen firmly and comfortably in your hand. Dip the pen in the ink and wipe off the excess. (If it is a new point, first wipe it with water before dipping it in ink; this helps wash off the oily film on the point.) Take a deep breath and get ready to write.

For most alphabets, it is suggested that you hold the pen at approximately a 45-degree angle to the surface of the paper. Try to find a comfortable angle for yourself, but you will find that a 45-degree angle has advantages to it.

Procedure

Breathing is important. Good breathing adds rhythm to your writing and helps keep your strokes steady and even. Inhale before starting a stroke; hold your breath while writing; exhale when finished with the stroke.

Try some practice strokes. If your pen doesn't write at first, try moving the point sideways to draw ink from the pen. Hold the point so that the entire edge of the point is in contact with the surface of the paper. This insures even strokes. Get the feel of your pen. Let it become an extension of your hand and fingers, of your mind. Keep writing until you feel the pen become alive. Try straight and curved strokes.

Line of writing →
Good
Not so good; line ragged.
Some practice strokes.

There are many different styles of Hebrew alphabets. But most of them have several basic strokes in common. Mastery of these basic strokes means mastery of the alphabet. A good alphabet to begin with, one that is both simple and beautiful and has easy basic strokes, is shown below. (Thanks are due to David Moss.)

← Line of writing
Direction of strokes

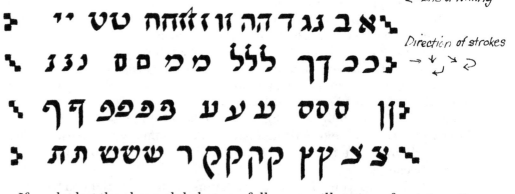

If you look at the above alphabet carefully, you will notice a few interesting things.

The Hebrew letter is basically divided into three parts: top, middle, and bottom. This tends to give proportion and emphasis to the various different strokes. Note the emphasis on horizontal and vertical strokes. Note that Hebrew is a "top-heavy alphabet"; most letters have long horizontal strokes on top. Also notice the variety of forms possible for each letter and that each form of letters is still consistent with the style of the alphabet. (Of course, that's a matter of taste; I have a bias, I wrote the alphabet.) Some more important things to notice are the proportions and shapes of the letters. Each letter is written holding the pen at the same angle to the line of writing—45 degrees (see diagram). And each letter is also three nib units high. (To obtain this height, hold the pen at 90 degrees to the line of writing and draw three widths of the pen, as shown in the diagram. This is the only time the pen is held at 90 degrees for this alphabet; its normal angle is 45 degrees.)

Holding the pen at a forty-five degree angle.

3 nib units in height.

Sometimes 3½ or 4 nib units of height are used, depending on the style desired.

Another thing to notice is the similarities and differences between the following groups of letters.

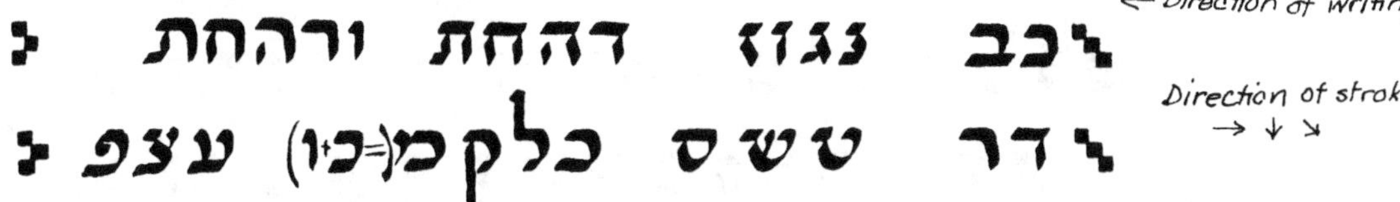

Grouping the letters in this way serves to highlight the basic strokes of the alphabet. Practice the following basic strokes. Try them on ruled paper (graph paper, if possible), using a B-4 Osmiroid nib (or Speedball C-2 or a nib that is approximately 3/32″ wide). The line of writing should be 3 nib units high; the pen should be held at a 45-degree angle to the line of writing.

← Direction of line of writing

Basic strokes.
(Arrows indicate direction of strokes)

To a certain extent this selection of strokes is arbitrary, but it does contain all the strokes necessary to write the previous alphabet. What is important in writing Hebrew is consistency of form, and this is gained through practice.

Here are most of the letters grouped by their basic strokes (or by combinations of these basic strokes).

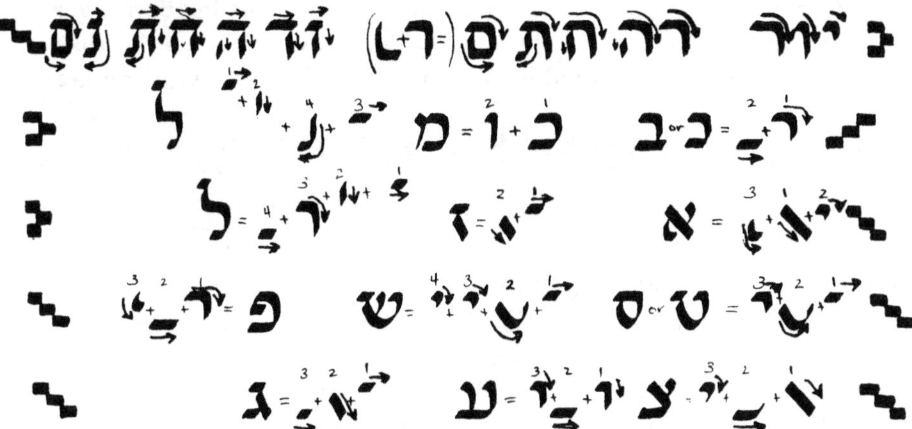

An additional note: In the writing of Hebrew letters, width must be considered. Below are the letters of the practice alphabet grouped by width.

These width groupings are approximate and done to show comparisons; occasionally one letter may not be written the width I suggest. One important fact to note concerning letter width—and this also relates to spacing—is that certain letters in Hebrew may be elongated.

These letters are

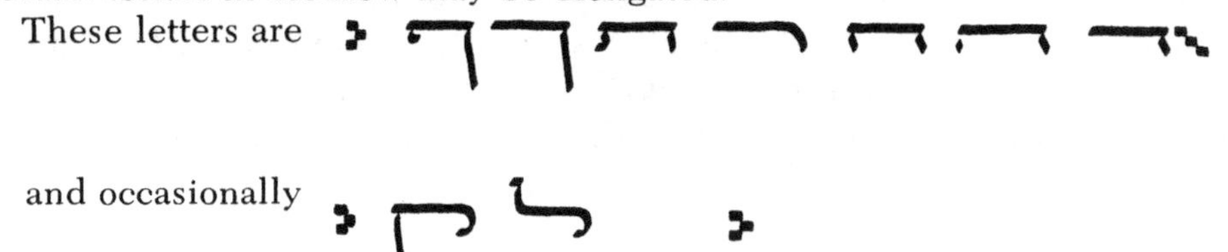

and occasionally

This is about all one needs to know in order to begin to do Hebrew calligraphy. For balance and perspective I would like to show you a few more alphabets. The one below is also written holding the pen at a 45-degree angle, but it is a little more decorative. (Thanks are due to Mark Loeb.)

אבגדהוזחטי
כךלמםנןסעפצףץ
קרשת

The following alphabet I call the modified stam because it bears similarity to the Torah script of a sofer stam (see below, The Calligraphy of the Classic Scribe). It is written holding the pen at a 90-degree angle, except for a few strokes where the angle is changed slightly; thus it is a little more difficult.

אבג ד הוזחטיכך ללמם
נןסעפףצץקקרשתת

You will notice that the modified stam requires much more control and practice than the previous two. The basic strokes, however, remain the same, just at a different angle. These are the basic strokes for the modified stam:

done at 45° angle — Basic strokes (arrows indicate direction)

[Joel recommends a tool of great simplicity and economy: a nylon felt- or bamboo-tipped pen. Art supply stores and five-and-dime stores sell packets of these pens, in a variety of colors, for a dollar or two. They are somewhat inflexible for stroke writing, but have a great variety of uses in adorning, as we shall see in connection with the ketubbah (see below). You can, for that matter, get off a pretty decent alphabet with it, if you are persuasive enough:

אבגדהוזחטיכלמנסעפצקרשת
םןץףך

The Rashi Script (so called not because Rashi himself used it, but because his commentaries to the Bible and the Talmud, like most other commentaries, are printed with it, thus making it a kind of Hebrew equivalent of our mechanical italic alphabet), which is intended to be quite severe and unadorned, lends itself effectively to the nylon (felt, bamboo) tip pen:

אבגדהוזחטיכךלמםנןסעפףצץקרשת]

Thus you have the fundamentals. By practicing and using the basic strokes and combinations of strokes, you build your alphabet. Practice until you can consistently get each lamed or shin or any one letter you write to look the same. Write something. Your name. My name. Transliterate the title of this book into Hebrew and practice. Through practice you will soon find your own style emerging; you will develop flourishes, strokes, and alphabets that express you.

Good luck.

Uses

With a working knowledge of Hebrew calligraphy you can transcend the bounds of the written word. Or you can use the written word for artistic expression, to make a beautiful manuscript or gift.

Here are some suggestions: ketubbot (see below and Weddings), shivvitim, mizrahim, (see Symbols of the Home), favorite Hebrew verses or quotes, wedding invitations, Bar Mitzvah invitations, birth announcements, Rosh ha-Shanah cards, greeting cards, note cards, bookplates, etc.

In writing such manuscripts, good design is extremely useful. Plan ahead. Make rough drafts. Measure the length of lines. Rule in or score in lines. Even pencil in the letters. Whatever you choose to do, try some preliminary designing.

The lovely art of ketubbah-making: *David Moss*

Let's face it—doing Hebrew calligraphy is a painstaking, time-consuming, laborious task. This task can either be a tremendous bore or a sheer delight. In order to make it delightful, I would suggest to you, aspiring calligrapher, that you try your hand at ketubbot—Jewish marriage contracts. Whatever you do, make your first ketubbah for friends or for yourselves. There is no comparison between sitting and practicing rows of letters and writing something meaningful for someone you love. The hours really fly by when you are working on something you know will be used, appreciated, and cherished; and believe me, a hand-done ketubbah will be!

Lines pulled black on white
Intend a dual unity,
Drawing separate lives together.
A golden rainbow garland,
Surrounding the ancient amulet,
Surrounding the aramagic letters,
Makes a beaming brideheart
beauty-beat;
Makes a pridegroom glow
Hot and happy.

Ketubta da—he reaches out to her;
Nedunya dane—and she to him;
Vetosefta da—adding mutual joys
and sorrows.

Kehilchot guvrin yehudain
And he lifts up a handkerchief
Denahagin bevanot yisrael
To wipe a love-tear from her eye.

What is the ketubbah?

The ketubbah is the standard Jewish marriage contract which every bride must be given according to Jewish law. The ketubbah was originally instituted (at the time of the Babylonian exile) to protect the rights of the Jewish married woman and to lend more dignity to the marriage. The text itself dates back to the second century B. C. E. and is written in Aramaic. It assures the woman that her husband will take care of her, provide for her, and cherish her, "as is the way of Jewish husbands." The ketubbah text assures her that if the husband dies or divorces her she will not be left without financial support.

Today, there are basically two ketubbah texts in use. The Orthodox text may be found in *Hamadrich,* published by Hebrew Publishing Co., N.Y., 1939; the Conservative text may be found in *A Rabbi's Manual,* published by the Rabbinical Assembly. The Conservative text differs from the Orthodox one in that it adds some clauses which give permission to a bet din—religious court—to go through civil authorities to force the husband to give his wife a Jewish divorce writ if the marriage is dissolved under civil law and the husband refuses to go through Jewish divorce proceedings. Another ketubbah, known as the Berkowitz Ketubbah, is in the process of being formulated and considered by various Orthodox authorities. This ketubbah would provide a sort of "conditional" marriage which would be annuled under certain circumstances. This is being suggested to avoid a great many serious legal problems involved in marriage and divorce. Reform rabbis do not generally use a ketubbah, though they are usually very willing to use one if the couple requests it. (I have done several ketubbot for Reform couples.)

Why make an artistic hand-done ketubbah? The writing of a Torah scroll, a mezuzah, or tefillin is governed by certain very strict laws. All of these must be done by hand; all must be done on parchment. The form of the letters is carefully prescribed. These texts may contain no embellishments. Special pens, inks, rulings, etc., must be used.

Not so with the ketubbah! The halakhah provides considerable latitude in the making of ketubbot. A ketubbah does not have to be on parchment, nor does it have to be printed by hand; it need not be written with special pens or inks. It may be embellished and any form of lettering may be used. The result of all this is both good and bad. It is bad because it has given rise to the horrible mass-produced "dimestore" ketubbot with which most people are now getting married. It is good because it allows you and me to create ketubbot that are original, meaningful, creative, and beautiful—and still are strictly valid according to halakhah.

The ketubbah has traditionally been one of the prime objects of Jewish artistic expression. Magnificent examples of hand-written and illuminated (decorated) ketubbot have come down to us from many centuries and from around the world: ornate Italian ketubbot; geometrical ketubbot from North Africa; ketubbot resembling oriental carpets from Persia; simple, folk-art ketubbot from Israel. When you pick up your pen to begin your own ketubbah, you will be engaging in a very traditional and authentic form of Jewish graphic expression.

There is also an important Jewish concept which you will be fulfilling when you make your ketubbot. It is the concept of hiddur mitzvah. This means "adornment of a commandment." The principle of hiddur mitzvah suggests that when a joyous commandment requires a physical object for its performance, that object should be as beautiful as possible. This is why we prefer to use a lovely silver becher (Kiddush cup) for Kiddush rather than a Dixie cup, which technically may be used to fulfill the mitzvah of Kiddush. In much the same way, the concept of hiddur mitzvah urges us to make the required ketubbah a beautiful, hand-done work of art.

Finally, there is a special mitzvah which you can perform when you make a ketubbah. We are commanded to make a bride and groom joyous on the day of their wedding. For me, this is one of the best reasons for writing ketubbot. The added joy which you can give a bride and groom on this most special day of their lives takes the writing of a ketubbah out of the realm of drudgery and makes it a delightful experience—that of performing this beautiful mitzvah. [The maker of the ketubbah, moreover, has the experience—a fragment of the experience—of participating in the cosmic wedding, that which happened at Mount Sinai, when Moses, the first ketubbah scribe, wrote down the words of the marriage contract between God and Israel, and, by extension too complicated to go into here, between heaven and earth. Every earthly wedding is a commemoration of that event.—Joel]

Writing the text To begin your ketubbah, select the size pen you wish to use. This will determine the size of the text and ultimately the size of the ketubbah. Using this pen, write a line or two (three to four pen widths high) from the ketubbah on a piece of scrap paper. Use the style of lettering you intend for the ketubbah. Count the words you have written and measure the area it required. From this you can figure what the overall area of the ketubbah text will be. (Figure the Orthodox text to be 270 words.) Using this area you can adjust the proportion accordingly and know you won't run out of room. Or you can fit your text into a circle ($A=\pi r^2$), or an ellipse ($A=\frac{1}{2}M \cdot \frac{1}{2}m \cdot \pi$), or whatever. A little effort and some minimal geometry at this stage can save a lot of headaches later.

Before you actually start working, make sure you have all the information you need: bride and groom's Hebrew names (including their fathers' Hebrew first names.) Be sure to include הלוי or הכהן after the father's name if he

נוסח שטר כתובה

ב______ (1) ______ בְּשַׁבָּת ______ (2) ______ ______
לְחֹדֶשׁ ______ שְׁנַת חֲמֵשֶׁת אֲלָפִים וּשְׁבַע מֵאוֹת (3) ______
לִבְרִיאַת עוֹלָם לְמִנְיָן שֶׁאָנוּ מוֹנִין כָּאן ______ (4) ______
בִּמְדִינַת אֲמֵרִיקָה הַצְּפוֹנִית אֵיךְ הֶחָתָן ______
______ בַּר ______
הַמְכוּנֶּה ______ אֲמַר לָהּ לַהֲדָא (6)
______ בַּת ______ (5)
וְהַמְכוּנָּה ______ הֲוַאי לִי לְאִנְתּוּ כְּדַת מֹשֶׁה
וְיִשְׂרָאֵל וַאֲנָא אֶפְלַח וְאוֹקִיר וְאֵיזוּן וַאֲפַרְנֵס יָתִיכִי לִיכִי
כְּהִלְכוֹת גּוּבְרִין יְהוּדָאִין דְּפָלְחִין וּמוֹקְרִין וְזָנִין וּמְפַרְנְסִין
לִנְשֵׁיהוֹן בְּקוּשְׁטָא וְיָהֵיבְנָא לִיכִי (7) וּמְזוֹנַיְכִי
וּכְסוּתַיְכִי וְסִפּוּקַיְכִי וּמֵיעַל לְוָתַיְכִי כְּאוֹרַח כָּל אַרְעָא
וּצְבִיאַת מָרַת ______ (6) דָּא
וַהֲוַת לֵיהּ לְאִנְתּוּ וְדֵין נְדוּנְיָא דְּהַנְעֵלַת לֵיהּ מִבֵּי ______ (8)
בֵּין בִּכְסַף בֵּין בִּדְהַב בֵּין בְּתַכְשִׁיטִין בְּמָאנֵי דִלְבוּשָׁא
בְּשִׁימּוּשֵׁי דִירָה וּבְשִׁימּוּשֵׁי דְעַרְסָא הַכֹּל קִבֵּל עָלָיו ______
חָתָן דְּנָן (9) זְקוּקִים כֶּסֶף צָרוּף ______
וּצְבִי ______ חָתָן דְּנָן וְהוֹסִיף לָהּ מִן
דִּילֵיהּ עוֹד (10) זְקוּקִים כֶּסֶף צָרוּף אֲחֵרִים כְּנֶגְדָּן
סַךְ הַכֹּל (11) זְקוּקִים כֶּסֶף צָרוּף וְכָךְ אֲמַר
______ חָתָן דְּנָן אַחֲרָיוּת שְׁטַר כְּתוּבְּתָא
דָּא נְדוּנְיָא דֵין וְתוֹסֶפְתָּא דָא קַבְּלִית עֲלַי וְעַל יָרְתַי בָּתְרַאי
לְהִתְפָּרַע מִן כָּל שְׁפַר אֲרַג נִכְסִין וְקִנְיָנִין דְּאִית לִי תְּחוֹת כָּל
שְׁמַיָּא דִּקְנָאִי וּדְעָתִיד אֲנָא לְמִקְנֵא נִכְסִין דְּאִית לְהוֹן אַחֲרָיוּת
וּדְלֵית לְהוֹן אַחֲרָיוּת כֻּלְּהוֹן יְהוֹן אַחֲרָאִין וְעַרְבָאִין לִפְרוֹעַ
מִנְּהוֹן שְׁטַר כְּתוּבְּתָא דָא נְדוּנְיָא דֵין וְתוֹסֶפְתָּא דָא מִנַּאי
וַאֲפִילּוּ מִן גְּלִימָא דְּעַל כַּתְפַּאי בְּחַיֵּי וּבְמוֹתִי מִן יוֹמָא דְנָן
וּלְעָלַם וְאַחֲרָיוּת וְחוֹמֶר שְׁטַר כְּתוּבְּתָא דָא נְדוּנְיָא דֵין
וְתוֹסֶפְתָּא דָא קִבֵּל עָלָיו ______
חָתָן דְּנָן כְּחוֹמֶר כָּל שְׁטָרֵי כְּתוּבּוֹת וְתוֹסֶפְתּוֹת דְּנָהֲגִין בִּבְנוֹת
יִשְׂרָאֵל הָעֲשׂוּיִין כְּתִקּוּן חֲכָמֵינוּ זִכְרוֹנָם לִבְרָכָה. וּצְבִיאוּ
מַר ______ בַּר ______ חָתָן
דְּנָן וּמָרַת ______ בַּת ______ (6)
דָּא לְמִשְׁבַּק דֵּין לְדָא וְדָא לְדֵין לְמִנְהַג כָּל יוֹמֵי חַיֵּיהוֹן
בְּאוֹרְחָא דְאוֹרַיְיתָא כְּהִלְכוֹת גּוּבְרִין יְהוּדָאִין. וּצְבִיאוּ בִּרְעוּת
נַפְשֵׁיהוֹן וְאַסְכִּימוּ לְקַבָּלָא עַל נַפְשֵׁיהוֹן בֵּית דִּינָא דִּכְנִישְׁתָּא
דְּרַבָּנָן וּדְבֵית מַדְרְשָׁא דְּרַבָּנָן דְּאַרְעָתָא דְקַיָּימָא, אוֹ מַאן
דְּאָתֵי מִן חֵילֵהּ, הֵיךְ רְשׁוּ יְחִידָאָה לְאַלָּפָא יָתְהוֹן לְמֵיזַל
בְּאוֹרְחָא דְאוֹרַיְיתָא וּלְמִרְחַם וּלְאוֹקָרָא דֵּין לְדָא וְדָא לְדֵין
כָּל יוֹמֵי מִיגַּד נִישּׂוּאֵיהוֹן. וְקַבִּילוּ עַל נַפְשֵׁיהוֹן כָּל חַד מִנְּהוֹן
לְאַרְשָׁאָה לְחַבְרֵיהּ לְזַמָּנָא יָתֵהּ לְבֵי דִּינָא דְּאִידְּכַר מִן עֵילָּא,
אִן יִתְרְמֵא תִּגְרָא בֵּינֵיהוֹן, בְּדִיל דְּיִכּוּל לְמֵיחֵי כָּל חַד דְּיִרְעֵי
מִנְּהוֹן בְּדִינֵי דְאוֹרַיְיתָא כָּל יוֹמֵי חַיּוֹהִי. וְאַרְשִׁיאוּ לְבֵי דִּינָא
דְּאִידְּכַר לְמִרְמֵא פִּיצּוּיִין עַל כָּל חַד מִנְּהוֹן, אִן לָא יִצְבֵּי
לְמֵיזַל קֳדָמוֹהִי בְּדִינָא אוֹ אִן לָא יִצְבֵּי לְצַיָּיתָא לְפִסְקָא
דְּדִינֵיהּ. דְּלָא כְּאַסְמַכְתָּא וּדְלָא כְּטוֹפְסֵי דִשְׁטָרֵי. וְקָנִינָא
מִן ______ חָתָן ______ בַּר ______
דְּנָן לְמָרַת ______ בַּת ______ (6) דָּא
וּמִן מָרַת ______ בַּת ______ (6)
דָּא לְמַר ______ בַּר ______ חָתָן
דְּנָן עַל כָּל מַה דִּכְתוּב וּמְפוֹרָשׁ לְעֵיל בְּמָנָא דְּכָשַׁר לְמִקְנֵא
בֵּיהּ וְהַכֹּל שָׁרִיר וְקַיָּם.

נְאוּם ______ עֵד
נְאוּם ______ עֵד

(1) בְּאֶחָד בְּשֵׁנִי בַּשְּׁלִישִׁי בָּרְבִיעִי בַּחֲמִישִׁי בְּשִּׁשִּׁי

(2) באחד לחדש, בשני ימים לחדש, בשלשה ימים, בארבעה ימים, בחמשה ימים, בששה ימים, בשבעה ימים, בשמנה ימים, בתשעה ימים, בעשרה ימים, באחד עשר יום, בשנים עשר יום, בשלשה עשר יום, בארבעה עשר יום, בחמשה עשר יום, בששה עשר יום, בשבעה עשר יום, בשמונה עשר יום, בתשעה עשר יום, בעשרים יום, באחד ועשרים יום, בשנים ועשרים יום, בשלשה ועשרים יום, בארבעה ועשרים יום, בחמשה ועשרים יום, בששה ועשרים יום, בשבעה ועשרים יום, בשמונה ועשרים יום, בתשעה ועשרים יום, בשלשים יום לחדש ______ שהוא ראש חדש ______ ______.

(3) ועשרים וחמש .The feminine form is used e. g

(4) .City

(5) הכהן, הלוי.

(6) בְּתוּלְתָּא, אַרְמַלְתָּא (widow), מְתָרְכְתָּא (divorcee), גִּיוֹרְתָּא (proselyte), אִיתְּתָא (others).

(7) Select appropriate line
מוֹהַר בְּתוּלַיְכִי כְּסַף זוּזֵי מָאתָן דְּחָזֵי לִיכִי מִדְּאוֹרַיְתָא.
כְּסַף אַרְמְלוּתַיְכִי זוּזֵי מְאָה דְּחָזֵי לִיכִי מִדְּרַבָּנָן.
כְּסַף מְתָרְכוּתַיְכִי זוּזֵי מְאָה דְּחָזֵי לִיכִי.
כְּסַף זוּזֵי מְאָה דְּחָזֵי לִיכִי.

(8) .If father is living: אֲבוּהָ; if deceased: נשא

(9) בתולה: בְּמֵאָה. אחרת: בַּחֲמִשִּׁין.

(10) בתולה: מֵאָה. אחרת: חַמְשִׁין.

(11) בתולה: מָאתַיִם. אחרת: מֵאָה.

The above ketubbah is the one commonly used by the Conservative movement.

is a kohen or levi. Write ז"ל if the father is deceased. Get the Hebrew day and date. Note: the masculine form of the number is used for the day of the week and day of the month; the feminine form is used for the year. Beware of weddings starting after sundown—they are on the next Hebrew day (example: a wedding late Sunday night is on שני בשבת . Get the proper Hebrew spelling for the city in which the wedding will occur. If the bride has been married before, some changes have to be made in the text.

If you are going to spend ten to thirty hours on a ketubbah, it is worth doing it on a material that will last and not discolor. Use parchment or good paper, or something else that has longevity. Real parchment is available from sofrim (Torah scribes); tell them you want it for writing a ketubbah. Also, real parchment, usually much thinner than that used by sofrim, is available at the larger art supply stores. Do not confuse this with parchment papers, which are simply oiled papers used to simulate real parchment. If you do use paper, use only 100% rag content paper. This will last for centuries and will not yellow. I use Strathmore two-ply in a dull finish. This paper is also available in one- and three-ply weights. I have also used acetate for ketubbot. If you do this it is a good idea to cover the writing with another piece of acetate to protect the lettering. Make sure it is framed before it is handled a lot (a good idea in general).

Now you are ready to begin. Take the paper or parchment or whatever you are going to work on. Draw in guide lines lightly with a very sharp, soft pencil. Don't draw in too many guide lines at once because your hand will be rubbing them out as you are writing. Try to write the entire text in one sitting. This makes for consistent lettering because you will maintain constant angles and inclines, and your inking will be the same. When you get about halfway through the text, check your overall spacing. If you need to condense or expand your writing begin doing it, but do it *gradually*. The full names of the bride and groom only need be written the first and last time they appear; all other places require only the first name(s). Do not write out the word וקנינא , though be sure to leave space for it; this word is usually written in by the rabbi at the time the document is actually ready to be used. Beware of homoeoteleuta and other beasties of their ilk! This is especially important if you go away from the text (even if only mentally) and return to it. If you do leave, check and double-check where you are in the text when you come back. Most of my mistakes are caused by some kind of interruption.

[Joel adds that erasure can be made with a double-edge razor blade. If you make a mistake (and mistakes are common, so the text of the ketubbah should be checked many times to make sure it is flawless), you should scratch VERY LIGHTLY in TWO DIRECTIONS with the blade, and brush the dust away. Writing over the erased area is difficult, and should be done very lightly, since the ink will tend to spread. The corrected letter will, in any case, be slightly

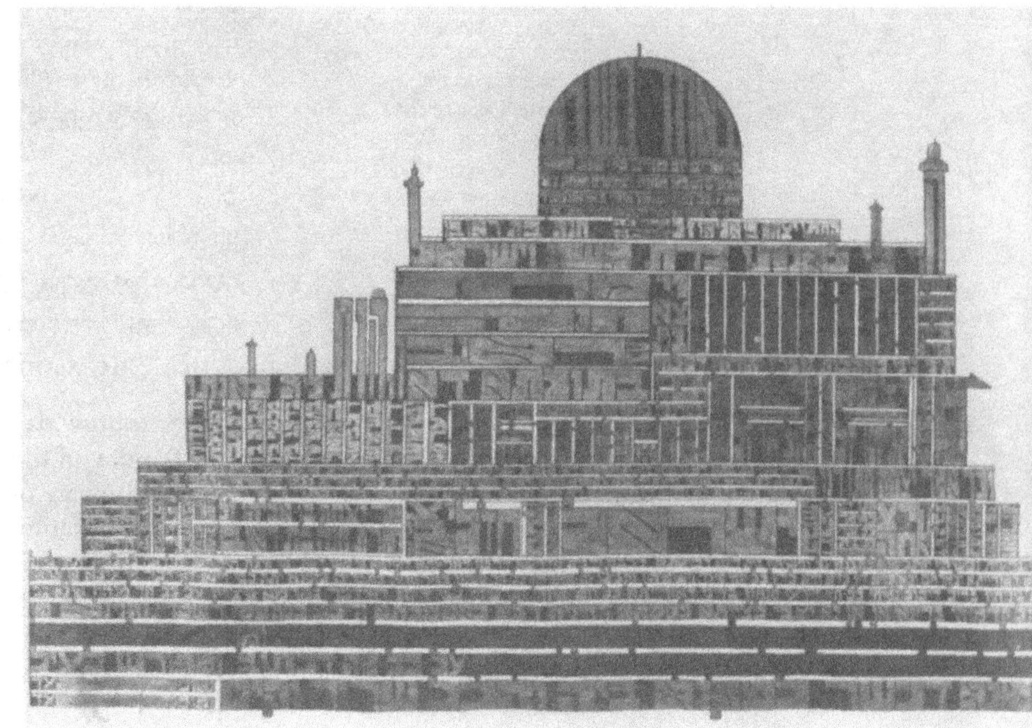

different in color from the original. He is studying possible ways to prevent this, and if anyone has any suggestions, he welcomes them. However, TAKE MISTAKES IN STRIDE. Do not panic, no matter how serious the mistake. Most mistakes can be corrected. Panic only prevents further accuracy of execution. By the way, some people recommend (mistakes or no mistakes) taking periodic breaks for meditation and light recreation, but NOT eating because it might cause food smears on the paper, and will, in any case, cloud your senses and smear the formation of letters from WITHIN.]

Illumination You need not illuminate your ketubbah. A carefully and nicely lettered ketubbah is in itself a beautiful thing. In fact, in the Middle Ages, when illumination was in its heyday and all books were handwritten, calligraphy and illumination were two very separate arts. The scribe was responsible for the overall manuscript and of course for the writing. After he had planned the page and written in the text he would give it to the illuminator, who would decorate it according to the scribe's instructions. Today, since we are not so specialized (at least in this one area!), you will have to do your own illumination if you want a decorated ketubbah; so here's some information you might need.

Colors Most any sort of colors can be used for ketubbot. Considerable research has been done in the field of recapturing the formulas used to make the wonderful colors developed in the Middle Ages. Most of what I have found in this area is from England, and the excellent work done there at the beginning of this century in reviving calligraphy and illumination. However, their "modern" equivalents of colors, bases, sizings, gessos, leaves, temperas, etc., seem nearly as inaccessible as their medieval counterparts. So I use commercially available watercolors and inks almost exclusively. But I would certainly encourage you to try different colors and techniques. And please inform me of what you discover if you do venture into these.

Bright red-letter words mixed in with a black text are very striking. Sometimes I put the names of the bride and groom in red. This use of red is, of course, very traditional in manuscripts and early book printing. That's what rubrics are all about; and if you think that *miniatures* have anything to do with *mini,* check out your dictionary—and miniate to your heart's content.

Blues, especially deep ones, look very nice with reds. These are the classical two colors (along with gold) for illumination and will give your ketubbah quite a traditional look if you use them together.

Outlining color or gold areas with a very thin black line makes them stand out.

The whole idea of "illuminated" manuscripts developed as a result of the shining, brilliant effect given them by the commonly used gold. Gold was generally used to represent light in the Middle Ages. You will certainly want to experiment with the use of gold on your ketubbot. Again, the literature is quite extensive as to how to use and apply golds of various types. Basically, there are two ways to apply gold: paint and leaf. About paint—the best, I think, is Testor's Pla-enamel, found at any hobby shop and many variety stores in little 15c bottles. Let it settle out until all the gold is at the bottom and the oil on top; pour off about ¾ of the oil, recap the bottle and shake it vigorously. Then apply it to your ketubbah with a little brush. Shake it from time to time, for it settles out quickly. Be careful of rubbing over any area you have already painted because it dries very slowly. The gold you will get with this method is very bright and nice, though it will not shine very well.

[Another method: This is what Jay does when he wants to illuminate a word or letter in gold. Instead of putting the gold on directly, he usually inks the letters in black. If he wants color surrounding the letter or word, he then paints that in with watercolors. Then he takes a small bottle of model gold paint (*not* gold ink), lets it stand so that the gold settles to the bottom, pours off most of the oil, and then dips a fine brush in the gold and paints over the blacked-in letters. This prevents the oil from soaking through the paper, since it is absorbed by the black ink.

Here is a design of the first word of a ketubbah to show you what he means.]

1. Black in letters
2. Paint in watercolor background
3. Paint gold over black ink

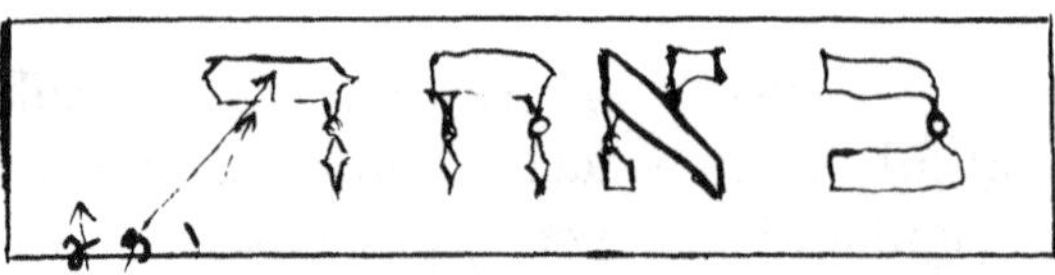

Gold leaf is tricky but fun. Prepare yourself for lots of time-consuming work and a good measure of frustration. First you must build up a base which will hold the size. Many coats of shellac are good for this. If you want raised lettering, use something more substantial, like Elmer's Glue-all or a gesso. This technique of raised lettering, by the way, was the original medieval ersatz gold. The fat raised gold areas on medieval manuscripts are supposed to (and in fact still do) look like solid gold; they are, of course, all made of some cheap gesso cleverly covered over with a thin coat of gold leaf. Once you have your area to the proper height and to a shiny finish, make sure it is dry and hard; then apply gold size. This comes in a regular (12 hour) and a quick-dry (2-3 hour) version. After the size is still tacky but not still wet, apply the gold leaf, using a camel's hair brush. (You cannot pick up gold leaf with your fingers because it disintegrates when you touch it.) Make sure the whole area is covered; don't worry about overlaps in the leaf. Let the size get completely dry and brush away the excess gold leaf. Burnish if you dare.

NOTE: All "writing" or design to be done in gold must be done with the size; wherever the size appears there will be gold, wherever there is no size, no gold will stick. It is often useful to add some oil paint to the size so it shows up better as you're working.

On illuminating letters Since Hebrew contains no capital letters, the Latin convention of using a highly decorated initial letter at the beginning of a text is generally discarded in Hebrew illumination; instead, the entire first word or words are illuminated.

[Joel adds: One may use one or more colors of ink. One should keep the letters as simple as possible, remembering that serifs and unnatural variations in thickness are artifices of mechanical printing. With this exception: certain formulas, such as the Aramaic headnote, be-simna tava u-ve-mazzala ma'alya ("with the good sign and the favorable constellation"), and certain letters (such as the bet, meaning "in," beginning the first line of the text) may be written with all of the resources of your imagination and may be conceived as colorfully and as wildly as you like, within spatial limitations and the demands of coherence. I have gotten a great many ideas from the calligraphy of Ben Shahn, in his book *Love and Joy about Letters;* for example:

This is *not* Shahn, but my inferior invention after his manner; if you try to copy his style long enough, you will find yourself invariably breaking away from it and inventing your own. That's because Shahn knew how to make Hebrew letters come alive, to dance like animals. And dancing animals can only be copied so far. Eventually, they break away and dance for themselves.

That is the way of letters.]

On copying Copying is not very well thought of today; neither in art nor in school, nor anywhere. All calligraphy and illumination manuals, whether they are from the Middle Ages or from modern times, however, seem to agree on the value of copying good examples. So if you can throw off your cultural prejudice, find good examples of fine calligraphy and illumination, and copy them. This will teach you more about the techniques and design required for these arts than all the reading you could do (or for that matter, all the writing I could do).

Conclusion I hope I have given you enough information to get started on the lovely art of ketubbah-making. Since great leeway is allowed in the making of ketubbot, the possibilities of materials, designs, formats, patterns, themes, etc. are limitless. Once you have acquired the skills needed for making the more or less traditional ketubbot which I have described here, you will find yourself able to explore and expand this exciting medium. Use your imagination. Now your hands are ready to do what your spirit and mind dictate.

Above all, enjoy making your ketubbot. Fill them with warmth and love. SHALOM

Fill them with you.

THE CALLIGRAPHY OF THE CLASSIC SCRIBE: Stuart Kelman

Introduction

The prohibition against graven images may have been a blessing in disguise for the Jewish artist. His attention no longer on human figures, he had the opportunity to show expression and creativity in the written letter and its accompanying illumination. One need only examine the book *Hebrew Alphabets* by Reuben Leaf or one of the newer volumes on Jewish manuscripts to see the ingenuity and creativity exhibited by these skilled craftsmen. Enormous importance was placed by the Talmud upon the art of writing. In Mishnah Avot 5:6 we are told that included among the ten things which were created on the eve of the Sabbath (of creation) is "ha-ketav ve-ha-makhtev" (writing and the instrument of writing). An interpretation states that this refers to the entire art of writing as a whole which was important enough to be included at this crucial moment in creation.

The sofer

The craftsman (sofer or professional scribe) was considered a special person because he had to master a vast amount of halakhic detail and because he had to follow a very precise ritual. The Talmud tells us that the scribe was recognizable in the street by the pen behind his ear (Shab. 11a). [See following page for list of abbreviations.] Before he could begin his daily writing of a Torah scroll, he had to begin with a ritual ablution in a mikveh.

Before commencing, the scribe tested the feather and ink by writing the name "Amalek" and crossing it out [*cf.* *Deuteronomy 25:19*]. *He then made the declaration, "I am writing the Torah (tefillin, mezuzah) in the name of its sanctity and the name of God in its sanctity." The scribe then looked into the* Tikkun [*explained below*], *read the sentence aloud, and proceeded to write it. Before writing the name of God the scribe repeats, "I am writing the name of God for the holiness of His name."*

—*Encyclopaedia Judaica, 14:1101*

If he errs in writing of God's Name, the entire sheet must be replaced. No word can be written from memory.

Aesthetics as well as Law played a crucial role in the development of this art. When a document was necessary for the fulfillment of a commandment, it was deemed proper that it be done in the nicest way possible. "This is my God and I will enshrine Him" (Exodus 15:2) was taken to mean that one should use and prepare *beautiful* objects to be used in Jewish ritual. This notion was concretized in the phrase hiddur mitzvah—enhancement of a mitzvah.

In general, the sofer engaged in his art within the framework of ritual objects. This category included the Sefer Torah, tefillin, and mezuzah, which are objects used in the continuing ritual of Judaism. (The sofer who wrote these was called a Sofer **STaM** (**STaM** being an abbreviation for **S**efer **T**orah, **T**efillin, and **M**ezuzah.) On the other hand, gittin (divorce) and ketubbah (marriage) documents were considered legal documents. (The sofer who wrote these acted as a notary public and a court secretary.) Although there are clear halakhic and ritual differences between the two categories, both were the subject of the sofer's artistic skills.

ABBREVIATIONS USED IN TEXT

Talmud (the Babylonian Talmud, unless otherwise indicated)

Av. Zar.	Avodah Zarah
BM	Baba Metzia
Er.	Eruvin
Git.	Gittin
Kel.	Kelim
Meg.	Megillah
Men.	Menahot
Mik.	Mikvaot
MK	Moad Katan
Sanh.	Sanhedrin
Shab.	Shabbat
Shek.	Shekalim
Sot.	Sotah

Miscellaneous

EJ	Encyclopaedia Judaica
Gen. R.	Genesis Rabbah (Midrash)
JE	Jewish Encyclopedia
Jos. Ant.	Josephus, Antiquities
Lev. R.	Leviticus Rabbah (Midrash)
Sh. Ar. OH	Shulhan Arukh, Orah Hayyim (Code of law)
Song R.	Song of Songs Rabbah (Midrash)
Sof.	Sofrim
Targ. Jon.	Targum Jonathan
TJ	Talmud Jerusalem
Tosef. Kel. BB	Tosefta, Kelim, Baba Kama
Tosef. Kel. BM	Tosefta, Kelim, Baba Metzia
Yad.	Rambam—Mishneh Torah (Code of Law)
Yal.	Yalkut
Yal. E.	Yalkut to Book of Exodus
Yal. Num.	Yalkut to Book of Numbers

The Sefer Torah (and tools of the trade)

The tools and materials used by the sofer are parchment, quill, ink, stylus and ruler, and Tikkun, *(guide), a book with the Torah text. The Torah is written on parchment made from specified sections of the hide of a kosher animal (though not necessarily slaughtered according to Jewish ritual). The hide consists of three layers, but only the flesh side of the inner layer and the outer side of the hairy layer may be used for Torah parchment* (kelaf) *(Shab. 79b).* Gewil *is the plain hide with hair scraped off (i.e., leather);* kelaf *is parchment;* doksostos *is another form of parchment (vellum). The method of cleaning and softening the hide, which must be of the best quality, has changed throughout the centuries. During talmudic times, salt and barley flour were sprinkled on the skins, which were then soaked in the juice of gallnuts (*Meg. *19a). There is, however, a reference to the use of dog's dung for this purpose (*Yal. E. *187). Nowadays the skins are softened by soaking them in clear water for two days, after which the hair is removed by soaking the hides in limewater for nine days. Finally, the skins are rinsed and dried and the creases ironed out with presses. The processor must make a verbal declaration when soaking the skins that his action is being performed for the holiness of the Sefer Torah.*

A differentiation is made between permanent writing materials and nonpermanent ones. In the former the Mishnah *enumerates olive leaves and a cow's horn, to which the* Tosefta *(*Shab. *11 [12:8]) adds carob leaves or cabbage leaves. It is difficult to see how they could be used widely. Non-*

permanent writing materials are given as leaves of leeks, onions, vegetables, and the sorb apple tree.

*Owing to the scarcity and high cost of paper, particularly parchment, it was used more than once, by rubbing out the writing with stone and superimposing new writing. It is this palimpsest which is referred to in the dictum of Elisha b. Avuyah, who compares learning as a child to "ink written on clean paper" and learning is one's old age to "ink written on erased paper" (*Avot *4:20;* Git. *2:4, where erased paper is equated with* diftera, *hide which has been treated with salt and flour, but not with gallnuts).*

Whereas reeds were used as pens in the days of the Talmud, quills are used today, the quill of the turkey feather, which is sturdy and long lasting, being preferred. The sofer *cuts the point of the feather to give it a flat surface, which is desirable for forming the square letters, and then slits it lengthwise.*

The inkwell of the scribe, called the bet deyo *(ink container) had a cover (*Tosef. Kel. BM *4:11) and mention is made of the "inkwell of Joseph the Priest which had a hole in the side" (*Mik. *10:1).*

A similar distinction is made between permanent and non-permanent inks. To the former belong ink proper (deyo), *caustic, red dye, and gum (*Shab. *12:4;* Sot. *2:4). The* Tosefta *(*Shab. *11*[*12*]*:8) adds congealed blood and curdled milk, as well as nutshells and pomegranate peel, which were widely used for making dyestuffs. Ink was made from a mixture of oil and resin, which hardened and to which water was added. Any oil or resin could be used, but the best quality was of olive oil and balsam (*Shab. *23a, 104b). The most permanent ink, however, was made by adding iron sulphate or vitriol (*kankantum *or* kalkantum, *properly* קלקנתים *to the ink, which made it a deep black, and it was therefore also used as boot-blacking (*Git. *19a). This admixture made the ink completely indelible and was therefore prohibited for use in writing the passage of the* Sotah *(*Er. *13a). Non-permanent inks were made from "taria water" (juice of wine), fruit juices, and juice of gallnuts (*Git. *19a). There is an interesting reference to invisible writing: "These people of the East are very cunning. When one of them wishes to write a letter in secret writing to his friend he writes it with melon water and when the recipient receives it he pours ink over it and is able to decipher the writing" (*TJ, Shab. *12:4; 13d;* Git. *2:3, 44b).*

[*In writing a Sefer Torah*] *the ink must be black, durable, but not indelible. During talmudic times a viscous ink was made by heating a vessel with the flame of olive oil, and the soot thus produced on the sides of the vessel was scraped off and mixed with oil, honey, and gallnuts (*Shab. *23a). Ink is now made by boiling a mixture of gallnuts, gum arabic, and copper sulfate crystals. Some scribes also add vinegar and alcohol.*

*It would appear originally the custom to use gold lettering for the writing of the Sefer Torah, since the Midrash (*Song R. *1:11; cf. ibid. 5:11) applies the verse "we will make the circlets of gold, with studs of silver" (Songs 1:11) to the writing and the ruled lines respectively. According to the letter of Aristeas, the Sefer Torah presented by Eleazer the high priest to Ptolemy Philadelphus was written in letters of gold (cf. Jos.* Ant. *12:89). However, such ostentation was later forbidden and tractate* Soferim *(1:9) states: "It is forbidden to write* [*a Sefer Torah*] *in gold."*

*Pen, paper, and inkstand are referred to as "things of honor" in a peculiar context. Rabban Simeon b. Gamaliel states that any idol which bears something in its hand is forbidden. The Jerusalem Talmud makes an exception in the case of "something of honor" and specifies "paper, pen, and inkwell"; (*Av. Zar. *3:1, 42c bottom). The word* kalmarin *is also used for the pencase (*Yal. Num. *766). Among the other instruments of the scribe were the* olar, *the* *pen-knife used for cutting the reed to make the quill (*Kel. *12:8,* Tosef. Kel. BB *7:12; the* izmel, *a knife for cutting the paper (*Targ. Jon. *to Jeremiah 36:23; Heb.* ta'ar, *cf. Targ. Jon. to Ps. 45:2); and the* sargel, *a sharp instrument for drawing the lines on the parchment or paper. For sacred writings the sargel had to be made from a reed (*TJ, Meg. *1:11, 71d;* Sof. *1:1). "Writer's sand" was used to dry the ink (*Shab. *12:5). To ensure that the letters will be straight and the lines equally spaced, 43 thin lines are drawn across the width of the parchment with a stylus or awl and ruler. [A pencil is forbidden.] Two additional longitudinal lines are drawn at the end of the page to ensure that all lines end equally. To enhance the appearance of the printing on the parchment a four-inch margin is left at the bottom, a three-inch margin at the top, and a two-inch margin between the columns.*

Although there is no law regulating the number of pages of columns a Torah must have, from the beginning of the 19th century, a standard pattern of 248 columns of 42 lines each was established. Each column is about five inches wide, since by tradition there must be space enough to write the word למשפחתיהם*(Gen. 8:19), the longest occurring in the Torah, three times (or 30 letters). The sheet (*yeriah*) must contain no less than three and no more than eight columns. A sheet of nine pages may be cut in two parts, of four and five columns respectively. The last column of the Sefer Torah may be narrower, and must end in the middle of the bottom line with the three concluding words of the Torah (*Men. *30a). Some* soferim *were careful to begin the columns of the Sefer Torah with a word commencing with a* "vav," *allowing an equal number of lines to every column. Such columns were known as* "vav ha-'ammudim."

There must be a space between the letters, a greater space between the words, and a nine-letter gap between the portions. A four-line separation is made between each of the Five Books of Moses.

To avoid mistakes, talmudic soferim *copied from another scroll, and according to one tradition there was a copy of the Torah kept in the Temple which scribes used as the standard (Rashi to* MK *3:4,* T.J, Shek. *4:3, 48a). Today a* tikkun *(guide) is used. The most popular is that published by Ktav (N. Y. in 1946).*

After the copying of the Torah has been completed, the sheets of parchment are sewn together with giddin, *a special thread made of tendon tissue taken from the foot muscles of a kosher animal. Every four pages are sewn together to form a section or yeriah. These sections of parchment are sewn on the outer side of the parchment, with one inch left unsewn both at the very top and bottom. To reinforce the* giddin, *thin strips of parchment are pasted on the top and bottom of the page. After connecting the sheets the ends are tied to wooden rollers, called* azei hayyim, *by inserting the* giddin *in holes in the rollers. The* ez hayyim *consists of a center pole, with handles of wood and flat circular rollers to support the rolled-up scroll. Besides serving as a means of rolling the scroll, the* azei hayyim *also prevent people from touching the holy parchment with their hands. In oriental and some Sephardic communities, the flat rollers are not employed, since the Torah scrolls are kept in an ornamental wooden or metal case* (tik).

Mistakes in the Torah scroll can generally be corrected, since the ink can be erased with a knife and pumice stone. However, a mistake in the writing of any of the Names of God cannot be corrected since the Name of God may not be erased, and such faulty parchments must be discarded. When a mistake is found in a Sefer Torah, the wimple is tied round the outside of its mantle as a sign that it should not be used until the mistake has been corrected. According to the Talmud, a Sefer Torah which has less than 85 correct letters is to be discarded (Yad. *3:5;* Shab. *116a). This number is the number of letters in Numbers 10:35–36, which is sometimes regarded as a separate book (hence the references to seven instead of five books of the Torah:* Gen. R. *64:8;* Lev. R. *11:3). However, it was later laid down that too extensive corrections rendered the scroll unsightly and therefore invalid. If a scroll is beyond repair, it is placed in an earthenware urn and buried in the cemetery.* [*It was customary to bury such scrolls alongside the resting place of a prominent rabbi* Meg. *26b).*]

It is regarded as a positive biblical commandment for every Jew to possess a Sefer Torah, the word "song" in Deuteronomy 31:19, "Now therefore write ye this song for you" being interpreted to apply to the Torah as a whole. Even if he has inherited one from his father he is still obliged to have one of his own (Sanh. 21b). He may write it himself, or have it written on his behalf by a sofer, *or purchase one, but "he who writes it himself is regarded as though it had been given to him on Mt. Sinai"* (Men. *30a).*

On the basis of the statement of the Talmud (ibid.) to the effect that he who corrects even one letter in a Sefer Torah is regarded as though he had himself written it, a custom has developed which both gives every Jew a portion in a Sefer Torah and symbolically regards him as having fulfilled the command of writing one. The sofer *writes only the outlines of the words in the first and last passages of the Sefer Torah and they are completed at a ceremony known as* Siyyum ha-Torah *("the completion of the Torah"). Those present are honored by each being invited to fill in one of the hollow letters, or formally authorize the* sofer *to do so.*

—EJ 14:1100–1104; 16:669–72; JE 11:126–34

Tefillin

Tefillin contain, in each of the two black leather boxes, four passages of the Bible (Exodus 13:1–10; 11–17; Deuteronomy 6:4–9; and 11:13–21). Each of these passages contains similar phrases which mention the requirement that a Jew put on "these words" (of the Law) for "a sign on your hand and as a symbol on your forehead." In the tefillah of the hand, the four passages are written on one piece of parchment, in the order of their occurrence in the

Bible, and are inserted into one compartment. The tefillah of the head is divided into four compartments. Each of the four passages is written on a separate piece of parchment, rolled, tied, and inserted into one compartment. As with the Sefer Torah, the tefillin must be written on parchment which comes from the skins of ritually clean animals and the scriptural passages must be written in Assyrian script and in black ink. Throughout the writing of the tefillin the attention of the sofer must not be diverted: "Even if the King of Israel should then greet him, he is forbidden to reply." If he omits even one letter, the whole inscription becomes unfit. If he inserts a superfluous letter at the beginning or at the end of a word, he may erase it, but if it is in the middle of a word, the whole becomes unfit. In writing the selections it is customary to devote seven lines to each paragraph in the hand tefillah and four lines to each paragraph in the head tefillah. (See Sh. Ar. OH 32-35.) Unlike the Sefer Torah, tefillin may be written from memory (Meg. 18b).

(See Tefillin.)

Mezuzah

שמע ישראל יהוה אלהינו יהוה אחד ואהבת את
יהוה אלהיך בכל לבבך ובכל נפשך ובכל מאדך והיו
הדברים האלה אשר אנכי מצוך היום על לבבך ושננתם
לבניך ודברת בם בשבתך בביתך ובלכתך בדרך
ובשכבך ובקומך וקשרתם לאות על ידך והיו לטטפת
בין עיניך וכתבתם על מזזות ביתך ובשעריך
והיה אם שמע תשמעו אל מצותי אשר אנכי
מצוה אתכם היום לאהבה את יהוה אלהיכם ולעבדו
בכל לבבכם ובכל נפשכם ונתתי מטר ארצכם בעתו
יורה ומלקוש ואספת דגנך ותירשך ויצהרך ונתתי
עשב בשדך לבהמתך ואכלת ושבעת השמרו לכם
פן יפתה לבבכם וסרתם ועבדתם אלהים אחרים
והשתחויתם להם וחרה אף יהוה בכם ועצר את
השמים ולא יהיה מטר והאדמה לא תתן את יבולה
ואבדתם מהרה מעל הארץ הטבה אשר יהוה נתן לכם
ושמתם את דברי אלה על לבבכם ועל נפשכם וקשרתם
אתם לאות על ידכם והיו לטוטפת בין עיניכם ולמדתם
אתם את בניכם לדבר בם בשבתך בביתך ובלכתך
בדרך ובשכבך ובקומך וכתבתם על מזוזות ביתך
ובשעריך למען ירבו ימיכם וימי בניכם על האדמה
אשר נשבע יהוה לאבתיכם לתת להם כימי השמים
על הארץ

A mezuzah, the third of these ritual objects, is the parchment scroll affixed to the doorpost of a Jewish home. Here, too, the parchment must be made from the skin of a clean animal.

On this parchment the two passages in which the above-mentioned verses occur (Deut. 6:4–9 and 11:13–21) are written in square (Assyrian) characters, traditionally in 22 lines. The parchment is then rolled up and inserted in a case with a small aperture. On the back of the parchment the word שדי *, "Almighty," but also represents the initial letters of* שומר דלתות ישראל *(Guardian of the doors of Israel) (Kol Bo, 90, 101:4) is written, and the parchment is so inserted that the word is visible through the aperture. At the bottom of the obverse side there is written the formula* כוזו במוכסז כוזו *, a cryptogram formed by substituting the next letter of the alphabet for the original; it thus being the equivalent of* יהוה אלהינו יהוה *("the Lord, God, the Lord"). This is already mentioned by Asher b. Jehiel in the 13th century in his commentary to the* Hilkhot Mezuzah *of Alfasi (Romm-Vilna ed., p. 6b).*

–EJ, 1475, 1476

While a Sefer Torah must always be written from a copy, the mezuzah may be written from memory (Men. 32b). If but one letter is missing, the mezuzah is invalid (Men. 28a).

Given the nature and the use of these three ritual objects, the texts must be regularly inspected to make certain the writing is still kosher (i.e., not rubbed out or unfit because of use, pressure, or age).

(See Symbols of the Home.)

Ketubbah and get

Other documents which have been the subject for the skills of the sofer have been the ketubbah and the get (plural, gittin). Unlike the Sefer Torah, tefillin, and mezuzah, the get—the bill of divorce—did not have to be written on parchment. It could be executed on papyrus. One entire tractate of the Talmud deals exclusively with gittin, and contains the detailed discussions about the laws of divorce. Before undertaking the writing of gittin, the sofer had to be grounded in the minutiae of the law, and only a few select sofrim actually practiced this art.

Because of the happiness of the occasion, the ketubbah or marriage contract has been the object of much artistic creativity, embellishing the calligraphy of the verbal formula it contains. The fact that the ketubbah must always be *written* (as opposed to an oral agreement) gave rise to many lovely illuminated ketubbot, including numerous ones from Italy with elegant artistry in European style as well as Persian ones decorated like rose gardens. Not infrequently, a stylized representation of the Holy City was depicted at the top, so as to implement literally the psalmist's resolve to place Jerusalem at the head of all his joy (Psalms 137:6).

Most of the laws governing ketubbot are to be found in the talmudic tractate Ketubbot.

The letters

The Torah is written in the square script known as Ketav Ashuri, of which there are two different types: the Ashkenazic, which resembles the script described in the Talmud (Shab. 104a), and the Sephardic, which is identical with the printed letters of the Hebrew alphabet currently used in sacred texts.

There are many different laws detailing these letters. They should be made precisely as pictured. Each letter must be written beginning from the left, with the initial stroke being (generally) a curved line ⁾ produced by using just the point of the quill. Next, using the entire surface of the pen, the letter is drawn ב

אבגדהוזח
טיכךלמם
נןסעפף
צץקרשת

אוזעצץש

אבגדהוזחט
יכלמםנןסע
פףצץקרשת

The thickness of the letters varies and it is often necessary for the sofer to make several strokes to form a letter. The scribe holds the feather sideways to make thin lines, and flat, so that the entire point writes, to make thick lines. Particular care must be given to those letters that are similar in appearance (e.g., dalet *and* resh*) so that they can be easily distinguished. Each letter must be complete, with the exception of the "split* vav*" in the word* shalom *in Numbers 25:12. Although Hebrew is read from right to left, each individual letter in the Sefer Torah is written from left to right. Six letters are written particularly small (e.g., the* alef *in the first word of Lev. 1:1) and 11 letters are written very large (e.g., the bet in the first word of Gen. 1:1).*

–EJ, 14:1101

Tagin *(Aramaic)*—תגין—*(sing.,* tag*), special designs resembling crowns placed by a scribe on the upper left-hand corner of seven of the 22 letters of the Hebrew alphabet in a Torah, tefillin, or mezuzah scroll.* A tag *is generally composed of three flourishes or strokes, each of which resembles a small* "zayin"*–thick on top with a thin line extending downward to the letter. The center stroke is slightly higher than the two end ones. The letters which receive the* tagin *are* שעטנזגצ *(Men. 29b), including the final* ן *and* ץ *(Rashi ad loc.) According to Maimonides the omission of* tagin *does not invalidate the scroll since its inclusion is considered as an "exceptionally beautiful fulfillment of the mitzvah" (Yad. Sefer Torah 7:9). Ashkenazi custom, however, holds that the scrolls are invalid without the appropriate* tagin *(Magen Avraham and Ba'er Heitev to Sh. Ar., OH 36:3).*

Kabbalah places great stress on the mystical meanings of the tagin. *Together with the letters and words of the Torah, every additional stroke or sign is a symbol revealing extraordinary secrets of the universe and creation. The importance of the* tagin *is already emphasized by the Talmud in its vivid description of Moses ascending on high to find God engaged in affixing* tagin *to the letters of the Torah (Men. 29b).*

–EJ, 15:700

Not only did the rabbis seek to detail the exact way in which these letters are to be drawn, but they also ascribed special sanctity to them. In Jewish mysticism, there is an entire genre of literature dealing with the letters of the alphabet. The belief that the alphabet had mystical significance is based on the idea that the 22 letters of the alphabet are spiritual essences which came into being as emanations from God. For example, it was held that bet was chosen as the proper letter with which to begin the creation since it is also the initial letter of the word berakhah—blessing. "Even the way the letters are to be written has significance. R. Ashi declares, 'I have observed that scribes who are most particular add a vertical stroke to the roof of the letter het.' This stroke signifies that 'He lives in the height of the world' since the het is the initial letter of the word hai, 'He lives.' The stroke above the letter indicates that the abode of the living God is on high" (EJ 2:748).

Similarly, each letter, its origin, and its place in the sequence of the alphabet have become the subject of some of the loveliest midrashim and commentaries.

The following are a number of people who do personalized calligraphy. The list is by no means exhaustive.

1. **Sam Beizer**
   2 W. 47th St.
   4th Floor
   New York, N. Y. 10036
2. **Janet Berg**
   3741 Midvale Avenue
   Oakland, Cal. 94602
3. **Lea Fankushen**
   11 Webb Hill Rd.
   Great Neck, N. Y. 11020
4. **Rabbi Gordon Freedman**
   74 Eckley La.
   Walnut Creek, Cal. 94598
5. **Jay Greenspan**
   299 Riverside Drive, Apt. 5E
   New York, N. Y. 10025
6. **Marcia Kaunfer**
   17 Meadowbrook Rd.
   Toronto, Ontario M6b 2S3
7. **Rabbi Stuart Kelman**
   1140 S. Alfred St.
   Los Angeles, Cal. 90035
8. **Sam Koltun**
   860 United Nations Plaza
   New York, N. Y. 10021
9. **Mark Loeb**
   185 Claremont St.
   New York, N. Y. 10027
10. **David Moss**
    c/o Bet Al-pha
    2911 Russell Street
    Berkeley, Calif. 94705
11. **Eric Ray**
    3911 Franklin Ave.
    Los Angeles, Cal. 90027
12. **Joel Rosenberg**
    113 College Ave.
    Somerville, Mass. 02144
13. **Oren Ben-Katool**
    610 Briarwood St.
    Abilene, Tex. 79603

Wear me as a seal
close to your heart
Wear me like a ring
upon your hand
שימני כחותם על לבך
כחותם על זרועך

I will betroth thee unto me
forever — I will
betroth thee unto me
in faithfulness
(HOSEA 2:21-22)

וארשתיך לי לעולם
וארשתיך לי באמונה
(הושע ב׳)

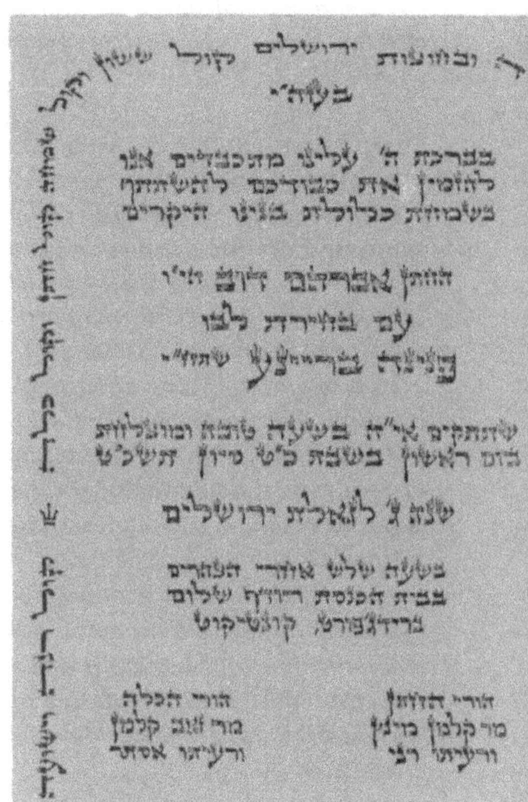

הלל אמר: במקום שאין
אנשים השתדל להיות איש.

Mr. and Mrs. Eric Ray
cordially invite you to worship with them
at nine o'clock on Shabbat morning
May fifth ג אייר תשל״ג
nineteen hundred and seventy three
when their son יעקב שאול
Jason Saul
will be called to the Torah
as a Bar Mitzvah

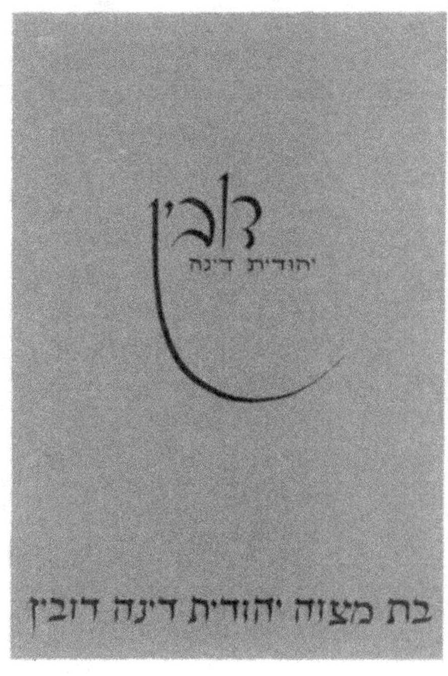

Today, there is a wave of modern sofrim whose artistic abilities have taken them beyond the Sefer Torah, tefillin, and mezuzot (although many still specialize primarily in the traditional three). Along with the value concept of hiddur mitzvah, many sofrim lend their traditional skills to beautifying Bar Mitzvah and wedding invitations, engagement and birth announcements, art posters, bookplates, illuminated Siddurim, Mahzorim and Haggadot, cards for Rosh ha-Shanah, as well as individual texts for framing.

BIBLIOGRAPHY FOR SCRIBAL ARTS

Davidovitch, David. *The Ketuba: Jewish Marriage Contracts through the Ages.* Tel Aviv: E. Lewin-Epstein Ltd., 1968.

Diringer, David. *The Story of the Aleph Bet.* New York: Thomas Yoseloff, 1960.

Leaf, Reuben. *Hebrew Alphabets.* New York: Reuben Leaf Studio, 1950.

This book is currently out of print, but plans are being made for a new printing by Bloch Publishing.

Narkiss, Bezalel. *Hebrew Illuminated Manuscripts.* Jerusalem: *Encyclopaedia Judaica,* and New York: Macmillan, 1969.

Shahn, Ben. *The Alphabet of Creation.* New York: Schocken, 1954.

———. *Love and Joy about Letters,* New York: Grossman Publishers, 1968.

———. *The Shape of Content.* New York: Vintage Books, paperback.

Toby, L. F. *The Art of Hebrew Lettering.* 4th enlarged edition. Tel Aviv, 1970.

Bowler, B. "The Word as Icon." *Typographica 16* (London), December 1967.

An interesting article, although difficult to locate.

Check both the *Encyclopaedia Judaica* and *The Jewish Encyclopedia* for additional information and illustrations.

שלום

Gematria

This is one of the haggadic hermeneutical rules for interpreting the Torah by which a word or phrase is explained on the basis of numerical equivalents. There is a basic kabbalistic myth that the essence of a thing is its name (in Hebrew) since the world was created through speech, i.e., as the name was spoken the thing came into being (see Genesis 1). Since at root the word is composed of letters, and since the letters have numerical equivalents, two words having the same value are considered integrally and fundamentally related.

The basic correspondence is:

70	60	50	40	30	20	10	9	8	7	6	5	4	3	2	1
ע	ס	נ	מ	ל	כ	י	ט	ח	ז	ו	ה	ד	ג	ב	א

400	300	200	100	90	80
ת	ש	ר	ק	צ	פ

There are several different ways of calculating numerical values, however.

1. The standard. Write out a word. Figure out its letter-by-letter equivalents. Compare the value to another word.

Example: אלהים —the name for God used in the creation story—is equal to הטבע —nature.

2. Variation. Sometimes when this does not work out exactly, you have the option to add "one" for the word itself.

Example: Why some do not eat nuts on Rosh ha-Shanah—because אגוז (nuts) equals (almost) חטא (sin).

3. Eliminate zeros. Thus ב =2, ר =2. By reducing the number to its essential integer אדם (man)= אמת (truth).

4. Square the letter and add, or square the word.

Example: The four-letter Name of God squared $(5+6+5+10)^2 = 186 =$ מקום (Place—another Name of God).

5. Rather than take the simple value of the letter, spell out the name of each letter and take its value. Thus ב becomes בית and ל becomes למד. Some letters have various spellings—such as the ה הי, הא, הה and ו וו, ואו.

The last three are rarer forms. There are, however, even more specialized styles. Work with these for a while until you get a feel for the process. Try taking your Hebrew name and seeing what it is equivalent to.

A rare but fascinating form of letter play—virtually a code—is At-Bash את בש. It simply involves substituting the letter at the other end of the alphabet for the letter of a word. Thus א exchanges with ת and ב exchanges with ש.

א ב ג ד ה ו ז ח ט י כ
ת ש ר ק צ פ ע ס נ מ ל

An example of using this in interpretation is in transfering the word מצוה (commandment) into the four-letter Name of God in that מצ exchanges for יה.

Both *The Jewish Encyclopedia* and *The Encyclopaedia Judaica* have excellent articles on gematria—virtually the only material on the subject written in English.

Music

"Song opens a window to the secret places of the soul" (Habad).

There is so much "Jewish music" in the air that one hardly knows where to begin. Somehow the most difficult of situations, the most hidden person, the most complex idea finds a clear expression in simple song that unlocks all its mysteries. Everywhere we turn there is music—what makes it specifically Jewish is often hard to define without a framework. Accordingly, I have grouped Jewish music according to certain ethnic considerations—Hasidic, Yiddish, Israeli, Yemenite, contemporary pop, and contemporary religious. The realms of cantorial, classic liturgical, and instructional music will not be included. This is not meant to be an exhaustive list of all Jewish music, but simply notations to certain Jewish musical things that excite me.

A general note first—you have ears; hearing is the first step. Second, your body senses rhythm—you can be a receptor for musical vibrations if you attune yourself. But to know music is to know how to hear and express it. You have a body that moves to sound. If you are blessed with a voice, learn where it is within you, discover how to bring it out to express yourself in song. If you play an instrument, make that a part of your musical self—use it to sing in ways your body and voice cannot. When all these aspects of yourself are coordinated through the mediating influence of a song, a melody, a musical idea, then you can begin to *know* that music and to make it your own.

HASIDIC MUSIC

If you have never heard Hasidim singing their own music, betake yourself to the Lubavitch or Bobov or Modzitz synagogues, located mainly in New York City and (at least for Lubavitch) also elsewhere, and get into the music as well as the entire scene. The best time for singing and dancing is Simhat Torah or, if possible, a wedding or some such simha in the Hasidic community. At Lubavitch in New York, contact:

Rabbi Shalom Ber Hecht
Machaneh Yisrael House
President St. corner Kingston Ave.
Brooklyn, N. Y. 11213

The essence of Hasidic music centers around the niggun, melody, sometimes simple, sometimes with words, more often starting with words and transcending them. Singing a niggun is the kind of total experience of body and voice that can lift you beyond yourself. It may take thirty or forty repetitions, moving in and out of the words and melody, before you get to *know* a niggun. Beginning with the words, you may soon (fifth or sixth time) pass beyond them into ay ay ay, da da da, and around the tenth to fifteenth time back into the words which suddenly fit completely with the song. This type of singing needs a community, unless you have the ability to stick with it by yourself. Do not give up! You can only discover a niggun when you are ready for it. Place, mood, company, and situation all play roles in this discovery. A niggun you pass over fifty times may suddenly light you up on the fifty-first time. Before that moment, it is work, an effort to move the lips, a strain upon the vocal cords. The music is sometimes so simple or so complex that it eludes you time and again. Finally, you may come to know it in its deepest sense. Once you have felt a niggun in such a way, a simple repetition of it at a later time may enable you to return to that moment of recognition.

Second best to an actual visit to a Hasidic gathering are recordings. These can be difficult to relate to, because the arrangements are often coarse, the niggun is repeated only five or six times, and a certain sameness may pervade the whole record. In order to discover a niggun from a record, you may have to play the record twenty times in various situations —until you suddenly catch youself singing strains of melody. Something has caught you; return to the record, learn the whole niggun, and master it.

The most extensive set of records are those of Lubavitch. They have some seven or eight records which first appeared on Guild recordings and now appear under their own label, Nichoach (Nigunei Hasidei Habad). The first record is my favorite but each of the others have gems of their own. Number four, side one, band two, is a long and beautiful dveikus niggun that is very difficult to master, but very rewarding. Side two has the "Shamil" and the incredible "Stav Yapitu"—a mixture of Hebrew, Yiddish, and Russian which you must learn. Record six has another Russian song that has now become well known—"Nye Bayusia." Buy, beg for, or borrow these records for a great introduction to Hasidic music.

The first two records of the Bobover Hasidim on Collector's Guild are very different in tone and style from Lubavitch record. Bobover Hasidim come from an Austro-Hungarian background, as the pronunciations on the record quickly reveal. Their niggunim are often in a major key and display a good deal more overt assimilation of niggunim from secular sources. Listen to the "El Adon" in all its amazing complexity, the exciting "Hamavdil," and "Bruder Bruder"—which is sometimes called the Hasidic Song of Songs, but may actually simply be a wine song!

Also to be noted are the records of the Modzitz, Gerer, and Viznitz dynasties, and a record of the Bostoner Rebbe's. Ben Zion Shenker records tend toward the cantorial, but have some lovely melodies, such as his "Mizmor L'David."

There are two main books of Hasidic music. Velvel Pasternak's *Songs of the Chassidim* in two volumes (Bloch Publishing, New York, 1971) is a wonderful collection that draws from the entire corpus of Hasidic music; it contains an adequate introduction about Hasidic song, some four hundred niggunim (with guitar chords) and a discography of whatever songs are available on record. The only bad thing about the set is its $25 to $27 price; but recently an abridged paperback edition has come out which is well worth owning. Also worthwhile is the Lubavitch work in two volumes, *Nigunei Chabad* (Hebrew). It has a great twenty-five page introduction on Hasidic music and many niggunim that are not available on records. The major difficulty here is not the price, which is relatively cheap, but the fact that music reads from left to right and Hebrew from right to left (no transliterations are used), so that learning an unfamiliar niggun can be difficult.

YIDDISH SONGS

Yiddish song has, at present, two expressive forms—show music and folk music. The boundary between the two is thin, since much of what we now consider to be old ethnic lullabies and love songs originated in the Yiddish theater. There is still some musical Yiddish theater in lower Manhattan, but mostly one must rely upon the personal appearances and records of the best singers. My two favorites are Theodore Bikel and Ruth Rubin. Bikel has been acting and singing in a million places and if you've never caught him—GO!!! He has a few Yiddish song albums. *Yiddish Folk Songs* and *Yiddish Theatre Songs* (both on Electra) are beautifully arranged and well performed.

Ruth Rubin is a folk musicologist from Montreal who has at least four records that I know of (mostly on Folkways) and two books of Yiddish song—*Jewish Folk Songs* (Oak Publishing) and *A Treasury of Jewish Folksong* (Schocken) which recently appeared in paperback. But seeing her perform, either a capella or with guitar, is a wonderful experience, for the records cannot convey the facial and tonal expressions that help make each one of her songs an intensive experience.

Other Yiddish records worthy of note are those by Nechama Lifschitz, a Russian singer who now lives in Israel. Others include a Folkways record, *The Wall,* which is a collection of songs from an adaptation of John Hersey's novel about the Warsaw Ghetto, ably performed with a few children's songs beautifully sung by Rochelle Horowitz. A record of songs about Vilna produced in Israel, *Songs of the Vilna Ghetto,* while sometimes overorchestrated, has the most moving versions of "Vilna Vilna" and "Dremlen Feygl Af di Tzvaygen" that I have ever heard. Two records entitled *Jewish Music,* by Benedict Solomon on Capitol Records, must be mentioned. They consist of familiar Yiddish songs without any singing; but the orchestrations are so sensitively done that those records have to be considered perfect for just plain listening, for background music if you want to do any readings, or for any other kind of Jewish program. I cannot leave off without mentioning a group of seven women singers called The Pennywhistlers, who have two records on Nonesuch and one with Bikel on Electra. While they mostly sing folk songs of Russia, Hungary, and the Balkans, the few Yiddish songs they do on each record are exciting enough to give me an excuse to mention them and urge you to hear them. Yiddish songs with Balkan harmonies—WOW!!!

ETHNIC JEWISH MUSIC

In other areas of ethnic Jewish music little has been done in the way of recordings. There are two volumes on Westminster called *In Israel Today*—collected "field renditions" of Armenian, Moroccan, Yemenite, and Kurdish melodies—not polished but very exciting rhythmically and melodically. One record has part of the Moroccan Torah trope for Bereshit which is fascinating. It is painful to acknowledge the dearth of Yemenite recordings, especially in Israel. I have found only one ancient ten-inch recording by the Inbal singers, entitled *Yemenite Songs and Dance.*

By all means see the Inbal dance troupe. They tour the United States frequently and perform music and dance that is beautifully choreographed, modern yet acutely sensitive to the tradition of Yemenite culture. This is very refreshing after the cultural distortions passed off in Israel as the "Yemenite Song Festival" and the "Hasidic Song Festival," which are coarse, heavily Westernized imitations of real folk cultures. Ladino music similarly has been victimized—Yehoram Gaon's *Ladino Songs* are overorchestrated and very stagey. The Parvarim's record of Ladino songs is recast in almost a flamenco mold, though the harmonies are pleasing. Best arranged is *Ladino Folk Songs,* sung by Raphael Yair Elnadav on Collectors Guild, though the singing is too cantorial or operatic for my own taste.

One of my all-time favorite albums is *Songs of Yemen and Israel* sung by Itamar on Vanguard. Though unpopular in Israel because of the feminine tenor qualities of his voice, he possesses a range and tonal control in his singing that is nothing short of electrifying. Nearly every song is a gem, both in the singing and the accompaniment by Walter Reim and Ruth Ben-Zvi. In Yemenite chants like "Chus Elohai" and "Nidom Kol Aytz" Itamar's voice is truly astounding—a must to hear. But his second album of pop Israeli songs is a sorry follow-up to this stunning beginning; such, alas, is the occasional fate of a performer who attempts to combine nightclub talent with ethnic material. The same is true of Jo Amar, a Yemenite Israeli, who has produced at least five albums in Israel. While these contain a few songs of true beauty, the vast majority are pop, watered-down versions of an ethnic style. Nonetheless, Jo Amar is worth listening to either live or on records.

DANCE

For Israeli dance music, the main record company is Tikva Records in New York. They have produced some nine or ten records of Israeli dance music with good arrangements and fair singing. The records have been produced with the help of Fred Berk, the famed dance teacher at the 92nd Street YMHA in New York. Included with each record are complete written instructions to all the dances. A Tikva collection is a must for any student or teacher of Israeli dance.

ISRAELI MUSIC

For general Israeli folk music, my favorite records are two well-arranged recordings by the Karmon singers on Vanguard which can also be used for dancing. Bikel has a record of old-time Israeli songs on Electra that is very lovely.

As for pop Israeli music, I can recommend little as I do not enjoy most contemporary Israeli music. There are many records of the yearly song festivals, performances by some of the army entertainment groups, but nothing outstanding. The recording of *Ish Hasid Hayah*, an amalgam of Hasidic tales and songs, has a few fine moments but is generally bland and tasteless. The recordings of *Six-Day War Songs* has my favorite performance of "Yerushalayim Shel Zahav," which, despite its overpopularization, still remains one of the finer Israeli songs of the past decade.

The songbook entitled *All My Songs (Almost)*, published by *Yidiot Acharonot* in 1967, contains forty-two songs by Naomi Shemer, one of the best songwriters in Israel. Such favorites as "Mahar" and "Yerushalayim Shel Zahav" are included, and the volume is highly recommended.

For the nostalgic halutz—pioneer—there is a two-volume record set called *Hayu Zmanim*, which catalogs in story and song the founding of Israel from the early pioneering days to the War of Independence. There is an integrity to the music of that period that has been lost in recent Israeli music. New Israeli songs are slavish and trite in their imitation of Western pop music. They pay occasional lip service to Yemenite, Spanish, or Hasidic influences, but treat those traditions with a marked lack of sensitivity to their uniqueness.

JEWISH RELIGIOUS MUSIC

New Jewish religious music owes a great debt to Shlomo Carlebach. Shlomo has been performing, recording, and teaching around the world for the past twelve or fifteen years. He has a large number of excellent songs to his credit that have been accepted as "traditional" in many Jewish circles. His records on Zimrani and other labels are well arranged and convey some of the excitement of his performances. Since he travels a great deal, it is relatively easy to get to one of his concerts almost anywhere in the United States or in Israel. He has recently put out a songbook with guitar arrangements published by Zimrani. Like any prolific song writer, some of his material is repetitive, but with songs like "Esa Eynai," "Pitchu Li," and "Haneshama Lach" to his credit, who can complain?

Also worth hearing are two records by the Pirchei boys' choir of Agudah which appear on Tikva Recordings. The songs are forceful, tuneful, and very singable. The songs of Boruch Chait as performed by The Rabbi's Sons on Emes Records are generally enjoyable and occasionally brilliant. Since most of the songs of these new writers are drawn from the Siddur, they can be used within the context of a religious service with little or no adaptation. By being aware of new songs, one can try to implement a theology of shir hadash, a new song, into our prayer life. The Gerer Rebbe has stated: "Were I blessed with a sweet voice, I would sing you new hymns and songs every day, for with the daily rejuvenation of the world, new songs are created." New songs can rejuvenate a familiar prayer or verse in such a way as to re-create the original moment in which that prayer was conceived.

We have dealt here with specifically Jewish song, but new songs are everywhere waiting for the proper setting and time for their use as niggunim. For anyone involved in leading group tefillot, prayers, the introduction of a new niggun can be a momentous event that can transform an entire service. A new "L'Kha Dodi" culled from a niggun with other words, or a new "El Adon" taken from a nonreligious setting remove an air of "tiredness" from oft-repeated prayers. Kavvanah is restored and real prayer in the language of the neginah, the real language of the soul, is expressed. Here are a number of different melodies from other settings I have used or heard used for "L'Kha Dodi":

1. "Scarborough Fair" (Simon and Garfunkel)
2. Israeli folk songs like:
   "Ma Avarech"
   "Ma Navu al Hehorim"
   "L'or Chiyuchech"
3. "Anim Zmiros"
4. "Hashmi-i-ni et Koleh"
5. "Ki Anu Ameho" (from Lubavitch)

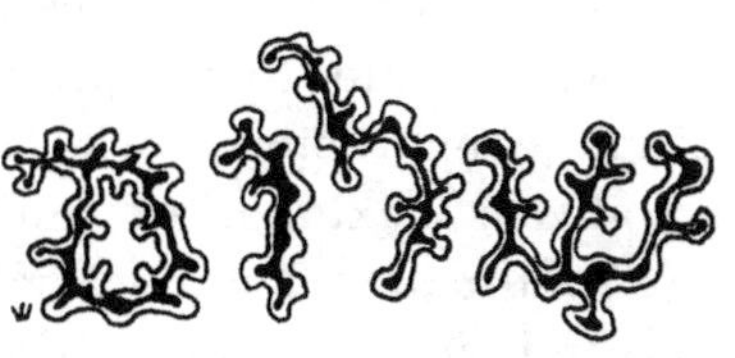

This process has been going on with "Adon Olam" for a long time—it should be transferred to other familiar prayers as well. In this way, Jewish music grows organically from the peoples and cultures within and around Judaism. Discrimination and sensitivity are necessary components in choosing niggunim for new situations; e.g., "The Yellow Rose of Texas" is grating for "L'Kha Dodi"—but "Those Were the Days" is very fitting for "Hashivenu Alecho" upon returning the Torah to the ark.

"How do you pray to the Lord? Is it possible to pray to the Lord with words alone? Come, I will show you a new way to the Lord—not with words or sayings, but with song. We will sing, and the Lord on high will understand us"(Rabbi Nahman of Bratzlav).

The Jewish Music Council offers information, catalogs, and resources on Jewish music to individuals and groups. Write them at:

National Jewish Welfare Board
15 E. 26th St.
New York, N. Y. 10010

שלום

Film

One of the major reasons that the Renaissance succeeded in Italy during the fifteenth and sixteenth centuries to the extent that it did was the availability of patronage from the church and wealthy guilds. Willing to pay the going rate, they enabled artists and sculptors to transform their creative energies into works of art. Through this medium, the greatest craftsmen in the history of Western civilization were commissioned to create.

In our day we are not quite so fortunate. Even if there is talent available it may, sadly, never see the light of day or the darkness of a movie theater because of the absence of patronage. Whereas a lack of money is a problem in all the creative arts, it is particularly debilitating in the area of film because of the tremendous expense of film-making. A good rule of thumb is that every minute of documentary footage that you see costs between $750 and $1,250. If a film-maker is lucky, or if he is not so picky, he might be able to come slightly under the $750 per minute amount.

The independent Jewish film-maker finds himself at a dead end even before he starts. He can't turn to the Jewish organizational structure or to local rabbis because film is not a priority item.

It has been demonstrated over and over again that film and TV are the major communication media to vast segments of the population, including the young and the collegiate. Yet the primary focus of the Jewish community is still, to a large extent, the printed word. Sadly, the leadership of the Jewish community is not willing to risk an expenditure of a few thousand dollars on the chance that a good film will be produced.

This does not refer to organizational films such as those made specifically for a single constituency. UJA, Hadassah, and the Eternal Light, to name a few, are always making films, but the film-maker is limited to producing "the message" of the organization. Such films are generally noncontroversial, nonpolitical, and lacking in original creativity. This is not the fault of the artist; generally, and perhaps understandably, the review boards of such organizations prefer to deal with subjects in a simplistic manner.

So where does that leave the independent film-maker who wishes to make a film on a Jewish subject that does not smell of institutionalism?

He could contact:

Encounter Films
254 W. 54th St.
New York, N. Y. 10019

the only independent company offering grants to young film-makers to make films that are primarily addressed to a collegiate audience. In the two years of Encounter Films' existence, over one hundred proposals for films have been offered, but less than five have been granted. This is not because of lack of good ideas, but because of a lack of funds. But don't be discouraged from contacting Encounter; who knows . . . if you have a good idea, they might try to come up with some funds. Their limit is generally $10,000, sometimes less, rarely more.

On a long shot you might contact National Educational Television (NET) or even, a longer shot, one of the major networks.

It is rather depressing but that is the story. Except for Encounter, you're pretty much on your own.

Out of this horror, though, have emerged a few creative films which are certainly worth viewing. I have noted their approximate length and included a short annotation. Their rental fees are generally under $50. They can be rented by contacting

J. J. Goldberg
American Jewish Congress
15 E. 84th St.
New York, N. Y. 10029

The AJC, the most sympathetic organization to the new Jewish media, will do the legwork for you in getting the film.

Also, a new organization:

New Jewish Media Project
c/o Elaine Slackman or Bernie Timberg
Judah Magnus Museum
20911 Russell St.
Berkeley, Cal. 94705

is in the process of assembling resource archives. They are also interested in fostering communication between artists involved in Jewish media and stimulating experimental projects. They have a catalog called *B'rashet* which appears three times a year. It can be obtained by writing to:

Rich Phillips
c/o Saguaro Blossom Press
819 N. First Ave., # 102
Tucson, Ariz. 85719

LIST A

1. *Shalom, Israel.* Joe Goldberg. 11 min. color.
An exciting kaleidoscopic view of Israel, good sound, good photography.
2. *It Goes.* J. Greene. 11 min. color.
Why young Americans are interested in aliyah, interesting interviews.
3. *Chusid.* J. Greene. 35 min. b/w.
A sensitive film on the Hasidim of Williamsburg.
4. *Carlebach.* J. Green. 25 min. color.
A behind-the-scenes portrait of Shlomo Carlebach in concert.
5. *Never Again.* Giora Neiman. 25 min. b/w.
An unsympathetic critical look at JDL activities and a visit to Camp JDL.
6. *Black Jews of Elmont* (New Jersey). Avi Goren. 25 min. color.
A fascinating look at a fascinating community—unusual.
7. *Zieglerville, An Encounter in Elul.* WUJS 25 min. b/w.
A view of the radical Jewish community in caucus—an important document.
8. *Aba.* Bernie Timberg. 20 min. color.
A warm portrayal of an old Israeli Jew.
9. *Bar Mitzvah.* Bernie Timberg. 20 min. color.
Tongue-in-cheek impression of the Bar Mitzvah ceremony as viewed by thirteen-year-olds.
10. *Milk and Honey Experience.* Yehuda Neeman. 35 min. color.
Funny film about American college students on their junior year at the Hebrew University.

The following list of films was produced for general audiences but the subject matter is either significantly or partially Jewish. The best thing to do is to write for the catalogs of the two largest film rental agencies:

1. Audio Brandon (depending on location)—ask for catalog of Jewish films.

34 MacQuesten Pkwy. South
Mt. Vernon, N. Y. 10550

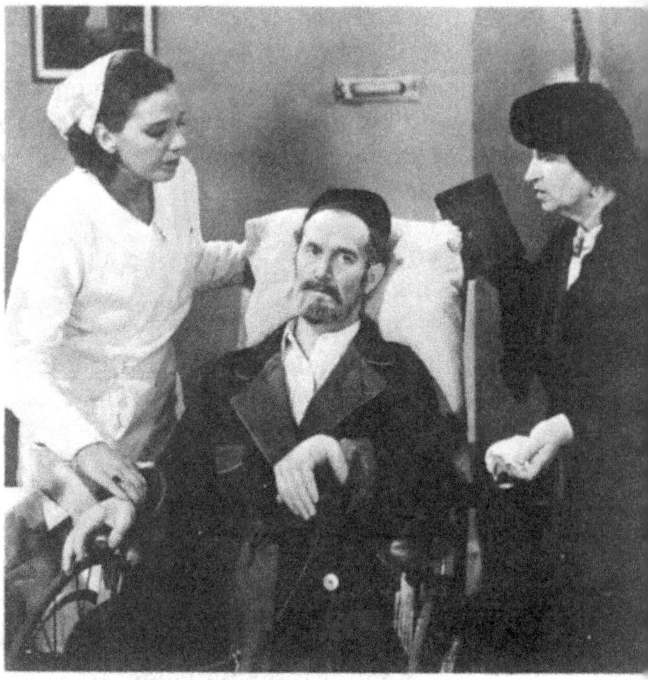

406 Clement St.
San Francisco, Cal. 94118

1619 N. Cherokee
Los Angeles, Cal. 90028

8615 Directors Row
Dallas, Tex. 75247

512 Burlington Ave.
La Grange Ill. 60525

2. Contemporary Films

Princeton Rd.
Hightstown, N. Y. 08520

828 Custer Ave.
Evanston, Ill. 60202

1714 Stockton Street
San Francisco, Cal. 94133

RECOMMENDED AUDIENCE KEY
H—Heavy
L—Light
TA—Teenage or Adult
PT—Young children
For any further information regarding who distributed any film ever made call:
Motion Picture Association of America
Research Dept.
522 Fifth Ave.
New York, N. Y. 10036
(212-TN7-1200)

From out of the thousands of possible films, the following thirty are suggested. I have asterisked my personal favorites, but don't take my word for it. Order the catalogs and make up your own mind.

LIST B

	Feature films	*Distributors*
	ISRAELI	
TA,L	*Sallah	*Brandon*
TA,L	Impossible on Saturday	*Brandon*
	My Father's House	*East Coast Productions* *16 W. 46th St.* *New York, N. Y. 10036*
TA,H	Matzor	*Cannon Releasing Corp.* *405 Park Ave.* *New York, N. Y. 10022*
TA,H	Dreamer	*Cannon*
	Every Bastard a King	*Continental Distributors & Walter Reade Corp.* *241 E. 34th St.* *New York, N. Y. 10016*
	CZECH	
TA,H	*The Shop on Main Street	*JWB* *15 E. 26th St.* *New York, N. Y. 10010*

TA,H	*Transport from Paradise	*Grove* *53 E. 11 Street* *New York, N. Y. 10003*
TA,H	Diamonds of the Night	*Grove*
TA,H	The Fifth Horseman Is Fear	*Brandon*
TA,H	Closely Watched Trains	*Brandon*
TA,H	Sweet Light in a Dark Room	*Brandon*
FRENCH		
TA,H	The Golem	*JWB*
TA,L	The Two of Us	*Cinema V* *595 Madison Ave.* *New York, N. Y. 10022*
TA,L	*The Confession	*Paramount Pictures* *1 Gulf & Western Plaza* *New York, N. Y. 10023*
POLISH		
TA,H	Border Street (Ulica Granicza)	*Brandon*
YIDDISH		
TA,H	*The Dybbuk	*Cinema Service Corp.* *106 West End Ave.* *New York, N. Y. 10023*
ITALIAN		
TA,H	Kapo	*Brandon*
TA,H	The Condemned of Altona	*Brandon*
TA,H	*In the Garden of the Finzi-Continis	*Cinema V*
GERMAN		
TA,H	The Black Fox	*Brandon*
AMERICAN		
PT,TA	A Wall in Jerusalem	*Eyr Corp.* *78 E. 56th St.* *New York, N. Y.*
PT,TA	Cast a Giant Shadow	*United Artists* *729 7th Avenue* *New York, N. Y.*
PT,TA	*Exodus	*United Artists*
TA	Gentlemen's Agreement	*ADL* *315 Lexington Avenue* *New York, N. Y.*
TA	The Pawnbroker	*Brandon, JWB*
TA	The Song and the Silence	*JWB*
TA	*The Fixer	*Films, Inc.* *3501 Queens Blvd.* *Long Island City, N. Y. 11101*
TA	The Last Angry Man	*Brandon*
PT	Me and the Colonel	*Brandon*
PT,TA	*Diary of Anne Frank	*Films, Inc.*
TA	*Judgment at Nuremberg	*United Artists*
TA	Ship of Fools	*Contemporary*
TA	House of Rothschild	*Films, Inc.*
TA	I Accuse	*Films, Inc.*

Other lists of Jewish films

1. The catalog of the Jewish Audio-Visual Materials Committee which can be purchased for a couple of dollars from:

The American Association for Jewish Education (AAJE)
114 Fifth Ave.
New York, N. Y. 10011

It lists just about every institutional film made in the last ten years with a heavy emphasis on Israel. Out of the hundreds of films listed, you might find a number that will suit your purpose. This listing would be particularly valuable for the Jewish educator who might be interested in an assembly program for his/her Hebrew school. Read the comments on each film carefully before deciding.

2. The film catalog of:

Jewish Chautauqua Society
838 Fifth Ave.
New York, N. Y. 10021

They will rent films on a variety of subjects including Soviet Jewry. Most of their films are also listed in the comprehensive catalog of the AAJE.

3. **National Bnai Brith Hillel**
1640 Rhode Island Ave. N. W.
Washington, D. C. 20036

They have an extensive catalog of full-length feature films of Jewish interest with lists of distributors and annotations. They include excellent suggestions for utilizing these films programmatically.

Filmstrips

1. The largest selection of educational filmstrips is available from:

Union of American Hebrew Congregations
838 Fifth Ave.
New York, N. Y. 10021

Dr. Samuel Grand must have made a hundred filmstrips on subjects ranging from the holidays to Bible stories. I would consider this listing a must for anyone interested in elementary Jewish education.

2. Another resource for filmstrips is:

The Eternal Light
3080 Broadway
New York, N.Y. 10027

They, too, have a variety of subjects and their work is an important resource for Jewish educators.

The Jewish press and periodicals

This is intended as a brief, highly subjective list of significant Jewish publications in America. It would have made sense to begin with an authoritative and quality Jewish newspaper, daily or weekly, that gives the news and provides analysis. It is a strange and unfortunate irony that American Jews, who read so many newspapers and magazines, have failed to establish such a publication. In its absence, we can do worse than read the *New York Times*, whose coverage of both American and foreign Jewish concerns is quite good. There is a lot of Jewish material these days in the *Village Voice*, while there is good editorial coverage of the scene (though it is often harsh on Israel) in the *Christian Science Monitor*, a daily published in Boston.

Without any doubt, the most important Jewish periodical published in America is *Commentary*. Founded and sponsored by the American Jewish Committee, *Commentary* began in 1945 as a monthly and is still going strong under the powerful guiding hand of Norman Podhoretz, editor since 1960. *Commentary* sees itself as far more than a Jewish magazine, and is involved in most societal and political concerns. Specifically Jewish material accounts for only about one-quarter of the magazine's content. In the last few years many readers have noticed a shift from *Commentary's* liberal and frequently avant-garde nature ten years ago to a more defensive and conservative posture in both Jewish and general matters. Even at its worst—and *Commentary* has a reputation, especially these days, for cynicism, great aloofness, and the capacity to be both stuffy and boring—it is almost always intelligent, responsible, and thoughtful; occasionally it is brilliant. It does, to be sure, speak for much of the "Jewish Establishment" in terms of public policy and social issues in both Jewish and general realms. Almost every significant Jewish writer and thinker of mainstream thought has appeared in its pages.

Commentary
165 E. 56th St.
New York, N. Y. 10022

If *Commentary's* chief rival on the general scene is the *New York Review of Books*, on Jewish matters it is, in some sense, *Midstream*. *Midstream* has always been *Commentary's* poor cousin and is the recipient and publisher of many articles which *Commentary* rejects. Some of these can be quite good. Unlike *Commentary*, *Midstream* is a completely Jewish magazine and is especially interested in problems concerning Israel, Zionism, and the Middle East. It is sponsored by the Herzl Foundation of the Jewish Agency, appears monthly, and is edited by Ronald Sanders.

Midstream
515 Park Ave.
New York, N. Y. 10022

Next follow three independent magazines, which contain most of the intelligent writing about American Jewish life that can be found these days, especially when it is of a critical nature. The oldest and biggest of these is *The Jewish Spectator*, which, under the editorship of Trude Weiss-Rosmarin, publishes a hodgepodge of material on Jewish life and scholarship. Unfortunately, the quality of the articles is generally weak; they are frequently thin, unsubstantial, and even careless. What makes *The Jewish Spectator* indispensable are its monthly editorial columns, written by Dr. Weiss-Rosmarin, which constitute the only continuous commentary on American Jewish affairs that is lively, courageous, and not hesitant about calling individuals and organizations into account when need be.

The Jewish Spectator
250 W. 57th St.
New York, N. Y. 10019

Next comes *Response*, which was begun in 1967 by a group of Columbia undergraduates, under the leadership of Alan Mintz. It began as a stuffy and esoteric little magazine, and has grown into a regular quarterly. Although it has other functions, *Response* is also as close as one can come to a Jewish literary magazine. Originally a student publication, *Response* now attracts lively and intelligent writers of all ages who are concerned not only with the critique of American Jewish life, which by now comes naturally to so many of us, but who are dedicated also to creating alternatives to what currently exists. Often informal, sometimes ludicrous, occasionally obscene or outrageous, *Response* is rarely boring. It is edited by Bill Novak.

Response
Box 1496
Brandeis University
Waltham, Mass. 02154

Sh'ma is the newest publication on the Jewish scene. It appears twice a month, is very small, and provides commentary on Jewish issues. It is published by a group of dissident and articulate intellectuals whose primary allegiance is to the Jewish community, but so far it is a mouthpiece for various viewpoints. Unfortunately, its format rarely allows for more than brief comments on particular viewpoints. Edited by Eugene Borowitz.

Sh'ma
Box 567
Port Washington, N.Y. 11050

Other independent Jewish periodicals include one magazine *(Davka)* and various Jewish student newspapers, of which there are about fifty as this is being written. The best and most regular of these is Boston's

Genesis Two
298 Harvard St.
Cambridge, Mass. 02138

Less regular but no less interesting are *The Jewish Radical* (Berkeley) and the *Jewish Liberation Journal.* For information about the Jewish student press since its inception several years ago, see Bill Novak and Robert Goldman, "The Rise of the Jewish Student Press," in *Conservative Judaism,* Winter 1971.

Since things change so fast among the Jewish student press, the reader is advised to contact the Jewish Student Press Service for up-to-date information. Their address is

36 W. 37th St.
New York, N. Y. 10018

The JSP-S serves virtually all independent Jewish student publications in North America, which presently number over fifty and represent a combined monthly press run of four hundred thousand. In addition, twenty periodicals are served in England, Italy, Germany, Uruguay, and Israel. The JSP-S plays an essential role for these newspapers by providing them with original features and research material. This service is essential to those papers which suffer from a lack of time and/or resources. By establishing contacts abroad and maintaining an Israeli Bureau, the JSP-S has become a recognized link between Israel and the Jewish students on American campuses. In addition, they publish a complete guide to the Jewish student press. This guide is periodically updated and also contains information on how to begin and run a Jewish student paper. The editor at this time is David DeNola; the administrator is Hannah Koevary. The JSP is an independent agency (legally and structurally) and an affiliate of the North American Jewish Student Appeal.

Judaism, a quarterly, first appeared in 1952. Published by the American Jewish Congress, it is as serious as you can get without quite crossing the boundary into pure scholarship. It always contains something of interest, although it tends to be rather specific and technical. But even for the beginner it can be a useful plunge into the world of Jewish thought. Edited by Robert Gordis.

Judaism
15 E. 84th St.
New York, N. Y. 10028

For those interested in the history of American Jewry, there are two fine quarterlies available:

American Jewish Historical Quarterly
2 Thornton Rd.
Waltham, Mass. 02154

and **American Jewish Archives**
3101 Clifton
Cincinnati, Ohio 45220

Each of the four major branches of Jewish life in America publishes a magazine. Except for the

Reconstructionist
15 W. 86th St.
New York, N. Y. 10024

which appears monthly, they are all quarterlies. The most generally diverse is the *C.C.A.R. Journal,* published by the

Central Conference of American Rabbis
790 Madison Ave.
New York, N. Y. 10021

which contains a fair amount of speculative material on theological and biblical subjects. The strongest of the four is probably

Conservative Judaism
3080 Broadway
New York, N. Y. 10027

which is published by the Rabbinical Assembly. The Orthodox quarterly is

Tradition
220 Park Ave. South
New York, N. Y. 10003

Younger readers may want to consult a fine monthly magazine, written for high school students, and published by the Reform Movement. *Keeping Posted* appears monthly.

Keeping Posted
838 Fifth Ave.
New York, N. Y. 10021

There are dozens of Jewish newspapers in America, most of them intended for local consumption in the various communities in which they are published. The largest of these are probably the Boston

Jewish Advocate (weekly)
251 Causeway
Boston, Mass. 02114

Detroit's
Detroit Jewish News
17515 W. 9 Mile Road
Southfield, Mich. 48075

Los Angeles's
B'nai Brith Messenger
2510 W. 7th St.
Los Angeles, Calif. 90057

Philadelphia's
Jewish Exponent (weekly)
1513 Walnut St.,
Philadelphia, Pa. 19102

and
Jewish Week and American Examiner (weekly)
3 E. 40th St.
New York, N. Y. 10016

All three of these contain the usual stuff that is common to all of the papers, but also some decent news coverage and a few intelligent articles as well. Also significant is the nationally circulated
Jewish Post and Opinion (weekly)
611 N. Park Ave.
Indianapolis, Ind. 46204

which contains articles and columnists of some interest. Also of note is the Jewish Telegraphic Agency, a news service which sends out dispatches five times a week, dealing with national and international Jewish matters.
Jewish Telegraphic Agency
660 1st Ave.
New York, N. Y. 10016

Monthlies of some note and varying degrees of interest and quality include
Hadassah Magazine
65 E. 52nd St.
New York, N. Y. 10022

and **Jewish Currents**
22 E. 17th St.
New York, N. Y. 10003

Israel Magazine
110 E. 59th St.
New York, N. Y. 10022

All are good, and deal respectively with general Jewish and Zionist issues, Israel (especially through photographs), and Old Left Jewish concerns. Two Zionist-oriented monthlies include
Jewish Frontier
45 E. 17th St.
New York, N. Y. 10003

and the **American Zionist**
145 E. 32nd St.
New York, N. Y. 10016

Other monthlies include Bnai Brith's
National Jewish Monthly
1640 Rhode Island Ave. N.W.
Washington, D. C. 20036

and the **Jewish Digest**
P. O. B. 153
Houston, Tex. 77001

There are many other magazines, but they are all house organs and of little interest to the general reader. A complete list of Jewish publications (except for student publications) can be found in each issue of the ***American Jewish Year Book***, an annual summary and guide to Jewish life in America.
165 E. 56th St.
New York, N. Y. 10022

Creating a Jewish library

AM HA-SEFER: NOTES ON CREATING A TRADITIONAL JEWISH LIBRARY

There is nothing more uniquely characteristic of the style of Jewish religious life than the great love Jews have for holy books. Customs such as kissing books, not leaving books open when not in use, keeping books in proper places, being sure that closed books are placed face up—all these point to a sense of the holy book as a living being, one who is to be treated with the honor you would give to a beloved friend and teacher.

Perhaps the most basic assertion of Jewish spirituality is that God speaks to man through the ongoing process of the Word as found in our sacred texts. Both prayer and study, the two basic forms of Jewish spiritual expression, find their source in the encounter that takes place in the presence of the printed page.

The notes which follow, recommending particular books in various areas of Jewish study, have a particular Jew in mind. You are neither a yeshivah student nor an aspiring academic Jewish scholar. You have studied Hebrew, can handle (i.e., understand with relative ease) the Bible and Siddur, have perhaps studied a bit of Talmud or Midrash, and want to become involved in more serious Jewish study, on your own or with friends. You are interested in owning some traditional Hebrew texts, but find yourself overwhelmed by the extent of the literature and the great number of editions of each text that the bookseller can present to you. What follows, then, is a beginner's guide to selecting Jewish texts for study in the various areas of traditional learning.

A few general warnings to book-buyers

Hebrew religious books are generally priced quite cheaply, especially when compared with English hardbacks of the same size. However, the quality of printing, binding, etc., especially regarding books published in Israel, is very poor by comparison, so that special precautions should be taken. Make sure the book is well bound, especially if it's a large, heavy volume. In any case, open the pages carefully, bit by bit, as your elementary school librarian must have shown you, or you will probably break the binding. Flip through the book quickly before you buy it to make sure there aren't pages missing, that some pages aren't bound in upside-down, etc. Most traditional texts published today are photo-offsets; make sure there aren't any blank pages where the machine didn't take, and the like.

Hebrew booksellers are not the most gracious of all people. They will often try to sell you an edition other than the one you want; stick to your guns. If you are in a city like New York or Jerusalem, where one guy does not have a monopoly, it often pays to compare prices. Bargaining is acceptable, especially in Israel. I have found that ordering traditional texts through Hayyim Ben-Arza, on Rehov ha-Gai in the Old City of Jerusalem, is about as nice a way as any to get these books.

NOTE: Following each division is a full bibliography of the English works mentioned in this article. Also, capital letters are used (e.g., RaDaK) to show that only those letters are used in Hebrew to form the acronym (e.g., רד"ק).

Bible

The Masoretic text of the Hebrew Bible is available in any number of reasonable editions. Since your one-volume Hebrew Bible will be a constant reference point for any kind of Jewish study, you want one small enough to carry around conveniently, but large enough to have very clear print. See the JPS Bibles, particularly the new translations of the Torah, Psalms, Isaiah, etc.

For understanding the meaning of the biblical text (peshat), modern commentaries are generally more valuable than traditional sources. Such Jewish scholars as E. A. Speiser, Nahum Sarna, Robert Gordis, and others have written commentaries in English which will be of great help in dealing with the biblical text. There is no reason to avoid the modern critical commentaries written by Christian scholars as well; most of the volumes of the *Anchor Bible* series are quite good. A Jewish-sponsored series of that type is due for publication within the next few years, and should be most exciting. Of the modern Jewish commentaries written in Hebrew, those of A. Ehrlich *(Mikra ki-Feshuto)*, David Zvi Hoffmann *(Perush al Sefer va-Yikra, Devarim*, etc.), Yehezkel Kaufmann *(Joshua, Judges)*, Moshe Weinfeld *(Devarim)*, Umberto Cassuto *(Me-Adam ad Noah, Mi-Noah ad Avraham, Perush . . . Shemot)*, M. Z. Segal *(Samuel)*, and Z. P. Chayes *(Psalms)* are particularly worthy of your attention. For a simple and direct attempt to understand the text, while avoiding serious critical problems, the commentary of A. S. Hartom on the entire Bible is quite usable. It is written in vocalized simple modern Hebrew, which will be a great blessing to the beginner. But do check it out against a more scholarly commentary, perhaps in English.

The best introduction to an understanding of the traditional Jewish Bible commentators is the work of Nehama Liebowitz, available in many recensions, both in Hebrew and English. Ms. Liebowitz has a great feeling for the questions raised by commentators, and her works are a fine anthology of traditional Hebrew commentaries.

If you want to begin working your way through Rashi's commentary on the Torah, which is a great compendium of traditional Jewish understanding of the text, you will find the Rosenbaum-Silbermann edition of Rashi (Hebrew Publishing Company) a good place to start. That gives you the full text of Rashi in vocalized square characters, as well as a full English translation and some worthwhile notes. You can now begin to do the same with the RaMBaN's commentary, fascinating particularly as a *theological* understanding of the text, using the edition by Chavel *(Perush Ha-RaMBan*, published by Mosad ha-Rav Kuk in two volumes) and Chavel's English translation of RaMBaN, now published on Genesis.

The traditional Hebrew Bible with commentaries is known as *Mikraot Gedolot*. There are many editions available; make sure the one you get is easily legible. A good *Mikraot Gedolot* should at least contain Rashi, Ibn Ezra, RaMBaN, RaSHBaM, Seforno on the Torah. The best editions will also have RaDaK, a very valuable commentary on Bereshit. On Neviim and Ketuvim, look for Rashi, RaMBaN, Ibn Ezra, and RaLBaG as the basic commentaries in a good set. The commentary of RaDaK on Psalms, usually printed separately and now available in a modern edition, is very valuable. The commentary of Rabbenu Bahya on the Torah, now also available in a modern Mosad ha-Rav Kuk edition, follows the medieval fourfold interpretation of Scripture, and is a very beautiful work, filled with both rationalist and kabbalistic readings of the Torah.

Beware of those editions of the Bible which may be billed as Mikraot Gedolot, but in fact contain only Rashi and various nineteenth-century parables and homilies, usually in Yiddish, unless you are particularly interested in that sort of material.

Anchor Bible. Garden City, N.Y.: Doubleday, 1964.

Chavel, Charles B. *Ramban: Commentary on the Torah: Genesis.* New York: Shilo, 1972.

Rosenbaum, M. and Silbermann, A.M. *Pentateuch with Targum Onkelos, Haphtaroth and Rashi's Commentary.* 5 vols. New York: Hebrew Publishing Co, 1934.

Sarna, Nahum. *Understanding Genesis*. New York: McGraw-Hill, 1966. New York: Schocken, paperback.

Mishnah and Talmud

For the study of Mishnah, the seven-volume edition by H. Albeck (Mosad Bialik) gives you a clear vocalized text and a simple commentary in modern Hebrew. You may combine this with the one-volume English edition of Danby, which is generally thought to be a reliable translation. For a summary of the talmudic discussion on the Mishnah, without going through the Talmud itself, the traditional commentary of Ovadiah of Bertinore (Bartenura, to your Hebrew bookseller) is useful. Good study of Mishnah should also involve study of the Tosefta, which is a larger collection of contemporary materials that were not included in the Mishnah itself. If your Hebrew skills are good, the edition of the Tosefta by Saul Lieberman, with his compendious commentary *Tosefta Ki-Feshutah* (published by the Jewish Theological Seminary), is an invaluable guide.

You may also want to consult the halakhic midrashim when you study the Mishnah. Here you will find materials parallel to the Mishnah and Tosefta, but arranged according to biblical verses, rather than the "systematic" mishnaic order. The main texts here are the Mekhilta to Exodus, the Sifra to Leviticus, and the Sifrei to Numbers and Deuteronomy. Use the editions of Horowitz-Rabin for the Mekhilta (along with the Lauterbach–Jewish Publication Society translation and M. Kadushin's *A Conceptual Approach to the Mekhilta),* and for Sifrei to Numbers, the Isaak Hirsch Weiss edition of the Sifra, and the Finkelstein edition for the Sifrei to Deuteronomy.

Study of the Talmud has been very much facilitated these days by a number of modern editions of various tractates. The most impressive of the modern editions is that of Adin Steinsaltz, currently available to the first six tractates, and coming out over the next decade or so on the entire Talmud. Here you will find a fully vocalized and punctuated text, a punctuated Rashi, and a commentary in clear modern Hebrew. This edition obviates many of the old difficulties in Talmud study, such as determining whether a particular statement is a question or an answer, finding the end of a sentence, etc. Of course, scholars do not always agree with Steinsaltz's determinations of the formerly fluid text, but for the student it is an invaluable boon.

If you are interested in buying a more traditional edition of the entire Talmud (usually published in twenty folio volumes), there are several things to watch out for. First and perhaps foremost, check the bindings. Bindings have to be very strong to bear the weight of these tomes, especially if they are to do more than decorate your shelves. The Israeli editions are particularly notorious for weak bindings. Next, make sure that the print is large enough for comfortable reading. To check this out, take a look at the Hiddushei Haggadot in the MaHaRSHA, published at the back of each volume. If you can read that without killing your eyes, you're doing well. Make sure your Talmud is a reprint of the Vilna edition, by far the most careful of the Talmud printings, and that it contains the RIF (Isaac Alfasi's abbreviated version of the Talmud), with its own commentaries at the back of the volume.

If you have a rich and pious father-in-law who's willing to foot the bill, the deluxe edition of the Vilna Talmud, reprinted by the Shulsinger Brothers in New York, is a thing of beauty.

Albeck, H. and Yalon, H. *Shisha Sidre Mishnah.* 6 vols. Jerusalem: Bialik Institute; Tel Aviv: Dvir, 1952–56.

Danby, H. *The Mishnah.* Oxford: Oxford University Press, 1933.

Horovitz, H.S. and Rabin, A. *Mechilta d'Rabbi Ismael.* Frankfurt on the Main: J. Kauffmann, 1928–31; reprinted, Jerusalem: Bamberger and Wahrmann, 1960.

Finkelstein, Louis and Horovitz, H.S. *Sifre d'be Rab.* Berlin: Gesellschaft zur Forderung der Wissenschaft des Judentums, 1939; reprint. New York: JTS, 1969.

Kadushin, Max. *A Conceptual Approach to the Mekilta: A Basic Text for the Study of the Midrash.* New York: JTS, 1969. New York: J. David, paperback.

Lauterbach, J.Z. *Mekilta de-Rabbi Ishmael.* 3 vols. Philadelphia: JPS, 1933–35.

Lieberman, Saul. *The Tosefta,* 3 vols. to date. New York: JTS, 1955–.

Lieberman, Saul. *Tosefta ki-Feshutah,* 11 vols. to date. New York: JTS, 1955–.

Steinsaltz, Adin, ed. *The Babylonian Talmud.* 6 vols. to date. Jerusalem: Israel Institute of Talmud Publications, 1969–.

Weiss, Isaak Hirsch. *Sifra deve Rav: Hu sefer torat kohanim.* Vienna: J. Schlossberg, 1862; reprinted New York: Om, 1946.

Midrash Haggadah

The great storehouse of rabbinic thought on nonlegal matters is found in the many volumes of the Midrash, as well as in the haggadic passages in the Talmud. For a list of the major midrashim and the best editions, see below.

The best way to begin studying midrashic literature is not to read straight through a midrashic text, as one traditionally does with Talmud, but rather to deal with a particular theme, and try to trace it through midrashic literature. You might take a favorite biblical story, for example (try something like the creation of man, the akedah, the burning bush, etc.), and trace it through midrashic literature. For this type of work, the various compendiums of midrashic literature are often more valuable than the texts themselves. You might begin with Louis Ginzberg's *Legends of the Jews,* and, using his footnotes, track down the original sources. For those who want to deal immediately with Hebrew texts, M. M. Kasher's *Torah Shelemah* is of tremendous value and contains all the basic haggadic sources, with many notes by Kasher himself. You will need another rich relative to buy this set for you. Something like twenty-three volumes now out have not quite made it to the beginning of Leviticus!

A briefer and highly readable midrashic collection is the *Midrash ha-Gadol,* a thirteenth-century Yemenite text on the first four books of the Torah, now published in modern editions.

Much of the mythical, kabbalistic, and demonological material absent from the more "classical" texts is to be found in the *Yalkut Re-ubeni,* published, like the others, following the order of the Torah.

If you want to study midrashic texts as they were first collected, you might do well with the edition of the Rabbah Midrashim to the Torah, edited in a vocalized text with a semicritical commentary by Mirkin. For more careful research, you should compare that text with the critical editions listed below. Of these texts, Bereshit Rabbah will probably be the most rewarding for study. A text which is particularly interesting for the rabbis' rereading of biblical stories, and containing much interesting mythic material, is the *Pirkei de-Rabbi Eliezer.* Get the edition with the commentary of David Luria, and use the English translation by Friedlander for reference.

Two other midrashim, that on Psalms and the *Pesikta Rabbati,* are also available in English translation by Braude in the Yale Judaica Series. While no midrashic text reads well in translation alone, these translations will be valuable guides if you come across difficulties in the Hebrew text. The same is true for the Soncino translation of all the Rabbah Midrashim.

The most reliable editions of some basic midrashim:

Bereshit Rabbah—Theodore Albeck (critical)

Wa-Yikra Rabbah—Margaliot

Devarim Rabbah—Lieberman

Tanhuma—All editions are uncritical; the text edited by S. Buber is an entirely different work

Pesikta de-Rav Kahana—Mandelbaum (critical)

Midrash Tehillim—S. Buber

Pesikta Rabbati—M. Friedmann (Ish-Shalom)

Seder Eliyahu—M. Friedmann (Ish-Shalom)

The various short midrashim, often of a later date, published by A. Jellinek in *Bet ha-Midrash* and by A. Wertheimer in *Batei Midrashot,* contain some of the most interesting material in all of midrashic literature, and should not be overlooked.

The large folio editions of *Midrash Rabbah im kol ha-Meforeshim* are still valuable, especially for the midrashim on the Megillot. The two most highly respected commentaries are the *Mattenot Kehunnah* and the *Perush MaHaR-ZaV.*

Braude, William G., ed. *Pesikta Rabbati: Discourses for Feasts, Fasts and Special Sabbaths.* 2 vols. New Haven: Yale University, 1968.

Braude, William G. *The Midrash on Psalms.* 2 vols. New Haven: Yale University, 1959.

Ginzberg, Louis, *Legends of the Jews.* 7 vols. Philadelphia: JPS, 1946.

Halakhic codes

The three basic codes of Jewish law which are used for study and halakhic decision-making are the *Mishneh Torah* of Maimonides, the *Arbaah Turim* of Jacob ben Asher, and the *Shulhan Arukh* of Joseph Karo. All of these are valuable additions to a Jewish library; they are published in standard editions with certain major commentaries. In the case of the *Shulhan Arukh,* the section entitled Orah Hayyim (dealing with prayer, the Sabbath, and holidays) is also published separately with the commentary *Mishnah Berurah* by the Hafetz Hayyim. This latter work serves as a basic guide to ritual practice in those areas for contemporary Orthodox Jews.

The most readable of the codes is the *Mishneh Torah.* Among the most interesting sections for study are the philosophical introduction (Sefer ha-Madda)—though one should bear in mind that Judaism is generally unreceptive to the somewhat dogmatic formulations found there, and Maimonides was severely criticized for them—and the Laws of Kings (Hilkhot Melakhim), which contain some provoking material on political philosophy. The *Mishneh Torah* has been translated as *The Code of Maimonides,* and is available to your rich uncle in the Yale Judaica Series.

Intelligent students of Judaism should *avoid* using the *Kitzur Shulhan Arukh* of Shlomo Ganzfried, a collection of ultrastringent views often without firm basis in halakhic sources.

Guides to contemporary Orthodox practice can be found in such works as *Shemirat Shabbat ke-Hilkhatah* by Yehoshuah Neuwirth and *Ha-Moadim ba-Halakhah* by S. Y. Zevin, which also contain some fascinating theoretical discussions.

Hasidism

The vast literature of Hasidism is basically divisible into two types: the tales and the teachings.

Hasidic tales make very beautiful reading, and are often written in rather straightforward and unproblematic Hebrew. The legends around the Baal Shem Tov and his circle are collected in the *Shivhei ha-BESHT* (edited by Hordezky) and also available in English translation (*In Praise of the Baal Shem Tov*).

Two volumes of Hasidic tales have been edited by S. Y. Zevin (*Sipurei Hasidim),* and they contain some interesting material, especially from HaBaD sources. The Hebrew edition of Buber's *Tales (Or ha-Ganuz)* contains source indications missing in the English version, and will lead to interesting study. Primary Hasidic collections of tales are often in a mixture of Hebrew and Yiddish; two particularly valuable collections are the *Eser Orot* and the *Siah-Sarfei Kodesh.*

Unique in the literature of Hasidic tales are those by Rabbi Nahman of Bratzlav, available both in traditional Hebrew-Yiddish editions, and in a somewhat modernized reworking by Yehudah Yaari.

Modern introductions to the world of Hasidic teachings and theological literature can again be a great help. Hasidic theological ideas are clearly explained by Louis Jacobs in his *Seeker of Unity*. Rivka Schatz's *Ha-Hasidut ke-Mistikah* is a gold mine of startling and exciting Hasidic texts, especially on prayer and the contemplative life. The various articles by Joseph Weiss, soon to appear in book form, are perhaps the most penetrating critical studies of Hasidic thought.

For the beginner who has read Scholem's *Major Trends* and Jacobs's book, three Hasidic texts come to mind as good places to begin an actual dive into the literature. The *Degel Mahaneh Efraiim* is a collection of short pieces on the weekly Torah reading, containing much authentic material by the Baal Shem Tov, the grandfather of the author. Somewhat longer passages, but also relatively easy in style and highly rewarding in content, are to be found in the *Meor Einayim*, by Menahem Nahum of Chernobyl. The basic book of HaBaD Hasidism, the *Tanya*, is also highly readable. The second section of that work is particularly interesting, if one learns to skip certain abstruse digressions.

The entire *Tanya* is available in English translation, published by Kehot in Brooklyn.

For those prepared to read more difficult sources of Hasidic literature, the works of the Maggid of Mezritch (now edited as *Torat ha-Maggid*, in two small volumes) and especially of Nahman of Bratzlav *(Likutei Moharan*, edition with the index by N. Z. Koenig) will be highly rewarding.

Jacobs, Louis. *The Seeker of Unity: The Life and Works of Aaron of Starosselje*. New York: Basic Books, 1966.

Mintz, Jerome R. and Ben Amos, Dan. *In Praise of the Baal Shem Tov (Shivhei ha-Besht): The Earliest Collection of Legends about the Founder of Hasidism*. Bloomington, Ind.: Indiana University, 1970; also in paperback.

Schneur Zalman of Ladi. *Tanya*. 5 vols. Brooklyn, N.Y.: Kehot, 1962.

Jewish philosophy and ethics

The great classics of Jewish philosophical literature such as the works of Saadia, Maimonides, and others need no special attention here. It should be said, however, that many of these writings were translated from the Arabic into a highly technical version of medieval Hebrew, and the Hebrew texts are not at all easy to read. One might do better to begin with them in English. The complete text of Saadia's *Emunot ve-Deot* is available in the Yale Judaica Series; Yehudah Halevi's *Kuzari* is available in an old translation by H. Hirschfeld. Both of these are adequately excerpted in the paperback edition of *Three Jewish Philosophers* (along with selections from Philo of Alexandria). For Maimonides' *Moreh Nevukhim*, use the translation by S. Pines published by the University of Chicago. Joseph Albo's *Iqqarim* is available in a bilingual edition by JPS. For further translations of Jewish philosophical classics, consult the bibliography in Julius Guttmann's *Philosophies of Judaism*.

Jewish ethical literature is also blessed with translations and bilingual editions of some of the most important classics. Bahya's *Hovot ha-Levavot* [Duties of the heart], Jonah Gerondi's *Shaarei Teshuvah* [Gates of repentance], and Moses Hayyim Luzzatto's *Mesillat Yesharim* [The path of the upright] are all available in English. A beautiful short treatise on the ethics of Kabbalah can be studied in Moses Cordovero's *Tomer Devorah*, also translated as *The Palm Tree of Deborah*. Two other ethical treatises also by leading kabbalists, which have not been translated but are highly worthy of study and are not terribly difficult, are Elijah De Vidas's *Reshit Hokhmah* and the *Sefer*

Haredim of Eleazar Azikri.

For an introduction to the Musar literature of nineteenth-century Eastern Europe, the basic work is Katz's four-volume *Tenuat ha-Musar*. A prior introduction to that world is the English biography of Israel Salanter by Menahem Glenn.

Albo, Joseph. *Sefer ha-Ikkarim: Book of Principles*. 4 vols. Philadelphia: JPS, 1929–30.

Bahya B. Joseph ibn Pakuda. *Duties of the Heart*. Translated by Moses Hyamson. 5 vols. New York: Bloch, 1925–47; reprinted 2 vols. Jerusalem: Boys Town, 1962.

Cordovero, Moshe. *The Palm Tree of Deborah*. Translated by Louis Jacobs. London: Vallentine, Mitchell, 1960.

Gerondi, Jonah. *Shaarei Teshuvah* [Gates of repentance]. Translated by Shraga Silverstein. Torah Classics Series. Jerusalem: Boys Town, 1967.

Glenn, Menahem. *Israel Salanter: Religious-Ethical Thinker; The Story of a Religious-Ethical Current in Nineteenth Century Judaism*. New York: Bloch, 1953.

Guttmann, Julius. *Philosophies of Judaism: The History of Jewish Philosophy from Biblical Times to Franz Rosenzweig*. New York: Holt, Rinehart & Winston, 1964.

Judah Halevi. *Kuzari: The Book of Proof and Argument*. Oxford: Oxford University Press, 1947. New York: Schocken, paperback.

Lewy, Hans et al., eds. *Three Jewish Philosophers: Philo, Saadya Gaon, Jehudah Halevi*. New York: Atheneum, 1960.

Luzzatto, Moses Hayyim. *Mesillat Yesharim* [The path of the upright] Translated by Mordecai M. Kaplan. Philadelphia: JPS, 1966.

Maimonides. *Guide of the Perplexed*. Edited and translated by Shlomo Pines. Chicago: University of Chicago, 1963.

Saadia Gaon. *The Book of Beliefs and Opinions*. Translated by Samuel Roseblatt. New Haven: Yale University, 1948.

Kabbalah

The world of kabbalistic literature, was, until recently, closed to all but initiates due to its difficult and abstruse use of symbolic language. Fortunately, the efforts of modern scholars, primarily at the Hebrew University in Jerusalem, have made this literature more available today to the intelligent reader. If a reading of Scholem's works in English has turned you on to a study of Kabbalah, and your modern Hebrew is fairly good, get hold of Isaiah Tishbi's two-volume *Mishnat ha-Zohar*. This work presents the main ideas of the Zohar in systematic subject order, illustrating each point with extensive selections from the text, translated into lucid modern Hebrew, and explicated in a brief commentary. When you have read through a few sections of this work, and are comfortable with the Hebrew translations, begin to study the Hebrew texts in Tishbi along with the Aramaic original in the Zohar itself. (The most usable edition of the Zohar text is that of Reuven Margaliot, published by Mosad ha-Rav Kuk in three volumes.) You will find the Aramaic less of a problem than you thought; the real difficulty in Zohar study is the symbolism, not the language.

For other modern works which will help you into the world of kabbalistic thought, consult the extensive bibliography following the article "Kabbalah" in the *Encyclopaedia Judaica*.

As to works written by the kabbalists themselves which are meant to serve as more or less introductory texts, the following are worthy of your attention:

Shaarei Orah by Joseph Gikatilia (new edition by Professor Ben-Shlomo).

Avodat ha-Kodesh by Meir Ibn Gabbai, a beautifully written text which is also a great encyclopedia of the kabbalists' rereading of biblical and rabbinic sources (available only in a reprint of the more-or-less illegible Warsaw edition).

Shenei Luhot ha-Berit by Isaiah Horowitz, the book which popularized Kabbalah in Eastern Europe.

It should be added that all these works, while relatively "easy" as compared to much of kabbalistic literature, are still far beyond the grasp of one whose command of rabbinic Hebrew and literature is only at a beginner's level. But keep studying—you'll get there!

A few reference works

In working with Hebrew texts, proper use of dictionaries, etc., can be most important. DO NOT try to use a modern dictionary for biblical or rabbinic

Hebrew; the language has changed sufficiently so that the results you come up with could be quite astounding!

For the Bible, the Brown-Driver-Briggs Lexicon is the generally accepted reference tool in English. The Kohler-Baugarten Lexicon is also good. Better than any lexicon, however, is the concordance called *Hekhal ha-Kodesh* by S. Mandelkern. In listing all places in the Bible where each word is used, this tool will set you on the road to real scholarship.

For critical work in Bible, the basic text is the edition of the *Biblia Hebraica* by Rudolf Kittel. Be sure you also get the little pamphlet which tells you how to use the symbols in that book.

For rabbinic texts of all kinds, you will need a good *Luah Rashei Tevot,* as abbreviations are the major hurdle to be crossed in deciphering this material. (A special little volume on *Rashei Tevot* used in kabbalistic and Hasidic writings, compiled by Adin Steinsaltz, is also available.) The best dictionary to use for rabbinic Hebrew and Aramaic is that of M. Jastrow. His etymologies are often not valid, but the book is a good working tool for students. The concordances compiled by the Kosovsky family in Jerusalem for the Mishnah, Targum, and various other sources can be valuable; work still goes on to complete the great concordance to the Talmud, which will add greatly to critical study.

To find a full treatment of a particular halakhic subject which may come up in the course of Talmud study, the *Enziklopedyah Talmudit* is very useful. For searching out the haggadic statements on a particular theme or person, the *Ozar ha-Aggadah* by Gross is also a valuable tool. If you do decide to tackle philosophical or ethical treatises in Hebrew, you will need to use J. Klatzkin's *Ozar Munahim Pilosofiim,* a lexicon of Hebrew philosophical language.

For introductory essays and further bibliography in all areas, you would do well to consult the new and generally excellent *Encyclopaedia Judaica.* For more detailed bibliography to use in research papers in various areas, you should know of Shunami's massive *Mafteah ha-Maftehot,* a listing of Judaica bibliographies for each subject area. A recent book edited by Jacob Neusner entitled *The Study of Judaism: Bibliographical Essays* (Ktav, 1972) may prove to be a highly valuable aid.

A BASIC ENGLISH BIBLIOGRAPHY

Introduction

Much of being a Jew depends on knowledge. Fortunately, almost everything you might ever want to know about Judaism can be found in books. This list is a place to start. Some of the books are basic introductions in areas of Judaism; others are scholarly or specialized. All Jewish books contain information and all have their limitations.

This list is necessarily subjective and selective. We have tried to choose outstanding items in many areas of Judaica, given the limitations of space and time. Although we have generally tried to include books in print, where there was no in-print equivalent, out-of-print items were listed. Naturally, we have left out many titles which may be useful and of interest to some readers. Hopefully, you will be led to some of these through our listing of bibliographies. We have omitted sections on biblical archeology, fiction, poetry, and biography as either too specialized or too broad.

In some sections we include annotations like "popular," "introduction," "scholarly," or "photographic essay," to differentiate between similar-sounding titles and to point up special features. Specialized book lists can also be found at the ends of the following sections: The Jewish Establishment, Festivals, Death and Burial, Weddings, Kashrut, Shabbat, Music, Scribal Arts, Jewish Women's Activities, A First Step, Jewish Travel.

Building your own Jewish library

We have, wherever possible, noted the paperback edition of the book. New paperback books are issued all the time. Check *Paperback Books in Print* at your local bookstore frequently for newer items. A list of some Jewish bookstores is also included. Other money-saving strategies:

1. **Jewish Publication Society**
1930 Chestnut Street
Philadelphia, Pa. 19103

JPS, the publisher of this catalog, is a nonprofit organization having various subscription plans which can save you a considerable amount of money on their publications. For different amounts of dues ($7.50 to $100), you can select 2 to 35 book units. Most books are one unit; most paperbacks are ½ unit. You can fill your subscription with new or backlist books, adult and juvenile titles. Write for an application and complete catalog. In addition, JPS has a yearly pre-Hanukkah sale in which most of their books are greatly reduced.

2. **Commentary Library/Jewish Book Club**
165 E. 56th St.
New York, N. Y. 10022

This Jewish book club offers many current books of Jewish interest, in addition to some records and artwork at savings up to 35%. You must order four books per year; after these, each book purchased earns bonus credit toward free books. Differing introductory offers are available at different times of the year. All offer enormous savings. Check *Commentary* magazine, which usually runs the current offer or write directly to them.

3. **Bloch Publishing Co.**
915 Broadway
New York, N. Y. 10010

is a mail-order bookstore as well as a publisher and has frequent sales of Jewish books by all publishers. Get on their mailing list.

4. Many Jewish bookstores offer discounts of 10%–30% to religious school and rabbinical students. Try to arrange something for yourself or through an eligible friend.

5. Most publishers offer 20% discounts on books to schools or libraries. If you work for a religious school or synagogue or have friends who do, befriend the librarian, school secretary, or whoever orders school books and order your books through the institution at discount prices.

6. Many synagogues and Jewish organizations have book fairs, usually during Jewish Book Month (around November each year). These often feature used books collected from the community and sold for almost nothing. This is a great way to pick up cheap books and often the only way to find out-of-print items. If your local synagogue or campus doesn't have such a sale, it's not hard to organize one. The Hillel Foundation would probably donate space on campus. Many people have books they would gladly donate, especially if the money goes to a worthy cause.

7. **Marboro Bookstores**
56 West 8th St.
New York, N. Y. 10011

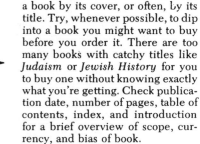

and various branches, sell remaindered books at great reductions. Get on their mailing list. Other remainder bookshops in your city are worth visiting to pick up very cheap books.

A NOTE OF CAUTION: You can't tell a book by its cover, or often, by its title. Try, whenever possible, to dip into a book you might want to buy before you order it. There are too many books with catchy titles like *Judaism* or *Jewish History* for you to buy one without knowing exactly what you're getting. Check publication date, number of pages, table of contents, index, and introduction for a brief overview of scope, currency, and bias of book.

It is hoped that most libraries will have most of these books. If they do not, there is something that you can do about it:

1. You can suggest that your library buy it/them.
2. Ask the library if they have taken your suggestion. You have a right to know.
3. If the library says no, remember this: the closer you are to an institution, the more power you have. You can change things close to home. For example, if you suggest that the library buy the *Encyclopaedia Judaica* for $500 and they say no because of budget considerations, then get up a petition for the purchase. A library must serve the community and it does not want to get a reputation for doing otherwise. A handful of people in a library can effect change. You will be surprised at how much power you have if you use it.
4. Remember that the same thing applies to magazines. Chances are that your library gets *Commentary* and nothing else Jewish. Use your influence. Remember: the public library must always justify its existence by public use—or no more funds.

One more thing about libraries and Judaica. Learn the few places to browse. Most libraries miscatalog Judaica. You may find Jewish history on the Israel shelves, the Judaism shelves, the ethnic group shelves, and the history shelves. Use the card catalog for locations, because browsing is not fully effective. For example, Jewish poetry will be with poetry, not with Judaica, and so on.

SHALOM

Basic Judaism

Agus, Jacob B. *The Evolution of Jewish Thought*. New York: Abelard-Schuman, 1959.

Hertzberg, Arthur. *Judaism*. New York: Braziller, 1961; New York: Washington Square, paperback.

Neusner, Jacob. *The Way of Torah: An Introduction to Judaism*. Belmont, Cal.: Dickenson, paperback.

Silver, Abba Hillel. *Where Judaism Differed*. New York: Macmillan, 1956; also in paperback.

Steinberg, Milton. *Basic Judaism*. New York: Harcourt Brace & World, 1947; also in paperback.

History (general)

Baron, Salo W. *Social and Religious History of the Jews*. 15 vols. to date. New York: Columbia; and Philadelphia: JPS, 1952–. Comprehensive, organized topically, not strictly chronologically.

Baron, Salo W. *The Jewish Community, Its History and Structure to the American Revolution*. 3 vols. Westport, Conn.: Greenwood, 1942.

Ben-Sasson, H.H. ed. *Jewish Society through the Ages*. New York: Schocken, 1972; also in paperback. Essays.

Dubnow, Simon. *History of the Jews*. 5 vols. New York: Yoseloff, 1967–. Stress on Eastern Europe.

Finkelstein, Louis, ed. *The Jews: Their History, Culture and Religion*. 4 vols. Philadelphia: JPS, 1949, out of print; 3 vols. New York: Schocken, paperback. Comprehensive. Excellent selection of essays.

Graetz, Heinrich. *History of the Jews*. 6 vols. Philadelphia: JPS, 1891–98. Old but standard.

Grayzel, Solomon. *A History of the Jews*. 2nd ed. Philadelphia: JPS, 1968; New York: NAL, paperback. Basic introduction.

Margolis, Max and Marx, Alexander. *A History of the Jewish People*. Philadelphia: JPS, 1960; also in paperback. Factual but dry.

Roth, Cecil. *A History of the Jews*. New York: Schocken, 1961, out of print; rev. ed. 1966; also in paperback. Popular.

Schwarz, Leo W., ed. *Great Ages and Ideas of the Jewish People*. New York: Random House, 1965. Collection of survey essays on important periods.

The World History of the Jewish People. 5 vols. to date. New Brunswick, N. J.: Rutgers University Press, 1964–.
- I. Speiser, E. A., ed. *At the Dawn of Civilization*.
- II. Mazar, Benjamin, ed. Part I. *The Patriarchs*.
- III. Mazar, Benjamin, ed. *Judges*.
- IV. Schalit, Abraham, ed. *The Hellenistic Age*.
- XI. Roth, Cecil, ed. *The Dark Ages: Jews in Christian Europe*.

Each volume composed of essays by noted historians.

Special history

Abrahams, Israel. *Jewish Life in the Middle Ages*. New York: Macmillan, 1896; Philadelphia, JPS, paperback. Standard introductory.

Baer, Yitzchak F. *Galut*. New York: Schocken, 1947.

Baer, Yitzchak. *History of the Jews in Christian Spain*. 2 vols. Philadelphia: JPS, 1961.

Bickerman, Elias. *From Ezra to the Last of the Maccabees: Foundations of Post-Biblical Judaism*. New York: Schocken, paperback. Standard.

Blau, Joseph L. and Baron, Salo W. *The Jews of the U.S., 1790–1840: A Documentary History*. 3 vols. New York: Columbia, 1963.

Dubnow, Simon. *History of the Jews in Russia and Poland: From Earliest Times until the Present Day*. 3 vols. Philadelphia: JPS, 1916, out of print.

Elbogen, Ismar. *A Century of Jewish Life*. Philadelphia: JPS, 1944.

Goitein, S.D. *Jews and Arabs: Their Contacts through the Ages*. New York: Schocken, 1955; also in paperback.

Hertzberg, Arthur. *The French Enlightenment and the Jews*. New York: Columbia University Press, and Philadelphia: JPS, 1968. New York: Schocken, paperback.

Josephus, Flavius. *Complete Works of Flavius Josephus*. Translated by William Whiston. Grand Rapids: Kregel, 1970; also in paperback.

Katz, Jacob. *Exclusiveness and Tolerance: Jewish-Gentile Relations in Medieval and Modern Times*. New York: Oxford, 1961; New York: Schocken, paperback.

Katz, Jacob. *Out of the Ghetto: The Social Background of Jewish Emancipation, 1770-1870*. Cambridge, Mass.: Harvard University Press, 1973.

Katz, Jacob. *Tradition and Crisis: Jewish Society at the End of the Middle Ages*. New York: Free Press of Glencoe, 1961; New York: Schocken, paperback.

Mahler, Raphael. *A History of Modern Jewry, 1780–1815*. New York: Schocken, 1971. Marxist interpretation.

Marcus, Jacob R. *The Jew in the Medieval World; A Source Book, 315–1791*. Cincinnati: UAHC, 1938; New York: Atheneum, paperback. Standard.

Meyer, Michael A. *The Origins of the Modern Jew: Jewish Identity and European Culture in Germany, 1749–1824*. Detroit: Wayne State University Press, paperback. Introductory.

Pfeiffer, Robert H. *History of the New Testament Times*. Westport, Conn.: Greenwood, 1949; reprint, 1972.

Roth, Cecil. *A History of the Mar-*

ranos, Philadelphia: JPS, 1932, out of print.

Rubens, Alfred. *A History of Jewish Costume.* New York: Funk & Wagnalls, 1967.

Rudavsky, David. *Modern Jewish Religious Movements.* New York: Behrman, 1972; also in paperback.

Sachar, Howard M. *The Course of Modern Jewish History.* Cleveland: World, 1958. New York: Dell, paperback. Introduction.

Sanders, Ronald. *The Downtown Jews: Portraits of an Immigrant Generation.* New York: Harper, 1969.

Schechter, Solomon. *Studies in Judaism.* Philadelphia: JPS, paperback.

Schoener, Allon, ed. *Portal to America: The Lower East Side 1870–1925.* New York: Holt Rinehart & Winston, 1967; also in paperback. Photographic essay.

Schurer, Emil G. *A History of the Jewish People in the Time of Jesus.* New York: Schocken, paperback. Standard.

Tcherikover, Victor. *Hellenistic Civilization and the Jews.* Philadelphia: JPS, 1966; also in paperback.

Vishniac, Roman. *Polish Jews: A Pictorial Record.* New York: Schocken, 1947; also in paperback. Photographic essay.

Bibles and biblical period

TEXT

Anchor Bible, Garden City, N.Y.: Doubleday, 1964. New translation and commentaries by biblical scholars. Recommended are Speiser's *Genesis* and Bright's *Jeremiah.*

Fox, Everett. *In the Beginning: A New English Rendition of Genesis.* Waltham, Mass.: *Response #14,* Summer 1972. Based on Buber-Rosenzweig translation of the Bible. Sensitive to language and sound. Exciting.

Isaiah. Philadelphia: JPS, 1972. A new translation available in two editions: the more expensive has handsome illustrations by Chaim Gross.

The Five Megillot and Jonah. Philadelphia: JPS, 1969. Excellent translation and introductions. *Esther* is available separately.

The Holy Scriptures According to the Masoretic Text. Philadelphia: JPS, 1917. Standard, one-volume translation of the Bible, available at various prices.

The Soncino Books of the Bible. London: Soncino, 1950. Hebrew and English texts and selections from classical commentaries.

The Torah: The Five Books of Moses. Philadelphia: JPS, 1962. A new translation in modern English.

BIBLICAL PERIOD

Adar, Zvi. *The Biblical Narrative.* New York: Jewish Agency, 1960. Humanistic approach to Bible as literature.

Aharoni, Yohanan, and Avi-Yonah, Michael. *Macmillan Bible Atlas.* New York: Macmillan, 1968.

Albright, William. *From the Stone Age to Christianity: Monotheism and the Historical Process.* Baltimore: Johns Hopkins University Press, 1940.

Bright, John. *A History of Israel.* 2nd ed. Philadelphia: Westminster, 1972.

Buber, Martin. *Moses.* Oxford: East and West Library, 1946.

Buber, Martin. *On the Bible: Eighteen Studies.* Edited by Nahum Glatzer. New York: Schocken, 1968.

Buber, Martin. *Prophetic Faith.* Translated by Carlyle Witton-Davies. New York: Macmillan, 1949.

Eissfeldt, Otto. *The Old Testament: An Introduction.* Translated by Peter Ackroyd. New York: Harper & Row, 1965. Especially good for bibliographies.

Frankfort, Henri, and others. *Before Philosophy: The Intellectual Adventure of Ancient Man.* New York: Penguin, paperback. Essays on religion of ancient Near East.

Gaster, Theodore, trans. *The Dead Sea Scriptures.* Garden City, New York: Doubleday, 1964.

Glatzer, Nahum N. *The Dimensions of Job: A Study and Selected Readings.* New York: Schocken, 1969; also in paperback.

Gordis, Robert. *The Book of God and Man: A Study of Job.* Chicago: University of Chicago, 1965.

Gordis, Robert. *Koheleth—The Man and His World.* New York: JTS, 1951. New York: Schocken, paperback.

Heschel, Abraham Joshua. *The Prophets.* Philadelphia: JPS, 1962.

Kaufman, Yehezkel. *The Religion of Israel: From its Beginnings to the Babylonian Exile.* Chicago: University of Chicago Press, 1960; New York: Schocken, paperback. Classic interpretation.

Levine, Moshe. *The Tabernacle: Its Structure and Utensils.* London: Soncino, 1969. Color plates and diagrams of reconstruction of desert tabernacle, with text.

Mazar, Benjamin, and Avi-Yonah, Michael. *Views of the Biblical World.* 4 vols.: *The Law; Early Prophets; Later Prophets; Writings; Hagiographa.* Jerusalem: International Publishing Co., 1960.

Pedersen, Johannes. *Israel—Its Life and Culture.* 2 vols. London: Oxford University, 1953–54. Nonsystematic phenomenological approach, beautifully written.

Pritchard, James. ed. *Ancient Near Eastern Texts.* Princeton, N.J.: Princeton University Press, 1955. A standard collection of texts parallel to the Bible, in translation.

Pritchard, James. *An Anthology of the Ancient Near East: Texts and Pictures.* Princeton, N.J.: Princeton University Press, paperback. Abridgment of hard cover above.

Sarna, Nahum N. *Understanding Genesis.* New York: McGraw-Hill, 1966; New York: Schocken, paperback.

See "Am ha-Sefer."

Rabbinic Judaism

Adler, Morris. *The World of the Talmud.* Washington, D.C.: Bnai Brith Hillel, Hillel Little Book Series, 1958; 2nd ed. New York: Schocken, paperback. Introductory.

Cohen, A. *Everyman's Talmud.* New York: Dutton, 1949. Introductory.

Finkelstein, Louis. *Akiba: Scholar, Saint and Martyr.* New York: Covici Friede, 1936; Philadelphia: JPS, 1962; Cleveland: Meridian, paperback; New York: Atheneum, paperback.

Finkelstein, Louis. *The Pharisees: The Sociological Background of Their Faith.* 2 vols. Philadelphia: JPS, 1938, out of print; 3rd ed. Philadelphia: JPS, 1962. Classic work.

Ginzberg, Louis. *Legends of the Jews.* 7 vols. Philadelphia: JPS, 1954. Translation of Midrash. Classic.

Ginzberg, Louis. *On Jewish Law and Lore.* Philadelphia: JPS, 1955, New York: Atheneum, paperback. Essays.

Ginzberg, Louis. *Students, Scholars and Saints.* Philadelphia: JPS, 1928 and 1958; New York: Meridian, paperback.

Glatzer, Nahum N., ed. *Hammer on the Rock: A Midrash Reader.* New York: Schocken, paperback.

Herford, R. Travers. *The Ethics of the Talmud: Sayings of the Fathers.* New York: Schocken, paperback.

Herford, R. Travers. *The Pharisees.* New York: Macmillan, 1924. Boston: Beacon, 1962, paperback.

Kadushin, Max. *Organic Thinking: A Study in Rabbinic Thought.* New York: JTS, 1938.

Kadushin, Max. *The Rabbinic Mind.* New York: JTS, 1952; New York: Bloch, paperback.

Kohler, Kaufmann. *Jewish Theology Systematically and Historically Considered.* New York: Macmillan, 1918.

Lauterbach, Jacob Z. *Rabbinic Essays.* Cincinnati: HUC, 1957.

Mielziner, Moses. *Introduction to the Talmud.* New York: Bloch, 1926; reprint 1969, with new bibliography. Excellent introduction and guide.

Montefiore, C.G., and Loewe, H. *A Rabbinic Anthology.* Philadelphia: JPS, 1960.

Moore, George Foote. *Judaism in the First Centuries of the Christian Era.* 3 vols. Cambridge, Mass.: Harvard University Press, 1954; 2 vols. New York: Schocken, paperback. Classic.

Neusner, Jacob. *History of the Jews in Babylonia.* 5 vols. Leiden: Brill, 1965–70.

Neusner, Jacob. *There We Sat Down: Talmudic Judaism in the Making.*

Nashville: Abingdon, paperback.
Neusner, Jacob. *A Life of Rabban Yochanan ben Zakkai.* Leiden: Brill, 1962.
Schechter, Solomon. *Aspects of Rabbinic Theology.* New York: Macmillan, 1909; New York: Schocken, paperback.
Strack, Hermann L. *Introduction to the Talmud and Midrash.* Philadelphia: JPS, 1931; New York: Meridian, paperback. Dry style, but valuable.

Jewish philosophy and thought

Bamberger, Bernard J. *The Story of Judaism.* New York: UAHC, 1957; 3rd rev. ed. New York: Schocken, paperback.
Blau, Joseph L. *The Story of Jewish Philosophy.* New York: Random House, 1962.
Glatzer, Nahum. *The Judaic Tradition.* Boston: Beacon, paperback. Anthology of primary sources.
Guttmann, Julius. *Philosophies of Judaism: The History of Jewish Philosophy from Biblical Times to Franz Rosenzweig.* Philadelphia: JPS, 1964. Standard.
Halevi, Judah. *The Kuzari: The Book of Proof and Argument.* Oxford: Oxford University Press, 1947; New York: Schocken, 1964; also in paperback.
Husik, Isaac. *A History of Medieval Jewish Philosophy.* New York: Macmillan, 1916. Philadelphia: JPS, paperback. Standard.
Moses ben Maimon (Maimonides). *Guide to the Perplexed.* Translated by M. Friedlander. New York: Dover, paperback.
Three Jewish Philosophers: Philo, Saadya Gaon, Jehuda Halevi. Edited by Hans Lewy, and others. New York: Atheneum, paperback.
Wolfson, Harry A. *Philo: Foundations of Religious Philosophy in Judaism, Christianity and Islam.* 2 vols. Cambridge, Mass.: Harvard University Press, 1947.
Wolfson, Harry A. *The Philosophy of Spinoza: Unfolding the Latent Processes of His Reasoning.* 2 vols. New York: Schocken, paperback.
See "Am ha-Sefer."

Mysticism, messianism, and occultism

Klausner, Joseph. *The Messianic Idea in Israel from Its Beginning to the Completion of the Mishnah.* New York: Macmillan, 1955.
Mowinckel, Sigmund. *He That Cometh.* Nashville: Abingdon, 1956.
Scholem, Gershom G. *Jewish Gnosticism, Merkavah Mysticism and Talmudic Tradition.* New York: Ktav, 1960; 2nd ed. New York: Bloch, 1965.
Scholem, Gershom G. *Major Trends in Jewish Mysticism.* New York: Schocken; 3rd rev. ed. New York: Schocken, paperback. Classic.
Scholem, Gershom G. *On the Kabbalah and Its Symbolism.* New York: Schocken, 1965; also in paperback.
Scholem, Gershom G. *Sabbatai Sevi.* 2 vols. Princeton, N.J.: Princeton University Press, 1973.
Scholem, Gershom G. *The Messianic Idea in Judaism and Other Essays on Jewish Spirituality.* New York: Schocken, 1971; also in paperback.
Scholem, Gershom G. *Zohar: The Book of Splendor—Basic Readings from the Kabbalah.* New York: Schocken, 1949; also in paperback.
Schrire, Theodore. *Hebrew Amulets: Their Decipherment and Interpretation.* New York: Fernhill, 1966.
Silver, Abba Hillel. *A History of Messianic Speculation in Israel: From the First through the Seventeenth Centuries.* New York: Macmillan, 1927, out of print; Boston: Beacon, paperback, out of print.
Sperling, Harry, and Simon, Maurice, trans. *The Zohar.* 5 vols. London: Soncino, 1933. Difficult to read without Hebrew text.
Trachtenberg, Joshua. *Jewish Magic and Superstition: A Study in Folk Religion.* New York: Behrman, 1939; New York: Temple, paperback. Fascinating.
For additional material see "Am ha-Sefer."

Hasidism, Eastern Europe

Buber, Martin. *For the Sake of Heaven.* Philadelphia: 1945; New York: Atheneum, paperback. Historical novel.
Buber, Martin. *Hasidism and Modern Man.* New York: Horizon, 1958; New York: Harper Torchbooks, paperback.
Buber, Martin. *Origin and Meaning of Hasidism.* New York: Horizon, 1960; also in paperback.
Buber, Martin. *Tales of the Hasidim: The Early Masters.* New York: Schocken, 1947; also in paperback. Collection of tales.
Buber, Martin. *Tales of the Hasidim: The Later Masters.* New York: Schocken, 1948; also in paperback.
Cohen, Arthur A., and Garvin, Philip. *A People Apart: Hasidism in America.* New York: Dutton, 1970. Photographic essay.
Davidowicz, Lucy S., ed. *The Golden Tradition.* New York: Holt Rinehart & Winston, 1967. Boston: Beacon, paperback. Source material on Eastern Europe.
Dresner, Samuel H. *The Zaddik: The Doctrine of the Zaddik According to the Writings of Rabbi Yaakov Yosef of Polnoy.* New York: Abelard-Schuman, 1960.
Heschel, Abraham Joshua. *The Earth Is the Lord's: The Inner World of the Jew in East Europe.* New York: Abelard-Schuman, 1960. Cleveland: World (Meridian), paperback. Lyrical essay.
Jacobs, Louis. *Hasidic Prayer.* New York: Schocken, 1973.
Jacobs, Louis. *Seeker of Unity: The Life and Works of Aaron of Starosselje.* New York: Basic, 1966.
Langer, Jiri. *Nine Gates to the Chassidic Mysteries.* New York: David McKay, 1961.
Levin, Meyer. *The Golden Mountain: Marvelous Tales of Rabbi Israel Baal Shem Tov and of His Great-grandson, Rabbi Nachman.* Retold from Hebrew, Yiddish and German sources. New York: Behrman, 1932, out of print; *Classic Hasidic Tales.* New York: Citadel, paperback, out of print.
Minkin, Jacob S. *The Romance of Hassidism.* New York: Macmillan, 1935. Alhambra, Cal.: Borden, paperback.
Mintz, Jerome. *In Praise of the Baal Shem Tov (Shivhei ha-Besht): The Earliest Collection of Legends about the Founder of Hasidism.* Bloomington, Ind.: Indiana University Press, 1970; also in paperback.
Mintz, Jerome. *Legends of the Hasidim: An Introduction to Hasidic Culture and Oral Tradition in the New World.* Chicago: University of Chicago Press, 1968.
Newman, Louis I., ed. *The Hasidic Anthology: Tales and Teachings of the Hasidim.* New York: Scribners, 1934. New York: Schocken, paperback.
Rubin, Israel. *Satmar: An Island in the City.* Chicago: Quadrangle, 1972. Sociological study.
Schneerson, Joseph I. *Memoirs.* 2 vols. Brooklyn: Otzar HaChassidim, 1956–60. Lubavitcher rabbi's memoirs.
Schneerson, Joseph I. *On Learning Chassidus.* Brooklyn: Kehot, 1959.
Wiesel, Elie. *Souls on Fire: Portraits and Legends of Hasidic Masters.* New York: Random House, 1972. Newly available in paperback edition.
Zborowski, Mark, and Herzog, Elizabeth. *Life Is with People: The Culture of the Shtetl.* New York: International Universities, 1962. New York: Schocken, paperback.
For additional material see "Am ha-Sefer."

Modern Jewish Thought

Agus, Jacob. *High Priest of Rebirth: The Life, Times and Thought of Abraham Isaac Kuk,* 2nd ed. New York: Bloch, 1972. The late chief rabbi of Palestine.
Baeck, Leo. *The Essence of Judaism.* Rev. ed. New York: Schocken, 1948; also in paperback.
Baeck, Leo. *Judaism and Christianity.* Philadelphia: JPS, 1958; New York: Atheneum, paperback.
Bergman, Samuel H. *Faith and Reason: An Introduction to Modern Jewish Thought.* Washington, D. C.: Bnai Brith Hillel, Hillel Little Book Series; 1961. New York: Schocken, paperback. Excellent introduction to Cohen, Rosenzweig, Buber, Kuk, A. D. Gordon,

and Magnes.
Buber, Martin. *Between Man and Man.* London: Routledge & Kegan Paul, 1947; New York: Macmillan, 1948; New York: Macmillan, paperback.
Buber, Martin. *Eclipse of God: Studies in the Relation Between Religion and Philosophy.* New York: Harper, 1952; New York: Harper Torchbook, paperback.
Buber, Martin. *I and Thou.* Translated by Walter Kaufmann. New York: Scribners, 1970; also in paperback. Buber's central work.
Buber, Martin. *Pointing the Way: Collected Essays.* New York: Harper, 1957.
Cohen, Arthur A., ed. *Arguments and Doctrines: A Reader of Jewish Thinking in the Aftermath of the Holocaust.* Philadelphia: JPS, 1970.
Cohen, Arthur A., *The Natural and Supernatural Jew: An Historical and Theological Introduction.* New York: Pantheon, 1962.
Cohen, Hermann. *Reason and Hope: Selections from the Jewish Writings of Hermann Cohen.* Translated by Eva Jospe. New York: Norton, 1971.
The Condition of Jewish Belief: A Symposium [from *Commentary*]. New York: Macmillan, 1966; also in paperback.
Deutscher, Isaac. *The Non-Jewish Jew and Other Essays.* New York: Oxford, 1968.
Fackenheim, Emil. *Quest for Past and Future: Essays in Jewish Theology.* Bloomington, Ind.: Indiana University Press, 1968; Boston: Beacon, paperback.
Friedman, Maurice S. *Martin Buber: The Life of Dialogue.* Chicago: University of Chicago Press, 1955; New York: Harper Torchbook, paperback.
Glatzer, Nahum N. *Franz Rosenzweig; His Life and Thought.* New York: Schocken, 1953; also in paperback.
Herberg, Will. *Judaism and Modern Man: An Interpretation of Jewish Religion.* Philadelphia: JPS, 1951; New York: Atheneum, paperback.
Heschel, Abraham Joshua. *God in Search of Man: A Philosophy of Judaism.* New York: Farrar Straus, 1955; New York: Harper, paperback.
Heschel, Abraham Joshua. *Man's Quest for God.* New York: Scribners, paperback.
Hirsch, Samson Raphael. *The Nineteen Letters of Ben Uziel.* New York: Funk & Wagnalls, 1899; New York: Feldenheim, 1960.
Kaplan, Mordechai M. *Judaism as a Civilization: Toward a Reconstruction of American-Jewish Life.* New York: Reconstructionist Press, 1934; also in paperback.
Kaplan, Mordechai M. *Questions Jews Ask: Reconstructionist Answers.* New York: Reconstructionist Press, 1956; also in paperback.
Memmi, Albert. *The Liberation of the Jew.* New York: Orion, 1966.
Memmi, Albert. *Portrait of a Jew.* New York: Orion, 1962; New York: Viking, paperback.
Noveck, Simon, ed. *Contemporary Jewish Thought: A Reader.* Washington, D.C.: Bnai Brith, 1963.
Noveck, Simon, ed. *Great Jewish Thinkers of the Twentieth Century.* Washington, D.C.: Bnai Brith, 1963. Introductory.
Petuchowski, Jacob. *Ever Since Sinai: A Modern View of Torah.* New York: Scribe, 1961; also in paperback.
Plaut, W. Gunther. *The Rise of Reform Judaism: A Sourcebook of Its European Origins.* New York: World Union for Progressive Judaism, 1963.
Rosenzweig, Franz. *The Star of Redemption.* New York: Holt, Rinehart & Winston, 1970; Boston: Beacon, paperback.
Roth, Leon. *Judaism: A Portrait.* New York: Viking, 1961; New York: Schocken, paperback.
Rothschild, Fritz A., ed. *Between God and Man: An Interpretation of Judaism from the Writings of Abraham J. Heschel.* New York: Harper, 1959; New York: Free Press-Macmillan, paperback.
Rubenstein, Richard. *After Auschwitz: Essays in Contemporary Judaism.* Indianapolis: Bobbs-Merrill, 1966; also in paperback.
Rubenstein, Richard. *The Religious Imagination: A Study in Psychoanalysis and Jewish Theology.* Indianapolis: Bobbs-Merrill, 1968; Boston: Beacon, paperback.
Steinberg, Milton. *The Making of the Modern Jew: From the Second Temple to the State of Israel.* New York: Behrman, 1949.
Weiner, Herbert. *9½ Mystics: The Kabbala Today.* New York: Holt Rinehart & Winston, 1969; New York: Macmillan, paperback.
Wolf, Arnold J., ed. *Rediscovering Judaism: Reflections on a New Theology.* Chicago: Quadrangle, 1965.

Holocaust

Arendt, Hannah. *Eichmann in Jerusalem: A Report on the Banality of Evil.* New York: Viking, 1963; also in paperback. Controversial analysis of responsibility for the Holocaust.
Arendt, Hannah. *Origins of Totalitarianism.* Cleveland: World, 1966. Rev. ed. New York: Harcourt, paperback.
Bettelheim, Bruno. *The Informed Heart: Autonomy in a Mass Age.* Glencoe, Ill.: Free Press, 1960; New York: Avon, paperback.
Cohen, Elie A. *Human Behaviour in the Concentration Camp.* New York: Grosset & Dunlap, out of print.
Feingold, Henry L. *The Politics of Rescue: The Roosevelt Administration and the Holocaust, 1938–1945.* New Brunswick, N.J.: Rutgers University Press, 1970.
Frankel, Viktor E. *Man's Search for Meaning: An Introduction to Logotherapy.* Rev. ed. Boston: Beacon, 1963; New York: Washington Square Press, Simon & Schuster, and others, paperback. Fascinating.
Friedlander, Albert H., ed. *Out of the Whirlwind: A Reader of Holocaust Literature.* Garden City, N.Y.: Doubleday, 1968.
Glatstein, Jacob, ed. *Anthology of Holocaust Literature.* Philadelphia: JPS, 1969.
Green, Gerald. *Artists of Terezin.* New York: Hawthorne, 1969. Artwork by artists of Terezin-Theresienstadt concentration camp.
Hilberg, Raul. *Destruction of the European Jews.* Chicago: Quadrangle, 1961; also in paperback.
Hilberg, Raul. *Documents of Destruction: Germany and Jewry 1933–1945.* Chicago: Quadrangle, 1971; also in paperback.
Kaplan, Chaim. *Scroll of Agony.* New York: Macmillan, 1965.
Levin, Nora. *The Holocaust: The Destruction of European Jewry 1939–1945.* New York: Thomas Y. Crowell, 1965; New York: Schocken, paperback.
Morse, Arthur D. *While Six Million Died: A Chronicle of American Apathy.* New York: Random House, 1967; New York: Ace, paperback.
Mosse, George L., ed. *Nazi Culture.* New York: Grosset & Dunlap, paperback.
Ringlebaum, Emmanuel. *Notes from the Warsaw Ghetto.* New York: McGraw-Hill, 1958.
Roskies, David. *Nightwords: A Midrash on the Holocaust.* Washington, D.C.: Bnai Brith Hillel, paperback. A liturgy for Yom ha-Shoah (Holocaust Remembrance Day).
Schwarz-Bart, André. *The Last of the Just.* New York: Atheneum, 1960. Novel.
Trunk, Isaiah. *Judenrat: The Jewish Councils in Eastern Europe under Nazi Occupation.* New York: Macmillan, 1972.
Volakova, Hana, ed. *I Never Saw Another Butterfly.* New York: McGraw-Hill, 1969. Children's poems and drawings from Terezin-Theresienstadt concentration camp.
Wiesel, Elie. *Night.* New York: Hill and Wang, 1960; New York: Avon, paperback, Autobiographical novel.
Wiesel, Elie. *The Gates of the Forest.* New York: Holt Rinehart & Winston, 1966; New York: Avon, paperback.
Wiesel, Elie. *The Town beyond the Wall.* New York: Holt Rinehart & Winston, 1964; New York: Avon, paperback.

Contemporary Jewish community

Chertoff, Mordechai. *The New Left and the Jews.* New York: Putnam's, 1971.

Glazer, Nathan. *American Judaism.* Chicago: University of Chicago Press, 1957; also in paperback.

Glazer, Nathan, and Moynihan, Daniel P. *Beyond the Melting Pot: The Negroes, Puerto Ricans, Jews, Italians and Irish of New York.* 2nd ed. Cambridge, Mass.: MIT Press, 1970; also in paperback.

Neusner, Jacob, ed. *Contemporary Judaic Fellowship in Theory and Practice.* New York: Ktav, 1972. Essays about Havurot.

Porter, Jack Nusan, and Dreier, Peter, eds. *Jewish Radicalism: An Anthology.* New York: Grove, 1972; also in paperback.

Sklare, Marshall. *Conservative Judaism: An American Religious Movement.* Glencoe, Ill.: Free Press, 1955; New York: Schocken, paperback.

Sklare, Marshall, ed. *The Jews: Social Patterns of an American Group.* New York: Free Press, 1958.

Sleeper, James A. and Mintz, Alan, eds. *The New Jews.* New York: Random House, paperback. Collection of essays.

Waskow, Arthur I. *The Bush Is Burning: Radical Judaism Faces the Pharaohs of the Modern Superstate.* New York: Macmillan, 1971; also in paperback.

Zionism and Israel

Alon, Azariah. *The Natural History of the Land of the Bible.* New York: Paul Hamlyn, 1969.

Bauer, Yehuda. *From Diplomacy to Resistance: A History of Jewish Palestine 1939-1945.* Philadelphia: JPS, 1970; also in paperback.

Bettelheim, Bruno. *Children of the Dream.* New York: Macmillan, 1969; New York: Avon, paperback. Study of child-rearing on kibbutz.

Capa, Cornell. *Israel: The Reality.* Cleveland: World, 1969. Photographic essay.

Collins, Larry, and Lapierre, Dominique. *O Jerusalem.* New York: Simon and Schuster, 1972; New York: Pocket Books, paperback. Narrative about the 1948 War of Independence.

Elon, Amos. *The Israelis: Founders and Sons.* New York: Holt Rinehart & Winston, 1971; New York: Bantam, paperback.

Halpern, Ben. *The Idea of the Jewish State.* Cambridge, Mass.: Harvard University Press, 1961; rev. ed. 1969. Standard.

Hertzberg, Arthur. *The Zionist Idea: A Historical Analysis and Reader.* Garden City, N.Y.: Doubleday, 1959; Philadelphia: JPS, paperback. Features excellent introduction.

Heschel, Abraham Joshua. *Israel: An Echo of Eternity.* New York: Farrar Straus, 1969; also in paperback.

Hurewitz, J.C. *The Struggle for Palestine.* New York: Norton, 1950.

Kollek, Teddy, and Pearlman, Moshe. *Jerusalem: A History of Forty Centuries.* New York: Random House, 1968.

Kurzman, Dan. *Genesis 1948.* New York: NAL, 1971; also in paperback.

Laqueur, Walter. *A History of Zionism.* New York: Holt Rinehart & Winston, 1972.

Laqueur, Walter, ed. *The Israel-Arab Reader: A Documentary History of the Middle East Conflict.* New York: Bantam, paperback.

Livni, Israel. *Encyclopedia of Israel Stamps.* Tel Aviv: Sifriat Maariv, 1969. Distributed in the U. S. by Bloch.

Orni, Ephraim, and Efrat, Elisha. *The Geography of Israel.* 3rd rev. ed. Philadelphia: JPS, 1972.

Prittie, Terence. *Israel: Miracle in the Desert.* Rev. ed. New York: Praeger, Rev. ed. New York: Penguin, paperback.

Sachar, Howard M. *Aliyah: The Peoples of Israel.* New York: World, 1961.

Sachar, Howard M. *From the Ends of the Earth: The Peoples of Israel.* New York: World, 1964; New York: Dell, paperback.

Shapira, Avraham, ed. *The Seventh Day: Soldiers Talk about the Six-Day War.* New York: Scribners, paperback.

Sokolow, N. *History of Zionism 1600–1918.* New York: Ktav, 1969. Complete, scholarly.

Spiro, Melford E. *Kibbutz: Venture in Utopia.* Rev. ed. New York: Schocken: also in paperback. Standard but dated.

Wiener, Herbert. *The Wild Goats of Ein Gedi: A Journal of Religious Encounters in the Holy Land.* Garden City, N. Y.: Doubleday, 1961; Philadelphia: JPS, paperback.

Weintraub, D., and others. *Moshava, Kibbutz and Moshav: Patterns of Jewish Rural Settlement and Development in Palestine.* Ithaca, N. Y.: Cornell University Press, 1969.

Soviet Jewry

Baron, Salo W. *The Russian Jew under the Czars and Soviets.* New York: Macmillan, 1964.

Cang, Joel. *The Silent Millions.* New York: Taplinger, 1970.

Cohen, Richard, ed. *Let My People Go: Today's Documentary Story of Soviet Jewry's Struggle to Be Free.* New York: Popular Library, paperback.

Dubnow, S. M. *History of the Jews in Russia and Poland.* 3 vols. Philadelphia: JPS, 1916, out of print.

Gilboa, Yehoshua. *The Black Years of Soviet Jewry 1939-1953.* Boston: Little Brown, 1971.

Goldberg, Ben-Zion. *The Jewish Problem in the Soviet Union: Analysis and Solution.* New York: Crown, 1966.

Kochan, Lionel, ed. *Jews in Soviet Russia since 1917.* New York: Oxford, 1970.

Rosenberg, Louise Renée. *Jews in the Soviet Union: An Annotated Bibliography 1967–1971.* New York: American Jewish Committee, paperback.

Rothenberg, Joshua. *The Jewish Religion in the Soviet Union.* New York: Ktav, 1971.

Rusinek, Alla. *Like a Song, Like a Dream: A Soviet Girl's Quest for Freedom.* New York: Scribners, 1973. Moving autobiography of young woman's growing Jewish identity, and her liberation.

Wiesel, Elie. *The Jews of Silence: A Personal Report on Soviet Jewry.* New York: Holt Rinehart & Winston, 1966; New York: NAL, paperback.

Literature–history and criticism

Band, Arnold. *Nostalgia and Nightmare: A Study in the Fiction of S. Y. Agnon.* Los Angeles: University of California Press, 1968.

Ben Shalom, Benzion. *Hebrew Literature between the Two World Wars.* New York: Jewish Agency, 1953.

Burnshaw, S., Carmi, T., and Spicehandler, E. *The Modern Hebrew Poem Itself.* New York: Holt Rinehart & Winston, 1965; New York: Schocken, paperback.

Fiedler, Leslie A. *The Jew in the American Novel.* New York: Herzl, 1967.

Gaer, Joseph. *The Legend of the Wandering Jew.* New York: NAL, paperback, out of print.

Guttmann, Allen. *The Jewish Writer in America: Assimilation and the Crisis of Identity.* New York: Oxford, 1971.

Halkin, Abraham S. *Zion in Hebrew Literature.* New York: Herzl, 1961.

Halkin, Simon. *Major Trends in Modern Hebrew Literature.* New York: Schocken, 1970.

Halkin, Simon *Modern Hebrew Literature, from the Enlightenment to the Birth of the State of Israel: Trends and Values.* New York: Schocken, 1950; also in paperback.

Liptzin, Sol. *A History of Yiddish Literature.* New York: Jonathan David, 1972.

Liptzin, Sol. *The Flowering of Yiddish Literature.* New York: Yoseloff, 1963.

Liptzin, Sol. *The Jew in American Literature.* New York: Bloch, 1966.

Madison, Charles A. *Yiddish Literature.* New York: Ungar, 1968; New York: Schocken, paperback.

Patterson, David, ed. *Studies in Modern Hebrew Literature Series.* Ithaca, N. Y.: Cornell University Press, in progress.

Patterson, David. *Abraham Mapu.* 1964.

Yudkin, Leon I. *Isaac Lamdan.*

1971.
Silberschlag, Eisig. *Saul Tschernichowsky.* 1968.
Preil, Gabriel. *Israeli Poetry in Peace and War.* New York: Herzl, 1959.
Ribalow, Menachem. *The Flowering of Modern Hebrew Literature.* New York: Twayne, 1959.
Schurer, Emil. *The Literature of the Jewish People in the Time of Jesus.* New York: Schocken, paperback.
Silberschlag, Eisig. *Hebrew Literature: An Evaluation.* New York: Herzl, 1959.
Spiegel, Shalom. *Hebrew Reborn.* Cleveland: World, 1962.
Wallenrod, Reuben. *The Literature of Modern Israel.* New York: Abelard-Schuman, 1956.
Waxman, Meyer. *A History of Jewish Literature.* 5 vols. New York: Yoseloff, 1960.
Zinberg, Israel. *A History of Jewish Literature.* 12 vols. Cleveland: Case Western Reserve, 1972. Translated from the Yiddish. Three volumes published so far.

Customs and ceremonies

Donin, Hayim Halevy. *To Be a Jew: A Guide to Jewish Observance in Contemporary Life.* New York: Basic, 1972.
Freid, Jacob, ed. *Jews and Divorce.* New York: Ktav, 1968.
Hirsch, Samson Raphael. *Horeb.* 2 vols. New York: Soncino, 1962
See also book lists at ends of following sections: Death and Burial, Festivals, Kashrut, Shabbat, Weddings.

Shmuel Rubinstein has published a series of pamphlets and manuals on various aspects of Jewish ritual and ceremony. In general, these present clear, comprehensive, and useful information from a highly Orthodox perspective. A selection of the topics covered so far include tallit, shatnez, Sefer Torah, shofar, matzot, and mikveh. The cost varies, but is generally under $2. Write to him directly for a complete list of the pamphlets published or to order:
2260 Olinville Ave.
Bronx, N. Y. 10467

Prayer and liturgy

Arzt, Max. *Justice and Mercy.* New York: Holt Rinehart & Winston, 1963, out of print; also in paperback, out of print. High Holidays commentary.
Glatzer, Nahum. *Language of Faith: A Selection from the Most Expressive Jewish Prayers.* New York: Schocken, 1947.
Idelsohn, A. Z. *Jewish Liturgy and Its Development.* New York: HUC-JIR Sacred Music Press, 1932; New York: Schocken, paperback. Scholarly introduction; structural analysis.
Jacobs, Louis. *Hasidic Prayer.* New York: Schocken, 1972.
Jacobs, Louis. *Jewish Prayer.* London: Jewish Chronicle, 1962, out of print.
Millgram, Abraham E. *Jewish Worship.* Philadelphia: JPS, 1971. Basic introduction; popular style.
Munk, Elie. *The World of Prayer.* Vol. 1, *Daily Prayers;* Vol. 2, *Sabbath and Festival Prayers.* New York: Feldheim, 1963. Commentary on prayers. Thorough.
Petuchowski, Jakob J. *Understanding Jewish Prayer.* New York: Ktav, 1972.

Music, dance

Berk, Fred. *Ha-Rikud: The Jewish Dance.* New York, UAHC, 1972. Includes instructions for dances.
Eisenstein, Judith Kaplan. *Heritage of Music.* New York: UAHC, 1972.
Idelsohn, Abraham Zevi. *Jewish Music in Its Historical Development.* New York: Tudor, 1929; New York: Schocken, 1967; also in paperback. Standard introduction.
Sendrey, Alfred. *Music in Ancient Israel.* New York: Philosophical Library, 1969, out of print.
Sendrey, Alfed. *Music of the Jews in the Diaspora.* New York: Yoseloff, 1970.
Soltes, Avraham. *Off the Willows.* New York: Bloch, 1970, out of print.
See also Music.

Art

Cockerell, Sydney C. *Old Testament Miniatures.* New York: Braziller, 1969.
Davidovitch, David. *The Ketuba: Jewish Marriage Contracts through the Ages.* Tel Aviv: Lewin-Epstein, 1968. Features color plates of illuminated ketubbot with text.
Goodenough, Edwin R. *Jewish Symbols in the Greco-Roman Period.* 13 vols. Princeton: Princeton University Press, 1953-1969.
Gutfeld, Ludwig. *Jewish Art from the Bible to Chagall.* New York: Yoseloff, 1968.
Guttmann, Joseph, ed. *Beauty in Holiness: Studies in Jewish Customs and Ceremonial Art.* New York: Ktav, 1970.
Kampf, Avram. *Contemporary Synagogue Art.* New York: UAHC, 1966; Philadelphia: JPS, 1966.
Kanof, Abram. *Jewish Ceremonial Art and Religious Observance.* New York: Abrams, 1969.
Katz, Karl, and others. *From the Beginning: Archeology and Art in the Israel Museum, Jerusalem.* New York: Morrow, 1968.
Landsberger, Franz. *A History of Jewish Art.* Cincinnati: UAHC,

1946.

Narkiss, Bezalel. *Hebrew Illuminated Manuscripts.* New York: Macmillan, 1969.

Roth, Cecil. *Jewish Art: An Illustrated History.* New York: McGraw-Hill, 1961; rev. ed. Greenwich, Conn.: New York Graphic Society, 1971.

BIBLIOGRAPHIES

Jewish Book Council Booklists
15 E. 26th St.
New York, N. Y. 10010

A Booklist for the Jewish Adult. 1970. 18pp. 20c

A Book List for the Jewish Child. 1972. 57pp. 75c

Selected Paperbound Books of Jewish Interest. 2pp. 30c

Selected Books on Israel. 15pp. 25c

Sephardic and Oriental Jewry: Selected Reading List of Books in English. 7pp. 15c

Jewish Life in Many Lands: A Selected Bibliography. 11pp. 15c

Historical Fiction on Jewish Themes. 7pp. 10c

Selected Yiddish Books for a Library (in Yiddish). 15pp. 5c

The Jewish Press: A Selected Listing. 1971. 6pp. 10c

Jewish Reference Books: A Selected List. 1970. 16pp. 25c

Jewish Bookland. Monthly publication, Jewish Book Council. Subscription: $2 per year. Reviews of recent books in English, Yiddish and Hebrew, plus juveniles, list of recent paperbacks and reprints.

Jewish Book Annual. Jewish Book Council. vol. 30 (1972-73); vol. 29 (1971-72); vol. 28 (1970-71); vol. 25 (1967-68); available from Jewish Book Council, $6 each volume. Earlier volumes are distributed by Krauss Reprint Corp.
16 E. 46th St.
New York, N. Y. 10017
Each volume contains articles and bibliographies of current Jewish books in English, Hebrew and Yiddish, plus essays on Jewish literature.

Neusner, Jacob, and others. *The Study of Judaism: Bibliographical Essays.* New York: Ktav for the ADL, 1972. 229pp. $12.50. Contains bibliographical essays on the following topics: Judaism in New Testament times; Judaism on Christianity; Christianity on Judaism; modern Jewish thought; the contemporary Jewish community; the Holocaust.

Guide to the Study and Practices of Judaism. Yavneh
156 Fifth Ave.
New York, N.Y. 10010
50c. List of source materials on various areas of halakhic Jewish life.

A Bibliography on Judaism and Jewish-Christian Relations. New York: ADL
315 Lexington Ave.
New York, N. Y. 10016
1965. 62pp. $1. 1300 entries.

Recommended Books of Jewish Interest. 1968. Hadassah
65 E. 52nd St.
New York, N. Y. 10022
50c

The Atid Bibliography: A Resource for the Questioning Jew. Atid
218 E. 70th St.
New York, N. Y. 10021

Judaica Book News. Published twice a year by Book News, Inc.
303 W. 10th St.
New York, N. Y. 10014
May be purchased at 50c each from various local Jewish bookstores around the country and directly from the publisher. Lists and ads for new and forthcoming Jewish books, paperbacks, and juvenile books. Also contains essays on Jewish book industry and Jewish authors.

Bibliographies available from:
Publications Dept.
Jewish Agency
515 Park Ave.
New York, N. Y. 10022

Bibliography of Israel and Jewish Folk Dances by Fred Berk. 1960. New York Jewish Agency, Youth and Hechalutz Dept. 50c. All books and records available at time of publication.

A Bibliography on Teaching Hebrew to Adults by Ben-Zion Fischler. New York Jewish Agency, Dept. of Education and Culture, 1964. 50c

Bibliographies available from:
The American Jewish Committee
Institute of Human Relations Press
165 E. 56th St.
New York, N. Y. 10022

Jews in the Soviet Union 1967–1971: An Annotated Bibliography by Louise Renée Rosenberg. 1971. 60pp. $1.25. Almost three hundred books and articles.

In the Jewish World: Views and Reviews of Current Jewish Writings. Quarterly. 50c each; annual subscription $2. Summaries of articles from Jewish and non-Jewish journals here and abroad.

What We Know about Young American Jews. 1970. 20pp. 35c. Annotated bibliography on current generation of Jewish teenagers and college youth.

Writings on Jewish Ḥistory. 1970. 32pp. 35c. Annotated list of books for students in grades 5–12.

Children of One Father. 1966. 28pp. 25c. Bibliography of inexpensive pamphlets on Jewish-Christian relations.

Bibliographies available from:
Anti-Defamation League
315 Lexington Ave.
New York, N. Y. 10016

Jews in American Life: A Selected Bibliography. Free.

Israel: A Bibliography. Compiled by Iva Cohen. 70pp. $2.50. Over 100 titles listed.

Jewish Music: A Guide and Bibliography. 20c

Bibliography of American and Canadian Jewish Memoirs and Autobiographies in Yiddish, Hebrew and English. New York: YIVO, 1970. $2

Glanz, Rudolf. *The German Jew in America: An Annotated Bibliography Including Books, Pamphlets and Articles of Special Interest.* Cincinnati: HUC, 1969. 192pp.

Schlesinger, Benjamin. *The Jewish Family: A Survey and Annotated Bibliography.* Toronto: University of Toronto Press, 1971. 175pp.

Goldberg, Ira S., comp. *Bibliography of Instrumental Music of Jewish Interest.* Rev. ed. New York: National Jewish Music Council, 1970.
part 1. Orchestra and Band
part 2. Ensemble and Solo.

Reference

INDEXES

Leikind, Miriam ed. *Index to Jewish Periodicals.* Cleveland: College of Jewish Studies, 1963–. Indexes about 50 periodicals of Jewish interest from U. S. and England.

Marcus, Jacob, and Bilgray, Albert. *An Index to Jewish Festschriften.* Cincinnati: HUC, 1937. Indexes 53 Festschriften through 1936, except those limited to philology and linguistics.

Berlin, Charles, ed. *Index to Festschriften in Jewish Studies.* New York: Ktav, 1971. Picks up where above titles leave off. Indexes 243 Festschriften.

Marcus, Jacob R. *An Index to Scientific Articles on American Jewish History.* New York: Ktav, 1971. Indexes 13 journals specializing in American Jewish history.

DIRECTORIES

Frenkel, Louis, ed. *American Jewish Organizations Directory.* New York: Frenkel Mailing Service, 1971. All Jewish organizations of U. S. and Canada with addresses and phone numbers.

American Jewish Year Book. New York: American Jewish Committee. Yearly survey, arranged by country, of Jewish vital statistics, demography, year's events. Includes list of Jewish periodicals and organizations, plus topical essays on world affairs.

Fraenkel, Josef. *The Jewish Press of the World.* London: World Jewish Congress, 1967. Newspapers, listed by country.

The Jewish Communities of the World. Institute of Jewish Affairs, 1971. Includes short essays about Jewish life in each country, plus statistics and leading institutions.

ENCYCLOPEDIAS

Roth, Cecil, and Wigoder, Geoffrey, eds. *Encyclopaedia Judaica.* 16 vols. Jerusalem: Keter (distributed in U. S. A. by MacMillan), 1972. The latest major Jewish reference book index contained in volume 1. Excellent maps, charts, and illustrations.

Patai, Raphael, ed. *Encyclopedia of Zionism and Israel.* 2 vols. New York: Herzl Press, 1971. Useful and thorough.

Roth, Cecil, and Widoger, Geoffrey, eds. *New Standard Jewish Encyclopedia.* New York: Doubleday, 1970. Good one-volume encyclopedia for home use. Often offered as introductory inducement by Commentary Library (see introduction to this section).

BIOGRAPHIES

Who's Who in Israel. Tel Aviv: 1972. Brief biographical information.

Who's Who in World Jewry, 1972. New York: Pitman, 1972. A biographical dictionary of outstanding Jews. 10,000 biographies; all countries except USSR and Arab lands.

ATLASES

Aharoni, Yohana, and Avi Yonah, Michael. *Macmillan Bible Atlas.* New York: Macmillan, 1968.

Gilbert, Martin. *Jewish History Atlas.* New York: Macmillan, 1969. Excellent collection of 112 pages of maps. Manageable size.

Vilnay, Zev. *New Israel Atlas.* New York: Sabra, 1970.

MISCELLANEOUS

Kolatch, Alfred J. *Names for Boys and Girls.* New York: Jonathan David, paperback.

Spier, Arthur. *The Comprehensive Hebrew Calendar 1900-2000.* New York: Behrman, 1952.

Spalding, Henry D. *Encyclopedia of Jewish Humor, from Biblical Times to the Modern Age.* New York: Jonathan David, 1969.

Baron, Joseph L. *A Treasury of Jewish Quotations.* New York: Crown, 1965.

DICTIONARIES

Alcalay, Reuben. *The Complete Hebrew-English Dictionary. The Complete English-Hebrew Dictionary.* Hartford: Prayer Book Press, 1965.

Weinrich, Uriel. *Modern English-Yiddish, Yiddish-English Dictionary. New York: YIVO, 1968.*

Some Jewish bookstores

New York

J. Biegeleisen Co.
83 Division St.
New York, 10002
(212) WO 6-5916

Bloch Publishing Co.
915 Broadway
New York, 10010
(212) 673-7910

Theodore S. Cinnamon Ltd.
420 Jerusalem Ave.
Hicksville, L. I. 11801
(516) WE 5-7480

Philipp Feldheim, Inc.
96 E. Broadway
New York, 10002
(212) WA 5-3180
Excellent stock of used and out-of-print sefarim.

The Jewish Museum Bookshop
1109 Fifth Ave.
New York, 10028
(212) RI 9-3770

Lazar's Sefer Israel, Inc.
156 Fifth Ave.
New York, 10010
(212) WA 9-6411
Specializes in Israeli publications.

J. Levine Co.
58 Eldridge St.
New York, 10002
(212) WO 6-4460

Louis Stavsky Co.
147 Essex St.
New York, 10002
(212) 674-1289

M. Wolozin, Inc.
38 Eldridge St.
New York, 10002
(212) WA 5-4289

Zion Tallis Book Division
48 Eldridge St.
New York, 10002
(212) 925-8558
Specializes in tallit, tefillin, etc.

California

Harelick and Roth
1070 South La Cienega Blvd.
Los Angeles, 90035
(213) 655-9877

Steven L. Maimes, Bookseller
224 Judah St. No. 1
San Francisco, 94122
Sells and distributes Judaic books. Mail order. Specializes in Kabbalah and hasidut.

Illinois

Hamakor Judaica Inc.
6112 N. Lincoln Ave.
Chicago, 60659
(312) 463-4455

Rosenblum's Hebrew Book Store
3443 W. Lawrence Ave.
Chicago, 60625
(312) IR 8-2278

Schwartz's-Goodman Bros. Hebrew Bookstore
2611 W. Devon Ave.
Chicago, 60645
(312) BR 4-0286 or SH 3-9779

Maryland

Abe's Jewish Book Store Inc.
11250 Georgia Ave.
Wheaton, 20902
(301) 942-2218

Central Hebrew Book Store
228 Reistertown Rd.
Baltimore, 21208
(301) 653-0550

Goodman's Hebrew Books and Gifts
2305 University Blvd. West
Wheaton, 20902
(301) 949-8100

Massachusetts

Israel Book Shop Inc.
410 Harvard St.
Brookline, 02146
(617) 566-7113

Mayan
P. O. Box 246
Sudbury, 01776

Melvin's
197–199 Main St.
Great Barrington, 01230
(413) 528-0822

Michigan

Borenstein's Book and Music Stores
25242 Greenfield
Oak Park, 48237
(313) DI 1-0569; *and*
13535 West 7 Mile Rd.
Detroit, 48235
(313) DI 1-0569 or DI 1-3268

Spitzer's Hebrew Book and Gift Center
24900 Coolidge Highway
Oak Park, 48237
(313) 542-7520

Minnesota

Brochin's Book and Gift Shop
4813 Minnetonka Blvd.
Minneapolis, Minn. 55416

New Jersey

Skybook Associates, Inc.
1923 Springfield Ave.
Maplewood, 07040
(201) 763-4244-5

Ohio

Frank's Hebrew Book Store
1647 Lee Rd.
Cleveland, 44118

Pennsylvania

Piotrkowski's Judaica Center
289 Montgomery Ave.
Bala Cynwyd, 19004
(215) MO 4-1303; *and*
115 Old York Rd.
Jenkintown, 19046
(215) TU 6-6062

Rosenberg Hebrew Book
4939 North Broad St.
Phila., 19141
(215) DA 9-0947; *and*
6408 Castor Ave.
Phila., 19149
(215) PI 4-5205

Canada

Book Center, Inc.
5168 Queen Mary Rd.
Montreal 248, P. Q.
(514) 481-5609

Negev Importing Co. Ltd
House of Judaica
3509 Bathurst St.
Toronto 392, Ont.
(416) 781-0071

Rodal's Hebrew Book Store and Gift Shop
4685 Van Horne St.
Montreal, P. Q.
(514) 733-1876

Zucker's Books and Art
3453 Bathurst St.
Toronto 392, Ont.
(416) 781-2133

CHILDREN'S BOOKS

The Jewish children's book scene is a bleak one. Books seem to be published mainly to instruct rather than to delight. There are very few books that are just plain fun to read or that communicate that being Jewish is fun at all. The moralistic note predominates.

Children's books usually fall into one of the following categories: Bible stories, holiday stories, books on Israel, biographies, and fiction.

The greatest number of acceptable books, especially for preschoolers, are found among the Bible stories. Here are books which are a pleasure to look at and which convey something of authentic Jewish heritage with minimal moralizing. Many of the best books are published by non-Jewish houses, which can afford to hire talented artists and designers because they seek a wider clientele than synagogue libraries and Jewish schools. Among the Bible stories, Noah and David have the lion's share of the market, the former, probably, because both illustrators and children love animals.

Among the Israeli books, most are aimed at older children and seem to be designed for use in the public or religious school social studies curriculum. They therefore tend to be instructional rather than imaginative in style. We have many books summarizing the history, geography, and economy of Israel and hardly any conveying what life is like for an Israeli child. Needless to say, most of these books are written by Jews and are totally one-sided in their presentation of Israel's past and present. The only current problem dealt with is security and defense, and all other aspects of present-day life are glossed over without any serious examination.

The holiday stories are, for me, the most deficient area of Jewish children's literature. Here, the teachy-preachy tone is ubiquitous and imagination is minimal. Over and over, the books tell the history of the holiday and instruct in today's observances. The historical treatments are, on the whole, much more acceptable and well written than the customs and ceremonies books. There are practically no attempts, in any sense, to show how children today approach the holidays. There are no problems in these books. The model children (always, it seems, a brother and sister) celebrate joyously or ask purely informational questions which stimulate parental preaching. Never is there a conflict, for example, about staying home from school or not going to synagogue. Of the fifty or so Hanukkah books available, only one deals intelligently with the conflict felt in many American homes between Christmas and Hanukkah. Of the score or more Passover books, not one talks about the difficulties a modern child might experience, for example, eating only kosher-for-Passover foods during the holiday. Of all Shabbat books, not one relates any negative feelings toward the restrictions on his freedom. Never is a resentful feeling about Sunday school expressed. Little David and Debbie and their counterparts are always mere cardboard figures, acting out the rituals with great cheer and family solidarity. Where might an older child learn to deal with the conflicts he must certainly face at some time in his life with accepting traditional patterns and rituals? Certainly not in any of these customs and ceremonies books. In addition, and certainly understandable in the context of showing traditional practices, these books are sexist, almost without exception. Mother is always cleaning or cooking for the holidays and little Debbie is usually at her side, learning to be the Jewish Homemaker of Tomorrow and earning Daddy's praises for her housewifely achievements. One can only hope that the new Jewish feminists will exert their efforts in creating some new Jewish books for their younger sisters and daughters to read.

In the area of fiction, fortunately, all is not so grim. Although, again, the negative or questioning note is rarely sounded, we at least have some books which show Jewish children as real people with problems in the social, familial, and academic aspects of their lives, if not in the religious. The only religious problem dealt with is anti-Semitism, and the Jewish children in these books usually come off as much more saintly characters than they do in books which deal with other aspects of growing up Jewish. In the fictional works, also, we get a more realistic picture of Israeli life and culture, especially in the recent books translated from Israeli originals. Unfortunately, there are still no books which deal realistically with children grappling with their Jewish identity. The most enjoyable and well-written books are those which deal positively with Judaism. Any which show conflict deal with it only in terms of the prejudices of the non-Jews.

The biographical works constitute a fairly healthy area, although there are still many eminent men and women about whom there is nothing available on a child's level.

The books in the following list are ones which I consider outstanding. With the limitations described above, these books are the best written and least objectionable available.

The Jewish Book Council
15 E. 26th St.
New York, N. Y. 10010

published a *Book List for the Jewish Child* at 75c which evaluates and annotates all children's books in print through June 1971. This booklet, an excellent comprehensive guide that should be consulted for a survey of the field, is also a source for beginning and building a children's library. Our list includes many of these items and adds new books published since the list and, in some cases, out-of-print items which are classics and still available in many libraries.

Now for omissions. I have omitted most books on Jewish thought and ethics as being outside the category of literature. Second, I automatically reject any books which feature talking dreidels, runaway matzot, and crying Kiddush cups. I am also turned off by any book whose plot consists of little David or Debbie being taken in a dream through Jewish history, Israel, or anywhere else. These are personal literary prejudices of mine which have influenced this list.

History

Charry, Elias, and Segal, Abraham. *The Eternal People: The Story of Judaism and Jewish Thought through the Ages.* New York: United Synagogue, 1967. (12–16). Stimulating presentation.

Karp, Deborah. *Heroes of Jewish Thought.* New York: Ktav, 1965. *Heroes of Modern Jewish Thought.* New York: Ktav, 1966. (10–14). Selected thinkers and their contributions.

Pearlman, Moshe. *The Zealots of Masada: The Story of a Dig.* New York: Scribners, 1967; also in paperback.

Pilch, Judah. *The Jewish Catastrophe in Europe.* New York: American Association for Jewish Education, 1968. (12–16). The Holocaust.

Yadin, Yigal. *The Story of Masada.* Retold by Gerald Gottlieb. New York: Random House, 1969. (10–14). Children's edition of author's report on the excavation.

Suhl, Yuri. *An Album of the Jews in America.* New York: Watts, 1972. (8 and up). Fascinating photographs from archival collections illustrate a brief history of Jewish immigrants and their contributions.

Biography

Appel, Benjamin. *Ben Gurion's Israel.* New York: Grossett & Dunlap, 1967. (12–16). The life of Israel's first prime minister.

Baker, Rachel. *Chaim Weizmann: Builder of a Nation.* New York: Messner, 1950. (12–16). Readable biography of the first president of Israel.

Berkman, Ted. *Cast a Giant Shadow: The Story of Mickey Marcus, a Soldier for All Humanity.* Philadelphia: JPS, 1967. (11–14). Young people's edition of adult biography of the American soldier who died fighting for Israel in the War of Independence, 1948.

Cone, Molly. *Hurry Henrietta.* Boston: Houghton Mifflin, 1966. (10–13). Biography of the younger years of Henrietta Szold.

Falstein, Louis. *The Man Who Loved Laughter.* Philadelphia: JPS, 1968. (11–14). Well-written biography of Sholem Aleichem.

Fast, Howard M. *Haym Solomon: Son of Liberty.* New York: Messner, 1941. (11–14). Life story of a Jewish patriot of the American Revolution.

Frank, Anne. *The Diary of a Young Girl.* Garden City, New York: Doubleday, 1967. (12–15). Diary of a Dutch Jewish girl in hiding with her family from the Nazis.

Greenfield, Howard. *Marc Chagall.* Chicago: Follett, 1968. (10–14). Life of the artist with reproductions of his work.

Klaperman, Libby. *Saadia Gaon: The Fighter Scholar.* Philadelphia: JPS, 1961. (11–14). Biography of the tenth-century philosopher.

Marcus, Rebecca B. *Moses Maimonides: Rabbi, Philosopher and Physician.* New York: Watts, 1969. (11–14). The Rambam and his thinking.

Merriam, Eve. *Emma Lazarus: The Voice of Liberty.* Philadelphia: JPS, 1959. Story of the American Jewish poet.

Morris, Terry. *Shalom, Golda.* New York: Hawthorn, 1971. Biography of the prime minister of Israel.

Omer, Deborah. *Rebirth: The Story of Eliezer Ben-Yehudah and the Modern Hebrew Language.* Philadelphia: JPS, 1972. (11–14).

Rothschild, Sylvia. *I. L. Peretz: Keys to a Magic Door.* Philadelphia: JPS, 1959. (11–14).

Simon, Charlie May. *Martin Buber: Wisdom in Our Time.* New York: Dutton, 1969. (12–16).

Singer, Isaac Bashevis. *A Day of Pleasure: Stories of a Boy Growing Up in Warsaw.* Photos by Roman Vishniac. New York: Farrar, 1969. (10 and up). Sensitive, beautifully written vignettes from the author's boyhood.

Stadtler, Bea. *The Adventures of Gluckel of Hameln.* New York: United Synagogue Commission on Jewish Education, 1967. Young people's edition of the classic memoirs of a seventeenth-century Jewish woman in Germany.

Vineberg, Ethel. *Grandmother Came from Dworitz: A Jewish Story.* Montreal: Tundra, 1969. (10–14). Loving tribute to the author's family as she recounts her ancestor's life in the shtetl and emigration to North America.

Fiction and fictionalized history

Burstein, Chaya M. *Rifka Bangs the Teakettle.* New York: Harcourt Brace & World, 1970. (9–11). Little shtetl girl longs for education.

Cohen, Barbara. *The Carp in the Bathtub.* New York: Lothrop, 1972. (6–10). Great story of children who can't bear to see their pet carp made into gefilte fish for Passover.

Cone, Molly. *A Promise Is a Promise.* Boston: Houghton Mifflin, 1964. (9–13).

Cone, Molly. *You Can't Make Me If I Don't Want to.* Boston: Houghton Mifflin, 1971. (10–14). Realistic family tensions. Boy runs away because he doesn't want to move to Israel with his family.

Feder-Tal, Karah. *The Ring.* New York: Abelard-Schuman, 1965. (9–12). Realistic story of development town in Israel.

Forman, James. *My Enemy, My Brother.* New York: Meredith, 1969. (12–16). Excellent novel of illegal immigration to Palestine.

Gold, Sharlya. *The Potter's Four Sons.* New York: Doubleday, 1969. (9 and up). Beautiful story of four boys' journey through life. Connected with Hanukkah.

Hautzig, Esther. *The Endless Steppe: Growing Up in Siberia.* New York: Thomas Y. Crowell, 1968. (10–16). Based on author's childhood experiences. Beautiful book.

Ish-Kishor, Sulamith. *Boy of Old Prague.* New York: Pantheon, 1963; Oceanside, N. Y.: Blue Star, paperback. Medieval history. Classic.

Ish-Kishor, Sulamith, *Master of Miracle: A New Novel of the Golem.* New York: Harper, 1971. (10–14).

Ish-Kishor, Sulamith. *Our Eddie.* New York: Pantheon, 1969. (12–16). Sensitive problem novel of family difficulties.

Kerr, Judith, *When Hitler Stole Pink Rabbit.* New York: Coward-McCann, 1972. (9–13). Moving story, based on the author's childhood of German family's escape to wander in Europe during Hitler's regime.

Konigsburg, E. L. *About the B'nai Bagels.* New York: Atheneum, 1969. (9–13). Amusing, very real story of American boy's life, featuring his Bar Mitzvah and Little League.

Levitin, Sonia. *Journey to America.* New York: Atheneum, 1970. (9–12). Jewish family escapes from Nazi Germany.

Levoy, Myron. *The Witch of Fourth Street and Other Stories.* New York: Harper, 1972. (8–12). Sensitive, unstereotyped stories of different ethnic groups on New York's Lower East Side. Several stories feature Jewish characters.

Moskin, Marietta. *I Am Rosemarie.* New York: John Day, 1972. (12–16). Author tells the story of her childhood in Nazi Germany, including her life in concentration camp.

Nathan, Dorothy. *The Shy One.* New York: Random House, 1966; Oceanside, N. Y.: Blue Star, paperback. Only peripherally Jewish in content, this is a sensitive story and does have positive feeling toward Jewishness.

Neville, Emily Cheney. *Berries Goodman.* New York: Harper, 1965. Story of non-Jewish boy confronting suburban anti-Semitism. Excellent book; very real family situations.

Richte, Hans Peter. *Friedrich.* New York: Holt Rinehart & Winston, 1970. (10–14). Holocaust story; excellent.

Sholem Aleichem. *Tevye. Oh a Miracle!* New York: Fleet, 1971. (7–10). How Tevye becomes a milkman. Colorful illustrations, simple text.

Shulevitz, Uri. *The Magician.* Adapted from Yiddish of I. L. Peretz. New York: Macmillan, 1973. (5–8). Story of Elijah's visit to a poor shtetl family on Passover.

Taylor, Sydney. *All-of-a-Kind Family.* Chicago: Follett, 1951; New York: Dell, paperback. *More All-of-a-Kind Family.* Chicago: Follett, 1954; New York: Dell, paperback. *All-of-a-Kind Family Uptown.* Chicago: Follett, 1958; New York: Dell, paperback. *All-of-a-Kind Family Downtown.* Chicago: Follett, 1972. (9–12). Wonderful, real, appealing stories of New York Jewish family in the early 1900s.

Taylor, Sydney. *A Papa like Everyone Else.* Chicago: Follett, 1966. Warm story of Jewish life in Czechoslovakia.

Bible stories

Allstrom, Elizabeth. *Songs along the Way.* Nashville: Abingdon, 1961. Selected psalms, strikingly illustrated.

Armstrong, William H. *Hadassah: Esther, the Orphan Queen.* Garden City, N. Y.: Doubleday, 1972. (8–12)

Bollinger, Max. *Daniel.* New York: Dell, 1970. (8–12)

Bollinger, Max. *David.* New York: Dell, 1967. (8–12)

Bollinger, Max. *Noah and the Rainbow.* New York: Thomas Y. Crowell, 1972. Beautiful illustrations, simple text.

Bulla, Clyde Robert. *Jonah and the Great Fish.* New York: Thomas Y. Crowell, 1970. (6–10)

Bulla, Clyde Robert. *Joseph the Dreamer.* New York: Thomas Y. Crowell, 1971. (7–10)

Davis, Moshe, and Levy, Isaac. *Journeys of the Children of Israel.* Hartford: Hartmore House, 1967. Bible atlas.

De Regniers, Beatrice. *David and Goliath.* New York: Viking, 1965. (5–8)

Eisenberg, Azriel, and Elkins, Dov Peretz. *Worlds Lost and Found: Discoveries in Biblical Archeology.* New York: Abelard-Schuman, 1964. (12–16)

Farb, Peter. *The Land, Wildlife, and Peoples of the Bible.* New York: Harper, 1967. (11–16)

Freehof, Lillian S. *Stories of King David.* Philadelphia: JPS, 1952. (8–12). Midrash retold.

Freehof, Lillian S. *Stories of King Solomon.* Philadelphia: JPS, 1955. (8–12). Midrash retold.

Freehof, Lillian S. *Third Bible Legend Book.* New York: UAHC, 1956. Midrashic stories of biblical personalities, Samuel to Esther.

Kummel, Sara B. *Esther Becomes a Queen.* New York: UAHC, 1955. (5–8). Unfortunately, out of print. The best telling of Purim story for young readers. Maybe UAHC will reprint it if pressure is put on them.

Lenski, Lois. *Mr. and Mrs. Noah.* New York: Thomas Y. Crowell, 1948. (4–7)

MacBeth, George. *Jonah and the Lord.* New York: Holt Rinehart & Winston, 1970. (4–8). Bold illustrations.

Malvern, Gladys. *The Foreigner.* New York: McKay, 1954. (10–13). Good retelling of the story of Ruth.

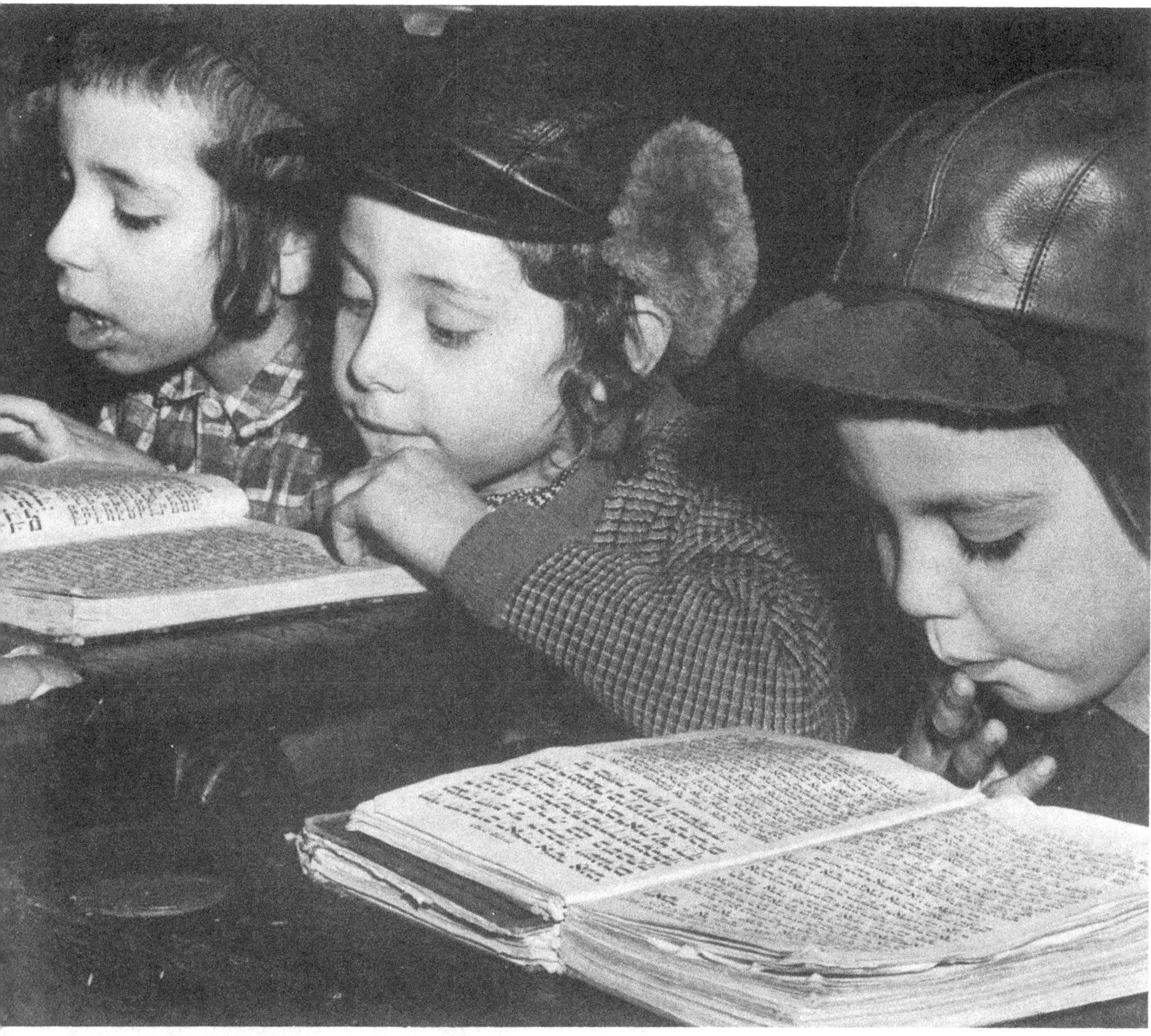

Mazar, Amihay, and Trone, Alexander. *Voices from the Past.* Irvington-on-Hudson, New York: Harvey House, 1968. Biblical archeology.

Miyoshi, Sekiya. *Oldest Story in the World.* Valley Forge, Pa.: Judson, 1969. (4–7). The creation told pictorially.

Miyoshi, Sekiya. *Singing David.* New York: Watt, 1970. (3–7). David the shepherd rescues a lamb.

Neurath, Marie. *They Lived like This in Ancient Palestine.* New York: Watts, 1965. (10–12). Clear reconstruction of everyday life in Bible times.

Newman, Shirley. *A Child's Introduction to Torah.* New York: Behrman, 1972. (8–10). The Melton approach to teaching the Bible, applied to an elementary textbook for Genesis.

Noble, Iris. *Treasure of the Caves: The Story of the Dead Sea Scrolls.* New York: Macmillan, 1971. (12–16). The finding, decipherment, and meaning of the scrolls. Exciting.

Palazzo, Tony. *A Time for All Things: Ecclesiastes III. 1–8.* New York: Walck, 1966. (5–8). "For everything there is a season," illustrated with animal pictures.

Petersham, Maud. *David; Joseph and His Brothers; Moses;* and *Ruth.* New York: Macmillan. Bible stories well told, well illustrated.

Rappaport, Uriel. *The Story of the Dead Sea Scrolls.* Irvington-on-Hudson, New York: Harvey House, 1968. (11–14). Featured is daily life in the time the scrolls were written.

Reeves, James. *The Angel and the Donkey.* New York: McGraw-Hill, 1970. The story of Balaam and his donkey.

Rose, Anne K. *Samson and Delilah.* New York: Lothrop, 1968.

Saporta, Raphael. *Basket in the Reeds.* Minneapolis: Lerner, 1964. (7–9). Moses' childhood. Good for Passover.

Skulsky. S. *Legends of Abraham; Legends of Joseph and His Brothers; Legends of Joshua; Legends of Judah the Maccabee; Legends of King David; Legends of King Solomon; Legends of Moses, the Lawgiver; Legends of Queen Esther; Legends of Ruth; Legends of Samson.* New York: Shulsinger, 1961. Blending of biblical stories plus midrash. Popular with children.

Taslitt, Israel I. *At the Walls of Jericho.* New York: Bloch, 1961. (10–14). Story of Joshua amplified fictionally.

Taslitt, Israel I. *Thunders over Tabor.* New York: Sabra, 1970. (9–12). Story of Deborah in the form of a novel.

Waddell, Helen. *The Story of Saul the King.* Abridged by Doreen Roberts and Elaine Moss. New York: David White, 1966. (10–14). Well illustrated, very close to biblical narrative.

Wagoner, Jean Brown. *The Shepherd Lad.* Indianapolis: Bobbs-Merrill, 1953. (9–12). David's childhood.

Wahl, Jan. *Runaway Jonah and Other Tales.* New York: Macmillan, 1968. (6–8). Cute illustrations and witty stories of Jonah, Noah, and Daniel.

Wengrow, Charles. *Tales of the Prophet Samuel.* New York: Shulsinger, paperback. (6–10). Well-told synthesis of biblical narrative and Midrash.

Wiesner, William. *The Tower of Babel.* New York: Viking, 1968.

Legends and folk tales

Barash, Asher, ed. *A Golden Treasury of Jewish Tales.* Translated from Hebrew by Murray Roston. New York: Dodd Mead, 1966. (10–14)

Elkin, Benjamin. *The Wisest Man in the World: A Legend of Ancient Israel.* New York: Parent's Magazine Press, 1968. (6–9). A legend about King Solomon and a bee.

Goldin, Hyman E. *Book of Legends.* 3 vols. New York: Hebrew, 1937. (12–14). Legends from Talmud and Midrash.

Ish-Kishor, Sulamith. *The Carpet of Solomon.* New York: Pantheon, 1966. (9–12). King Solomon learns humility.

Meckler, David L. *Miracle Men: Tales of the Baal Shem Tov and His Chassidim.* New York: Bloch, 1964. (12 and up).

Serwer, Blanche. *Let's Steal the Moon.* Boston: Little Brown, 1970. (6–10). Ancient and recent tales.

Simon, Solomon. *The Wise Men of Helm.* New York: Behrman, 1945. (9–12); *More Wise Men of Helm.* New York: Behrman, 1965. (9–12); *The Wandering Beggar.* New York: Behrman, 1942. (9–12). All three are classics of humor and warmth. Loved by children of all ages.

Singer, Isaac Bashevis. *Elijah the Slave.* New York: Farrar Straus & Giroux, 1970. (4–8). Tale of Elijah, with magnificent illustrations.

Singer, Isaac Bashevis. *Mazel and Shlimazel or The Milk of a Lioness.* New York: Farrar Straus & Giroux, 1967. (6–10). Good and bad luck influence a young man. Beautiful illustrations.

Singer, Isaac Bashevis. *The Fearsome Inn.* New York: Scribners, 1967. (9–14). Three maidens freed by young men from bondage to a witch.

Singer, Isaac Bashevis. *Zlateh the Goat and Other Stories.* New York: Harper, 1966. (7–12). Yiddish folktales. Very funny.

Tenebaum, Samuel. *The Wise Men of Chelm.* New York: A. S. Barnes, 1965; New York: Collier paperback. Another version of Chelm stories.

Holidays

Cedarbaum, Sophia N. *First Holiday Books.* New York: UAHC, 1961–62. (5–7). Simple well-illustrated little books on each holiday, including *The Sabbath, Chanuko, Purim, Passover, Shovuous, Rosh Ha-Shono, and Yom Kippur, Sukos and Simchas Torah, Tu Bi-Sh'vot.*

Chanover, Hyman and Chanover, Alice. *Happy Hanukkah Everybody; Pesach Is Coming, Pesach Is Here.* New York: United Synagogue Commission on Jewish Education, 1954–56. (5–8). Family activities surrounding these holidays.

Charles, Freda. *The Mystery of the Missing Chalah.* New York: Jonathan David, 1959. (5–8). Delightful family story of preparations for Shabbat.

Cohen, Lenore. *Came Liberty beyond Our Hope: A Story of Hanukkah.* Los Angeles: Ward Ritchie, 1963. (10–13). Thorough retelling of Hanukkah story.

Edelman, Lily. *The Sukkah and the Big Wind.* New York: United Synagogue, 1956. (4–8). Charming story of family sukkah.

Gersh, Harry. *When a Jew Celebrates.* New York: Behrman, 1971. (11–14). Clear, modern approach to Jewish life cycle and Jewish year.

Jaffe, Leonard. *The Pitzel Holiday Book.* New York: Ktav, 1962. (5–9). Imaginative appealing stories of how the Pitzels (tiny creatures) celebrate the holidays.

Purdy, Susan Gold. *Jewish Holidays: Facts, Activities and Crafts.* Philadelphia: Lippincott, 1969. (6–adult). A craft project for each holiday with information about holidays.

Rosenblum, William and Robert J. *Eight Lights: The Story of Chanukah.* Garden City, N. Y.: Doubleday, 1967. Shraga Weil's illustrations enhance this exciting retelling of the Hanukkah story.

Simon, Norma. *Hanukkah, Passover.* New York: Thomas Y. Crowell, 1965–66. (5–8). Beautiful illustrations by Symeon Shimin bring the stories alive.

Weilerstein, Sadie Rose. *Adventures of K'tonton.* New York: Bloch, 1964. (4–8). Classic tales, one for each holiday, plus some about a "Jewish Tom Thumb." Loved by children. The sequel, *K'tonton in Israel* (same publisher and date), is not as good.

Weilerstein, Sadie Rose. *Molly and the Sabbath Queen.* New York: Behrman, 1949. (5–9). Unfortunately out of print. This classic is about a little girl's preparations for Shabbat. Wonderful.

Weilerstein, Sadie Rose. *What the Moon Brought.* Philadelphia: JPS, 1942. (5–7). Time-tested classic. How two sisters celebrate holidays.

Israel (fiction)

Banai, Margalit. *Yael and the Queen of Goats.* New York: Sabra, 1968. (8–12). Much information about Israel woven into a story of a little girl and her pet goat.

Biber, Yehoash. *The Treasure of the Turkish Pasha.* New York: Scribners, 1968; Oceanside, N. Y.: Blue Star, paperback. (12–16). Exciting novel about hidden treasure.

Cone, Molly. *The House in the Tree: A Story of Israel.* New York: Crowell, 1968. (5–8). Young American boy and his adjustment to Israel.

Eisenberg, Azriel and Globe, Leah Ain, eds. *Sabra Children: Stories of Fun and Adventure in Israel.* New York: Jonathan David, 1969. (8–12). Short stories, some classics.

Goldberg, Lea. *Little Queen of Sheba.* New York: UAHC, 1959. (10–13). Moroccan girl learns to adjust to life in Youth Aliyah village.

Edwardson, Cordelia. *Miriam Lives in a Kibbutz.* New York: Lothrop, 1971. (7–9). Little Moroccan girl adjusts to kibbutz life. Illustrated with photographs.

Gur, Morra. *Azeet, Paratrooper Dog.* Nashville: Thomas Nelson, 1972. (9–12). Exciting stories, based on fact, of a German shepherd, member of an Israeli paratrooper unit.

Hamory, Laszlo. *Flight to the Promised Land.* New York: Harcourt Brace & World, 1963. (10–14). Yemenite boy becomes an Israeli pilot.

Nurenberg, Thelma. *My Cousin, the Arab.* New York: Abelard-Schuman, 1965. (12–16). Palestinian kibbutz during preindependence time. Arab-Jewish relations.

Ofek, Uriel. *The Dog that Flew and Other Favorite Stories from Israel.* New York: Sabra, 1969. (9–13). Israeli short stories.

Omer, Devorah. *Journey to the Land of the Rain.* Tel Aviv: Massada, 1969. (6–9). Unusual story of a little girl on kibbutz. Illustrated with photographs.

Omer, Devorah. *The Gideonites: The Story of the Nili Spies in the Middle East.* New York: Sabra, 1968. (10–16). Excellent story of the heroic Aronson family and halutzim of the early twentieth century.

Omer, Devorah. *The Path beneath the Sea.* New York: Sabra, 1969. (9–14). Moroccan boy becomes an Israeli frogman.

Reit, Seymour. *A Week in Hagar's World: Israel.* New York: Crowell-Collier, 1969. (4–8). Daily life on a kibbutz. Illustrated with photographs by Louis Goldman.

Spector, Shoshannah. *Five Young Heroes of Israel.* New York: Shengold, 1970. Kibbutz children during an Arab attack.

Watson, Sally. *Other Sandals.* New York: Holt Rinehart & Winston, 1966. (10–13). Two cousins live in the city and on kibbutz in Israel.

Israel (nonfiction)

Comay, Joan and Pearlman, Moshe. *Israel.* New York: Macmillan, 1964. (11–15).

Essrig, Harry and Segal, Abraham. *Israel Today.* Rev. ed. New York: UAHC, 1968. (12–16). Textbook, good photography.

Fine, Helen. *Behold the Land.* New York: UAHC, 1968. (10–14). Well-written textbook. Could be used for collateral reading.

Gidal, Sonia. *My Village in Israel.* New York: Pantheon, 1959; paperback. Oceanside, N. Y.: Blue Star, paperback. Natural, appealing story of boy on kibbutz. Great photography.

Golann, Cecil Paige. *The Taming of Israel's Negev.* New York: Messner, 1970. (10–12)

Goldberg, Lea, and Riwkin-Brick, Anna. *Eli Lives in Israel.* New York: Macmillan, 1965. (6–8). Photo essay about the life of a little boy on kibbutz.

Grand, Samuel, and Tamar. *The Children of Israel.* New York: UAHC, 1972. (8–12). Photographic book of the life of children all over Israel. Text introduces Hebrew words.

Klein, Mina C. *Temple Beyond Time.* History of the Temple Mount, with photography.

Rutland, Jonathan. *Looking at Israel.* Philadelphia: Lippincott, 1970. (10–14). Succinct history of Israel. Well illustrated with photographs.

Sasek, M. *This Is Israel.* New York: Macmillan, 1962. (All ages). Witty illustrations of Israel, quick visual survey.

Shamir, Gabriel, and Maxim. *The Story of Israel in Stamps.* New York: Sabra, 1970, Oceanside, N. Y.: Blue Star, paperback.

Werstein, Irving. *All the Furious Battles: The Saga of Israel's Army.* New York: Meredith, 1968. (11–16).

Jewish practices, ethics

Arian, Philip, and Eisenberg, Azriel. *The Story of the Prayer Book.* Hartford: Prayer Book, 1968. (12–15). History of Siddur and synagogue services.

Brichto, Mira. *God around Us: A Child's Garden of Prayer.* New York: UAHC, 1969. (5–8). Beautifully illustrated; simple prayers in Hebrew and English.

Chanover, Human, and Zusman, Evelyn. *My Book of Prayer.* Vol. 1. Weekdays and Sabbath; vol. 2. Holidays. New York: United Synagogue Commission on Jewish Education, 1966. (6–9). Simple Hebrew and English prayers; beautiful illustrations.

Freeman, Grace, and Sugarmen, Joan G. *Inside the Synagogue.* New York: UAHC, 1963. (7–9). The synagogue and its ritual objects, illustrated with photos.

Levin, Meyer, and Kurzband, Toby K. *The Story of the Jewish Way of Life.* New York: Behrman, 1959. (10–12). Jewish thought through the ages; very well written.

Vorspan, Albert. *To Do Justly: A Junior Casebook for Social Action.* New York: UAHC, paperback (11–14). Children's edition of the author's *Jewish Values and Social Crisis.* Judaism's attitude to current social and political problems.

Miscellaneous

Ben-Asher, Naomi, and Leaf, Hayim. eds. Rev. ed. *Junior Jewish Encyclopedia.* New York: Shengold, 1970.

Freund, Miriam. *Jewels for a Crown: The Story of the Chagall Windows.* New York: McGraw-Hill, 1963. (10–16).

Meshi, Ita. *A Child's Picture Hebrew Dictionary.* New York: Sabra, 1970. (4–8).

Postal, Bernard. *Encyclopedia of Jews in Sports.* New York: Bloch, 1965. (10–15).

Rieger, Shay. *Our Family.* New York: Lothrop, 1972. (8 and up). Sculptress explains how she tries to convey the spirit of her Jewish ancestors through her sculpture. Moving illustrations.

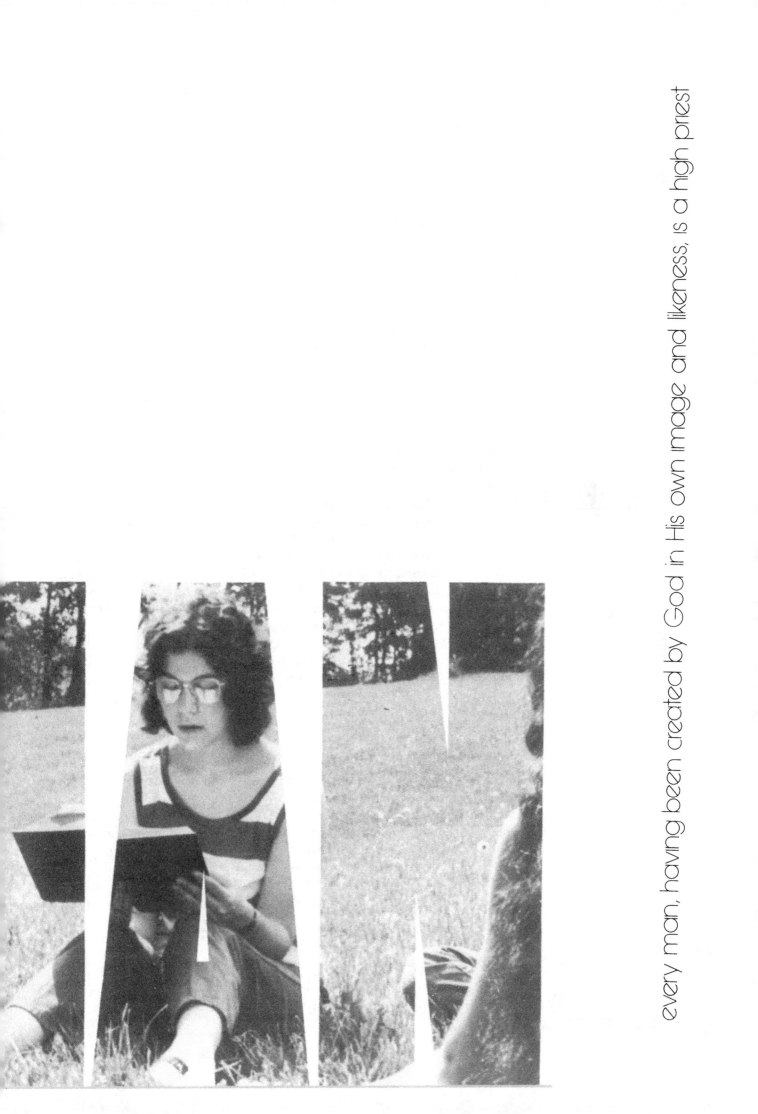

every man, having been created by God in His own image and likeness, is a high priest

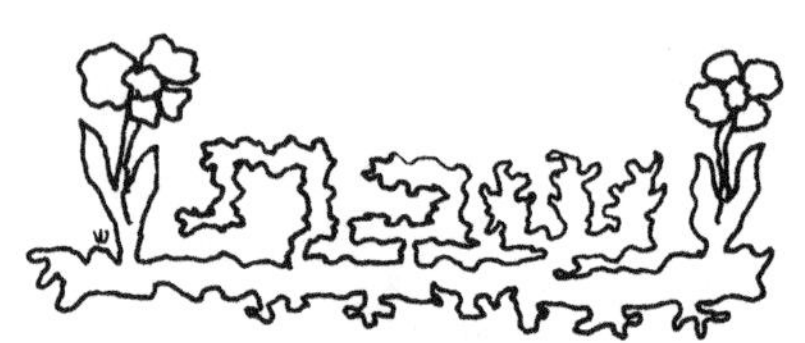

How to bring Mashiah

1. "If you're planting a tree and you hear Mashiah has come, first finish planting and then run to the city gates to tell him Shalom" (Yochanan Ben Zakkai).

THEREFORE: Plant a tree somewhere as a small tikkun olam—fixing up the world—wherever the olam most needs it. Plant a tree in Vietnam in a defoliated former forest. *Go there to plant it* if possible (even if difficult); if not, send money to:

Abraham Heschel Memorial Forest
Trees and Life for Vietnam
Glengary Road
Croton on Hudson, N. Y. 10520

Plant a tree in Appalachia where the strip mines have poisoned the forests. *Go there to plant it; start a kibbutz there and grow more trees.* Plant a tree in Brooklyn where the asphalt has buried the forest. *Go back there to plant it* and live with some of the old Jews who still live there. If policemen come to save the asphalt, keep planting. Offer everybody a turn with the shovel.

2. "Mashiah will come when the whole Jewish People keeps/remembers Shabbat twice in a row" (Talmud, Shabbat 118b).

THEREFORE: Forget about all the things you *mustn't* do on Shabbat, and instead think of all the things you would most *like* to do on Shabbat (and forever). Do them. Read Torah with some friends and talk about it; walk on grass barefoot; look very carefully at a flower without picking it; give somebody something precious and beautiful without asking him to pay you; give love. Since it's not enough to do this alone (see the prediction), pick out a few Jews on the street, tell them it's Shabbat, and dance a horah with them (or the kazatsky, if you're into Yiddish).

3. "The nations . . . shall beat their swords into plowshares. . . . They shall never again know war" (Isaiah 2:4).

THEREFORE: Get together a minyan and travel up to West Point. Take along ten swords and a small forge. Put the small forge in the main entrance, start it glowing, and beat the swords into something like a digging tool. Dig holes for ten trees, and plant the trees in the roadway. Meanwhile, sing "Lo yisah goy" and "Ain't Gonna Study War No More" alternately, and if any West Pointers stop to see what's going down, offer them a reworked sword to dig with.

4. "Mashiah will come when one generation is either wholly innocent or wholly guilty" (Talmud, Sanhedrin 98a).

THEREFORE: Analyze the tax system of the United States, and publish a detailed answer to these two questions: (a) Are United States taxes used largely for purposes prohibited by Torah (e.g., oppressing the poor, destroying

trees, etc.)? (b) Are any Jews in the United States successfully avoiding payment of all taxes? If the answer to (a) is "Yes" and to (b) is "No," proclaim that the entire generation is guilty *in fact,* regardless of their personal opinions. Ask all shuls to include the proclamation in their Shabbat prayers with strong kavvanah: "HaShem, we are at last *all* guilty: send him!"

5. "And a woman shall conceive and bear in the same day [i.e., without pain]" (Midrash on Jeremiah). "See whether a man doth travail with child; wherefore do I see every man with his hands on his loins, as a woman in travail. . . Alas! for that day is great, so that none is like it" (Jeremiah 30: 6–7).

THEREFORE: If you're a man, practice having a baby. Whether you're a man or woman, take a class in the Lamaze method of trained, fully awake childbirth. Learn and practice the exercises. If you're an expectant father, take as much time off from work as your wife/lover does (before and after the birth), and try to experience fully what giving birth and baby care mean.

6. "For the Lord hath created a new thing in the earth: a woman [nekevah] shall court a man [warrior]" (Jeremiah 31:22).

THEREFORE: If you're a woman, surround the nearest warrior type with a ring of laughing, singing women. If he threatens you with a gun, ask seventeen of your sisters to join you in taking it away from him—gently. But more important, whether you're a man or a woman let the female *within you* encompass the warrior *within you.* Let that soul of yours which is open, receptive, enveloping, envelop that soul of yours which is angry, threatening, thrusting.

7. "In that day shall the Lord [Adonai] be one [Ehad], and His name one" (Zechariah 14:9).

THEREFORE: When you pray and come to "Adonai" in the prayer, either *think* "Ehad" with full kavvanah at the same time you are saying "Adonai," or *say* "Ehad" while you think "Adonai."

8. Rabbi Joshua ben Levi found Elijah the prophet, disguised as a leper, begging at the gates of Rome. "When will you come to proclaim the Mashiah?" he asked. " *'Today, . . . if you will hear his voice,'* " replied Elijah (Talmud Babli, Sanhedrin 98a).

THEREFORE: Hear his voice. Open yourself to hear it. Practice saying, "Hineni"—"Here I am"—in a sense of total openness.

9. "In the days to come . . . instruction shall come forth from Zion" (Isaiah 2:1-3). Not out of Sinai. "Behold, the days come, saith the Lord, that I will make a new covenant with the house of Israel, . . . not according to the covenant that I made with their fathers in the day that I [led] them out of . . . Egypt. . . . [Instead,] I will put My law [Torah] in their inward parts, and in their hearts will I write it. . . . They shall teach no more every man his neighbour and every man his brother, saying: 'Know the Lord'; for they shall all know Me" (Jeremiah 31:31-34).

THEREFORE: Stop teaching. Listen inward, inward to your own heart, for the new covenant: the covenant of the Torah from Zion. Listen especially for what is new about it.

10. Said a poor tailor one Yom Kippur, "I have committed only minor offenses; but You, O Lord, have committed grievous sins: You have taken away babies from their mothers, and mothers from their babies. Let us be quits: may You forgive me, and I will forgive You." Said Reb Levi Yitzhak of Berditchev to the tailor, "Why did you let Him off so easily? You might have forced Him to redeem all of Israel!"

THEREFORE: Do not let God off so easily. Hear His/Her voice, but challenge His/Her answer. Wrestle mightily; like Yaakov, you may win. *Keep on wrestling!*

A guide to Jewish women's activities

The Jewish women's movement is still very young and its "membership" is of an undetermined number. This is both because of the lack of a unifying Jewish women's organization and because a system of communication among various small groups with varying objectives has not yet been established.

The following is an introduction to the projects being organized in different parts of the country. It will hopefully serve both to clarify a sometimes fuzzy issue and to provide encouragement to those who are eager to be actively involved in the movement but until now did not know what was available. This guide, it must be emphasized, is *only* a set of general guidelines and a presentation of the reality of the Jewish women's movement as seen from the eyes of a New Yorker. We are still fumbling to determine what is the most crucial issue to tackle first, what our objectives should be, and what strategy is to be used.

Take this introduction as a jumping-off point, not a set of policy statements. We are all united by our sense of frustration, anger, and bewilderment at being treated like second-class citizens within both halakhic and institutional Judaism; we are tired of being shuttled into certain jobs and roles only because we are female.

But we are by no means a homogeneous movement, and we present no uniform ideology. This was aptly demonstrated (very positively, too) at the first National Jewish Women's Conference held in February 1973 in New York City. Over 500 Jewish women of all ages met for four nonstop days, attending panels and workshops dealing with the multifaceted life of a Jewish woman. Many of the activities and projects listed below as suggested areas of priorities for interested Jewish women are the result of the conference.

All inquiries and suggestions about any topic discussed (or not discussed) should be directed to:

North American Jewish Students Network
36 W. 37th St.
New York, N. Y. 10018

They will answer you directly or refer your inquiry to the suitable group.

CONSCIOUSNESS-RAISING

There is no reason to exclude CR groups from the framework of a Jewish women's group. Whether they come from religious or secular backgrounds, at some point in their lives most Jewish women have experienced certain pressures that stem from the fabric of Jewish culture. Learning from the experience of general CR groups, we suggest that if you intend to do this type of thing, limit your group to about 10. Intimacy and trust are the desired results, and for practical reasons a larger group becomes unwieldly. There has been much literature recently about how to run a rap group (see practically any copy of *MS.* magazine), so there is no need to go into that here.

"Jewish" and "non-Jewish" topics for discussion are not mutually exclusive; therefore, do not necessarily exclude a topic because it doesn't seem to fit in with a "Jewish theme" (unless everyone in your group also belongs to a general CR group). Topics found to be especially pertinent to most Jewish women and that are suggested supplements to general topics are:

1. Success and failure: Do parents, and Jewish parents in particular, push an ambiguous or even contradictory success ethic on their daughters—i.e., to do well in school (better than anyone else) and go far in school, but know when to turn off the brains, etc.? If we have children, do we do the same thing? How do we relate to potential success?

2. How do we relate to our mothers? Are we sensitive to the pressures on them to be "Jewish mothers"?

3. Pressure to get married and have children: Because of the deaths of so many Jews, how much are we affected by the psychology of the Holocaust? If we do/do not choose to marry and have children, are our reasons healthy? What kinds of decisions are made out of guilt feelings? If you want children, how many? Are Jews still obliged to "be fruitful and multiply"?

WOMEN AND HALAKHAH

The halakhic questions involving women's rights, obligations, and limitations are the subject of much controversy. The literature listed in the bibliography goes into the issues at length; only a brief presentation of the basic halakhic stance and women's objections to it will be given here.

Legally, women were exempted from practically all positive, time-bound mitzvot (mitzvot aseh she-hazman geramah) because the rabbis recognized their obligation to their families. Women married early, had many children, and spent most of their lives rearing small children. They did not have the time to attend the synagogue and fulfill the ritual functions that developed in it: praying in a minyan, reading the Torah, being a shaliah tzibur (one who leads the congregation). Indeed, women did not even have to pray three times a day. A primary principle in halakhah applying in these cases is that one who is not obligated to do something cannot fulfill someone else's obligation to do that thing; thus women are not only exempt from these commitments but also may not perform these functions where there are men present, for the man is still obliged to do it himself. Another problematic principle very much related to the first is that of kvod ha-tzibur, loosely translated as the honor of the community; this has to do with the idea that if a woman gets up to fulfill a

ritual function in public, aspersion is cast on that congregation, for the implication is that there is no man present who is capable of doing it. This is the reason that's often given for prohibiting women from being called to the Torah and from participating in other synagogue ritual functions.

Briefly, it should be mentioned that with regard to the question of all-women congregations, there are Orthodox rabbis who will sanction a woman's minyan in which women participate in the service either in most or in all the ways men do. This is a potential "out" for Orthodox women and for rabbis who don't want to change the halakhic status quo but want to see it applied fairly. For some, a woman's minyan is an end in itself; for others, it is only a temporary resting place. (If you are interested in organizing something like this, talk to your rabbi or write to Network.)

An extremely vocal element of educated Jewish women, most of them young, has cropped up; they cannot sit quietly and accept the fate most Orthodox rabbis offer them today. Starting in 1972, groups have been emerging around the country to study the position of women in Judaism in different periods in history, and to use their knowledge to push for change. They argue that though the restrictions placed on women were once a blessing and are acknowledged as such, the changing sociology of the times necessitates a vast attitudinal change on the part of those whose decisions legitimize changes in halakhah, an institution which in the past has been responsive to needs of the Jewish community. Women no longer marry at an early age, have many children, or live short lives. The phenomenon of the independent woman, be she single, divorced, or widowed, has never been taken into account in halakhah. The growing number of working women who are not tied down to their homes is also a new development to be reckoned with.

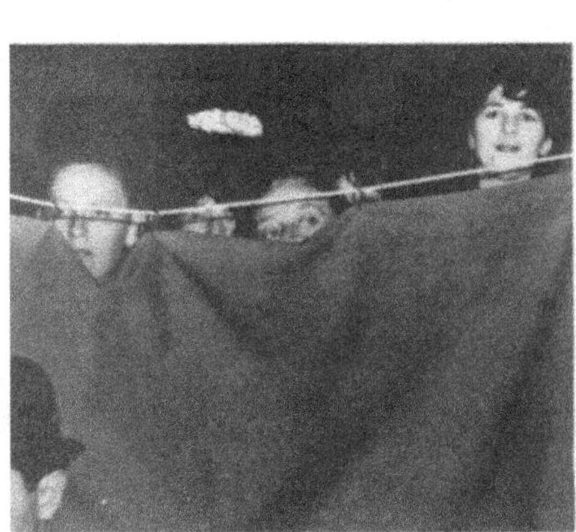

In the area of communal ritual, which has had a very high status in Judaism, many women who have the knowledge, skills, and intellectual and spiritual desire to participate are excluded because of conditions that no longer exist. There are other halakhic areas in which women are discriminated against because of their sex: a woman may not initiate a Jewish divorce; if her husband refused to grant her one, she may not remarry (see T. Weiss-Rosmarin, "The Unfreedom of the Jewish Woman," listed in the bibliography); nor can she be a witness in most cases in a Jewish court. The former problem has caused severe problems in Israel (it is connected to the problem of mamzerut, bastard children), but steps to correct the situation have not been as intensive or extensive as they should be. Most attempts focus upon trying to find loopholes in the law rather than upon a reevaluation of the very basis of the law itself.

It must be mentioned that the Reform and Reconstructionist movements already have, in policy and generally in action, ameliorated these sore points. The Conservative movement has made advances but moves very cautiously—its congregations have the individual rights to institute the changes that would affect the above problems as each sees fit. The Orthodox movement has done almost nothing. Again, to some women, none of the above areas create personal problems; to others, they are all sources of frustration and create feelings of rejection by a beloved tradition as well as anger at the refusal of rabbis to deal with issues that alienate much of half of the Jewish population.

If you are concerned about any/all of these issues, the following are suggested activities you can start in your community to push for change. It is important to remember that no rabbi will give a legal opinion that is not popular in the tradition (or new to it) unless there is substantial need for change; halakhah does not evolve in a vacuum. In other words, until women demonstrate that their needs as Jews are not being met and that they have valid reason to complain, nothing will be done; that is the nature of halakhah, which is basically a conservative institution.

1. Organize a group. Other women will lend much weight to any arguments you might present.

2. In your group study, make a top priority of traditional sources that deal with "women's questions": most importantly, Talmud and responsa literature. This is an ambitious endeavor but crucial if you are to influence rabbis. If you cannot find a woman to teach you (and there are pitifully few—as of now —qualified to teach Talmud), ask your rabbi for help in choosing source material and guiding your study (or use the halakhic bibliography printed here). If you cannot read original sources, either get an English translation or browse extensively through the Jewish religion and law bibliography. Knowledge is crucial.

3. Pressure the power-holders. How you do this depends on you. In Conservative communities you must not only get to the rabbi but also to the synagogue ritual committee. A Conservative synagogue will often respond to the pressure of a significant group of female (or any other) members, especially of the Sisterhood, which can be quite a powerful bloc. In Orthodox communities the task is harder and requires much endurance and patience. Knowledge of the issues is especially important here if a rabbi is to be moved enough to consider the issue seriously. If there is a posek—one who delivers halakhic opinions—call him, or camp on his doorstep until he is ready to give you an answer to your problem(s). If you are sincere, determined, and educated you have a chance.

4. Once you have a group organized, go to neighboring Sisterhoods, Hadassah chapters, Mizrahi groups, and appeal to the women there. Explain your goals to them; it is crucial to remember that many women will never even consider the issue until it is presented to them. Use autobiographical material to illustrate how a Jewish feminist is created. Never threaten a woman by rejecting the role of wife and mother. This is *not* our purpose. The objective is to enable a woman to choose the spiritual life that is right for her.

5. An area ripe for reconsideration is that of theology and prayer. Does the image of God presented in the Bible and Siddur as King, Father, Shepherd, etc. affect the way women view God? Have you ever thought of God as a woman? Do you think sexually about God? What does the prayer "L'Kha Dodi" convey to a man? To a woman? Should we strive for all-inclusive sexual imagery or asexual imagery in our attempts to relate to God? The prayers in the Siddur are not necessarily the last words in prayer; there are different versions of many prayers, and different communities often used and still use different Siddurim. If you are inspired, try creating new prayers.

WOMEN IN JEWISH INSTITUTIONS

Religious

1. The synagogue has traditionally been the focal point of the community as a community; it still is in America. Women have participated actively in the synagogue, but until now only in certain capacities—mainly Sisterhood and PTA. According to the result of a poll of Conservative synagogues taken by Ezrat Nashim, a woman's group in New York, there are very few women who act as officers in the synagogue; those who are officers are, more often than not, secretaries, and there are only one or two Conservative congregations that have a woman as president. There are in fact congregations that outlaw a

woman president in their bylaws, but this restriction has very recently been rendered inoperative by the United Synagogue. There is female representation on boards of trustees, but often only in the capacity of president of the Sisterhood rather than as independent women. The all-important ritual committee, mentioned before, is almost without exception devoid of women. Many synagogues will not allow an adult single woman to become a member of the congregation.

Women who are concerned about the future of their synagogues should run for office, put up their own slates if women are not put up by the nominating committee, and be stubborn about defending their interests. This may even mean withholding Sisterhood funds from the synagogue until legitimate demands are met, be they about membership, admissions policy, or who does what in any given synagogue service. A "Sisterhood Sabbath" once or twice a year should not become the means by which men ease their consciences by showing that "women can participate." This event is a mere token. The only clear indication that men recognize women's rights in the synagogue should be a woman's ability to participate equally with men on *any* Sabbath or holiday. Again, this is almost impossible to achieve in Orthodox synagogues but not difficult in Reform congregations. Recently the Committee on Jewish Law and Standards of the Conservative movement's Rabbinical Assembly rendered a decision that men and women should be counted equally for a minyan—synagogue quorum. This is a welcome change. How effectively it will be instituted in local Conservative synagogues remains to be seen.

One area that affects almost all women (Conservative, Reconstructionist, Reform) is the Bat Mitzvah. If the ceremony is to regain dignity and meaning, it has to be revamped. The only suggestion that will be made here is a structural one: insist that the Bat Mitzvah be celebrated on Saturday morning when the Torah is read (and it should be read by the girl), as is done with the Bar Mitzvah. Relegating the girl to Friday night with part of a haftarah (which is never recited on Friday night anyway) is an example of second-classism and is bound to be picked up by the girl as a sign of the unimportance of her "special day." This change will by no means cure the malaise of the Bat Mitzvah, but it is an important step.

2. Jewish education is perhaps the most important area in which to concentrate your efforts. It touches all women (men, too, of course) regardless of religious affiliation. There are several ways to get involved where very little has been done and much is needed.

The first and most crucial step is to take a good look at the textbooks and children's books being used in all Jewish schools (day schools, Talmud Torahs, Sunday schools). In all of them, Mommy is seen lighting candles and making gefilte fish while the little girl helps set the table; at the same time, father goes to synagogue and the little boy accompanies him. This is the typical message of the literature; it is a surefire way of teaching Jewish girls that they belong at home in the kitchen preparing to become good balabustes while boys prepare for the task of carrying the spiritual burden of the Jews. It is a wonder that girls show up in synagogue at all.

In the area of Bible and Jewish history, there is another serious lack of role models that allow for freedom of choice. Almost all Bible stories are uniformly about men and their spiritual greatness, leadership abilities, and intellectual prowess; men are not presented in one way only, but run the gamut of personality characteristics. The exceptions with regard to women are Deborah and perhaps Esther (though Esther's claim to great respect is dubious to some). The other women in the Bible are not played up and are often not even dealt with on their own merits; the matriarchs seem important because they mar-

ried important men, Miriam because of her brothers, etc. Even granting an antifeminist overtone to the Bible, possibilities for new development of female characters are not nil. Later Jewish history mentions even fewer women, but they are there, waiting to be rediscovered. The situation need not remain as it is now. What is needed are new perspectives and the willingness to work on new texts that are psychologically more suited to raising children who will not grow up with fixed images of what a Jewish man/woman should or should not be.

Another area that involves women is that of Jewish education. Most elementary schoolteachers are women, many of whom, unfortunately, are proponents of the abba-ima school of Jewish education. In the high schools there are very few women, and in general there are practically no female principals. All these problems can be rectified, some more quickly than others. One of the main problems is that elementary schoolteaching has a very low status (and low pay) and therefore does not attract men. Another is that there still is prejudice against hiring a woman for a "disciplinarian's" job, one that requires toughness and administrative ability: that of principal. Women must start badgering school boards to seek out male teachers for younger grades, to hire women for older grades and as principals. They must push for educational reform as talked about above, e.g., use of new and better textbooks. Again, these must not be idle expressions of annoyance; you can send your child to another school or organize a boycott if the educational policy of your present school is offensive to you.

A further area of concern for Jewish women motivated intellectually by Judaism is that of higher Jewish learning. Though women can study Jewish history, philosophy, and literature on a university level, they still cannot always learn Talmud if they want to. This is especially true in Orthodoxy, where an old taboo which has no legal basis anymore still governs education. Talmud is not only the area of highest prestige in Jewish learning but also one of the most challenging and exciting. Orthodox women can push for the end to exclusively male Gemara-Mishnah classes in their schools and expect positive results (though you may have to settle for segregated classes). Again, a good halakhic reason will not be given to oppose you, and an emotional argument about "It's never been done like this" has no leg to stand on.

A further, related problem is that of women rabbis, already dealt with positively by the Reconstructionist and Reform movements. There does not seem to be a good halakhic reason for keeping women from being rabbis, but the status quo will not change in Conservative and Orthodox Judaism until women demand to be included. Attitudinal changes take time to settle in.

Secular

The problem of women in secular Jewish institutions has to do with power. Jewish women participate actively and in large numbers in fund-raising and volunteer work. Both these activities (and they overlap) are necessary but by now are taken for granted by the community and are of very low status. Women in these capacities keep many of our institutions going on a day-to-day basis, but have very little or no say in how the money collected is to be used, or in what areas their volunteer efforts are most needed. There are few women in decision-making positions in major Jewish organizations, such as the federations, Bnai Brith, and UJA. Even more ironic is the fact that some Jewish women's organizations have men who represent them, either as officers or press liaisons, etc. Again, a suggested way to combat this type of discrimination is, first, to disseminate the facts among the organization's supporters and, second, to lobby for representation. Women have quite a bit of untapped power potential.

Just a word about the news media. In the past year or two there has been growing discussion of the Plight of the Jewish Woman in many newspapers and journals, both Jewish and secular. Authors have represented all points of the political and religious spectrum. There have been several issues of publications dedicated specifically to the various aspects of this area: *Off Our Backs* (published in Washington, D. C.); the March 1973 issue of *Sh'ma* (published in New York City); the summer 1973 *Response* (published in Boston); *Genesis 2* (April 1972, Boston); the summer 1971 issue of *Davka* (published in Los Angeles); and a 1972 edition of the *Jewish Free Press* (published by Columbia University students); this is just a partial listing.

The issues and activities discussed here hopefully will be completely irrelevant in the very near future. They are not all only in the theoretical state—there are groups and individuals all over the country working on various aspects of this complex issue. Look around, ask questions, write to Network for help, be creative. . . .

BIBLIOGRAPHY FOR JEWISH WOMEN'S ACTIVITIES

*indicates that the periodical is a constituent of the Jewish Student Press Service; address, etc. can be obtained from

JSP
36 W. 37th St.
New York, N. Y. 10018

Books

ISRAEL

Ben-Zvi, Rachel Yanait. *Coming Home*. New York: Herzl, 1964. Autobiography of a pioneer of the second aliyah period.

Cohen, Guela. *Woman of Violence*. New York: Holt Rinehart & Winston, 1966. Autobiography of her years in the Stern group.

Lindheim, Irma L. *Parallel Quest*. New York: Yoseloff, 1962. Autobiography of a woman from an assimilated German-Jewish family who becomes a Zionist and settles on a kibbutz.

Kaznelson-Rubashow, Rachel. *The Ploughwoman: Records of Pioneer Women of Palestine*. New York: Brown, 1932, out of print. Personal accounts and testimonies.

Maimon, Ada. *Women Build a Land*. New York: Herzl, 1962. Excellent and important history of the working women's movement in prestate Israel from the early 1900s; first feminist wave.

HISTORY AND SOCIOLOGY

Weiss-Rosmarin, Trude. *Jewish Women through the Ages*. New York: The Jewish Book Club, 1940, out of print.

Zbrowski, Mark, and Herzog, Elizabeth. *Life Is with People: The Culture of the Shtetl*. New York: University Press, 1952; New York: Schocken, paperback. Anthropology of Eastern Europe.

HOLOCAUST AND RESISTANCE

Birenbaum, Halina. *Hope Is the Last to Die*. New York: Twayne, paperback. Testimony. Quintessential Jewish mother and sisterhood in ghettos and camps.

Dribben, Judith Strick. *A Girl Called Judith Strick*. New York: Pyramid, paperback. Autobiography of how she spied for partisans in wartime Poland and survived.

Langfus, Anna. *The Whole Land Brimstone*. New York: Pantheon, 1962. Fictionalized or semifictionalized testimony.

Rosen, Donia. *The Forest, My Friend*. New York: Federation of Bergen-Belsen Associations, 1971. Testimony.

Senesch, Hannah. *Letters, Diary, Poems*. New York: Herzl, 1972.

Suhl, Yuri. *They Fought Back*. New York: Crown, 1967. Biographical accounts include Zofia Yamaika, Mala Zimetbaum, Rosa Robota, Niuta Teitelboim (Wanda).

Syrkin, Marie. *Blessed Is the Match*. Philadelphia: JPS, 1947, out of print. Accounts of resistance: Hannah Senesch, Zivia Lubetkin, etc.

NOTE: Two more books in this category are expected soon: a biography of Hannah Senesch by Anthony Masters, *The Summer that Bled*, to be published in England; and an autobiography by Vladka Mead about a Bundist leader in the Warsaw ghetto revolt.

AMERICA

Drinnon, Richard. *Rebel in Paradise: A Biography of Emma Goldman*. Chicago: University of Chicago, 1961.

Fineman, Irving. *Woman of Valor: Life of Henrietta Szold*. New York: Simon & Schuster, 1961.

Goldman, Emma. *Living My Life*. 2 vols. New York: Dover, paperback.

Jacob, H. E. *The World of Emma Lazarus*. New York: Schocken, 1949.

Lebeson, Anita. *Recall to Life: The Jewish Woman in America*. South Brunswick, N. J.: Yoseloff, 1970. Excellently researched accounts of Jewish women from the 1960s.

Merriam, Eve. *The Voice of Liberty*. New York: Farrar Straus & Giroux, and Philadelphia: JPS, 1959. Emma Lazarus biography.

Morton, Leah. *I Am a Woman—and a Jew*. New York: Arno, 1961. Autobiography of a Jewish feminist of the 1930s, written then.

Schwartz, G. and Wyden, B. *The Jewish Wife*. New York: Paperback Library. Popular sociology based on in-depth interviews.

Good despite the author's value judgments.

Suhl, Yuri. *Eloquent Crusader: Ernestine Rose.* New York: Julian Messner, 1970. Biography of Polish-born, feminist comrade of Stanton and Anthony, all but forgotten.

Wald, Lillian. *The House on Henry Street.* New York: Henry Holt, 1915, out of print.

Yezierska, Anzia. *Red Ribbon on a White Horse.* New York: Scribner's, 1950. Autobiography of the novelist of the immigration period.

Special issues on the Jewish woman

*Davka**, Summer 1971. 900 Hilgard Ave., Los Angeles, Cal. 90024.

*Genesis 2**, March 25, 1971. 298 Harvard St., Cambridge, Mass. 02138.

*Kadima**, *May 1972.*

Keeping Posted, April 1972. Nat. Fed. Temple Youth, 838 5th Ave., New York, N. Y.

Off Our Backs. March 1972. Rm. 1013, 1346 Connecticut Ave. NW, Washington, D. C. 20036.

*Response**, Summer 1973. P. O. Box 1496, Brandeis University, Waltham, Mass. 02154.

Articles, papers, accounts in books

ISRAEL

Aloni, Shulamit. "Israel's Women Need Women's Lib." *Israel Magazine* April 1971. Attorney emphasizes problems arising from the rabbinate's control.

Beauvoir, Simone de. "Israeli Women." *New Outlook,* May 1967.

Ben-Yosef, Avraham C. "The Woman on Kibbutz." *Israel Horizons,* Feb. 1957.

Bondy, Ruth. "Granddaughter Wants Conservative Femininity." *Hadassah,* May 1972. Critical of work situation in Israel today but puts much blame on women for accepting old roles.

Kahanoff, Jacqueline. "Grandmother Was a Militant Feminist." *Hadassah,* May 1972. About pioneer women of the second aliyah period.

Horowitz, Emi. "Women and Family in the Kibbutz"; Gerson, Menachem. "The Family in the Kibbutz"; and Golan, Yona. "The Woman in the Kibbutz." *Kibbutz: A New Society.* Tel Aviv: Ichud Habonim, 1971. Available in pamphlet from Kibbutz Aliyah Desk, 575 6th Ave., New York, N. Y. 10011. About women and family on kibbutz.

Meir, Golda. "My First Days in Kibbutz Merhavia." *Midstream,* May 1970.

"Women on Kibbutz." *Mishmar.* Tel Aviv: Hashomer Hatzair, April 1967. Excerpts from discussions and resolutions of a special conference held on the problem.

HISTORY AND SOCIOLOGY

Noble, Shlomo. "The Jewish Woman in Medieval Martyrology." *Studies in Jewish Bibliography: History and Literature in Honor of I. Edward Kiev.* Charles Berlin, editor. New York: Ktav, 1971. Available from the author, YIVO Institute for Jewish Research, 1048 5th Ave., New York, N. Y. Historical research on the crucial survival role played by Jewish women during the era of the Crusades and forced conversions in the Middle Ages.

Rakowski, Puah. "A Mind of My Own." *Golden Tradition* by Lucy Davidowicz. New York: Holt Rinehart & Winston, 1967. Autobiography of Zionist leader.

Schneider, Sarah. "Mother of the Beth Jacob Schools." *Golden Tradition* by Lucy Davidowicz. New York: Holt Rinehart & Winston, 1967.

Zuckoff, Aviva Cantor. "The Real Story of Esther." *Off Our Backs* 2, no. 6. Analysis of the role Jewish women play in galut (exile) as the life force of the culture.

HOLOCAUST AND RESISTANCE

Benkler, Rafi. "Haviva Reik." *Israel Horizons,* April 1964. Remembrances of the other (forgotten) woman parachutist from Hashomer Hatzair movement.

Birman, Tzippora. "From the Bialystok Ghetto." *Jewish Spectator,* Sept. 1971.

"Diary of Justina (Gusta Davidson)." *A Tower from the Enemy* by Albert Nirenstein. New York: Orion, 1959. The Cracow resistance.

Farstendiger-Navon, Sylvia. "Hannah Senesch." *Jewish Liberation Journal,* Nov. 1970.

Grossman, Chaika. "Revolt in the Bialystok Ghetto." *The Massacre of European Jewry.* Tel Aviv: Hashomer Hatzair, 1963. Also in *The Fighting Ghettoes* by Meyer Barkai. New York: Tower, paperback.

Klibanski, Bronya. "Bialystok Underground." *Jewish Spectator,* Nov. 1969.

Korczak, Ruzka. "A Shomer Pesach in the Ghetto (Vilna)." *The Massacre of European Jewry.* Tel Aviv: Hashomer Hatzair, 1963.

———. "Flames out of Ashes: Vilna Uprising." *Israel Horizons,* April 1967.

Melamed, Aliza. "From the Diary of a Young Fighter (Warsaw Ghetto)." *Israel Horizons,* April 1967. Also in *The Massacre of European Jewry.* Tel Aviv: Hashomer Hatzair, 1963.

Miedzyrzecka, Wladka Peltel. "Underground Activity on the Aryan Side of Warsaw." *Yad Vashem Bulletin* 22.

Rozycka, Eugenia. "Looking through My Window." *Yad Vashem Bulletin* 18. Book review of testimony of an Orthodox woman and her form of resistance.

Zdrojewicz, Malka. Excerpts from testimony given at Yad Vashem by the woman in the famous picture (*Davka* cover and poster). *Yad Vashem Bulletin* 22.

SOVIET JEWISH WOMEN

Bershadskaya, Lyuba. "Twenty-four Years in the Life of Lyuba Bershadskaya." *New York Times Sunday Magazine,* March 14, 1971. Available from SSSJ. Autobiographical account.

AMERICA

Baron, Sheryl. "National Liberation and the Jewish Woman." *Davka,** Summer 1971.

Bart, Pauline. "Portnoy's Mother's Complaint." *Transaction,* Nov.-Dec. 1970.

———. "Depression in Middle Aged Women." *Woman in Sexist Society.* Edited by V. Gornick and B. Moran. New York: Basic Books, 1971.

Berman, Louis A. "Sex Role Patterning in the Jewish Family." Chap. 8. *Jews and Intermarriage.* New York: Yoseloff, 1968.

Bronznick, Shifra. "Jewish Women's Liberation." *Alliance**, April 1972.

Brown, Laura. "Jewish Women: Mothers, Princesses or Sisters?" *Hashofar,* Oct. 1972.

Dworkin, Susan "Henrietta Szold: Liberated Woman." *Hadassah,* Feb. 1972. Interesting and sad.

Garson, Sascha. "On Re-Becoming a Jew." *Village Voice,* Nov. 25, 1971. Beautiful account of the development of her Jewish consciousness.

Gold, Doris B. "Women and Voluntarism." *Woman in Sexist Society.* Edited by V. Gornick and B. Moran. New York: Basic Books, 1971.

———. "Jewish Women's Groups: Separate—But Equal?" *Congress Bi-Weekly,* Feb. 6, 1970. Oppressive nature of the division of labor in the Jewish community.

"Jewish Women: Life Force of a Culture." *Brooklyn Bridge* 1.

Snitow, Virginia, and Levine, Jacqueline. "Role of Jewish Women." *Congress Bi-Weekly,* June 18, 1971.

Timberg, Judy. "Are Jewish Women Oppressed?" *The Jewish Radical* (Berkeley), Spring 1971.

Weiss-Rosmarin, Trude. "Women in the Jewish Community." *Jewish Spectator,* Feb. 1972.

Whelton, Clark. "The Triangle Fire." *Village Voice,* March 25, 1971. Also in Louis Levine, *The Women's Garment Workers.* New York: Huebsch, 1924, pp. 153-54, out of print. Account of Jewish women strikers.

Yezierska, Anzia. "One Thousand Pages of Research." *Commentary,* July 1963. Writer of the period of great immigration tells of growing old in New York City.

Zuckoff, Aviva Cantor. "The Oppression of the Jewish Woman." *Ort Reporter,* Sept.-Oct. 1972, JSP feature. Theoretical analysis of the historic role of Jewish women in galut (exile), and the specific nature of their oppression in America.

NOTE: Various clippings on Jewish women are available from:

Women's History Library
23-25 Oak St.
Berkeley, Cal. 94708

Fiction

ISRAEL

Dayan, Yael. *New Face in the Mirror.* New York: World, 1959; also in paperback.

Oz, Amos. *My Michael.* English translation, New York: Knopf, 1972. Beautiful, sensitive novel of the crackup of a Jerusalem student/housewife/teacher in the 1950s.

Viertel, Joseph. *The Last Temptation.* New York: Simon & Schuster, 1955. A young woman, raised to be clinging and dependent, survives the Holocaust, is forced to conduct an independent struggle, and then faces the choice of giving in to her upbringing or continuing an independent life.

HOLOCAUST AND RESISTANCE

Field, Herman, and Mierzenski, Stanislaw. *Angry Harvest.* New York: Crowell, 1958. Searing story of a Jewish girl who escapes from a burning ghetto and is sheltered by a Polish family.

Goldworth, Bella. *Across the Border.* New York: UKUF, 1971. Sentimental, old-fashioned, but still moving short stories, mostly about pre-Holocaust Europe, many about women. See especially "New Days."

Karmel-Wolfe, Henia. *The Baders of Jacob Street.* Philadelphia: Lippincott, 1970. Traces the lives of three Jewish women in Cracow under the Nazis.

Levin, Meyer. *Anne Frank.* Published privately. Available in pamphlet from the author, Kfar Shmaryahu, Israel. Emphasizes her Jewish consciousness, unlike the commercial Hackett version which was the "universalist" one.

Tennenaus, Hanna. *Eva.* Bathurst, N. Br.: Aire, 1959. Novel based on a survivor's true story; much revolves around women's friendships in the camp.

AMERICA

Asch, Sholem. *The Mother.* New York: Liveright, 1930. Immigrant mother versus second-generation daughter.

Epstein, Seymour. *Leah.* Boston: Little Brown; 1964, New York: Pocket Book, paperback. Sensitive portrait of a single thirty-seven-year old Jewish woman living in New York.

Parent, Gail. *Sheila Levine Is Dead and Living in New York.* New York: Putnam, 1972. A Jewish girl who wants to get married and can't, tries suicide.

Yezierska, Anzia. *All I Could Never Be.* New York: Brewer Warren & Putnam, 1932.

———. *The Arrogant Beggar.* New York: Doubleday, 1927.

———. *Bread Givers.* New York: Doubleday, 1925.

———. *Children of Loneliness.* New York: Funk & Wagnalls, 1932.

———. *Hungry Hearts.* Boston: Houghton Mifflin, 1920.

———. *Salome of the Tenements.* New York: Boni & Liveright, 1927. All these are novels or collections of short stories dealing with the struggles of young Jewish women in the 1920s. *Salome* draws on the story of Rose Pastor Stokes, a radical Jew who married a rich Christian liberal.

Jewish religion and law

Adler, Rachel. "The Jew Who Wasn't There: Halacha and the Jewish Woman." *Davka,* Summer 1971, pp. 6–11.

Blumenthal, Aaron H. "An Aliya for Women." *Proceedings of the Rabbinical Assembly* 19: 168–81.

Davidowicz, Lucy S. "On Being a Woman in Shul." *Commentary* 45 (July 1968): 6.

Epstein, Isadore. "The Jewish Woman in the Responsa: 900 C.E.–1500 C.E." *The Jewish Library, 3: Woman,* edited by Leo Jung. London: Soncino, 1970.

Feldman, David M. *Birth Control in Jewish Law.* New York: New York University, 1968.

Greenberg, Simon. "And He Writes Her a Bill of Divorcement." *Conservative Judaism* 24 (Spring 1970): 75–141.

Gendler, Mary. "Male and Female Created He Them." *Jewish Heritage,* Winter 1971–72, pp. 24–29.

Gittelsohn, Roland B. "Women's Lib and Judaism." *Midstream* 17 (Oct. 1971): 51–58.

Guttmacher, Alan. "Traditional Judaism and Birth Control." *Judaism* 16: 159–65.

Hauptman, Judith. "Women's Liberation in the Talmudic Period." *Conservative Judaism.* Summer 1972.

Hyman, Paula. "The Other Half: Women in the Jewish Tradition." *Conservative Judaism,* Summer 1972.

Levinas, Emmanuel. "Judaism and the Feminine Element." *Judaism* 18 (Winter 1969): 30–38.

Miller, Deborah. "Equal Only When Obligated." *Sh'ma,* Nov. 1971.

Moses ben Maimon. *The Book of Women.* New Haven: Yale University, 1972.

Patai, Raphael. *The Hebrew Goddess.* New York: Ktav. 1968.

Rackman, Emmanuel. "Ethical Norms in the Jewish Laws of Marriage." *Judaism,* Summer 1954.

Schachter, Zalman. "Modern Covenants Need Modern Ketubah." *Sh'ma,* Oct. 8, 1971.

Solevechik, Aaron. "The Jewish View of the Higher Nature of Women." *Jewish Horizon,* Nov.–Dec., 1969.

Weisbart, Gladys. "Experiencing the Shekinah." *Reconstructionist* 13 (April 14, 1967): 13–17.

Weiss-Rosmarin, Trude. "The Unfreedom of the Jewish Woman." *Jewish Spectator,* Oct. 1970. Available from 270 W. 57th St., New York, N. Y. Excellent.

Excerpted from a 6-page annotated bibliography on the Jewish woman published by the Jewish Liberation Project, 150 5th Ave., Room 700C, NYC 10011. Can be ordered from JLP for 50c.

Notes on Sources

Herzl Press and ***Midstream***
515 Park Ave.
New York, N. Y. 10022

On sale in their bookshop. Addresses of all Jewish organizations and periodicals are listed in *American Jewish Year Book,* published annually by the American Jewish Committee and JPS.

Israel Horizons, New Outlook, and ***Hashomer Hatzair***
150 Fifth Ave.
New York, N. Y. 10011

Many books are out of print. Let's get them reprinted!

SHALOM

Selected halakhic bibliography

Study of this material should follow the order listed.

General Source

„מחניים" (כתב עתי של הרבנות הראשית של הצבא הגנה לישראל) מוקדש לנושא האשה במקורות היהדות, מס' צ"ח, תשכ"ה, תל-אביב.

Sources for particular issues

א בעניני ברכת המזון וברכת הזימון אצל האשה

1 משנה ראש השנה כט. דה"מ זה הכלל

2 קיצור פסקי המרדכי על הנ"ל דה"מ הרי שתוקעים להם

3 ירושלמי על המשנה הנ"ל דה"מ תני אבל אמרו אשה מברכת

4 פני משה על הנ"ל דה"מ אבל אמרו

5 משנה ברכות כ. דה"מ נשים עבדים וקטנים פטורים מק"ש

6 המחלוקת בין רש"י ותוס' שם בתוס' דה"מ נשים, וע' ג"כ ערכין ג. רש"י דה"מ מזומנות לעצמן

7 ירושלמי על משנה הנ"ל (הל' ג)

8 מראה הפנים על הנ"ל דה"מ ובברהמ"ז

9 משנה ברכות מה. דה"מ נשים וכו' אין מזנין

10 הגמ' שם ופירוש הרמב"ם שם

11 גמ' ערכין ג. דה"מ הכל חייבין בזימון לאתויי

12 תוס' שם דה"מ מזומנות לעצמן

13 גמ' ברכות מ"ה: דה"מ ת"ש נשים מזומנות לעצמן

14 המחלוקת שבין רש"י ותוס' על הנ"ל וסברת הרא"ש על ענינו ובפרט דבריו בקיצור פסקיו דה"מ נשים מזומנות

15 רמב"ם הל' ברכות פ"ה ה"א, ה"ו, ה"ז

16 ש"ע א"ח קפ"ו ס"א, קצ"ט ס"ו, ומ"א וט"ז על זה

17 ש"ע הרב א"ח קפ"ו ס"א, וס"ב, וס"ג, וס"ד

18 שם קצ"ט ס"ו

19 משנה ברורה קפ"ו ס"ק ג'

ב בענין מצות עשה שהזמן גרמא

1 משנה קידושין כ"ט, והגמ' על זה בירושלמי

2 גמ' שם ל"ה: דה"מ אמר רבא פפונאי

3 גמ' מנחות מ"ג. דה"מ ת"ר הכל חייבין בציצית

4 סיפרי דבי רב פיסקא קט"ו

5 גמ' על משנתינו בקידושין דה"מ אמר ר"י אין לומדין מן הכלל

6 ויכוח על מצב הירושלמי בכל זה במאמר הרב גורן בחיבור „מחניים" הנ"ל

7 רמב"ם פירוש המשניות על משנתינו בקידושין

ג בענין עדות בנשים

1 משנה וגמ' שבועות ל.

2 משנה וגמ' ראש השנה כ"ב דה"מ אלו הן, ורש"י ותוס' שם שהביאו קצת הפרטים היוצאים מכלל זה

3 רמב"ם הלכות עדות פ"ט ה"ב ומחלוקת הכ"מ על דבריו

4 ספר זכר יצחק לרבינו יצחק יעקב רבינוביץ ז"ל דפוניבז', סוף ההקדמה

5 שלטי הגבורים הנמצא אצל הר"ן על ראש השנה ל"ב: (בהר"ן דף ט:) דה"מ אין מעכבין את התינוקות—וכל זה לטובת ענין קבלת מצוות האינן מצוות באשה

6 ועל הנ"ל ע' באנצ' תלמודית ב„אשה"

ד Women, Marriage, Divorce & Property

NOTE: The preceding bibliography is intended largely as a sequence of footnotes for a course. What follows, since a similar series of notes on primary sources would be too huge to be of value, is a listing of secondary material of much more recent vintage. Unless indicated, they are published by Mosad h-Rav Kuk in Jerusalem.

1 Kahana, K. *The Theory of Marriage in Jewish Law, Leiden:* E. J. Brill, 1966

2 רפאל, יצחק. תורה שבעל פה, חלק י"ב, תש"ל

3 ברקוביץ, א. תנאי בנשואין ובגט, תשכ"ז

4 כהנא, ק. ברכת כהן, תשל"ב

5 רקובר, ג. השליחות וההרשאה במשפט העברי, תשל"ב

6 פריימן, א. ח. סדר קידושין ונשואין מאחרי חתימת התלמוד ועד ימינו, תשכ"ה

Using the Jewish Establishment-a reluctant guide

This section should seem anomalous in a book which aims at enabling the individual Jew to build his own Jewish life. One of our assumptions is that hardly anyone should have to resort to organizations, professional "experts," or service agencies in the normal course of creating and enjoying a fulfilling Jewish life. With this book, a teacher, friends (perhaps in a real community), study, and imaginative effort, almost anyone can create a richer and more satisfying Jewish life than any organization offers.

There are, however, many Jewish organizations, agencies, congregations, associations, and the like which offer access to tools and resources useful in the creation of a Jewish life. Locally many social, recreational, health, welfare, religious, and cultural services are offered by such organizations as synagogues, Jewish community centers, family agencies, fraternal societies, etc. Nationally, dozens of Jewish organizations serve the Jewish blind, Orthodox Jewish scientists, victims of anti-Semitic discrimination, veterans, researchers of the Jewish past, students trying to live Jewishly away from home, lovers of Jewish music, scholars in search of funds, potential travelers in search of Jewish experiences, friends of Israel, defenders of Soviet Jewry, and many others.

Those people who enjoy organizations can find many opportunities to become joiners, cause-followers, committee members, and even machers (L*E*A*D*E*R*S). But Jewish organizations are like most others in America—better at doing specific jobs than in providing community, identity, inspiration, leadership, or profound understanding. It is more helpful to approach them as specialized tools than to turn to them for personal fulfillment.

A brief, sympathetic picture of Jewish organizational life is presented in S. P. Goldberg's *The American Jewish Community* (see bibliography, Section Six). The diversity of the thousands of Jewish organizations in America, however, makes it impossible to know local resources without personal inquiry. The best guides are likely to be a rabbi or the nearest Jewish federation or welfare fund (called by various names around the country).

The following pages give a partial guide to organizational resources. Abbreviations (except for organizational names) are explained below. Section One gives an organizational profile of a typical Jewish settlement. Section Two is a selective listing and brief description of national Jewish organizations. Section Three catalogs organizational sources for various services. Section Four offers a schematic view of the organization of American Jewish religious life. Section Five charts the allocation of funds by organized local campaigns. Section Six provides a bibliography for further information.

America's Jewish organizations reflect, perpetuate, and, to a considerable extent, structure Jewish life in America. Those Jews who have lost access to traditional models and textual sources for Jewish living must rely on the establishment's monopolization of the sources of information about things Jewish. Yet Jewish life is not synonymous with the Jewish organizations which have objectified and subdivided it for piecemeal appropriation. The eternal sources of Jewish meaning—awe and love of God and man, humility, prayer, practice, Torah, teachers, friends, family, community, peoplehood, and a shared heritage—are the inalienable possessions of every Jew. If we live them, they are ours. They are dispensed by no organization.

Section One: *Typical Jewish organizations from which services may be obtained in cities with more than 20,000 Jews*

( )= 50,000 or more
[ ]= 100,000 or more

1. Synagogue
2. Jewish federation
3. Jewish hospital
4. Jewish Community Center, Young Men's/Women's Hebrew Assn.
5. Family Agency
6. (Hebrew Free Loan Society)
7. Home for aged
8. (Employment and guidance service)
9. Bureau of Jewish Education
10. Camp
11. Hillel
12. Day school or yeshivah
13. Jewish Community (Relations) Council
14. AJCe, AJCo, ADL, Had, National Council of Jewish Women, (JWV), ZOA, BB, (LZA), (WC)
15. Board of Rabbis
16. [UAHC], [USA]
17. [Israel Aliyah Center]
18. [Habad House]
19. [Israel Consulate]

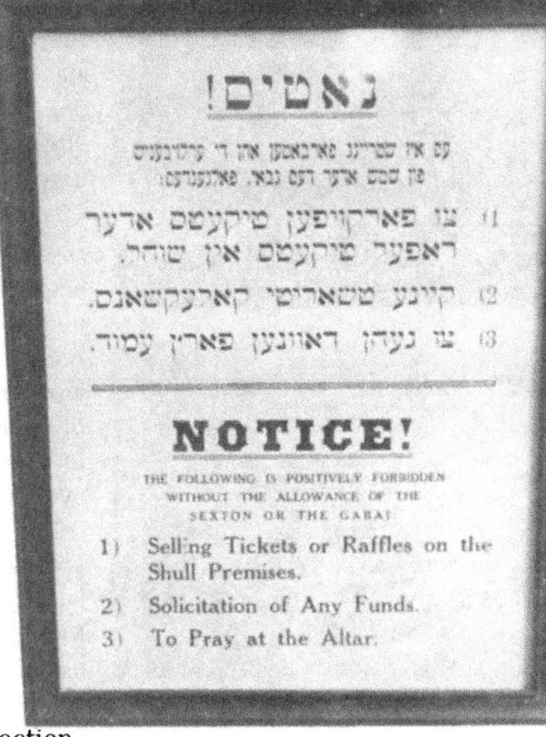

Many cities offer guides to Jewish agencies and their services (see Section Six). They are usually available from the local Jewish federation. The use of the word community to describe a Jewish settlement is a convention and does not imply the existence of any real communal ties among the Jews of any city.

1. Synagogues vary widely in quality and concern for individuals, especially strangers. Apart from religious services, they may offer men's and women's clubs, youth groups, singles clubs, religious classes, adult education programs, gift shops, communal meals on Jewish holidays, newsletters, libraries, etc. Most synagogues are listed in the yellow pages under "Churches (and Synagogues)." There are three major religious groupings in American Judaism: Orthodox (which attempts to preserve all traditional religious beliefs and practices), Conservative (which attempts to maintain or adapt traditional religious practices to suit contemporary circumstances and encourages belief in a historically evolving Judaism), and Reform (which is generally a setting for cultural Judaism with religious overtones and little formal ideology). Reconstructionism is an ideology which encourages traditional practices without a supernatural rationale. The right wing of Orthodoxy attempts to preserve intact most of the social and cultural life of European Jewry. Hasidism is a pietistic and communal Orthodoxy centered on the person of a rebbe, and, whether emotionally ecstatic or highly rational, is generally mystical and re-

ligiously intense. Sephardic Jews are generally those who derive cultural identity, at some point in their history, from predominantly Moslem countries; their practices are distinct from those of most others, i.e., Ashkenazic Jews. Reform synagogues are usually called temples. Many Conservative and some Orthodox synagogues call themselves centers. Orthodox synagogues are often referred to colloquially as shuls.

Some pulpit rabbis are disappointing people, but if one looks he will find those who will be helpful. If one is looking for deep religious experience, it is generally best to avoid large synagogues. Like anything else, there are good and bad synagogues. If you don't like any in your area, you and your friends should start your own congregation. (See Communities, "Blueprint for a Havurah," page 281.)

2. There are more than 200 communities which conduct combined fund-raising campaigns for operating expenses of nonreligious Jewish institutions and organizations locally, nationally, and internationally. Jewish federations may be called by various names, including Welfare Fund, Welfare Federation, Community Council, Federation Council, Combined Jewish Philanthropies, United Jewish Appeal (except in New York, where the Federation of Jewish Philanthropies allocates almost all its funds for local needs and UJA almost all its funds for foreign ones; most national agencies fend for themselves in New York fund-raising). Each federation has generally acquired a central planning function in its community and supervises local agencies which provide for health care, social welfare, community relations, nonsectarian Jewish education, etc. It is generally run by professional administrators and large donors. Although few people involved in the running of a federation are likely to know much about Judaism or living Jewishly, a federation is usually an excellent source of information about services available from local agencies.

3. Most major Jewish communities partially support at least one hospital. Indigent Jews can usually receive free or inexpensive health care in such a facility. For information, check with the local federation. Do not expect that Jewish facilities will be any more available at Jewish hospitals than at nonsectarian or Catholic ones.

4. Most Jewish communities support a center, or YM/YWHA, for recreational, social, educational, or cultural activities, programs for the young and old, classes in various arts, crafts and skills, and often for more distinctively Jewish programs. Most are staffed by trained social workers. Many house social service programs for underprivileged or aged Jews and community resources such as libraries, gymnasiums, pools, nurseries, Hebrew schools, etc. Most are open only to members who pay fees (often scaled to income).

5. The central social service agency in a city is usually called a Family (or Family and Children's) Agency or Service and probably offers counseling and referral services for most personal or familial difficulties, including adoptions, big brothers/sisters, marriage counseling, the consequences of divorce, emotional disturbances, physical handicaps, legal problems, drug addiction or dependence, unwanted pregnancies, simple material needs, etc. It can usually provide full information about local welfare rights. Few such services are sensitive to the Jewish religious or cultural needs of clients, but they are often excellent agencies and scale fees according to ability to pay.

6. Many communities maintain a Hebrew (or Jewish) Free Loan Society (often as part of the Family Agency), which extends interest-free loans to those in need.

7. Since most Jews have all but abandoned personal responsibility for their elders, Jewish nursing homes and other facilities for the aged usually have

long waiting lists. Jewish homes tend to be no worse than most and often quite good, although their sensitivities to needs for self-dignity and a Jewish environment are often poor. Large cities often maintain facilities for chronic and terminal care.

8. Most large communities maintain a service to aid people in choosing careers and getting jobs. They are generally better, more personal, and cheaper than commercial or public agencies, especially if one has special needs, such as physical or emotional handicaps, or religious requirements. Bnai Brith also maintains vocational counseling offices in some cities.

9. The local Bureau (or Board) of Jewish Education (sometimes called the Jewish Education Committee) can provide information about instruction in Jewish religion, culture and history, and the Hebrew and Yiddish languages for children and sometimes adults. Many maintain good public libraries. They can usually give advice about tuition and scholarships.

10. Most Jewish communities operate day camps, and sizable ones usually run residential camps. Some are good. Ideological (usually Zionist) or religious camps are often more stimulating and educational alternatives.

11. Most colleges and universities with sizable Jewish enrollments are served by a Hillel Foundation. Hillels are often staffed by the best young rabbis in the country and optimally offer many opportunities for young Jews to create and develop their own Jewish lives. Hillels generally offer religious services, classes, entertainment, lectures, social functions, kosher meals, libraries, meeting facilities, etc. Even if one is not a student, he will rarely be turned away from any Hillel activity. Hillel directors are usually excellent rabbinical counselors. They are generally the best available for Jewish counseling of people worried about the draft, conversion, marriage, unwanted pregnancies, and other life crises.

12. Day schools and yeshivot are institutions for intensive Jewish learning, the latter usually being more traditional than the former. They can offer, if not direct services to adults, at least a staff of well-informed Jews who may be able to give intelligent advice. Most such schools adjust their fees to parental income. Hardly any will accept a minor without his parents' consent and financial support. Some offer evening and Sunday classes in Jewish texts and practices for beginners.

13. A Jewish Community Council (or Community Relations Council) is usually an umbrella agency in larger cities for most local Jewish organizations—including local affiliates of national agencies—coordinating local communal activities which relate to non-Jews or the defense of general Jewish interests. CRC's coordinate nationally through the NJCRAC and provide local sources of information about national Jewish organizational policy (often synonymous with Israeli policy). The JCRC is generally a good source of information about local affiliates of national agencies. It probably carries large quantities of informational and propagandistic literature about Jewish political issues, especially touching on Israel and the Middle East, Soviet Jewry, Jews in Moslem lands, discrimination against Jews, and interfaith activities. It is generally a poor source of information about any aspect of Jewish religion, culture, or personal life.

14. There are likely to be local affiliates of national Jewish organizations in your city. All vary widely in character in different parts of the country. All are professionally run membership organizations, share concern for and offer propaganda and programs about Israel, Soviet Jews, and other subjects beyond controversy or consideration among Jews. AJCe, AJCo, and ADL are likely to be most helpful with the above, but especially so in cases of discrimination against Jews or protection of what is left of the name (if not the

substance) of the Jewish community. The National Council of Jewish Women is only marginally Jewish. Hadassah and ZOA are nominally Zionist and represent, respectively, one of the most and one of the least effective Jewish organizations in America. BB is the largest American Jewish fraternal organization and often has good local programing. RZA is a religious Zionist organization for sedate people. LZA tends to be liberal-labor oriented Zionist. WC is aging, Yiddishist, and leftist. The women's divisions of most Jewish organizations are likely to offer more possibilities for personal involvement than the men's division. Policy in most organizations comes from the top (i.e., the rich or powerful members and the Israeli Establishment).

15. The local interdenominational rabbinical body can provide information about kashrut (the observance of Jewish dietary laws), religious services (notably conversion and divorce), and religious facilities. It may, in addition, offer such services as adult education classes, Jewish adjudication services, Passover meals, draft counseling, a good Jewish library, etc.

16. The regional offices of the Reform and Conservative movements can provide films, literature, program assistance in various areas of Jewish educational interest.

17. Regional offices to encourage and assist in aliyah (emigration to Israel) are maintained in many cities. Before you leave, independently corroborate all the information on which you are basing your future—e.g., with AACA (see Jewish Travel, "Aliyah"). No one will help the majority who try it, fail, and return to America.

18. In many large cities the Lubavitch Hasidic organization maintains youth facilities which provide the experience of an intense form of traditional Judaism (see Communities). They offer classes in Jewish texts and practices, personal counseling, and a friendly atmosphere.

Abbreviations for Sections Two and Three

a—agency
AJYB—*American Jewish Year Book*
assn—association
BJE—Bureau of Jewish Education
Bkln—Brooklyn
BR—rabbi or Board of Rabbis
C—Conservative
cat—(publishes) catalog of publications
CJFr—the Council of Jewish Federations and Welfare Funds can refer inquiries to the nearest Jewish agency providing service
coord—coordinating body
cr—community relations organization, concerned primarily with protecting Jewish rights and interests, but likely to dabble in many areas
CRC—Jewish Community Relations Council
cult—cultural (resources)
ed—educational
esp—especially
f—family
fa—family agency
fed—Jewish Federation, welfare fund, or community council
frat—fraternal organization, nonspecific goals, primarily social
g—general program, offers resources in many areas
incl:—includes the following:
info—information
J—Jewish
JCC—Jewish Community Center, Young Men's/Women's Hebrew Association
L—local
l—literature/central resource for printed materials
lib—library
M—major organizational resource
m—maintains or sponsors
mem—member
n—has field offices and personnel providing services around the country
nat—national
NYC—New York, New York (Manhattan)
0—Orthodox
org—organization
p—publishes material on the subject in question
proj—project
r—will refer inquiries to appropriate agencies
R—Reform
rab—rabbinical
rel—religious, dealing with matters that focus on Jewish religious practices and life-styles, study, prayer and related areas
s—student
serv—national service agency for other groups as well as individuals
syn—synagogue
w—women
y—youth
Z—Zionist
$—source of funds

Section Two:
Selective listing of national Jewish organizations providing direct services
(for further descriptions, see AJYB)

(AACA) Association of Americans and Canadians for Aliyah
515 Park Ave.
NYC 10022
Aids and advises prospective emigrants to Israel

(AAJE) American Association for Jewish Education
114 Fifth Ave.
NYC 10011
[M, ed, serv]. "Transideological" ed advisory a

(ADL) Anti-Defamation League of Bnai Brith
315 Lexington Ave.
NYC 10016
[M,n,g,cr,r,cat]. Silences critics of Jews, Judaism, and Israel

(AH) Agudas Harabonim—Union of Orthodox Rabbis of the United States and Canada
235 E. Broadway
NYC 10007
[O, rab]. Very traditional O rab assn

(AIA) Agudath Israel of America
5 Beekman St.
NYC 10038
[M, O, Z, m y&w orgs]. Central lay body and service office for very traditional O Judaism, affiliated with "ultra-Orthodox" party in Israel

(AIPAC) American Israel Public Affairs Committee
1341 G St. NW
Washington, D. C. 20005
[M, serv]. Israel's lobby, offering pro-Israeli information and legislative recommendations

(AJA) American Jewish Archives
3101 Clifton Ave.
Cincinnati, Ohio 45220
Records of American Jewry, especially good periodical collection

(AJCe) American Jewish Committee
165 E. 56th St.
NYC 10022
[M, n, g, cr, r, cat]. Highly professionalized, wealthy, and influential, with offices around the world and fingers in many pots

(AJCo) American Jewish Congress
15 E. 84th St.
NYC 10028
[M, n, g, cr, r, cat]. Liberal, politically and legally active with diverse programs

(AJHS) American Jewish Historical Society
2 Thornton Rd.
Waltham, Mass. 02154
Records of American Jewry, good reference service, many organizational archives

(AJS) Association for Jewish Studies
Brandeis University
Waltham, Mass. 02154
Professional society for scholars and graduate students

(API) Americans for Progressive Israel—HaShomer HaTzair
150 Fifth Ave.
NYC 10011
[Z, m y org]. Socialist Zionist organization

(APPEAL) North American Jewish Students Appeal
36 W. 37th St.
NYC 10018
[s, $]. Raises and allocates money for national student activities, incl: Network, JSP-S, SSSJ, *Response* magazine, Yavneh, Yugntruf

(AZF) American Zionist Federation
515 Park Ave.
NYC 10022
[M, Z, coord, r]. Umbrella org for American Zionists (except ZOA) incl: Had, LZA, Pioneer Women, Bnai Zion, American Jewish League for Israel, United Zionists Revisionists, RZA, Mizrahi Women's Organization, Americans for Progressive Israel, Women's Organization of HaPoel-HaMizrahi, and Association of Americans and Canadians for Aliyah; promotes Zionism

(AZYF) American Zionist Youth Foundation
515 Park Ave.
NYC 10022
[M, Z, s, r]. Central agency for Israel and Zionist programing for youth and students, maintains representatives around the country, funds student projects

(BB) Bnai Brith
1640 Rhode Island Ave. NW
Washington, D. C. 20036
[M, n, g, frat, r, cat, m y, s&w orgs]. The largest Jewish membership organization with many kinds of programs around the world

(BONDS) State of Israel Bond Organization
215 Park Ave. S.
NYC 10003
[$]. Sells bonds to finance Israel

(BUND) International Jewish Labor Bund
25 E. 78th St.
NYC 10021
Aging non-Zionist Yiddish socialists and a small student group with excellent archives of East European radical Jewish history

(CCAR) Central Conference of American Rabbis
790 Madison Ave.
NYC 10021
[M, R, rab]. The Reform rabbinical body, issues some interesting policy studies

(CJC) Canadian Jewish Congress
1590 McGregor Ave.
Montreal 109, Quebec Canada
[M, n, g, r, cat]. Unlike the U.S. alphabet-soup Jewish waste and chaos, Canada has a central Jewish organization; this is it

(CJF) Council of Jewish Federations and Welfare Funds
315 Park Ave. S.
NYC 10010
[M, serv, coord, r, cat]. The service agency for all community fund-raising organizations in America, it can answer inquiries about services supported by Jewish communal funds

(COLPA) National Jewish Commission on Law and Public Affairs
66 Court St.
Bklyn, NY 11201
The legal arm of Orthodox Judaism, protects Jewish rights

(CUJS) Canadian Union of Jewish Students
754 Sherbrooke St. W.
Suite 7
Montreal 110, Quebec, Canada
[M, serv, coord, s, r]. The central Canadian Jewish student organization

(HABAD) Lubavitch Hasidic Organization
770 Eastern Pkwy.
Bklyn, NY 11213
[M, O, n, m y&w orgs]. The most highly organized and hospitable of Hasidic groups, offering spiritual services around the country through schools, publications, youth programs, and personal encounter

(HAD) Hadassah, the Women's Zionist Organization of America
65 E. 52nd St.
NYC 10022
[M, Z, n, g, w, m y org]. The largest and busiest of women's or Zionist organizations

(HI) Histadruth Ivrith of America
120 W. 16th St.
NYC 10011
[cat]. Fosters use of Hebrew

(HILLEL) Bnai Brith Hillel Foundations
1640 Rhode Island Ave. NW
Washington, D. C. 20036
[M, n, s, g, Z, rel, serv, r, cat]. Worldwide network of Jewish student centers and services

(IJL) Institute for Jewish Life
65 Williams St.
Wellesley, Mass. 02181
[$, r]. Created by CJF to renew Jewish life cheaply and painlessly, has money and does research to foster innovative Jewish projects

(ISO) Israel Students Organization
515 Park Ave.
NYC 10022
For Israelis in America and their friends; provides speakers, programs, literature

(ISRAEL) Embassy of the State of Israel
1621 22nd St. NW
Washington, D. C. 20008
(consulates in New York, Philadelphia, Boston, Chicago San Francisco, Los Angeles, Atlanta, and Houston. The Embassy in Canada is in Ottawa and consulates in Montreal and Toronto). Representing the biggest Jewish organization
Embassy of Israel
1621 22nd St. NW
Washington, D. C. 20008

Consulate General of Israel
800 2nd Ave.
NYC 10017

805 Peachtree St.
Atlanta, Ga. 30308

Park Sq. Bldg.
31 St. James Ave.
Boston, Mass. 02116

111 E. Wacker Dr.
Chicago, Ill. 60611

1 Greenway Plaza East
Houston, Tex. 77046

225 S. 15th St.
Philadelphia, Pa. 19102

105 Montgomery St.
San Francisco, Cal. 94104

659 S. Highland Ave.
Los Angeles, Cal. 90036

Canada: Embassy of Israel
45 Powell Ave.
Ottawa, Ontario

Canada: Consulate General of Israel
1555 McGregor St.
Montreal 25, Quebec

101 Davisville Ave.
Toronto 295, Ontario

(ISRAEL—ALIYAH OFFICES)

1. 515 Park Ave.
   NYC 10022
   (212 PL 2-0600)
   98-120 Queens Blvd.
   Forest Hills, NY 11374
   (Queens and L.I.)
   (212-459-5600)
   1416 Avenue M
   Brooklyn, NY 11230
   (212-336-1215)
2. 31 St. James Ave.
   Park Sq. Bldg., Suite 450
   Boston, Mass. 02116
   (617-423-0868)
3. 225 S. 15th St.
   Suite 1530
   Philadelphia, Pa. 19102
   (215-KI6-2088)
4. 2027 Massachusetts Ave. NW
   Washington, D.C. 20036
   (202-387-8224/5)
5. 13947 Cedar Rd.
   Room 202
   Cleveland, Ohio 44118
   (216-321-0757)
6. 230 S. State St.
   Chicago, Ill. 60604
   (312-922-5938)
7. 111 S. Meramec
   Suite 309
   St. Louis, Mo. 63105
   (314-PA1-5922)
8. 805 Peachtree St. NE
   Room 629
   Atlanta, Ga. 30308
   (404-872-1967,
   875-5166)
9. 46 Kearny St.
   San Francisco, Cal. 94108
   (415-392-8998,
   392-3970)
10. 590 N. Vermont Ave.
    Los Angeles, Cal. 90004
    (213-662-2181)
11. Ainsley Bldg., Suite 1401
    14 NE First and Flagler St.
    Miami, Fla. 33132
    (305-358-6540)
12. Fountainside Office
    17520 W. Twelve Mile Rd.
    Suite 111 (Detroit)
    Southfield, Mich. 48076
    (313-559-6755)
13. 11300 N. Central Expressway
    Suite 218
    Dallas, Tex. 75231
    (214-369-5506)
14. 1310 Greene Ave.
    Montreal, 215 P.Q.
    Canada
    (514-934-0804, 931-1804)
15. 788 Marlee Ave.
    Toronto, 395, Ontario
    Canada
    (416-781-4660, 781-4353)

(JBC) Jewish Book Council of America
15 E. 26th St.
NYC 10010
[serv, r, cat]. Fosters publication and use of Jewish books

(JBI) Jewish Braille Institute of America
110 E. 30th St.
NYC 10016
Aids Jewish blind, esp in Jewish texts

(JDL) Jewish Defense League
144 W. 27th St.
NYC 10001
[n, g, cat]. Varied services

(JLC) Jewish Labor Committee
25 E. 78th St.
NYC 10021
[M, n, sec, cr, coord, r, cat]. Politically active umbrella org for Jewish labor groups

(JPF) Jewish Peace Fellowship
420 Riverside Dr.
NYC 10025
[s, r, cat]. Promotion of pacifism, counseling Jewish CO's, related activities

(JPS) Jewish Publication Society of America
222 N. 15th St.
Philadelphia, Pa. 19102
[cat]. Publishes books of Jewish interest

(JRF) Jewish Reconstructionist Foundation
15 W. 86th St.
NYC 10024
[M, rel, r, cat]. Parent body for the Reconstructionist ideological movement

(JSP-S) Jewish Student Press-Service
36 W. 37th St.
NYC 10018
Services Jewish student publications and distributes them

(JTA) Jewish Telegraphic Agency
165 W. 46th St.
NYC 10036
Publishes daily and weekly reports of Jewish news

(JWB) National Jewish Welfare Board
15 E. 26th St.
NYC 10010
[M, serv, g, r, cat]. Services community centers, camps, Jews in armed forces, conducts cultural and entertainment programs

(JWV) Jewish War Veterans of the United States of America
1712 New Hampshire Ave. NW
Washington, D. C. 20009
[M, n, frat, cr, m w org]. Aside from the titles and funny hats, a very effective force for Jewish interests

(LZA) Labor Zionist Alliance
575 Sixth Ave.
NYC 10011
[M, n, Z, g, frat, m y&w orgs]. Incl: Poale Zion, Farband Labor Zionist Order and Pioneer Women, liberal-oriented Zionists affiliated with Mapai party in Israel, responsive to inquiries

(LUBAVITCH) See (Habad)

(MFJC) Memorial Foundation for Jewish Culture
215 Park Ave., S.
NYC 10003
[$]. Largest international source of funds for Jewish cultural and scholarly purposes, financed by German reparations

(MIZRAHI) See (RZA)

(NCAJL) National Council for Art in Jewish Life
c/o AJC, 15 E. 84th St.
NYC 10028
[serv, r, cat]. The only (tiny) effort to promote Jewish arts in general

(NCJPS) National Center for Jewish Policy Studies
1320 19th St.
Washington, D.C., 20036
Study and advisory group patterned on Nader's Raiders

(NCSJ) National Conference on Soviet Jewry
11 W. 42nd St.
Rm. 1860
NYC 10036
[M, serv, coord, r]. Umbrella agency for Soviet Jewry matters

(NETWORK) North American Jewish Students' Network
36 W. 37th St.
NYC 10018
[M, serv, g, coord, s, r]. Umbrella org and spokesperson for Jewish students

(NFJC) National Foundation for Jewish Culture
408 Chanin Bldg.
122 E. 42nd St.
NYC 10017
[$, r, serv]. Created by CJF to foster Jewish scholarship cheaply and quietly

(NJCRAC) National Jewish Community Relations Advisory Council
55 W. 42nd St.
NYC 10036
[M, serv, coord, cr, r, cat]. Central intelligence and advisory agency for Jewish organizations concerned with intergroup relations and defense of Jewish interests

(NJMC) National Jewish Music Council
15 E. 26th St.
NYC 10010
[serv, r, cat]. Fosters Jewish music

(RA) Rabbinical Assembly
3080 Broadway
NYC 10027
[M, C, rab]. The Conservative rabbinical association

(RAA) Rabbinical Alliance of America —Igud HaRabonim
156 Fifth Ave.
NYC 10010
[M, O, rab]. Very traditional Orthodox rabbinical association

(RCA) Rabbinical Council of America
200 Park Ave. S.
NYC 10003
[M, O, rab]. "American-style" Orthodox rabbinical association

(RZA) Mizrahi-HaPoel HaMizrahi—Religious Zionists of America
200 Park Ave. S
NYC 10003
[M, O, Z, n, frat, m y&w orgs]. Orthodox Zionists with educational and practical projects

(SCA) Synagogue Council of America
432 Park Ave. S.
NYC 10016
[M, serv, coord, rel, r]. Coordinating body for the major rabbinical and congregational organizations (see Section Four); doing impressive policy studies

(SSSJ) Student Struggle for Soviet Jewry
200 W. 72nd St.
NYC 10023

[serv, s, r, cat]. Promotes activity to aid Soviet Jews
(TuM) Torah Umesorah—National Society for Hebrew Day Schools
156 Fifth Ave.
NYC 10010
[M, O, serv, ed, cat]. Central body for Orthodox day schools and yeshivot ketanot
(UAHC) Union of American Hebrew Congregations
838 Fifth Ave.
NYC 10021
[M, n, R, serv, g, m y, s, w orgs, cat]. Central congregational body and service agency for Reform Judaism
(UJA) United Jewish Appeal
1290 Ave. of the Americas
NYC 10019
[$]. Raises money for United Israel Appeal (to fund projects of Jewish Agency for Israel), American Jewish Joint Distribution Committee (including ORT and Malben), United HIAS Service, and New York Association for New Americans
(UOJCA) Union of Orthodox Jewish Congregations of America
116 E. 27th St.
NYC 10016
[M, O, serv, g r, m y&w orgs, cat]. Central congregational body and service agency for most American-born Orthodox Jews
(USA) United Synagogue of America
3080 Broadway
NYC 10027
[M, n, C, serv, g, r, m y, s, w orgs, cat]. Central congregational body and service agency for Conservative Jews
(WZO) World Zionist Organization —American Section
(formerly Jewish Agency—American Section)
515 Park Ave.
NYC 10022
[M, Z, serv, g, r, cat]. Programs, publications, services, and information about Israel, Zionism, Hebrew, Jewish religious and cultural studies
(YAVNEH) Yavneh—Religious Jewish Students Association
84 Fifth Ave.
NYC 10011
[M, O, n, s, serv, r, assn, cat, cult, ed, g, rel]. Fosters traditional Judaism on campus
(YI) National Council of Young Israel
3 W. 16th St.
NYC 10011
[M, O, serv, r, cat, m y, s, w orgs]. National organization of Young Israel Orthodox synagogues with many central services
(YIVO) YIVO Institute for Jewish Research
1048 Fifth Ave.
NYC 10028
[M, serv, ed, r, cat]. Primary institution fostering study of Eastern European culture and Yiddish language, offering publications, archives, courses
(YUGNTRUF) Yugntruf—Youth for Yiddish
3328 Bainbridge Ave.
Bronx, NY 10467
[s, r]. Fosters Yiddish among youth
(ZOA) Zionist Organization of America
145 E. 32nd St.
NYC 10016
[M, Z, n, g, frat, r, m y org, cat]. Middle-class, middle-aged Zionists, vaguely rightist ideology

Section Three: Subject guide to resources offered by Jewish organizations

ACADEMICIANS (in Jewish studies): AJS
ADOPTION: L fa, L fed, CJFr
AGED: L fa, L fed, CJFr
ALIYAH: L Israel Aliyah office, Israel, Aliyah Dept. WZO, AACA, Kibbutz Aliyah Desk,
575 Sixth Ave.
NYC 10015
AMERICAN JEWS (history): AJHS, AJA
ANTI- AND NON-ZIONISM: Bund, American Council for Judaism
309 Fifth Ave.
Suite 303-6,
NYC 10016
ANTI-SEMITISM: See *Discrimination*
ARAB-JEWISH RELATIONS: Committee on New Alternatives in the Middle East
339 Lafayette St.
NYC 10012
all J orgs offer propagandistic l on the subject
ARCHIVES: AJHS, AJA, Zionist Archives at WZO, AJCe, AJCo, BB, Jewish Theological Seminary at USA, Bund
ARMED FORCES: (religious needs): JWB or religious orgs (see Section Four), YI p *Guide for the Orthodox Serviceman*
ART: NCAJL
BIBLIOGRAPHIES: JBC: see Bibliography
BLACK JEWS: SCAr
BLIND: JBI
BOOKS: JPS JBC, See also Bibliography
CAMPS: JWB, (see Section Six for cat); camps are run by many feds and rel and Z orgs, incl: AIA, Habad, Had, JDL, LZA, WC, USA, YU, HI
CANADA: CJC and CUJS are the central J and J s orgs in Canada
CHAPLAINS: (in armed forces) JWB, (in hospitals) L fed. LBR, (on campus) Hillel, (in prisons) LBR
CHRISTIANS AND CHRISTIANITY (relations with): AJCe, ADL, SCA, UAHC
CLOTHING: L fed, L fa r
COLLEGES: Hillel publishes a *Directory* evaluating Jewish life on many campuses (see Section Six), Network publishes a guide to student groups and can give advice.
COMMUNITY RELATIONS (organizations dealing with): L CRC, NJCRAC, AJCe, AJCo, ADL, etc.
CONSERVATIVE JUDAISM: See Section Four
CONVERSION: L BR. Those considering life in Israel for themselves or their descendants or possibilities of marrying religiously observant Jews now or in coming generations should consult an O rabbi or rab assn
COUNTERCULTURE: Network r
DEAF: UAHC helps in establishing R syns for the deaf
DEATH: L Hevra Kadisha; BR; syn, UOJCA p. Many Jewish frat orgs offer death benefits or burial services
DISCOGRAPHY: NJMC
DISCRIMINATION (problems of): AJCe (especially in executive hiring and promotion), ADL (esp overt anti-Semitism), COLPA (esp for rel observance), AJCo (esp class actions), JDL (esp physical threats), L CRC
DIVORCE: L BR. An improperly divorced Jew renders children by a subsequent marriage mamzerim, and unable to marry a religiously observant Jew. Avoid the problem; consult a rabbi
EDUCATION (adult): L BJE, National Association on Advanced Jewish Education of AAJE; BB, JDL, Had, USA, UAHC, UOJCA, YU, L syns, L JCC
EDUCATION (children): L BJE, AAJE cat (Section Six), TuM cat (Section Six), L syns. If you won't trust a teacher with your head, why with your child's?
EDUCATION (instruction): L BJE: AAJE provides good practical assistance to teachers; TuM. Consult educational departments of religious movements (Section Six); Sholem Aleichem Folk Institute, 41 Union Sq., NYC 10003 (for seculiar Yiddish culture); Merkos L'inyonei Chinuch
770 Eastern Parkway
Bklyn., NY 11213
(for Hasidism)
ELECTIONS: AIPAC provides info on congressional voting records about Israel, NCSJ on Soviet Jewry, NCJPS on other Jewish issues.
ENTERTAINMENT (hiring): JWB
FAMILY (programs for): BB, IJL
FILMS: AAJE p *Jewish Audio Visual Review* and supplements covering films of most J orgs. See Film; $ for J filmmaking from Encounter Films
254 W. 54th St.
NYC 10024
films available from L and nat offices of most J orgs incl: L BJE, L CRC, Israel, ADL (good film lib), AJCe,

Section Three continues on page 272.

	RECONSTRUCTIONIST	REFORM	CONSERVATIVE
Congregational & Coordinating Bodies	Federation of Reconstructionist Congregations & Havurot Jewish Reconstructionist Foundation	Union of American Hebrew Congregations	United Synagogue of America
			SYNAGOGUE COUNCIL OF AMERICA[2]
Rabbinical Bodies		Central Conference of American Rabbis	Rabbinical Assembly
Major Seminaries	Reconstructionist Rabbinical College	Hebrew Union College—Jewish Institute of Religion (Cincinnati, N.Y.)	Jewish Theological Seminary of America (N.Y.) University of Judaism (L.A.)
Youth Movements (College)	(T'hiyah)	National Federation of Temple Youth	United Synagogue Youth (Atid)
Major Publications			
Scholarly		*CCAR Journal*	*Conservative Judaism*
Popular	*Reconstructionist*	*Reform Judaism*	*United Synagogue Review*
Sisterhoods	Women's Organization of the JRF	National Federation of Temple Sisterhoods	Women's League for Conservative Judaism
Brotherhoods		National Federation of Temple Brotherhoods	National Federation of Jewish Men's Clubs
Educational Organizations			
Educators' Associations		National Association of Temple Educators	Educators' Assembly
Administrators' Associations		National Association of Temple Administrators	National Association of Synagogue Administrators
Cantors' Associations		American Conference of Cantors	Cantors' Assembly
Miscellaneous Bodies			

ORTHODOX				
Union of Orthodox Jewish Congregations of America	National Council of Young Israel	Mizrachi-HaPoel HaMizrachi—Religious Zionists of America[1]	Agudath Israel	
Rabbinical Council of America	Council of Young Israel Rabbis	Rabbinical Alliance (Igud HoRabbonim)	Union of Orthodox Rabbis (Agudath HoRabbonim)	Hisachdus HoRabbonim
Rabbi Isaac Elchanan Theological Seminary of Yeshiva University (N.Y.) Jewish University of America–Hebrew Theological College (Chicago)			Rabbi Jacob Joseph Yeshiva (N.Y.), Torah VoDas Yeshiva (N.Y.), Ner Israel (Baltimore), Mirer Yeshiva (N.Y.), Tiferes Yerushalayim (N.Y.), Telshe Yeshiva (Cleveland), Bais Medrosh Gavohah (Lakewood, N.J.), Lubavitch Yeshiva (N.Y.), Satmarer Yeshiva (N.Y.), Chaim Berlin (N.Y.)	
National Conference of Synagogue Youth (Yavneh)	Yisrael Hatzair (Young Israel Intercollegiates)	Noam[1] Bnei Akiva[1]	Pirchei Agudath Israel Bnos Agudath Israel Bachurei Agudath Israel (Zeirei Agudath Israel)	Pirchei Habad Bnos Habad
Tradition *Jewish Life*	*HaDarom* *Young Israel Viewpoint*		*Allgemeine Journal*, *Jewish Press*, *Jewish Observer*, *Dos Yiddishe Vort*, *Der Yid*	
Women's Branch of the UOJCA	Women's League of National Council of Young Israel	Mizrachi Women[1] Women's Organization of HaPoel HaMizrachi[1]	Neshei Agudath Israel	Neshei Habad
National Commission on Torah Education of Yeshiva University		Vaad HaChinuch Ha Torani[1] (Mizrachi)	Torah U'Mesorah-National Association of Hebrew Day Schools	Merkos l'Inyonei Chinuch (Habad)
Educators' Council of America			National Conference of Yeshiva Principals of Torah U'Mesorah	
National Organization of Synagogue Administrators				
Cantorial Council of America				
National Jewish Commission on Law and Public Affairs Community Service Division at Yeshiva University		Young Israel Employment Bureau Association of Orthodox Jewish Scientists Commission on Legislation and Civic Action of Agudath Israel National Association of Jewish Traditional Social Workers		

[1] Zionist and educational organization
[2] Coordinating body for the six largest congregational & rabbinic bodies

AJCo, AZYF, BB, CVJC, Had, Hillel, American Trade Union Council for Histadrut
33 E. 67th St.
NYC 10021
ISO, American Jewish Joint Distribution Committee
60 E. 42nd St.
NYC 10017
JWB, Habad, RZA, LZA, SCA, TuM, UAHC, United Israel Appeal
515 Park Ave.
NYC 10022
UJA, USA, YIVO, ZOA

FOOD: L fa, L fed r

FUND-RAISING: CJF can give information on orgs that raise funds, careers in fund-raising, where fund-raising orgs exist

GRADUATE STUDIES IN JUDAICA (info): AJS, Hillel p

HASIDISM: Habad. See also Communities, "Hasidic Communities"

HEBREW: HI, Israel. See *Education*

HOLOCAUST (info and ed lit): AAJE, YIVO (esp scholarly), Department of Contemporary Jewish Studies
Brandeis U
Waltham, Mass. 02154
r, L BJE

INSURANCE: Many J orgs offer various kinds of insurance to mems at reduced premiums

INTERGROUP RELATIONS: AJCe, UAHC, SCA, JLC, JWV, L CRC, NJCRAC

ISRAEL (info): Israel, WZO. Almost every J org offers more or less propagandistic l about Israel

ISRAEL: (programs): WZO; (for youth and students) AZYF most y and s orgs sponsor or refer to Israel programs

ISRAEL (travel to): See *Tours*. Tour leaders often get free trips

ISRAEL (helpful orgs for Americans in Israel): Association of Americans and Canadians in Israel, Zionist House, Jewish Agency r, ISTA. Many orgs m offices in Israel. If you are a mem, ask the nat office. American Embassy, National Union of Israeli Students

ISRAEL (settling): See *Aliyah*

ISRAEL (products from): For Israeli products in various parts of the United States: Oded Erez, Israel Government Office
850 3rd Ave.
New York, N. Y. 10022
(212)-752-5600

ISRAELIS (in America): Israel, ISO

JEWISH ISSUES (analyses of): SCA, CCAR. See *Publications*. Few Jewish orgs consider anything more profound than immediate crises and self-perpetuation

JEWISH NEWS: JTA, JSP-S. See *Publications*

JEWISH STUDIES: AJS, Hillel p

JEWS IN MOSLEM/ARAB LANDS: Committee of Concern, 1 Williams St., NYC, Israel, AJCe, AJCo, ADL, NJCRACr

KASHRUT (Jewish dietary laws and their observance): UOJCA (p and product guides); L BR, USA p, YI and Yavneh help set up kosher kitchens on university campuses

KIBBUTZ: Kibbutz Aliyah Desk
575 6th Ave.
NYC 10011

LECTURERS (hiring): JWB, BB, Jewish Chautauqua Society of UAHC

LEGISLATIVE ADVICE: NCJPS; (on legislation affecting real practices) COLPA; (on church-state problems) AJCo (secularist), COLPA (rel); (affecting Israel) AIPAC; (affecting Soviet Jewry) NCSJ

LIBRARIES: Section Six. L BJE, L syns, L JCC, ; see *Archives;* cultural listings in AJYB. Good J libs attached to all seminaries and yeshivot, most major universities and public libs

LOANS: L Hebrew/Jewish Free Loan Society, L fa, L fed

MAPS: WZO, AAJEr, L BJE

MARRIAGE: L syn, L BR

MEDICAL CARE: L J hospital, L fed, CJFr

MONEY (for J cultural, ed, or scholarly projects): IJL, MFJC, NFJL, L fed (for student or youth projects): AJCo, AZYF, CJF, Appeal, Hillel, L feds in various cities have set up special funds for student projects

MUSIC: NJMC

ORAL HISTORY: AJCe

ORTHODOX JUDAISM: Section Six

PACIFISM: JPF

PASSOVER: Some feds distribute food or $ to poor Jews for Passover

PERIODICALS: See *Publications*. AJA m extensive collection of American J periodicals. Other good collections in major J libraries

PSYCHOLOGICAL/PSYCHIATRIC COUNSELING: L fa, L fed, L J hospital. Most rabbis have training and experience in counseling and can refer.

PUBLICATIONS: Most J orgs publish prodigiously. For useful guides see Section Six. Many J orgs issue their own periodicals. Most are dull and propagandistic or dull and statistical. The best organizational periodicals of general interest incl: AIPAC (*Near East Reports*—Israel propaganda), AJCe (*Commentary*—partially Jewish, totally highbrow), AJCo (*Congress Bi-Weekly*—issues and current affairs—and *Judaism*—fine readable scholarship), BB (*National Jewish Monthly*—light and general), CCAR (*CCAR Journal*—lightly intellectual), Had (*Hadassah*—excellent and varied), HI (*LaMishpaha*—easy Hebrew and *HaDoar*—American Hebrew journalism), JRF (*Reconstructionist*—lively J issues), LZA (*Jewish Frontier*—Left Zionist thinking), Network (*Network*— national J s affairs), RCA (*Tradition*—Orthodox thought and scholarship), SCA (*Analysis*—excellent studies of J issues), UOJCA (*Jewish Life*—O schmaltz and some meat), ZOA (*American Zionist*—good propaganda), AIA (*Jewish Observer*—for the very traditional). The Herzl Institute, at WZO p *Midstream,* which is consistently intelligent and interesting

RABBINICAL SEMINARIES: Section Four

RABBIS (Associations of): Section Four; CCAR (R), RA (C), RCA (O), RAA (O), AH (O)

REFORM JUDAISM: Section Four

RELIGIOUS COUNSELING AND ADVICE: L rabbi, Habad; (s) Hillel; (y) National Conference of Synagogue Youth of UOJCA, Torah leadership seminars of YU, some youth group leaders

RELIGIOUS INFO: Religious bodies, lay and rabbinical (Section Six)

SCHOLARSHIPS (in Jewish studies): NFJCr, MFJC (advanced only), (communal and social work) CJFr. No yeshivah will reject a student for lack of funds

SCIENTISTS: Association of Orthodox Jewish Scientists
84 Fifth Ave.
NYC 10011

SELF-DEFENSE (lessons): JDL, L JCC

SEPHARDIC JEWS: World Institute for Sephardic Studies
135 Central Park West
NYC 10023
American Sephardic Federation of WZO; Sephardic Foundation for Jewish Culture
17 Grenfell Dr.
Great Neck, NY 11020
YU p *American Sephardi*

SEX: Many J orgs sponsor singles' programs, "young leadership" divisions, etc. Most such groups attract singles from mid-twenties to mid-forties looking for marriage or sex. Sometimes the groups have good programs in addition to social and fund-raising activities

SHABBAT HOSPITALITY: L syns; more traditional hosts offer more hospitality

SHALIHIM: (community representatives from Israel): Israel, WZO, AZYF, L CRC

SHELTER: L fa, L fed

SOCIOLOGY: Association for the Sociological Study of Jewry
C/o Dr. Norman L. Friedman
Dept. of Sociology
California State U.
Los Angeles, Cal. 90032

SOVIET JEWRY: L CRC; many L Soviet Jewry orgs exist; NCSJ, SSSJ; most major orgs have info, programs or refer

STUDENTS: Section Six; Hillel; many L feds m agencies which aid and fund J s programs; Network, Hillel; see Network guide (Section Six)

SYNAGOGUES (association of): Section Six; UAHC (R), USA (C), UOJCA (O), YI (O), AIA (O)

TEACHERS (in Jewish schools): Associations in each rel movement (Section Six)

TEACHERS (secular): Jewish Teachers Association
11 W. 42nd St.
NYC 10036

TEACHING: See *Education (instruction)*

THEATER: NCAJL
TOURS: AJCo, BB, UJA. Many other J orgs offer inexpensive group tours, particularly to Israel and other places of J interest, for members. Savings are much more than dues
TRAVEL: Section Six
UNIONS: JLC
VETERANS: JWV
VOCATIONAL GUIDANCE: L J vocational service, L fed, CJF r; BB; YI m nat office for Sabbath observers
WOMEN: On a local level many J women's orgs are interchangeable. There are Sisterhoods attached to most syns. Some women's orgs have as their primary activities, fundraising. Some, like National Council of Jewish Women, are only marginally Jewish. Few offer direct services. Major organizations with good women's divisions incl: AJCo and BB. Other outstanding women's orgs incl: Had; Mizrahi Women's Org
817 Broadway
NYC 10003
Women's Org of HaPoel HaMizrahi at RZA; Pioneer Women at LZA; Women's American ORT
222 Park Ave. S.
NYC 10003
YIDDISH: YIVO, WC, LZA, Yugntruf, Bund; for teaching, see *Education*
YOUTH: L syns, LCRC, LJCC; see Network student guide (Section Six); Nat orgs incl: BB (Bnai Brith Youth Org—nonideological) RZA (Bnai Akiva—very O, very Z and NOAM—similar but less intense). AIA (Bnos Agudath Israel—O for girls; and Zeirei Agudath Israel—O for boys) Dror, 2091 Broadway, NYC 10023 (independent Z), Had (HaShachar—Young Judea—Zionist), Americans for Progressive Israel
150 Fifth Ave.
NYC 10011
(HaShomer Ha Tzair—Left Zionist), LZA (Ichud HaBonim—Left Zionist), UOJCA (National Conference of Synagogue Youth—O), UAHC (National Federation of Temple Youth—R), USA (United Synagogue Youth—C); Yavneh (O,s)
ZIONISM: WZO, AZF (see entry for names of orgs); most maintain y and women's affiliates stronger than the parent body

For further information, consult S. P. Goldberg, "Jewish Communal Services: Programs and Finances" in *American Jewish Year Book* (or available as a pamphlet from CJF).

*Section Five: Allocations of Jewish federations and welfare funds**

LOCAL[1] (41%)

Family Service (14.1)
Hospitals (10.7)
Aged Care (6.1)
Jewish Community Centers (YMHA-YWHA) (36.2)
Community Relations (NA)[5]
Jewish Education (9.7)
Employment and Vocational Service (NA)
Jewish Camps (NA)
Youth and Student Services (NA)

NATIONAL[2] (4%)

AJCe (952)
ADL (1149)
AJCo (472)
JLC (210)
JWV (92)
NJCRAC (289)
JWB (1842)
JWB (211)
BBYSA (includes Hillel) (NA)
NFJC (179)
NCSJ[6]
SCA (32)
Jewish cultural institutions, seminaries, teachers' colleges, etc.

INTERNATIONAL[3] (55%)

Israeli universities
America-Israel Cultural Foundation
Israeli religious institutions
Hadassah
HIAS

UNITED JEWISH APPEAL (except IEF)[4] funds
1. Joint Distribution Committee (ORT, Malben, etc.)
2. New York Association for New Americans
3. HIAS
4. United Israel Appeal[4] funds

JEWISH AGENCY FOR ISRAEL

*In 1970 approximately $140,000,000 was allocated by over 200 federations; 55.3% or $77,414,000 went to overseas agencies, of which 52.9% or $74,050,000 went through UJA. An *additional* $127,500,000 in IEF monies was also transferred to Israel by UJA.

1. For 1970, in millions of dollars.
2. For 1970, in hundred of thousands of dollars.
3. For 1971, in millions of dollars.
4. The Israel Emergency Fund (IEF) goes, after expenses, to the United Israel Appeal, which is UJA's funding agent for the Jewish Agency for Israel (or vice-versa, depending on one's perspective). Including the IEF, UJA represents approximately two-thirds of all federation allocations. In addition, $209,161,000 in State of Israel Bonds were sold in the United States in 1971. American voluntary aid for Israel, excluding bonds, totaled $281.1 million in campaigns authorized by the Jewish Agency (i.e., federated campaigns and independent organizations such as Hadassah, National Council of Jewish Women, and "American Friends of" various Israeli institutions of higher learning). Many unauthorized campaigns also collect funds for Israeli (mostly religious) institutions. Government and foundation grants to Israeli institutions represent millions of additional dollars.
5. NA—Not Available
6. Not funded in 1970

Section Six: Bibliography

Aside from local federation listings of local service agencies, the following detailed community guides, describing local organizations, are available:

Jewish Boston and New England Supplement: A Guide, 233 Bay State Rd., Boston, Mass. 02215 ($1)
A Guide to Jewish Chicago, American Jewish Congress, 22 W. Monroe St., Chicago, Ill. 60603 ($2)
Thy Source: A Guide to Jewish Cleveland for Young Adults, Jewish Community Federation of Cleveland, 1750 Euclid Ave., Cleveland, Ohio 44155
A Guide to Jewish Los Angeles, Youth Department, Jewish Federation Council of Greater Los Angeles, 590 North Vermont Ave., Los Angeles, Cal. 90004 (50c)
Jewish New York, Box 399, Planetarium Station, NYC 10025 ($5)
Jewish Philadelphia, PUJS, 401 S. Broad St., Philadelphia, Pa., 19147 ($1).

Other community guides are or may soon be available. The best short description of American Jewish organizations is:

Goldberg, S. P., *The American Jewish Community: Its Structure, Role, and Organization*, Women's American ORT, 222 Park Ave. S., NYC (35c)

The two best general directories of American Jewish organizations are:

American Jewish Year Book, published annually by AJCe and JPS ($12 from either). It contains a section of "Directories and Lists," including national organizations (with an information puff, including publications, founding date, current officers, and subsidiaries, on each), Jewish periodicals, etc., "Jewish Communal Services: Programs and Finances" by S. P. Goldberg (an overview of how American Jewry spends its public funds), and often carries interesting articles on organizational issues.

Directory of American Jewish Organizations, Frankel Mailing Service, 14 Rutgers St., NYC 10002 ($10). A city-by-city listing with no explanations

A more ambitious directory with less on the United States is:

Jewish Organizations: A Worldwide Directory, International Conference of Jewish Communal Service, 31 Union Sq. W., NYC 10003

Useful for teaching is:

Efron, Benjamin. *Multimedia Resources on the Jewish Community*, AAJE ($3.50). The AAJE has other materials on the subject

Literature on the subject is catalogued in:

Linzer, Norman. *Jewish Communal Services in the United States: 1960–1970, A Selected Bibliography*, Commission on Synagogue Relations, Federation of Jewish Philanthropies of New York, 130 E. 59th St., NYC 10022 ($5)

More specialized directories include the following:

CAMPS

Directory of Resident Summer Camps under the Auspices of Jewish Communal Organizations, Camping Services Dept., JWB ($2)

COMMUNITY CENTERS

Directory, Jewish Community Centers and Young Men's and Young Women's Hebrew Associations JWB ($2)

COMMUNITY RELATIONS

National Jewish Community Relations Advisory Council Directory of Constituent Organizations NJ. Lists national staff and assignments and local offices of AJCe, AJCo, BB, ADL, JLC, NCJW, UAHC, UOJCA, USA, and most local Jewish community relations councils

EDUCATION

Jewish Education Directory AAJE. Lists central educational agencies, teacher training schools, Jewish schools in U.S. and Canada, public high schools teaching Hebrew

Directory of Day Schools in the United States and Canada TuM ($5). Orthodox day schools and yeshivot ketanot

Jewish Studies at American Colleges and Universities: A Catalogue Hillel ($2)

FEDERATIONS

Directory of Jewish Federations, Welfare Funds and Community Councils. Published annually by CJF ($3.50). Lists national staff and officers of CJF and local lay and professional leadership of fund-raising bodies

HEALTH AND WELFARE

Directory of Jewish Health and Welfare Agencies CJF ($3.50)

HILLEL

Directory Hillel. Lists Hillel foundations and discusses Jewish life on many campuses

LIBRARIES

Guide to the Jewish Libraries of the World. World Jewish Congress, 55 New Cavendish St., London, W 1, England. Out of date but useful

Mimeographed list of members, Association of Jewish Libraries, AJHS, 2 Thorton Rd., Waltham, Mass. 02154

PRESS

The Jewish Press of the World. World Jewish Congress (10 shillings, 6 pence)

See also *American Jewish Year Book* (above)

Joseph Jacobs Organization, *The Joseph Jacobs Directory of the Jewish Press in America* (2nd ed., 1972)

STUDENTS

A Guide to Jewish Student Groups Network ($1)

A useful book of international scope is

The Jewish Communities of the World: Demography, Political and Organizational Status, Religious Institutes, Education, Press Institute of Jewish Affairs/World Jewish Congress, 15 E. 84th St., NYC 10028 ($2.95)

Various Jewish travel guides give information about Jewish organizations in specific cities. The most popular is:

The Jewish Travel Guide. Jewish Chronicle/Hartmoor House, Inc. of Media Judaica, Inc. 1363 Fairfield Ave., Bridgeport, Conn. 06605 ($3.45)

Other useful guides are:

INTERNATIONAL

Freedman, Warren. *The Selective Guide for the Jewish Traveller: A World Guide to Restaurants, Hotels, Communal Organizations, Landmarks and Scenery, Synagogues and More.* Macmillan, 866 Third Ave., NYC 10022 ($6.95)

UNITED STATES

Postal, Bernard and Koppman, Lionel *A Jewish Tourist's Guide to the U.S.* JPS (out of print)

Postal, Bernard and Koppman, Lionel *Jewish Landmarks in New York: An Informal History and Guide* Hill and Wang ($2.45 paper). Includes descriptions of major organizations based in New York

LATIN AMERICA

Comunidades Judias de Latino America AJCe

Postal, Bernard and Stern, Malcolm. *A Jewish Tourist's Guide to the Caribbean.* American Airlines

EUROPE

Postal, Bernard and Abramson, Samuel *The Traveler's Guide to Jewish Landmarks of Europe.* Fleet Press, 156 Fifth Ave., NYC 10010 ($3.95)

European Travel Guide for Jews Belgisch Israelitisch Weekblad, 106–108, Pelikaanstraat—2000 Antwerp, Belgium. Concise, especially good for Belgium

Guide Juif de France. Roger Berg, 31 bis Faubourg Montmartre, Paris 9e, France

ISRAEL: See Jewish Travel, bibliography

Hakhnasat orhim-hospitality

"Great is hospitality; greater even than early attendance at the house of study or than receiving the Shekhinah" (Talmud, Sabbath, 127a).

When I was a kid, our family never had a lot of guests. We didn't have much space at home and, besides that, a home was thought to be a rather closed corporation. Eighteen years ago in Safed, a friend and I were desperately looking for a hotel room late one Friday afternoon. There were none to be found. A young schoolteacher, whom I remember today only as Judah, witnessed our consternation as we vainly sought accommodations. He approached us and said, "It is unthinkable that Jews should be without a place to stay on Shabbat. You will come home with me." That was when I began to learn about hakhnasat orhim—the mitzvah of bringing guests into the house.

Since that time my life was saved by a Jewish doctor who took me into his home in southern India; I was invited home for lunch by a lady in Rome because she heard me speaking Hebrew with someone; as a student, I schnorred my way across the country never paying for lodging because there was always the home of a friend of a friend of a friend to stay at; I have eaten with a Quebec farmer who offered me dinner because he knew how far I must have had to walk uphill with my bicycle in order to reach the part of the road where his farm was located. I could multiply the stories endlessly.

I will never be able to reciprocate these people's hospitality. All that I can do is give to guests what some other hosts have given to me and hope that they will do the same for others.

Our family now places guests into two categories. The less gratifying are usually the people who just got stuck and need a place to stay overnight or for a few days. They never come from the same place twice and each guest's story is unlike the preceding one. If you want to continue to enjoy such people over a period of time, don't flutter over them too much. Chat as long as you find that good things are happening between you, and then only if you are not pressed with other urgent responsibilities. Beyond that, show them where the linens are, let them stow their belongings, and point out what's around for breakfast. When the time comes, they'll be on their way. Perhaps we have been fortunate, but we have almost never been seriously imposed on by our guests. In general, our guests have given us far more than we have given them.

There must have been occasional moments of desperation in some ancient rabbinic households or else the rabbis would not have suggested that there are realistic limitations to what one can legitimately be expected to do for a guest: "It sometimes happens that when a person receives a guest, he feeds him fowl on the first day, more ordinary meat on the second day, fish on the third, cheese the day after that, vegetables the next day, until he finally feeds him no more than greens" (Pesikta 31).

We find that we generally "specialize" in a second variety of guests—guests for Shabbat and holidays. At these times we are not pressed by outside concerns and can really be present to enjoy and learn from those who come into our home. Somewhere I read that children who live in homes that house boarders are more adaptable and better adjusted than those that live only within their nuclear families. I realize that the causal factors producing such data may not have a simple explanation, but I have enough data from the life of our own family to know how much my wife, our children, and I have gained from those who have come into our home.

Over the years they have included hundreds of students (mostly from the days when I was Hillel director at Yale), and lots of faculty too. Now it is primarily friends we have chanced to meet in any number of casual ways. We invite people we would like to know better, people we suspect might be feeling lonely, people who will bring us special joy, people who would like to learn something about Shabbat or yom tov, people to whom we would like to teach something about Shabbat or yom tov, people who know really good Shabbat songs, neighbors, people who drop in, and people for whom we can find no particular rationale at all.

Every now and then we get a few duds—guests who pretend that they are visiting anthropologists come to watch our quaint oriental rites. We are also burdened with a problem that many readers of this book happily will not face: those people who are terrified by being in the house of a rabbi for the first and only time in their lives. They don't know how they are "supposed" to act and are sure that they will inadvertently do something dreadfully gauche. If they are sufficiently on edge, there is really very little we can do except heave the same sigh of relief that they do once they are out the door.

Far more often, however, we have fun. We learn about different kinds of people. We learn about different parts of the country or the world; we learn of the activities of long-lost friends through the "Do you know . . . ?" game. Our children meet new styles of Jewishness. (It is our children, in fact, who are usually most disappointed when we do not have guests.)

Guests can pick us up when we are in the doldrums. If there are squabbles afoot anywhere in the family, the presence of outsiders forces us to behave for a while and frequently takes enough edge off the incident that started the trouble that we can reestablish contact with much greater ease than would otherwise have been possible. Even the "company behavior" of children is a nice thing (although we can't count on it consistently—alas).

"It is said that there was a custom in Jerusalem to spread a napkin over the doorway. All the time the napkin was spread, guests [travelers] could enter; when the napkin was removed, wayfarers were not allowed to enter" (Tosefta, Berakhot, IV,4a).

"A man must not press his fellows to be his guest when he sees that person does not wish to accept" (Talmud Yerushalmi, Dema'i, IV, 6).

HAKHNASAT ORHIM: SOME PRACTICES

1. Offers of hospitality should always be given wholeheartedly and with sincerity. That is—if you don't mean it, don't say it!

2. Sometimes for very good reasons, someone to whom you would like to open up your home simply cannot accept your offer. For his own comfort and yours, drop the subject.

3. It can be tempting for me to sit and entertain the guests while my wife straightens up and sends the children off to bed. It is obviously far more satisfactory for everyone if we all pitch in—guests, too. There is no reason for not enlisting the help of guests in clearing away food, cleaning up, etc. It usually makes them feel more relaxed about being with you and makes your life a little easier, too. Besides, guests have responsibilities, too.

"A guest who unduly troubles his host is considered unworthy" (Derech Eretz Zuta, 8).

4. Try to avoid a trap I fall into too frequently. I come rushing home at the last minute and try to pull a Clark Kent, flinging off my workaday frenetics to zip into my fresh Super-Jew Shabbat clothes and mood. It never works. When you have guests, the whole family should prepare for them. Otherwise, the burden will fall on one member of the family, who may not only be too busy to enjoy guests but may even come to resent them.

5. One way to avoid extending yourself beyond your abilities is to keep the food simple. It is better to offer straightforward, uncomplicated cooking to many guests than Cordon Bleu goodies to only a select few. At least we find it more fun that way.

"Let your house be wide open to guests. Receive people graciously. Lavish hospitality accompanied by a sour disposition means far less than modest hospitality which is extended cheerfully" (Avot d'R. Nathan, 1).

6. Finally—Do Not Overdo!! By the end of the spring we often feel ourselves overguested. We want to have a bit more privacy to do our family thing alone. Then it is time to stop for a few weeks or even for the season. Sometimes we tend to overextend ourselves by our feeling of responsibility for showing hospitality to the whole world. That is silly. And so we say, "Enough!" Come fall, we will begin to feel that things have been too quiet and that we are once again ready to get into the mitzvah of hakhnasat orhim.

Communities

With the conception of Havurat Shalom in 1968, a new idea developed among Jews disenchanted with the synagogue. That idea was that it was possible, here in the Diaspora, to resurrect in some way the old Jewish idea of community and join together to work, learn, pray, and live. We are including a list of some of these communities, what we know about them, etc. By the time this catalog is published this list will, almost inevitably, contain some misinformation. New communities may have come into existence; others (God forbid!) may have disbanded. The important thing is that something new, exciting, and creative is happening—something good.

1. **Havurat Shalom**
   113 College Ave.
   Somerville, Mass. 02144

The alter zaydeh of the movement, the havurah is something deeply important to all of us who are or have been its members. It's a community of people who study, pray, retreat, fight, talk, sing, dance, and love each other. The world is invited to services every Saturday morning at 10:30. The services are led by a different haver every week. In addition, adult education courses ranging from Moses and Freud to holy men and hallah-baking are offered. A distinct and close community has arisen between haverim and those people who join us in prayer, celebration, and study.

2. **House of Love and Prayer**
   1456 9th Ave.
   San Francisco, Cal.
   (415-731-2261)

A group started by Shlomo Carlebach; a very open community that encourages people to join and participate. There's a Shabbos Love and Prayer every Friday evening at sundown and Saturday morning beginning between 10 and 11; also prayers every morning at 6:30. They get together for classes in Hebrew, Talmud, Humash, etc., and anyone is invited. In addition, they have a prayer room and a library, both of which are open all day. A Jewish book service is run by:

Steven Maimes
Judaic Book Service
224 Judah St. #1
San Francisco, Cal. 94122

He offers books from all publishers; mail order at good discounts.

3. **The Fabrangen**
   4500 Connecticut Ave., N. W.
   Washington, D. C. 20008
   (202-667-7829)

The Fabrangen focuses on the building of a holistic Jewish life process in the Diaspora. They try to bring religion, politics, work, "fun," and relations among women, men, and children into a Jewish relationship. It is an open-ended community which celebrates Shabbat together and studies Torah and Talmud in relation to their own lives. It assumes the full and equal participation of women and men in davening, making dinners, etc. and tries to see beyond this toward discovery of what new forms of Jewish life the full participation of women should lead to. The Fabrangen also tries to shape a "politics" of tzedek—justice—out of religious concern. It runs a Sunday cheder which takes children seriously and good-humoredly. Send self-addressed envelope for the newsletter, etc.

4. **Chavurat Aviv**
   1676 E. 117th St.
   Cleveland, Ohio 44106

Chavurat Aviv is in its second year of existence and has become a very active, open community. Its members are involved in a free Sunday school which they run for kids in the community. They hold open house periodically and run other programs to which everyone is invited.

5. **Beit Ephraim (The Bayit)**
535 W. 112th St.
New York, N. Y. 10025

A new group which began in 1971. There are thirty people who encompass a wide range of Jewish interests. They live together in a big six-story building where they daven, eat, study, etc. They have a library and lounge. Two services are held on Shabbat—traditional and creative. There are once-a-week lectures to which everyone is invited and which have featured such interesting personalities as Rabbi Shlomo Riskin and Dr. Yitzchak Greenberg.

6. **New York Havurah**
299 Riverside Drive, Apt. 3D
New York, N. Y. 10025

A group of thirty to forty people who form a community of study, celebration, and prayer. Services, which are held every Shabbat and holiday, are open to the general community. In addition, open forums are held once a month with presentations by haverim or noted guest speakers. Again, once a month the New York Havurah goes to the country for a Shabbat retreat. It is first cousins with Havurat Shalom but has somewhat different religious, intellectual, and communal orientations—due partly to the composition of its membership and partly to its being in Manhattan.

7. **Kibbutz Langdon**
142 Langdon St.
Madison, Wis. 53703

Kibbutz Langdon is a heterogeneous group of Jewish students who experiment with living together in a Jewish community. Combining the broad range of backgrounds and interests, they find a common ground to celebrate Shabbat and holidays together.

In addition, there are several havurot which are fairly new as of this writing. Among these are:

Chevra
213 University Dr.
Tempe, Ariz. 85281

Ithaca Chavurah
522 Stewart Ave.
Ithaca, N. Y. 14850

Talmidei Aharone
428 S. 42nd St.
Philadelphia, Pa. 19104

The Georgetown Chavurah
3612 N St. N. W.
Washington, D. C. 20007

Havurah House
25 Andrews Memorial Dr.
Rochester, N. Y. 14623

Hebrew House
1606 West Ave.
Austin, Tex. 78701

For a more detailed list, Network publishes a *Guide to Jewish Student Groups,* which is available for $1 from:

North American Jewish Students' Network
36 W. 37th St.
New York, N. Y. 10018

HOW TO START A HAVURAH

Burt Jacobson, one of the earliest members of Havurat Shalom, has written "Blueprint for a Havurah." It is a comprehensive statement on what a havurah is and how to start one. We are including this blueprint because we think it is an important statement about a way we can find the roots of our past and adapt those roots so as to help us discover new meaning and a new sense of community in the Jewish people.

Introduction

Many of us are lonely and hunger for meaning beyond our limited selves. We seek genuine fellowship and joy with others, the excitement of encounter with the Transcendent, and the discovery of our roots in the past.

One answer to our quest seems to be emerging from the youth culture—the creation of a new form of extended family: communes, co-ops, and, in the Jewish counterculture, the havurah.

A havurah is a core community of individuals who care for one another personally, and strive to attain a shared human and Jewish consciousness through shared activities and experiences. In this way a community structure is gradually built, and the havurah becomes a meaningful center in the lives of its haverim.

The task of creating a havurah is most difficult, given the individualistic and institutional conditioning that is at the root of American living patterns. A havurah cannot be built overnight. A group that wishes to become an interdependent community must accept the fact that this will require change in both the outer and inner patterns of living. And such change—if it is to become genuine change—can only come about over a prolonged period of time, and possibly with a great deal of the tension that comes with growth.

Such a community can only develop through compromise. But compromise and consensus should not be attained through the mere repression of individual conscience. We should attempt to create a structure that retains the polarity of individual and community, rather than merely seeking a framework in which the individual escapes from his autonomy and becomes dependent upon the will of the group.

The Components of Havurah

The following articulation of elements that might go into building a core community is based primarily, though not exclusively, on the experiences of Havurat Shalom during 1969–71. A number of the ideas discussed are adapted or quoted from a pamphlet called *Making Communities* written by an anonymous Canadian commune.

1. You begin with a shared dissent from existing Jewish institutions and their modes of participation, and a group decision to initiate an alternative model.

2. You must have a personal compatability of members, or at least an initial agreement to work together in areas of mutual concern. It is difficult to measure in advance how well people will get along once the havurah becomes more intensive. Yet one of the goals of the community should be the development of a sense of generosity, care, and responsibility toward one another. For only through a sense of giving can you put another's interest before your own, which is so necessary to community-building. From the very beginning members should have mutual respect, a sense of humor, and the ability to compromise. The size of the havurah should be limited so that superficial relationships can become truly genuine, and so that every member bears some active responsibility toward the community.

3. Haverim should make responsible personal commitments to the new community for a set period of time (perhaps two years) despite the problems and tensions that might occur.

4. If at all possible, the group should have a committed, Jewishly learned leader

a. whose leadership role is accepted;

b. who fosters leadership potential among other members so as to eventually minimize or eliminate the need for his own leadership role;

c. who does not have a holier-than-thou attitude toward other members and is thus open to criticism.

Such a leader may be found among Jewish professionals in the city, or may be found in a nearby city. This leader should work directly with

a. aiding work-group chairmen;

b. changing community coordinators;

c. teaching the entire community.

As a teacher he should give members a sense of the geography of Jewish values as embodied in the tradition, as well as methods of access and inquiry into Jewish source material. Thus some members can eventually become teachers themselves. The length and times of work-group leadership roles should be short in duration—perhaps four or six months—giving everyone a chance to lead different work groups and coordinate communal activities. All members should serve in at least one work group.

"Have *specific* community goals. This is extremely important! It is on these goals that all future agreements must be based. The more specific the goal, the better. The goal can be as abstract as a search for a better way of living or as concrete as the promulgation of an idea. Without a common goal you cannot have common values; without common values there can be no agreements. . . . Take your time. Spend as much time as you can rapping with your brothers before you talk about where to build or how to build. During this time of talking, work toward the making of specific agreements. These basic agreements are the most important. They must be *real* agreements. Don't give in on an important issue to preserve community harmony at this point; there will be plenty of opportunity for that later. Write the agreements down so you won't forget them. Talk about them as long as the subject is interesting to you. It's during these months that you will decide if you can live with your brothers" *(Making Communities).*

This emerging vision can be embodied in a community covenant which would be amended as the havurah develops and changes.

5. Every healthy individual has a conscious set of goals and values that give him a sense of wholeness. In like manner, a community must slowly develop a shared consciousness—shared values, attitudes, and ideas, and a vision of the goals of the havurah. But such a communal consensus can only be built where individual goals and values overlap. Such a consensus will widen slowly as members get to know each other, and learn from one another through shared experiences. At the very beginning, each haver should examine his own life and try to determine which values and goals are most important to him. The members can share these things with one another and find out where their individual goals overlap.

6. The havurah should be involved in a step-by-step development of exciting shared experiences and activities which will implement the specific community goals.

The creative power that the community exerts upon personal and interpersonal development will stem, to a great extent, from the amount of willingness that the members have toward sharing, in terms of time and energy. In this fashion the community can develop bonds of love and responsibility and become a true center. These experiences can lead to a true community structure and discipline.

The following is a list of the kinds of experiences and activities which might become part of the havurah structure. Each area would be planned by one work group and the community as a whole would accept or modify the work group's proposals. The following structure is quite full and detailed, and again it must be stressed that such a structure will be developed slowly over a period of years. A new havurah will create its own order of priorities out of a large number of possibilities.

a. *Education*

(1) Shared day care for the children.

(2) Classes for youngsters—formal or free; taught by the Jewishly learned leader and/or other willing and capable haverim. (If this is impossible, the havurah will have to seek help from the "outside" community.) Classes may be developed by age bracket, interest, etc. The "little red schoolhouse" approach might be used when the ages of youngsters differ, and older students can help teach younger students. The youngster-teacher relationship

should be emphasized. Kids should be involved in at least 2–3 hours of classes a week.

(3) Classes for parents/adults. Parents should study some of the same areas of subject matter which their youngsters are learning, perhaps together with their youngsters at times. In this connection, parents should study with their children's teacher. Possible areas of study might include traditional and modern sources on the following: Who Is Man?; Man and His Fellowman; Experiences and Ideas of God; Social Justice; The Basis and Nature of Jewish Tradition; Family Relationships; Eretz Yisrael; Myth and Ritual in Religion; Particular Rituals (the Sabbath, kashrut, traditional life-style).

The community could also study the history and literature of a particular period of time, e.g., the biblical period, the rabbinic period, etc. Also, traditional commentaries on the portion of the week. Other areas of study might include Comparative Religion; Religion, Science and Technology; Religion and Politics; Yiddish and Hebrew Literature; Conversational Hebrew; The Thought of Modern Jewish Thinkers. The number of study areas for each semester or year will depend on the resources of the community.

(4) In line with this, the community should develop a communal library of Jewish and other books and records. If the community has its own building, the library could be located there. If not, a listing of books and records from each member's home could be compiled by a havurah librarian and this list given to each member. The havurah should also purchase books which can be of benefit to all members, such as the new *Encyclopaedia Judaica.*

b. *Celebration* The havurah should experiment with traditional religious observances and rites of passage, as well as create its own new forms of celebration and commemoration. The havurah can compile its own loose-leaf prayer book. Shared times of celebration could include:

(1) The Sabbath: Friday night services and a communal meal; Saturday morning services, Kiddush or luncheon; the third meal and Havdalah.

(2) Holy day celebrations: a community Seder, an all-night Tikkun on Shavuot, a havurah sukkah, Rosh Hodesh celebrations.

(3) Midweek communal meals with singing, storytelling, guest speakers. These meals could be potluck or elegantly planned.

(4) Weekend retreats of celebration and study at nearby Jewish camps, Christian retreat houses.

(5) Forms of meditation.

c. *Social and political justice* A haver could research a particular problem in the Jewish or general community at large, and a specific work group could explore various tactics to deal with the problem. One area that should be considered is the development of ongoing personal programs for Jewish old-age homes. The havurah should consider strategies for taking over positions of power on the federation, synagogue, center boards, and city council. Professionals in the havurah—doctors, lawyers—could donate their services and time to youth-culture centers, free clinics, and halfway houses.

d. *Encounter* Encounter sessions are times when members can confront one another openly and honestly on a feeling level. This can be very important, especially for haverim working so closely together, since tensions often build up. Encounter means the lowering of the defense mechanisms, the airing of gripes and criticism; but it also means mutual encouragement and complement. Encounters can take place as frequently as members feel the need for

TWO CONCLUDING REMARKS

"Visions have a way of magnetizing those committed to them. And yet somehow a vision is elusive. For a vision is not a goal or a set of goals. A goal is attained; a vision constantly calls for self-transcendence. A community is not built; it is always being built.

Good luck. Making a community is making a life-style; take responsibility for your life in your own hands. Like any major human undertaking, it requires courage, the solidity of character that comes from being on friendly terms with yourself, limitless patience and occasional heroism. But the rewards are great in accordance with the sacrifices. You will learn a great deal about yourself and about people, and grow in proportion to your willingness to suffer for love. And it's a very exciting game to play. May God bless you" *(Making Communities).*

this activity. There should also be times set aside when members can share with the community what they are doing and experiencing on an individual level.

e. Meetings Meetings should be held only when there are issues and problems that the havurah as a whole must resolve. They should never last longer than two hours. Every thirty minutes or so, haverim should stand up and laugh.

f. Fun Socializing, open house, plays, dancing, choir, sports, picnics, Jewish and other crafts, Jewish cooking, creating magazines, theater parties, etc.

g. Economy The havurah should consider having, in some sense, a shared economic base, which can also add to its solidarity. Such economic sharing can be of various kinds: a food-buying co-op, shared group insurance, shared Israeli bonds, a community treasury fund for members in need, shared income, communal philanthropy, shared stockholding. (If all members own stock in a particular corporation, they may wield greater control over company policies through combining their proxies and getting other stockholders in the company to do the same.)

7. A decision regarding the special needs of the havurah: whether homes and apartments can suffice, or whether a special building is necessary. If the community has enough funds for a building, it should consider one that is located in a semirural area (perhaps an old farm) which could offer a greater seclusion and closeness to nature. It could also be used for retreats and as a campsite—during the summer and during holy day vacations—for a havurah family camp. Eventually the farm could possibly become a Jewish retreat center for other havurot (which are now developing as a result of your activity!) and for local synagogues (and the havurah will be the host!). Some of the farm acreage could actually be used to grow vegetables, and families might come out on weekends to work on the garden. The farmhouse and the property would probably need a good deal of work to be put in shape, and this work should be done by the members themselves.

8. The havurah should develop a policy of relations to the Jewish and general community, a visitor's policy, and a policy of new admissions—including a set of criteria for membership.

9. Do not be frightened by the magnitude of the task. Every act that brings the community closer to realizing its vision—no matter how seemingly insignificant—is real and important. No community has yet become the Ultimate Utopia. And a community that feels secure because it has truly achieved its vision begins to stagnate. For man cannot be man without some insecurity, and without creating problems to knock his head against. The constant revolutionary process of growth is perhaps more important than the goals that have been achieved.

HASIDIC COMMUNITIES

Introduction

No section on Jewish communities would be even remotely complete without mention of the Hasidic centers in New York (and sometimes, especially in the case of Lubavitch, elsewhere as well). Each differs from the next in very major ways, including spiritual direction, custom, ritual, etc.

Before visiting any of these places, check them out. Some are more hospitable than others. Some pointers:

1. Dress appropriately. Men should wear a kippah, and either a sports jacket or a suit. Married women should wear a head covering. All women should wear a dress (at least knee length) with sleeves (preferably elbow length) as well as stockings. This fulfills Hasidic standards of modest attire.

   To dress in a way that you do not normally dress may seem strange to you, but it is important to care about the feelings of your host, who might be offended if you wear jeans and a T- shirt. Also, standard dress will make the community more accessible to you.

2. There are certain particularly auspicious occasions during which to visit. Among these are the holidays—especially Purim and Simhat Torah. Of special note are the fabrengens—joyous gatherings at Lubavitch. The rebbe speaks, the Hasidim sing, and everyone drinks. These are held on the evening following a special Shabbat or holiday and can last well into the early morning. The 19th day of Kislev is an additional festive occasion at Lubavitch and marks the day that the first Lubavitcher Rebbe was released from a Russian prison. Finally, Lubavitch also holds pegishas—weekends at various times throughout the year to which students are invited.

A WORD OF CAUTION: Despite all its positive aspects, Lubavitch maintains a clearly articulated goal to convert Jews to the halakhic and specifically Hasidic way of life.

3. Beware of the laws regarding segregation of the sexes. Men can participate in these events more fully than women can. The experience for women can, nonetheless, be valuable and enjoyable.

4. If you are beginning to get the feeling that Lubavitch is the most hospitable, the best organized, and the most outgoing of all the groups, you are right. Lubavitch is a highly organized Hasidic community with branches all over the world. They support facilities around the country for study (from any level and background), prayer, meeting, etc. The central people to call or write with regard to visits or other contacts with Lubavitch (internationally) are:

Rabbi Shalom Ber Hecht
Machaneh Yisrael House
President St. and Kingston Ave.
Brooklyn, N. Y. 11213

Rabbi Kasriel Kastel
770 Eastern Parkway
Brooklyn, N. Y. 11213
(212) PR 8-4270

Alabama:
Birmingham. Rabbi M. Stern, c/o
Knesset Israel
3225 Montevalo Rd.
Mountain Brook, Birmingham
35210

Arizona:
Phoenix. Rabbi B. Field
730 E. Monticello 85014

California:
Berkeley. Rabbi C. I. Drizin,
1930 Vine St., 94709
or
Chabad House,
2340 Piedmont, 94704

Los Angeles. Rabbi S. Cunin
11058 Strathmore Dr., 90024
or
Chabad House
741 Gayley,
Westwood, L. A., 90024

Long Beach. Rabbi E. Piekarski,
3723 Lewis Ave., 90807
or
The Long Beach Hebrew
Academy
3981 Atlantic Ave., 90807

San Diego. Rabbi J. Kranz
455 S. Sherbourne Dr.
or
Chabad House
6115 Montezuma, 92115

Connecticut:
New Britain. Rabbi Okolico
44 Chamberlain St., 06052

New Haven. Rabbi M. Hecht
Director of School
111 Alden Ave., 06511

Bridgeport-Trumbull. Rabbi I. Stock
77 Mt. Pleasant Dr., 06611

Florida:
Miami Beach. Rabbi A. Korf
1257 Alton Rd., 33139

Rabbi S. B. Lipskar
Director of Schools
3917 N. Meridan Ave.
Apt. 17, 33140

Georgia:
Atlanta. Rabbi B. Steifel
1168 Biltmore Dr. N. E., 30329

Savannah. Chaim Capland
5543 Camelot Dr., 31405

Illinois:
Chicago. Rabbi S. Z. Hecht
5916 N. St. Louis Ave., 60645

Rabbi H. Shusterman
6227 N. Albany, 60645

Maine:
Portland. Rabbi C. Yaffee
94 Noyes St., 04103

Maryland:
Baltimore. Naftali Berg
3901 Clarinth Rd., 21215
Silver Spring. Dr. J. Sinsky
University of Md.
1701 E. W. Hgwy., 20910
College Park. Rabbi M. Silverman
4812 B. College Ave. #4B, 20740
Massachusetts:
Boston. Rabbi D. Wichnin
Contact for School
51 Cottage Farm Rd.
Brookline, 02146

Rabbi M. Bergstein
46 Euston Road
Brighton, 02135

Rabbi J. Polak
159 Coolidge
Brookline, 02146

Rabbi E. Wenger
38 Embassy Road
Brighton, 02135
Springfield. Rabbi D. Edelman
Contact for School
15 Elwood Dr., 01106
Worcester. Rabbi H. Fogelman
Contact for School
69 Morningside Rd., 01602

Hebrew Day Academy
22 Newton Ave., 01609

Y. Blotner, Youth Contact
17 Kensington Rd., 01602
Michigan:
Detroit. Rabbi M. Gasthalter
18041 North Lawn, 48221
Oak Park. Rabbi S. B. Shem Tov
14100 W. Nine Mile Rd., 48237
Lubavitch Center
14000 W. Nine Mile Rd. 48237
Farmington and Oak Park
Rabbi Y. M. Kagan
23080 Park Lawn, 48237
Minnesota:
Minneapolis. Dr. V. Greene
1601 N. Spring Valley Rd., 55422
St. Paul. Rabbi A. Zeilengold
1731 Saunders St., 55116

Rabbi G. Grossbaum
15 Montcalm Ct. (Estate)

Rabbi M. Feller, Area Contact
1955 Pinehurst St., 55116
Missouri:
Kansas City. Rabbi Weinberg
8243 Virginia, 64131
Nebraska
Omaha. B. Garb
1513 N. 48th St., #38, 68104
New Jersey:
Elizabeth. Dr. Y. Levine

142 Bellvue St., 07202
Highland Pk. J. Hanoka
338 N. 4th Ave., 08904
Hillside. Rabbi E. Carlbach
250 Williamson Ave., 07205
Maplewood. Rabbi S. B. Gordon
12 Wellesley Rd., 07940
Morristown. Rabbi A. Lipsker
226 Sussex Ave., 07940
Newark. Rabbi S. Bogomilsky
250 Mt. Vernon Pl., 07160
Norma. Rabbi N. Weinstein
P. O. B. 128, 08346 (696-1432)
Livingston. Rabbi M. Kasinetz
12 Beverley Rd., 07039
Passaic. Rabbi S. Bobrowsky
175 Hope Ave., 07055
Patterson. Rabbi M. Greenberg
438 Park Ave., 07504
W. Orange. Rabbi Herson
24 Schmitt Rd., 07702
Wanamassa. Rabbi Simon
2202 Sunset Ave., 07712
New York:
Albany. Dr. Luchins
SUNY at Albany
53 Fordham Ct., 12209
Buffalo. Rabbi Gourary
Buffalo Chabad House, 77 Niagara Falls Blvd., 14214
Monsey. Rabbi Werner
1 Hopal Lane, 10952
Syracuse. Alon
108 Haterly Rd., 13224
New York. Rabbi Kasriel Kastel
770 Eastern Pkwy.
Brooklyn 11213
Ohio: Cincinnati. Rabbi S. Sharfstein
1542 Beaverton, 45237
Cleveland, Rabbi L. Alevsky
4481 University Pkwy., 44118

Columbus. Rabbi Y. Seigel
2228 N. High St., 43215
Pennsylvania:
Philadelphia. Rabbi A. Shem Tov
1712 Griffith St., 19111
Pittsburgh. Rabbi K. Weiss
Director of School
5614 Forbes Ave., 15217
S. Katzen
5835 Nicholson St., 15217
Yeshiva Achei Tmimim
2408 5th Ave., 152135
Scranton. Rabbi Silverstein
612 N. Irving Ave., 18510
Rhode Island:
Providence. Dubovick
39 Taft Ave., 02904
Tennessee:
Nashville. Rabbi Z. Posner
3317 Fairmount Dr., 37203
Texas:
Dallas. Rabbi Alperowitz
5930 Harvest Hill, 75230
Houston. Rabbi S. Lazaroff
3832 N. Braeswood Blvd., 77025
Washington:
Seattle. Rabbi S. Levitin
5215 S. Holly St., 98118
Wisconsin:
Milwaukee. Rabbi I. Smotkin
2943 N. Summit, 53211
Virginia:
Norfolk. Rabbi N. Kaplan
1912 Hampton Blvd., 23517
Richmond. Rabbi D. Nelkin
5207 Monument Ave., #6, 23226
Rabbi S. Capland
901 F. N. Hamilton Ave., 23226

CANADA:
Winnipeg, Manitoba:
Rabbi A. Altien
480 Charles, Apt. 104
Toronto, Ontario:
Rabbi D. Schochet
10 Romney Rd., Downsview
Rabbi J. I. Schochet
55 Charles Wood Dr., Downsview
E. Lipsker
145 York Downs Dr., Downsview
London, Ontario:
Dr. Y. Block
1059 Williams St.

EUROPE:
England:
Rabbi Shmuel Lew
Lubavitch Fndn.
109-115 Stamford Hill, London N16
France:
Jewesse Loubavitch
8 Rue Lamarine, 75009, Paris
Mula Asimov
27 Rue Fauxbourg, Paris, 10
Holland:
Rabbi D. Kahn
Bentincklaan 21, Rotterdam, 3004
Italy:
Gorelick
Via Carlo Poerio 16, Milano

ISRAEL:
Jerusalem:
Habad House
Beit Knesset Tsemach Tzedeck
Rehov Habad, Old City
Kfar Habad, near Lod

Other Hasidic communities in New York City vicinity which are open and receptive to visitors

Bobover:
Rabbi Halberstam—The Bobover Rebbe
Yeshiva Bnai Zion
1533 48th Street
Brooklyn (Boro Park), N. Y. 11219
(excellent for Melaveh Malkah, Saturday nights)
Bostoner:
Rabbi Moshe L. Horowitz
983 48th Street
Brooklyn (Boro Park), N. Y. 11219
Rabbi Levi Horowitz
The New England Chassidic Center
1710 Beacon St.
Brookline, Mass. 02146
(highly receptive to students)
Bratslaver:
16th Ave., between 55th and 56th, Brooklyn.
Try to contact either Gedalia Fleer
1738 E. 4th St., Brooklyn, 11225
or Rabbi Leo Rosenfeld (212-DE 9-1851)
(a small, somewhat anonymous community, but if you can get into it, Bratslav offers an interesting alternative to Lubavitch)
Squarer–New Square:
New Square, N. Y. 10977
(the entire town is composed of the Squarer Hasidim)

Where to learn in your ghetto

Quite often there is greater accessibility to Hebrew classes, study groups, and Jewish courses in your own hometown than you would imagine. There are some obvious places to search out and we're including a short list of them.

1. The first place to start is your own synagogue. There might be lots of classes you never even knew about—principally because no one ever reads temple bulletins!
2. You might try calling your local Jewish Community Center; most centers across the United States offer a variety of classes in everything from Hebrew to Yoga.
3. Most major cities (and many not-so-major cities) have a Bureau of Jewish Education. These generally offer Hebrew courses; if the one in your town doesn't, it can certainly direct you to a place that does.
4. Try calling the Hillel chapter at your local university. Many Hillel units have a "free university" which offers a huge variety of courses; those that don't usually have some other kind of study course built into their program.
5. Find out whether the local university itself gives courses in Hebrew (try Language Department, Near Eastern Languages, Semitic Languages), Judaica (try Judaic Studies, Religion). Also look for appropriate courses in related fields (i.e., politics, history, theology, humanities, etc.).

JEWISH STUDY IN UNIVERSITIES

The Bnai Brith Hillel Foundations puts out a catalog called *Jewish Studies in American Colleges and Universities*. Every Hillel unit has this guide and you can get your own copy by sending two dollars to:

Bnai Brith Hillel Foundations
1640 Rhode Island Ave., N.W.
Washington, D. C. 20036

We're including a list (arranged according to states) of those universities and colleges offering eight or more courses in Judaica, as well as those schools having undergraduate or graduate majors in such fields. Those schools with one asterisk offer an undergraduate major; those with two asterisks offer graduate programs in some field of Jewish study.

School	*Courses Offered*
California	
California State College at Fullerton	13
California State College at Northridge	8
University of Cal. at Berkeley	23
University of Cal. at Los Angeles	25
University of Cal. at Riverside	8
University of Cal. at Santa Barbara	11
Los Angeles Valley College (A.A. degree only)	*6
University of Southern California (has agreement with Hebrew Union College and accepts courses taken there)	*39

Stanford University 13
Colorado
University of Denver 8
Connecticut
University of Connecticut 9
Wesleyan University 9
Yale University **21
District of Columbia
American University 8
Florida
University of Miami 9
Illinois
University of Chicago **12
Roosevelt University *26
Indiana
Indiana University **11
Iowa
University of Iowa **8
Maryland
University of Maryland 9
Massachusetts
Boston University 9
Boston College (students may cross register for courses at Hebrew College and receive credit) *4
Brandeis University **36
Harvard University **25
University of Massachusetts (Amherst) (students may receive credit for courses taken at Amherst, Mt. Holyoke and Smith) *6
Smith College *6
Michigan
University of Detroit 8
University of Michigan **13
Wayne State University **21
Minnesota
University of Minnesota *6
Missouri
Washington University 10
New Jersey
Princeton University *6
Rutgers University—Newark 13
Rutgers University—New Brunswick **34
New York
Adelphi 14
City University of New York:
Bernard Baruch College 10
Brooklyn College **49
City College of New York *23
Hunter College **29
Herbert H. Lehman College 20
Queens College *28
Columbia University (grants credit for courses taken at Teachers' Institute of Jewish Theological Seminary) **13
Cornell University **20
Hofstra University *16
Long Island University 9
New School for Social Research 8
New York University **28
University of Rochester 10
State University of New York:
at Albany *41
at Buffalo 9
at Oneonta 11
Kingsborough Community College 11
Vassar College 13
North Carolina
Duke University **8
Ohio
Case-Western Reserve University 11
Ohio State University **29
Pennsylvania
Bryn Mawr College 8
Dickinson College *8
University of Pennsylvania **14
Temple University **42
Rhode Island
Brown University **10
Tennessee
Vanderbilt University **4
Texas
University of Texas **16
Washington
University of Washington **8
Wisconsin
University of Wisconsin—Madison **19
University of Wisconsin—Milwaukee *24

There are lots of places that offer Jewish studies on a concentrated level. We're including a list of Jewish seminaries and yeshivot as well as a list of colleges of Jewish studies. This list is taken from the Hillel booklet on *Jewish Studies in American Colleges and Universities* mentioned earlier.

1. Academy for Jewish Religion
61 Elmwood Drive
Elmwood Park, N. J. 07407
Combines students and teachers from Orthodox, Conservative, and Reform backgrounds and gives ordination.

2. Baltimore Hebrew College
5800 Park Heights Blvd.
Baltimore, Md. 21215
College program in Judaica and teacher training.

3. Cleveland College of Jewish Studies
2030 South Taylor Rd.
Cleveland Heights, Ohio 44118
College program with credit accepted at Cleveland State. Teacher training.

4. Dropsie University
Broad and York Sts.
Philadelphia, Pa. 19132
Postgraduate degrees in Judaica and Semitics; nonsectarian and nontheological.

5. Gratz College
10th St. and Tabor Rd.
Philadelphia, Pa. 19141
Teacher training for religious schools; college-level Judaica courses.

6. Hebrew College
43 Hawes St.
Brookline, Mass. 02146
Teacher training program with diploma awarded. College program in Judaica. Courses transferable to U. S. colleges. Cooperative programs with Simmons College and Boston College.

7. Hebrew Theological College
7135 North Carpenter Rd.
Skokie, Ill. 60076
Traditional Jewish study, training for rabbis and teachers, advanced degrees in Hebrew literature.

8. Hebrew Union College-Jewish Institute of Religion
3101 Clifton Ave.
Cincinnati, Ohio 45220
40 W. 68th St.
New York, N. Y. 10023
8745 Appian Way
Los Angeles, Cal. 90046
Prepares students for Reform rabbinate, cantorate, teaching, and community service. Offers baccalaureate and graduate degrees.
New York: Cooperative arrangement with Hunter College. Runs School of Education and Jewish Music, which trains cantors and music personnel for all movements. Also trains educational personnel for Reform religious schools.
California: Cooperative arrangement between HUC and U. of Southern Calif. Runs School of Jewish Communal Service, which offers graduate work in Jewish psychological, sociological, cultural, historical, and valuation material.

9. Herzliah Hebrew Teachers Institute
69 Bank St.
New York, N. Y. 10014
Undergrad and grad degrees given for work in Jewish teaching, research, and community service. Co-op arrangement with several N. Y. colleges.

10. Jewish Reconstructionist Foundation Rabbinical College
2308 North Broad St.
Philadelphia, Pa. 19132
Prepares rabbis for service in synagogue leadership, educational administration, community organizations, counseling, pastoral and chaplaincy work. Provides academic qualifications for university teaching of Jewish studies.

11. Jewish Theological Seminary of America
Teachers' Institute Seminary
College of Jewish Studies
3080 Broadway
New York, N. Y. 10027
Trains rabbis and teachers. Gives Bach. of Hebrew Lit. and Bach. of Religious Ed. degrees; college program in Judaica. Also masters and doctoral programs. Joint program with School of General Studies, Columbia University.

12. Mesivta Yeshiva Rabbi Chaim Berlin Rabbinical Academy

1593 Coney Island Ave.
Brooklyn, N. Y. 11230
Ordains rabbis and supports a kollel (an intensive postgraduate study of traditional rabbinic scholarship, generally with an emphasis on Talmud).

13. Midrash College of Jewish Studies
21550 W. Twelve Mile Rd.
Southfield, Mich. 48076
College program in Judaica and teacher training. Cooperative program with Oakland University.

14. Mirrer Yeshiva
1791–5 Ocean Pkwy.
Brooklyn, N. Y. 11223
Rabbinical college and kollel.

15. Ner Israel Rabbinical College
400 Mount Wilson Ln.
Baltimore, Md. 21208
Ordains rabbis, trains teachers. Emphasis on talmudic and halakhic study.

16. Rabbinical College of Telshe, Inc.
28400 Euclid Ave.
Wickliffe, Ohio 44092
Traditional study with emphasis on Talmud and rabbinics. Trains teachers, maintains a kollel.

17. Spertus College of Judaica
72 E. 11th St.
Chicago, Ill. 60605
Teacher training. Co-op arrangement with colleges in Chicago area. Serves as Dept. of Judaica for some. Degrees in Bach. of Hebrew Lit. and Bach. of Judaic Studies.

18. University of Judaism–College of Jewish Studies
6525 Sunset Blvd.
Los Angeles, Cal. 90028
Trains teachers. Graduate studies. Credit granted by U. of Calif., U. of Southern Cal., and State U. of Cal.

19. West Coast Talmudical Seminary, Yeshiva Ohr Elchonon Inc.
851 North Kings Rd.
Los Angeles, Cal. 90069
Orthodox rabbinical training. Conducts graduate talmudical division on a college level.

20. Yavne Hebrew Theological Seminary Inc.
510 Dahill Rd.
Brooklyn, N. Y. 11218
Trains rabbis and teachers. School for higher Jewish learning.

21. Yeshiva University
500 West 186th St.
New York, N. Y. 10033
Undergraduate, graduate, and professional programs. Awards thirteen different degrees. Offers study in medicine, science, social work, education, and psychology in graduate schools. Runs Rabbi Isaac Elchanan Theological Seminary, which trains rabbis. Also Cantorial Training Institute, which awards cantor's certificate and cantorial diploma.

22. Yeshivath Chachmey Lublin
P. O. Box 236
Southfield, Mich. 48075
Religious school and rabbinical seminary.

23. Yeshivath Torah Vodaath and Mesivta Rabbinical Seminary
425 E. 9th St.
Brooklyn, N. Y. 11218
Both Hebrew and secular education through ordination. Has a kollel and teachers institute.

24. Yeshivath Torah Vodaath–Beth Midrosh Elyon (Academy of Higher Learning and Research)
73 Main St.
Monsey, N. Y. 10952
Postgraduate courses and study in higher Jewish studies. Kollel.

25. Shor Yoshuv Yeshiva
1284 Central Ave.
Far Rockaway, N. Y. 11691
For people with little Jewish background who want an intense introduction to Orthodoxy.

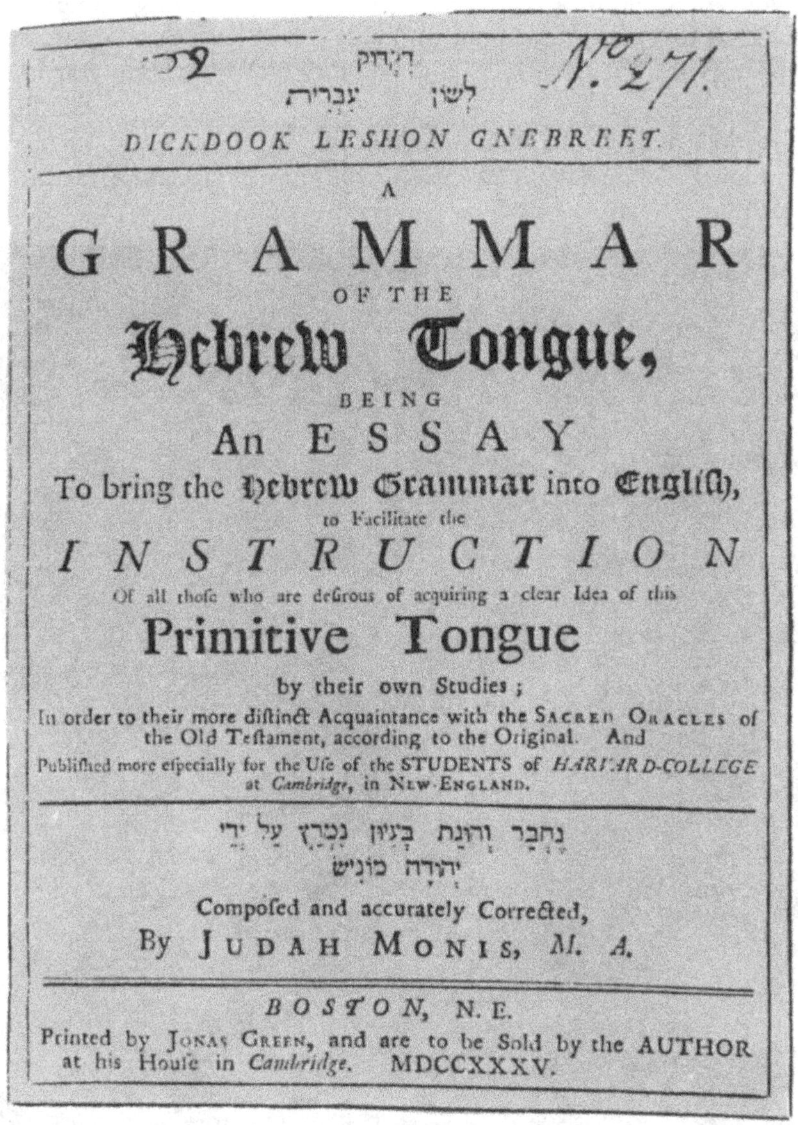

דִקְדוּק לְשׁוֹן עִבְרִית

DICKDOOK LESHON GNEBREET.

A

GRAMMAR

OF THE

Hebrew Tongue,

BEING

An ESSAY

To bring the Hebrew Grammar into English, to Facilitate the

INSTRUCTION

Of all those who are desirous of acquiring a clear Idea of this

Primitive Tongue

by their own Studies; In order to their more distinct Acquaintance with the SACRED ORACLES of the Old Testament, according to the Original. And Published more especially for the Use of the STUDENTS of HARVARD-COLLEGE at Cambridge, in NEW-ENGLAND.

נחבר והוגה בעיון נמרץ על ידי
יהודה מוניש

Composed and accurately Corrected,
By JUDAH MONIS, M. A.

BOSTON, N. E.
Printed by JONAS GREEN, and are to be Sold by the AUTHOR at his House in Cambridge. MDCCXXXV.

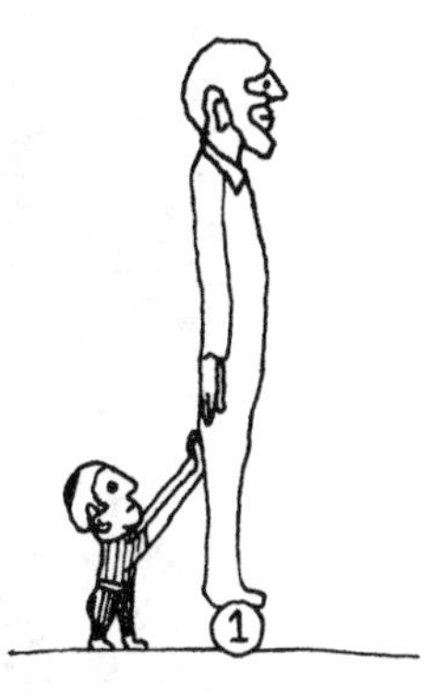

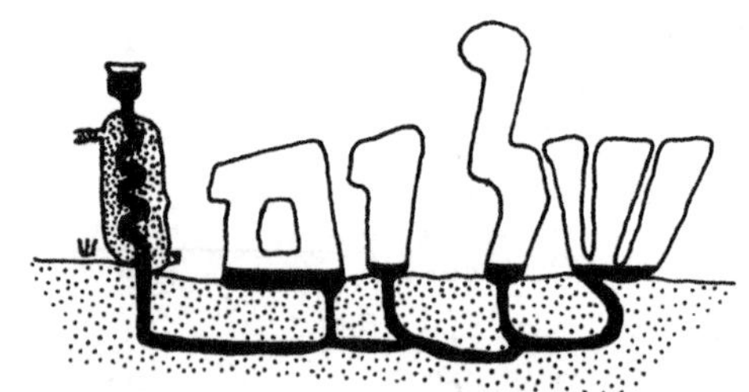

Teachers

"Who is wise? He who learns from everybody" (Pirkei Avot, 4.1).

Ideally it is possible to learn from everybody and everything. Our sages even tell us that it is possible to learn industriousness from the ant and modesty from a cat. Perhaps such learning is learning from models. Perhaps such learning requires a special way of perceiving your environment, a special vision of the world.

A less radical approach to learning from everybody is simply meeting people, asking them questions, and listening to them. Have you ever picked up an elderly Jew and heard fascinating stories about his East European boyhood? Such pickups can be very simple. They begin with, "Shalom Aleichem. Where do you come from?"

If you are seeking a teacher to teach you something specific, then it is reasonable to begin by asking yourself questions. Your questions will be unique to you, but here are some examples of questions you may need to confront.

—What do I really want from a teacher?

—Who am I? Where am I at? Is this an appropriate time for me to have a teacher?

—Could I really be open with a teacher?
—Am I serious in my search for a teacher? If I have failed to find a teacher, does that reflect on the seriousness of my desire for a teacher?

There are three kinds of teachers in the American Jewish community. First, there are public figures. Such people teach us in large groups, at public lectures. Although they may be accessible to a few students, they are inaccessible to most of us. They are busy people, deeply committed to a variety of projects, and seeking them out for private conversation raises serious ethical questions about imposing on their time.

Second, there are private teachers. The public does not know about such people. They are hidden. A person you may least suspect of having anything to say to you may turn out to be such a teacher. You may discover a person you have known for years can be a teacher for you. There is no list of such people. Discovering such a person depends on the earnestness of your search, on coincidence of timing (someone you might have discovered as a teacher a few years ago may not be appropriate now and vice versa), and on divine providence.

Third, there are semipublic or semiprivate teachers. Like teachers of the first and second groups, individuals within this third group may possess widely differing interests and skills. Listed below are a few such people; add names of people you know to the list. It is by no means exhaustive. It is a list of a few teachers who are known to the editors of this book and whose addresses are relatively permanent. It is a list of a few people seriously involved in Jewish religious pursuits who sometimes teach publicly and will talk with you—despite busy schedules. Although some of the teachers listed are scholars of Judaism, many significant scholars and academicians are absent from the list. They are named in other sections of the catalog and can also be found through universities and through books and articles they publish.

You may find a teacher and work with him/her many years. Or you may find someone who can be your teacher temporarily. Perhaps someone who is a teacher for others and not for you will be able to give you the name of someone more appropriate for you. Natan of Nemirov, who became a disciple of the great Hasidic master Nahman of Bratzlav, sought a teacher many years. He visited several of the holy men of Eastern Europe. He stayed a long time, learning from Levi Yitzhak of Berdichev. Finally he found Nahman and said later that only Nahman could tell him step by step how to draw close to God. Levi Yitzhak was a great teacher, but only Nahman was right for Natan.

About annotations

All of the people listed below are good people to talk with. Some people's names are annotated with references to their specific interests. That does not mean that their interests are confined to the particular areas listed here. Other people have been listed without annotations. This does not mean that they have no special areas of concern. It means that their interests are far ranging, and the editors of this book leave the discovery of their particular concerns to you.

About the list itself

This list is not definitive; it is coincidental. It is a list of people whom the editors of this book coincidentally know, with some additional recommendations by people on the list. There are, without doubt, many other people who should be on the list but whom we don't know. We apologize for these omissions and urge you to send in recommendations for future additions.

NEW ENGLAND

Axelrad, Albert, Rabbi
Brandeis U. Hillel
Usdan Student Center
Suite 133
Waltham, Mass. 02154
peace; Judaism and social responsibility; liturgical renewal

Birnbaum, Michael
Wesleyan University
Dept. of Religion
Middletown, Conn. 06457

Fishbane, Michael, Dr.
Brandeis U.
Dept. of Near Eastern and Judaic Studies
Waltham, Mass. 02154
Bible scholarship

Gendler, Everett, Rabbi
Temple Emanuel of Merrimack Valley
101 W. Forest St.
Lowell, Mass. 01851
social action; ecology; liturgical renewal

Gold, Ben-Zion, Rabbi
Harvard U. Hillel
1 Bryant St.
Cambridge, Mass. 02138
Eastern European Jewish culture; Yiddish language and literature

Goldstein, Baruch, Rabbi
6 Tohanto Rd.
Worcester, Mass. 01602

Horowitz, Levi, Grand Rabbi
New England Chassidic Center
1710 Beacon St.
Brookline, Mass. 02146
Bostoner Rebbe

Israel, Richard, Rabbi
Hillel
233 Bay State Rd.
Boston, Mass. 02215

Kushner, Lawrence, Rabbi
Congregation Beth El
Hudson Rd.
Sudbury, Mass. 01776
alef-bet

Matt, Daniel
113 College Ave.
Somerville, Mass. 02144
Midrash and hitchhiking

Polak, Joseph, Rabbi
Boston U. Hillel
233 Bay State Rd.
Boston, Mass. 02215
Hasidism and halakhah

Strassfeld, Meyer, Rabbi
Temple Sinai
1 Community Rd.
Marblehead, Mass. 01945

Wolf, Arnold, Rabbi
Yale U. Hillel
1904 A Yale Station
New Haven, Conn. 06520
contemporary theology and social concern

MIDDLE ATLANTIC

Berman, Saul, Rabbi
Stern College
253 Lexington Ave.
New York, N. Y. 10016
halakhah and modern problems

Carlebach, Shlomo, Rabbi
888 7th Ave., Rm. 400
New York, N. Y. 10019
Hasidic singer and storyteller

Feld, Edward, Rabbi
Hillel Foundation
Princeton University
Princeton, N. J. 08540
modern theology; religious dimensions of the interpersonal

Feld, Merle
Hillel Foundation
Princeton University
Princeton, N. J. 08540

Frimer, Norman, Rabbi
Hillel
2901 Campus Rd.
Brooklyn, N. Y. 11210
Orthodoxy and existentialism

Green, Arthur, Rabbi
Dept. of Religious Thought
U. of Pennsylvania
Philadelphia, Pa. 19104
Hasidism and theology

Green, Kathy
Dept. of Religious Thought
U. of Pennsylvania
Philadelphia, Pa. 19104
Hasidism; devotion and contemplation

Greenberg, Blu
Religious Studies Dept.
College of Mount St. Vincent
Riverdale, N. Y. 10471
women's issues and Judaism; Jewish-Christian relations

Greenberg, Yitzchak, Rabbi
Jewish Studies Dept.
City College
Convent Ave. and 138th St.
New York, N. Y. 10022
halakhah and moral development; human development and Jewish models

Jospe, Alfred, Rabbi
Hillel
1640 Rhode Island Ave. N. W.
Washington, D. C. 20036
modern Jewish theology; religion on the college campus

Jospe, Eva
Hillel
1640 Rhode Island Ave. N. W.
Washington, D. C. 20036
modern Jewish thought

Monson, Michael, Rabbi
U. of Penn. Hillel
202 S. 36th St.
Philadelphia, Pa. 19104

Paltiel, Eliezer, Rabbi
1109 Englewood
Philadelphia, Pa. 19111

Riskin, Shlomo, Rabbi
Lincoln Square Synagogue
Amsterdam Ave. and 69th St.
New York, N. Y. 10023

Sachs, Leonie, Dr.
160 West End Ave.
New York, N. Y. 10023
Spanish and Jewish mysticism

Saks, Robert, Rabbi
U. of Maryland Hillel
P. O. Box 187
7505 Yale Ave.
College Park, Md. 20740
Musar movement (Jewish ethics and spiritual growth)

Shaw, Steven, Rabbi
Dept. of Jewish Studies
City College
Convent Ave. at 138th St.
New York, N. Y. 10031

Siegel, Richard
115 North Country Rd.
Port Jefferson, N.Y. 11777
devotional life

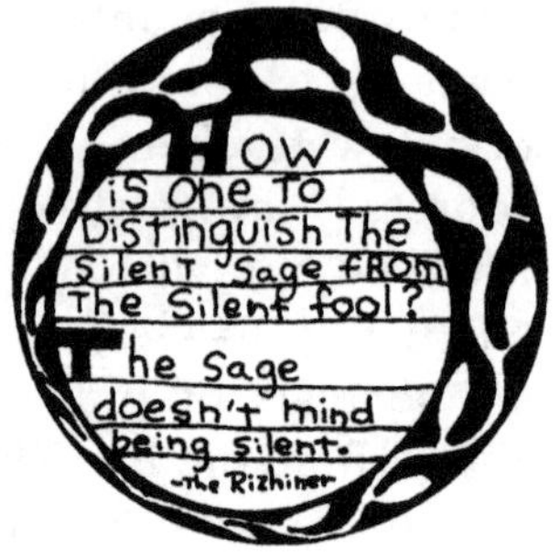

Ticktin, Esther
Hillel
1640 Rhode Island Ave. N. W.
Washington, D. C. 20036
psychology and theology

Ticktin, Max, Rabbi
Hillel
1640 Rhode Island Ave. N. W.
Washington, D. C. 20036

Waskow, Arthur, Dr.
Institute for Policy Study
1520 New Hampshire Ave. N.W.
Washington, D.C. 20036
political activism and exploration of Jewish symbols

Weiner, Herbert, Rabbi
Temple Israel
432 Scotland Rd.
South Orange, N.Y. 07079
search for spiritual teachers; author of 9½ *Mystics*

MIDWEST

Brooks, Michael
2163 Medford
Ann Arbor, Mich. 48104

Diamond, James, Rabbi
Hillel at Washington University

6300 Forsyth
St. Louis, Mo. 63105

Gellman, Mark
Northwestern U.
Evanston, Ill. 60201
Jewish theology and Jewish radicalism

Leifer, Daniel, Rabbi
U. of Chicago Hillel
5715 S. Woodlawn Ave.
Chicago, Ill. 60637
Midrash; Israel-Arab relations; ritual innovation

Lettofsky, Alan, Rabbi
U. of Wisconsin Hillel
611 Langdon St.
Madison, Wis. 53703

Poupko, Joel, Rabbi
U. of Michigan Hillel
1429 Hill St.
Ann Arbor, Mich. 48104
search for meaning in the Holocaust; change within halakhah

Riemer, Jack, Rabbi
Beth Abraham Synagogue
1306 Salem Ave.
Dayton, Ohio 45406

Schaalman, Herman, Rabbi
5959 N. Sheridan
Chicago, Ill. 60660

Schwarzschild, Steven, Dr.
Dept. of Philosophy
Washington U.
St. Louis, Mo. 63110

Shusterman, Harold, Rabbi
Congregation Bnei Reuven
6350 N. Whipple St.
Chicago, Ill. 60659
Lubavitcher Hasid

Zisenwine, David, Rabbi
Tifereth Israel Synagogue
1354 E. Broad St.
Columbus, Ohio 43205

SOUTHEAST

Gross, Rita
New College
Dept. of Religion
Sarasota, Fla. 33577
history of religions

Posner, Zalman, Rabbi
3317 Fairmont Dr.
Nashville, Tenn. 37203

FAR WEST

Adler, Moshe, Rabbi
Hillel Council
Los Angeles Valley College
13164 Burbank Blvd.
Van Nuys, Cal. 91401

Adler, Rachel
Hillel Council
Los Angeles Valley College
13164 Burbank Blvd.
Van Nuys, Cal. 91401
women's issues within halakhic Judaism

Berner, David, Rabbi
Hillel Council of U.C.L.A.
900 Hilgard Ave.
Los Angeles, Cal. 90024
Judaism and Christianity on the current scene

Levy, Richard, Rabbi
Hillel Council of U.C.L.A.
900 Hilgard Ave.
Los Angeles, Cal. 90024

Rosenberg, Joel
205 Jackson St.
Santa Cruz, Cal. 95060
Jewish mysticism; Midrash and rabbinic literature; religious foundations of creative imagination

Rottenberg, Ephraim, Rabbi
219 S. Alta Vista
Los Angeles, Cal. 90024
authentic Hasidic teacher open to other disciplines

Vernoff, Charles
U. of Calif.
Dept. of Religious Studies
Santa Barbara, Cal. 93106

CANADA

Epstein, Seymour (Epi)
3511 Peel St.
Montreal H3A 1W7, Que.
Canada
Jewish education

Feder, Herbert, Rabbi
5715 Waldwood St.
Montreal, Quebec
Canada

Rose, Carol
349 Matleson
Winnipeg 4, Manitoba
Canada

Rose, Neal, Rabbi
Judaics Dept.
U. of Manitoba
Winnipeg, Manitoba
Canada
neo-Orthodoxy and Hasidism

Schachter, Zalman, Rabbi
Judaics Dept.
U. of Manitoba
Winnipeg, Manitoba
Canada
author of *A First Step*, phenomenology of religious experience

A first step: a devotional guide

INTRODUCTION
Much of Judaism concerns relationships, especially the relationship between God and human beings. The Bible contains so many descriptions of human and divine encounters, of God seeking out a person or of a person seeking God. Our traditional liturgy seems to assume that God and any and all Jews have a relationship. When we speak the words of the prayer book, we often find ourselves saying things to God, telling God: You are praised, You are holy. Sometimes the words of the prayer book seem to describe particular ways we are supposed to relate to God; for example, we are told that we should love God. Modern (and not so modern) Jewish theologians provide us with a variety of opinions on the matter of relating to God. But reading Bible, liturgy, and theology can lead to a real sense of conspiracy; all those sources conspire to tell us that we ought to relate to God, and none seems to tell us how or where to begin.

Jewish mystics (kabbalistic and Hasidic) have always tried to address "how-to" questions. Sometimes they preferred to deal with these questions in face-to-face meetings with their students, but sometimes they or their students wrote books. Texts which concern such questions as how to experience the Divine Presence, how to love and fear God, how to worship, how to enter into a relationship with God do exist. The problem is that these texts exist in Hebrew and Aramaic; relatively few of them have been translated into English.

A First Step by Zalman Schachter is not a translation. It was first written in English. It is a contemporary attempt to make accessible spiritual and devotional techniques from classic, Jewish sources, sources on which the pamphlet was based. We reprint part of it here for you in the hope that it may prove useful.

TO WHOM THIS MAY CONCERN:

This guide intends to give you practical information in the area of spiritual discipline and resources. I imagine you, the reader, in the following way. You are a "seeker." This means (to me) that you are trying to find a *way* to express some spiritual stirrings in yourself and to develop that holy source within you, so that it may begin to flow freely. You have for some time searched for the *way*. You have read some Jewish books, which have succeeded only in increasing your need for this search. You have also read some non-Jewish material. You have become further convinced that somewhere, somehow, there is a greater reality, and you have from time to time made efforts in the direction of finding it. I take it that these efforts proved disappointing to some degree, that you have many times cast this search aside, only after some time to take it up again. This cycle has repeated itself. You are perhaps now looking for a practical way, which will show you some measure of advance. I also take it that you are concerned enough to spend some time and effort at working with discipline and resources.

You need not have a clearly crystallized philosophy. All you need is a willingness to test some of your already held beliefs, and those which you wish to hold, in the laboratory of your experience.

All this I take for granted. You will consider it only fair if you are required to spend at least a half hour each day, and an additional two hours each week, at this work. You will have to be honest with yourself. You cannot do this work alone. You need a trusted friend with whom you can work together and with whom you can freely discuss your work. Spiritual work in loneliness, without the possibility of sharing and comparing, can be harmful. Be prepared to let the work affect you fully, and take you into its own direction. Be prepared to have your mode of living profoundly changed in all its aspects. Read this manual time and time again. Do not proceed with a new exercise before you have the previous one under full control and can *at will* duplicate it any time you desire.

If any of the above does not apply to you, you need not read further. It will only be a waste of time. This guide takes your motivation for granted, and also the fact that you do follow and apply it.

This is not an inspirational text, nor does it contain anything *new*. It is deliberately dry. To add a number of very charming illustrations and stories might divert you from *working*.

But even if you do follow this guide honestly and conscientiously, it will not take you *all* the way. It will only introduce you to some *elementary techniques* of the spiritual laboratory. When you will have reached the last of the exercises in your own practical experience, and when you can "control" your actions as outlined here, you will need a *teacher* and *guide* to prescribe the specific and very personal other steps for you. Let me assure you that there *are* teachers who can take you further. Further steps cannot be given to you in a manual, since it cannot speak to your own specific differences from other people. Your own very individual further development will need individual guidance.

This primer is the result of experience with a limited group; but for you your own progress will be the decisive factor. You will soon come to realize that, in order to make progress in this work, a certain levelheaded sobriety is immensely necessary. Anyone thinking that rapture awaits him instead of hard work will soon be disappointed.

Let me explain to you the function of kavvanah. Kavvanah means intention. Our intention is always free. There is nothing that can obstruct your intending. Even if the whole world coerces you into a pattern of actions, you can always "intend" whatever you want. For instance, you sit in the dentist's chair. He drills and you feel a sting of pain, but you can "intend" this pain as an offering of love. You offer to God the moment of pain, intending to suffer it for Him. You might put it in somewhat this way: "Ribbono Shel Olam!—You are good and Your universe is good. The All is filled with Your mercy and goodness, as is the pain I feel. I cannot bring You any other sacrifice. Please accept this moment of pain as a love offering from me." Or you work in your day-by-day endeavor. You do whatever you must do, and you intend: "God of law and order, You have ordained work for man. In doing, I intend to do Your will, I wish to cleave to You in this action." Or you travel and time is taken up by it. You lean back and wink at Him in your mind as if to say, "Sweet Father, I enjoy Your presence! The rhythm of the wheels, the fleeting scenery, we are all nothing but You. You contain me and my vehicle. I will be careful in travel, for this is Your will. Guard my going out and my coming back. I am secure in You."

You see, these "arrows of awareness" are rather simple to practice. You will soon find that placing yourself in His presence will come with some practice.

Especially when engaged in doing a mitzvah, you will want to put your intention to use. On the Sabbath, when eating, you can intend, "Likhvod

ha-Shabbat—May I eat this food and enjoy it for Your sake, for this is the mitzvah of the Shabbat."

When putting on the tefillin, or lighting the candles, you can intend: "Lovely Lord, take my body as an instrument of Your will. My limbs are prepared, and are at Your disposal. Use them!" And then you say the blessing.

It is helpful to have a visual image in the kavvanah. You picture the will of God flowing into your body and soul, becoming united with the limbs, organs, senses, brain, and nerves, and moving—make sure at this point to feel them moving by His will—to execute the mitzvah. This should become very familiar to you. Do not go on to the next point until the practice of kavvanah has become firmly established in your habit pattern.

On the examination of one's conscience and going to sleep Deliberateness and watchfulness over your actions and motives now becomes important. You will find yourself failing persistently. At this point study the *Mesillath Yesharim* by M. L. Luzzatto (Jewish Publication Society, 1948). For encouragement, also read Rabbi Milton Steinberg's Yom Kippur sermon entitled, "Our Persistent Failures," in *The Believing Jew* (pp. 213–28).

You will then have come across Rabbi Levi Yitzhak's Heshbon ha-Nephesh—Reckoning of the Soul—before going to sleep. This is what we will begin to work on now.

Before going to sleep start out by fully and completely forgiving anyone who wronged or hurt you, and pray for the welfare of that person. Continue by affirming the Oneness of God, and your longing to love Him, and then read the Shema.

Finally, take a short tally of your actions during the day. Begin with the first thought upon awakening. (This thought is of tremendous power, it exerts influence on the rest of the day. Make sure to think a good first thought and last thought every day.) Don't spend more than five minutes on this tally to begin with. Just check through your actions to see if they are as you planned them. If you are sure that you did not do the right thing, hold the thought, word or action up to God and, with a short arrow prayer, ask Him to remove this kind of thing from your life. Again, much will depend on the sobriety and tenacity you show every night.

Once a week (Thursday night might be best) you must set aside more time than usual. Do this when you are still fresh. If you leave this until you are too worn out, you cannot expect to succeed. Therefore, plan the evening accordingly. Let us say you are now alone and not too tired. At first, you slip into the "life" meditation, and then, when you come to feel His presence in your being, you begin to judge yourself in His sight, not harshly, not carelessly, but justly. Do this in great detail; look at your motivations in great detail; don't condemn or convict yourself, but visualize yourself before God, and listen to His judgment.

This does not mean that you will not get anywhere. It *does* mean that your *real effort* will be rewarded.

This manual is intended as a laboratory guide, to help you on your way. In order to keep you from confusion, it is suggested that, for the time being, you stop any further outside reading in this area. Later on, when you will have some real experience behind you, further reading will prove to be a joy instead of a hindrance. The many states described will be familiar to you, and serve as a further validation of the rightness of your own experience. But until you gain positive experience, refrain from further reading, in order to find the way.

On the other hand, inspirational (instead of *how-to-do-it*) reading is of

immense importance. You will find a bibliography in the back. Choose one of those books but do not read it in one sitting. Rather, find time (it need not be very much—in this you suit yourself to your own schedule and inclination) and hold on to this time as something very precious. Address God and ask Him that your reading may inspire your *continued effort*. Then read for a while. Before you put the book away, close it and think back to fasten what you have read in your memory. You need a *model* to sustain you in this work. Your reading ought to give *this* to you. Anything describing the thoughts and lives of tzaddikim makes, therefore, very necessary reading. However, do not, at this point, look for functional aspects of that literature. You must work quite a bit before some of the formulas shown there will apply to you. A certain amount of responsibility for your progress can be taken by the compiler of this guide, only if you see fit to trust it from the outset. If you make up your mind to do so, this manual will be of help to you. (Scholarly documentation of sources can be supplied. For your practical work this is not necessary, and at this point would only be intrusive.)

The approach used here is that of classical Jewish mysticism, as refined by Hasidism and, in particular, by the Habad school.

This approach seeks to get you to work on yourself and to help you achieve something.

Many prayers have been offered for your success.

On meditation

You want to grow spiritually, to grow a soul. The Zohar has it: "Each one is given a nephesh" (meaning the lowest of the five soul stages. The others are ruach, neshamah, chavah, yechida; nephesh corresponds to the action aspect, ruach to the emotive, and neshamah to the intellective). "If one so merits [by refining oneself], one is granted ruach, etc."

This nephesh can become a functioning and active force within you, but it has to be aroused. The best way to rouse nephesh is by meditation (because it shifts your identity from the body to the nephesh), coupled with the active observance of the mitzvot (because it asserts itself as the "self" in the active fulfillment). Perhaps you have tried to meditate. Do this *now.* Take ten minutes for meditation. Meditate upon God. Continue your reading later. Go on, meditate, and put the book away!

Being honest with yourself, you will have observed several things:

1. You had some trouble finding enough material to think about.
2. You were beset by many distractions.

There are, of course, a large number of "outer" distractions, such as sounds, sights, and other sense impressions, that want to keep claiming your attention. You can look for a quiet spot, find yourself a comfortable chair, and close your eyes. But having done this, your other troubles seem to begin. There is an onrush of thoughts and inner sensations. Before your closed eyes a host of images seem to present themselves. You hear yourself breathe and you may even sense your heartbeat. You remember all sorts of trite things you must do. (For this it is best to keep a pad and pencil at your side, and to write these down for your postspiritual work period.) You feel all sorts of itches and twitches. It is quite difficult to settle your mind.

It will become important at a later stage to do something about these distractions, but for the time being the problem of content is the more important one. What did you meditate on?

You have read about God's immanence, His indwelling in creation; it is called His being m'malleh kol almin, His filling of all the worlds with light and life. If you are acquainted with some literature on this point, make it your business to study it again and learn to *rethink it in sequence.* If you are not, any of the following might be of help: Psalms 104 and 147; Gate 2, *Duties of the Heart,* by Bahia Ibn Pakuda; *Some Aspects of Chabad Chasidism,* by N. Mindel, 3:19; *The Commandments,* by N. Mindel, 4:25–28, or chapters 2, 20, 33; *Tanya,* by Rabbi Shneur Zalman.

At first you study the thought and you do this in an academic objective way. You want to fully understand the entire image, to its very last detail.

However, when you have mastered the thought sequence in detail and in richness, you must give it all a twist into another dimension—that of situational thinking. Let me give you two illustrations: You can, for instance, study the toxic effects of carbon monoxide on the various cells. You learn to understand in great detail the process of the poisoning, which makes it impossible for the vital organs to keep functioning. The patient dies. Now the twist from the conceptual mode to the situational mode occurs when you realize that it is not air that you breathe, but carbon monoxide, and that you are about to die. This situational mode of thought we shall henceforth call ada–ata d'nafshey thinking. It fills you with an immediate emotional awareness, in this case, with horror and anxiety. It also produces behavior, in this case escaping behavior.

Or, as another example, you can fully understand what a large sum of money could mean to someone. The beneficiary can do many things he could not do up to now. You can picture the economic and social effects of a sudden acquisition of money. Now you twist that ada–ata d'nafshey, and you are the beneficiary. You are filled with an emotion of enlargement and this too begets behavior—in this case approach behavior.

All this is applicable to meditation. All meditation that has gone beyond the sequence thinking stage ought to be ada–ata d'nafshey thinking.

So you meditate on God filling the universe with life and you do this ada–ata d'nafshey: you are now, here, filled with life—with God. . . . When you finally face this tremendous fact, you feel something in your heart. But the feeling is not as important as whom you feel. When you have reached that point in your meditation, fasten on to it for a few moments. Nothing, neither your thought sequence nor your emotional response, is as important as He whom you are facing and who fills you with life. So hold on to this confrontation for a while. When you do this, you need not do anything else except face and behold Him.

You may want to do this only once or twice and then to proceed to another thought. But here you must be cautioned. There is no benefit in rushing ahead. You must work on this one thought for at least twenty times. If you do this more often, you will benefit even more.

Of course you will have problems. You might become bored by the one thought, but this only shows that you have not sufficiently deepened your thinking. How many times have you indulged ada–ata d'nafshey in some nonspiritual thought and desire and not gotten bored by it? It won't do to move on. This moving on from thought to thought, this kind of scanning, can give you only information. Meditation is precisely the working with the information you already have.

One can really live a whole life with just one meditation. So you subdue the boredom and here is where it becomes work—until you break through. You will know that you have broken through by the fact that your subconscious has, in this area, become slightly reoriented. Life, filling the All, will have become a real factor in your living.

Shivviti and kavvanah

God's presence and your intention You have learned how to meditate on God's immanence, and His indwelling is now a part of your mental and emotional life. You now wish to live your active life in His presence. You want to be able to practice the presence of God. This discipline will become the mainstay of your spiritual life. This is not too difficult at first, but it does take remembering. You will from time to time remember that you stand before Him. You sort of wink at Him, while engaged in whatever function you are busy with. You eat and enjoy your food, and you remember Him. You might recite a blessing over the food. It need not take long, a short moment is all that is necessary.

Then offer all your "sins" and guilts up to Him. Ask Him to take these from you and wash you clean. (You need at this point an image in which you can bring yourself to arouse His infinite mercy. This arousing of God's mercy is called hithorruth rachmim rabbim. Each person finds himself comfortable in his own image. You may find one of the following useful: the image of the prince, all dirty, facing his father, the king—the image of the prisoner, who is made to help his oppressors—the image of the spark which wants to return to the flame, but is bottled up—the image of the prince, who, in love with a princess (or vice versa), has been robbed of the hard-earned money, saved penny by penny, for ransoming the beloved—the image of the child who has lost his parents in the crowd because he looked at some puppies in the window—the image of the amnesiac exiled prince, who suddenly remembers that he is a prince. The purpose of this image is for you to feel the need of His mercy, to feel so helpless in His presence that out of your inability to do anything to help yourself you implore Him in your own language. This utter helplessness before God is not a theological and theoretical dogma, but a functional attitude appropriate to this moment of your spiritual development. Identify with one of these and implore Him for mercy.) Make sure to use everyday language in doing this.

Now, at this point you might step into the even higher motive of being sorry for what you have done to Him: how you abused His presence and *life* in you, in order to do the very opposite of His plan of love for you; how you took His very head and heart and soiled them foolishly. How you are more pained for what you did to your Beloved than for the reversal of your own progress. Read any of these Psalms—6, 25, 51, 73, or 130—*a few times.* Then renew your covenant with Him and prepare for bed.

When you are all ready for sleep, lift your soul in your hands, as it were, and give it to Him, saying, "In Thy hand do I hide my soul—for the night. Thou has—doest, and wilt redeem me. YHVH, God of truth." Visualize your tensions walking out of you, one by one, beginning from your toes—become all limp—out from between your eyes. At last—repeating the verse and asking Him to wake you refreshed at —o'clock, and to take over your breathing and rest, feeling at the same time caressed by His hand—visualize your mattress as His arms.

On other nights, after the short examination, screen yourself off from sounds and cares by visualizing an angel—a spiritual force field—of grace at your *right,* this force field being impenetrable by care and worry; at your *left,* an angel of power and strength; *before* you, an angel of soft light and luminousness; and *behind* you, an angel of healing. Over your head, picture the very presence of the loving God. As you visualize this, you say:

In the name of YHVH
The God of Israel:
At my right hand Michael
At my left Gabriel
Ahead of me Oriel
Behind me Raphael
Above my head the Shekhinah of God!

Imagine yourself plugging into Michael for love—so that you can love more the next day; Gabriel for strength—to fill you for the next day; Oriel filling you with the light of the mind; Raphael healing all your ills.

Again let me ask you not to give up. These are new practices which you must acquire, and their real power begins to show well only after you can control the sequence of thought and feeling. The first time it *may* come a bit easy, but after that it takes a great deal of persistence. You are rebuilding some intangibles inside yourself. Years of habit must be fought. But you will succeed if you persist. Only then should you continue with the other points outlined here.

The Shabbat, hospitality to God

The Shabbat is the fulfillment of what you began on Thursday night (see above). The Shabbat has two aspects. The *outer* aspect is the refraining from "servile" work, as defined by the Mishnah (Shabbat 7:2) and subsequently by the codes of Jewish law. The *inner* aspect is the one great effort in the direction of God, in Torah, and in prayer. In other words, work of another kind is indicated for Shabbat.

Instead of working with *things* on the outside, one must work with the *self* on the inside. After having been in a state of soul reckoning, and therefore of bitterness, the Shabbat becomes a day of enjoying the Lord.

Just a few thoughts to give you a framework for thinking about the Shabbat. The world is continually being created by God. His will makes the world, but there are many levels of the divine will. The many dimensions of His will are better understood from the standpoint of man's soul.

You will something in your innermost being. This *inner* will works toward fulfillment, but often it has to be contravened by the *outer*—instrumental—will, which sets up the mechanics toward the fulfillment of the *inner.* Let us say man wills to be in the state of sanctity and rest. In order to gain this *inner* will he must work and hunger, to acquire the means of eating and relaxing. So the *outer* will, which works toward fulfilling the *inner* will, is in exact opposition to the stated purpose, in order to gain it.

Now picture God's majesty willing on the *inner* level to dwell with man in the Shabbat-like manner. In order to gain this, He creates a world with innumerable details to sustain man, and He sustains innumerable men in order to have among them those who will invite Him to dwell within themselves. During the week, the *outer* will is in ascendance, the *inner* will is only active in a hidden way. Comes Shabbat, the *inner* will moves to the foreground and the *outer* will retreats to the background. The goal of this *inner* will, the real purpose of creation, is to dwell with God. So here we have a framework for kavvanah. Every action in the Shabbat must not be merely instrumental—preparing for His dwelling—but must be an *act of hospitality* toward Him.

Now, you will first of all have to study the laws of the Shabbat, in order to know the framework. You will attend the synagogue (see below) and learn your way about the twenty-six hours of the Shabbat. (For the sake of *intending,* remember that the twenty-six hours of the Shabbat correspond to the twenty-six which is the numerical value of the YHVH.) The Shabbat is particularly difficult to experience and to *work out* in the absence of a friendly, intimate group engaged in the same work. But we will concern ourselves here with you as an individual.

The first thing to remember again and again is to curb your conversations on the Shabbat. You must move *inward.* Only that which pertains to Torah and prayer is proper conversation. Any other areas are to be shunned. In refraining from *doing,* you will be able to *do* inwardly. Of course the first few times the observances of silence will be stifling, but if you proceed in silence, you will find other things speaking to you. Your prayer, too, will become more alive.

You may try another mode of meditating on the Shabbat. Instead of programing your thought you might, after some study, sit quietly—place yourself in His presence—address God and say to Him, "Give me a gift of insight today." Then you clear your mind from preoccupations, by an act of offering them up. You wait upon Him. There is no need to force any experience at this time. It is enough to visit with Him in silence, as one visits with a very good friend; one need not talk. It is a sort of trusting, good-to-be-with-You quietude. If He will want to take it further, be grateful, but there is no need to force Him. Your mind will still be acrawl with all sorts of petty thoughts and you will probably find it difficult to banish them. Invite God to see into your thoughts—in His presence they will hide. But to keep His presence in your mind is also difficult at first. Thank Him after a period for His patience, and offer your frustration on His behalf as an offering to Him. Then take the prayer book and, standing up, permit yourself to sway (don't force yourself) as you *chant* His praises. Don't just read in silence. Prayer is not gaining *new information.* You address God in praise; or if you can't feel yourself addressing Him, address the world in its vastness, telling it of His wonderful goodness. If you feel like injecting some of your own ideas of praise—in particular, of His kindness to you—by all means, do so.

After you have finished your prayers, and you sit down to eat, intend to feed *Him* (you have made the Kiddush and ha-Motzi over the loaf) by eating. Or reverse it, and intend that He feed you. Sing at the table; between courses you can talk or think about a Torah idea. Psalm 23 is especially recommended for this. The grace after meals is especially rich for kavvanah. Then spend some time in study. Visualize Him facing you and teaching you through the text. Say a short prayer of both petition for insight and thanksgiving for the opportunity of studying His will and wisdom.

You will find that the Shabbat was all too short when you will have to part from it on Saturday night. At Havdalah you might ask for a spiritual "hangover"into the week.

You notice the full Shabbat pattern was purposely not given here. You must make your own particular pattern which will fit into your specific interpersonal situation. *The patterns of mealtime and prayer observance by the other members of your family have to be taken into consideration in planning your day.* You might have to forsake the silence in order to *be with* the others in your home. But then you can steer conversation to something valuable. You might tell a story, sing a niggun, read an excerpt from a good book and begin to delve into it. But whenever possible, the less spoken, the better.

A word of caution is in order. Don't give anyone in your family a reason to object to your search for God, and thus turn the Shabbat into a battlefield. Remember that you are ever *free* to "*intend.*" If you live with friends who are *with* you in this, you might discuss and plan beforehand. Perhaps you and a few others might conduct a retreat on a Shabbat. At other times, any outward signs of your devotion before others who are not with you in this are highly undesirable. There is plenty of room for yourself on the *inside*. Thus, structure your Shabbat around your own given situation.

How He can be found where He is sought

This brings us to the corporate worship at a regular synagogue. By this time you will have become aware of additional valuable and uplifting material in the synagogue service. On the other hand, you will perhaps be impatient with some of the human factors. The officiating rabbi and cantor, the choir, and the other worshipers might make your synagogue attendance something less than inspiring. Let us see how we can make the service a resource in our lives.

Before leaving for shul, you should decide that you are not going in order to *"get something out"* but rather to *serve* Him. The getting is not at all important when you come to serve. You serve by *active participation* in the reading, chanting, and listening. You intend that these activities *are* pleasing to Him. As you enter the shul you avoid any conversation. Your time before the service is best used in active and passive meditation, petition, intercession, and preparation. As soon as the minyan is assembled, you are *assured* that He is present. Don't worry about the problem of His particular presence, in the face of His omnipresence. Someday you will know what the difference is. Just be assured that there *is* a real difference, and that with the minyan He *is* here in a manner approximating His presence in the holy of holies in the Temple. With this presence, you can do quite a bit. You address Him in His Shekhinah and grow in worship. But you also remember that His Shekhinah is contingent on the other worshipers. They are the ones who bring His presence to you, and you must love them. You, therefore, affirm your love for all the worshipers at the beginning of the service. If you find this difficult, you affirm your wish to love them.

Now that the service has begun, you enter into the spirit of the worship-as-it-ought-to-be. You might read the prayers as an actor reads his lines, putting feeling and conviction into your chanting. In worship it need not be you who speaks; you can become David's mouthpiece. The liturgy speaks for you, with you *acting* as an instrument. Make sure that you know the often used congregational responses; then you can actually partake with your amens, etc.

The first-person plural which you use in the liturgy may represent not only the congregation but also the many levels of your own awareness. Thus the liturgy becomes effective as a unitive power. The ark as the specific sanctuary should be your focus. Visualize the Presence there. When it is opened, you might send arrow prayers in that direction.

Study the liturgy with a teacher or friend and learn to dilate its meaning to accommodate a higher level of kavvanah. By becoming aware of the many levels of insightful kavvanah, you enlarge your intention repertoire. A person with a diversified repertoire of kavvanah can serve in many moods and spiritual "keys." The liturgical year of the Siddur and Mahzor makes demands on one's ability to sing in the "key" which the time and season demand. This holds true not only concerning the chant but also concerning the *inner* mood and approach. *Be sure to pray in private, and before corporate worship, that God may grant you the resources you need for serving Him at worship.*

During the Torah reading you will pay attention, intending to hear from it the solution to your problems. Follow the reading in the Humash, and hope for at least one sentence or part per week to speak to you. Treasure this sentence for that week.

When hearing the sermon, pray to God that there may be something important in it for you. Your sympathetic attention and expectation to hear a *living* word will have its own effect on the preacher. Any word which you feel to be useful to you, remember it and treasure it, for God did send it to you through the (sometimes unwitting) preacher. You might, when hearing some statements which you affirm, shout aloud, *inside yourself,* "Amen."

After the service you might wish to remain seated for another few moments, and "tarry awhile." You need not become conspicuous. It takes at least a few minutes for the congregation to file out. Do visit the shul from time to time in order to meditate. Despite the fact that it may be empty, or perhaps because of it, you may gain something worthwhile.

Obedience and criteria

There is no need here to go into detail about the particulars of your home observances and your business dealings. They are up to you and the kind of commitment you make. But there is an important characteristic of the *how*.

There is the intention of obedience. It makes little sense to wear yourself out in a selfish desire for inner growth for its own sake. With this motivation alone, no one survives the rigors of development. Some people only flirt for a little while with this and leave it. In order to really progress you need a different motivation, and that is loyal obedience to Him. This motivation, however, refuses to serve as a mere means to progress. One has to give in to the whole meaning of obedience and surrender one's own will to His. In the course of being obedient, one can expect the real purpose of one's own life to be achieved. While the servant image seems so prosaic, and you might much rather see yourself as a *child* or *lover* of God, you will not really be able to relate to Him as a child or lover unless, at least for a time, you have served Him as a *servant.* When service in obedience is a real dimension in your life, you might get orders to move toward the other areas.

Obedience can be established in many ways. Here is one of the many. (I think that until your commitment and thinking have become clearer, and the criteria of His will have become known to you, this one might be the best.) Remember, you were asked to share this work with a friend. Hopefully, up to now you have done this, step by step. Here the friend becomes instrumental, as you will see.

At three periods during the day listen awhile for orders. By that is meant that you sit, empty yourself of thought, and jot down the orders you receive. As you proceed, you will see that they are generally not of a religious nature.

They might have to do with some of the simpler things in life. But no one knows how *you* will be led; it is up to you and to Him.

There are many times that you will be in doubt as to the *origin* of the order. The simple way about it is to see if the orders are not against (a broad reading of) the Ten Commandments. If you are still in doubt, check with your friend. When two friends talk on such matters, there are two inclinations for good fighting one inclination for evil.

Of course then, when you are sure of the order, do not fail to carry it out. You must also, before "listening" to the orders, pray a short prayer for guidance, especially asking for criteria upon which to base your checking.

This is what is meant by the *acceptance of the heavenly yoke*. It is borne when you fulfill your orders in both decision and action. You will find that in the measure that you fulfill them, greater and higher tasks will eventually become yours. He has a way of bestowing little favors along the way which you will treasure.

As you proceed to follow the "order," send a little arrow of added awareness His way, offering your obedience to Him in a flash of warm feeling. Find your own stirring term of endearment for Him (this you need not even share with your friend).

Shalom

As it is about time to take leave of you, there are a few things you must still be told. You will now need a teacher who will begin to direct you in details. You must learn to breathe, eat, drink, sleep, and so much about prayer. This teacher must get to know you as an individual and further prescribe to you for your own physical and psychological bent.

By this time you will also have discovered the ups and downs of progress, the subtle shifts in your moods, and the especially meaningful or meaningless things that are your very own. Books cannot help you much at this stage; the teacher can.

When you are really ready, you will find yourself directed to him/her. Of course you must do a great deal of praying for this to happen. If it does not happen so soon, this might be a sign that you still have to check your past progress and inspect your whole pattern of having followed this manual. It is also possible that you will find a temporary teacher who will help you a bit further on the way, and then you will have to search again. Ultimately, you will find him/her.

Also, you must prepare yourself to be able to read and understand Hebrew. When you can understand some, you will find a tremendous literature for further guidance and have the means of penetrating into the glory of our Siddur and Tehillim. Also, when you do know some Hebrew, your teacher will have a deeper means of communication to your soul.

May His blessed Name be with you until you get to Him.

What is a meditation?

Perhaps a meditation is a daydream, a daydream of the soul as the beloved and God, the lover, their meeting in the tryst of prayer, their yearning for one another after parting; a daydream of their being united again.

Or perhaps a meditation is the becoming aware of the human soul of its loneliness and the anticipation of its being united with the One who transcends the All and is able to come past one's own defenses.

Or perhaps, again, it is a standing back with the whole of the cosmos before one's mind's eye as one's heart is being filled with the sheer joy of seeing the balance of the All and one's own self as part of it.

Or perhaps a searching into one's own motives, values, and wishes, with the light of the Torah against the background of the past.

Or perhaps . . .

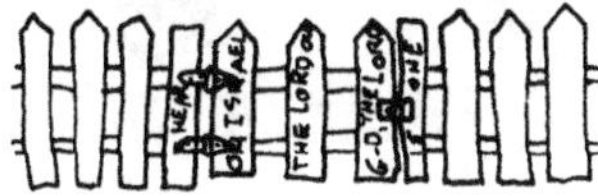

BIBLIOGRAPHY FOR A FIRST STEP

Agnon, Samuel Joseph. *The Days of Awe.* New York: Schocken, 1948.

Ben Zion, Raphael. *The Way of the Faithful.* Los Angeles: Raphael Ben Zion, 1945.

Dresner, Samuel H. *Prayer, Humility and Compassion.* Philadelphia: Jewish Publication Society, 1957.

Glatzer, Nahum N., ed. *Hammer on the Rock: A Midrash Reader.* New York: Schocken, 1948.

———. *In Time and Eternity.* New York: Schocken, 1946.

Goldin, Judah. *The Living Talmud.* Chicago: University of Chicago, 1957.

Heschel, Abraham Joshua. *God in Search of Man.* New York: Farrar, Straus, and Young, 1951.

———. *Man Is Not Alone.* New York: Farrar, Straus, and Young, 1951.

———. *Man's Quest for God.* New York: Scribners, 1954.

———. *The Sabbath.* New York: Farrar, Straus, and Young, 1951.

———. *The Earth Is the Lord's.* New York: Schuman, 1952. (The last two were published together in paperback by Harper and Row in 1968.)

Krantzler, George. *Rabbi Shneur Zalman of Ladi.* New York: Otzar HaChassidim, 1957.

Luzzatto, Moses Hayyim. *Mesillath Yesharim.* Philadelphia: Jewish Publication Society, 1948.

Mindel, Nissan. *The Commandments.* New York: Otzar HaChassidim, 1949.

———. *The Lubavitcher Rebbe's Memoirs.* New York: Otzar HaChassidim, 1949.

———. *Some Aspects of Chabad Chasidism.* New York: Otzar HaChassidim, 1957.

Minkin, Jacob S. *The Romance of Hasidism.* New York: Yoseloff, 1955.

Newman, Louis I. *The Hasidic Anthology.* New York: Schocken, 1963.

Steinberg, Milton. *The Believing Jew.* New York: Harcourt Brace and Co., 1951.

If you read French, try:

Schaya, Leo. *L'Homme et L'Absolu.* Paris: Buchet-Chastel, Corrêa, 1958.

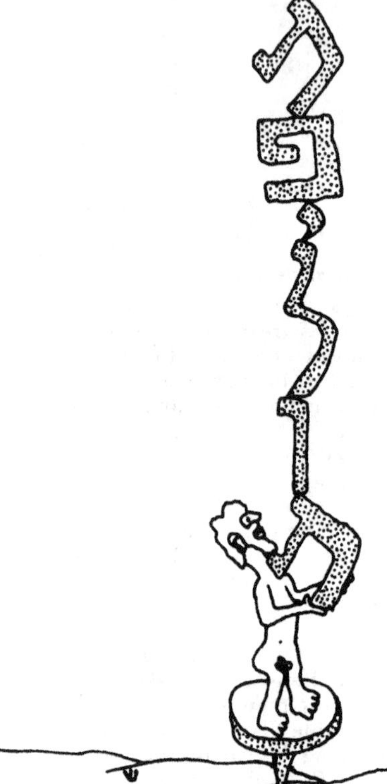

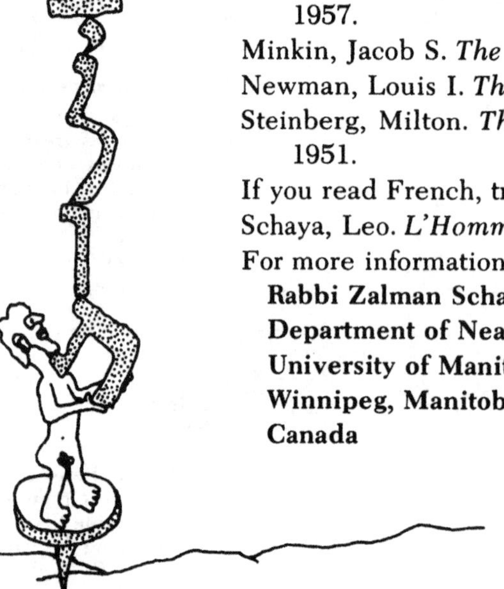

For more information, contact:

Rabbi Zalman Schacter, Chairman
Department of Near Eastern and Judaic Studies
University of Manitoba
Winnipeg, Manitoba
Canada

Our thanks to the following for their kind permission to use copyrighted material:

Bloch Publishing Co.: an illustration from Reuben Leaf, *Hebrew Alphabets,* 1951, page 34.

Encyclopaedia Judaica: Keter Inc., with permission of Keter Inc., 104 E. 40th St., New York 10016, for use of material from *Encyclopaedia Judaica* (1972), volume 1, columns 136-137; volume 6, columns 1239-1240; volume 14, columns 1100-1104; and volume 16, columns 667-672.

Harcourt Brace Jovanovich, Inc.: Reprinted from T. S. Eliot, "East Coker,"

The Four Quartets (New York: Harcourt Brace Jovanovich, Inc., Harvest Paperbacks, 1943), lines 1; 101-2; T. S. Eliot, "Little Gidding," *The Four Quartets* (New York: Harcourt Brace Jovanovich, Inc., Harvest Paperbacks, 1943), lines 214-15; 225-31.

New Directions Publishing Corporation: Dylan Thomas, "And death shall have no dominion," *The Poems of Dylan Thomas.* Copyright 1943 by New Directions Publishing Corporation. Reprinted by permission of New Directions Publishing Corporation.

Response magazine, vol. 13 (Spring 1972), for the chapter on Hallah, which appeared there in somewhat different form.

Photo Credits

American Jewish Historical Society
front cover and pages 36, 74, 127, 224, 252, 299

Cinema Service Corporation, N. Y. C.
pages 218, 219, 220

Gingold, Barbara (from her exhibit "On View: The New Jews")
front cover and pages 43, 86, 89, 98, 109, 110, 117, 213, 222, 251, 253, 257, 274, 279, 284, 285, 288

Goldberg, Joseph R.
pages 214, 217, 264

Green, Jeff
back cover and pages 7, 297

Herzberg, Irving I.
back cover and pages 22, 38, 41, 44, 56, 61, 78, 123, 127, 129, 131, 136, 140, 141, 144, 162, 169, 239, 245, 254, 256, 286, 287, 292, 295

Jewish Student Press Service
pages 91, 133, 149, 213, 284

Konikoff, Sid
pages 44, 277, 284

National Ramah Commission, Camp Ramah, Wisconsin
endpapers

The Photographic Archive of the Jewish Theological Seminary of America, New York Frank J. Darmstaeder
pages 12, 14, 16, 17, 70, 94, 95, 134, 198, 199

Polen, Nehemiah
pages 127, 283

Pollitzer, Eric
page 110

Rosenfeld, Dina
page 177

Shumack, Sharon
back cover and pages 10, 11, 51, 239, 248, 249, 281, 284, 297, 299

Sobol, Richard
pages 30, 31, 85, 89, 90

Vishniac, Roman
back cover: children at heder

YIVO Institute for Jewish Research
back cover and pages 38, 55, 77, 109, 123, 129, 130, 144, 160, 175, 177, 186, 279

Zabari, Moshe; Tobe Pascher Workshop, Jewish Museum, N. Y. C.
pages 45, 46, 58, 110, 113, 127, 135, 141, 163

Calligraphy credits

Courtesy Barton's Candy Company
page 99

Berg, Janet
page: 185

Greenspan, Jay
pages 196, 200

Harlow, Jules, ed. *A Rabbi's Manual,* 1965, by the Rabbinical Assembly, reprinted with the permission of the Rabbinical Assembly
page 197

Kelman, Rabbi Stuart
pages 204, 209

Kelman, Vicky
page 187

Koltun, Sam
page 125

Leaf, Reuben
page 189

Moss, David
pages 195, 196, 198, 199

Ray, Eric
pages 187, 205, 208, 209

CPSIA information can be obtained
at www.ICGtesting.com
Printed in the USA
LVHW061916070821
694812LV00013B/583